Exploring
Art

GLENCOE
Macmillan/McGraw-Hill

Understanding
Art

Picture the perfect art course:

STUDENT EDITIONS

Exploring Art

Media Intensive The media experience energizes students to discover how artists are inspired and why they choose a particular medium of expression. From drawing and painting to architecture, graphic design and photography, chapters interweave studio production with narrative lessons on the elements and principles of art, techniques, art history and criticism. This curriculum yields a first-hand appreciation for artists' skills as well as the basis to evaluate the art itself.

Every lesson integrates:
aesthetics • art history
art criticism • studio production

Narrative Lessons illustrate chapter objectives in accessible, easy-to-understand language, using relevant examples from art, daily life or history. Many include a "hands-on" Studio Experience. Check Your Understanding provides a mini-review for each lesson.

Studio Lessons Learning intensifies as students actually create their own works of art in each medium. Lessons are **illustrated** by intriguing examples of fine art shown full frame and in detail. Features: Examining Your Work (applied art criticism), Other Studio Ideas, Safety Tips.

Whether your focus is hands-on . . .

Understanding Art

Art & Culture   From earliest time to the contemporary, this student text blends art history with the religious, political, geographical, and social events which make each culture's art unique. Traditions of Western Europe are augmented by those of China, Japan, India and Africa. Each narrative lesson includes a studio experience to heighten understanding. And studio lessons build active involvement while balancing aesthetic and critical values.

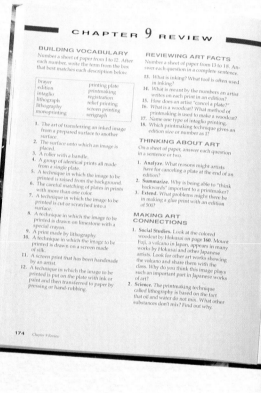

- **Chapter Openers** link large full color fine art reproductions and thought-provoking discussion. This interactive format engages students' thinking and provides activities to reinforce each chapter's primary goal.

- **Chapter Reviews** include <u>Building Vocabulary</u>, <u>Reviewing Art Facts</u>, <u>Thinking About Art</u>, <u>Making Art Connections</u>, and <u>Looking At The Details</u>.

- **50-page handbook** (uniquely developed to support each text) enriches learning with <u>Artist Profiles</u>, <u>Career Spotlights</u>, <u>Studio Extensions</u> and <u>Technique Tips</u>.

- **Features ethnic, women and minority artists.**

- **Representative student work** builds interest, motivation and confidence.

. . . or discussion . . .

TEACHER'S WRAPAROUND EDITION

The first middle school/ junior high art textbooks to offer a Teacher's Wraparound Edition.
Sized-down Student Text pages surrounded by teaching materials save you time and effort while enhancing every lesson.

. . . it simplifies the planning . . .

Side panels provide daily lesson plans:

On Chapter Pages you'll find <u>Chapter Scan</u> (helps you allocate time), and <u>Using the Chapter Opener</u> (artist's background for opening works of art, with suggestions for introducing, examining, and discussing).

<u>Answers to the Chapter Review</u> and <u>Using the Chapter Detail</u> are page-specific, <u>Building Self-Esteem</u> enhances each student's artistic and personal development, and <u>Evaluation Techniques</u> monitor progress and success.

Lesson Pages give you <u>Lesson Objectives</u>, <u>Teacher's Resource Binder Resources</u>, a daily <u>Motivator</u> that sparks interest in lesson content, plus defined <u>Vocabulary</u> and exercises.

<u>Exploring Aesthetics</u> encourages discussion and thinking skills, and <u>Art Criticism</u> relates to the text's art or activity. <u>Art History</u> activities build interest in research. <u>Appreciating Cultural Diversity</u> helps you develop a sensitive multicultural art program.

Bottom margins are filled with special studio emphasis and annotations:

<u>Background Information</u> on artists' lives and art styles plus media techniques are strategically placed to correlate to text.

You'll also find <u>Classroom Management Tips</u> from other classroom art teachers, <u>Cooperative Learning</u>, a <u>Cross-reference to Handbook</u> and <u>Answers to Review Questions</u>.

TEACHER'S RESOURCE BINDER

For the first time, an art course offers a Teacher's Resource Binder— separate for each text. Tabbed to correspond to chapters, there's a wealth of supplementary handouts, teaching strategies and resource materials to complement the skill level, time framework and interest level of your class:

TEACHER'S RESOURCE BINDER

Exploring Art

CHAPTER 3
Art Criticism, Aesthetics, and Art History
Table of Contents

CHAPTER 4
Art of Earliest Times
Using the
Teacher's Resource Binder

CHAPTER 1
CHAPTER 5
The Language of Art

CHAPTER 6
CHAPTER 2
The Media of Art

- **Reproducible masters**   Planned for each lesson, these provide supplementary material for your students.

- **Cooperative Learning Activities**   Each has been selected to promote teamwork, cooperation and responsibility.

- **Aesthetics/Art Criticism**   As aestheticians and art critics, students explore, theorize and apply principles to practical situations.

- **Art History**   Activity sheets relate to each chapter.

- **Studio Lessons**   Additional lessons supplement or replace those in texts. Field-tested by classroom teachers and selected to reinforce and extend chapter contents.

- **Appreciating Cultural Diversity**   In the ideal setting of the art classroom, students celebrate their ethnicity and gain understanding for global views.

- **Evaluation Techniques**   A reproducible objective testing program is provided for each chapter.

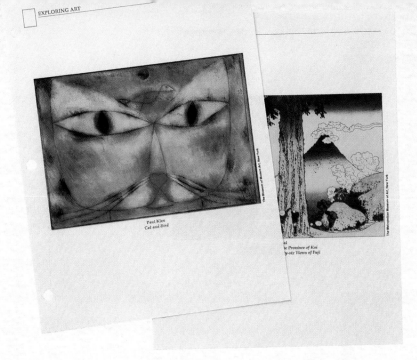

OVERHEAD COLOR TRANSPARENCIES

- Two color transparencies for each chapter
- Transparencies project large enough for detail examination
- Accompanied by Instructor's Guide

FINE ART PRINTS

- 20 masterworks for each text; no duplications from the textbook
- 22-1/2" x 28-1/2", the largest practical classroom size
- Printed on sturdy self-supporting stock
- Laminated to resist wear and tear
- Reinforced corner holes
- Presented in a handsome and durable portfolio
- Top quality fine art pieces differ from text
- Includes an extensive Instructor's Guide and Resource Book

. . . so you have more time for the art!

PROGRAM COMPONENTS

Exploring Art

STUDENT TEXT	0-02-662281-5
TEACHER'S WRAPAROUND EDITION	0-02-662282-3
TEACHER'S RESOURCE BINDER	0-02-662283-1
FINE ART PRINTS	0-02-662284-X
OVERHEAD COLOR TRANSPARENCIES	0-02-662293-9

Understanding Art

STUDENT TEXT	0-02-662286-6
TEACHER'S WRAPAROUND EDITION	0-02-662287-4
TEACHER'S RESOURCE BINDER	0-02-662288-2
FINE ART PRINTS	0-02-662289-0
OVERHEAD COLOR TRANSPARENCIES	0-02-662294-7

GLENCOE
Macmillan/McGraw-Hill

936 Eastwind Drive • Westerville, Ohio 43081

1. NORTHEAST REGION
GLENCOE
17 Riverside Drive
Nashua, NH 03062
603-880-4701

2. MID-ATLANTIC REGION
GLENCOE
Princeton-Hightstown Road
P.O. Box 409
Hightstown, NJ 08520
609-426-7356

3. ATLANTIC-SOUTHEAST REGION
GLENCOE
Brookside Park
One Harbison Way, Suite 101
Columbia, SC 29212
803-732-2365

4. SOUTHEAST REGION
GLENCOE
6510 Jimmy Carter Boulevard
Norcross, GA 30071
404-446-7493

5. MID-AMERICA REGION
GLENCOE
4635 Hilton Corporate Drive
Columbus, OH 43232
614-759-6600

6. MID-CONTINENT REGION
GLENCOE
846 East Algonquin Road
Schaumburg, IL 60173
708-397-8448

7. SOUTHWEST REGION
GLENCOE
320 Westway Pl., Suite 550
Arlington, TX 76018
817-784-2100

8. TEXAS REGION
GLENCOE
320 Westway Pl., Suite 550
Arlington, TX 76018
817-784-2100

9. WESTERN REGION
GLENCOE
610 E. 42nd St. #102
Boise, ID 83714
208-378-4002
Includes Alaska

10. CALIFORNIA REGION
GLENCOE
15319 Chatsworth Street
Mission Hills, CA 91345
818-898-1391

FOR CANADIAN ORDERS
Maxwell Macmillan Canada
1200 Eglinton Ave., East, Suite 200
Don Mills, Ontario M3C 3NI
Telephone: 416-449-6030
Telex: 069.59372
Telefax: 416-449-0068

FOR HAWAII
Donald Hosaka, Rep.
Macmillan/McGraw-Hill International
1613 Kanalui Street
Honolulu, HI 96816
Telephone: 808-734-6971
Telefax: 808-735-4590

FOR ALL OVERSEAS K-12 SCHOOLS
Macmillan/McGraw-Hill International
866 Third Avenue
New York, NY 10022-6299
Telephone: 212-702-3276
Telex: 225925 MACM UR
Telefax: 212-605-9377

Exploring Art

Rosalind Ragans, Ph.D.
Associate Professor Emerita
Georgia Southern University

Jane Rhoades, Ph.D.
Teacher Educator
Georgia Southern University

GLENCOE
Macmillan/McGraw-Hill

Lake Forest, Illinois   Columbus, Ohio   Mission Hills, California   Peoria, Illinois

Send all inquiries to:
Glencoe Division, Macmillan/McGraw-Hill
15319 Chatsworth Street
P.O. Box 9609
Mission Hills, California 91346-9609

ISBN 0-02-662281-5 Student Text
ISBN 0-02-662282-3 Teacher's Wraparound Edition

 2 3 4 5 6 7 8 9   95 94 93 92

CONTENTS

Introduction   TM-5

Teaching with **Exploring Art**   TM-5

    The Student Text   TM-6

    The Teacher's Wraparound Edition   TM-8

    The Teacher's Resource Binder   TM-10

    Overhead Color Transparency Packet   TM-10

Recognizing the Importance of a Quality Art Program   TM-11

    Benefits of a Quality Program   TM-11

Planning the Course   TM-13

    Pacing Chart   TM-13

    Scope and Sequence Chart   TM-18

    Designing a Quality Art Program   TM-27

Creating a Positive Learning Environment   TM-30

    Teaching Students with Varying Ability Levels and Learning Styles   TM-30

    Teaching Art to Students From All Cultural Backgrounds   TM-31

    Teaching Critical Thinking in the Art Classroom   TM-32

    Implementing Cooperative Learning   TM-33

    Relating Art to Other Content Areas   TM-34

    Providing Sources of Inspiration   TM-35

    Evaluating Performance   TM-35

Classroom Environment and Management   TM-38

    Classroom Organization   TM-38

    Safety in the Classroom   TM-38

    Resources in the Community   TM-44

Public Relations   TM-45

    Public Relations Strategies   TM-45

CONTRIBUTORS

Carol M. Burris
Art Teacher
Columbus East High School
Columbus, Ohio

Vicki D. Hatfield
Art Teacher
Beechcroft High School
Columbus, Ohio

Ann E. Heintzelman
Art Teacher
Daleville Elementary School
Daleville, Indiana

Josephine Julianna Jones
Art Teacher
Booker T. Washington High School
for the Performing Arts
Dallas, Texas

Bruce E. Little
Art Educator
Georgia Southern University
Statesboro, Georgia

Virginia Little
Counselor
Myers Middle School
Savannah, Georgia

Nancy Miller
Art Teacher
Booker T. Washington High School
for the Performing Arts
Dallas, Texas

Rebecca Robertson
Art Teacher
W. W. Samuell High School
Dallas, Texas

Carolyn Sollman
Art Teacher
Eminence School
Eminence, Indiana

William Zeigler
Art Teacher
New Castle Chrysler High School
New Castle, Indiana

Introduction

The experience of watching students involved in the process of exploring, understanding, and producing works of art is exciting and professionally rewarding. Today's art classroom fosters this instructional climate by providing a place where students can express artistic talent and develop creative thinking; a forum where students are encouraged to ask questions and challenged to find answers to their questions; an environment that encourages students to think, to learn, and to create.

Exploring Art has been designed to meet the needs of today's art classroom and to address in a systematic and integrated fashion the major goals of art education. These goals include:

- The development, expression, and evaluation of ideas and processes;
- The ability to produce, read, and interpret visual symbols;
- The assimilation of information needed to recognize and understand the artistic achievements and expectations of various societies.

By achieving these goals students gain an awareness and sensitivity to the humanmade and natural environment and develop the skills to become visually literate.

The *Exploring Art* program has been written and designed specifically for middle school/junior high students. Its motivational appeal and high-interest, interactive approach stems from the philosophy that *all* students benefit from a well-planned and sequentially articulated art program. *Exploring Art* is based on the belief that a quality art program allows for discovery and creative problem solving, and in the process, cultivates learners who are able to make positive contributions to society.

Teaching with Exploring Art

Exploring Art is a middle school/junior high textbook written collaboratively by Dr. Rosalind Ragans and Dr. Gene Mittler. Both of these experienced art specialists, teachers, and writers recognized the need for developing a quality middle school/junior high textbook program based on an integrated approach of aesthetics, art criticism, art history, and studio production. Throughout the development of the textbook, material was reviewed and field tested in classrooms across the United States by middle school/junior high teachers. These combined efforts bring you an innovative art program that both students and teachers will find meaningful and rewarding.

Exploring Art is based on the assumption that the following features are an essential part of an effective art program.

- **Program articulation and flexibility.** A quality art education program provides students with experiences that are sequentially planned, building on previous art concepts and skills. At the same time the program must fit the configuration and topic emphases of the middle school/junior high program, which vary from school district to school district. *Exploring Art* meets these needs. The program builds sequentially on content giving students experiences in the various aspects of an art program. Its short, self-contained lessons, which are appropriate for 45-minute class periods, have built-in flexibility allowing the teacher to adapt the content to a 6-week, 9-week, 18-week, or 36-week course.

- **Visual perception and creative problem solving.** *Exploring Art* is a visually oriented program, incorporating reproductions of masters' work and other art works so that students can develop an appreciation and understanding for various artists, works of art, and artistic styles. Each illustration in the text is discussed and explored within the narrative and studio lessons. After examining the works of art, students explore concepts related to these works and apply specific techniques in the hands-on Studio Experiences and Studio Lessons. The art production segments allow for personal expression, encourage discovery, and promote creative problem solving.

- **Integration of aesthetics, art criticism, art history, and studio production.** *Exploring Art* successfully weaves aesthetics, art criticism, art history, and studio production throughout the narrative and studio lessons and in the correlated program components. Each lesson discusses works of art from aesthetic viewpoints and provides teaching strategies which deal with the steps of art criticism and art history. In each narrative lesson a Studio Experience is included to provide hands-on application of the material. In each studio lesson, students are encouraged to critique their works of art. This assists the teacher in providing a unified program that meets today's curriculum direction in art education.
- **Appreciation of cultural diversity.** *Exploring Art* addresses a variety of cultural and ethnic groups. This attention to cultural diversity is represented in works of art, teaching strategies, and curriculum content.

Exploring Art consists of the following components:

- **Student Text.** The 352-page book introduces students to a solid art program, laying the foundation for lifelong art appreciation and art production skills.
- **Teacher's Wraparound Edition.** This edition provides a complete teaching program, including lesson plans, teaching suggestions, classroom management tips, and supplemental information—conveniently wrapped around the outside column of a reduced student page. A 48-page Teacher's Manual is included in the wraparound edition, which is designed to assist the teacher in setting up his or her classroom and listing effective teaching techniques.
- **Teacher's Resource Binder.** This separate component includes reproducible masters, handouts, and student activity sheets, which emphasize aesthetics and art criticism, art history, evaluation techniques, cooperative learning, and appreciation for cultural diversity. Also included are additional studio lessons and teacher-ready overhead color transparencies.
- **Overhead Color Transparencies.** Ready-to-use color transparencies are an effective way to introduce and reinforce concepts. This separate package of overhead color transparencies can be used to extend the lessons and develop higher-level thinking skills as students compare, analyze, and evaluate works of art.

The Student Text

Exploring Art offers a broad range of visual art experiences based on the elements and principles of art and using various art media and techniques. The concepts of aesthetics, art criticism, art history, and art production are applied and reinforced throughout the program.

After students are introduced to the elements and principles of art, students learn about art criticism and art history. Next they explore in depth the various art media, such as printmaking, painting, graphic design, sculpture, architecture, and photography. Studio lessons appear throughout the text and as a model for each studio lesson a work of a master is included. Each studio lesson also involves creating works of art using a range of art media and techniques. Exemplary age-appropriate student art work is displayed in the text to be used as a source of inspiration and motivation for the student.

The structure of the textbook provides for flexibility to accommodate the varied configuration of the middle school/junior high program. By consulting the pacing chart and the scope and sequence chart, the teacher can tailor a course that is appropriate for his or her specific teaching methods and the local, state, and national art education framework.

Organization of the Text

The text is divided into 15 chapters. Chapters 1 and 2 pose the question, "What is Art?" and introduce students to different aesthetic theories. Three aesthetic viewpoints are presented, and students are encouraged to see the value of all three viewpoints and realize the benefit of using several theories when evaluating works of art. In Chapter 3 students are introduced to and experiment with various art media. Chapters 4 and 5 introduce students to the elements and principles of art. This helps them understand the importance of developing a visual vocabulary. In Chapters 6 and 7 students learn about art criticism and art history, enabling them to apply these operations when critiquing and evaluating works of art. Chapters 8 through 15 present information and studio lessons dealing with specific art media.

Chapters

Exploring Art is divided into chapters, which are further divided into self-contained narrative or studio lessons. In each chapter the following recurring learning aids and textbook features are integrated:

- **Chapter Opener.** Each chapter begins with a two-page spread that includes:
  — **Full-color reproduction of a work of art** to provide visual motivation for the student.
  — **Chapter learning objectives** to help students identify the behavioral goals of the chapter.
  — **Vocabulary terms** to help students develop an art vocabulary, enabling them to understand and participate in class discussion.
  — **Artists You Will Meet** to introduce students to the artists whose art works appear within the chapter.
- **Chapter Review.** The two-page chapter review includes:
  — **Building Vocabulary** to check comprehension of vocabulary terms.
  — **Reviewing Art Facts** to help teachers monitor the recall and comprehension of the material.
  — **Thinking About Art** to provide exercises involving higher-level thinking skills.

— **Making Art Connections** to suggest other interdisciplinary activities.
— **Looking at the Details** to enable students to apply the information that they have learned in the chapter to a segment of the work of art that appears on the chapter opener.

Lessons

Each chapter is divided into self-contained lessons. There are two types of lessons: narrative and studio. Both types of lessons use a work of art as point of departure for explanation of content and studio production. The narrative lessons present art concepts and help increase cognitive learning. The studio lessons provide manipulative experiences that build on previous studio exercises and give students the opportunity to use various media and techniques.

Features found in the lessons include:

- **Studio Experience.** A studio experience in each narrative lesson provides immediate hands-on application of the content.
- **Check Your Understanding.** Comprehension questions enable the teacher to quickly assess students' understanding of the narrative lessons.
- **Examining Your Work.** This section guides students in applying the process of art criticism to their own works of art.
- **Safety Tip.** Where appropriate, a note alerts students to take precautions when dealing with certain items, such as utility knives, paints, and glues.

Handbook

A 40-page handbook, which appears at the end of the Student Text provides resource and reference information for students.

- **Technique Tips.** Step-by-step procedures or techniques that pertain to drawing, printmaking, painting, sculpting, and other production skills are presented and illustrated.
- **Artist Profiles.** This handy reference material gives students additional information about the lives of artists. The section can be used as a separate art history unit or used in the context of the Student Text and presented as the artist's work is presented in the text.

- **Career Spotlights.** The purpose of the career spotlights is to acquaint students with a variety of career opportunities within the field of art. This section can be covered as a separate unit or assigned as extra credit.
- **Additional Studios.** Additional studio lessons provide enrichment and extension. These optional studio activities are designed for cooperative learning and/or the creatively gifted student.

Other Features

- **Student Art Work.** Exemplary student art work of middle school/junior high students is displayed within the studio lessons.
- **Artists and Their Works.** All artists and the names of their works are previewed on the chapter opening page. A comprehensive listing of all artists and the titles of their art works and page references appears in the section, Artists and Their Works.
- **Glossary.** Every vocabulary term (identified in boldface type) is listed and defined in the Glossary. Where needed, a pronunciation guide is also provided. Page references assist students in locating where the word is introduced and defined in context within the text.
- **Index.** A comprehensive index is provided as a study aid and to assist students in finding particular topics.

The Teacher's Wraparound Edition

Exploring Art is the first middle school/junior high art textbook program that offers a Teacher's Wraparound Edition. The Teacher's Wraparound Edition differs from the Student Text in the following ways: (1) material from the Student Text is reproduced in a slightly smaller size to allow more room for the teaching material, which fills the side and bottom columns; (2) a 48-page Teacher's Manual (the section you are reading now) is bound into the book.

Teacher's Manual

To assist in course planning and to increase teacher effectiveness, a Teacher's Manual is included in the Teacher's Wraparound Edition. This manual explains the program components and how to use them. Other parts of the Teacher's Manual include:

- **A Pacing Chart** to help you decide how much time to spend on each lesson.
- **A Scope and Sequence Chart** to help you identify topics and where they appear in each chapter and lesson.
- **A Teaching Methods Manual** to help articulate the criteria of a quality art education program, explain how to teach students with varying ability levels, and suggest ways to create a positive classroom environment. This mini-manual also discusses classroom organizational and management techniques.

Lesson Plans

In the Teacher's Wraparound Edition the lesson plans fill the outside column of the Student Text page. The consistent, easy-to-follow lesson plans give the teacher a variety of teaching strategies to motivate students, to introduce, teach, and reinforce concepts, and to provide enrichment and extension ideas.

Chapter Pages

On the two-page spreads that begin and end each chapter, these elements are provided:

- **Chapter Scan.** In the left column a listing of the lesson titles that appear in the chapter is provided. The quick scan enables you to see the scope of the chapter at a glance and helps decide how much time you will spend on each lesson.
- **Using the Chapter Opener.** This information helps the teacher effectively use the chapter opening work of art. Background information about the artist is given along with suggestions for introducing, examining, and discussing the art work.
- **Answers to the Chapter Review and to Looking at the Details.** Answers to all questions are provided on the same page as the questions themselves.
- **Building Self-Esteem.** At the beginning of each chapter a teaching strategy designed to build students' self-esteem and to show students the relationship between art and self-esteem is provided. In using some of the self-esteem strategies, it is suggested that the art teacher invite the school counselor into the classroom to team teach the lesson. An effective team teaching program may be developed between

the counselor and the art teacher, thus providing the strongest possible experience for the students, in terms of both their personal and artistic development.

- **Evaluation Techniques.** At the end of each chapter there are at least three evaluation techniques that help to monitor students' progress and evaluate students' success with the material.

Lesson Pages

On the various lesson pages these elements are provided:

- **Lesson Objectives.** Student objectives for the lesson are provided.
- **Supplies.** A listing of supplies that the teacher will need for implementing the art production experiences and for following the lesson plan are listed.
- **Teacher's Resource Binder.** This is a list of student handouts and activities from the Teacher's Resource Binder that are correlated to the chapter and lesson.
- **Motivator.** This short motivational teaching strategy is designed to spark students' interest in the content of the lesson.
- **Vocabulary.** The vocabulary is identified in boldface type within the lesson and defined in italics. To help students grasp concepts, a vocabulary exercise is given in the lesson plan.
- **Exploring Aesthetics.** This teaching strategy is based on the aesthetic viewpoints presented in the text. These types of activities lend themselves well to classroom discussion and help students develop critical thinking skills.
- **Using Art Criticism.** This type of activity challenges students to apply the steps of art criticism to the work of art that appears within the text or to a related activity.
- **Understanding Art History.** These teaching activities provide additional information for the students in relationship to art history. Many of the art history activities develop research and language art skills.
- **Developing Studio Skills.** This section offers a variety of activities that help students develop and practice art production skills.
- **Appreciating Cultural Diversity.** To help the teacher develop a sensitive multicultural art

program, various multicultural teaching strategies are provided.

- **Closure.** Suggestions for bringing closure to the instructional period are presented.
- **Evaluation.** An important part of any curriculum area is the evaluation process. There are many ways to evaluate students. Of course, objective testing is one method and a testing program is included in the Teacher's Resource Binder. Other evaluation methods are listed at the end of each lesson and at the end of each chapter.
- **Reteaching/Enrichment.** These activities are suggested so that the teacher has easily accessible teaching suggestions to meet the needs of all students. The enrichment strategy can be used to keep gifted students challenged and make it possible for the instructor to spend time with students who need more instruction time.

Annotations

Annotations appear at the bottom of the pages. These include: Background Information, Note, Handbook Cross-Reference, Classroom Management Tip, Cooperative Learning, Developing Perceptual Skills, and Answers to "Check Your Understanding."

- **Background Information.** Background information about an artist, art style, medium, and technique is listed so that you have supplemental information at your fingertips.
- **Note.** This annotation is directed to the teacher as a reminder of where important concepts are presented in the program, or as a reminder of information that you may wish to share with students.
- **Handbook Cross-Reference.** Bound into the student text is a 40-page handbook that lists Technique Tips, Artist Profiles, Career Spotlights, and Additional Studios. This handy resource manual is cross-referenced in the bottom-page annotations.
- **Classroom Management Tips.** These helpful suggestions have been written by classroom art teachers as ideas that might help organize or manage an art classroom.
- **Cooperative Learning.** Teaching strategies that encourage teamwork and cooperative interaction among all levels of students are provided.

- **Developing Perceptual Skills.** Suggestions for improving perceptual skills and enhancing students' observational skills are provided.
- **Answers to "Check Your Understanding."** Answers to the factual recall questions are provided on the same page as the questions.

The Teacher's Resource Binder

A separate *Exploring Art* Teacher's Resource Binder is designed to provide you with a correlated supplemental resource for *Exploring Art*. The purpose of the Teacher's Resource Binder is to provide a wealth of additional handouts, teaching strategies, and resource material designed for more effective teaching. You can choose the materials that complement the skill level, time framework, and interest level of your class. Most of its pages are designed to be reproduced for classroom use. The Teacher's Resource Binder is organized into chapters. The following types of teaching materials have been provided for each chapter:

- **Reproducible Master.** Reproducible masters have been planned for each lesson to provide supplementary material for your students. They can be used to create an overhead transparency master, which visually introduces or reinforces information, or they can be used as black-line masters and distributed as handouts to students.
- **Cooperative Learning Activities.** Cooperative learning activities have been developed to promote teamwork, cooperation, and responsibility. They require students to work in small groups or teams of three or four. Each team member is responsible not only for his or her own learning but also for the learning of the other team members. Students assist and help each other master skills, solve problems, and find creative solutions. In this type of learning environment students are encouraged to share ideas, interpret material, and cooperate to help each other learn. Working in small groups gives all students the opportunity to experience

success. In addition, the active participation of the students and the group creates a positive, stimulating classroom environment.
- **Aesthetics/Art Criticism.** These student worksheets are designed to make the teaching and application of aesthetics and art criticism meaningful and enjoyable to middle school/junior high students. As aestheticians and art critics, they explore, theorize, and apply the principles learned in the text to practical situations.
- **Art History.** Every chapter contains an activity sheet pertaining to art history. Although *Exploring Art* is not an art history text, the text introduces students to art history by illustrating specific concepts with works of art from various periods and styles. The activity sheets in the Teacher's Resource Binder reinforce and extend the information.
- **Studio.** The Teacher's Resource Binder offers a variety of studio activities that help students develop and practice art production skills. These activities can be used in place of or in addition to the studio lessons in the Student Text. Each lesson has been field tested by classroom teachers and selected for its ability to reinforce and extend chapter content.
- **Appreciating Cultural Diversity.** Worksheets are presented for each chapter to help students celebrate their cultural diversity and understand various global views.
- **Evaluation Techniques.** To help teachers measure students' performance and attest to accountability, a reproducible objective testing program is provided for each chapter.

Overhead Color Transparency Packet

The ready-to-use overhead color transparency packet is provided as a way to introduce, reinforce, or extend the chapter. The package contains 30 full-color overhead transparencies along with a 32-page instructional manual to assist the teacher in guiding discussion.

Recognizing the Importance of a Quality Art Program

Young people learn about the visual arts outside of school through their family and friends, through the mass media, and perhaps even by teaching themselves. Sometimes the information learned this way is valuable, but it should not be relied upon to always give correct and adequate information about art. Our schools are the most available and most effective place for giving students the opportunity to learn about the visual arts.

Benefits of a Quality Art Program

A quality art education program taught by a qualified art specialist benefits every adolescent student. If art educators teach their subject matter in a systematic, coherent, and meaningful fashion, students will acquire knowledge about art that will benefit them throughout their life. Such a program promotes growth in many areas. Some of these areas are noted below.

- **Art Teaches Effective Communication.** In order for students to become visually literate, they need to understand that the visual symbols developed by artists and designers transmit information that cannot be disclosed through other modes of communication. Adolescent students should be encouraged to learn visual literacy by looking, understanding, talking, writing, and, of course, creating images. Through a quality art education program, students should be able to discuss and create images—images that convey knowledge, create new knowledge, reveal opinions and shape opinions, disclose the depths of human emotion, and impart the most profound values.
- **Art Teaches Creativity.** All people possess creative intelligence. When a quality art

program is implemented, creativity in all students is nurtured and stimulated. Through an art program, students learn to solve problems creatively. Every time a student creates an art work, he or she has to make creative decisions. Research has shown that experiences in art are ideal for cultivating, exercising, and stimulating the imagination and for developing creative problem-solving abilities.

- **Art Teaches About Civilizations.** Through a quality art program, students develop a sensitivity and understanding of the history of humankind. For many periods in history it is only through visual remains or material culture that a societies' culture can be pieced together. A study of art history reveals varied world views, concepts, symbols, styles, feelings, and perceptions. Experiences that adolescent students have with these art objects from the past teach them respect for others, challenge their minds, and stimulate not only the intellect but also the imagination.
- **Art Teaches Critical Thinking.** A quality art program encourages a variety of critical thinking skills. Students are asked to identify and recall information; to organize select facts and ideas; to use particular facts, rules, and principles; to be able to figure out component parts or to classify; to combine ideas and form a new whole; and to make critical judgments and develop their own opinions.
- **Art Teaches Perceptual Sensitivity and Aesthetic Awareness.** As a result of a quality art program, students develop a keen sense of awareness and an appreciation for beauty. Art experiences help cultivate an aesthetic sensitivity and respect for the natural and humanmade environment. Art classes are the

only place in the school curriculum where students learn about what constitutes quality design—about harmony, order, organizations, and specific design qualities (such as balance, movement, and unity).

- **Art Teaches Personal Expression.** Art is an effective way to express emotions. The adolescent years are often filled with emotional turmoil—frustrations, tensions, and irritations. Art experiences permit the expression of ideas, feelings, and perceptions in a healthy, socially acceptable way. Although art educators are not trained art therapists, they understand that art experiences help adolescents release emotions in a positive way. Through their art, students sometimes begin to discover their own identity and build self-esteem. Personal expression is encouraged and the result is often a statement in visual form that is both inventive and filled with personal meaning.

- **Art Teaches the Value of Work.** Through a quality art program, students learn the meaning and joy of work. Working to the best of one's ability is a noble expression of the human spirit. Students learn the satisfaction and excitement that comes from developing their art skills and craftsmanship when they have successfully completed an art production project.

Planning the Course

To implement a quality art education program there is no standard formula or format that will work for every program. The content of the lessons in *Exploring Art* draws upon the fundamental disciplines that contribute to the understanding and making of art—art production or studio art, art criticism, aesthetics, and art history. Goals and objectives will be developed by the professional art teacher and will be dependent upon the interests, ability levels, learning styles, and instructional time allotted for the individual program.

To assist with the planning and development of individual courses, a Pacing Chart, Scope and Sequence Chart, and overall suggestions are included in this section. These are only intended as suggested guidelines. Individual teachers will need to make necessary adjustments and modifications as required by their local, state, and national curriculum guidelines, and by the ability level and learning styles of their students.

Pacing Chart

		6 wk	9 wk	18 wk	36 wk
	Total Days	30 days	45 days	90 days	180 days
Chapter 1 *Art in Your World*					
Lesson 1 The Art Experience		1/2 day	1/2 day	1/2 day	1 day
Lesson 2 Examining Art Works		1/2 day	1/2 day	1/2 day	1 day
Lesson 3 Artists and Ideas		1 day	1 day	1 day	1 day
Lesson 4 Making a Content Collage				1 day	2 days
	Total	2 days	2 days	3 days	5 days
Chapter 2 *Enjoying Art*					
Lesson 1 Understanding Art		1 day	1 day	1 day	1 day
Lesson 2 Aesthetics		1 day	1 day	1 day	2 days
Lesson 3 Torn Paper Face				1 day	2 days
	Total	2 days	2 days	3 days	5 days

	Total Days	6 wk 30 days	9 wk 45 days	18 wk 90 days	36 wk 180 days
Chapter 3 *Exploring Art Media*					
Lesson 1 Drawing		1 day	1 day	1 day	2 days
Lesson 2 Printmaking		1 day	1 day	1 day	2 days
Lesson 3 Painting		1 day	1 day	1 day	2 days
Lesson 4 Experimenting With Pigment			1 day	1 day	1 day
Lesson 5 Sculpture		1 day	1 day	1 day	2 days
Lesson 6 Creating with Mixed Media		1 day	1 day	2 days	2 days
Total		5 days	6 days	7 days	11 days
Chapter 4 *The Elements of Art*					
Lesson 1 The Language of Art		1/2 day	1/2 day	1 day	1 day
Lesson 2 Color		1 day	1 day	1 day	2 days
Lesson 3 Using Color Combinations			1 day	1 day	2 days
Lesson 4 Line		1 day	1 day	1 day	1 day
Lesson 5 Shape, Form, and Space		1 day	1 day	1 day	1 day
Lesson 6 Paper Sculpture Forms			1 day	2 days	2 days
Lesson 7 Texture		1/2 day	1/2 day	1 day	1 day
Lesson 8 Painting a Landscape		1 day	1 day	1 day	2 days
Total		5 days	7 days	9 days	12 days
Chapter 5 *The Principles of Art*					
Lesson 1 The Language of Design		1/2 day	1/2 day	1 day	1 day
Lesson 2 Formal Balance Cityscape		1 day	1 day	1 day	1 day
Lesson 3 Variety, Harmony, Emphasis, and Proportion		1 day	1 day	1 day	1 day
Lesson 4 Abstract Painting			1 day	1 day	2 days
Lesson 5 Movement and Rhythm		1 day	1 day	1 day	1 day
Lesson 6 Creating Visual Movement		1 day	1 day	1 day	2 days
Lesson 7 Unity in Art		1/2 day	1/2 day	1 day	1 day
Total		5 days	6 days	7 days	9 days

	Total Days	6 wk 30 days	9 wk 45 days	18 wk 90 days	36 wk 180 days
Chapter 6 *You, the Art Critic*					
Lesson 1 Describing Art Works		1/2 day	1/2 day	1 day	1 day
Lesson 2 Using Descriptive Techniques		1/2 day	1/2 day	1 day	1 day
Lesson 3 Analyzing Art Works		1 day	1 day	1 day	1 day
Lesson 4 Interpreting Art Works		1 day	1 day	1 day	1 day
Lesson 5 Mood Chalk Painting				1 day	2 days
Lesson 6 Judging Art Works		1 day	1 day	1 day	2 days
Lesson 7 Using Art Criticism		1 day	1 day	1 day	2 days
Total		5 days	5 days	7 days	10 days
Chapter 7 *Art History and You*					
Lesson 1 Describing—Who, When, and Where		1/2 day	1/2 day	1 day	1 day
Lesson 2 Making a Mixed-Media Self-Portrait			1 day	1 day	2 days
Lesson 3 Analyzing Artistic Style		1/2 day	1/2 day	1 day	1 day
Lesson 4 Painting in the Fauve Style			1 day	1 day	2 days
Lesson 5 Interpreting Time and Place		1/2 day	1 day	1 day	2 days
Lesson 6 Time and Place Collage		1 day	1 day	1 day	2 days
Lesson 7 Judging Historical Importance		1/2 day	1 day	1 day	2 days
Total		3 days	6 days	7 days	12 days
Chapter 8 *Drawing*					
Lesson 1 The Art of Drawing		1 day	1 day	1 day	1 day
Lesson 2 Gesture Drawing			1 day	1 day	2 days
Lesson 3 Contour Drawing			1 day	1 day	2 days
Lesson 4 Presentation Drawing				1 day	3 days
Lesson 5 Fantasy Jungle				1 day	3 days
Total		1 day	3 days	5 days	11 days

	Total Days	6 wk 30 days	9 wk 45 days	18 wk 90 days	36 wk 180 days
Chapter 9 *Printmaking*					
Lesson 1 The Art of Printmaking		1 day	1 day	1 day	1 day
Lesson 2 More About Printmaking			1 day	1 day	1 day
Lesson 3 Monoprints			1 day	1 day	1 day
Lesson 4 Glue Prints				1 day	1 day
Lesson 5 Linoleum Block Prints					3 days
Lesson 6 Silk Screen Prints					3 days
Total		1 day	3 days	4 days	10 days
Chapter 10 *Painting*					
Lesson 1 The Art of Painting		1 day	1 day	1 day	1 day
Lesson 2 Watercolor Painting			2 days	1 day	2 days
Lesson 3 Non-objective Painting				1 day	3 days
Lesson 4 Expressive Painting				2 days	4 days
Total		1 day	3 days	5 days	10 days
Chapter 11 *Graphic Design*					
Lesson 1 The Art of Graphic Design			1 day	1 day	1 day
Lesson 2 Designing a Logo			1 day	2 days	2 days
Lesson 3 Drawing a Comic Strip				2 days	3 days
Lesson 4 Designing a Poster					4 days
Lesson 5 Illustrating a Story					4 days
Total			2 days	5 days	14 days
Chapter 12 *Sculpture*					
Lesson 1 The Art of Sculpture				1 day	2 days
Lesson 2 Carving a Plaster Relief				2 days	3 days
Lesson 3 Modeling in Clay				2 days	4 days
Lesson 4 Abstract Sculpture					4 days
Total				5 days	13 days

	Total Days	6 wk 30 days	9 wk 45 days	18 wk 90 days	36 wk 180 days
Chapter 13 *Crafts*					
Lesson 1 The Art of Crafts				1 day	1 day
Lesson 2 Clay Bowl				2 days	3 days
Lesson 3 Slab Container					3 days
Lesson 4 Making a Weaving				3 days	3 days
Lesson 5 Jewelry Art				1 day	2 days
Total				7 days	12 days
Chapter 14 *Architecture*					
Lesson 1 The Art of Architecture				1 day	1 day
Lesson 2 Building a Clay Model				2 days	4 days
Lesson 3 Drawing Floor Plans				2 days	4 days
Lesson 4 Clay Entrance Relief					4 days
Total				5 days	13 days
Chapter 15 *Photography, Film, and Video*					
Lesson 1 The Art of Photography				1 day	1 day
Lesson 2 Making a Photogram				2 days	2 days
Lesson 3 The Art of Film				1 day	1 day
Lesson 4 Making a Silent Movie				3 days	4 days
Lesson 5 The Art of Video				1 day	1 day
Lesson 6 Designing a Video Game					4 days
Total				8 days	13 days
Handbook				10 days	20 days

Scope and Sequence Chart

	Chapter 1 *Art in Your World*	Chapter 2 *Enjoying Art*
Elements and Principles of Art	• Defining **perception** (L1) • Understanding **point of view** (L1) • Artist defined (L2) • **Fine art** vs. **applied art** (L2) • Types of applied art (L2)	• Defining **work of art** (L2) • Introduction of **composition** of elements (L1) • **Elements and principles** related to composition (L1)
Aesthetics/ Art Criticism	• Examining Homer's *Right and Left* (L1) • Examining art works (L2) • Where artists get ideas (L3) • Examining Your Work (L4)	• Identifying **properties of art** (L1) • Defining **non-objective art** (L1) • Introducing **subject, composition, content** (L1) • Reading a **credit line** (L1) • **Aesthetics** defined (L2) • Describing aesthetic views (L2) • **Super-realism** (L2) • Examining Your Work (L3)
Art History	• Learning from artists of the past (L3) • Explaining Greek Muses (L3) • Patrons of the arts (L3)	• Reading the credit line (L1) • Super-realism (L2)
Media and Techniques	• **Collage** defined (L4) • **Titling** a work of art (L4) • Pencil drawing (L1) • Collage materials (L4)	
Studio Production	• Drawing details from a point of view (L1) • Developing an idea bank (L3) • Creating a collage (L4)	• Applying aesthetic views to works of art (L2) • Making a torn paper face (L3)
Safety	• Glue safety (L4)	
Career Exploration	• Patrons of the arts (L3)	
Artists	• Rockwell, Homer (L1) • Miró, Houser (L2) • Wilgus, Dali, Bonheur, Murillo, Willson (L3) • Dvorak (L4)	• Goncharova, Cassatt, Motherwell, Hopper (L1) • Harnett, Hanson, Stella, Cannon (L2) • Manet (L3)

	Chapter 3 *Exploring Art Media*	Chapter 4 *Elements of Art*
Elements and Principles of Art	• Finding 4 colors in a painting (L2) • Dimension of sculpture (L5)	• Introducing **elements of art** (L1) • Examining the color wheel (L2) • Understanding traits of **color** (L2) • Defining types of hue (L2) • Value: tints and shades (L2) • Intensity defined (L2) • Complementary colors defined (L2) • Monochromatic and analogous (L2) • Warm vs. cool colors (L2) • Understanding **line** (L4) • Describing line quality (L4) • Defining the variation (L4) • Describing **shape** (L5) • Defining **form** (L5) • Defining **shape** (L5) • Examining **texture** (L7)
Aesthetics/ Art Criticism	• Identifying **style** (L3) • Examining Your Work (L4, L6) • Explaining different results in painting media (L4)	• Understanding visual language (L1) • Examining Your Work (L3, L6, L8) • How lines affect mood (L4)
Art History	• Köllwitz, social statement in sculpture (L5)	• Cézanne's subjects (L1) • Van Gogh's use of line (L4) • Brancusi's use of shape (L5) • Mondrian's use of the elements of art (L5)
Media and Techniques	• Defining **medium** (L1) • Mixed media defined (L1) • Importance of **drawing** (L1) • Examples of drawing media (L1) • **Printmaking** vs. **reproduction** (L2) • Tools for printmaking (L2) • Steps in printmaking (L2) • Edition defined (L2) • Types of printmaking plates (L2) • Types of **painting** described (L3) • Identifying painters' tools (L3) • Ingredients of paint (L3) • Defining **sculpture** (L5) • 3 dimensional vs. 2 dimensional (L5) • Types of sculptural media (L5) • Sculptor defined (L5) • Freestanding vs. relief (L5) • Describing sculpture types (L5) • Additive vs. subtractive (L5)	
Studio Production	• Drawing a leaf (L1) • Making a gadget print (L2) • Experimenting with pigment (L3, L4) • Creating a freestanding sculpture (L5) • Creating a mixed-media picture (L6)	• Painting tints and shades (L2) • Painting bright and dull colors (L2) • Using complementary colors (L3) • Drawing a continuous line (L4) • Creating a paper sculpture (L6) • Making a multi-texture design (L7) • Painting an unusual landscape (L8)
Safety	• Scissors and knife safety (L5)	
Career Exploration	• How fashion designers, architects and painters use drawing (L4)	
Artists	• Steen, Hopper, Chernow (L1) • Cassatt, Toulouse-Lautrec (L2) • Kandinsky, Manguin, O'Keeffe (L3) • Hopper (L4) • Graves, Köllwitz, Escobar (L5) • Williams (L6)	• Cézanne, Köllwitz, Giacometti (L1) • Schapiro, Orozco (L2) • Murray (L3) • Van Gogh (L4) • Salemme, Dove, Brancusi (L5) • Stella (L6) • Mondrian (L8)

Scope and Sequence Chart

	Chapter 5 *Principles of Art*	Chapter 6 *You, the Art Critic*
Elements and Principles of Art	• Introducing the **principles of art** (L1) • Understanding **balance** (L1) • **Variety** vs. **harmony** (L3) • Defining **emphasis** (L3) • Understanding **proportion** (L3) • Following **movement** (L5) • Feeling **rhythm** (L5) • Defining **unity** (L7) • Using a design chart (L7)	• Describing art works (L1) • Describing elements (L1) • Analyzing art works (L3) • Judging art works (L6)
Aesthetics/ Art Criticism	• Interpreting balance (L1) • Examining Your Work (L2, L6) • Seeing the principles of art in a painting (L6) • Seeing how visual movement is created in art (L6)	• Defining **art criticism** (L1) • Steps in art criticism (L1) • **Describing** defined (L1) • Describing objective and non-objective art works (L1) • Examining Your Work (L2, L5) • **Analyzing** art works (L3) • **Interpreting** art works (L4) • Ways of **judging** art works (L6) • Criticizing Wyeth's *Christina's World* (L7)
Art History	• Examining *Poor Man's Cotton* (L1) • Balance: Monastery of Oliva (L1) • Balance: Sittow's *Assumption* (L1) • Glackens's emphasis (L1) • O'Keeffe's use of elements (L1) • Matisse's use of color (L3) • Kandinsky's harmony (L3) • Pater's emphasis (L3) • Emphasis of Daddi, Jawlensky (L3) • Gwathmey's use of proportion (L4) • Boccioni's movement (L5) • Lawrence's harmony (L6)	• Examining Raphael's *St. George and the Dragon* (L2) • Analyzing *St. Martin and the Beggar* (L3) • Pollack's use of elements (L4)
Media and Techniques		
Studio Production	• Creating a formal balance city scene (L2) • Using the principles of art in an abstract painting (L4) • Creating patterns of movement and rhythm in a drawing (L5) • Using visual rhythm in a construction paper design (L6)	• Describing your own art work (L1) • Extending Raphael's *St. George and the Dragon* (L2) • Analyzing line in a photo (L3) • Creating a chalk painting (L5)
Safety		• Avoid inhaling chalk dust (L5)
Career Exploration		
Artists	• Woodruff, Sittow, Glackens (L1) • O'Keeffe (L2) • Matisse, Kandinsky, Pater, Daddi, Jawlensky (L3) • Gwathmey (L4) • Boccioni, Johns (L5) • Lawrence (L6) • Van Gogh (L7)	• Morisot, de Hooch, Hartigan (L1) • Raphael (L2) • El Greco, Resnick (L3) • De Hooch (L4) • Ryder (L5) • Estes, Panton, Hepworth (L6) • Wyeth (L7)

Scope and Sequence Chart

	Chapter 7 *Art History and You*	Chapter 8 *Drawing*
Elements and Principles of Art	• Using elements of art in a self-portrait (L2) • Using elements of art in Impressionist style (L3) • Using elements in imitating Fauve style (L4) • Using principles of art in a collage (L6)	• Importance of drawing (L1) • Use of line in contour drawing (L3) • Using elements and principles in designing a gate (L4) • Using elements and principles in designing a jungle (L5)
Aesthetics/ Art Criticism	• Examining Your Work (L2, L4, L6) • Art historian vs. art critic (L1) • Expressing personality in a self-portrait (L2) • Analyzing artistic style (L3) • Judging for technique (L7)	• Examining Your Work (L2, L3, L4, L5) • Improving **perception** (L1) • Choosing a theme (L7)
Art History	• Defining art history (L1) • Art critics vs. art historians (L1) • Steps used by art historians (L1) • How art historians **describe** art (L1) • **Analyzing** an artist's style (L3) • **Art movement** defined (L3) • Describing the **Fauves** (L3) • Introducing **Impressionism** (L3) • **Interpreting** style and subject (L5) • **Renaissance** (L5) • Madonna defined (L5) • Artists role in Renaissance (L5) • **Judging** historical importance (L7) • Judging style and technique (L7) • Giotto's Madonnas vs. traditional (L7)	• Calles's shadows (L1) • Rembrandt's action (L2)
Media and Techniques	• **Collage** defined (L6) • **Technique** defined (L7)	• Three uses of drawing (L1) • Improving perception (L1) • Planning projects (L1) • Making a finished art work (L1) • **Shading** defined (L1) • Basic **shading** techniques (L1) • Understanding **gesture drawing** (L2) • **Contour drawing** defined (L3) • **Presentation drawing** defined (L4)
Studio Production	• Making a mixed-media portrait (L2) • Imitating Impressionist style (L3) • Creating a Fauve style painting (L4) • Making a time and place collage (L6)	• Creating shaded rectangles (L1) • Making gesture drawings (L2) • Creating contour drawings (L3) • Making a presentation drawing (L4) • Creating a fantasy jungle (L5)
Safety		• Water vs. permanent markers (L4)
Career Exploration		
Artists	• Picasso, Inness, Renoir (L1) • Leyster (L2) • Cropsey, Derain, Renoir, De Vlaminck, Monet (L3) • Matisse (L4) • White, Degas, Vigée-Lebrun, Raphael, Lippi (L5) • Braque (L6) • Giotto, Seurat, Epstein (L7)	• Calle, da Vinci, Goncharova (L1) • Rembrandt, Vigée-Lebrun (L2) • Gris (L3) • Mills (L4) • Rousseau (L5)

Scope and Sequence Chart

	Chapter 9 *Printmaking*	Chapter 10 *Painting*
Elements and Principles of Art	• Using elements and principles of art in a monoprint (L3) • Using elements and principles of art in screen printing (L6)	• Comparing paint hues (L1) • Using line and color in a painting (L2) • Delaunay's use of color and rhythm (L3) • Working with shapes (L3) • Using color and line to express mood (L4)
Aesthetics/ Art Criticism	• Examining Your Work (L3, L4, L6) • Interpreting Munch's *The Kiss* (L2)	• Examining Your Work (L2, L3, L4) • Using social issues as subject matter (L4) • Expressive painting (L4)
Art History	• History of printmaking (L1) • Dürer, Hokusai prints (L1) • Examining Lee's serigraph (L2) • Stayton's *Yellow Promenade* (L3)	• History of painting (L1) • Encaustic used by Greeks and Romans (L1) • Delaunay's use of color (L3) • Examining Neel's social statement (L4)
Media and Techniques	• **Printmaking** defined (L1) • **Brayer** defined (L1) • Describing a print **edition** (L1) • Techniques of printmaking (L2) • **Relief** printmaking described (L2) • **Intaglio** technique explained (L2) • **Engraving** vs. **etching** (L2) • **Lithography** explained (L2) • Introducing **screen printing** (L2) • Defining serigraph (L2) • **Monoprinting** described (L3)	• Ingredients of paint (L1) • Describing painting media (L1) • **Encaustic** (L1) • **Fresco** (L1) • **Tempera** (L1) • **Oil Paint** (L1) • **Acrylic** (L1) • Synthetic paint defined (L1) • **Water Color** (L1) • Palette defined (L1)
Studio Production	• Making a letter stamp print (L2) • Creating a monoprint (L3) • Making a glue print (L4) • Cutting a linoleum block print (L5) • Making a silk screen print (L6)	• Creating a paint comparison display (L1) • Painting a Kingman style watercolor (L2) • Making a non-objective painting (L3) • Creating an expressive painting (L4)
Safety	• Using linoleum blades (L5)	
Career Exploration		
Artists	• Dürer, Hokusai (L1) • Munch, Lee (L2) • Stayton (L3) • Picasso (L5) • Warhol (L6)	• Thomas, Rivera, Wyeth, Fontana, Homer, Siquieros, Hockney (L1) • Kingman (L2) • Delaunay (L3) • Neel (L4)

Scope and Sequence Chart

	Chapter 11 *Graphic Design*	Chapter 12 *Sculpture*
Elements and Principles of Art	• Using elements and principles of art to design a logo (L2) • Using line and shape to add rhythm (L3) • Using elements and principles of art in illustration (L5)	• Hogue: creating feeling of space (L1) • Blending elements and principles of art for action (L1) • Using elements and principles of art to design flowers (L2) • Examining Clodion's sculpture (L2) • Adding texture to sculpture (L3)
Aesthetics/ Art Criticism	• Examining Your Work (L2, L3, L4, L5) • Promoting products (L1) • Examining style (L4)	• Examining Your Work (L2, L3) • Studying O'Keeffe's flowers (L3) • Capturing the personality in sculpture (L3) • **Abstract art** defined (L4)
Art History	• Graphic design in the 1500s (L1) • Colonial sign makers (L1) • Toulouse-Lautrec: combining words and pictures (L1) • Sign making (L1) • Explaining comic strips (L3) • Examining Wyeth's illustration (L5)	• The beginning of sculpting (L1) • Examining Moore's *Family Group* (L1) • Carpeaux: *Neopolitan Fisherboy* (L1) • Great Sphinx (L1) • Effect of background: Nevelson (L1) • Chinese casting (L1)
Media and Techniques	• **Graphic artist** defined (L1) • Defining **logo** (L2) • Explaining **comic strips** (L3) • Art media used by illustrators (L3) • Collage materials (L1)	• Introducing basic techniques of sculpting (L1) • **Carving** (L1) • **Casting** (L1) • **Modeling** (L1) • **Assembling** (L1) • Addition vs. subtraction (L1) • **Relief sculpture** defined (L2) • **Low relief** vs. **high relief** (L2) • **Freestanding** defined (L3) • **Slip** defined (L3) • **Abstract art** defined (L4)
Studio Production	• Making a typeface collage (L1) • Designing a logo (L2) • Creating a comic strip (L3) • Designing a poster (L4) • Illustrating a story (L5)	• Carving a plaster relief (L2) • Modeling a clay animal (L3) • Creating an abstract sculpture (L4)
Safety	• Choosing watercolor markers (L2)	• Using a safety mask for dust (L2) • Spray painting outdoors (L4)
Career Exploration	• Using media in commercial art (L1) • Exploring the field of **graphic design** • **Editorial design** (L1) • **Illustration** (L1) • **Advertising design** (L1) • **Sign making** (L1)	
Artists	• Bourke-White, Brady, Lange, Stieglitz (L1) • MacNelly, Schulz (L3) • Moscoso (L4) • Wyeth (L5)	• Moore, Hogue, Carpeaux, Smith, Nevelson (L1) • O'Keeffe (L2) • Clodion (L3) • Gabo (L4)

Scope and Sequence Chart

	Chapter 13 *Crafts*	Chapter 14 *Architecture*
Elements and Principles of Art	• Examining Tafoya's pottery (L2) • Decorating with pattern (L2) • Using texture and color in weaving (L4) • Using elements and principles of art in designing jewelry (L5)	• Using elements and principles of art in architecture (L1) • Proportion of Greek temples (L1) • Line and balance in Europe 1200s and 1300s (L1) • Using elements and principles of art to design a shopping mall (L3) • Using value and texture in design (L4)
Aesthetics/ Art Criticism	• Examining Your Work (L2, L3, L4) • Harmonizing jewelry with the wearer (L5)	• Examining Your Work (L2, L3, L4) • Feeling openness in church (L1) • Examining Wright's museum (L1) • Goals of architecture (L1) • Creating an ideal setting (L1) • Designing an entrance (L4)
Art History	• **Craftsperson** defined (L1) • Pottery in ancient times (L1) • Early weaving (L1)	• The first architects (L1) • Greek Temples (L1) • Roman architecture (L1) • Sullivan: modern architecture (L1) • Wright: famous modern architecture (L1)
Media and Techniques	• Defining **crafts** (L1) • Introducing **weaving** (L1) • Weaving fiber on a **loom** (L1) • **Warp** vs. **weft** (L1) • **Ballooning** defined (L4) • **Glassmaking** described (L1) • Glassblowing defined (L1) • **Ceramics** described (L1) • **Pottery** defined (L1) • Conditions of clay (L1) • **Pinching** vs. **coiling** or **slab building** (L1) • **Greenware** vs. **bisqueware** (L1) • **Throwing** and **firing** clay (L1) • Defining **glaze** (L1) • Clay and materials (L1)	• **Architecture** defined (L1) • Purposes of architecture (L1) • Structures for **prayer** (L1) • Structures for **business** (L1) • Structures for **recreation** (L1) • **Basilica** defined (L1) • **Amphitheater** defined (L1) • **Post and lintel** defined (L2) • Floor plan described (L2) • **Elevation** defined (L2) • **Facade** defined (L2)
Studio Production	• Making a clay bowl using the pinch method (L2) • Designing a slab cylinder (L3) • Making a weaving (L4) • Creating a piece of jewelry (L5)	• Sketching a building and setting (L1) • Building a clay model (L2) • Drawing a floor plan (L3) • Creating a clay entrance relief (L4)
Safety	• Choosing a nontoxic glaze (L2) • Using polyurethane sprays (L5)	
Career Exploration		
Artists	• Garrison, Weaver, Mann, Keats, Tiffany, Kimiko, Owens (L1) • Tafoya, Nampeyo (L2) • Pleak (L3) • Scanlin (L4) • Lee, Weaver (L5)	• Sullivan, Wright (L1)

Chapter 15
Photography, Film, and Video

Elements and Principles of Art	• Using elements and principles of art in designing a photogram (L2) • Cinematography: use of light and color (L3) • Planning a film (L4) • Using color and sound effects (L5)
Aesthetics/ Art Criticism	• Examining Your Work (L3, L4, L6) • Expressing mood in a design (L2) • Effects in film (L3) • Planning a film (L4)
Art History	• Understanding a photo of Ghandi (L1) • History of photography (L1) • Describing the first film (L3) • History of video games (L5)
Media and Techniques	• **Photography** defined (L1) • Describing **daguerreotypes** (L1) • The **wet-plate** method (L1) • **Negative** defined (L1) • **Calotype** defined (L1) • Describing a **photogram** (L1) • Introducing **film** (L3) • **Motion picture** defined (L3) • Describing the **director, producer** and **cinematographer** (L3) • Adding sound and color to film (L5) • Defining **video game** (L5) • Designing video games (L5)
Studio Production	• Making a photogram (L2) • Making a silent film (L4) • Designing a video game (L6)
Safety	• Avoiding ammonia fumes (L2)
Career Exploration	
Artists	• Bourke-White, Daguerre, Brady, Lange, Steiglitz (L1) • Talbot (L2) • Griffith, Lang, Welles, Burton (L3) • Lloyd (L4)

Scope and Sequence Chart

Handbook

Aesthetics/ Art Criticism

- Examining Your Work (L1, L2, L3, L4, L5, L6, L7, L8, L9)

Technique Tips

Drawing Tips
- Making gesture drawings
- Making contour drawings
- Drawing with oil paints
- Drawing thin brush lines
- Making an enlarging grid
- Using shading techniques
- Using sighting techniques
- Using a viewing frame
- Using a ruler

Painting Tips
- Cleaning a paint brush
- Making natural earth pigments
- Mixing paint: value and color
- Working with poster paints
- Working with watercolors

Printmaking Tip
- Making a stamp printing

Sculpting Tips
- Working with clay
- Joining clay
- Making a clay mold
- Mixing plaster
- Working with papier mâché
- Making a paper sculpture

Other Tips
- Measuring rectangles
- Making a mat
- Mounting a two-dimensional work
- Making rubbings
- Scoring paper
- Making a tissue paper collage
- Working with glue

Studio Production

- Designing gift wrap (L1)
- Creating an action painting (L2)
- Creating a wall mural (L3)
- Making a cityscape (L4)
- Designing a banner (L5)
- Constructing a wire sculpture (L6)
- Creating a freestanding mobile (L7)
- Painting to tell a story (L8)
- Building a pinhole camera (L9)

Safety

- Safely working with wire (L6)
- Using spray paint safely (L9)

Career Exploration

- Advertising artist, animator, architect, corporate art adviser, art director for performing arts, art teacher, art therapist, city planner, display designer, fashion designer, interior designer, industrial designer, landscape designer, museum curator

Artists

- Cassatt, Dürer, Homer, Hopper, Kandinsky, Matisse, O'Keeffe, Picasso, Raphael, Renoir, Toulouse-Lautrec, van Gogh, Vigée-Lebrun, Wyeth

Designing a Quality Art Program

Teachers need to be keenly aware and responsive to the physical, intellectual, and social-emotional development of the middle school student in order to appropriately plan for instruction. The following strategies are suggested to help the teacher organize the chapters and lessons in the order that best meets the needs of their students.

- **Set goals.** The key to a quality art program is knowing your students and then deciding what you want them to learn. The Pacing Chart and the Scope and Sequence Chart in *Exploring Art* highlight topical emphases and suggest sequential development of material. In addition *Exploring Art* outlines specific objectives at the beginning of each chapter, which tells students what they will be learning. Teachers need to plan specific objectives to meet the general goals of a quality art education program. It is best if the objectives are behaviorally written. Use the curriculum guides developed by your school, school district, and/or state to create your own specific program.

- **Create lessons that divide the entire period.** Subdivide the time available for classroom instruction into a number of modules. These modules can vary in length and will of course, depend on the activity to be completed. For example, introduce a new concept through slides or give a short demonstration, give an assignment, have students participate in a summary of the lesson, and assign a homework assignment before dismissing the class.

- **Offer a concise and clearly formulated structure for all activities.** Students must know exactly what is required of them for each specific activity. Give them as many "clues" as possible; for example, write instructions on the board, have them repeat your directions, give a handout, show a completed example, and so on. Do not assume that students can see the interrelationships between steps. Give students detailed step-by-step instructions and then show them how the steps are connected.

- **Provide variety within the class time.** Variety is achieved by having the various phases of the art program accomplished within the given period.

For instance, the lesson can include slides or a portion of a video combined with a studio production activity and concluding with class discussion. You must recognize that providing variety maintains student enthusiasm and interest.

- **Give explanations for each activity.** Students must know what they can expect to learn from a certain activity.

- **Provide motivation and readiness techniques.** Once students know what is expected of them, you must make an extra effort to provide motivational techniques to get students involved in the lesson focus. In his book *Emphasis Art* (1985), Wachowiak suggests the following motivational resources:
  — Reproductions of paintings, sculpture, prints, and crafts that can supplement, illuminate, and intensify the objectives of the lesson.
  — Photographs, in color or black and white, that can extend the students' visual repertoire of experiences.
  — Color slides of paintings, drawings, sculpture, prints, architecture, and crafts; of design elements in nature and constructed objects; of creative work by children worldwide; of examples illustrating technical stages in a project; of people in active work, in sports, and in costume; and of animals, birds, fish, insects, and flowers.
  — Filmstrips and video tapes on artists, art history, and art techniques.
  — Films, TV films, and tapes that relate to the art project undertaken.
  — Books (stories, plays, poems, and biographies) and periodicals that can help both teachers and students toward a richer interpretation of the art project undertaken.
  — Recordings (disk or tape) of music, dramatizations, poetry, sounds of geographic regions—city and country, nature's forces, forest and jungle—and sounds of machines, planes, ships, trains, rockets, circuses, and amusement centers.
  — Guests invited to art class as inspiration, such as police officers, fire fighters, and nurses; performers such as clowns, dancers, pantomimists, and musicians with their

instruments; and scuba divers, pilots, athletes in uniform, and, if possible, an astronaut outfit.

— Resource and sketching trips to science, natural, and historical museums; art museums; university and college art studios; farms; factories; wharves; airports; observatories; bus and train stations; bridge and dam sites; national parks; zoos; shopping malls; boat marinas; air shows; amusement parks; and historical monuments. Be sure field trips are planned in advance. Visit the sketching site beforehand, if possible, to check on hazards and permits. Clear permission with the school principal so that parental approval can be obtained and travel arrangements can be expedited. If necessary, arrange for parent chaperones.

— Models for art-class drawing projects may include animals, birds and fish, flowers and plant life, dried fall weeds, beehives, bird's nests, insect and butterfly collections, terrariums, pets, rocks and pebbles, fossils, coral, seaweed and seashells, skeletons of animals, and assorted still-life material: fruits and vegetables, including gourds; lanterns; kettles; teapots; vases; old clocks; bottles; fish net; old lamps; assorted fabrics for drapery; musical instruments; bicycles and motorcycles; and old hats, shoes, and gloves. Vintage automobiles can be sketched in school parking lots.

— Artifacts from other cultures and countries: masks, wood carvings, costumes, textiles, ceramics, toys, dolls, puppets, kites, armor, fans, and paper umbrellas.

— Examples of children's art in varied media from worldwide sources.

— Demonstrations of art techniques by teacher and students.

— Introduction of a new art material or tool or a new use for commonly employed art materials.

— Planned exhibits and bulletin board displays that relate to the art project in process.

— Assorted devices and equipment to help expand the students' awareness and visual horizons: microscopes, prisms, kaleidoscopes, touch-me kinetics, magnifiers, color machines, liquid light lamps, telescopes, microscopic projectors, computers, mirrors, and black light.

- **Use recall and transition strategies.** Help students connect material they have already learned with new material. Open-ended questions are a particularly effective technique. An effective lesson for pupils is to provide several activities designed to accomplish an objective. For example, if students were to learn about van Gogh, show a video about his art; have them study about the time period and cultural context of his life; have them learn about color, color mixing, and painting techniques by viewing his art; and then maybe have them create a painting in his style or of a similar subject matter.

- **Within the class structure, be flexible.** Middle school/junior high art teachers are most often structured and organized. They spend a great deal of time preparing challenging art lessons, but they need to be flexible. Sometimes it may be necessary to reteach a concept, or a conflict may arise, or some interesting question is asked that needs further exploration. Be flexible within the prescribed time limits.

- **In the concept development process, move from concrete to abstract.** Always begin with the specific or concrete examples, and then move to the more abstract, general, or theoretical. Concrete examples are exact and can often be something students can touch—a reproduction of an art work, a model, an advertisement, various media, or objects.

- **Ask effective questions to reach the objectives of each lesson.** Teachers should refine their questioning techniques. In preparation for teaching, plan several key stimulating questions that serve to promote students' critical thinking skills and to maintain student interest. You may want to evaluate your questions by asking:
  — Do the questions I ask elicit concepts?
  — Are the questions focused on the lesson objectives?
  — Are they clear?
  — Do I ask questions only one time?
  — Do the questions promote critical thinking skills?
  — Do I wait enough time after asking each question?

- **Provide an evaluation or summary.** There should be a summary at the end of each activity and also at the end of the class. You should help students see what they learned during the lesson and prepare them for the next step. This also provides an opportunity for students to ask questions.

Creating a Positive Learning Environment

Exploring Art provides a variety of activities to help the teacher create a positive learning environment and to support the concepts presented in the text. You will need to select those activities that best suit your teaching methods and the needs, and interests, maturity level, and artistic abilities of your students.

The following suggestions can help art teachers structure the classroom to create a positive learning environment for all students.

- Accept students as they are and encourage students to reach their maximum level of potential.
- Become familiar in detail with the specific learning styles of your students and employ media that will help them achieve success.
- Find out about the students' previous art education programs.
- If possible, obtain assistance from a teacher's aide to help with individual or organizational problems that may occur in the art classroom.
- Art teachers are often required to write and implement an individualized educational plan for students with special needs. Find out if this is the case in your school.

Teaching Students with Varying Ability Levels and Learning Styles

In most art classrooms there is a wide range of ability levels and learning styles. It becomes critical that teachers identify the various abilities within the classroom and adapt instructional materials to meet the needs. Below are additional suggestions for teaching students with varying ability levels and learning styles.

The Hearing Impaired
- Learn sign language—at least a few basic words.
- Use the chalkboard or other visuals to highlight key art concepts, vocabulary words, or terms.
- Give the students your lecture notes or ask a good student to make copies of his or her notes.
- Speak normally and look directly at a hearing-impaired student when you are speaking.

- Write instructions for activities on the chalkboard, or hand out written instructions.
- Encourage as much verbal interaction as possible.

The Visually Impaired
- Emphasize art experiences that promote kinesthetic manipulation and multisensory stimulation.
- Assign student helpers.
- Provide opportunities for students to tape-record assignments or to complete them orally.
- Tape-record each chapter of the textbook for the students' use.
- Administer tests orally.
- Let students move around the art classroom freely so that they can get close to displays or three-dimensional visuals located in the room.

The Learning Disabled
- Provide an organized environment.
- Make expectations and directions clear and realistic.
- Give large amounts of positive reinforcement that indicate the students' strengths.
- Encourage small-group participation.
- Encourage students to participate in discussions.
- Avoid assigning these students to seats around distracting students.
- Provide positive feedback whenever possible.

The Physically Challenged
- If necessary, rearrange the classroom to accommodate the students' needs.
- Encourage these students to participate in physical activities whenever possible.
- Allow sufficient time for completion of a task.
- Plan studio projects that can be broken down into sequential and manageable tasks.

The Gifted and Talented
- Be patient and nurture these youths' playfulness because this contributes to their cognitive development.

- Avoid overstructuring of tasks and time for gifted students; they need the freedom to come up with solutions.
- Demand and challenge these students. It is always good to give verbal positive reinforcement, but they should work for it.
- Encourage students to think about and use metaphors in their art work.
- Establish an art honorary society as an effective way for gifted students to receive special recognition.
- Expose these students to quality art work created by others. Do not let these students be content to compare their work with that of peers.
- The general consensus regarding teaching the gifted is to let them work independently. So-called gifted students should be given the same assignments the other students are given, but they should be challenged to stretch the possibilities of the assigned project or theme to the fullest.

The Limited-English Proficiency Student

Students with limited English proficiency may not have problems with mastering art content. Their difficulty may be only with the English language. The following teaching strategies will help you provide a welcoming positive learning environment:

- Allow students to become familiar with the structure of English. Even if students make grammatical mistakes, praise their efforts. Provide a classroom environment in which students can experiment with English.
- Students can often understand more than they can say. Students may be able to construct simple sentences but have difficulty with idioms, figures of speech, and words with multiple meanings. Take time to explain yourself, or involve the other students in the explanation.
- If you assign art reports or other writing assignments, expect to see a mixture of English with their native language. Bear in mind that at this stage, helping an adolescent gain confidence

and building self-esteem are valuable educational goals.
- Provide peer learning by grouping English-proficient students with students who have a limited proficiency. Encourage students to work in small groups or in pairs to teach one another various art skills.

Teaching Art to Students From All Cultural Backgrounds

Art teachers are faced with the challenge of teaching art and all its cultural contexts to a changing wide range of ethnic groups. Art teachers respect and appreciate ethnic diversity and whenever possible should adapt teaching strategies, curriculum content, and the classroom environment to best meet individual student's needs. The teacher should be committed to multicultural education and to a culturally pluralistic view. In cultural pluralism people with different ethnic backgrounds retain many of their cultural traditions but also adapt to predominant North American social values, the English language, and many other aspects of life. Within this view people can possess their particular ethnic perspective and still identify with the general policies of this society.

A quality multicultural-sensitive art program should begin to help students do the following:

- Celebrate the diversity of individuals and cultures as seen through their art.
- Understand different world views and concepts expressed through art in various cultures.
- Understand how the cultural mores affect art.
- Understand the different subcultures within a core culture and explore the differences in the ways those subcultures express themselves through art.
- Understand the roles of artists in different cultures.
- Understand how art affects changes within a culture and also how it sometimes maintains the status quo.
- Understand how the physical environment has affected the visual arts.

- Understand the support (for example, financial, educational, and so on) given for the visual arts and the impact made within a culture.
- Help students make connections with other subjects (such as social studies, religion, history, or economics).
- Understand both *what* art is and *why* it was made.

The following are some sample activities that could be used in getting students to explore cultural contexts:

- Visit an art museum and have students pretend they are cultural anthropologists. They could work individually or in a group. Have them pick three or four art works and compare them and the cultures they represent.
- Have students pick a theme such as nature, color, religion, wooden objects, life/death, utility and find related works of art through library research or by visiting a museum. Ask students to compare and contrast the expressions of the theme in the various works.
- Have students pick a particular aspect of one culture and compare it with the same aspect of another culture. For example, students could compare the fiber arts of two cultures.

Below is a series of specific questions that can be helpful in exploring the cultural contexts of art works.

- What are the ideas, emotions, values, and/or qualities being transmitted through the art work?
- What does the work tell the viewer about the person who created it (that is, rank, status or role in his or her culture)?
- What does this piece tell the viewer about the culture it was created in?
- Does the art work tell the viewer anything about the style of the culture?
- Is the art form now extinct?
- Is the art considered popular, traditional, or avant-garde?
- Was this art produced because of ethnic revitalization or simply as an economic response to the perceived desires of the consumer?
- Was this work an innovation? If so, why did it come about?

- Why would one culture put more emphasis on the shape of a bowl, another on the pictorial decoration, another on size, another on texture, and so on?
  1. Does this difference indicate specific availability of materials, knowledge of tools, or specific needs of their personal, social, or religious life?
  2. Are these differences related to date, climate, or trade patterns?
  3. To what degree do differences depend on the skills and dedication of the individual artist?
- What evidence can be found that one culture has learned from (been acculturated with) another culture?
  1. Is there a similarity in utilitarian objects or pictorial subject matter?
  2. Is there a similarity in the treatment of materials?
  3. Is there a similarity in emphasis on the depiction of the human figure or of other subject matter?

Teaching Critical Thinking in the Art Classroom

Helping students to think critically is one of the major goals of education. Critical thinking can be defined generally as the process of logically deciding what to do, create, or believe.

Creative thinking requires the ability to identify and formulate problems, as well as the ability to generate alternative solutions. Fluency (quality of ideas), flexibility (variety of ideas), originality (unusual or unique ideas), and elaboration (details for the implementation of ideas) are necessary components of creative thinking.

The following assumptions underlie the teaching of thinking:

- All students are capable of higher-level thinking.
- Thinking skills can be taught and learned in the art classroom.
- Appropriate expectations for logical thinking are based on physiological maturation, social experiences, and the knowledge level of the students.

- Students can be taught to transfer thinking skills from the art content area to an internalized process applicable to a variety of new learning.

How do you teach thinking skills in the art classroom? Teachers need to reflect on their instructional strategies used in daily art lessons and include opportunities for students to reason and think about what is being learned.

Bloom's taxonomy is generally the most widely recognized scheme for levels of thinking. Each of Bloom's categories includes a list of various thinking skills. Here are some examples:

- **Knowledge:** define, recognize, recall, identify, label, understand, examine, show, collect.
- **Comprehension:** translate, interpret, explain, describe, summarize.
- **Application:** apply, solve, experiment, show, predict.
- **Analysis:** connect, relate, differentiate, classify, arrange, check, group, distinguish, organize, categorize, detect, compare, infer.
- **Synthesis:** produce, propose, design, plan, combine, formulate, compose, hypothesize, construct.
- **Evaluation:** appraise, judge, criticize, decide.

The art class is a fertile content area to help students develop critical and creative thinking skills. Begin by knowing the cognitive level of the students in your classroom and realize that not all questions or interactions need to be initiated by the teacher. Dialogue among peers is a way to promote critical thinking. Having students discuss, debate, explain, decide, or creatively solve problems increases critical thinking skills. Encourage students to generate answers to solve their own problems, create their own projects, and be responsible for their own learning.

The following are some examples of critical thinking questions:

- **Knowledge**—the identification and recall of information:
  — Who, what, when, where, how . . . ?
  — Describe an art work.
- **Comprehension**—the organization and selection of facts and ideas:
  — Retell in your own words . . .
  — What is the main idea of . . . ?
  — Create an art work that demonstrates . . .

- **Application**—the use of facts, rules, principles:
  — How is . . . an example of . . . ?
  — How is . . . related to . . . ?
  — Demonstrate through . . . art activity . . .
- **Analysis**—the separation of a whole into component parts:
  — What are the parts or features of . . . ?
  — Classify . . . according to . . .
  — How does . . . compare/contrast with . . . ?
- **Synthesis**—the combination of ideas to form a new whole:
  — Construct a . . .
  — What would you predict/infer from . . . ?
  — What might happen if you combined . . . with . . . ?
  — Design a . . .
- **Evaluation**—the development of opinions, judgments, or decisions:
  — What do you think about . . . ?
  — Prioritize . . .
  — Criticize this art work.

Implementing Cooperative Learning

In the same way that society is made up of groups such as sports teams, families, and political parties, learning in the classroom is most effective when students cooperate to achieve a common goal within an art lesson.

Cooperative learning is when students are assigned to work in small heterogeneous groups of four or five. Student groups are chosen by the teacher. The major difference between cooperative learning and traditional group projects is that the completion of a project and mastery of a lesson are dependent upon each student's contributions to the team effort. When graded, each group is given a team score based on an average of each individual's grade.

The recognition of teams that clearly meet the goals and criteria set by the teacher is an important aspect of cooperative learning. Students that are lazy cannot easily get by with utilization of this teaching strategy. The situation is designed so that the *group* may achieve recognition and success as a team—individual members encourage each other to complete the specific tasks at hand.

Cooperative learning is an ideal strategy to employ in the art classroom. Not only are the learning experiences effective with studio activities, but they can also be used to teach art history, art criticism, and aesthetic concepts.

Relating Art to Other Content Areas

Interdisciplinary teaching is central to the middle school/junior high concept. Efforts to integrate and interrelate the many areas of the school curriculum have a long history and are supported by a large amount of research. Interdisciplinary programs are organized in many different ways and involve various degrees of curriculum integration. Below is a listing of a few ways that art teachers can encourage and participate in such approaches.

- **Total staff approach.** This involves a school-wide theme approach to interdisciplinary learning. In this format art teachers must seek ways to relate both instruction and curriculum to the chosen theme.
- **Interdisciplinary teams.** Having an interdisciplinary event or course of study undertaken by a team of three to five teachers is the approach used most often. Because few teachers have been prepared for this type of planning and teaching, the following list of steps outlined in *Interdisciplinary Teaching in the Middle Grades*, (1990) by Gordon F. Vars, may be helpful.
  1. Review goals and objectives for that grade level and/or subjects.
  2. Review curriculum scope and sequence. Determine degree of flexibility.
  3. Determine the type of interdisciplinary unit that will be attempted: correlated, fused, or purely problem-centered without restriction as to subjects covered.
  4. Brainstorm themes, topics, or problem areas that: (a) fit the given curriculum, (b) are interdisciplinary, and (c) appear to be relevant to students.
  5. Seek student reactions and input.
  6. Select one or two themes, topics, or problem areas for further development.
  7. Explore the contributions of each subject area to the unit, including pertinent content, skills, and learning activities.
  8. Develop an overall framework or outline for the unit.
  9. Locate learning materials and other sources. Invite students to help.
  10. Plan procedures for evaluating student learnings.
  11. Determine logistics:
      a. Time frame; full-time or part-time each day?
      b. Student groupings.
      c. Rooms and other facilities needed.
      d. Equipment needed.
  12. Carry out the unit, seeking student involvement along the way and at its conclusion.
  13. Evaluate the unit.

- **Self-contained and block-time classes.** This approach gives one teacher responsibility for the so-called academic subjects, with students traveling to art and other similar classes. Whenever possible, art teachers should work with self-contained classroom teachers to interrelate appropriate content. Block-time teachers should also work closely with art teachers to make connections whenever possible.

There are basically three ways to interrelate different subject areas.

- **Correlation.** Correlation arises out of cooperative planning among teachers even if they are not officially members of a team. Correlation only requires that teachers try to present related material at the same time. Through merely a change in the sequence of their materials, students can benefit from reinforcement of learning. This approach shows students how various subjects are related.
- **Fusion.** Fusion, or unified studies, as it is sometimes referred to, is often organized around a theme. For example, a class called "World History" may be offered, which would include art, music, literature, and dance.
- **Core.** Core is a type of curriculum that focuses on helping students deal with their immediate problems or issues of significance to them.

Both students and their teachers vary in their needs and characteristics, so schools should use a variety of approaches. Art teachers need to be aware of the various approaches and actively participate in the interdisciplinary process.

Teachers or teams inevitably develop interdisciplinary units in their own unique ways, but they can benefit from examining units developed by others. Teachers are urged to keep informed of new developments through reading professional journals and attending workshops and conferences.

A few sources especially appropriate for middle school teachers are described below:

1. National Resource Center for Middle Grades Education, University of South Florida, EDU 115, Tampa, FL 33620. Reproducible interdisciplinary units available for purchase. Write for current list. As new units become available, they are announced in the Resource Center's newsletter, *Middle Grades Network*.

2. National Association for Core Curriculum, Inc. 404 White Hall, Kent State University, Kent, OH 44242. Units of various lengths are sold at cost.

3. ERIC Document Reproduction Service, Computer Microfilm Corporation, 3900 Wheeler Avenue, Alexandria, VA 22304. Units occasionally appear in this source and are available in either microfiche or photocopy form. Titles are listed in *Resources in Education*, under the descriptor "Teaching Guides (for Teachers)" (052).

4. Association for Supervision and Curriculum Development, 125 North West Street, Alexandria, VA 22314. Resource units and interdisciplinary units occasionally appear among the curriculum materials displayed at the annual ASCD convention.

5. National Middle School Association, 4807 Evanswood Drive, Columbus, Ohio 43229-6292. How to design quality units may be found in their publication.

Providing Sources of Inspiration

Art teachers are generally receptive to a variety of resources that are available to them to help in the development of new units or lesson plans or to augment existing lessons. The following is a list of ideas that may serve as sources of inspiration:

- **Artist-in-residence programs.** These programs provide students with the rare opportunity to witness an artist at work.

- **Arts councils.** Art councils provide many educational programs that may offer unique possibilities.

- **Art teacher associations.** By becoming a member of your state association or the National Art Education Association you will have the opportunity to make interesting contacts. These associations sponsor conferences and seminars that offer a mixture of workshops, visits to schools, lectures, exhibitions, and social events.

- **Museums and galleries.** Both offer the opportunity to view various exhibitions. Museums also often offer educational services, slide presentations, and special docent tours. You can even find interesting inspirational materials in their gift shops.

- **Inservice training.** Many school districts offer special workshops on art education. Organize these yourself; have an idea-sharing session with teachers in your area.

- **Multicultural or cross-cultural experiences.** Learn about or visit an area in North America you are not familiar with, or travel to another country and visit art education programs, museums, and the like there.

- **Environment.** From the natural and human-made environment you can get many ideas.

- **Other.** Book stores, antique shops, junk stores, shopping malls, parks, historic homes, industries (especially those related to the art field), interesting speakers, poetry, music, dance, theatre, and so on.

Evaluating Performance

Many schools require written tests as well as performance grades. Although written tests should be only one part of the total evaluation of the art student's performance, the art teacher should approach testing as creatively as possible. Below are some guidelines to follow if you want to use test items other than those included in this program.

- Always build some success into each test. Place a few simple items that everyone will be able to answer at the beginning of the test. The positive reinforcement received from answering the first questions correctly may overcome students' fear of tests.

- The test items should span a range of cognitive levels instead of being limited to the recall of facts. The following list gives examples related to visual art for each level.
  - **Knowledge:** This level requires the recall of facts, terminology, dates, events, or titles of art works. It also involves the recall of simple processes such as cleaning a brush, mixing colors, and/or classifying works according to style. The highest level of knowledge required is knowledge of universals and abstractions.
  - **Comprehension:** In visual art this level may include diagramming, explaining, summarizing, and/or predicting outcomes.
  - **Application:** This level relates to the proper use of materials. It can be tested, for example, by asking students to describe how to make a glue print or what steps must be followed to join clay.
  - **Analysis:** An example of this level of cognitive learning is the analysis step in art criticism. Analysis can deal with the students' work as well as with reproductions of works by master artists.
  - **Synthesis:** At this level students display their ability to use a combination of concepts or elements to solve a visual problem. This creative level can be tested by asking students to produce designs expressing a particular emotion. Synthesis is much more open-ended than the previous levels. In art, it is usually tested in an art production activity rather than by a verbal problem.
  - **Evaluation:** Critically examining an art work requires judging and giving reasons for the judgment.

By using various cognitive levels in designing tests, you will be able to distinguish the achievement levels of students.

- Keep the reading level of tests low so that you are testing art knowledge and not reading ability. Make your tests as visual as possible, using drawings and reproductions. For example, you can test knowledge of color theory in several ways that do not require reading. You may put three reproductions on a bulletin board, number each work, and ask the students which one contains cool colors. This question is a better test of the student's understanding of cool colors than asking them to name these colors. Ask the students to describe how to change the value of a hue, to use paint to mix a light value of a hue, or to find a magazine picture showing a light value of a specific hue.
- You could also display several reproductions identified with numbers and ask the students to recognize different color concepts by listing which reproduction uses high-intensity colors, which shows a large area with a light value of red, or which uses a complementary color scheme.
- Essay tests require high-level thinking in which students must reorganize knowledge. Be sure to make expectations for the answers clear for these tests. For example, ask for at least four works of art using a technique, or similarities and differences between two artists' works. Ask essay questions about the students' work as well as works of the masters.

Other Evaluation Methods

The following suggestions are based on classroom practices of experienced teachers. Not all of them are appropriate for every situation. Try the ones you think will work for you.

1. Daily participation grades: As the class works, quickly give each student a check in your roll book for satisfactory participation, a check-plus for exceptional work, a check-minus for below average participation, and a minus or zero for inadequate work.
2. Anecdotal records: At the end of the day, take a few minutes to record any outstanding student behavior, either positive or negative.
3. Daily journals: Have students record what they have done in class each day. These journals may be part of the students' notebooks. At the end of the grading period, they will help you

remember what students have accomplished. The entries in the journals do not have to be elaborate. For example, they might be as simple as "I helped Joe mix colors to make a color wheel," or "Continued working on my expressive painting."

4. Performance criteria for creative work: Grading criteria should be planned and explained to students before they start an activity. One way to grade an art work is to assign percentages out of a total of 100 to each item in the "Examining Your Work" feature in the text (plus others you want to add). Although the subjective aspect of grading art cannot be eliminated, it can be reduced by using performance criteria. You might decide to give A's for exceeding objectives, B's for meeting all of them, C's for completing a certain number, and so on.

5. Written evaluations: When you grade major works, whether they are verbal or visual, take the time to write evaluations of strengths and weaknesses.

Finally, remember that students' talent should not influence evaluation. Each student should be graded on his or her specific achievements. A student with little natural ability who struggles to draw a still life should be recognized for his or her effort. However, a talented student who does not finish the assignment or turns in careless work should not be given a high grade. (At the same time, don't penalize the gifted student for being able to produce work in little time.) Since most art classes are a good place to practice mainstreaming, they will often contain students with a wide range of abilities. Tailor your expectations to fit the different levels of your students' capabilities.

Classroom Environment and Management

Although they tend to be taken for granted, a classroom's environment and organization are a part of the instruction process for the art teacher. Teachers working with his junior high students are confronted daily with problems of discipline. By providing an effectively designed physical environment, many problems can be prevented and students will have the opportunity to learn responsible behavior. Researchers in the areas of environmental psychology, architecture, interior space design, communications theory, and sociology have developed a large body of information that can assist the art teacher in guiding environmental decisions. Art teachers need to understand that the spatial arrangement of the art classroom has a major impact, not only on discipline, but also on the effectiveness of teaching in general.

Classroom Organization

Quality art programs continue the traditional studio experiences, which include diverse laboratory activities. Pupils learning about art production need to be provided a safe, comfortable, and organized area in which to work in these various media.

In addition, the classroom needs to be designed so that quality learning outcomes may be achieved in the study of art history, art criticism, and aesthetics. Every art teacher develops her or his own style for organizing, arranging, and effectively using classroom space. The following points are suggested in order to have a quality art education program:

- Organize the room so that there are distinct areas where certain activities always take place.
- Pay attention to the amount of space needed by pupils so that they may work effectively.
- When students are required to clean up by using the sink, the proximity of student work areas should be considered.
- Map out specific procedures to expedite cleanup.
- Cluster storage and work areas so that travel around the room by students is limited.

- Arrange your supplies, and label shelves where materials are to be stored.
- Provide the least restrictive setting for the activities you plan.
- Pay attention to your floor plan—where storage is located and general traffic flows.
- Tell students your classroom rules, such as where supplies are stored, to put away things where they found them, and so on.
- Make sure the desks or tables are arranged so that the teacher can easily view each student.
- Arrange the room so that there is easy movement around the room. Try to prevent congestion around sinks, door, or other areas.
- Emphasize order and respect for equipment and materials; have students apply the "golden rule."
- Have students avoid unnecessary trips around the room. Be clear as to where you want them to be in the room.
- Make sure you can have eye contact with everyone in the class.
- Set up a "home base" location for student tables or desks. If student desks or tables are moved around for a particular activity mark the original location in some way, such as with tape or paint on the floor, so that they can be easily returned.
- Make your room interesting and aesthetically pleasing! A carefully designed room sends a message to students that you care about art and about their learning experiences.
- Have a wide variety of items around your room to make it interesting (for example, plants; shells; fossils; artifacts from other cultures; lots of visuals; still-life materials; interesting garage sale, junk store, or junk yard finds, and so on).

On the following pages are suggested floor plans for a classroom, a darkroom, and storage/kiln room.

Safety in the Classroom

Because there are many potential health hazards in the art classroom, the art teacher must be particularly careful. It is *very important* that every

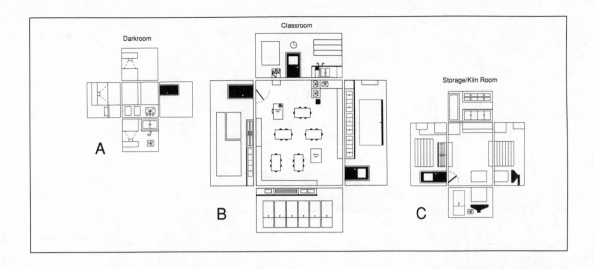

Darkroom

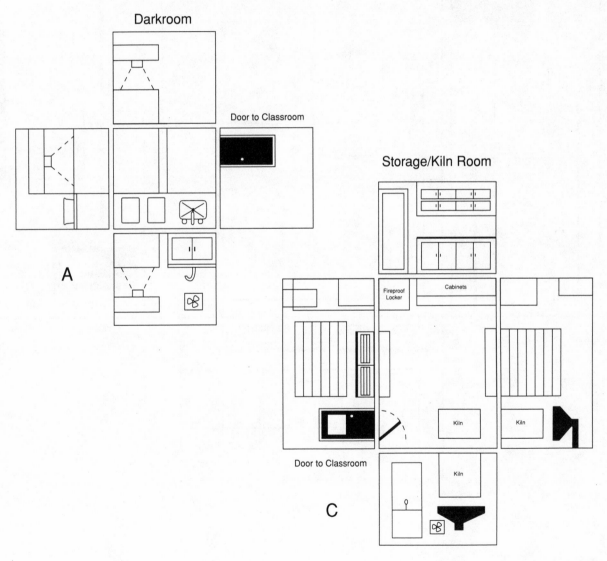

A

Door to Classroom

Storage/Kiln Room

Fireproof Locker

Cabinets

Kiln

Kiln

Kiln

Door to Classroom

C

Classroom

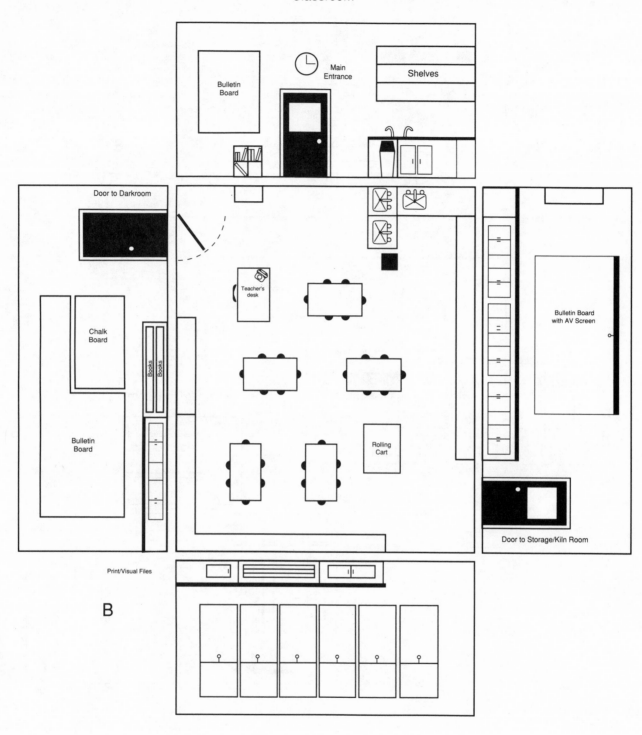

Bulletin Board

Main Entrance

Shelves

Door to Darkroom

Chalk Board

Books
Books

Bulletin Board

Teacher's desk

Rolling Cart

Bulletin Board with AV Screen

Door to Storage/Kiln Room

Print/Visual Files

B

teacher become aware of how to minimize health risks in the art classroom. Listed below are the major routes by which hazardous materials enter the body.

- **Skin contact.** This is a common route of entry into the body. Substances such as acid, bleach, and organic solvents destroy skin upon contact. There are certain chemicals that go even deeper and may even enter the bloodstream (for example, turpentine and methyl alcohol).

- **Inhalation.** The inhalation of toxic fumes, dust, smoke, spray mists, and vapors may cause serious problems—damaging lungs and airways, and sometimes affecting the whole body through the blood stream.

- **Ingestion.** Serious problems result from ingesting toxic materials directly or indirectly (such as through mouth contact with hands, drawings, implements, food, and the like that have come into contact with such materials). Do not let young adults chew on pencils, paintbrushes, and the like.

Labeling

Labeling can provide information on any potentially dangerous art supplies, but teachers need to be aware of what various labels mean. The label "non-toxic," for example, does not guarantee a product's safety. According to federal regulations, toxicity means that a single exposure can be fatal to adults. The effect on children, who are more likely to be harmed by dangerous substances, is not considered in this definition. Also, the chance of developing chronic or long-term illnesses is not addressed by the legal definition of toxicity. Repeated exposure to non-toxic materials is not always safe. Many dangerous substances, such as asbestos, can legally be defined as non-toxic. Also, some art supplies, particularly those manufactured by small or foreign companies, may be improperly labeled as non-toxic.

Not all products whose labels provide chemical components but have no warnings or list no information at all are safe to use. Since manufacturers are not required to disclose ingredients, products without this information or warnings are potentially hazardous.

For more complete information on the presence of hazardous substances in art supplies, teachers may request a Material Safety Data Sheet (OSHA Form 20) from the manufacturer. This sheet provides information on potential health and fire hazards, a list of chemicals that might react dangerously with the product, and a list of all ingredients for which industrial standards exist. The manufacturer should supply this sheet on request, and a local public health official or poison control center technician can help interpret the information.

Art teachers can also take advantage of voluntary labeling standards developed by the art materials industry. The Art and Craft Materials Institute (ACMI) administers a voluntary testing and labeling program that helps to ensure the safety of those who work with art materials. This system uses the labels CP, AP, and HL.

CP (Certified Product) and AP (Approved Product) labels are used mainly on products

MEETS PERFORMANCE STANDARDS

Saftey labels approved by the Art and Craft Materials Institute (ACMI).

designed for younger children, while HL (Health Label) is used on products intended for older children and adults. Products labeled CP, AP, or HL are certified in a program of toxicological evaluation by a medical expert to contain no materials in sufficient quantities to be toxic or injurious to humans or to cause acute or chronic health problems. Products labeled CP, in addition, meet specific requirements of material, workmanship, working qualities, and color. HL means that the product is certified to be properly labeled in a program of toxicological evaluation by a medical expert. The Art and Craft Materials Institute makes available a list of institute-certified products. For a copy, or for more information on the Institute's certification program, write to:

The Art and Craft Materials Institute
715 Boylston Street
Boston, MA 02116

Common Toxic Processes and Materials

As shown above, many techniques and materials art teachers use are *very* dangerous. For the elementary level a restriction to AP- or CP-approved products is fine, but middle school/junior high art teachers will want to provide their students with more challenging techniques and media. Be aware of the potential risks in such offerings and take heed of the following:

- **Paint.** Some paints that are commonly used may be carcinogenic (for example, chromate and cadmium). The dangers of using lead pigments are well known and documented. If possible, do not use these inorganic pigments.

  Turpentine and other solvents, especially the ones used for varnishes and lacquers are *very* toxic. These should only be used with extreme caution and proper ventilation. Acrylic emulsions contain small amounts of formaldehyde and ammonia. Without proper ventilation, they may cause throat and lung irritations.

- **Ceramics.** Clay itself may be toxic. If people inhale silica dust or Kaolin dust over a prolonged period of time, it may cause silicosis. Whenever possible, use talc-free clay and asbestos-free talcs.

When mixing clay from powder, make sure to use an exhaust system and/or a toxic dust respirator. If clay dust is covering the studio, *never* try to sweep up the clay. Use a wet mop or HEPA-type vacuum cleaner.

When mixing glazes, wear a toxic dust respirator. Spraying glazes should be done only with a spray booth exhausted to the outside. It is important to stress to students to keep glazes off their skin.

- **Jewelry.** Local ventilation is a must. Teachers should purchase only lead-free enamels. Heated enamels give off infrared radiation, so teachers should require students to use infrared goggles to protect their eyes from injury.

- **Printmaking.** Local exhaust is required to prevent the accumulation of dangerous toxic vapors. Whenever possible, use water-based inks for all silk screening.

  With intaglio and lithography, the major danger is contact with the acids and the toxic gases given off when etching copper or zinc. Students should *never* mix acid baths. Rubber gloves, aprons, and face protectors should be worn when working with acids. Acid baths should have proper ventilation hoods over them.

- **Photography.** It requires proper ventilation. Hands should never be put into developer, stop-baths, or fixers. Use tongs. Kodak recommends at least ten changes of room air per hour for black-and-white processing.

- **Art materials in general.** Rubber cement contains large amounts of toxic hexane, which causes many serious health problems. Substitute other adhesives whenever possible. If students use a spray fixative, they should use it outside or in a spray booth.

  Over-heated wax for batik or encaustic may release dangerous fumes and formaldehyde. Watch for explosions or fires when using a hot plate, open flame, or iron.

- **Equipment.** Students should be carefully instructed in the proper use of drills, potters' wheels, paper cutters, printing presses, grinders, air brushes, knives, etc. Items should be labeled as dangerous. Require students to learn the proper procedures of equipment use, and make them take a test before using the equipment.

General Safety

There are certain guidelines to be followed in selecting art supplies to be used in the classroom. Perhaps the most important is to know what the materials are made of and what potential hazards exist. If a material is improperly labeled, or if adequate information cannot be obtained about it, don't use it. The following rules are also helpful:

- Be sure that all materials used by younger students (age 12 and under) have the CP or AP label and that materials used by older children and adults are marked HL.
- Don't use acids, alkalies, bleaches, or any product that will stain skin or clothing.
- Don't use aerosol cans because the spray can injure lungs.
- Use dust-producing materials (such as pastels, clays, plasters, chalks, powdered tempera, pigments, dyes, and instant papier-mâché, except the premixed cellulose type) with care in a well-ventilated area. Better yet, avoid using them at all.
- Avoid using solvents (including lacquers, paint thinners, turpentines, shellacs, solvent-based inks, rubber cement, and permanent markers) in the art room.
- Avoid using found or donated materials unless the ingredients are known.
- Avoid using old materials. Many art supplies formerly contained highly dangerous substances, such as arsenic, or raw lead compounds, or high levels of asbestos. Older solvents may contain chloroform or carbon tetrachloride.

Working conditions in the art room also affect safety. A disorderly, confused art room leads to unsafe conditions, particularly when there are many people working close to each other. Controlling the buildup of litter and dust, ensuring that tools are in good condition, and keeping the work space reasonably organized not only help prevent common accidents but also make it easier to recognize and eliminate other hazards. An orderly art room is absolutely essential to the students' and teacher's safety.

Following the above measures will provide a safe and healthy art environment. However, some students who, for one reason or another, run a higher risk of injury will need special precautions. It's a good idea to identify high-risk students at the beginning of each school term by sending questionnaires to parents and checking school records. Teachers are urged to plan programs with these students' limitations in mind.

The safety of students with some physical impairments must also be considered. Visually impaired students, for example, tend to get closer (sometimes within one or two inches) to the work in order to see it and are more likely to inhale fumes or dust. Also, they are less likely to notice spills. Some activities that create noise, such as hammering or using machinery, may be unsuitable for the hearing impaired. Asthmatics already have difficulties in breathing and should not be exposed to dust or fumes. Students with motor impairments may manipulate materials with their feet or mouths, making accidental ingestion or absorption more likely and cleanup more difficult.

Students who are mentally impaired may have trouble understanding rules for art room safety and may require extra supervision. Some students with emotional disturbances might deliberately abuse art supplies. Students who are taking medication or undergoing chemotherapy should be medically evaluated for possible interactions between their medications and art materials.

More information on safety in the art environment is available from The Center for Occupational Hazards, a national nonprofit clearinghouse for research and information on health hazards in art. For more information, or to subscribe to their newsletter, which covers a variety of topics on art safety, write to:

The Center for Occupational Safety
5 Beekman Street
New York, NY 10038

Resources in the Community

The community is an excellent resource for the art teacher. There are a wealth of opportunities available for enriching art instruction through the use of community resources. Every art teacher should create a notebook of resources.

The following are suggested contents for a resource notebook. Under each topic list the place, address, telephone number, contact person, hours, cost, topics covered, recommended group size, and grade-level suitability.

- **Museums/Galleries.** An obvious resource would be art museums and galleries. They often offer many educational programs. Larger museums often have an educational staff that will perform a variety of services for you.
- **Historical Sites.** Historic homes or buildings are particularly useful in teaching architectural concepts.
- **State and National Parks and Monuments.** State and national parks provide wonderful educational services.

- **Public and Social Services.** Public recreation areas may be used in a variety of ways. Various parks, lakes, and riverfront areas may be used also for picnic lunches while on a field trip.
- **Institutional Services.** College and university art departments will be an invaluable resource.
- **Industry and Business.** Think of each one in your community, and see how each could be useful to you. Your local newspaper and Chamber of Commerce are good resources.
- **Government Resources.** City or state art councils are an excellent resource for you. Check to see whether your city has an Office of Cultural Affairs. Many cities put out a cultural events list.
- **People.** There are many people in your local area who would be happy to come to your class or let you visit their studio. Include, of course, artists of every kind. Think about craftspeople, for example, quiltmakers, basketmakers, potters, or furniture makers.

Public Relations

It is important that a quality art program is visible to those in the school, school district, and community. If you desire strong support for your program, consider the following:

- Are you committed to the idea of public relations and convinced of its importance?
- Have you recruited the proper people (for example, parents, school board members, key community figures, etc.) for support?
- Have you planned a public relations program for the school year (for example, exhibitions, Youth Art Month activities, etc.)?
- Have you prepared hand-out materials to tell about your art program accomplishments, goals, how your program contributes to the community, etc?
- Have you committed at least a small portion of your art budget to "selling" your program so that you can eventually get more financial and other types of support?
- Does your art program have an image problem? Have you outlined steps that could be taken to improve this image?
- Do your colleagues, board members, media, and community leaders know about your quality art program? Have you personally contacted these individuals?
- Are other media contacts, local art museum or art councils familiar with the exciting things happening in your program?
- Do you work with other teachers in your school, county, or district to promote art education?
- When you hold special events (such as exhibitions, special field trips, etc.) do you contact the radio, newspaper, or television to offer suggestions for stories or photos?
- Have you contacted local community businesses or community organizations for support for your program? Many companies and organizations will give you free materials or money—they sometimes like taking on a special project (for example, helping send children to a special art exhibit).

Public Relations Strategies

One of the most effective public relations strategy is to display your students' art works. The following are teacher-tested ideas for displaying art work both within the school and throughout the community and creating support for the program.

- Use bulletin boards and display cases in halls at school as concept teaching boards. You could display projects from a "Studio Experience" activity with the title "Art Concepts." Type a brief explanation of the activity, and mount it to accompany the display. You will be surprised at how many people will take the time to read the explanation of the concept that is illustrated.
- Have a "teacher's choice" work selected each year by a panel of judges, frame it, and place it on permanent display in the office. In a few years you will have an interesting collection.
- Get permission to hang framed students' work in high-traffic areas around the school building, such as offices, the lunchroom, the teachers' lounge, the library, and entrance halls. These pieces could be products of the Studio Lessons that students have had time to carefully plan and finish. These art works can be changed several times throughout the school year.
- Hold an exhibit at the end of each semester or at the end of the year. Send out invitations, have a guest book, and invite honored guests. Take photos and send them to the local newspaper.
- Contact local banks, other businesses, and government offices to display framed pieces. Volunteer to have your students paint store windows for special occasions.
- Hold an exhibit at the local mall.
- Encourage your students to participate in community art festivals and exhibits.
- Create public art to make community members notice your program. Paint a mural on the walls around a construction site, make relief tiles and mount them on a wall, stitch some banners, or weave wall hangings.

- Join and actively participate in the local art association. It can be a valuable source of contacts, information, and possible funding for special programs.
- Get a local art association or art-related business to sponsor your class. Its members or employees could not only donate money but also help you collect found items such as magazine pictures and fabric scraps for projects, hang art works for shows, or go with your class on a weekend trip to a museum.
- Organize a parents' support group. Even if you don't hold meetings, send out newsletters. Although everyone is busy, some parents will be interested enough in art education to volunteer help with your class.
- Speak to community groups in order to develop an interest in your art program; for example, the PTA, garden clubs, civic groups. Show slides of students' works, have students tape a narrative to accompany the slides explaining how and why they created their art works, or make a videotape of yourself teaching the class.
- Be involved with Youth Art Month activities. Contact the National Art Education Association, 1916 Association Drive, Reston, VA 22091-1590, for further information.

Notes

Notes

Exploring Art

Exploring Art

Gene Mittler, Ph.D.
Professor of Art
Texas Tech University

Rosalind Ragans, Ph.D.
Associate Professor Emerita
Georgia Southern University

GLENCOE
Macmillan/McGraw-Hill

Lake Forest, Illinois   Columbus, Ohio   Mission Hills, California   Peoria, Illinois

Send all inquiries to:
Glencoe Division, Macmillan/McGraw-Hill
15319 Chatsworth Street
P.O.Box 9609
Mission Hills, CA 91346-9609

ISBN 0-02-662281-5 (Student Text)
ISBN 0-02-662282-3 (Teacher's Wraparound Edition)

2   3   4   5   6   7   97   96   95   94   93   92

Editorial Consultants

Nancy C. Miller
Booker T. Washington High School
for the Performing and Visual Arts
Dallas, Texas

Jean Morman Unsworth
Art Consultant to Chicago
Archdiocese Schools
Chicago, Illinois

Contributors/Reviewers

Josephine Julianna Jones
Booker T. Washington High School
for the Performing and Visual Arts
Dallas, Texas

Rebecca Robertson
W.W. Samuell High School
Dallas, Texas

Anne Nicholson
Our Lady of Grace Elementary School
Encino, California

Carolyn F. Sollman
Eminence School
Eminence, Indiana

Studio Lesson Consultants

Acknowledgments: The authors wish to express their gratitude to the following art coordinators and specialists who participated in the field test of the studio lessons.

Janette Alexander, Denver City Junior High, Denver City, TX; Nan Ball, Camp Creek Middle School, College Park, GA; Wendy Bull, Colonial High School, Memphis, TN; Isabelle Bush, Crabapple Middle School, Roswell, GA; Ann Campoll, Sauk City, WI; Pam Carsillo, Floyd Middle School, Marietta, GA; Kellene Champlin, Fulton County Art Supervisor, Fulton County, GA; Michael Chapman, Treadwell Junior High School, Memphis, TN; Fay Chastain, Hilsman Middle School, Athens, GA; Greg Coats, Havenview Junior High School, Memphis, TN; Rebecca Crim, Holcomb Bridge Middle School, Alpharetta, GA; Jeannie Davis, Hallsville Junior High, Hallsville, TX; Lane Dietrick, Freedom Junior High School, Freedom, WI; Jean Carl Doherty, Sandy Springs Middle School, Atlanta, GA; Joan Elsesser, Beaver Dam, WI; Linda Eshom, Corpus Christi Intermediate School District, Corpus Christi, TX; Eva Fronk, Hales Corners, WI; Kay Godawa, Savannah Country Day School, Savannah, GA; Dr. Nadine Gordon, Scarsdale High School, Scarsdale, NY; Thomas Healy, Canutillo Middle School, El Paso, TX; Garlan Hodgson, Tapp Middle School, Powder Springs, GA; Florence Kork, Harold Wiggs Middle School, El Paso, TX; Nellie Lynch, Duval County Art Supervisor, Jacksonville, FL; Kelly Mann, All Saints Episcopal School, Lubbock, TX; Theresa McDaniel, Towson High School, Towson, MD; Barbara Merritt, Canyon Hills Middle School, El Paso, TX; Bunyan Morris, Marvin Pittman Laboratory School, Statesboro, GA; Jimmy Morris, Clarke County Fine Arts Supervisor, Clarke County, GA; Perri Ann Morris, Jenkins County High School, Millen, GA; Mary Lee Nance, Harris Middle School, Shelbyville, TN; Jackie Norman, East Middle School, Tullahoma, TN; Susan R. Owens, Haynes Bridge Middle School, Atlanta, GA; Robert M. Perry, Jr., Paxon Middle School, Jacksonville, FL; Eunice Plieseis, West Allis, WI; Dr. Marilyn Ragaty, Burney-Harris-Lyons Middle School, Athens, GA; A.P. Register, Bassett Middle School, El Paso, TX; M. Joi Roberts, Stanton High School, Jacksonville, FL; Julia Russell, Art Supervisor, Memphis City Schools, Memphis, TN; Karen Sandborn, Metter High School, Metter, GA; Wandra Sanders, Mandarin Middle School, Jacksonville, FL; Russ Sarasin, Green Bay, WI; Dr. Barbara Shaw, Cobb County Art Supervisor, Marietta, GA; Linda W. Smith, Jenkins County Elementary School, Millen, GA; Ellen Stanley, All Saints Episcopal School, Lubbock, TX; Linda Strong, La Pietra School, Honolulu, HI; Ola Underhill, Chula Vista Academy of Fine Arts, Corpus Christi, TX; A. Villalobos, Guillen School, El Paso, TX; C. Waites, Guillen School, El Paso, TX; Shirley Yokley, Tennessee Visual Arts Consultant, TN; Barbara Zelt, Reistertown, MD.

Photography Credits

Contents

viiT, *Ara fittile con Achille e Agamennone.* Argrigento, Museo Archeologico.

viiB, Stuart Davis. *Owh! In San Paõ.* Collection of Whitney Museum of American Art, New York, New York.

viiiB, Douglas Mazonowicz. Cave painting. Lascaux, France.

ixT, Janet Stayton. *Ravello.* Pat Heesy Gallery.

xT, Rembrandt van Rijn. *Portrait of a Lady with an Ostrich-Feather Fan.* National Gallery of Art, Washington, D.C. Widener Collection.

xB, Laura Lynn Weber. *Starfish.* Private Collection.

xiT, Torii Kiyotada. An actor of the Ichikawa clan. The Metropolitan Museum of Art, New York, New York. Harris Brisbane Dick Fund.

xiB, Jacob Lawrence. *Toussaint L'Overture Series.* Fisk University.

xiiB, Donald Harvey. *Huaka'i.* Kamehameha School, Hawaii.

xiiiT, American-South Peru. Coastal Huari-Tiahuanaco. Shirt section. The Metropolitan Museum of Art, New York, New York. The Michael C. Rockefeller Collection. Bequest of Nelson A. Rockefeller.

xiiiB, M. Richards. TransAmerica Building. San Francisco, California.

xivT, Dr. Harold Edgerton. *Milk-drop Coronet.* Palm Press.

Text

Daniel Alonzo, 302; American Weaving Association, 224L; Ansel Adams, 318; Art Resource, 190; Atari Games Corp., 263T; Craig Aurness/WestLight, 72; Margaret Bourke-White, 250, 267; Mathew Brady, 253B; Robert Brenner/PhotoEdit, 295R; D&R Bretzfelder/PhotoEdit, 194R; California State University, Northridge (materials courtesy of), 34; Jeffrey Clements, 107R; Paul Conklin/PhotoEdit, 294L, 297R; Laima Druskis, 295L; Marcel Eskanazy/PhotoEdit, 242; Tony Freeman/PhotoEdit, 291; Rick Fowler, selected student works; Ann Garvin, 290; Beryl Goldberg, 139L; David Heald, 241; Dr. Jesse Lovano Kerr, 240B; Dorothea Lange, 254; Eric Lessing/PhotoEdit, 236R; Lossen Foto, 161 (courtesy of Heidelberg West, Brisbane, CA); Douglas Mazonowicz, 54; Stephen McBrady/PhotoEdit, 296R; Guy Motil/WestLight, 73; William Nettles, 181L; John Neubauer/PhotoEdit, 152R; Michael Newman/PhotoEdit, 31T, 293R; Dr. Denny Pett, 238; PhotoEdit, 236, 249; Gene Plaisted OSC, 5; M. Richards, 244R, 294R; Sandak, 240T; Scala/Art Resource, 244L; Rhoda Sidney, 292L; Alfred Stieglitz, 255; William Henry Fox Talbot, 256; Tektronix, 296L; Texas Software, Inc., 262T; The Art Store, Pasadena, CA (materials courtesy of), 32T, 38, 45; Susan Van Etten, 30; Lorin D. Whittaker, 209B; David Young-Wolff, 261, 292R, 297L; Anna E. Zuckerman, 293L.

Illustrations

Michael Rowley

CONTENTS

CHAPTER 1

Art in Your World   1

Lesson 1 The Art Experience   2
• Studio Experience   3
Lesson 2 Examining Art Works   4
Lesson 3 Artists and Ideas   6
• Studio Experience   9
Lesson 4 Making a Content Collage   10
• Examining Your Work   11
• Safety Tip   11
Chapter 1 Review   12
• Looking at the Details   13

CHAPTER 2

Enjoying Art   15
Lesson 1 Understanding Art   16
Lesson 2 Aesthetics   20
• Studio Experience   23
Lesson 3 Torn Paper Face   24
• Examining Your Work   25
Chapter 2 Review   26
• Looking at the Details   27

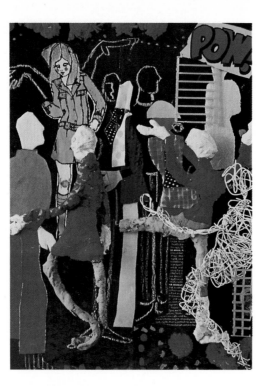

CHAPTER 3

Exploring Art Media   29

Lesson 1 **Drawing**   30
• Studio Experience   33
Lesson 2 **Printmaking**   34
• Studio Experience   37
Lesson 3 **Painting**   38
• Safety Tip   41
• Studio Experience   41
Lesson 4 **Experimenting with Pigment**   42
• Examining Your Work   43
Lesson 5 **Sculpture**   44
• Safety Tip   47
• Studio Experience   47
Lesson 6 **Creating with Mixed Media**   48
• Examining Your Work   49

Chapter 3 Review   50
• Looking at the Details   51

CHAPTER 4

The Elements of Art   53

Lesson 1 **The Language of Art**   54
Lesson 2 **Color**   56
• Studio Experience   57
• Studio Experience   59
Lesson 3 **Using Color Combinations**   60
• Examining Your Work   61
Lesson 4 **Line**   62
• Studio Experience   65
Lesson 5 **Shape, Form, and Space**   66
• Studio Experience   69
Lesson 6 **Paper Sculpture Forms**   70
• Examining Your Work   71
Lesson 7 **Texture**   72
• Studio Experience   73
Lesson 8 **Painting a Landscape**   74
• Examining Your Work   75

Chapter 4 Review   76
• Looking at the Details   77

The Principles of Art 79

Lesson 1 **The Language of Design** 80
Lesson 2 **Formal Balance Cityscape** 82
• Examining Your Work 83
Lesson 3 **Variety, Harmony, Emphasis,
             and Proportion** 84
Lesson 4 **Abstract Painting** 88
• Examining Your Work 89
Lesson 5 **Movement and Rhythm** 90
• Studio Experience 91
Lesson 6 **Creating Visual Movement** 92
• Examining Your Work 93
Lesson 7 **Unity in Art** 94

Chapter 5 Review 96
• Looking at the Details 97

You, the Art Critic 99

Lesson 1 **Describing Art Works** 100
• Studio Experience 103
Lesson 2 **Using Descriptive Techniques** 104
• Examining Your Work 105
Lesson 3 **Analyzing Art Works** 106
• Studio Experience 107
Lesson 4 **Interpreting Art Works** 108
Lesson 5 **Mood Chalk Painting** 110
• Safety Tip 111
• Examining Your Work 111
Lesson 6 **Judging Art Works** 112
Lesson 7 **Using Art Criticism** 114

Chapter 6 Review 116
• Looking at the Details 117

CHAPTER 7

Art History and You 119

Lesson 1 Describing—Who, When, and Where 120
Lesson 2 Making a Mixed Media Self-Portrait 122
• Examining Your Work 123
Lesson 3 **Analyzing Artistic Style** 124
• Studio Experience 127
Lesson 4 **Painting in the Fauve Style** 128
• Examining Your Work 129
Lesson 5 **Interpreting Time and Place** 130
Lesson 6 **Time and Place Collage** 134
• Examining Your Work 135
Lesson 7 **Judging Historical Importance** 136
• Studio Experience 139

Chapter 7 Review 140
• Looking at the Details 141

CHAPTER 8

Drawing 143

Lesson 1 **The Art of Drawing** 144
• Studio Experience 147
Lesson 2 **Gesture Drawing** 148
• Examining Your Work 149
Lesson 3 **Contour Drawing** 150
• Examining Your Work 151
Lesson 4 **Presentation Drawing** 152
• Examining Your Work 153
• Safety Tip 153
Lesson 5 **Fantasy Jungle** 154
• Examining Your Work 155

Chapter 8 Review 156
• Looking at the Details 157

CHAPTER 9

Printmaking   159

Lesson 1 **The Art of Printmaking** 160
Lesson 2 **More About Printmaking** 162
  • Studio Experience 165
Lesson 3 **Monoprints** 166
  • Examining Your Work 167
Lesson 4 **Glue Prints** 168
  • Examining Your Work 169
Lesson 5 **Linoleum Block Prints** 170
  • Safety Tip 171
  • Examining Your Work 171
Lesson 6 **Silk Screen Prints** 172
  • Examining Your Work 173

Chapter 9 Review 174
  • Looking at the Details 175

CHAPTER 10

Painting   177

Lesson 1 **The Art of Painting** 178
  • Studio Experience 181
Lesson 2 **Watercolor Painting** 182
  • Examining Your Work 183
Lesson 3 **Non-objective Painting** 184
  • Examining Your Work 185
Lesson 4 **Expressive Painting** 186
  • Examining Your Work 187

Chapter 10 Review 188
  • Looking at the Details 189

CHAPTER 11

Graphic Design   191

Lesson 1 **The Art of Graphic Design**   192
• Studio Experience   195
Lesson 2 **Designing a Logo**   196
• Examining Your Work   197
• Safety Tip   197
Lesson 3 **Drawing a Comic Strip**   198
• Examining Your Work   199
Lesson 4 **Designing a Poster**   200
• Examining Your Work   201
Lesson 5 **Illustrating a Story**   202
• Examining Your Work   203

Chapter 11 Review   204
• Looking at the Details   205

CHAPTER 12

Sculpture   207

Lesson 1 **The Art of Sculpture**   208
Lesson 2 **Carving a Plaster Relief**   212
• Examining Your Work   213
• Safety Tip   213
Lesson 3 **Modeling in Clay**   214
• Examining Your Work   215
Lesson 4 **Abstract Sculpture**   216
• Safety Tip   217
• Examining Your Work   217

Chapter 12 Review   218
• Looking at the Details   219

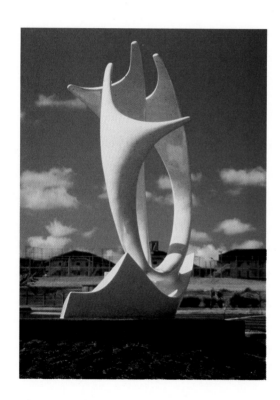

CHAPTER 13

Crafts   221

Lesson 1 **The Art of Crafts**   222
Lesson 2 **Clay Bowl**   226
- Safety Tip   227
- Examining Your Work   227

Lesson 3 **Slab Container**   228
- Examining Your Work   229

Lesson 4 **Making a Weaving**   230
- Examining Your Work   231

Lesson 5 **Jewelry**   232
- Safety Tip   233
- Examining Your Work   233

Chapter 13 Review   234
- Looking at the Details   235

CHAPTER 14

Architecture   237

Lesson 1 **The Art of Architecture**   238
- Studio Experience   241

Lesson 2 **Building a Clay Model**   242
- Examining Your Work   243

Lesson 3 **Drawing Floor Plans**   244
- Examining Your Work   245

Lesson 4 **Clay Entrance Relief**   246
- Examining Your Work   247

Chapter 14 Review   248
- Looking at the Details   249

Contents   **xiii**

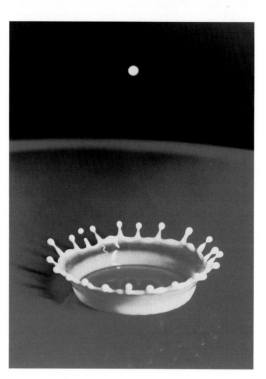

CHAPTER 15

Photography, Film, and Video   251

Lesson 1 **The Art of Photography**   252
Lesson 2 **Making a Photogram**   256
- Safety Tip   257
- Examining Your Work   257
Lesson 3 **The Art of Film**   258
Lesson 4 **Making a Silent Movie**   260
- Examining Your Work   261
Lesson 5 **The Art of Video**   262
Lesson 6 **Designing a Video Game**   264
- Examining Your Work   265

Chapter 15 Review   266
- Looking at the Details   267

Handbook

- Table of Contents   269
- Technique Tips   271
- Artist Profiles   283
- Career Spotlights   291
- Additional Studios   298
- Artists and Their Works   320
- Glossary   323
- Index   326

LISTING OF STUDIO LESSONS BY MEDIA

Acrylics and Oil Pastels

Expressive Painting 186
Illustrating a Story 202
Group Mural 302

Chalk

Mood Chalk Painting 110
Fantasy Jungle 154

Clay

Modeling in Clay 214
Clay Bowl 226
Slab Container 228
Building a Clay Model 242
Clay Entrance Relief 246

Fibers

Making a Weaving 230
Appliqué Banner 308

Mixed Media

Making a Content Collage 10
Creating with Mixed Media 48
Mixed Media Self-Portrait 122
Time and Place Collage 134

Paper

Torn Paper Face 24
Paper Sculpture Forms 70
Creating Visual Movement 92
Abstract Sculpture 216
Jewelery 232
Pop-up Cityscape 304
Freestanding Mobile 314

Pencil, Pen, Charcoal, and Markers

Using Descriptive Techniques 104
Gesture Drawing 148
Contour Drawing 150
Presentation Drawing 152
Designing a Logo 196
Drawing a Comic Strip 198
Designing a Poster 200
Drawing Floor Plans 244
Designing a Video Game 264

Printmaking

Monoprints 166
Glue Prints 168
Linoleum Block Prints 170
Silk Screen Prints 172
Print Motifs 298

Tempera

Using Color Combinations 60
Painting a Landscape 74
Formal Balance Cityscape 82
Abstract Painting 88
Non-objective Painting 184
Abstract Action Painting 300
A Picture that Tells a Story 316

Watercolor

Experimenting with Pigment 42
Painting in the Fauve Style 128
Watercolor Painting 182

Other

Carving a Plaster Relief 212
Making a Photogram 256
Making a Silent Movie 260
Wire Sculpture 312
Pinhole Camera Photography 318

Art in Your World

Chapter Scan

Lesson 1 The Art Experience
Lesson 2 Examining Art Works
Lesson 3 Artists and Ideas
Lesson 4 Making a Content
          Collage

TRB Resources
- 1-8 Chapter Test
- Color Transparency 1
- Color Transparency 2

TEACHING THE CHAPTER

Introducing the Art Work

Direct students' attention to Norman Rockwell's illustration entitled *Triple Self-Portrait.* Inform them that Norman Rockwell was an American artist and illustrator of the twentieth century. Many of his highly popular illustrations were used as magazine covers for the *Saturday Evening Post* in the 1930s. Rockwell celebrated Americana, giving a humorous but insightful view of daily life. His works are known for their illustrative quality, or ability to tell a story.

Examining the Art Work

Tell students that this painting is Rockwell's self-portrait. It shows the viewer a man who is analytical but who also has a sense of humor. His plain clothing, the handkerchief hanging out of his back pocket, and his pipe and glasses show a man who doesn't take himself too seriously. Instead, he considers himself just a "regular guy." Explain that the point of emphasis is Rockwell himself, looking at his own reflection in the mirror. Point out that he paints himself without his glasses. Explain to students that he painted himself from different views: mirror image, back image, and portrait. Point out that the viewer's attention is first drawn to the center of the picture and then travels around from left to right, focusing on the details.

▲ A self-portrait is an artist's painting of himself or herself. Do you know the artists in any of the self-portraits on the upper right of the artist's easel?

Norman Rockwell. *Triple Self-Portrait.* 1960. Oil on canvas. 113 x 87.2 cm (44½ x 34⅓"). Norman Rockwell Museum at Stockbridge, Stockbridge, Massachusetts. Norman Rockwell Art Collection Trust.

xvi

Art in Your World

You are about to begin a journey to an interesting and exciting place. This is a place where your curiosity and creativity will be stirred. It is a place where you will be invited to make discoveries and share feelings and ideas. It is the world of art.

Throughout your journey you will see many works of art like the one at the left. This is a painting both *of* and *by* an artist. What makes this picture art? What makes the person who did it an artist? In the pages that follow you will find answers to these and many other questions.

OBJECTIVES

After completing this chapter, you will be able to:
- Explain what can be learned by looking at art made by others.
- Explain what is meant by perceiving.
- Define the term *artist*.
- Name sources of ideas that artists might use.
- Make a collage.

WORDS YOU WILL LEARN

applied art
artists
collage
fine art

patrons of the arts
perceiving
point of view

ARTISTS YOU WILL MEET

Rosa Bonheur
Salvador Dali
Lois Dvorak
Winslow Homer
Allan Houser
Joan Miro

Bartolomé Esteban
  Murillo
Norman Rockwell
William John Wilgus
Mary Ann Willson

1

The Art Experience

Can you imagine what it would be like to play a new game without first learning the rules, or to read a story in a language that is not familiar to you? Neither of these activities can be carried out automatically. Both, and especially the reading, demand that you have some knowledge beforehand. Both require you to be prepared.

The same is true of art. Understanding art takes more than just looking at an object. It takes looking—and knowing *how* to look—to find meaning. It takes truly seeing, or perceiving the object. **Perceiving** is *looking at and thinking deeply about what you see.*

On your journey through the world of art, you will learn how to "see" art. You will learn how to perceive artistically.

A FIRST LOOK AT ART

You will begin your journey with the painting below (Figure 1–1). Look at this painting. If you were asked to write a description of what you see, what would you write? You might note that this is a skillfully made painting of two ducks. You might add that the ducks are flying above a stormy sea.

▲ **Figure 1–1   Notice the artist's use of different shades of gray. What mood does the color gray bring to mind? Why might he have chosen this color for this painting?**

Winslow Homer. *Right and Left.* 1909. Canvas. 71.8 x 122.9 cm (28¼ x 48⅜"). National Gallery of Art, Washington, D.C. Gift of the Avalon Foundation.

LESSON PLAN
(pages 2–3)

Objectives
After completing this lesson, students will be able to:
• Explain what is meant by *perceiving.*
• Define the term *point of view* and explain how it pertains to works of art.
• Explain what can be learned by looking at art made by others.
• Draw the same object from two different points of view.

Supplies
• Large photograph or display-sized reproduction of art work.
• Illustrated volume of *Gulliver's Travels* by Jonathan Swift.
• Drawing paper, pencils.

> **TRB Resource**
> • 1-1 *The Many Faces of Arts,* (appreciating cultural diversity)

TEACHING THE LESSON

Getting Started

Motivator. Begin with an activity to help students understand some of the differences between looking and perceiving. Choose a large photograph or reproduction of an art work that is probably not familiar to your students. Display it for only a few seconds. Then cover it and let students discuss what they saw. Display the photograph or reproduction again and leave it in view as students continue to discuss it. Finally, ask: How does being able to look closely help you understand what is in this photograph/art work?

Vocabulary. Ask students to brainstorm a list of terms or phrases they think of when they hear the word *perceiving.* Then focus students' attention on the prefix in *perceiving: per-* means "thoroughly." Ask students to suggest other words (such as *perform, perfect, persuade,* for example) that begin with the same prefix.

Background Information
Winslow Homer (United States, 1836–1910) is considered one of the most important painters of nineteenth century America. Though he devoted most of his life to art, his formal training was limited to an early apprenticeship to a lithographer. Homer spent nearly 20 years working as a magazine illustrator. His first significant paintings, depicting the Civil War.

Unlike many other American artists of his time, Homer did not go to Europe for an extended period of training. However, he did make two visits to France, and his work was apparently influenced by that of Édouard Manet.

Not long after finishing *Right and Left* (Figure 1–1), Homer completed a painting entitled *Driftwood.* It shows a small, solitary human figure observing the sea in a storm. It was Homer's final tribute—and his farewell—to the sea he loved. When the painting was finished, he set aside his easel and his brushes, never to paint again. Less than a year later, Winslow Homer died.

So far, so good. But this description only begins to scratch the surface. There is much more going on in this painting. Look again, and you will notice something strange about the duck on the right. Namely, it seems to be plunging downward into the sea. Searching for clues to explain this odd behavior, you might notice the boat in the picture. It is partly hidden by the feet and tail feathers of the other duck. Looking more closely still, you might see the red flash and smoke above the boat. There is a hunter in the boat, and he is shooting at the ducks. The duck on the right has been hit. Now, for the first time, you notice the small white feather floating nearby. It was set free when a shotgun blast struck the duck.

Curiosity mounts as you realize the flash you are now seeing is the second shot. (The first has already found its target.) Try to imagine that you can hear the noise of the gun. Will the duck on the left, its wings beating wildly, escape? Will it become the hunter's next victim?

Far from just a picture of ducks, this is an action-packed glimpse of a dramatic event. Notice, by the way, where the artist has placed you, the viewer. What point of view has the artist used? **Point of view** is *the angle from which the viewer sees the scene.* Are you watching this drama unfold through the eyes of the hunter? No, you are staring, like the hunter's targets, down the barrels of the shotgun.

LEARNING FROM ART

Art, as you have just seen, has the power to challenge our minds and stir up our feelings. The ability to see the kinds of things just described can be learned with practice. This book will prepare you to use your eyes and mind to understand many different kinds of art. As each new art experience unfolds, your ability to see or perceive art will increase.

STUDIO EXPERIENCE

Look once more at the painting in Figure 1–1. One of the most interesting things about this painting is its unusual point of view. Using an unexpected point of view can add interest to art.

Using a pencil, make a drawing of an object you know well. One possibility might be one of the shoes you are wearing right now. Draw the object as well as you can. Now draw the same object from the point of view of a bug looking up at it. What details might the bug see? Compare your two drawings. Which one do you consider more interesting?

You will also learn, through looking at art by others, ways of making your own art. Looking at art created by others will develop your powers of creative thinking. It will help you find fresh and exciting ideas and reveal different ways of expressing those ideas. It will highlight the many kinds of tools and techniques you can use. Studio experiences, like the one above, will give you a chance to practice what you have learned.

✔CHECK YOUR UNDERSTANDING

1. What is meant by the term *perceiving*?
2. What are some of the things to be gained by looking at art made by others?
3. Define *point of view*.

Lesson 1   *The Art Experience*   **3**

Answers to "Check Your Understanding"
1. Perceiving means looking at and thinking deeply about what you see.
2. Looking at art created by others can help you develop your ability to perceive art, explore ways of making your own art, develop your powers of creative thinking, find new ways of expressing your ideas, and learn about the many kinds of art tools and techniques.
3. Point of view is the angle from which the viewer sees the scene.

Developing Concepts

Exploring Aesthetics. Have students look at *Right and Left*, Figure 1–1. Help them discuss the message by asking: What feeling or idea does this painting give you? How would that feeling or idea change if it were painted from a different point of view?

Developing Studio Skills. After students have completed the Studio Experience, show students several illustrations of Lilliput from *Gulliver's Travels*. Help students discuss how the land, the Lilliputians, and Gulliver might have looked from two different points of view—the Lilliputians' and Gulliver's. Then have pairs of students draw the same person or object from those two different points of view.

Following Up

Closure. Go around the room and let each student answer this question: What can you do to become more perceptive of your environment?

Evaluation. 1. Review students' written responses to the "Check Your Understanding" questions. 2. Be sure each student can identify at least one way to become more perceptive.

Reteaching. Have students work with partners to improve their understanding of the term *point of view*. First let them look through the text or other sources and identify paintings and drawings done from a panoramic view (*The Lackawanna Valley*, Figure 7-1, for example), from a limited view (*Madonna and Child*, Figure 7-14, for example), from a distant view (*Christina's World*, Figure 6-16, for example), and from a magnified view (*The White Calico Flower*, Figure 12-7, for example). Then help all the students identify and discuss the art works they have found.

Enrichment. Have each student research the era during which Winslow Homer painted and identify at least three major world events of that period. Then have students work in groups to discuss the effect world events may have had on Homer's work.

LESSON 2

Examining Art Works

LESSON 2

*Examining
Art Works*

LESSON PLAN
(pages 4–5)

Objectives

After completing this lesson, students will be able to:
• Define the term *artist*.
• Identify the two basic kinds of art.
• Explain the difference between fine art and applied art.

Supplies

• Photographs of art works, representing both fine arts and applied arts, and photographs of common household objects.

TRB Resource

• 1-2 *Form Follows Function,* (aesthetics/art criticism)

TEACHING THE LESSON

Getting Started

Motivator. Display the photographs of art works (such as paintings, sculptures, jewelry, and pottery) and common household objects (such as a can opener and a stapler). Focus students' attention on each photograph in turn and ask: What do you see here? Is it art? Why, or why not? Encourage a variety of responses, and ask students to explain and support their opinions. After students have finished reading the lesson, have them review the photos and explain whether each is an example of fine art, an example of applied art, or simply a common household object. There may still be some differences of opinion; encourage discussion.

Vocabulary. Have students work in small groups to answer these questions: What is an artist? What does an artist do? Then ask a member of each group to share the group's ideas with the class. Finally, have students compare their ideas about artists with the definition given in the text.

When you see a great movie, do you keep the experience to yourself or do you tell friends all about it? This eagerness to share experiences and feelings with others is a typically human trait. It is also a reason why artists like to make art. **Artists** are *people who use imagination and skill to communicate ideas in visual form*. These ideas may represent experiences, feelings, or events in the artist's life.

Artists are creative thinkers. They combine a knowledge of art materials, tools, and methods with a rich imagination and deep sensitivity. They use this combination to present their reactions to the world around them.

◀ **Figure 1–2   Compare this painting with Figures 1–3 and 1–4. In what ways do the three pieces of art work seem alike? In what ways do they seem different?**

Joan Miro. *Three Women*. 1934. Pen and black ink with pink and brown pastel on laid paper. 63.2 x 46.8 cm (24⅞ x 18⁷⁄₁₆″). National Gallery of Art, Washington, D.C. Gift of Frank and Jeannette Eyerly.

ARTISTS AND THEIR WORK

All works created by artists are made to be viewed. Some are created with an added purpose; they are meant to be *used*. People who study art have a separate term for each of these two kinds of art. *Art made to be experienced visually* is called **fine art**. *Art made to be functional as well as visually pleasing* is called **applied art**.

Fine Art

A phrase sometimes used for fine art is "art for art's sake." This means the only use for fine art is to communicate the artist's feelings or ideas.

Fine art can be made from a number of different materials. Figures 1–2 and 1–3 show examples of these types. Figure 1–2 is a drawing. Do you know what kind of fine art is shown in Figure 1–3?

Background Information

The distinction between fine art and applied art has been made only in modern times. In Europe, until the later part of the Middle Ages, painters, sculptors, and others we now consider artists were regarded as skilled craftspeople. The rise of the guilds reinforced this distinction between fine art and applied art. Each kind of art or craft had its own guild and its own masters. During the Renaissance, these artists—and their works—gained new prestige; their "art" began to be distinguished from the "crafts" or applied arts.

Today the separation of fine art from applied art is still sometimes controversial. For example, some artists and critics regard certain paintings as "merely decorative" and therefore categorize these works as applied art. On the other hand, some artists and craftspeople take as their creed the usefulness of art; they insist that art is valid only if it can be used in daily life.

▲ **Figure 1–3   See caption for Figure 1–2.**

Allan Houser. *Waiting for Dancing Partners.* 1980. Tennessee marble. 76.2 x 53.3 cm (30 x 21). Museum of the Southwest, Midland, Texas.

Applied Art

Applied arts are usually found in our everyday lives. Objects of applied art may be either made by hand or with machines. What other kinds of applied art can you name?

Sometimes the small differences between applied art and fine art become confused over a period of time. Look, for instance, at the stained glass church windows shown in Figure 1–4. These windows were originally designed at a time in history when few people could read. One of their purposes was to teach stories from the Bible. Today these same windows are also enjoyed as fine art because of their great beauty.

✓CHECK YOUR UNDERSTANDING

1. What is an artist?
2. Name the two basic kinds of art.
3. What is fine art? What are two types of fine art shown in this chapter?
4. What is applied art?

◀ **Figure 1–4   See caption for Figure 1–2.**

Stained glass window. *Elijah and Chariot.* House of Hope, Presbyterian, St. Paul, Minnesota.

Lesson 2   *Examining Art Works*   📖   **5**

Answers to "Check Your Understanding"
1. An artist is a person who uses imagination and skill to communicate ideas in visual form.
2. The two basic kinds of art are fine art and applied art.
3. Fine art is art made to be experienced visually. Drawing and painting are two types of fine art.
4. Applied art is art made to be functional as well as visually pleasing.

Developing Concepts

Exploring Aesthetics. Have students work in small groups to discuss this question: How is a work of applied art similar to and different from a common useful object?

Using Art Criticism. Help students discuss their responses to these questions: How do you think critics judge the success of an example of fine art? How do you imagine they judge the success of an example of applied art? Should there be any differences? Why, or why not?

Understanding Art History. Have each student choose one of the artists whose work is shown in Figures 1–1, 1–2, and 1–3. Ask students to research and present short oral reports about the lives and works of the artists they choose.

Appreciating Cultural Diversity. Ask each student or pair of students to select a particular culture or society and research the applied art works of that group. Have students present their findings in brief reports to the rest of the class.

Following Up

Closure. Have students list at least three qualities in answer to this question: If a person wants to become an artist, what important qualities should that person have or try to develop?

Evaluation. 1. Review students' written responses to the "Check Your Understanding" questions. 2. Read students' lists of qualities important to someone who wants to become an artist.

Reteaching. Present photographs showing objects of fine art and objects of applied art. (Include photos of art works used in the "Getting Started" activity.) Have students work in pairs or small groups to distinguish between examples of fine art and examples of applied art.

Enrichment. Have individual students select specific art works that were created as applied art and are now considered works of fine art. (See Figure 1–4 for an example.) Have students research the creation of these art works and the reasons they are now considered fine art. Ask students to summarize their research in written or oral reports.

LESSON 3

Artists and
Ideas

LESSON PLAN
(pages 6–9)

Objectives
After completing this lesson, students will be able to:
- Name sources of ideas that artists might use.
- Create their own idea banks.
- Draw pictures based on subjects from their idea banks.

Supplies
- Envelopes, slips of paper.
- Copy of one of Aesop's fables or of another short tale.
- Drawing paper, pencils.
- Several books of haiku.

TRB Resources
- 1-3 *Myth—The Imagination's Answer,* (reproducible master)
- 1-4 *What Does "Fine Art" Mean?,* (art history)
- 1-5 *A Journey Into the Past,* (cooperative learning)

TEACHING THE LESSON

Getting Started
Motivator. Begin by holding up a blank sheet of drawing paper. Ask: What do you see here? Let several students respond. Then ask: Imagine that you are a professional artist. Now what do you see when you look at this piece of paper? Encourage a variety of responses. Then explain to students that they will be discussing one of the artist's greatest challenges—finding ideas.

Vocabulary. Let volunteers look up the word *museum* in dictionaries that include word derivations. Ask those volunteers to tell the rest of the class what the word *museum* means and where it comes from. Then let students share and discuss their own experiences of museums.

Artists and Ideas

What do you see when you look at a blank sheet of paper? An artist will look at the blank sheet and see a challenge. That challenge—to come up with an idea—may be one of the toughest an artist faces.

Through the ages artists have answered the challenge of finding ideas, or sources of inspiration, in different ways. In this lesson you will learn about some of these ways.

WHERE ARTISTS GET IDEAS

The ancient Greeks routinely prayed to special goddesses called Muses (**myooz-uhz**) to send them inspiration for ideas. They even built shrines to honor the Muses.

In more recent times artists in search of ideas have looked elsewhere for sources of inspiration. Here are some of the resources they have explored:

- **The world of myths and legends.** Some artists borrow ideas from famous works of literature. The artist of Figure 1–5 has brought to life characters from one of these literary works. Do you know these characters? Do you know the legend surrounding them?

▲ **Figure 1–5   Do you know what is about to happen in this scene? Do you know what the rider of the black horse is holding?**

William John Wilgus. *Ichabod Crane and the Headless Horseman.* c. 1855. Canvas. 53.3 x 76.7 cm (21 x 30¼"). National Gallery of Art, Washington, D.C. Gift of Edgar William and Bernice Chrysler Garbisch.

6   Lesson 3   *Artists and Ideas*

Background Information
Individual artists report finding inspiration in many different sources and under many different circumstances. For example, some artists use stream-of-consciousness techniques. Others rely on their surroundings, and others call upon a personal, often unidentified muse.

Max Ernst (Germany, 1891–1976), a painter, sculptor, and collagist, described this source of inspiration: "One rainy day in 1919, I was struck by the obsession which held under my gaze the pages of an illustrated catalog showing objects designed for anthropologic, microscopic, mineralogic, and paleontological demonstration. There I found brought together elements of figuration so remote that the sheer absurdity of the collection provoked a sudden intensification of the visionary faculties in me . . . thus I obtained a faithful fixed image of my hallucination and transformed into my revealing dramas what had been before only some banal pages of advertising."

- **The world of imagination.** Everyone has dreams and fantasies. Artists have the creative ability to turn dreams, and even nightmares, into the illusion of reality. Look at Figure 1–6. What message about the world of dreams might the artist be giving us?
- **Their own hearts and minds.** Personal beliefs, or feelings, are often a source of ideas for art. Sometimes artists will express those feelings in their work. Can you think of a good example of this kind of painting?
- **Real-world events and people.** People and events often turn up in art. Figure 1–7 offers a rare glimpse of Wild West hero Buffalo Bill Cody.

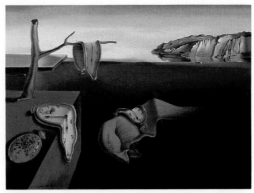

▲ **Figure 1–6** Has the artist painted a happy place or a forlorn, lonely place? What might he be telling us about time in the land of dreams?

Salvador Dali. *Persistence of Memory.* 1931. Oil on canvas. 24.1 x 33 cm (9½ x 13"). Museum of Modern Art, New York, New York. Given anonymously.

◀ **Figure 1–7** The artist did this painting of Buffalo Bill when he came to France to visit her.

Rosa Bonheur. *Buffalo Bill on Horseback.* 1889. Oil on canvas. 47 x 38.7 cm (18½ x 15¼"). Buffalo Bill Historical Center, Cody, Wyoming. Given in memory of Wm. R. Coe and Mai Rogers Coe.

Lesson 3   *Artists and Ideas*   📖   **7**

Developing Concepts

Exploring Aesthetics. Divide the class into five groups. Assign each group one of these art works from the lesson: Figure 1–5, Figure 1–6, Figure 1–7, Figure 1–8, Figure 1–9. Have the students in each group meet and discuss their reactions to the assigned work. They should also try to agree on an answer to this question: What may have been the source of inspiration for this work of art? Then have the members of each group share their ideas with the rest of the class.

Using Art Criticism. Let pairs of students choose and discuss one of the art works shown in this lesson. The partners should discuss their responses to these questions: What do you think the specific inspiration for this work could have been? What do you imagine the artist saw, did, or thought about before creating this work? How do you think the artist reacted to that experience? How successfully does the work communicate the artist's reaction to the experience? Then have each student write a short paragraph summarizing the discussion.

Understanding Art History. Have the students work individually or in groups to learn more about the Muses. Ask them to do research, looking for answers to questions such as these: What are the names of the nine Muses? Of which art form was each goddess a patron? When and how were the Muses first depicted? When and where were shrines built to honor them? Where and how have the Muses been depicted in more recent times? After the students have shared and discussed their findings, let each student draw his or her own version of one of the Muses.

Note
Tell students that Rosa Bonheur, the artist of Figure 1–7, worked in an age when few women were allowed to paint. She also lived at a time when trousers were off limits to women. Before she could attend horse fairs and cattle markets to sketch animals, she had to obtain police permission to wear overalls.

Cooperative Learning
Divide students into small groups and distribute Resource 1-5, *A Journey Into the Past* (cooperative learning activity). Challenge each group to research some part of mythology that interests them and design an original board-like game.

▲ Figure 1–8   Do you know the Biblical story told by these two paintings? Do you notice anything different about the clothing in the painting at the right? During what period of American history was clothing like this worn?

Bartolomé Esteban Murillo. *Return of the Prodigal Son.* 1667/70. Oil on canvas. 236.3 x 261 cm (93 x 102¾"). National Gallery of Art, Washington, D.C. Gift of the Avalon Foundation.

- **Ideas commissioned by employers.** Many artists are hired by individuals or companies to create works of art. In the past such employers of artists were called patrons. **Patrons of the arts** are *sponsors, or supporters, of an artist or art-related places and events.* For example the Catholic Church, as you will see, was at one time a major patron of the arts. It employed artists to create paintings and sculptures illustrating stories from the Bible.

- **Artists of the past.** Art is not made in a vacuum. Artists learn from and build on the work of artists who came before them. Sometimes artists base works directly on earlier pieces. (See Figures 1–8 and 1–9.) The artist of the painting that opened this chapter shows his appreciation to the past in a different way. Look back at that painting (page **xvi**). Do you know any of the artists in the small pictures at the upper right?

8   Lesson 3   *Artists and Ideas*

▲ **Figure 1–9   See caption for Figure 1–8.**

Mary Ann Willson. *The Prodigal Son Reclaimed.* c. 1815. Pen and black ink and watercolor. National Gallery of Art, Washington, D.C. Gift of Edgar William and Bernice Chrysler Garbisch.

IDEAS FOR YOUR OWN ART

In the coming chapters you will be asked to come up with ideas of your own. Like all other artists, you may at times find yourself stuck. At such moments, an idea bank may be just the answer. It may help boost your powers of creative thinking.

The following studio experience will explain how to make an idea bank for your classroom.

STUDIO EXPERIENCE

Find four envelopes. Label one *Noun*, one *Adjective*, one *Verb*, and one *Adverb*. Think up words for each part of speech. Use a dictionary for help. Avoid proper nouns (those beginning with capital letters). Write each of your words on a separate slip of paper. Place your slips in the correct envelope. Take turns choosing four slips, one from each type of envelope. Share envelopes with other class members to get more variety in the word combinations. These envelopes will be your idea bank for future art projects.

When you have a word combination that you like, arrange the slips on a table in this order: adjective–noun–verb–adverb. Make the words form an interesting idea.

On a sheet of white paper, 9 x 12 inch (23 x 30 cm), sketch your idea. The sketch should show the thing or object (noun) described doing the action (or verb) named.

✔ CHECK YOUR UNDERSTANDING

1. What are patrons of the arts?
2. List and describe four sources artists use for inspiration.

Classroom Management Tip

In addition to the idea bank, a filing system can be set up for students to use. Use four file folders and label them with the following: people, places, objects, and designs. When you or your students see an interesting magazine picture, cut it out and place it in the correct file. Later when students need another source of inspiration, they can use the file. Postcards, photos, or prints of art works can also be included.

Answers to "Check Your Understanding"

1. Patrons of the arts are sponsors, or supporters, of an artist or of art-related places and events.
2. These are some possible sources of an artist's inspiration: famous works of literature, including myths; the artist's own dreams and fantasies; the artist's own personal beliefs and feelings; real people and events; ideas and requirements of the artist's employer; the work done by other artists. (Students may identify any four.)

Objectives

After completing this lesson, students will be able to:
• Define the term *collage.*
• Use their idea banks to develop subjects for their own work.
• Make and describe collages.

Supplies

• Two examples of student art: one a painting, the other a collage (or reproductions of a painting and a collage).
• Pencils, sketch paper, magazines and newspapers, wallpaper scraps, scissors, white glue, colored construction paper.

> **TRB Resources**
> • 1-6 *Romare Bearden,* (artist profile)
> • 1-7 *Shadow Puppets,* (studio)

TEACHING THE LESSON

Getting Started

Motivator. To help students recognize both the similarities and differences between painting and collage, display the two examples of student art (painting and collage). If possible, show works that are similar in color and/or in subject. Ask: What do you see in each of these works? How was each work made? How do you think the different methods affected the artists? How do they affect you as viewers?

Vocabulary. Point out the collage on display, and ask students to describe other collages that they have seen. Have students work together to develop their own definition of the term *collage.* Then let them check their definition against the definition given in the text.

Making a Content Collage

This work of art by Lois Dvorak is made with handmade paper. Called a **collage** (kuh-**lahzh**), this is *art work arranged from cut or torn materials pasted to a surface.* The lizards are native to the New Mexico desert where she lives. (See Figure 1–10.)

WHAT YOU WILL LEARN

You will create a collage using a combination of drawn and found materials. You will combine natural materials that you find in your environment with your own drawings of insects and other small creatures from your local environment. (See Figure 1–11.)

▶ **Figure 1–10   Where did the artist go for ideas in this art work? Can you name the different materials the artist used?**

Lois Dvorak. *The Lizards.* Handmade paper assemblage. 81.3 x 101.6 cm (32 x 40″). Private collection.

Background Information

The first important collage art was created by Cubists and Dadaists.

Cubism was developed jointly by Pablo Picasso and Georges Braque around 1908. Cubists concerned themselves with the essence of a subject. They simplified planes and combined or superimposed many views of a single figure or object to express the idea of that figure or object. Eventually, Cubists began adding elements other than paint to their works—and began creating collages.

The Dada movement, which began in Europe around 1915, was anti-art. Dadaists created their works with the intention of shocking or outraging their viewers. One well-known Dada work by Marcel Duchamp was a re-creation of Leonardo da Vinci's *Mona Lisa*—embellished with a mustache. Then Duchamp began to make art of found objects. His role as an artist, as he perceived it, was to bring these different objects together.

WHAT YOU WILL NEED

- Pencils and sketch paper
- Small pieces of white paper
- Watercolor markers
- Natural, found materials such as leaves, twigs, pebbles, dirt, bark, wild flowers, and grasses
- White glue
- White paper, 9 x 12 inch (23 x 30 cm)

WHAT YOU WILL DO

1. Brainstorm with your classmates for ideas of what insects, spiders, frogs, and lizards you might find outdoors in your area. Look for pictures of these creatures in the library, and in science books. Notice the difference in body structure between insect and spider.
2. Collect natural materials from your outdoor environment. Look for leaves, twigs, grasses, bark, dirt and sand, wild flowers, and pebbles. If you live in a city, the florist might have old leaves and ferns to give away.
3. Make some rough sketches of the creatures. Then make finished drawings with pencil on white paper of the creatures for your work. Decide whether you want your creatures to contrast with the background or to blend in to the colors. Color them with watercolor markers.
4. Arrange your found objects with the creatures you drew. When you are satisfied with the composition glue everything down.
5. Display your work. Can you find similarities and differences?

OTHER STUDIO IDEAS

- Make the collage using construction paper for all the objects.

EXAMINING YOUR WORK

- **Describe** Tell about the creatures you selected and explain why you selected them. Describe the found materials you collected. Invent a title for your composition. Are you satisfied with your work? Explain.

SAFETY TIP

Make sure to use only ordinary household glue for your collage. Wallpaper paste and similar glues have poisons in them. These poisons can enter the body through the skin.

▲ **Figure 1–11   Student work. A content collage.**

- ●● Imagine that these little creatures have human characteristics such as expressive faces, and human hands and feet. Draw a scene of these imaginary creatures at home.

Lesson 4   *Making a Content Collage*   **11**

Developing Concepts

Exploring Aesthetics. Help students examine and discuss Figure 1–10. Ask: What do you see in this art work? What is happening in the scene? What feeling does the work convey? How does it convey that feeling?

Using Art Criticism. Have each student write a paragraph in response to these questions: Why do you think Lois Dvorak created *The Lizards* as a collage instead of as a painting? How would the work have been different if it had been a painting or a drawing?

Developing Studio Skills. Have students select one of their own collage works and create a painting or drawing inspired by that collage.

Following Up

Closure. Help students discuss their responses to these questions: How did you feel while you were working on your collage? What did you learn from making your collage? How do you plan to use collage in future art projects?

Evaluation. 1. Review students' written responses to the "Check Your Understanding" questions. 2. Listen to students' discussion about their own experiences in making collages.

Reteaching. Help students review collage as they discuss Figure 1–10. Explain that when objects from real life are simplified in an art work, the work is called an abstract. Then ask: Is the scene in *The Lizards* realistic or abstract? What specific details in the art work make you think that? Can collage works be realistic? Why, or why not?

Enrichment. Let students work in small groups to find and discuss reproductions of collage works by early Cubists (such as Georges Braque and Pablo Picasso) or Dadaists (such as Jean Arp and Kurt Schwitters). After their discussion, ask students to create their own collage works in the style either of Cubism or of Dada.

Note
Tell students that collages are well-planned designs, in which an artist suggests ideas by using pictures or objects as symbols that are suggestive of a mood, emotion, or intellectual response. Tell students that fabric can also be used as a collage material. Bring in various fabric samples—course, smooth, patterned, and plain. Suggest that students experiment with various fabric samples and arrange the fabric to create an interesting design. Have students describe the textural qualities of the collage. Point out the way that line, rhythm, and pattern are used in the fabric samples.

ANSWERS TO "CHAPTER 1 REVIEW"

Building Vocabulary

1. perceiving
2. point of view
3. artists
4. fine art
5. applied art
6. collage
7. patron of the arts

Reviewing Art Facts

8. Looking at art can help people develop their ability to perceive art, explore ways of making their own art, develop their powers of creative thinking, find fresh ways of expressing their ideas, and learn about the tools and techniques artists use.
9. Types of fine art include drawings, paintings, and sculptures.
10. Stained glass is a type of applied art.
11. The Muses were special goddesses to whom the ancient Greeks prayed for inspiration.
12. There are six sources to which artists turn for inspiration: the world of myths and legends; the world of imagination; their own hearts and minds; real-world events and people; ideas commissioned by employers; artists of the past.
13. Patrons of the arts are sponsors, or supporters, of artists or of art-related places and events. Patrons often employed artists to create certain art works or to create art works with specific messages.
14. An idea bank can expand your creative thinking by helping you think of objects and actions in new ways or in new combinations.
15. When Dvorak created her collage *The Lizards*, she turned to nature for a source of ideas.

Thinking About Art

1. Responses will vary; they should reflect students' understanding of these terms: *artists, fine art,* and *applied art.*
2. Responses will vary depending on the objects chosen and the details included in students' descriptions.
3. Responses will vary; they should reflect students' understanding of the differences that result from observing the same subject from different points of view.
4. Responses will vary; students should identify objects that are made to be both functional and visually pleasing.
5. Responses will vary; be sure students support whichever idea they present.

BUILDING VOCABULARY

Number a sheet of paper from 1 to 7. After each number, write the term from the box that best matches each description below.

applied art	patrons of the arts
artists	perceiving
collage	point of view
fine art	

1. Looking at and thinking deeply about what you see.
2. The angle from which viewers see the scene in a painting.
3. People who use imagination and skill to share ideas in visual form.
4. Art made purely to be experienced visually.
5. Art made to be both looked at and used.
6. Art made up of cut and torn materials pasted to a surface.
7. A sponsor, or supporter, of an artist or art-related places and events.

REVIEWING ART FACTS

Number a sheet of paper from 8 to 15. Answer each question in a complete sentence.

8. What are some of the things people can learn by looking at art?
9. Name two kinds of fine art.
10. Name a type of applied art.
11. What were Muses? How did the ancient Greeks use the Muses?
12. Name six sources to which artists turn for ideas.
13. What are patrons of the arts? What is the connection between art patrons and artists?
14. How can an idea bank expand your creative thinking?
15. When Dvorak created the collage, *The Lizards*, where did she turn for her idea?

THINKING ABOUT ART

On a sheet of paper, answer each question in a sentence or two.

1. **Extend**. Based on what you learned in this chapter, how would you define *art*?
2. **Analyze**. Write a description of some object in the art room without naming it. Mention as many details as you can. See whether anyone in your class can identify the object.
3. **Summarize**. How could changing the point of view in an art work help make it more interesting?
4. **Analyze**. Name three examples of applied art in your home. Tell how useful you find each of the objects.
5. **Extend**. Do you think makers of applied art and fine art turn to the same sources for ideas? Explain your answer.

MAKING ART CONNECTIONS

1. **Language Arts**. Look at Rockwell's self-portrait on page **xvi**. What does the art work tell about the artist other than how he looks? How has the artist shown other information? An autobiography, a story of one's own life, is a written self-portrait. Write an autobiography. Begin by describing your physical, mental, and social characteristics. Other details to include are: Where and when you were born. Where you have lived and traveled. What your favorite things are.
2. **Science**. Using books and field guides, try to identify the kind of ducks shown in Winslow Homer's painting, *Right and Left*, on page **2**. In what parts of the world can this species be found? Where do you think Homer might have observed these ducks? Can you tell what time of year it is? Reading about migration might help to answer the question.

CHAPTER **1** REVIEW

LOOKING AT THE DETAILS

The detail shown below is from Norman Rockwell's *Triple Self-Portrait*. Study the detail and answer the following questions.

1. What might hint to you that Rockwell was an artist who built on the works of artists who came before him?
2. How do you perceive the artist in this detail? Why?
3. Look at the entire portrait on page **xvi**. Does your perception change? Explain your answer.
4. Certain clothing, furniture, backgrounds, and props the artist chooses to show can also tell us about the subject's character, beliefs, and personality. What do you think Rockwell is trying to tell you if anything about his fellow self-portrait artists? About himself? What things in the painting helped you in forming your answer?
5. Is the entire work a more interesting perspective than if his portrait included only the face you see in the detail? Why? How do you think Rockwell was able to paint the back view of himself?
6. Why do you think Rockwell omitted painting a background or a floor?

Norman Rockwell. *Triple Self-Portrait*. 1960. Oil on canvas. (Detail.) 113 x 87.2 cm (44½ x 34⅓"). Norman Rockwell Museum at Stockbridge, Stockbridge, Massachusetts. Norman Rockwell Art Collection Trust.

Chapter 1 Review **13**

Enjoying Art

Chapter Scan

Lesson 1 Understanding Art
Lesson 2 Aesthetics
Lesson 3 Torn Paper Face

TRB Resources

- 2-9 Chapter Test
- Color Transparency 3
- Color Transparency 4

TEACHING THE CHAPTER

Introducing the Art Work

Direct students' attention to Natalia Goncharova's *Cats*. Inform them that Natalia Goncharova was a Russian artist during the early twentieth century. She came from a distinguished family in central Russia, who enabled her to study at the Moscow School of Painting, Sculpture, and Architecture, with a former pupil of Rodin. Her sculptures won many awards, but after 1900 Goncharova switched to painting and began experimenting with abstract painting. Her desire for exploring abstract art led her out of Russia to Paris in 1917, where she settled and continued to produce theatrical designs and abstract paintings.

Examining the Art Work

Tell students that *Cats* is considered to be part of some of Natalia Goncharova's most innovative work.

Inform them that Goncharova portrays light in the way it emanates from and is reflected by objects. Point out how in this work, movement is suggested by light radiating in many different directions at the same time. Explain to students that Goncharova quickly takes the viewer's eye to every part of the canvas not only with the use of light but also with the use of line. The many sharp edges going in various directions give the viewer a sense of action.

Describe for students how harmony is achieved in this work by the repetitive use of the same shapes and colors. Also tell them that the contrast in colors—black/yellow, white/fuchsia—gives the viewer a feeling of intensity and drama about the subject.

Explain how Natalia Goncharova has achieved a sense of balance in this work. The darker shapes to the right are balanced by the large white shape in the upper left part of the work.

▲ It is hard to tell what the subject of this painting is without reading the credit line. What do you think the inspiration for this painting was?

Natalia Goncharova. *Cats*. 1913. Oil on canvas. 84.4 x 83.8 cm (33¼ x 33"). Solomon R. Guggenheim Museum, New York, New York.

Enjoying Art

Imagine you were in the museum where the painting at the left hangs. You might overhear someone say he or she doesn't like the painting because there is not anything familiar or recognizable in it. That might even sum up your own feelings about the painting.

But is this all there is to say about a painting? Does art succeed as art *only* because of lifelike details? Are there other ways of looking at — and evaluating the success of — an art object? In this chapter you will find out.

OBJECTIVES

After completing this chapter, you will be able to:
- Explain how subject, composition, and content relate to works of art.
- Define the term *aesthetics*.
- Discuss three schools of thought on what is important in art.
- Make a torn paper face.

WORDS YOU WILL LEARN

aesthetics
aesthetic views
composition
content
credit line

non-objective
subject
super-realism
work of art

ARTISTS YOU WILL MEET

T. C. Cannon
Mary Cassatt
Natalia Goncharova
Duane Hanson
William Harnett

Edward Hopper
Éduoard Manet
Robert Motherwell
Frank Stella

15

Understanding Art

To praise a job well done, people sometimes borrow a term from art. That term is *work of art*. A well-cooked meal might be described as "a work of art." So might a neatly arranged clothes closet.

In the study of art, the term **work of art** has a specific meaning. It is *any object created or designed by an artist*. Works of art, however, are not all equally successful.

▶ **Figure 2–1 The opera and the theatre were often subjects of art work. Why do you think this is so?**

Mary Stevenson Cassatt. *At the Opera.* 1879. Oil on canvas. 80 x 64.8 cm (31½ x 25½"). Museum of Fine Arts, Boston, Massachusetts. Hayden Collection.

16 〣 Lesson 1 *Understanding Art*

LESSON PLAN
(pages 16–19)

Objectives
After completing this lesson, students will be able to:
• Define the term *work of art*.
• Explain how subject, composition, and content relate to works of art.
• Identify the information presented in a credit line.

Supplies
• Drawing paper in various sizes; crayons, markers, pencils, watercolors with brushes, and/or other media.
• Map of the world.
• Strips of paper, markers.
• Listings of local art museums and galleries in local Yellow Pages telephone books, brochures, or newspapers.

TRB Resources
• 2-1 *What is Art?,* (reproducible master)
• 2-2 *Every Culture Has It's Own Beauty,* (appreciating cultural diversity)

TEACHING THE LESSON

Getting Started

Motivator. Begin by having students look at Figure 2–1 (or at a reproduction of another art work of your choice). Ask this question: What do you see when you look at this work? Encourage discussion, but do not ask specific questions. Then explain that as students read and discuss this lesson, they will discover new ways to see and understand this painting and other works of art.

Vocabulary. To help students understand the term *non-objective,* guide them in recognizing its parts. What does the prefix *non-* mean? (*It means "not" or "absence of."*) What is an object? (*It is something that can be perceived by the senses.*) Does the suffix *-ive* change the meaning or only the form of the word? (*It changes only the form.*)

16

Handbook Cross-Reference

Tell students the painting in Figure 2–1 is the work of Mary Cassatt, one of America's best known artists. She used her skill to paint pictures of an experience she was never to enjoy herself—motherhood. As she grew older she began to lose her sight. This made it necessary for her to stop painting, but she remained active in the world of art by acting as an art advisor. She convinced many to buy and bring to the United States masterpieces created by many of the great French artists. These works are now on view in museums across the country.

Refer students to the Artist Profiles, *Handbook* page **283** to read more about this leading female painter. Give them time to compare both of her works on pages **16** and **35**. Encourage students to bring in additional examples of works of art by Mary Cassatt.

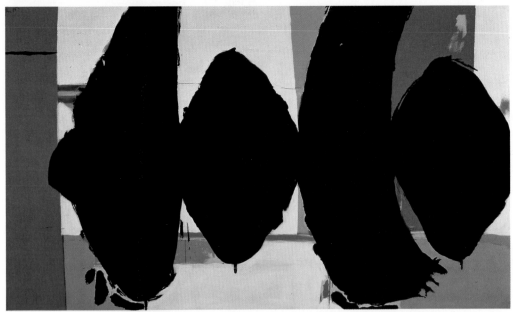

▲ Figure 2–2   An elegy is a speech or song of sorrow. How is sorrow expressed in this painting?

Robert Motherwell. *Elegy to the Spanish Republic 108*. 1966. Oil and acrylic on canvas. 213.4 x 373.4 cm (84 x 147"). Museum of Art, Dallas, Texas.

THE WORK OF ART

Works of art may be defined by three basic properties, or features. These properties are subject, composition, and content.

Subject

The subject answers the question "What do I see when I look at this art work?" The **subject** is *the image viewers can easily identify*. The subject may be a person or persons. It may be a thing, such as a tree. It may be a place. It may even be an event, such as a parade. The subject of the painting in Figure 2–1 is easily recognized. It is a woman seated in a theater box gazing through opera glasses.

In recent years some artists have chosen to create non-objective artwork. **Non-objective** means *there is no recognizable subject matter in the work*. The picture in Figure 2–2 is such a work.

Composition

All art works are made up of parts known as visual elements. These elements, which you will learn more about in Chapter 4, include color, line, shape, form, space, and texture. You will also learn that artists use certain guidelines, called principles of art, to organize these elements in their work. The principles of balance, variety, harmony, emphasis, proportion, movement, and rhythm will be discussed in Chapter 5. The **composition** of an art work is *how the principles are used to organize the elements*.

Look again at the picture in Figure 2–1. With your finger, trace the line of the railing beginning at the lower left edge. Where does this line take you? It carries you upward along the woman's right arm. From there the dark straps of her hat lead you to her lightly colored face. The woman's face is the most important part of the painting. The artist has skillfully used lines to direct your attention to it. Part of the picture's composition is how the artist uses the element of line and the principle of movement.

Content

Often a work of art communicates a message, idea, or feeling. This *message, idea, or feeling* is the art work's **content**. Look once more at Figure 2–1. Notice the man in the distance, leaning out of his theater box. He is using his own opera glasses, not to watch the show, but to stare at the woman. She, too, must be spying on people in other boxes. No-

tice where her glasses are pointed. Are they aimed downward, toward the stage?

Maybe the artist, Mary Cassatt, is trying to tell us something about human nature. Maybe she is saying that while we are busy looking at—and judging—others, we are being judged ourselves. This message is the painting's content.

Sometimes the content of a work is expressed as a feeling, such as love or hate. Can you identify the feeling expressed by the picture in Figure 2–3? What details of the picture give you a clue to that feeling?

▲ **Figure 2–3   What might this young woman be feeling? What clues do you have that she is feeling this way?**

Edward Hopper. *New York Movie.* 1939. Oil on canvas. 81.9 x 101.9 cm (32¼ x 40⅛"). Museum of Modern Art, New York, New York. Given anonymously.

Notice that even art works without recognizable subjects can show a feeling. Look again at Figure 2–2. The artist of this work depends on composition alone to express content. He uses scary dark shapes to communicate the terror and destruction of a civil war. These dark shapes overpower the brightly colored shapes behind, which stand for peace and happiness.

THE CREDIT LINE

Look once more at Figure 2–3. Do you see the name of the artist who created this work? Do you know the title of the work? Answers to these and other questions can be found in the credit line appearing alongside the work. A **credit line** is *a listing of important facts about an art work.*

Every art work in this book has a credit line. It is there to help you learn as much as you can about the work.

Reading a Credit Line

Most credit lines are made up of six facts. These facts, in the order in which they appear, are as follows:

- **The artist's name.** This information always comes first. Who is the artist of the work in Figure 2–1? Who is the artist of the work in Figure 2–2?
- **The title of the work.** Many titles give useful information about the subject or content. Some are meant to stimulate viewers' curiosity. Do you remember the title of the painting of the ducks back in Chapter 1 (Figure 1–1, page **2**)? Can you find a work in the present chapter with the title *New York Movie*? Who painted it?

- **The year the work was created.** Sometimes, in the case of older works, *c.* appears before the year. This is an abbreviation for *circa*, which means "around" or "about" in Latin. Which work in this lesson was created in 1966? What is its title?
- **The tools and materials used in creating the work.** Artists, as you will learn, use many different materials to create an art work. Watercolor paint is one of these materials. Pencil is another. How many works in Chapter 1 and in this chapter were made using oil on canvas?
- **The size of the work.** Size helps you imagine how the work would appear if you were standing before it. Height, in centimeters as well as in inches, is always listed first. The width is listed second. A third number refers to depth. What is the height of the painting in Chapter 1 by Bartolomé Esteban Murillo?
- **The location of the work.** Location includes the name of the gallery or museum where the work is housed and its city and state or country. Where would you go to view the painting in this chapter by Mary Cassatt? In what city is the National Gallery of Art located?

✔ CHECK YOUR UNDERSTANDING

1. What is a work of art?
2. What are three properties of art works?
3. Name four pieces of information given in a credit line.

Following Up

Closure. Help students recall the lesson title, and then pose this question: What have you learned about understanding art? Have students write short answers; then guide them in discussing their ideas.

Evaluation. 1. Review students' written responses to the "Check Your Understanding" questions. 2. Read students' explanations of what they have learned about understanding art.

Reteaching. Work with small groups of students to review the facts included in a credit line. Then have each student choose a work of art (either from the text or from a set of reproductions) and copy the credit line, writing each fact on a separate strip of paper. Let students mix up the strips of paper and then exchange sets. Give each student at least one opportunity to put the fact strips from a credit line in the correct order.

Enrichment. Ask volunteers to learn more about local art museums and galleries. (If there are no museums or galleries in the local community, students might research museums in the nearest large city.) Encourage all the students to read about museums and galleries in the community. Then let students volunteer to visit specific museums or galleries and report to the rest of the class on the collections and/or special exhibits on view there.

Answers to "Check Your Understanding
1. A work of art is any object created or designed by an artist.
2. The three basic properties of art works are subject, composition, and content.

3. A credit line presents these six pieces of information: the artist's name; the title of the work; the year the work was created; the tools and materials used in creating the work; the size of the work; the location of the work. (Students may identify any four of these pieces of information.)

Aesthetics

LESSON PLAN
(pages 20–23)

Objectives

After completing this lesson, students will be able to:
• Define the term *aesthetics.*
• Discuss three different aesthetic viewpoints.
• Use a chosen aesthetic view in planning and executing a drawing.

Supplies

• Collection of display-sized reproductions of various art works, or several art books with clear reproductions.
• Old magazines with black-and-white photographs, scissors, drawing paper, glue, pencils.
• Books or articles including information about and reproductions of works by T. C. Cannon and other Native American artists.
• Drawing paper, colored construction paper, scissors, thinned glue.

TRB Resources

• 2-3 *Duane Hanson,* (artist profile)
• 2-4 *What is Beauty?,* (aesthetics/art criticism)
• 2-5 *Explosion in the Art World,* (cooperative learning)
• 2-6 *Aesthetic Views,* (reproducible master)
• 2-7 *The Search for Beauty,* (art history)

TEACHING THE LESSON

Getting Started

Motivator. Review with students the definitions of the terms *subject, composition,* and *content* as they relate to works of art. During this review discussion, have several volunteers select (from a collection of large reproductions or from various art books) works of art that they find especially appealing. Then ask each volunteer to present his or her selection to the rest of the class and to describe what he or she especially likes about the work. After each brief presentation, have the other students identify whether the volunteer's choice was based primarily on subject, on composition, or on content.

Aesthetics

When you hear a new song on the radio, what do you listen for? Are you mostly interested in the words? Do you tune in, instead, to the beat? Maybe what matters to you most is the skill of the performers.

The question of what counts most in a work is not only a concern of listeners of music. It is a major concern of viewers and creators of every kind of art. This question is one art scholars have been wrestling with since earliest times.

In this lesson you will learn some of the ways they think about works of art.

AESTHETICS IN ART

You have probably heard the saying "beauty is in the eye of the beholder." People see beauty in different ways. Pinpointing the meaning of beauty is only one goal of the branch of learning called **aesthetics,** (ess-**thet**-iks) *the philosophy or study of the nature and the value of art.*

▶ **Figure 2–4   Notice how the objects in the painting seem to project out into space. Which object looks most lifelike to you?**

William Harnett. *My Gems.* 1888. Paint on wood. 45.7 x 35.6 cm (18 x 14"). National Gallery of Art, Washington, D.C. Gift of the Avalon Foundation.

Note

Explain to students that there are many definitions for the term aesthetics. Help them understand that one's own values and understanding of their personal likes and dislikes influence their appreciation and understanding of the art around them. Have students look around and think about who else dresses like them, or wears their hair the same length as theirs. Discuss whether these people would appreciate the same art, music, or clothing.

Tell students that what makes us more understanding of the art processes are our aesthetic understanding of shapes, lines, and colors. Ask students: What design makes a composition appealing to your aesthetic preferences? Have students use one word in which to describe themselves if they were a shape or object moving through space or time.

The chief goal of aesthetics is finding an answer to the question "What is art?" In their search for an answer, art scholars have put forth different views on what is important in art. *These ideas, or schools of thought, on what to look for in works of art* are called **aesthetic views**.

AESTHETIC VIEWS

Today, students of art recognize three main aesthetic views. These aesthetic views are based on the properties of an artwork: subject, composition, and content. One aesthetic view has to do with an art work's subject. The second view relates to composition. The third view is tied to content.

View #1: Subject

The first aesthetic view states that art should imitate what we see in the real world. A successful work in this view is one with realistic subject matter. Look at the painting in Figure 2–4. Notice how lifelike the objects in this work look. The image of the light-blue pitcher could pass for a photograph. Art scholars of this first school would praise this painting for being so true to life. Would you agree with them?

Modern artists have found ways of creating works with even more convincingly life-like subjects than the type found in Figure 2–4. A style of *art devoted to extraordinarily realistic works,* called **super-realism,** has come into being. Without being told, would you ever guess that Figure 2–5 is a photo of an art work and not a real person?

Vocabulary. Before students begin reading the lesson, direct their attention to the title and let volunteers suggest definitions for *aesthetics.* Then, after students have read the definition in the text, help them discuss fields other than visual arts in which aesthetics is an important branch of learning.

Developing Concepts

Exploring Aesthetics. Guide the class in discussing some of the art works selected by volunteers during the "Motivator" activity (or ask a few new volunteers to select new works). Display each reproduction in turn and ask: Do you consider this work true to life? What kind of design does this work present? Do you consider it unified and visually interesting? What message, idea, or feeling does this work communicate to you?

Encourage all the students to participate in the discussion, and emphasize that there are no right or wrong answers. Ask students to support their opinions by pointing out specific details in the works of art. Conclude the consideration of each work by returning to the basic question posed by aestheticians and asking: Is this art? Why?

Using Art Criticism. Have each student write a paragraph about Figure 2–5. Students should describe what they see in the work and how they react to it. Next, have students share and discuss their responses. Finally, help students focus on describing and evaluating the content of *Sunbather.* Explain that the work points out some of the artist's observations about modern society. Help students identify some of the conflicting ideas they find in the work. Ask: What message do you think Hanson wanted to communicate with this work? Do you think he succeeded in communicating that message? Why, or why not?

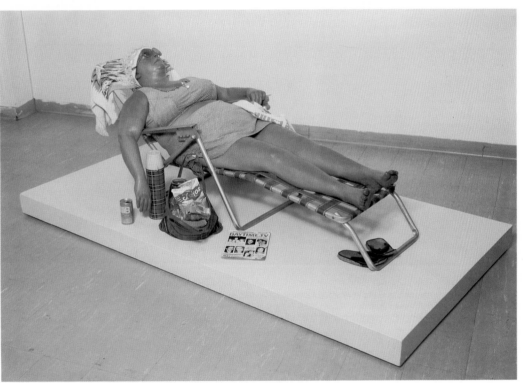

▲ **Figure 2–5** Notice the details the artist has included in this work. What message about certain American values might he be trying to express?

Duane Hanson. *Sunbather.* 1971. Polyester fiberglass polychromed in oil. Life-size. Wadsworth Atheneum, Hartford. National Endowment for the Arts/Gift of Roscoe Nelson Gray in memory of Roscoe Nelson Dalton Gray and Rene Gabrielle Gray.

Lesson 2   *Aesthetics*   **21**

Note
Tell students that the painter of Figure 2–4, William Harnett, is famous for his lifelike works. Explain that one of his works so amazed people in his day that they refused to believe it was a painting. Many, seeing it for the first time, tried to reach out and grasp objects in it. Have students compare the style of William Harnett to the super-realism style used by Duane Hanson in Figure 2–5.

View #2: Composition

The second aesthetic view or school of thought argues that what counts in art is composition. In this view a successful art work is one in which the artist has used the principles of art to skillfully combine the art elements. Look again at Figure 2–4. Supporters of this view would find much to admire in the painting. They might note the way the shapes have been arranged to balance the composition. They might explain how the contrast between light and dark emphasizes certain objects.

Some artists have paid more attention to composition than to any other feature. How would art scholars of the second school react to the work in Figure 2–6? What visual elements and principles might they refer to when discussing this work?

View #3: Content

The third aesthetic view holds that what is most important in an art work is its content. In this view a successful art work is one that sends a clear message or feeling. Look once more at Figure 2–4. Notice the work's title, *My Gems*. The artist seems to be giving us a peek at some of his most prized possessions. Note how worn some of these objects are. What feeling about favorite things might the artist be expressing? How would individuals taking this third aesthetic view react to that feeling? How do you react to it?

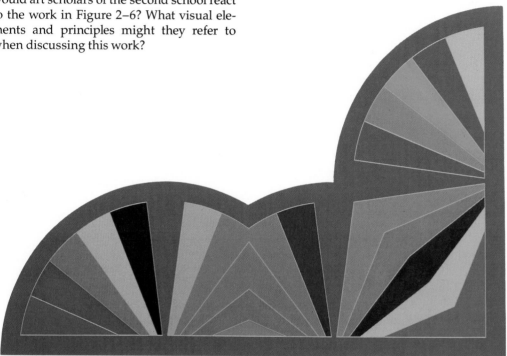

▲ **Figure 2–6** Many of this artist's works were not rectangular. He worked on a huge scale and painted designs that followed the unusual shapes of his canvases. This art work is called a "hard-edged painting." Why do you think it is called that?

Frank Stella. *Agbatana III*. 1968. Flourescent acrylic on canvas. 305 x 457 cm (120 x 180″). Allen Art Museum, Oberlin College, Ohio. Ruth C. Roush Fund for Contemporary Art and National Foundation for the Arts & Humanities Grant, 1968.

22   Lesson 2   *Aesthetics*

▲ Figure 2–7 **What is the subject of this painting? What is the composition? What is the content?**

T. C. Cannon. *Turn of the Century Dandy*. 1976. Acrylic on canvas. 152.4 x 132.1 cm (60 x 52″). Private collection.

AESTHETICS AND THE "BIG PICTURE"

It is important to note that few students of art accept just one aesthetic view. Most believe that to achieve a full understanding of art requires keeping an open mind. How might a person with all three views react to the painting that opened this chapter? (See page **14**.) Do you think the person would describe this work as true to life? Would you describe it that way? How have color, line, and shapes been used to create this work? Do you think they have been used effectively to create an unified and visually interesting design? Do you think the picture communicates a message, idea, or feeling? What might that message be? Look at the painting above. (See Figure 2–7.) Ask yourself the same questions regarding this art work.

✔CHECK YOUR UNDERSTANDING

1. What is the study of aesthetics? What is the chief goal of aesthetics?
2. Briefly describe the three main aesthetic views described.
3. What is super-realism?
4. Why do few students of art accept just one aesthetic view?

Torn Paper Face

STUDIO   LESSON 3   STUDIO

Torn Paper Face

LESSON PLAN
(pages 24–25)

Objectives
After completing this lesson, students will be able to:
- Make and discuss torn paper faces.
- Discuss how colors can help develop different moods in art works.

Supplies
- Pencils, notepads, scrap pieces of colored construction paper, sheets of construction paper, small brushes, slightly thinned white glue.

> **TRB Resource**
> - 2-8 *Collage Your Day,* (studio)

TEACHING THE LESSON

Getting Started
Motivator. Ask volunteers to use only their faces—no words or sounds—to express various emotions, such as anger, happiness, surprise, fear, disappointment, and confusion. Let each volunteer show a mood facially without first identifying it. Then ask the class: What mood do you think this is? Why? What color or colors does this mood make you think of?

Vocabulary. Ask volunteers to recall the definition of *content* introduced in the text. Let other volunteers give examples of different uses of the noun, and guide students in discussing the relationships among these various uses of *content.*

Developing Concepts
Exploring Aesthetics. Help students discuss Figure 2–8. Ask: What mood does this painting communicate to you? How does it communicate that mood? What story does it suggest to you? Then let students work with partners to write stories suggested by the painting.

Look closely at the woman in Figure 2–8. She sits in a garden overlooking the tracks of a railroad station. She stares off into space, lost in her own thoughts. What contrast do you notice between her and the young girl?

If you had to describe this woman's mood, what words would you use? If you were going to create a piece of art, how would you show this mood?

WHAT YOU WILL LEARN

This studio lesson will test your skill in creating a face as seen from the front. The face will express a mood. In your work, you will focus totally on content. No effort will be made to create a real-looking face. You will exaggerate the features in your face and select colors that will communicate a mood.

You will "build" your face of torn bits of construction paper. (See Figure 2–9.)

WHAT YOU WILL NEED

- Pencil and notepad
- Scrap pieces of colored construction paper
- Sheet of construction paper, 12 x 18 inch (30 x 46 cm)
- Small brush and slightly thinned white glue

WHAT YOU WILL DO

1. Working with a partner, practice acting out different moods. On your notepad, jot down notes about which facial expressions fit which moods. What happens to

▶ **Figure 2–8   What are the subjects in this painting? How does content differ from subject in art works?**

Édouard Manet. *Gare Saint-Lazare.* 1873. Canvas 93.3 x 114.5 (36¾ x 45⅛″). National Gallery of Art, Washington, D.C. Gift of Horace Havemeyer in memory of Louisina W. Havemeyer.

24   Lesson 3   *Torn Paper Face*

Background Information
Édouard Manet (France, 1832–1883) is often identified with the artists of French Impressionism. However, Manet did not care to be judged with the Impressionist painters and refused to exhibit with them.

Manet came from a wealthy, respectable family, and throughout his life he dressed and acted in an elegant manner. During his life Manet would have liked to be accepted by the Academie and/or critics of the time.

Manet's paintings seemed shockingly modern to the public. He had developed new ideas about both the subject and the composition of painting. He believed that a painting should show only what the eye can actually see and that the brushstrokes and the colors of a painting should be more important than the figures or objects represented. Because of these new ideas, Manet's work marked a turning point in the history of Western art.

your eyes, for instance, when you feel anger? What happens to your mouth when you feel sadness? Decide what mood your work will show and write this on your notepad.

2. Select one sheet of construction paper for the background. Choose colors of construction paper scraps that show up clearly against one another. Keep in mind that certain colors call to mind certain moods. Red is commonly thought of as a color connected with anger. Blue might be thought of in connection with sadness. (See Figure 2–9.)

3. Begin tearing your scraps into a variety of large and small shapes to represent features of a face. Exaggerate these features to capture the mood you have chosen. To show happiness, for example, make the mouth unusually large and smiling. Position your shapes on the sheet of construction paper to form a face seen from the front. Using the brush, apply a small amount of glue to the back of each scrap. (For information on applying glue, see Technique Tip **28**, *Handbook* page **281**.) Lightly press each scrap into place.

4. When the glue has dried, display your torn paper face. Compare your work with that of your classmates. See how many of your friends can tell immediately which mood your face shows. Try to guess the moods their faces show.

● **Describe**   Tell whether your work reveals a front view of a face. Point to the features you exaggerated. Tell what different colors you used for your torn paper face. Explain whether they helped capture the mood of your work. Tell what mood your work shows. Discuss what reactions members of your class had toward your work.

▲ Figure 2–9   Student work. A torn paper face.

OTHER STUDIO IDEA

● Create a non-objective picture to express another mood. Use brightly colored markers and draw a non-objective picture. Draw seven triangles, eight circles, and nine rectangles on a page. Have some of the shapes overlap. Color as you wish to create an interesting non-objective picture. If you choose to color the background, color it only one color for contrast.

Lesson 3   *Torn Paper Face*   **25**

Using Art Criticism. Explain that Édouard Manet did not consider subject or content the most important aspect of his work; he preferred an aesthetic view centered on composition and technique. For him, the subject and the mood were incidental to the actual application of paint. Manet wanted viewers to consider the painted surface of the canvas, not just to look beyond it to identify the subject or search for the work's message. Ask students to think about Manet's intentions as they look at Figure 2–8: When you view this work, what aspect of it do you consider most striking—its subject, its composition, or its content? Why?

Appreciating Cultural Diversity. After students have completed and discussed their torn paper faces, explain that many groups of Native Americans created masks for ceremonial and religious uses. For example, Alaskan Inuits made ceremonial masks from driftwood and feathers, and the Iroquois' False Face masks were made from basswood and horsehair. Ask volunteers to find and share photographs of such masks; help the class discuss the message each mask communicates.

Following Up

Closure. Give each student a turn to answer these questions: What do you like best about your own torn paper face? What did you learn as you planned, created, and examined this work?

Evaluation. Review students' torn paper faces, and consider their responses to the "Closure" questions.

Reteaching. Encourage students who express dissatisfaction with their torn paper faces to work with partners in creating new works using the same technique.

Enrichment. Have students read about and find photographs of African masks. Then guide students in discussing how these tribal masks are similar to and different from the Native American masks they studied. (See "Appreciating Cultural Diversity," above.)

Classroom Management Tip
Have students make an art portfolio in which to keep drawings, paintings, and other flat art work. Have them use two sections of cardboard measuring 24 x 36 inches (61 x 90 cm). These can be cut from an ordinary cardboard box. Space a series of holes along one side of each cardboard section. Use cord or yarn to lace the two sections together.
   Have students create an interesting design for the cover of the art portfolio and be sure they include their name in a prominent place on the cover.

BUILDING VOCABULARY

Number a sheet of paper from 1 to 9. After each number, write the term from the box that best matches each description below.

aesthetics	non-objective
aesthetic views	subject
composition	super-realism
content	works of art
credit line	

1. Objects created or designed by artists.
2. The image viewers see and can easily identify in an art work.
3. How the principles are used to organize the elements in an art work.
4. The message, idea, or feeling expressed by an art work.
5. A list of facts about an art work.
6. The philosophy or study of the nature and the value of art.
7. Ideas, or schools of thought, about what to look for in art.
8. Type of art devoted to creating works with convincingly lifelike subjects.
9. Art which has no recognizable subject.

REVIEWING ART FACTS

Number a sheet of paper from 10 to 15. Answer each question in a complete sentence.

10. What are three properties, or features, of art works?
11. Which property is concerned with how the principles of a work are used to organize the elements?
12. Name five pieces of information that appear on a credit line.
13. What is the abbreviation for circa? What does this term mean?
14. What is the key question asked by people who work in the field of aesthetics?
15. Why do many students of art accept more than one aesthetic view?

THINKING ABOUT ART

On a sheet of paper, answer each question in a sentence or two.

1. **Analyze**. Pick two works of fine art from Chapter 2 that have subjects. List the subjects found in each.
2. **Analyze**. Pick two works of fine art from Chapter 2 that you believe express a feeling. Identify the feeling of each. Explain how these feelings were shown.
3. **Extend**. Look around the room you are in at the moment. Try to imagine that you are looking at a very lifelike painting. Can you find a message in this scene? What is it?
4. **Compare and contrast**. In what ways is a painting like a short story or poem? In what ways is it different?
5. **Interpret**. Why do you think the final fact in a credit line includes the city and state or country in which a museum is found?

MAKING ART CONNECTIONS

1. **Drama**. Theater and television productions include the same features as works of visual art. The subject is represented by the characters, the content is represented by the script, and the composition determines how the characters and ideas are presented. Choose a play or television production that you have seen. Write a brief report identifying the subject, content, and composition.
2. **Music**. Music also has subject, content, and composition. Music may tell a story through instrumentation or through lyrics. Choose a type of music, such as rock, jazz, country, or classical and analyze the piece for its subject, content, and composition.

LOOKING AT THE DETAILS

The detail shown below is from Natalia Goncharova's *Cats*. Study the detail and answer the following questions.

1. Do the colors and shapes suggest a certain feeling? Explain.
2. Cover up the credit line. What is the subject of this painting? Look at the entire work on page **14**. Does this help? Explain.
3. Which aesthetic view or views would you take in judging this painting? Explain.
4. Do you think this work is successful as art? Why or why not?

Natalia Goncharova. *Cats.* 1913. Oil on canvas. (Detail.) 84.4 x 83.8 cm (33¼ x 33"). Solomon R. Guggenheim Museum, New York, New York.

Exploring Art Media

Chapter Scan

Lesson 1 Drawing
Lesson 2 Printmaking
Lesson 3 Painting
Lesson 4 Experimenting with Pigment
Lesson 5 Sculpture
Lesson 6 Creating with Mixed Media

TRB Resources

• 3-10 Chapter Test
• Color Transparency 5
• Color Transparency 6

TEACHING THE CHAPTER

Introducing the Art Work

Direct students' attention to Jan Steen's painting *The Drawing Lesson.* Inform students that Jan Steen was a Dutch painter in the mid-seventeenth century who helped form the painter's guild in his home city of Leyden. During that time it was fashionable to paint genre paintings, which depict ordinary people and situations. It was also popular to fill interior scenes with all sorts of objects that were symbolic clues about the story. Jan Steen's paintings are filled with detail, but unlike many of his contemporaries, he does not let detail overpower his main theme.

Examining the Art Work

Tell students that in the *Drawing Lesson* the viewer's attention is first drawn to the teacher and students in the center of the picture, and then radiates outward to include objects that further explain the story. Point out that the studio pictured here is filled with all the tools necessary for a busy artist. A canvas, painting and drawing supplies, an easel, and items used for still lifes are positioned about the studio. Decorating the room are plaster molds of classical figures and casts of body parts. Point out the realism of Steen's images and his use of color and light. Note how the light coming in through the window suggests the time of day.

▲ The artist is famous for his paintings of ordinary people and events. Here you see him showing a drawing technique to children. On the shelf, the sculpture of the ox stands for St. Luke, the saint who watched over artists.

Jan Steen. *The Drawing Lesson.* 1665. Oil on wood. 49.3 x 41 cm (19⅜ x 16¼"). J. Paul Getty Museum.

Exploring Art Media

Every profession has its "tools of the trade." Carpenters use hammers and wood. Plumbers use wrenches and pipes. Baseball players use bats and balls.

Artists, too, have their tools of the trade. One of these, shown in the painting at the left, is a pencil. How many tools of the artist's trade can you find in the painting? Can you think of any others that are not shown here?

In this chapter you will learn more about the materials used by artists.

OBJECTIVES

After completing this chapter, you will be able to:

- Define the term *medium of art*.
- Name the different kinds of media used in drawing, printmaking, painting, and sculpting.
- Experiment with drawing, printmaking, painting, and sculpting media.
- Use mixed media to create a work of art.

WORDS YOU WILL LEARN

binder	relief
edition	reproduction
freestanding	solvent
medium of art	style
mixed media	three-dimensional
pigment	two-dimensional
print	

ARTISTS YOU WILL MEET

Mary Cassatt	Henri-Charles
Ann Chernow	Manguin
Marisol Escobar	Georgia O'Keeffe
Nancy Graves	Jan Steen
Edward Hopper	Henri de Toulouse-
Wassily Kandinsky	Lautrec
Käthe Kollwitz	

Discussing the Art Work

Explain to students that his painting makes the viewer feel as if he or she is witnessing a private moment. Steen accomplishes this not only by his subject matter but also by the personal space of the room and by the position of the subject's faces. Point out how the teacher is engrossed in what he is doing and that the students are looking at him and his work. Refer to the title of the work; then ask students whether they think this teacher's art consists only of drawing. Point out the canvas and easel; then ask students to identify some other objects in the room which might suggest that this artist uses other media. Ask students to look closely at the man's face and discuss whether they think he is serious about his art. Point out the man's posture and the appearance of his studio. Ask students to think about whether this might be the man's home as well as his studio.

Ask students whether they think this painting tells us something about Jan Steen. Explain that a work of art tends to reflect the beliefs and the personality of the artist who creates it. Ask students whether this painting might tell us what an artist's life might have been like in Jan Steen's time.

Tell students that in this chapter they will learn about the different kinds of materials artists use to create their works, and they will create their own work of art using several of these media.

29

Building Self-Esteem

In this chapter, students will see how Henri de Toulouse-Lautrec became famous for his posters of the Moulin Rouge in the late 1800s. Today, one commonly-seen type of poster advertises movies. Tell the class they will now create a poster advertising a movie in which *they* star as the superhero or heroine. Discuss some characterics common to most superheros. Have students name their superhero along with the other stars in the supporting cast. Tell the class to make the superhero's picture much larger than the other subjects included and to give the movie an exciting title that would make people want to come and see it. Urge students to choose a subject area they like. Perhaps they draw jets or horses or dinosaurs well; tell them to draw a scene that will show off their best talents. Display the movie posters and give students a chance to discuss the superhero's role in the movie.

LESSON PLAN
(pages 30–33)

Objectives

After completing this lesson, students will be able to:
• Define the term *medium of art*.
• Name the different kinds of media used in drawing.
• Plan and execute a mixed-media drawing.

Supplies

• Sketch paper, wide variety of drawing media.
• Index cards, drawings (by other students, if possible) done in a single medium and in mixed media.
• Natural drawing tools, such as sticks, roots, grasses, pebbles; ink; drawing paper.
• Leaves (brought in by students, if possible), magnifying glasses, drawing paper, pencils and other drawing media.

TRB Resource
• 3-1 *Drawing Media*, (reproducible master)

TEACHING THE LESSON

Getting Started

Motivator. Begin by distributing sketch paper and various drawing media to the students. Have them work with partners to experiment with the media. What kinds of lines do they make? How does changing the angle change the kind of line? Which media move slickly across the paper? Which drag? Which make lines that bleed? Encourage the partners to discuss their reactions to each medium. Then, in a class discussion, give each student a chance to identify his or her own favorite drawing medium.

Drawing

Do you remember drawing or scribbling with crayons when you were a small child? Although you didn't know it at the time, you were using a medium of art. A **medium of art** is *a material used to create a work of art*. Crayons are one medium of art. Colored markers are another. Modeling clay is a third. When we talk about more than one medium at a time, we use the term media. Colored markers and modeling clay are two media that you have probably used.

Sometimes artists combine several media to create a work of art. This is called mixed media. **Mixed media** is *the use of more than one medium*. Can you find a work of art in this chapter that is created with more than one medium?

In this lesson you will learn about the different kinds of media used in drawing. In later lessons you will learn about media used in other areas of art. You will also get a chance to experiment with some of these art media.

THE IMPORTANCE OF DRAWING

Before a person can run or jump or pedal a bicycle, he or she must be able to stand and walk. Walking is a stepping-stone to all these other activities.

In much the same way, drawing is a stepping-stone to almost all types of art production skills. Fashion designers make drawings of a design before patterns can be made for cutting fabric (Figure 3–1). Architects need to draw sketches and blueprints before the actual building of a house can begin (Figure 3–2). Some painters make sketches, or studies, before they put a brush to canvas. Figure 3–3 shows a sketch made by Edward Hopper for his painting called *Gas*.

▶ Figure 3–1 Drawing is an important step in many designing professions. How many careers can you think of that might require drawing?

30 Lesson 1 *Drawing*

Background Information
Modern drawing techniques have their roots in the Italian Renaissance. The media of choice during that period included silverpoint (the forerunner of the lead pencil), pen, charcoal, and chalk. During the sixteenth century, wash drawings became popular. Peter Paul Rubens (Flanders, 1577–1640) drew with red and brown chalk. Rembrandt (Holland, 1606–1669) produced most of his sketches with reed pen. During the nineteenth century, the simple pencil became quite popular. It was the favorite drawing medium of Édouard Manet (France, 1832–1883) and Edgar Degas (France, 1834–1917).

The common pencil is still the most often used medium for drawing. Drawing pencils come in 17 degrees of hardness; they are made of graphite, carbon, or charcoal. Colored pencils are also widely used. Wax crayons are another popular choice for students and amateur artists. They come in a wide variety of colors and sizes, and can be used the way paints are used.

◀ Figure 3–2   Architects have to be careful and precise in their work. Why do you think this is so?

▲ Figure 3–3   Hopper made this sketch at the scene. Then he took the sketch back to his studio where he made a painting based on this drawing. Why do you suppose he didn't just rely on his memory?

Edward Hopper. *Gas (Study for Gas)*. 1940. Charcoal on paper. 38.1 x 56.2 cm (15 x 22⅛").
Whitney Museum of American Art, New York. Josephine N. Hopper Bequest.

Vocabulary. Explain that the word *medium* comes from the Latin *medius*, meaning "middle." Suggest that students can think of an art medium as the "middleperson" between the artist's idea and the viewer of the art work. Then, to provide practice in the use of the terms *medium* and *mixed media,* have each student write the two terms on opposite sides of an index card. Display one drawing at a time, and have students hold up their cards to identify each as a single-medium work or a mixed-media work. If students disagree or are uncertain about any drawing, help them discuss and identify it.

Developing Concepts

Exploring Aesthetics. As students consider Figures 3–1, 3–2, and 3–3, ask: Are the drawings made by fashion designers and architects works of art? Why, or why not? Are all sketches or studies made by all painters works of art? Why, or why not? What might make the difference between a sketch or study that is only a planning tool and one that is in itself a work of art?

Then, as students consider Figure 3–5 on page **32**, ask: Why do you think Chernow chose to draw this work rather than, for example, painting it? Would it have been more interesting or valuable if it had been painted? In general, do you think a work of art that has been drawn is as important and/or valuable as a painting or a sculpture? Encourage students to express individual opinions and to explain and support their responses.

Using Art Criticism. Write on the board this quotation from Edgar Degas: "Drawing is not a matter of shape, it is the way that shapes are seen." Let students discuss the quotation, restating Degas's ideas in their own words. Then ask them to consider the drawings in this lesson and their own "Studio Experience" drawings in light of this quotation. How do Degas's ideas apply to each work?

Handbook Cross-Reference
To help students understand the different uses of drawing and how different careers in art use drawing skills, refer them to the Career Spotlights, *Handbook* pages **291–297**. After they have read about the different careers ask them to discuss the importance of drawing. Stress that drawing is a skill that can be learned and improved with practice and concentration.

Refer students to the Artist Profile, *Handbook* page **284** for additional information about Edward Hopper.

Classroom Management Tip
Colored pencil markings are often difficult to erase with an ordinary rubber or plastic eraser. Try to purchase erasable colored pencils for art projects. A particularly erasable brand, which is available in a wide range of colors, is the Col-Erase series manufactured by FaberCastell.

THE MEDIA OF DRAWING

The media of drawing are many. You have already looked at some. Some others are shown in Figure 3–4. How many of these can you name? How many of them have you used?

Drawing media are used for planning a work of art and sometimes they are used to create a finished work of art. The drawing in Figure 3–5 is such a work.

Throughout this book you will have the opportunity to practice your drawing skills. Experiment with different drawing media to achieve the results you want. Learning to draw, like other skills, takes practice and concentration.

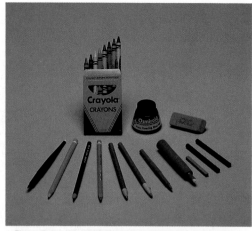

▲ **Figure 3–4** There are many kinds of drawing media. This picture shows a few. Can you name other media?

▲ **Figure 3–5** Compare Chernow's drawing to Hopper's sketch (Figure 3–3). You can see that Chernow spent a long time using a pencil and eraser to create this finished work.

Ann Chernow. *Lady of L.A.* 1984. Pencil on paper. 52.7 x 80 cm (20¾ x 31½"). National Museum of Women in the Arts, Washington, D.C. Gift of Mr. & Mrs. Edward P. Levy.

Note
Tell students that the name "pencil" comes from the Latin word pencillum, meaning a little tail, because the first pencils were actually fine brushes of hair or bristle. Today, the average pencil has enough lead in it to draw a line 35 miles long.

▲ Figure 3–6 Student work. Leaf drawing.

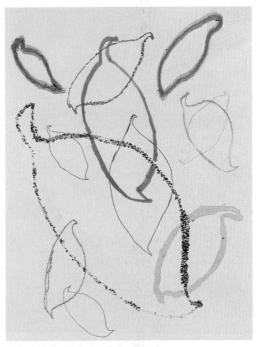

▲ Figure 3–7 Student work. Leaf drawing.

STUDIO EXPERIENCE

Select a leaf that you would like to draw. On a large piece of white paper, draw the leaf with a pencil. Next, draw the same leaf in different places on the paper, using a different drawing medium each time. Turn the paper so that you fill the paper with leaves. Draw some large ones and then draw some smaller ones to fill the smaller spaces. As you work, notice that some media make broad lines, while others make fine lines. Use your imagination to come up with new ways to make a line with each medium. (See Figures 3–6, 3–7.) Experiment with using broad-line media to make larger leaves and fine-line media to make smaller leaves.

Place the finished drawings up for study by the class. Can you tell what media other students used in their works? Does everyone's work look the same? Why or why not?

✔CHECK YOUR UNDERSTANDING

1. What is a medium of art?
2. Name three media that are used in drawing.
3. How is drawing used by an architect? How is drawing used by a painter?

Closure. Ask students to write short paragraphs about their own "Studio Experience" work. Their paragraphs should include responses to these questions: What media did you use? Which media and combinations of media are most effective? Why?

Evaluation. 1. Review students' written responses to the "Check Your Understanding" questions. 2. Read their paragraphs about the "Studio Experience" work.

Reteaching. Have students find and browse through books that include photographs of drawn works of art. Ask each student to choose at least three reproductions of art works drawn in different media. Let the students share their choices with the rest of the class, either by showing the photographs or by describing the drawings.

Enrichment. Ask students to find and bring in interesting leaves. Then have each student view a leaf from various distances and draw several versions of it. Have students view their leaves under magnifying glasses if possible. Also have them take close, unmagnified views, arm's-length views, and distance views. When they have finished their drawings, have them discuss their work, noting how the changes in distance affected what they saw and how they drew.

Answers to "Check Your Understanding"
1. A medium of art is a material used to create a work of art.
2. Media that are used in drawing include pencils, charcoal, charcoal buffers, pen, ink, conte crayons, pastels, silverpoint, and crayons. (Students may identify any three of these media.)
3. An architect draws sketches and blueprints of a house before building can begin. A painter may draw sketches before beginning to paint.

L E S S O N **2**

Printmaking

LESSON PLAN
(pages 34–37)

Objectives

After completing this lesson, students will be able to:

• Name the different kinds of media used in printmaking.
• Explain the difference between an original print and a reproduction.
• Identify the three basic steps in printmaking.
• Make and compare prints and rubbings.

Supplies

• Large sheets of construction paper, tempera paint in shallow dishes.
• Sheets of newsprint, pencils.
• Small, variously shaped objects, such as paper clips, erasers, clothespins, spools, corks, buttons; white paper; tempera paint and brushes; crayons.
• Large white potatoes, small knives or potato peelers, tempera paints and brushes, large sheets of newsprint.

> **TRB Resource**
> • 3-2 *Printmaking*
>   (reproducible master)

TEACHING THE LESSON

Getting Started

Motivator. Have students work in groups to experiment with printmaking. Give each group a large sheet of construction paper and two or three colors of tempera paint in shallow dishes. Ask the students in each group to work together to create a fingerprint and handprint design, dipping their fingers and hands into the paint and then pressing them onto the paper. Let each group share its design with the rest of the class, and encourage students to discuss the process. Then give students the definition of *print:* an image that is transferred from a prepared surface to paper or fabric. Ask: What images did you transfer? What surfaces did you prepare? How did you prepare those surfaces? What kind of art work have you created?

Have you ever made a fingerprint? A fingertip is pressed on an inked pad, and ink is transferred to the raised ridges of the skin. Then the fingertip with the ink on it is pressed on clean white paper. The print on the paper shows the pattern of lines made by the raised ridges of that finger.

An art print can be made in a similar way. Special printing ink is applied to a prepared surface. Then paper or fabric is pressed against the inked surface. An original art **print** is *an image that is transferred from a prepared surface to paper or fabric.* An artist who makes prints is known as a printmaker.

THE IMPORTANCE OF PRINTMAKING

Like other types of art, printmaking allows artists to produce an image on various surfaces. In printmaking, though, an artist can produce multiple copies of the original work. Each print is signed by the artist.

Notice that a print is not the same as a reproduction of an art work, such as those you see on these pages. A **reproduction** is *a photograph of a print.* Confusing original prints with a reproduction of an art work is a mistake many people make.

The printmaker uses a number of tools and materials in making a print. These are shown in Figure 3–8. How many of these media can you name? How many have you used?

THE STEPS OF PRINTMAKING

In making a print, the printmaker follows three basic steps. The first step is to make a plate. The printmaker creates a printing plate

by altering a surface to create an image. Next, the printmaker applies ink to, or inks, the plate. Finally, the printmaker transfers the ink to the paper or cloth by pressing the paper or cloth against the plate. Then the paper or cloth is pulled off the plate.

▲ **Figure 3–8   This picture shows printmaking media and tools. What are some of the similarities in drawing and printmaking? What are some of the differences?**

Background Information

Artists have been using printmaking techniques for thousands of years. Prehistoric cave art—some of which may have been created 25,000 years ago—incorporates printmaking.

Handprints have been found on the walls of a number of caves. The prints were formed simply—a hand smeared with paint was pressed against the wall. Negative prints were also formed by dotting paint on the wall around a hand. The handprints vary. Sometimes the back of the hand was pressed

against the wall; sometimes the palm. In some cases all the fingers were used; in others, only a few.

The meaning of these handprints remains unclear. Since a certain level of skill was involved in this printmaking, a shaman or healer might have been involved, and the prints may have been part of an initiation rite. Another possibility is that the prints are signatures or a form of identification.

This set of steps may be repeated many times for a given plate. *A series of prints that are all exactly alike* is called an **edition**. The printmaker signs his or her name, usually in pencil in the bottom margin, and writes the title on each print of an edition. He or she also writes on each print a number that has this form: 10/20. The second number tells how many prints there are in the edition. The first number tells which print you are viewing. A print labeled 10/20 means that you are looking at the tenth of 20 prints that were made from one plate.

THE PRINTMAKER'S MEDIA

Plates in printmaking are usually made of wood, stone, or metal. Sometimes, however, other materials are used. Often prints are done in color. To make a print with more than one color, the printmaker must use a separate plate for each color.

The final appearance of a print will depend on the media, colors, and techniques the printmaker used. Different combinations will give different results. When inked and printed, lines etched in metal will look different from lines drawn with grease crayon. Figures 3–9 and 3–10 show some of these differences.

◄ **Figure 3–9 A "drypoint" is made by scratching lines into a metal plate with a sharp pointed tool. When it is printed, a drypoint looks like a drawing. The difference is that the lines in the drypoint will be raised where the paper has been pressed into the scratches.**

Mary Cassatt. *Maternal Caress.* 1891. Drypoint, soft ground etching and aquatint printed in color. 36.5 x 26.8 cm (14⅜ x 10⁹⁄₁₆"). Metropolitan Museum of Art, New York, New York. Gift of Paul J. Sacks, 1916.

Understanding Art History.
Direct students' attention to Figures 3–9 and 3–10, and let volunteers identify any similarities they see between these two works. Explain that both Mary Cassatt and Henri de Toulouse-Lautrec were influenced by the work of Edgar Degas. Have students work in groups to research and discuss the lives of these three artists and the impact Degas had on the work of Cassatt and Toulouse-Lautrec.

Developing Studio Skills. Let students practice their printmaking skills by creating printing plates from potatoes. Give each student half of a large white potato. Have students use small knives, utility knives, or potato peelers to slice away parts of the flat cut surface, leaving a simple shape with which to print. Then have students brush tempera paints onto their printing plates and use them to print on sheets of newsprint. Encourage students to plan and create patterns as they print. (See "Making a Stamp Print" in the "Technique Tip" section of the *Handbook,* page **275**.) Some students may want to work with partners to combine two shapes in a single printed pattern. Display the finished works, and encourage students to compare and discuss them.

Appreciating Cultural Diversity. Explain to students that cloth can be decorated with printed designs. Point out, for example, that the Yoruba of southwest Nigeria make a special fabric called Adire on which they print designs and symbols. Each piece of cloth is hand-printed by one of the women and is given its own name. The people of Ghana make a cloth called Adrinka, which they print using carved gourds dipped in dye. South African people also make and print fabrics with special designs and symbols. Ask volunteers to learn more about some of these printed cloths and the people who make them; let the volunteers give brief presentations to the rest of the class.

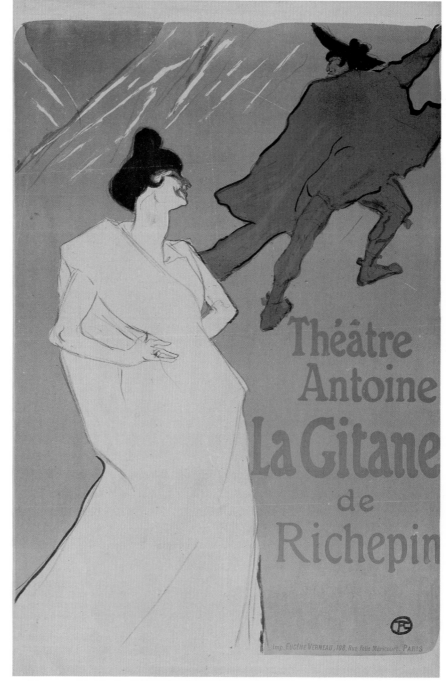

▲ **Figure 3–10** This print is made with four colors. Can you tell which ones?

Henri de Toulouse Lautrec. *La Gitane.* 1900. Lithograph. 160 x 65 cm (63 x 25⅝"). Los Angeles County Museum of Art. Gift of Dr. & Mrs. Kurt Wagner.

36 ■ Lesson 2 *Printmaking*

Note
Tell students that Henri de Toulouse-Lautrec liked to spend time at a Paris nightclub called the Moulin Rouge. As part of a plan to improve business, the owners asked him to create a poster. He designed one unlike any that Paris had ever seen. The colors were bright, and the figures were full of life. The Moulin Rouge became successful, as did the artist. Henri de Toulouse-Lautrec changed the world of graphic arts by including fine art as the important part of the overall design.

Handbook Cross-Reference
You may wish to refer students to the Artist Profile, *Handbook* page **283** for biographical information about Mary Cassatt.

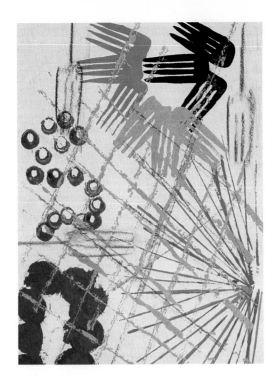

STUDIO EXPERIENCE

Gather small items with different shapes that might be dipped into paint to make a gadget print. Some possibilities are paper clips, erasers, clothespins, spools, cork, and buttons. Be as imaginative as you can. Brush tempera paint on each gadget, and press the gadget firmly on a sheet of white paper. Exchange gadgets with your classmates. (See Figure 3–11.)

Once the paint has dried, select one of the gadgets, and place it underneath the paper near a printed image of the same gadget. Make a crayon rubbing of the gadget. (See Technique Tip **25**, *Handbook* **280**.) Discuss your work with your classmates. Do the rubbings look like the prints? Why or why not?

▲ **Figure 3–11   Student works. Gadget prints.**

✔CHECK YOUR UNDERSTANDING

1. How does an original print differ from a reproduction?
2. Summarize the three basic steps in printmaking.
3. What is an edition? What is the meaning of the numbers an artist will write on a print?
4. Name two materials that can be used to make plates in printmaking.

Following Up

Closure. Let students work in small groups to compare and discuss their "Studio Experience" prints and rubbings. How are the prints of all the group members alike? How are they different? What are the most important differences between the prints and the rubbings?

Evaluation. 1. Review students' written responses to the "Check Your Understanding" questions. 2. Listen to the groups' discussions of their "Studio Experience" projects.

Reteaching. Work with small groups of students to reinforce their understanding of the difference between an original print and a reproduction. Display several of the students' "Studio Experience" prints and ask: What kind of art works are these? How can you tell? If we wanted to make reproductions of these prints, what would we have to do? Be sure students recognize that only by photographing the print can they make a reproduction of it.

Enrichment. Ask groups of students to work together in researching the development of printmaking in Japan. Ask students to find answers to questions such as these: When did Japanese artists begin making prints? Who are some of the most famous Japanese printmakers? What materials are used in Japanese prints? How have Japanese prints influenced European artists? Let the groups make oral presentations of their findings to the rest of the class.

Lesson 2   *Printmaking*   **37**

Answers to "Check Your Understanding"
1. An original print is an image that is transferred from a prepared surface to paper or fabric. A reproduction is a photograph of an art work.
2. The three basic steps in printmaking are making a plate, inking the plate, and transferring the ink from the plate to the paper or cloth.
3. An edition is a series of prints that are all exactly alike. The second number an artist writes tells how many prints are in the edition. The first number tells which print you are viewing.
4. The materials usually used to make plates in printmaking are wood, stone, and metal. (Students may identify any two of these materials.)

Painting

LESSON 3
Painting

LESSON PLAN
(pages 38–41)

Objectives

After completing this lesson, students will be able to:
• Name the different kinds of media used in painting.
• Identify the three basic ingredients found in all paints.
• Experiment with different painting media.

Supplies

• Finger paints, finger painting paper (other kinds of paper will not work with finger paints), water, pencils, sponges for cleanup.
• Various painting media, such as school acrylics and thick tempera paints; white paper; various tools for applying paint, such as brushes, painting knives, and twigs.
• Tape recorders (if available).
• Acrylic paints and brushes, palettes (or old plates, microwave trays, or styrofoam trays from meat packages), white paper.

TRB Resources
• 3-3 *Painting Media,* (reproducible master)
• 3-4 *Wassily Kandinsky,* (artist profile)
• 3-5 *Media Through the Ages,* (art history)

TEACHING THE LESSON

Getting Started

Motivator. Begin by having students create their own finger paintings. Remind them to write their names on the back of the finger painting paper before wetting it. As they work, ask: What is this art medium? When and how have you used it? What is special about it? Encourage students to share their personal responses and experiences. Then explain that students will learn more about this and other media of painting.

When students have finished their finger paintings, lay or hang the papers to dry. The following day give students a chance to share and discuss their finger paintings.

You have probably worked with paints at one time or another. The paints may have been the kind that you smear on wet paper with your fingers or paints you mix with water. These are just two of the media used in painting. In this lesson you will learn about others.

CHARACTERISTICS OF PAINTS

Painting is the process of covering a surface with color using a brush, a painting knife, a roller, or even fingers. Sometimes paint is made into a mist by being blown onto a surface with an airbrush. Some paints dry fast, some look bright, and some blend easily. Different effects can be achieved by using different types of paints.

THE PAINTER'S MEDIA

Like other artists, painters use a wide variety of tools and materials. Some of these are shown in Figure 3–12. How many of these can you identify? How many have you used?

Before a painter begins a work, he or she chooses a type of paint and an appropriate surface on which to work. The surface is the material to which the paint is to be applied. Canvas, paper, or silk are three examples. The look of a finished painting has much to do with the combination of media the artist chooses. A painting made by putting oil paint on canvas with a knife has a look very different from a painting made by putting watercolor on paper with a soft brush.

▶ Figure 3–12 Some painting tools and media are shown at the right. What other media can you think of that are not shown here?

Classroom Management Tip
Before using fingerpaints in the classroom, collect old shirts to be used as cover-ups. Always allow at least 15 minutes for clean-up and choose clean-up monitors to be in charge of different groups. Think about where to hang the wet paintings so that they can dry. When the fingerpainting experience is completed, have students hold up their art works and describe and discuss the physical and mental involvements associated with fingerpainting.

All paints used in art are made up of three basic ingredients:

- **Pigment** is *a finely ground, colored powder that gives paint its color*.
- **Binder** is *a liquid to which the dry pigment is added*. The binder makes it possible for the pigment to stick to a surface. Linseed oil is the binder for oil paints. Gum arabic (**ar-uh-bik**) is the binder for watercolors.
- **Solvent** is *a liquid that controls the thickness or thinness of the paint*. Turpentine is the solvent in oil paints. Water is the solvent in watercolors. Solvents are also used to clean brushes.

STYLES OF PAINTING

When painters finish works of art, they usually sign their names to them. In a way, the signature of the artist is already there, in his or her individual style. **Style** is *an artist's personal way of expressing ideas in a work*. Style is like a snowflake or a fingerprint. No two are exactly alike, just like no two people have exactly the same handwriting. Two artists may start off with exactly the same media and end up with works that look totally different. Compare Figures 3–13, 3–14, and 3–15. In what ways are these three works alike? In what ways are they different? How do you think the thickness of the paint affected each work? How might you describe the style of each artist?

▲ **Figure 3–13** This artist experimented with many different styles of art before he came up with his own style. How would you describe that style? Explain your answer.

Wassily Kandinsky. *Improvisation Number 27: The Garden of Love*. Oil on canvas. 120.3 x 140 cm (47⅜ x 55¼"). Metropolitan Museum of Art, New York, New York. The Alfred Stieglitz Collection, 1949.

Lesson 3 *Painting* 39

Vocabulary. Let students share and discuss various definitions of the noun *style*. Stimulate discussion with questions such as these: What is a musician's style? What contributes to a writer's style? What kinds of styles come and go? What special styles do you have? What do you hope your own fashion style or other style expresses? Then ask what an artist's style might be, and let volunteers check the Glossary definition. Ask: Why do you think different artists have different styles? How do you imagine an artist develops his or her own style?

Developing Concepts

Exploring Aesthetics. Help students identify Figure 3–13 as a non-objective painting. Explain that the subject is not a specific object or group of objects; in this way the painting differs from a landscape or portrait or still life, for example. Encourage students to share their own reactions and the reactions they have heard others express to non-objective art. Ask: Does an artist need more skill or talent to create representational art than to create non-objective art? Does a painting have to represent something or someone to be considered successful art? Why, or why not?

Using Art Criticism. Have pairs of students interview each other about Henri-Charles Manguin's painting shown in Figure 3–14 on page **40**. Ask each student to prepare several questions about the subject, composition, and content of the work and about the artist's success. If tape recorders are available, allow students to record their interviews. Then have each student write a newspaper article about the interview he or she conducted.

Background Information
Wassily Kandinsky (Russian-born, 1866–1944) was one of Europe's most famous Expressionist painters. He studied law and politics and became a lawyer in 1892. Three years later he went to Munich, Germany, and began to study painting. He was strongly influenced by the Fauves but created the first paintings which came to be known as non-objective art. His experiences as a painter led him to believe that the object got in the way of the painting. In 1910 Kandinsky made a sudden breakthrough with what is considered the first non-objective painting.

In 1921 Kandinsky began teaching art in Germany. His work with young artists—as well as his paintings and his theoretical writings—influenced painters throughout Europe and in the United States. The Nazis closed the Bauhaus school where Kandinsky was teaching in 1933, and his paintings were confiscated. The artist fled to Paris, where he lived and worked until his death.

Understanding Art History.
Have each student choose one of the artists whose paintings are reproduced in this lesson. Ask students to study examples of that artist's paintings and try to make generalizations about his or her artistic style. Then have students read about the influences on that style: How did the work of other artists influence that style? What was the influence of world and local events? What was the influence of technological developments? Let students summarize what they have learned in written or oral presentations.

Developing Studio Skills.
Give students an opportunity to mix paints on palettes. Give each student a palette; old white plates, microwave trays, or styrofoam trays can easily be used in place of palettes. Then let students use acrylic paints on their palettes. Have them work with partners to practice mixing paints before applying them to paper. Encourage partners to discuss and compare the colors and effects they can create.

Appreciating Cultural Diversity. Point out that though we are most familiar with paintings done on canvas or paper, other surfaces are also used for painting. Chinese artists have been painting on silk from 400 B.C., or perhaps even earlier. The people of the Pacific Islands make tapa cloth from the bark of particular trees and then paint the cloth with vegetable pigments. Artists of the Eastern Orthodox Church painted icons (religious images) on wood panels. Have students form three groups to research these different surfaces and the kinds of paintings that are created on them. Ask the members of each group to work together to find out about the surfaces, the kinds of paints used, the history and background of these paintings, and the style of painting usually used. Then have each group present its findings to the rest of the class.

▲ **Figure 3–14   Henri-Charles Manguin was known as an open-air painter. This means that he did most of his work outdoors. He is best known for scenes that are near water.**

Henri-Charles Manguin. *Port Saint Tropez, le 14 Juillet*. Oil on canvas. 61.3 x 50.2 cm (24⅛ x 19¾"). The Museum of Fine Arts, Houston, Texas. The John A. & Audrey Jones Beck Collection.

Background Information
Henri-Charles Manguin was known as an open-air painter, because he did most of his work outside. Among his artist friends were Matisse, Rouault, and Manet. Although he exhibited with the Fauves, his work was not distinctly of that school. Instead, he has been compared to van Gogh. He is best known for settings near the water's edge and many of his works were done around the Bay of St. Tropez.

Classroom Management Tip
When using tempera paint or other materials, make certain that the container or package bears one of the following safety labels: *AP* (Approved Product); *CP* (Certified Product); or *HL* (Health Label). The *AP* and *CP* labels certify that the product contains no material in sufficient amounts to be toxic or dangerous to the user. The *CP* label also indicates that the product meets specific quality standards. A *HL* seal is used to certify art products which are appropriate for older students.

✔CHECK YOUR UNDERSTANDING

1. What are the three types of ingredients found in every type of paint?
2. What is pigment?
3. What is an artist's style?

STUDIO EXPERIENCE

Experiment with different painting media. Gather an assortment of school acrylics and thick tempera paints, as well as tools for applying paint and a supply of white paper. In addition to different types of brushes, your painting tools might include painting knives, twigs with the ends bunched together into a brushlike effect, and even your fingers. Try one combination and then another, noting the effects of each. What kind of brush stroke do you get, for example, with a dry brush that has been dipped in thick paint? What happens when you use a wet brush dipped in the same paint? Does thinning the paint with water change its look on paper?

Share your observations with your classmates. Discuss similarities and differences in your results. Try to imagine how you could use these effects in a painting.

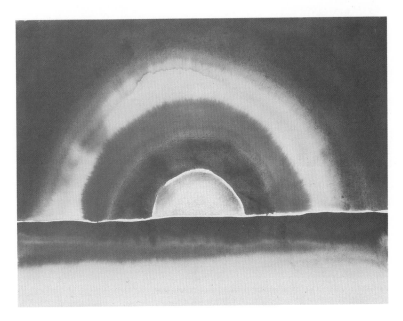

◄ **Figure 3–15 O'Keeffe "simplified" nature. Here she used a few wet watercolor shapes to capture the idea of sunrise over a desert.**

Georgia O'Keeffe. *Sunrise.* 1917. Watercolor. 22.5 x 30.2 cm (8⅞ x 11⅞"). Collection of Barney A. Ebsworth.

Experimenting with Pigment

LESSON PLAN
(pages 42–43)

Objectives

After completing this lesson, students will be able to:

• Make a painting with watercolors on paper, experimenting with changing the amount of solvent (water).

• Discuss the different effects painters are able to create using a single medium.

Supplies

• Tempera paint, water, three brushes, three large sheets of white paper.

• Watercolor paints and water, pencils, white paper, large and small watercolor brushes, trays or flat boards (larger than the sheets of white paper), paper towels, sponges.

• Reproductions of landscape or nature paintings by Georgia O'Keeffe, recording of "Painted Desert" movement from Ferde Grofe's *Grand Canyon Suite*.

> **TRB Resource**
>
> • 3-6 *Design Your Own Tapa Cloth*, (studio)

TEACHING THE LESSON

Getting Started

Motivator. Show students three containers of tempera paint, all the same color. Add a little water to the paint in one container; add more water to another; leave the third container of paint undiluted. Ask students to predict what the effects of the three different solutions will be. Then have three volunteers paint dots and lines with the three different solutions of tempera paint and discuss the effects.

Vocabulary. Review the definition of *solvent*, and have students identify the solvent used in the demonstration (see "Motivator"). Then write the words *strong* and *weak* on the chalkboard. Ask: What do these two words mean? How can they be applied to colors?

Experimenting with Pigment

Look again at the painting in Figure 3–15 on page **41** and at Figure 3–16 on this page. These were done by American artists, Georgia O'Keeffe and Edward Hopper. Notice from the credit lines that each painter used watercolor on paper. Yet the paintings look as if they were done with completely different media. In this studio lesson you will learn how one medium can be used to give such different results.

WHAT YOU WILL LEARN

You will be making a painting using watercolors on paper. You will experiment with changing the amount of solvent which, for watercolors, is water. Through this experiment, you will learn about the different effects painters are able to create using a single medium. (Figure 3–17 shows an experiment of this kind carried out by a student.)

WHAT YOU WILL NEED

• Watercolor paints and water
• Pencil and sheet of white paper, 9 x 12 inch (23 x 30 cm)
• Two watercolor brushes, one large and one small
• Tray or flat board larger than paper
• Paper towels and sponges

▲ Figure 3–16   Edward Hopper painted this scene in watercolor. What emotion do you feel when you look at this painting? Hopper is noted for the loneliness portrayed in his work.

Edward Hopper. *Cottages at North Truro, Massachusetts*. 1938. Watercolor. 51.3 x 71.4 cm (20³⁄₁₆ x 28⅛"). Collection of Barney A. Ebsworth.

Background Information
During her long life Georgia O'Keeffe (United States, 1887–1986) became renowned for her flower paintings. Her stylized flowers and abstracts of flowers are painted in extraordinarily vivid colors. As she herself said, "Whether the flower or the color is the focus, I do not know. I do know that the flower is painted large to convey to you my experience of the flower, and what is my experience of the flower if not color?" Later, when the desert became the focus of her work, the colors remained clear and vivid.

WHAT YOU WILL DO

1. Wet each cake of paint in the set with a few drops of water. This will allow the paint to begin to soften.
2. Write your name on the back of your paper with a pencil.
3. Using your large brush, wet the back of the paper with clear water. Make sure to wet the entire surface. Place the wet side of the paper on your tray or board. Now brush water on the front side of the paper. Be thorough, but do not let puddles form.
4. Load your small brush with color by rubbing it against one of the cakes of paint. Take time to dissolve the pigment. Then touch the paper in several places with the brush to make dots. What happens to the paint dots?
5. Clean your brush by swishing it around in the water. Blot it on a paper towel and load your brush with a second color. Draw lines on an unused wet area of the paper. What happens to the paint?
6. As your paper dries, add other colors to unused dry areas where the paint will not run. Concentrate on making some of your lines thick and some of them thin. (See Technique Tip **14**, *Handbook* **275**.) After a time, you will be able to paint over areas you have already painted since they have had time to dry.
7. When your paper is completely dry, share your work with your classmates. Discuss the different effects you have created.

OTHER STUDIO IDEAS

- On another piece of paper, make a geometric pattern using just one color. Plan your work using what you have learned from the experiment above.

EXAMINING YOUR WORK

- **Describe**   Point out areas in your work where the color is very weak. Describe the condition of the paper when you made these dots and lines. Point out dots and lines in your work where the color is very strong. Describe the condition of the paper when you made these dots and lines. Identify areas of your work where you painted over other colors.
- **Explain**   Tell what effect changing the amount of solvent will have in a painting. Tell how you think the artists of the works in Figures 3–15 and 3–16 arrived at such different results using the same medium.

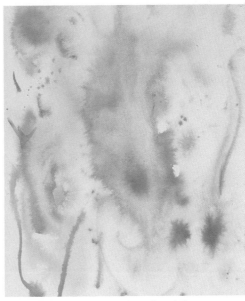

▲ Figure 3–17   Student work. Watercolor painting.

 Repeat the pigment experiment, but this time use school acrylics or tempera paints. Compare your results. (Both use water as a solvent.)

Lesson 4   *Experimenting with Pigment*   **43**

Sculpture

LESSON PLAN
(pages 44–47)

Objectives

After completing this lesson, students will be able to:

- Name the different kinds of media used in sculpting.
- Explain the difference between freestanding sculpture and relief sculpture.
- Identify the four basic methods for making sculpture.
- Use both additive and subtractive techniques to create a freestanding sculpture.

Supplies

- Drawing paper and colored pencils or markers, modeling clay or play dough.
- Styrofoam from recycled beverage containers, trays, and packing materials; straight pins, string, thumbtacks, yarn, and/or staplers; knives and scissors.
- Small objects from nature, such as pebbles, twigs, and leaves (collected by students, if possible); modeling clay or play dough.
- Photographs of totem poles.
- Various sculpture media, such as clay, plaster, wire, papier-mâché, and molds; books with photographs of a variety of sculptures.

> **TRB Resources**
> - 3-7 *Sculpture Media*, (reproducible master)
> - 3-8 *Meet the Artist*, (cooperative learning)

TEACHING THE LESSON

Getting Started

Motivator. Ask students to begin by drawing reptiles (alligators, crocodiles, lizards, snakes, turtles) or other animals. Then give each student a lump of clay or play dough; ask students to use this new medium to create the same animals they have just drawn. When they have finished, help students compare and discuss their two different kinds of works.

Sculpture

Have you ever made a sand castle or a snowman? If you have, then you have worked in sculpture. Sculpture is art that is made to occupy space. Sculpture is three-dimensional. **Three-dimensional** means *that an object has height, width, and depth.* (See Figure 3–18.) This is one way in which sculpture is different from the other kinds of art you have looked at so far. Although objects in a drawing or painting can look quite real, the work is flat, or two-dimensional. **Two-dimensional** means *that the work has height and width but not depth.*

▶ **Figure 3–18** This artist is both a painter and a sculptor. She often uses "found" objects as the basis for her art. Name some of the found objects you see in this sculpture.

Nancy Stevenson Graves. *Zaga.* 1983. Cast bronze with polychrome chemical patination. 182.9 x 124.5 x 81.4 cm (72 x 49 x 32"). Nelson-Atkins Museum of Art, Kansas City, Missouri.

44   Lesson 5   *Sculpture*

Background Information

Nancy Graves (United States, born 1940) is an American sculptor best known for her work *Camels*. This sculpture is a group of life-sized, furry camels. It caused quite a sensation when it was first shown in New York City.

The intended meaning of *Camels* is not readily apparent. We do know, however, that as a child Graves regularly visited the natural history museum in her hometown. There she developed a strong interest in science and the natural world; this

interest continues to be reflected in Graves' current work as an artist.

Camels may also be considered a statement of rebellion; it contrasts vividly with the non-objective works and the Pop Art culture of the time. The life-sized camels present a bold emphasis on the subject of the art work.

Graves' work continues to focus on her experience of the natural history museum and what she found there.

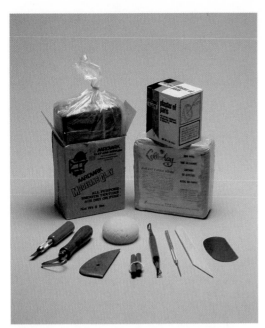

▲ Figure 3–19   There are many kinds of sculpture tools and media. Can you name some other kinds not shown in this picture?

THE MEDIA OF SCULPTURE

An artist who works in sculpture is called a sculptor. Sculptors work with a great many materials and tools. One sculpture medium that you have probably used is modeling clay. Some others are shown in Figure 3–19. How many of these can you name? How many have you used?

Most sculpture is freestanding, or in the round. **Freestanding** means *surrounded on all sides by space*. Statues of people are examples of freestanding sculptures. Every side of a freestanding sculpture is sculpted and finished. In order to see the work as the sculptor meant it to be seen, you have to move around it. Notice that each view of the boy in Figure 3–20 reveals something the other views do not.

▲ Figure 3–20   This young boy stands stiffly with his toys. This shows the stern rules of the tribe he belonged to. In a few years, he would be a soldier.

Unknown artist. *Figure of Standing Youth.* 400-300 B.C. Bronze and jade, Chinese Eastern Zhou Dynasty. 30 cm (11.8"). Museum of Fine Arts, Boston, Massachusetts. Maria Antoinette Evans Fund.

In addition to freestanding sculpture, there is relief sculpture. **Relief** is *a type of sculpture in which forms and figures are projected from the front only*. It is flat along the back. You can see large reliefs on buildings and small reliefs on items such as jewelry.

Understanding Art History.

Write the following sentence on the chalkboard: "The artist Michelangelo described the process of creating sculpture as `liberating the figure from the marble that imprisons it.'" Begin by letting students share and discuss their responses to Michelangelo's idea. Then ask students to tell what they know about Michelangelo. Explain that he is considered by many to be the most famous artist of Western civilization. He lived and worked in Italy from 1475 to 1564. A multitalented artist, he created paintings, architecture, and sculpture, and wrote letters and poems that are still read today; however, Michelangelo thought of himself primarily as a sculptor. Let students work with partners to read more about Michelangelo and find photographs of his art works. Finally, have each student write a brief description of one of Michelangelo's sculptures.

Developing Studio Skills.

Ask students to collect small objects found in nature, such as pebbles, twigs, and leaves. Then have students work with partners or in small groups to create relief sculptures from clay (or play dough) and their collected natural objects. Encourage students to share and discuss their sculptures; be sure they can identify the sculpture methods they used.

Appreciating Cultural Diversity.

Display photographs of several totem poles, and ask students to share and discuss what they know about these impressive carvings. Explain that Native Americans of the northwestern coast, particularly the Haida, the Tlingit, and the Tsimshian, traditionally carved these massive posts to mark important events, to honor the dead, or to show land ownership. Ask volunteers to read about the methods of carving, the symbolic meanings of the works, and the traditional beliefs of the people who created these totem poles. Then let the volunteers present their findings to the rest of the class.

▶ **Figure 3–21** Käthe Kollwitz produced powerful treatments of well-known subjects such as poverty and sorrow. She made social statements with her work. This is a self-portrait she executed when she was 69 years old.

Käthe Kollwitz. *Self-Portrait.* 1936. Bronze on marble base. 36.5 x 23.1 x 28.7 cm (14⅜ x 9⅛ x 11⅜"). Hirshhorn Museum, Smithsonian Institution, Washington, D.C. Joseph H. Hirshhorn, 1966.

▼ **Figure 3–22** What is the center of interest in this work? Why? What do you think it means?

Marisol Escobar. *Poor Family I.* 1987. Wood, charcoal, stones, plastic doll. 198.1 x 396.2 x 213.4 cm (78 x 156 x 84"). Sidney Janis Gallery, New York, New York.

Note

Have students refer to Figure 3–22 and ask them to notice how the artist has combined freestanding sculpture, relief sculpture, and two-dimensional drawing. Explain that the baby in the center is symbolic of the future, tomorrow, and hope for the family. Tell them that Marisol's work was very humorous during the Pop Art movement of the 1960's, but in the 1980's her work turned toward serious themes, such as religion and the human condition.

SCULPTING METHODS

There are four basic methods for making sculpture. These are:

- **Carving.** In carving, the sculptor starts with a block of material and cuts or chips a shape from it. Often a hard material like stone is used.
- **Casting.** In casting, the sculptor starts by making a mold. He or she then pours in a melted-down metal or some other liquid that will later harden. See Figure 3–21 for an example of bronze sculpture.
- **Modeling.** In modeling, the sculptor builds up and shapes a soft material. Clay and fresh plaster are two such materials.
- **Assembling.** In assembling, also known as constructing, the sculptor glues or in some other way joins together pieces of material. The sculpture in Figure 3–22 was made by assembling pieces of wood, charcoal, stones, and a plastic doll. This sculpture shows both additive and subtractive methods.

Modeling and assembling are known as additive methods of sculpting. In the additive method, the artist adds together or builds up the material. Carving is a subtractive method. In the subtractive method, the artist takes away or removes material.

SAFETY TIP

Be very careful when using cutting tools, such as scissors and knives. Pick these up only by the handle, never by the blade. When handing them to another person, offer the handle to the other person.

STUDIO EXPERIENCE

Using pieces of scrap styrofoam from beverage containers, trays, and packing materials, work in teams to create a freestanding sculpture. You may use both the additive and subtractive techniques to create this work. Use slots and tabs to hold the smaller pieces of your construction together. Straight pins, strings, and other joining devices can help you hold the larger pieces together. The size of these constructions depends upon the limits of your art room and the supplies you can collect. They may reach from floor to ceiling, or they may be 5 inches (13 cm) tall. If you are working with very large packing materials, you can carve them with scissors and utility knives. If you are making small sculpture pieces, you can cut the cups and trays with scissors into a variety of shapes.

✔ CHECK YOUR UNDERSTANDING

1. What is another term that has the same meaning as freestanding?
2. Name two media used by sculptors.
3. Briefly describe the four basic methods for making sculpture.
4. What is meant by the term additive as it is used in sculpture? Which two basic methods of making sculpture are additive?
5. What is meant by the term subtractive as it is used in sculpture? Which basic method of making sculpture is subtractive?

Closure. Have students write short paragraphs describing what they consider the most successful aspects of the sculptures they worked on in the "Studio Experience."

Evaluation. 1. Review students' written responses to the "Check Your Understanding" questions. 2. Read students' descriptions of their "Studio Experience" sculptures.

Reteaching. Work with small groups of students to review the four basic methods for making sculpture. Display as many different media of sculpture as you have available. Let volunteers explain, in their own words, what modeling, assembling, carving, and casting involve. Then have the other group members point out the media that can be sculpted by each method. Finally, ask students to browse through art books and select photographs of several different sculptures. Have group members discuss the pictured works and identify the sculpture methods used in creating them.

Enrichment. Ask students to look for and record examples of sculpture, many of which they probably pass—perhaps without noticing—every day. Students should take the time to notice freestanding sculptures, both indoors and outdoors. They should also look for large reliefs on buildings and for small reliefs on jewelry and similar items. Have students record their findings by taking photographs, makings sketches, and/or writing descriptions. Then have students collect and organize their records into a "Familiar Sculpture" booklet.

Answers to "Check Your Understanding"

1. The terms *freestanding* and *in the round* have the same meaning.
2. Media used by sculptors include clay, plaster, wire, papier-mâché, wood, stone, and bronze. (Students may identify any two of these media.)
3. These are the four basic methods of making sculpture: modeling, in which the sculptor builds up and shapes a soft material; assembling, in which the sculptor joins pieces of material; carving, in which the sculptor cuts or chips a shape from a block of material; and casting, in which the sculptor makes a mold and pours into it a melted metal or another liquid that will later harden.
4. Additive methods of sculpture involve adding together or building up the material. Modeling and assembling are additive methods.
5. The subtractive method of sculpture involves taking away or removing material. Carving is a subtractive method.

Objectives

After completing this lesson, students will be able to:
• Create mixed-media pictures that represent important aspects of their lives.
• Describe their own mixed-media pictures.

Supplies

• Pencils; sketch paper; white paper; variety of media, including markers, paints, colored pencils; old newspapers and magazines; wallpaper scraps; scissors; glue.
• Clay, wire, sticks and twigs, small found objects (collected by students, if possible).
• Sketch paper, pencils, large erasers, small sharp knives, printing ink.

> **TRB Resource**
> • 3-9 *Media—A Characteristic of a Culture,* (appreciating cultural diversity)

TEACHING THE LESSON

Getting Started

Motivator. Pose this question: What people, objects, and events have been most important in your life? Have students work independently to brainstorm as many responses as possible, listing their ideas. After several minutes, let students share and discuss their lists. Encourage them to add to or revise their lists during this discussion. Explain to students that they have begun gathering ideas for their mixed-media art work.

Vocabulary. Review with students the definitions of these terms: *media* and *mixed media*. Let volunteers give specific examples. Then ask: When you are creating an art work that represents your life, what are the advantages of using mixed media? How can your choices of media help reflect your own ideas about your life?

48

Creating with Mixed Media

The young artist who created the mixed media work in Figure 3–23 was creating a work of art which represented his life. He included objects and symbols that were important to him. The daffodil represents a summer spent studying art at the Daffodil Farm. The tiny figure of Pinocchio is from a drawing that his kindergarten teacher had framed for him. Near the center of the work there is a checkerboard. What do you think this might represent? Can you recognize any other symbols that give you more information about this young man?

He used different types of media to create this work. For example, graphite, colored pencil, and markers are some of the media he used. What others can you identify?

WHAT YOU WILL LEARN

You will create a mixed-media picture that represents something about your life. You may include a photo or sketch of yourself, but do not have it take up the whole work. As you create your work of art, experiment with a variety of media.

▲ **Figure 3–23   The artist worked on this mixed media piece for a year. It shows symbols of important events in his life. Can you identify some of the symbols?**

Herbert Andrew Williams. *A Year in the Life of Herbert.* 1988. Mixed media. Private collection.

Background Information
One result of the early Cubists' experiments with collage was the idea that "ready-made" objects could become art. In 1914, for instance, Marcel Duchamp (France, 1887–1968) bought a steel bottle rack and presented it as a work of art. His theory was that art was anything the artist called art.

During the 1950s and 60s, Robert Rauschenberg (United States, born 1925) resurrected this idea and helped pioneer a whole new era in art with his mixed-media works. His work in this period was strongly influenced by commercialism and advertising; it reflects images of everyday, popular life. A painter, sculptor, and printmaker, Rauschenberg combined such a variety of media in his works that they defy easy categorization. One of these works includes a stuffed ram within an automobile tire. With works such as these, Rauschenberg has enlarged the range of materials considered legitimate vehicles of artistic expression.

WHAT YOU WILL NEED

- Pencil and sketch paper
- Sheet of white paper, 12 x 18 inch (30 x 46 cm)
- Variety of media, including markers, paints, colored pencils
- Magazine, newspaper, and wallpaper scraps

WHAT YOU WILL DO

1. Make a list of people, places, objects and events that symbolize you and your life. Make rough sketches of these items. You may also add words. Notice that you can find the artist's name in Figure 3–23, but it is slightly hidden.
2. Look through magazines and newspapers for pictures and words that represent your interests, skills, and cultural background. If you decide to cut out a shape, cut neatly around the edge of the shape. Do you see the brown hand near the center of Figure 3–23? Notice how it has been carefully cut and outlined with colored pencil and black ink.
3. Select from the pieces you have cut and decide on the sketch you will use. Draw your final plan on the sheet of white paper.
4. Glue down the cut objects. Use any other media you wish to finish your work. (See Figure 3–24.)
5. Place your work on display with your classmates. Can you recognize your friends by the symbols they used?

OTHER STUDIO IDEAS

- Select one medium that gave you the most successful results. Determine a theme for your composition, such as a sporting event, school activity, or family outing. Plan the composition and complete it using the medium of your choice.
- ●● Create a mixed media work that represents your school, city, state, or country.

- **Describe** List the media that you used in this work. List the symbols you included and explain how each symbol relates to you. Identify the media that you enjoyed working with and explain why. Identify any media that did not produce the results you wanted. Explain why.

▲ **Figure 3–24 Student work. Mixed media.**

Developing Concepts

Exploring Aesthetics. Let students work in small groups to discuss Figure 3–23. What is the subject? How would they describe the composition? What do they consider the content of the work? Then have each student write a brief description of the work.

Using Art Criticism. Display the students' mixed-media pictures. Have each student select a work by another student and write about it, answering these questions: What media did the artist use? Would you suggest changes in the media? What message does the work convey to you? How could that message be more clearly communicated?

Following Up

Closure. Let each student explain how the media he or she chose contributes to the content of the mixed-media work. Would the work communicate a different message if it were created in a single medium?

Evaluation. Review students' mixed-media works, and consider their explanations of their own choices of media.

Reteaching. Let students work in small groups. Have each group plan and create a sculpture that represents the group and all its members. Make clay, wire, sticks, and twigs available; ask group members to bring in small objects that can be incorporated into their sculpture.

Enrichment. After students have shared and discussed their mixed-media works about themselves, let each student draw a personal symbol—a small, clear design that represents what is most important about himself or herself. Then have students make printing stamps showing their personal symbols; these stamps can be cut from large erasers. Let students use printing ink to print their personal symbols onto selected possessions.

Lesson 6 *Creating with Mixed Media* **49**

Cooperative Learning Activity
Discuss an environmental issue which directly affects students' home and/or life. Invite a speaker who represents a particular environmental issue to speak to the class and distribute literature. After the presentation, divide the class into small groups. Have each group develop a mixed-media piece of art that addresses the environmental issue.

Note
Before proceeding with the studio lesson, have students brainstorm about their own lives. On the chalkboard list words such as *family, friends, goals, fashion, music, work, hobby, sports,* and so forth. Have students think about how these words depict their lifestyle.

After students have completed their art work, classmates should try to recognize each others' works. Give students a chance to explain their personal interpretations and symbols.

BUILDING VOCABULARY

Number a sheet of paper from 1 to 13. After each number, write the term from the box that best matches each description below.

binder	print
edition	relief
freestanding	reproduction
medium of art	solvent
mixed media	style
pigment	three-dimensional
	two-dimensional

1. A material used to create an art work.
2. An image that is transferred from a prepared surface to paper or fabric.
3. Work that has height, width, depth.
4. A finely ground powder that gives paint its color.
5. Surrounded on all sides by space.
6. Use of more than one medium in art.
7. A work that has height and width.
8. A type of sculpture in which the image projects from only the front.
9. A photograph of a print.
10. An artist's personal way of expressing ideas in a work.
11. A liquid to which dry pigment is added.
12. A liquid that controls the thickness or thinness of the paint.
13. A series of prints all exactly alike.

REVIEWING ART FACTS

Number a sheet of paper from 14 to 18. Answer each question in a complete sentence.

14. Name two drawing media.
15. What is the first step in printmaking?
16. What is a group of identical prints called?
17. How is freestanding sculpture meant to be seen?
18. What type of sculpture is flat on the back?

THINKING ABOUT ART

On a sheet of paper, answer each question in a sentence or two.

1. **Summarize.** Look again at the photograph of the painting by Jan Steen on page **28**. How many painting media are shown in the work? How many sculpture media?
2. **Compare and contrast.** Compare the styles of the prints in Figures 3–9 and 3–10. What differences can you describe?
3. **Analyze.** Sculptors, like other artists, develop individual styles. How would you describe the styles of the sculptors for Figures 3–18 and 3–20?
4. **Analyze.** What method of sculpture would you be using if you whittled a tree branch? What method would you be using if you built a tower of building blocks that snapped together?

MAKING ART CONNECTIONS

1. **Language Arts.** Carefully study the Hopper painting in Figure 3–16. Try to imagine the mood of the event and what is happening in the painting. Describe the place and people shown. Use words such as color, line, shape, form, space, and texture. Write a few paragraphs about what is happening in the painting.
2. **Communication.** Find three examples of printmaking in your daily activities. Think about how this art form has developed into an important medium for communicating ideas. Share your examples with the class.
3. **Industrial Arts.** In 1440 a German printer named Gütenberg invented a printing press with movable type. The effect of this invention was profound. Trace the development of the printing industry from 1440 through the present.

CHAPTER 3 REVIEW

LOOKING AT THE DETAILS

The detail shown below is from Jan Steen's *The Drawing Lesson*. Study the detail and answer the following questions.

1. This painting is of ordinary people and an ordinary situation. What message do you think Jan Steen was trying to communicate? What do you think he is telling us about the artist?
2. Look at the entire work on page **28**. Does this change or add to your answers to the previous questions? Explain.
3. Locate examples of drawing, printmaking, painting, and sculpture in this work.
4. How would you describe this artist's style?
5. Why do you think Jan Steen chose the media of painting instead of sculpture to communicate his message?

Jan Steen. *The Drawing Lesson.* 1665. Oil on wood. (Detail.) 49.3 x 41 cm (19⅜ x 16¼"). J. Paul Getty Museum.

Chapter Evaluation

The goal of this chapter is to develop sensitivity to the distinct character of each medium and the variety of ways in which each artist uses it. Possible methods of evaluating include:

1. Assign a group of students to find all the new terms learned in the chapter and in the supplementary activities and make a set of cards with words and definitions. Play with them as a game, giving each student one or two cards. One calls out a definition or a term and its match comes forward.
2. Assign a team to collect reproductions of works in as many different media as they can and design a bulletin board display. Cards with identification of works and information about them can be in a box below the board. Students take a card and find the matching work.
3. Have students complete Chapter 3 Test (TRB, Resource 3–10).

The Elements of Art

Chapter Scan

Lesson 1 The Language of Art
Lesson 2 Color
Lesson 3 Using Color
          Combinations
Lesson 4 Line
Lesson 5 Shape, Form and
          Space
Lesson 6 Paper Sculpture Forms
Lesson 7 Texture
Lesson 8 Painting a Landscape

> **TRB Resources**
> • 4-10 Chapter Test
> • Color Transparency 7
> • Color Transparency 8

TEACHING THE CHAPTER

Introducing the Art Work

Direct students' attention to Paul Cézanne's *The Bay of Marseille*. Inform students that Cézanne was a French painter of the nineteenth century who studied in Paris and became part of the Impressionist movement. However, his work broke from that style and paved the way for modern painting, including Cubism and later schools of abstract painting. Cézanne's artistic development was slow and painstaking. However, because of his father's fortune, Cézanne did not need to earn a living through his art, allowing him the freedom to experiment. His determination earned him the title of one of the greatest painters of his time, but only after his death.

Examining the Art Work

Tell students that when this work was painted, it was considered revolutionary, primarily because of Cézanne's treatment of space. Point out that the artist's viewpoint is from high ground looking down onto the tops of the houses. Explain how the water seems to come forward rather than flow away. Because of Cézanne's use of color, there is no evidence of light to pull the viewer's eyes into the distance. Explain that the houses and trees are recognizable because of Cézanne's ability to portray form using color and linear perspective. However, there seems to be no illusion of space between the trees and houses. The cool colors of the water in this painting tend

▲ Cézanne is noted for the many landscapes he painted, but he also used people and everyday objects as sources of inspiration.

Paul Cézanne. *The Bay of Marseille, Seen from L'Estaque.* 1886–90. Oil on canvas. 80.8 x 99.8 cm (31⅞ x 39¼"). The Art Institute of Chicago. Mr. & Mrs. Martin A. Ryerson Collection.

The Elements of Art

When creating a work of art, an artist is faced with a number of questions. Look at the painting at the left. Think about how the artist answered the following questions:

- What colors will I use?
- Will the painting as a whole appear to be smooth or rough to the touch?
- Will the objects in the painting look flat and two-dimensional, or will they appear deep and realistic?

How an artist answers these and other questions determines how the finished work will look.

OBJECTIVES

After completing this chapter, you will be able to:

- Name the six elements of art.
- Identify the three properties of color.
- Use complementary colors in an art work.
- Name the different kinds of line.
- Explain the difference between shapes and forms.
- Explain the two ways we experience texture.
- Experiment with the elements of art.

WORDS YOU WILL LEARN

analogous colors
color wheel
complementary colors
form
hue
intensity
line
line quality

line variation
monochromatic colors
motif
shape
space
texture
value

ARTISTS YOU WILL MEET

Constantin Brancusi
Paul Cézanne
Arthur G. Dove
Alberto Giacometti
Käthe Kollwitz
Piet Mondrian

Elizabeth Murray
José Clemente Orozco
Attilio Salemme
Miriam Schapiro
Frank Stella
Vincent van Gogh

53

to grab the viewer's attention more strongly than the warm colors of the houses and land. Point out that Cézanne's use of the cool color green (in the form of trees and grass) and the touches of warm colors in the mountains unify the warm and cool color schemes to form a pleasing whole.

Discussing the Art Work
Point out that the painting is empty of people, roads, and shops. Ask students to find one place in the painting where they can identify some action. Note the smoke going out over the water from the smokestack. Ask students to think about what this place might sound and smell like.

Ask students whether they can tell where the sun is in this painting. Point out the light hues on the first row of houses and the way that the light hits only portions of the walls to indicate that the sun was to the artist's right.

Ask students to point out the soft and curved shapes as well as the geometric ones in this work. Ask them whether they think this combination is essential in a landscape. Explain to students that a landscape incorporates nature, whose shapes and forms are not necessarily geometric.

Tell students that in this chapter they will learn about the six elements of art. They will be able to use color and identify its properties. They will learn about lines, shapes, forms, and texture. They will also create their own art works using the elements of art.

Building Self-Esteem
The primitive cavemen told of successful hunts, strange and exciting happenings, and their own personal experiences by painting on their cave walls. Tell students to use the primitive style of the "Cavemen at Lascaux" to depict two or three events in which they have excelled. Or, give them the option of drawing events that they *want* to achieve in the future. Distribute lengths of butcher paper and instruct students to use it like a scroll. Tell them they can cut or tear the long edges to make the scroll look like an animal hide or a piece of parchment. When they have completed their drawings, give them the chance to share an experience that made them feel good about themselves. Let them speculate about what the cavemen at Lascaux might have done to feel good about their lives.

LESSON 1

LESSON PLAN
(pages 54–55)

Objectives
After completing this lesson, students will be able to:
- Discuss how artists use the visual elements of art to communicate with us.
- Name the six elements of art.

Supplies
- Drawing paper, crayons or colored markers.
- Examples of calligraphy, books with reproductions of works by famous calligraphers.

> **TRB Resource**
> - 4-1 *The Elements Chart,* (reproducible master)

TEACHING THE LESSON

Getting Started

Motivator. Write the following sentence on the chalkboard: "Everyone felt furious!" Point to the sentence, but do not read it aloud, and explain to the class that the written words on the chalkboard communicate a message. Ask students to show other ways in which the same message might be communicated. Volunteers might read the sentence aloud and say or write it in other languages. They might also pantomime the message, dance it, sing it, draw it, or find some other means of communicating it. Encourage as much participation—and as much variety—as possible.

Vocabulary. Introduce the names of the six art elements: color, line, shape, form, space, texture. Explain that students will learn the specific art-related definitions of these terms in the next lessons; now let them discuss and give examples of the familiar uses of these terms. Be sure students note the math-related meanings of several of the terms.

The Language of Art

When you talk to someone or write a letter, you communicate. You share your ideas and feelings. You use words—either spoken or written—to get a message across.

Artists do the same thing. They do not express their thoughts and feelings in ordinary words, however. Instead, artists use visual images—things that we can see and sometimes touch—to "speak" to us.

In this lesson you will learn about the special "language" artists use when they communicate. You will also begin to see that an artist's success in communicating depends partly on his or her skill in using this language.

THE VISUAL LANGUAGE

Since earliest times people have used the language of art to speak to each other. This is clear from the discovery of cave paintings like the one in Figure 4–1. Such early art works show that humans were writing in pictures some 12,000 years before the invention of the alphabet.

You have probably heard it said that a picture is worth a thousand words. In a very real sense, this saying is true. To understand the relationship between words and pictures, first read the following paragraph:

> The frightened mother was locked in a terrible struggle with the phantom, who greedily eyed her child. "No!" the mother's wide eyes protested. "No—you can never have him!" As her heart raced wildly, the mother clutched her little boy to her body with the strength of 10 men. But no matter how hard she fought, little by little she felt her grip weaken. Slowly—ever so slowly—the child was slipping from her fingers. In the end, she was no match for the phantom. Death, she knew in that awful final instant, would soon claim another helpless victim.

Now look at Figure 4–2 with the title *Death and the Mother*. Notice the look of sheer terror on the mother's face. Notice the power in her

▶ **Figure 4–1** Humans long ago painted pictures of animals on cave walls and ceilings. What reasons might they have had for doing this?

Unknown. Cave paintings. Gallery of Prehistoric Art, New York, New York.

Background Information

Thousands of years before they had written languages, people used visual images to record their experiences and ideas. The cave paintings and other works that remain from prehistoric times are a vivid reminder of this fact.

Cave art was created during the Paleolithic era in several different ways. Some images were engraved—or scratched—into the cave walls; others were painted onto the walls. Relief sculpture has been found near some cave openings.

Although it is clear that these works of cave art "speak" in visual images, interpretation of their intended meaning remains impossible. Some theorists suggest mystical, religious meanings for the cave paintings and other works. Others suggest they may comprise a record of events; still others regard these works as attempts to control the future. Whatever their original messages, today these visual images communicate to us at least part of the story of life in prehistoric times.

bulging arm as she holds fast to her child. What it took the writer 100 words to say, the artist has said in a single look!

▲ **Figure 4–2** How would you describe the look on the woman's face? Why is she terrified? Can you tell what she is clutching in her arms?

Käthe Kollwitz. *Death and the Mother*. 1934. Lithograph. Private collection.

THE VOCABULARY OF ART

You know that every language has its own word system, or vocabulary. Before a person can speak the language, he or she must know at least some of the words in its vocabulary.

The language of art, too, has a vocabulary all its own. Instead of words, however, the vocabulary of art is made up of six visual elements. An **element of art** is a *basic visual symbol an artist uses to create visual art*. These are color, line, shape, form, space, and texture. In much the way we put words together to form a sentence, the artist puts the visual elements together to make a statement.

▲ **Figure 4–3** Why might the artist have chosen to make the man so thin and angled?

Alberto Giacometti. *Man Pointing*. 1947. Bronze. 179.1 x 103.5 x 41.6 cm Base 30.5 x 33.1 cm (70½ x 40¾ x 16⅜" Base 12 x 13¼"). The Museum of Modern Art, New York, New York. Gift of Mrs. John D. Rockefeller III.

It is often hard to tell one element from another when you look at a work of art. When you look at Figure 4–3, for instance, you do not see the elements of line (long) and texture (rough). Instead, you see the sculpture as a whole. Your eye "reads" the elements of line and texture together. And yet, it is the very blending of these elements that permits you to see the art work as the artist meant you to see it: a man pointing.

"READING" THE LANGUAGE

When you first learned to read, you did not start with a book. You began by reading a word at a time. That is how you will learn the language of art: one element at a time.

Because these elements are so important, the remaining lessons of this chapter will be devoted to a discussion of them. Once you have studied these elements you will know a good part of the art vocabulary.

✔ CHECK YOUR UNDERSTANDING

1. In what way can art be said to be a language?
2. What is an element of art?
3. Name the six elements of art.

Lesson 1   *The Language of Art*   📖   **55**

Developing Concepts
Understanding Art History. Have students identify the year in which Käthe Kollwitz created *Death and the Mother* (Figure 4–2). Ask whether students know what was happening in Germany, Kollwitz's country, during that time. If necessary, explain that 1934 is the year in which Adolf Hitler proclaimed himself Führer, or supreme leader. Help students discuss possible connections between Kollwitz's art and the events and atmosphere in Germany.

Developing Studio Skills. Have each student create a drawing that communicates a specific mood or feeling. On the other side of their papers, have students write a word or sentence identifying the pictured feeling. Then let students work in small groups to share and discuss their drawings.

Following Up
Closure. Have students work in small groups to discuss their own ideas about the ways in which visual images can speak to them. Then have the members of each group choose a reproduction of one art work from the text; let them discuss the feeling or story that the work communicates to them. Finally, let the students in each group present that art work and their ideas about it to the rest of the class.

Evaluation. 1. Review students' written responses to the "Check Your Understanding" questions. 2. Listen to the presentation each group makes.

Reteaching. Help students discuss Figure 4–1 as an example of the language of art: What is the message?

Enrichment. Let students work with partners to learn more about the earliest cave paintings, such as the one shown in Figure 4–1. Have them look for answers to questions such as these: When were cave paintings made? Who made them? In what medium were they drawn? What purpose do we think the cave paintings served? How were the cave paintings discovered?

LESSON 2

The Element of Color

LESSON PLAN
(Pages 56–59)

Objectives
After completing this lesson, students will be able to:
- Identify the three properties of color.
- Use various values and various intensities of chosen hues in their own paintings.
- Define different kinds of color schemes.

Supplies
- Reproductions of paintings by Henri Matisse.
- Index cards, markers.
- Pencils, tempera paints and brushes, paper.
- Reproductions of art works from various time periods and from various cultures (such as European, African, Asian, Native American).
- Small pieces of red cellophane and green cellophane.

> **TRB Resources**
> - 4-2 *Color and the Artist,* (art criticism)
> - 4-3 *Color is a Symbol,* (appreciating cultural diversity)
> - 4-4 *What is Color?,* (art history)
> - 4-5 *"Discover" Color Yourself,* (cooperative learning)

TEACHING THE LESSON

Getting Started

Motivator. Display reproductions of paintings by Henri Matisse, and read aloud these quotes from the artist: "Color was not given to us to imitate nature. It was given to us to express our own emotions." "When I choose a color, it is not because of any scientific theory. It comes from feeling, from the innermost nature of the experience. Strong emotions call for vivid blues, reds, yellows—colors to stir the senses." Encourage students to discuss and react to these quotations. Ask: What ideas was the artist expressing? How do you see those ideas reflected in his paintings? What message or feeling do his paintings communicate? Do you think all other artists agree with Matisse's ideas? Why, or why not? Do you agree with his ideas? Why, or why not?

56

Color

Color is everywhere. It is in the orange-pink glow of the summer sky just before sunrise. It is in the rich reds and oranges of autumn leaves and in the long purple shadows that lay across the snow toward the close of a winter's day.

Color is even in our everyday language. "Green with envy," "feeling blue," and "red with rage" are English expressions that mention color.

In this lesson you will learn about the very important role color plays in art. You will learn how some artists have used color successfully. This knowledge of color can help you use it more creatively and effectively in your own art works.

TRAITS OF COLOR

Look up at the sun on a clear day and you see an almost blinding white light—or so your eye tells you. In reality, what you are looking at—but failing to see—are all the colors of the rainbow. When the sunlight shines on objects, some of the light is absorbed by the object. Some of the light bounces off. Color is what the eye sees when sunlight or some other light bounces off an object.

In the 18th century, Sir Isaac Newton organized the colors into a color wheel. The **color wheel** is *an arrangement of colors in a circular format.* See Figure 4–4. Later in this chapter you will learn more about the arrangement of the colors on the color wheel.

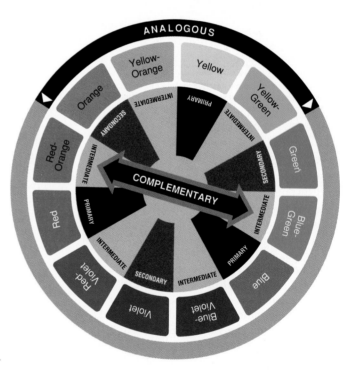

▶ **Figure 4–4   Color wheel.**

Background Information
For many artists color has been essential both to the experience of life and to the creation of art. This importance of color has led painters to discuss and write about the subject.

During a trip to Tunisia Paul Klee (Switzerland, 1879–1940) felt nearly overwhelmed by the intense light. He wrote: "Color has taken possession of me. No longer do I have to chase after it; I know that it has hold of me forever. That is the significance of this blessed moment. Color and I are one. I am a painter."

Henri Matisse (France, 1869–1954) explained his use of color this way: "To paint an autumn landscape, I will not try to remember what colors suit the season; I will only be inspired by the sensation that the season gives me. . . My sensation itself may vary, the autumn may be soft and warm . . . or quite cool with a cold sky and lemon-yellow trees that give a chilly impression and announce winter."

Sometimes artists use colors in bold and shocking ways (Figure 4–5). Sometimes they use them in quiet and serious ways (Figure 4–6 on page 58). To achieve different results, artists must understand the three properties or traits of color. These are hue, value, and intensity.

Hue

Hue is *a color's name*. Red, yellow, and blue are the primary hues. They are always equally spaced on the color wheel. (See Figure 4–4.) They are called primary, or first, because they can be used to mix all the other colors but cannot themselves be made by the mixing of other colors.

STUDIO EXPERIENCE

On a sheet of white paper, make pencil drawings of three or four objects in your classroom. Choose a hue from the color wheel. Paint one of the objects that hue, paint a second a tint of that hue, and a third a shade of that hue.

◀ **Figure 4–5** What makes this painting bold? Do you think this is a successful painting? Why or why not?

Miriam Schapiro. *High Steppin' Strutter I.* 1985. Paper and acrylic on paper. 203.2 x 138.4 cm (80 x 54½"). Bernice Steinbaum Gallery, New York. Given anonymously.

Lesson 2   *Color*   ▨   **57**

Vocabulary. Ask students to work in pairs to prepare 16 index cards. On each of 8 cards, have the partners write one of these terms: *hue, value, intensity, primary hues, secondary hues, intermediate hues, tint,* and *shade*. On each of the other 8 cards, have them write the definition of each of those terms. Then let the partners use their cards to play Art Concentration, turning over two cards at a time and trying to match a term with its definition.

Developing Concepts

Exploring Aesthetics. Help students discuss the art works shown in Figures 4–5 and 4–6. Ask: What is the subject of each painting? What message does each communicate? How is color used to help communicate that message? What hues do you recognize in each painting? What shades and tints of those hues do you recognize? What color schemes can you identify? After the discussion, ask each student to write a paragraph describing the use of color in one of the paintings.

Using Art Criticism. Have students work in small groups to compare and discuss their "Studio Experience" paintings. What similarities can they find among the paintings of objects in the same hue? How are those paintings different? How are the window/landscape paintings alike? How are they different? What messages or moods do the different color combinations express? Let each student explain to the rest of the group the techniques he or she used, and encourage students to note the most successful aspects of one another's work.

Cooperative Learning
For centuries people wondered what caused the rainbow, the change of color in the sky and on the water surface. In 1665, the answer was found. Isaac Newton was grinding lenses for a telescope when he found that one of his lenses made blurred rims of color around the edge. He stopped working on lenses and began his study of color. Distribute the cooperative learning handout, *Discover Color Yourself* (TRB, Resource 4–5). Have students work in small groups to complete the assignment.

Cooperative Learning
After discussing the color wheel and color schemes, bring in a chart of a permanent palette so students will recognize colors such as cadmium, cerulean, or manganese. Divide students into small groups and have each group research one manufactured permanent color. Have them find out what it is made of and how it is made. Ask them to present their findings to the class.

▶ **Figure 4–6   Why would this be considered a quiet painting? What gives it its serious quality?**

José Clemente Orozco. *Zapatistas.* 1931. Oil on canvas. 114.3 x 139.7 cm (45 x 55"). The Museum of Modern Art, New York, New York. Given anonymously.

The secondary hues are green, orange, and violet. The place of each on the color wheel — between the primary hues — tells which hues can be mixed to make it. To get orange, for example, you mix equal parts of red and yellow. Can you identify the colors that you would mix to obtain the remaining secondary hues?

Intermediate hues are made by mixing a primary hue with its neighboring secondary hue. When you mix the primary hue yellow with the secondary hue green, you get the intermediate hue yellow-green.

Value

You may have noticed that some colors on the color wheel seem lighter than others. The difference is one of value. **Value** is *the lightness or darkness of a hue.* Pale yellow is light in value and deep purple is dark in value.

You can change the value of a hue by adding black or white. In art, a light (or whiter) value of a hue is called a tint. Pink is a mixture of red and white. Pink could be called a tint. A dark (or blacker) value is called a shade. (See Figure 4–7.) Maroon is a mixture

of red and black. It could be called a shade. Be careful when using these terms. In everyday language, the word shade is often used to describe both light and dark values of a hue.

Intensity

Some hues strike the eye as bright and alive. Others appear dull or muddy. The difference is the color's intensity. **Intensity** is *the brightness or dullness of a hue.* A bright hue is said to be high in intensity. A dull hue is said to be low in intensity. Bright yellow is high in intensity. Mustard yellow is low in intensity.

Look again at the color wheel on page **56**. Notice that as you move away from green in the direction of red, the hue grows less intense. Red and green are **complementary colors,** *colors opposite each other on the color wheel.* Adding a hue's complementary color lowers the hue's intensity. (See Figure 4–7.) If you mix equal parts of two complementary colors, you get a neutral color such as brown or gray.

VALUES OF BLUE

SHADE   TINT

INTENSITIES OF BLUE

HIGH INTENSITY   LOW INTENSITY

▲ **Figure 4–7** **Value and intensity scales.**

COMBINING COLORS

Colors are like musical instruments. Just as each instrument has its own special sound, so every color has its own "personality." Combining colors in just the right way can lead to striking results. The following are some common color schemes that trained artists use:

- **Monochromatic color schemes.** Monochromatic (**mahn**-uh-kroh-**mat**-ik) **colors** are *different values of a single hue*. For example, dark blue, medium blue, and light blue is a monochromatic scheme. This type of scheme tightly weaves together the parts of an art work. A danger of a monochromatic scheme, however, is that it can bore the viewer.
- **Analogous color schemes.** Analogous (uh-**nal**-uh-gus) **colors** are *colors that are side by side on the color wheel and share a hue*. Violet, red-violet, red, and red-orange are analogous colors that share the hue red. Analogous colors in an art work can tie one shape to the next.

- **Warm or cool color schemes.** Red, yellow, and orange remind us of sunshine, fire and other warm things. For this reason, they are known as warm colors. Blue, green, and violet make us think of cool things, like ice and grass. They are known, therefore, as cool colors. When used in an art work, warm colors seem to move toward the viewer. Cool colors appear to move back and away.

✔ CHECK YOUR UNDERSTANDING

1. What are the three primary hues?
2. What is the difference between a tint and a shade?
3. What are complementary colors? Give an example.
4. What is a monochromatic color scheme?
5. Define an analogous color scheme.

LESSON PLAN
(pages 60–61)

Objectives
After completing this lesson, students will be able to:
• Use complementary colors in an art work.
• Describe the effect created by using complementary colors side by side.

Supplies
• Small pieces of construction paper in the primary and secondary hues, scissors.
• Pencils and erasers; sketch paper; sheets of white paper, 4 1/2 x 6 inches (11 x 15 cm); sheets of white paper, 9 x 12 inches (23 x 30 cm); tempera paint and brushes; paper towels.
• One or more reproductions of Paul Gauguin's paintings of Tahiti.
• Drawing paper, pencils, watercolor markers or colored pencils.
• Old magazines, scissors, construction paper, glue.

> **TRB Resource**
> • 4-6 *Analogous Painting,* (studio)

TEACHING THE LESSON

Getting Started
Motivator. Give each student (or each pair or group of students) six small pieces of construction paper, one in each of the primary hues and one in each of the secondary hues. Ask students to pair the complementary colors. Then have them cut a shape from each paper in a secondary hue and place it over its complement to make a simple design. Finally, encourage students to share and discuss their designs; let them identify their favorite complementary pairs and discuss reasons for their choices.

Vocabulary. Let volunteers discuss what they know about the use of the word *motif* in such fields as literature and music. Have others define *motif* as it is used in art, referring to the text if necessary. Then help students discuss the relationships between different uses of the word.

60

Using Color Combinations

Artists use color schemes to create special effects in works of art. Color schemes can make a painting vibrate or make colors look brighter.

Look at Figure 4–8. Notice how Elizabeth Murray has used the red and green complementary color scheme to create this work. To give it variety she has experimented with values. Can you find a tint and a shade of red?

WHAT YOU WILL LEARN

You will create a complementary color design. You will create a motif, based on your initials. A **motif** (moh-**teef**) is *a unit that is repeated in a pattern or visual rhythm*. Plan the motif so that it touches all four edges of the paper. Then arrange the motif to form an interesting pattern. Paint all the letters with one color. Paint all the negative spaces with its complement.

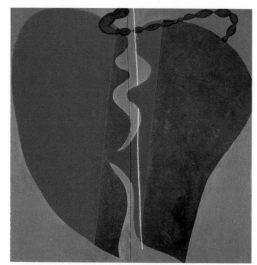

▲ **Figure 4–8   How does the artist's choice and placement of color affect the meaning of the painting?**

Elizabeth Murray. *Join*. 1980. Oil on canvas. 337.8 x 304.8 cm (133 x 120″). Security Pacific Bank Collection.

60   Lesson 3 *Using Color Combinations*

WHAT YOU WILL NEED

• Pencil, sketch paper, eraser
• White paper, 4½ x 6 inch (11 x 15 cm)
• White paper, 9 x 12 inch (23 x 30 cm)
• Masking tape
• Tempera paint and two small brushes
• Paper towels

WHAT YOU WILL DO

1. Using sketch paper, draw different arrangements of your initials. In this design, an interesting shape is more important than the readability of the letters.
2. Select your best design. Using double lines, draw the letters on the smaller sheet of white paper. Be sure that the letters touch all four sides of the paper. (See Figure 4–9.)
3. Hold the paper up to a glass window with the letters facing out. You will see them backwards through the paper. Carefully draw over the lines on the back with a soft lead pencil. The lines on the back must go directly over the lines on the front. These lines will act like carbon paper.
4. You may arrange the motif any way that fits on the larger sheet of paper.
5. Place your motif on the larger sheet of paper. Hold it in place with a small piece of tape. Transfer the image by drawing over the lines of the motif. If you wish, you may flip the motif over and trace the mirror image.
6. Select a set of complementary colors. You may use primaries and secondaries, or you may use a set of intermediates such as red-orange and blue-green.

Background Information
Several modern artists have experimented with unusual approaches to color. For example, Fernand Leger (France, 1881–1955), who contributed to the development of Cubism, used color simply as decoration. If he took a liking to a particular color, he used that color in his painting. Leger's use of color led to an art movement known as Orphism; members of this movement considered color the primary visual element. Robert Delaunay (France, 1885–1941) was the leading member of the Orphism movement. Delaunay painted with geometric patterns of color; his ideas and works influenced other painters both in Europe and in the United States.

For Wassily Kandinsky (Russian-born, 1866–1944) color and form were the only elements necessary to art. Kandinsky felt that color, like music, acted directly on the soul.

Another art movement, Suprematism, was founded on the element of color. For Suprematist painter Kasimir Malevich (Russia, 1878–1935), the reality of art was color itself.

4.5"

6"

- **Describe** Explain what set of complementary colors you selected. Did your motif touch all four sides of the paper? Describe the pattern you created with your motif. Show where you painted all the letters with one hue and all the negative spaces with its complement.
- **Explain** Describe the effect that is created by painting the complementary colors side by side.

▲ Figure 4–9 Letter motif arrangement.

7. Use one brush and one hue to paint all the letters in your pattern. Be sure the paint is dry before you paint the second color next to it.
8. Use a second brush to paint all the negative spaces with the complement of that hue. Nothing should be left white. If you do not have two brushes, clean your brush thoroughly before using another color. (See Technique Tip **10**, *Handbook* page **273**.)
9. Put your work on display with your classmates. Do all the complements have the same exciting visual effect? (See Figure 4–10.)

▲ Figure 4–10 Student work. Motif design.

OTHER STUDIO IDEA

- Select a sheet of construction paper of a primary color. Cut out objects from a magazine that have the complementary color of your paper. Organize them into a design and glue them to the background paper.

Lesson 3 *Using Color Combinations* **61**

Developing Concepts

Exploring Aesthetics. Display reproductions of some of Paul Gauguin's Tahitian paintings, and read aloud this quote from Gauguin: "I think colors have an emotional power which can convey a mood to the viewer." Point out that the artist often used flat areas of bright, intense complementary hues, creating emotional tension. Ask: What idea (in your own words) did Gauguin express in the quotation? How do you see that idea reflected in his paintings?

Developing Studio Skills. Let students make line drawings of landscapes, either real or imaginary. Make three photocopies of each student's drawing, and have students color all three pictures, using a different set of complementary colors for each. Then have the students compare and discuss their work. Ask: How does your feeling toward the scene change as a result of different color combinations? Which combination do you like best? Why?

Following Up

Closure. Have students write short paragraphs describing what they have learned about the uses and impact of complementary colors.

Evaluation. Check students' complementary-color designs, and read their paragraphs describing what they have learned.

Reteaching. Have students work in pairs or small groups to collect magazine pictures showing the use of complementary colors. Ask students to cut out the pictures they select, glue them onto construction paper, and label the complementary colors.

Enrichment. Ask students to research the use of complementary hues in the "official colors" of governments, holidays, or religious observances. (One example is the use of red and green during Christmas celebrations.) Be sure students do not limit their research to local governments, familiar holidays, or their own religions.

Classroom Management Tip
Explain to students about the proper care of brushes. Tell students that before they use a new brush, they should wash out any glue placed on the top to protect its shape.

While they are drawing, they should stop often to swish the brush around in water so that the medium doesn't dry in the brush hairs. Then blot the brush with a rag, tissue, or paper towel. By blotting the brush the medium won't be diluted when they begin to use the brush again.

When they are through with the brush for the day, they should wash it with soap and water until the rinse water comes out clear. Rinsing the brush will keep the medium from building up under the metal ring that holds the hairs. If ink or paint collects there, the brush hairs will fan out.

Line

Objectives

After completing this lesson, students will be able to:
- Define the term *line*.
- Name the different kinds of lines and describe the kinds of messages or feelings communicated by each.
- Draw a continuous line that creates a visually balanced composition.

Supplies

- Drawing paper, pencils, black markers, tracing paper.
- Old magazines, scissors, construction paper, glue.

TEACHING THE LESSON

Getting Started

Motivator. Ask students to draw simple outlines of objects, real or imaginary. Have them use dark markers on drawing paper. Next, have them place tracing paper (or other sheets of thin paper) over their drawings and convert them to dot-to-dot drawings. Then let students trade dot-to-dot pages and complete the drawings. Finally, let volunteers show their drawings and help students discuss this definition of a line: the path of a dot through space.

Think about how many times every day you see lines. You write words, numbers, and symbols with the help of lines. You use lines to draw pictures. The lines on a map help you find the best route from one place to another. You also feel lines—in the grain of a piece of wood or the veins of a leaf.

This lesson will focus on the importance of line as one of the six elements of art.

THE MEANING OF LINE

Take a pencil and move it across a sheet of paper. What happened? The moving point of the pencil made a path of connected dots on the paper. In other words, it made a line. This definition of **line**—*the path of a dot through space*—is a good one to remember. It reminds you that it takes movement to make a line. When you see a line, your eye usually follows its movement. A trained artist uses lines to control the movement of the viewer's eyes. Lines can lead the eyes into, around, and out of visual images in a work of art.

KINDS OF LINE

There are five main kinds of line: vertical, horizontal, diagonal, curved, and zigzag. When used in an art work, lines can communicate different messages or feelings to the viewer.

Vertical Lines

Vertical lines (Figure 4–11) move straight up and down. They do not lean at all. When you stand up straight and tall, your body forms a vertical line.

In art, vertical lines appear to be at attention. Artists use them to show dignity, formality, or strength.

Horizontal Lines

Horizontal lines (Figure 4–12) run parallel to the ground. They do not slant. When you lie flat on the floor, your body forms a horizontal line.

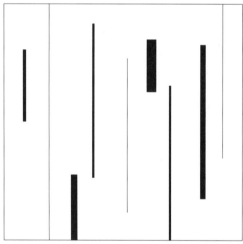

▲ **Figure 4–11**   Vertical lines move straight up and down.

▲ **Figure 4–12**   Horizontal lines lie parallel to the horizon.

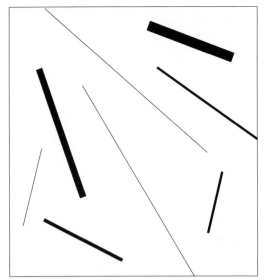

▲ Figure 4–13 Diagonal lines slant.

▲ Figure 4–14 Curved lines change direction gradually.

Horizontal lines in art seem at rest. Other words that come to mind in connection with them are quiet and peaceful. Horizontal lines make the viewer feel comfortable, calm, and relaxed.

Diagonal Lines

Diagonal lines (Figure 4–13) slant. They are somewhere between a vertical and a horizontal line. Imagine standing straight up and then, with your body stiff, falling to the floor. At any point during your fall, your body would form a diagonal line.

To the artist, diagonal lines signal action and excitement. Since they appear to be either rising or falling, diagonals sometimes make a viewer feel tense and uncomfortable. But when they meet and seem to hold each other up, as in the roof of a house, they appear firm and unmoving.

Curved Lines

Curved lines (Figure 4–14) change direction little by little. When you draw wiggly lines, you are actually linking a series of curves. Other forms that begin with curves are spirals and circles.

Like diagonal lines, curved lines, express movement, though in a more graceful, flowing way. The amount of movement in a curve depends on how tight the curve is. Notice how the painter, Vincent van Gogh suggests motion in his tree through the unusual use of curves (Figure 4–15, on page **64**).

Zigzag Lines

Zigzag lines (Figure 4–16, on page **65**) are made by combining different directions of diagonal lines. The diagonals form sharp angles and change direction suddenly.

Zigzag lines can create confusion. They suggest action and nervous excitement. Sometimes zigzags move in even horizontal patterns, like those at the top of a picket fence. These are less active than the jagged lines in a diagonal streak of lightning.

QUALITIES OF LINES

Lines may appear smooth or rough, continuous or broken, sketchy or controlled. The **line quality** describes *the unique character of any line*. Line quality is affected by either the tool or medium used to produce the mark, or by the particular motion of the artist's hands.

Vocabulary. Have students brainstorm a list of words they think of when they hear the word *line* (such as *path, trail, road, direction, row, curve, coil, slant*). Record their ideas on the board. Then ask students to discuss what all the words have in common; help them recognize that all suggest movement. Explain to students that lines can lead the eyes into, around, and out of visual images.

Developing Concepts

Exploring Aesthetics. Guide students in discussing Figure 4–15. Ask: What kinds of lines can you identify in this painting? What line qualities can you identify? How did van Gogh create the lines? What impression do the lines create? What message or mood do you think van Gogh wanted to create? Do you feel he succeeded? If so, how? If not, why not? Then ask students to compare this painting to other paintings of trees, to photographs of trees, and to their own perception of natural trees. How is this painting different? Why is it different? Finally, read students this quotation from van Gogh: "I believe in the necessity for a new art of color, of design, and of the artistic life." Let students discuss their understanding of van Gogh's words; then ask them to write short paragraphs telling how they think van Gogh's quotation helps explain his painting.

Using Art Criticism. Display students' "Studio Experience" drawings. Have students choose the drawings they like best and write paragraphs describing what makes those particular works successful.

Cooperative Learning

Divide students into groups of four to five. Tell them the assignment is as follows: As a group, they will select one of the kinds of line—vertical, horizontal, diagonal, curved, or zigzag. They will appoint one member to write down all the visual examples they can list in five minutes. For instance, if the group chooses curved lines, they might include sagging telephone wires, an eyebrow, the trail a snake would leave in the sand. The idea behind the exercise is to snowball ideas without censoring. At the end of the time limit, each group will read its list to the rest of the class. There will probably be some duplication, but that is less important than the fact that there will be many different examples. Stress the idea that every *individual* can snowball ideas in order to stimulate creativity when given an art assignment.

Understanding Art History.
Briefly discuss with the class the work of Albrecht Dürer and Paul Klee (see "Background Information"). Then have students read about and look at works produced by one of these artists. Ask students to write one or two paragraphs in response to these questions: From this research, what have you learned about the element of line? How do you hope to use what you have learned?

Developing Studio Skills.
Have partners work together to list at least five adjectives that describe moods or activities (*nervous, calm, bold, rippling,* and *spinning,* for example). Then have each student independently draw a line that expresses each adjective. Encourage them to show variations in their lines—thick/thin, long/short, heavy/light, smooth/rough. Have the partners compare and discuss their lines.

Appreciating Cultural Diversity. One fascinating way to learn about line is to explore—through photographs and the imagination—some of Japan's Zen gardens. Explain to students that Zen Buddhism is a religion that emphasizes meditation; Kyoto, Japan, is an important Zen center and the home of more than 2000 shrines and temples. One of these is the Ryoanji Temple, famous for its garden made entirely of rocks. The garden rocks are raked into straight rows, creating thousands of orderly lines. Zen Buddhists feel that this garden of lines facilitates meditation. Ask volunteers to read more about Ryoanji Temple and other gardens and to gather photographs, if possible. Then let volunteers present their findings to the rest of the class.

▲ **Figure 4–15** How do the lines in van Gogh's painting direct your eyes? How is van Gogh's tree different from the usual idea of a tree?

Vincent van Gogh. *Cypresses.* 1889. Oil on canvas. 93.3 x 74 cm (36¾ x 29⅛"). Metropolitan Museum of Art, New York, New York. Rogers Fund, 1949.

Handbook Cross-Reference
Tell students that few artists accomplished as much in so little time as Vincent van Gogh. His artistic career spanned just ten years. During this time, he received only one favorable review and sold only one painting. For more information about his life, refer students to the Artist Profile, *Handbook* page **288**.

Note
Visual elements are the ingredients of art. Explain to students that the elements have been analyzed, organized, and used in many ways, but they are not inventions of the artist. They are natural elements that artists have learned to use as an alternative language. Emphasize that the use of visual elements is common to all cultures. Helping students to understand the elements will give them new methods of applying them and new ways to perceive their environment.

▲ Figure 4–16　Zigzag lines are combinations of diagonals.

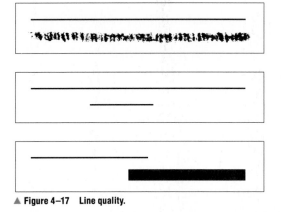

▲ Figure 4–17　Line quality.

Lines can also be varied. **Line variation** describes *the thickness or thinness, lightness or darkness of a line*. Thick and dark lines appear to be visually heavier than thin and light lines. Look at Figure 4–17 and identify the different quality of lines. What medium do you think was used to create each line?

✔CHECK YOUR UNDERSTANDING

1. What is the meaning of the term *line* as it is used in art?
2. Name five kinds of line.
3. Describe the way each of the five kinds of line causes a viewer of an art work to feel.
4. What affects line quality?

LESSON 5

Shape, Form, and Space

Shape, Form, and Space

LESSON PLAN
(pages 66–69)

Objectives

After completing this lesson, students will be able to:

• Explain the differences between shapes and forms.
• Explain the difference between geometric shapes or forms and organic shapes or forms.
• Define the term *space.*
• Use space-creating techniques in a drawing.

Supplies

• Collection of small common objects, such as keys, leaves, paper clips, buttons; construction paper; tempera paint in shallow dishes.
• Drawing paper, pencils.
• Reproductions of pre-Renaissance and Renaissance paintings.
• Construction paper, scissors.
• Photographs of the statues on Easter Island.

TRB Resources

• 4-7 *Symbolic Shapes,* (art history)
• 4-8 *The Elements in Functional Form,* (aesthetics/art criticism)

TEACHING THE LESSON

Getting Started

Motivator. Have students work in three or four groups. Give each group several small common objects, one sheet of paper, and tempera paint in shallow dishes. Ask group members to work together to dip the objects into the paint and then press them onto the paper, making prints. Then let the group members show their prints, and have other students try to guess which objects were used. Finally, help students compare the two-dimensional shapes with the three-dimensional forms.

The world we live in is made up basically of two things: objects and space. Each object — a car, an apple, a book, even you — has a shape or a form. Often you are able to pick out objects by their forms or shapes alone. Sometimes you can spot a friend in the distance just by recognizing his or her shape. With your eyes closed you could feel an object and tell that it has a round form.

Shape, form, and space are all closely tied to one another. In this lesson you will learn to read the meaning of these three elements.

SHAPE

In art a **shape** is *an area clearly set off by one or more of the other five visual elements of art.* Shapes are flat. They are limited to only two dimensions: length and width. A ball's shape is a circle. A shape may have an outline or boundary around it. Some shapes show up because of color. Others are set off purely by the space that surrounds them.

Shapes may be thought of as belonging to one of two classes:

▲ **Figure 4–18   What kind of unique worlds exist in your own imagination? Would you use geometric shapes in creating your unique world on paper?**

Attilio Salemme. *Inquisition.* 1952. Oil on canvas. 101.6 x 160 cm (40 x 63″). Whitney Museum of American Art.

Note
The difference between shape and form can be hard to remember. In the text, shape is defined as, "an area clearly set off by one or more of the other five elements of art. Shape is limited to two dimensions: length and width." Tell students they can think of shape as the *outline* of an object—"what you would trace if you drew a line around it." The two classifications of shape, geometric and organic, can be differentiated and remembered by pointing out that the root of the word "organic"

is *organ.* Our organs—heart, liver, kidney—have *curved* outlines. Most students will recognize the term "kidney-shaped pool" and will know what a kidney bean looks like. Ask them to suggest other organic shapes from nature; a flower petal, a raindrop, a puddle.

▲ **Figure 4–19** Do you like the organic shapes in this painting better than the geometric ones in Figure 4–18? Why or why not?

Arthur G. Dove. *Plant Forms*. 1915. Pastel on canvas. 43.8 x 60.6 cm (17¼ x 23⅞"). Whitney Museum of American Art, New York, New York. Purchased with funds from Mr. & Mrs. Roy R. Nueberger.

- **Geometric shapes.** These are precise shapes that look as if they were made with a ruler or other drawing tool. The square, the circle, the triangle, the rectangle, and the oval are the five basic geometric shapes. The strange world shown in Figure 4–18 is made up largely of geometric shapes.
- **Organic shapes.** These are not regular or even. Their outlines curve to make free-form shapes. Organic shapes are often found in nature. The objects in the painting in Figure 4–19 are based on organic, free-form shapes.

FORM

Like shapes, forms have length and width. But forms go a step further. They have depth. A **form** is *an object with three dimensions.* You are a three-dimensional form. So is a tree or a table.

Forms, too, are grouped as either geometric or organic. Examples of geometric forms are a baseball and a child's building block. Examples of organic forms are a stone and a cloud.

Shapes and forms are closely linked in art (Figure 4–20). The end of a cylinder is a circle. One side of a cube is a square. A triangle can "grow" into a pyramid.

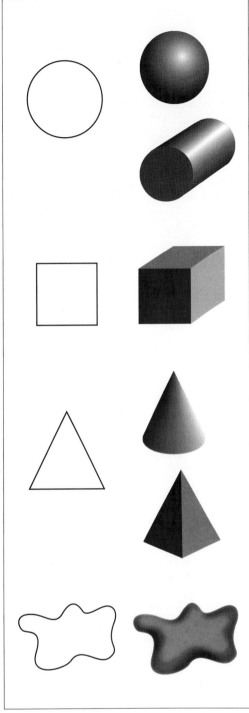

▲ **Figure 4–20** Form-shape correspondences.

Vocabulary. Have each student work with a partner to make a simple five-column chart with these headings: Geometric Shapes, Organic Shapes, Geometric Forms, Organic Forms, Space. Then name various items, and have students, working with their partners, record the items in the correct columns. Examples of items to name: sky, cloud, ice-cream cone, stop sign, softball, leaf, mountain, key. Finally, encourage students to compare and discuss their charts.

Developing Concepts

Exploring Aesthetics. Ask pairs of students to discuss Figure 4–18. What shapes can they identify? What forms can they identify? What is the subject of the work? What message or mood does the sculpture seem to communicate? Then have the partners work together to write a short description of the work.

Using Art Criticism. Have students work in discussion groups or as a class to compare and contrast Figures 4–18 and 4–19. Ask: What different feelings do you get from looking at these paintings? Why? What similarities do you see between the two paintings? What kinds of lines are used in the two paintings? Which kind of shape—geometric or organic—do you prefer? Why? Then have students write short descriptions of the painting they prefer.

Cooperative Learning

Form is defined as "an object with three dimensions." Help clarify the difference between shape and form by stressing that form refers to an object—something that can be held in the hand, picked up and moved, has weight and would occupy space. Pair students up and have them do this exercise: One student names a three-dimensional object, the other answers whether it is an organic or geometric form. Suggest a category to the class from which to select objects, such as toys.

Examples might include child's building block (geometric), puzzle piece (organic), marble (geometric), football (organic). After about two minutes, they can change sides. The goal is to clarify the distinction between the two types of form and shape using mental imagery and memory aids.

Understanding Art History.
Display reproductions of paintings created by European artists before the Renaissance. Then add to the display several reproductions of paintings by some of the great artists of the Renaissance, such as Leonardo da Vinci, Michelangelo, and Raphael. Help students contrast the flat figures and lack of depth in the first set of paintings with the rounded, more realistic figures and the illusion of depth created in the Renaissance paintings. Ask students to study the works by Renaissance artists and identify examples of specific techniques used to give the feeling of depth.

Developing Studio Skills.
Let students work with the same small objects from which they made shape prints (see "Motivator"). Have groups of students arrange several objects on a table and then make sketches of the arrangement, employing one or more depth-creating techniques. Encourage the members of each group to discuss and compare their sketches.

Appreciating Cultural Diversity. Encourage students to read and look at reproductions to discover how other, non-Western cultures show depth in their works of art. For example, in some Asian and African art, both front and side views of an object or figure are shown at the same time. Asian artists often show distance by using parallel lines to divide an area into foreground, middle ground, and background. Ancient Egyptian artists used a similar technique. Let volunteers work individually or with partners to research this aspect of art in other cultures and then report to the rest of the class.

▲ **Figure 4–21   Does seeing this sculpture make you want to walk around it and see it from different sides?**

Constantin Brancusi. *Mlle. Pogany II*. 1920. Polished bronze. 44.5 x 17.8 x 25.4 cm (17½ x 7 x 10"). Albright-Knox Art Gallery, Buffalo, New York. Charlotte A. Watson Fund, 1927.

Note
You may wish to introduce students to the concept of *linear perspective*. Linear perspective is the geometric system that shows artists how to create the illusion of depth on a flat surface. Using this system, an artist is able to paint figures and objects so that they seem to move deeper *into* a work rather than across it. Slanting the lines of buildings and other objects in the picture inwards makes them appear to extend back into space. If these lines are lengthened, they will eventually meet at a point along an imaginary horizontal line representing the eye level. The point at which these lines meet is called a vanishing point.

SPACE

Space is *the distance or area between, around, above, below, and within things.* Space is empty until objects fill it. All objects take up space. You, for instance, are a living, breathing form moving through space.

Some kinds of art are three-dimensional. You may recall from Chapter 3 that sculpture is this kind of art. When a piece of sculpture is freestanding, as in Figure 4–21, we can move completely around it and see it from different sides.

Although drawings and paintings are created in two dimensions, they can be made to appear three-dimensional. Artists have developed techniques for giving the feeling of depth in paintings and drawings. These include:

- **Overlapping.** Having shapes overlap one another.
- **Size.** Making distant shapes smaller than closer ones.
- **Focus.** Adding more detail to closer objects, less detail to distant objects.
- **Placement.** Placing distant objects higher up in the picture, closer ones lower down.
- **Intensity and value.** Using colors that are lower in intensity and lighter in value for objects in the distance.
- **Linear perspective.** Slanting lines of buildings and other objects so they seem to come together in the distance.

STUDIO EXPERIENCE

Imagine that the room you are sitting in is a painting. Look around the room. Be on the alert for the use of techniques that lead to a feeling of deep space. For example, which objects, if any, overlap? Which objects appear to be smaller than others? Now make a sketch of the room, replacing some real objects with ones from your imagination. Make sure that your new objects follow the same rules of space as the old ones. When you have finished, discuss your drawing with other members of the class. Can they identify all the space-creating techniques in your work?

✔CHECK YOUR UNDERSTANDING

1. What is shape?
2. What are the two types of shape? Give an example of each type.
3. What is form?
4. What are the two types of form? Give an example of each type.
5. Name two techniques that artists use for creating a feeling of space.

Lesson 5   *Shape, Form, and Space*   **69**

---

1. A shape is an area clearly set off by one or more of the other five visual elements of art.
2. The two types of shape are geometric, such as a circle, and organic, such as the shape of a leaf. (Students may give other examples of geometric shapes.)
3. A form is an object with three dimensions.
4. The two types of form are geometric, such as a baseball, and organic, such as a stone.
5. Techniques for creating a feeling of space include having shapes overlap each other; making distant shapes smaller than closer shapes; adding more detail to closer objects; placing distant objects higher in the picture; using colors that are lower in intensity and lighter in value for distant objects; and slanting lines of building and other objects so they seem to come together in the distance. (Students may identify any two of these techniques.)

Following Up

Closure. Have each student select one of the art works shown in this lesson and briefly describe the use of shape, form, or space in the work.

Evaluation. 1. Review students' written responses to the "Check Your Understanding" questions. 2. Review students' descriptions of shape, form, or space in art works.

Reteaching. Work with small groups of students. Ask each group member to cut two or three shapes from construction paper. Then have students work together to identify all the group's shapes as either geometric or organic. When the group members are confident of the distinction, have them each cut out two more shapes: one geometric and one organic. Finally, let the group members experiment with arranging the cut shapes into various designs.

Enrichment. To help students think further about form and space, show photographs of the mysterious statues of Easter Island in the Pacific Ocean. Explain that more than 600 of these statues were carved—with stone tools—at an undetermined time and under circumstances that have not been established. Most of the statues are between 10 and 12 feet (3 and 4 m) tall, but the tallest is more than 35 feet (11 m) high. Encourage students to speculate about the content of these statues: What message were they intended to communicate? What other messages do they—in their mystery—communicate to us now? Ask volunteers to read more about the statues and to share the information they gather with the rest of the class.

Paper Sculpture Forms

LESSON PLAN
(pages 70–71)

Objectives
After completing this lesson, students will be able to:
• Turn flat paper shapes into three-dimensional forms, using three paper sculpture techniques.
• Describe and explain their paper sculpture forms.

Supplies
• Construction paper.
• Simple examples of scored paper, pleated paper, and curled paper.
• Sheets of scrap paper; pencils; rulers; sheets of construction paper, 12 x 18 inches (30 x 45 cm); scissors; utility knives; staplers; white glue.
• Origami paper, books or pamphlets explaining simple origami techniques, examples of completed origami forms.

> **TRB Resource**
> • 4-9 *Frank Stella*,
>   (artist profile)

TEACHING THE LESSON

Getting Started
Motivator. Give each student a sheet of construction paper, and ask volunteers to identify the paper surface as a shape. Then ask students to experiment with changing these shapes into forms. Let students share and compare their efforts. Explain that students will learn about and use specific techniques for creating paper sculpture forms.

Vocabulary. Ask volunteers to look up these three verbs in dictionaries: *score, pleat, curl.* Have them read the definitions aloud, and ask students to select for each word the definition that applies to creating paper sculpture. Let them speculate about each technique, and then display your examples.

Paper Sculpture Forms

Study the work in Figure 4–22. From the credit line, you can tell what media the artist, Frank Stella, used. You can also tell the size of the piece. Try to imagine a work of this size in your classroom. Do you think it could have been made with paper? In this studio lesson you will explore some of the ways that paper can be used to make sculpture forms.

WHAT YOU WILL LEARN
You will alter a flat two-dimensional shape of paper into a three-dimensional form. You will use paper sculpture techniques to create an interesting paper sculpture form.

WHAT YOU WILL NEED
• Scrap paper for experimenting
• Pencil and ruler
• Sheets of construction paper, 12 x 18 inch (30 x 46 cm)
• Scissors, knife, stapler
• White glue

WHAT YOU WILL DO
1. Using scrap paper, experiment with a variety of paper sculpture techniques. (See Technique Tip **21**, *Handbook* **278**.) This will show you some ways of working with paper. These techniques can be used for your paper sculpture.

▶ **Figure 4–22   Frank Stella's art was often displayed by attaching it to walls with heavy bolts.**

Frank Stella. *St. Michael's Counterguard.* 1984. Aluminum, fiberglass and honeycomb. 396.2 x 342.9 x 274.3 cm (156 x 135 x 108"). Los Angeles County Museum of Art. Gift of Anna Bing Arnold.

70 Lesson 6   *Paper Sculpture Forms*

Background Information
Creating paper sculptures should not be considered an activity appropriate only to student artists. Naum Gabo (Russian-born, 1890–1977) created paper sculptures that have been exhibited in museums.

Gabo and several other Russian sculptors established the Constructivist movement; they intended to create non-objective art works suited to the new industrial age. Later in his career, however, Gabo tried to disassociate himself from Constructivism and adopted a more humanistic approach to non-objective art. In fact, he left the U.S.S.R. at least in part to distance himself from Constructivists with whom he disagreed. Eventually Gabo settled in the United States where he worked and taught.

Gabo created most of his sculptures from wood, glass, metal, and plastic. As a kind of preliminary sketch for each work, Gabo worked with paper. Before creating a final art work, Gabo usually made a complete model out of very stiff paper.

2. Using your large sheet of paper, begin your design. As you work, you may have to alter your plan to get the effect you desire. Include three paper sculpture techniques in your design.
3. You may cut into the paper, but do not cut it into two pieces. Use staples or glue to hold the paper in place.
4. Keep turning your sculpture so that it looks interesting from every point of view.
5. Display your paper form. (See Figure 4–23.)

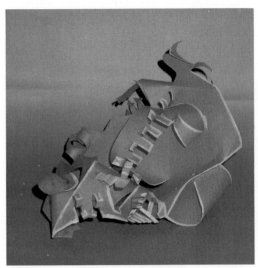

▲ Figure 4–23 Student work. Paper sculpture.

- **Describe**   Tell what paper sculpture techniques you used.
- **Explain**   Tell how your two-dimensional shape was altered into a three-dimensional form. Tell how you used the paper sculpture techniques to complete your design.

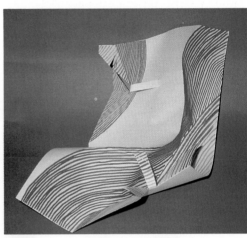

▲ Figure 4–24 Student work. Paper sculpture.

OTHER STUDIO IDEAS

- Experiment with scrap paper using the scoring and folding techniques you have learned to make a large bird. Attach a fine nylon filament to the center of the bird. You may have to attach more than one filament to position the bird the way you want. Suspend the bird from the ceiling or other high place so that it looks like it is flying.
- ●● Build a paper castle using the paper sculpture techniques you have learned so far.

Lesson 6   *Paper Sculpture Forms*   **71**

Developing Concepts

Exploring Aesthetics. Help students discuss Figure 4–22. How did the artist use color, line, shape, form, and space in this work? What idea or feeling does this work communicate to you?

Using Art Criticism. After students have described and explained their own paper sculpture forms, put all the sculptures on display. Let students compare and discuss the works. Then have each student choose one sculpture he or she especially likes and write a paragraph about it.

Developing Studio Skills. Let volunteers research other techniques for creating paper sculpture. Ask them to explain and demonstrate these techniques to the rest of the class.

Following Up

Closure. Have students suggest at least one way they might improve their own paper sculptures.

Evaluation. Consider each student's paper sculpture and his or her own evaluation of the project.

Reteaching. Have students plan and make new paper sculpture forms, this time working in assigned pairs or small groups. Be sure each student who seemed uncertain or dissatisfied with his or her first project is assigned to work with a more skilled—and helpful—partner.

Enrichment. Display several completed origami forms, and make booklets of origami instruction and sheets of origami paper available. Then let students work individually or in small groups to try creating their own folded paper forms. Encourage interested students to learn more about the development and the techniques of origami; have them share their findings with the class.

LESSON PLAN
(pages 72–73)

Objectives

After completing this lesson, students will be able to:
- Explain the two ways in which we experience texture.
- Create a design with examples of actual texture and visual texture.

Supplies

- Bags (one for each pair of students) containing scraps of textured material, such as rope, yarn, netting, lace, foil, cotton, sandpaper, sponge, tissue, waxed paper.
- Scraps of fabric and textured papers, old magazines, scissors, cardboard, glue.
- Textured materials and objects; cardboard; glue; drawing paper; markers, pencils, paints and brushes, and/or other media.
- Newsprint, crayons.

TEACHING THE LESSON

Getting Started

Motivator. Have students work with partners. Give each pair of students a bag containing a scrap of material. Ask the partners to take turns feeling the material inside the bag, describing it as fully as possible, and then trying to identify it.

Vocabulary. Ask students to define the word *texture.* Then have them brainstorm a list of adjectives that can be used to describe texture; record their adjectives on the chalkboard. Finally, ask students to suggest specific objects with textures that might be described by the listed adjectives.

LESSON 7

Texture

Rub your fingers lightly over this page. How would you describe the way it feels? **Texture** refers *to how things feel, or look as though they might feel, if touched*. No one needs to teach you about texture. You know what is rough and what is smooth. There are certain textures you find pleasant to the touch. Other surfaces you avoid touching because you do not like the way they feel.

In this lesson you will learn about the two ways texture works as an element of art.

TWO SIDES OF TEXTURE

Sandpaper, glass, a block of concrete—each has its own special texture, or feel. Have you ever tried on a piece of clothing—perhaps a sweater—that you thought looked itchy only to find it was not? Such things are possible because we experience texture through two of our senses. We experience texture with our sense of sight. We also experience it again—and sometimes differently—with our sense of touch.

▶ **Figure 4–25 How does your eye see the trees in this photograph? How do your fingers "see" them?**

Developing Perceptual Skills
Remind students that two senses, vision and touch, give us evidence when we experience texture. Most people have been fooled by the appearance of an object because of the way the light was hitting it, or because it was getting dark outside and they couldn't see clearly anymore. But we can also be fooled when the light is good unless we look at something carefully. Ask students if any of them have a magnifying glass at home. Ask if they have ever looked at the skin on the back of their hands or the skin of an orange. Although we think of some objects as smooth-textured, most have high and low spots that are visible when we examine them closely. Ask students to name some other common items that would generally be characterized as smooth but have a subtle texture. Remind students that careful observation of detail is necessary in order to paint and draw well.

When you look at a photograph of tree bark or a seashell, you see patterns of light and dark (Figures 4–25 and 4–26). These patterns bring back memories of how those objects feel. When this happens, you are experiencing visual texture. The photograph is smooth and flat. It is your eyes that add the splintery coarseness of the bark or the satiny smoothness of the shell. Actual, or real texture, on the other hand, is what you experience when you touch the object itself, not the photograph. It is the message your fingers send to your brain.

✔ CHECK YOUR UNDERSTANDING

1. What is texture?
2. Through which two of our senses do we experience texture?
3. What is visual texture? What is actual texture?

◀ **Figure 4–26** Why is the visual texture of the shell different from the actual texture of the photograph?

Painting a Landscape

LESSON PLAN
(pages 74–75)

Objectives

After completing this lesson, students will be able to:
• Use the elements of color, line, shape, space, and texture to create a unified painting.
• Describe and explain their landscape paintings.

Supplies

• Pencils, sketch paper, tempera paint, soft and stiff brushes, mixing tray, water, sheets of heavy paper or illustration board, paint cloths.

> **TRB Resource**
> • 4-1 *The Elements Chart*, (reproducible master)

TEACHING THE LESSON

Getting Started

Motivator. Let the students work in small groups to experiment with tempera paint, using different kinds of brushes and techniques. Ask students in each group to work together to find answers to these questions: How can you create rough textures? How can you create smooth textures? What effect do you create when you drag a soft brush across the paper? What effect do you create when you drag a stiff brush? What other kinds of effects can you create with the brushes and paints? Then have all the students share and discuss what they have discovered.

Vocabulary. Ask two or three students to prepare an art-related word search puzzle that includes these words: *color, line, shape, form, space, texture, hue, tint, shade, value, intensity, geometric, organic.* Also have them prepare a list of definitions of the words hidden in the puzzle. Check the puzzle carefully, and then make a photocopy of it for each student in the class. Let the rest of the students solve the puzzle independently; then discuss and evaluate it.

74

Painting a Landscape

Look at the painting of a tree by the Dutch artist Piet Mondrian (peet **mawn**-dree-ahn) in Figure 4–27. Does this look like a real tree? In this painting Mondrian used line quality and line variation to express the idea of a tree. Note how the artist also used color, shape, and texture to capture the idea of a tree.

WHAT YOU WILL LEARN

You will use the elements of color, line, shape, space, and texture to paint an unusual landscape. The landscape will have trees at different places in space. It will also show the underground roots of the nearest tree, plus different layers of soil and rock. (See Figure 4–28.)

WHAT YOU WILL NEED

• Pencil and sketch paper
• Tempera paint
• Soft and stiff brushes
• Mixing tray
• Water
• Sheet of heavy paper or illustration board, 12 x 18 inch (30 x 46 cm)
• Paper towels

WHAT YOU WILL DO

1. Take a walk outside or use your imagination to think of different landscapes. On scrap paper, make several pencil sketches of landscapes with trees. Show the branches clearly, but do not draw leaves.

▶ **Figure 4–27** Are warm or cool colors used in this painting? How would you describe the lines used? Are the shapes geometric or organic? What has been done to give the work a rich texture?

Piet Mondrian. *Blue Tree.* 1909–1910. Oil on composition board. 56.8 x 74.9 cm (22⅜ x 29½"). Dallas Museum of Art.

74 🎨 Lesson 8 *Painting a Landscape*

Background Information

Piet Mondrian (Holland, 1872–1944) was a member of the Dutch art movement known as De Stijl. The painters, sculptors, and architects in this group considered order and harmony the goal of life; they strove to create works reflecting this goal. The painters of De Stijl were non-objective artists. Many achieved only an arid uniformity; Mondrian was a clear exception. His style followed the Dutch style of austerity and clarity, but with a spark of humanity.

Horizontals and verticals are key in Mondrian's paintings. He used primary colors along with black, white, and gray. Using these same lines, shapes, and colors, he produced a great many works. Remarkably, each painting maintains its own identity. Mondrian's work shows that he was intent on shedding the unnecessary and keeping only the harmonious.

2. Divide your sheet of white paper or illustration board horizontally into three equal parts with light pencil lines. In the top part, redraw lightly the best of your landscape sketches. The lines of the tree branches should be designed to make an interesting pattern of shapes. (Look again at Figure 4–27 for ideas.) The branches of the nearest tree should run off the top of your paper.

3. In the center part, draw the underground roots of the nearest tree. Use your imagination. The lines of the roots should add other interesting shapes.

4. In the bottom part, draw different layers of soil and rock. Once again, be as imaginative as you can.

5. Before painting your final work, experiment on scrap paper using stiff and soft brushes to create different textures. Dip the tip of the stiff bristle brush into the paint. Dab lightly at the paper. You should see bunches of dots. Drag the same brush across the paper for a fuzzy rough effect. Dip your soft brush into the paint. Dab it onto the paper making brush prints. Experiment with other techniques and develop your individual style.

6. Using tempera paint, mix your colors with white and black and with their complements to create different values and intensities.

7. Share your work with your classmates. Look for differences and similarities between your own landscape and those of other students.

EXAMINING YOUR WORK

- **Describe** Point to the three trees and identify the roots of the nearest tree. Identify the different layers of rock and soil and describe how you made them different.
- **Explain** Tell why you chose the colors you did. Show different lines, shapes, and textures in your work, and explain what media you used to create the differences. Explain how you created the illusion of space in your work.

▲ **Figure 4–28   Student work. An unusual landscape.**

OTHER STUDIO IDEAS

- Think about the characteristics and structures of trees you see during the winter season. Practice sketching a variety of trees using combinations of loosely drawn lines to build up the tree structures. Build up the trunk, limbs, branches, and twigs with straight, curved, and/or angular lines.

- Think about parks or forests and sketch an arrangement of trees with quick and spontaneous strokes of colored chalk or paint. Select three colors for the trees. Use a sheet of colored paper that works well as a background.

Lesson 8   *Painting a Landscape*   **75**

Developing Concepts

Exploring Aesthetics. Have pairs of students work together to discuss Figures 4–27 and 4–28. Ask: What color combinations are used? How are the paintings divided? What types of lines are used? What kinds of shapes—organic or geometric—are used? Are certain types of shapes and lines repeated in each section? How? Do the paintings contain mostly crowded space or empty space? How many different textures are shown? After discussing both works, have each partner write a short description of one of the paintings.

Appreciating Cultural Diversity. Guide students in comparing and discussing landscape paintings from several cultures. Ask volunteers to find and browse through books with reproductions of landscapes painted in Japan, China, North America, and Europe. Let the volunteers share selected reproductions with the rest of the class, and help students compare and discuss the paintings. Which artists have tried to create a mirror of the natural world? Which have tried to evoke a sense of the landscape without just copying it?

Following Up

Closure. Give each student an opportunity to share and discuss his or her landscape with the rest of the class. Ask students to identify the element—color, line, shape, space, or texture—they feel they used most successfully in their own works.

Evaluation. Review students' landscapes, and consider their own evaluations of their work.

Reteaching. Give students an opportunity to experiment further with different brush techniques and various kinds of paints.

Enrichment. Have students examine various biological specimens under a microscope and sketch what they see, or have them find photographs of microscopic details from plants and animals. Encourage students to share these sketches or photographs and to discuss the abstract designs they see.

BUILDING VOCABULARY

Number a sheet of paper from 1 to 15. After each number, write the term from the box that best matches each description below.

analogous colors	line variation
color wheel	monochromatic
complementary	colors
colors	motif
form	shape
hue	space
intensity	texture
line	value
line quality	

1. Colors opposite each other on the color wheel.
2. An area clearly set off by one or more of the other five visual elements of art.
3. Different values of a single hue.
4. The name of a color and its place on the color wheel.
5. An object with three dimensions.
6. The brightness or dullness of a hue.
7. The lightness or darkness of a hue.
8. Colors that share a hue and are side by side on the color wheel.
9. The distance or area around, between, above, below, and within things.
10. How things feel, or look as though they might feel, if touched.
11. The path of a dot through space.
12. A pattern that repeats.
13. Arrangement of hues in a circular format.
14. The unique character of any line.
15. The thickness or thinness of a line.

REVIEWING ART FACTS

Number a sheet of paper from 16 to 22. Answer each question in a complete sentence.

16. What is a risk of using monochromatic colors?

17. What effect can be achieved by using complementary color schemes?
18. How does a trained artist use line?
19. What are some adjectives that could be used to describe horizontal lines?
20. What is the difference between line quality and line variation?
21. What is the relationship between shape and form?
22. Describe one way you can create different textures, using paints.

THINKING ABOUT ART

On a sheet of paper, answer each question in a sentence or two.

1. **Analyze.** Imagine that you are helping paint a mural for the new school gymnasium. You have just finished painting a happy-looking section in red. You notice a student moving toward the section carrying a jar of green paint. What words of caution about the blending of colors might you pass along to this student?
2. **Compare and contrast.** In what ways are the elements of form and shape alike? In what ways are they different?

MAKING ART CONNECTIONS

1. **Science.** One way artists develop new images from subject matter is to change the distance from which they view it. As an object is viewed through the microscope, greater detail is observed and the image changes. Try drawing leaves and other objects while looking through the microscope.
2. **Language Arts.** Think about the color expressions used on page **56.** Explain what is meant by these expressions and why certain colors are used. List other color expressions that you can think of.

CHAPTER 4 REVIEW

LOOKING AT THE DETAILS

The picture shown below is a detail from
Paul Cézanne's *The Bay of Marseille, Seen from
L'Estaque.* Study the detail and answer the
following questions.

1. What techniques did Cézanne use to
   turn shapes into forms?
2. What are some things that this landscape
   communicates to you? Is it a quiet place?
   Is it a modern city or resort? Talk about
   color hues, intensity and value when explaining your answer.

3. Cézanne used both warm and cool color
   schemes. What effect does this have?
   How are the schemes brought together to
   create a unified whole?
4. How does Paul Cézanne's use of space
   differ from Elizabeth Murray's on page
   60? What effect does it have?
5. What do you think are some of the different ways color can affect a painting?

Paul Cézanne. *The Bay of
Marseille, Seen from L'Estaque.*
1886–90. Oil on canvas. (Detail.)
80.8 x 99.8 cm (31⅞ x 39¼"). The
Art Institute of Chicago. Mr. &
Mrs. Martin A. Ryerson
Collection.

77

The Principles of Art

Chapter Scan

Lesson 1 The Language of Design
Lesson 2 Formal Balance Cityscape
Lesson 3 Variety, Harmony, Emphasis, and Proportion
Lesson 4 Abstract Painting
Lesson 5 Movement and Rhythm
Lesson 6 Creating Visual Movement
Lesson 7 Unity in Art

TRB Resources

- 5-9 Chapter Test
- Color Transparency 9
- Color Transparency 10

TEACHING THE CHAPTER

Introducing the Art Work

Direct students' attention to Hale Woodruff's *Poor Man's Cotton.* Inform students that Hale Woodruff was an African-American artist of the twentieth century. Born in Illinois, Hale Woodruff studied at some of the finest art schools both in America and in Paris. He also studied fresco painting in Mexico with Diego Rivera in 1936.

In the 1930s and 1940s Woodruff painted traditional still lifes, such as flowers and fruits, as well as landscapes that reflected the inspiration he felt in the quiet streets of Southern towns. In the 1940s his images began to take on a more stylized and abstract quality. Then in the 1950s and throughout the rest of his career Woodruff experimented using magnified brush strokes and fragmenting anatomical forms to create abstract images. His drawings were free interpretations of figures.

▲ How do the colors and shapes in this work make you feel? What do they remind you of? What do you suppose the title of the work means?

Hale Woodruff. *Poor Man's Cotton.* 1944. Watercolor on paper. 77.5 x 57.2 cm (30½ x 22½"). The Newark Museum, Newark, New Jersey. Sophronia Anderson Fund.

The Principles of Art

Have you ever looked at a work of art and found yourself wondering what the point of it was? Look at the painting at the left. Can you find any "rhyme or reason" to it? Why do you suppose the artist chose the colors, the lines, or the shapes he did?

If art has at times seemed puzzling to you, that is because every work of art is a "puzzle." Its "pieces" have been carefully combined. In this chapter you will learn about the guidelines artists use to make works of art.

OBJECTIVES

After completing this chapter, you will be able to:
- Define the term *principle of art*.
- Explain the three kinds of balance.
- Tell how artists use the principles of variety, harmony, emphasis, proportion, movement, and rhythm.
- Explain what unity does for an art work.
- Practice organizing elements and principles in original art works.

WORDS YOU WILL LEARN

balance
emphasis
harmony
movement
principles of art

proportion
rhythm
unity
variety

ARTISTS YOU WILL MEET

Umberto Boccioni
Bernardo Daddi
William Glackens
Robert Gwathmey
Alexei von Jawlensky
Jasper Johns
Wassily Kandinsky
Jacob Lawrence

Henri Matisse
Georgia O'Keeffe
Jean-Baptiste-Joseph
   Pater
Michel Sittow
Vincent van Gogh
Hale Woodruff

Examining the Art Work

Tell students that in this painting Hale Woodruff portrayed the figures with an overall quality of proportion, only slightly distorting certain parts to emphasize body movement. Point out the way the hips of the figures jut out and how the bodies are bent. Also note the way the first two hoes face in, then the next two face out, and the last one faces in again. Tell students that this creates a pattern using the element of line to create a rhythm and beat. Explain to students that curved lines of the bodies, the fact that the bodies themselves are diagonally stacked, and the hats work with this beat to further emphasize it.

Explain to students that although the viewer can identify the figures as human and can identify the action being portrayed, the work begins to enter the realm of abstraction. Point out how the figures' garments and faces lack detail and how Woodruff created an unrealistic sense of depth. Tell students that this helps focus the viewer's attention on the movement in the work.

Discussing the Art Work

Ask students to think about how Woodruff used color. Explain that he used different tonal qualities of the same hue to create unity. Ask students to look at the contrast between the dark, straight lines of the hoes and the curved lines and colors of the garments. Point out that this contrast emphasizes the gestures.

Discuss Woodruff's use of balance: how the figures occupy two vertical lines in the center of the canvas and the way color is used so that no one figure stands out more than the others.

Tell students that in this chapter they will learn about the various principles of art and will practice organizing those principles along with the elements of art in original art works.

Building Self-Esteem

In this chapter students will see the work of many people who have chosen art as a profession. Ask them to think about the future and imagine a profession *they* might enter. Ask what personal qualities an individual in that profession might need in order to be successful. Do they possess those qualities already? If not, what can they do to develop those qualities. Let them think about what kind of a building they would work in, what they would do, what tools they would use. Ask them to make a design showing the tools, type of uniform or dress, place of work, and types of people found in their desired profession. Tell them to use the principle of emphasis, making the most important symbol of their chosen profession the largest. Let students share their drawings. See if the rest of the class can determine what professions are being depicted. Ask what attribute is the most necessary in order to be a good doctor, librarian, or any other profession illustrated. Have them explain how these attributes would help them in their daily activities.

The Language of Design

LESSON PLAN
(pages 80–81)

Objectives

After completing this lesson, students will be able to:
• Define the term *principle of art*.
• Tell how artists use the principle of balance.
• Explain the three kinds of balance.
• Work with partners to paint designs that use informal balance.

Supplies

• Long, narrow piece of plywood or cardboard; 1-quart (1L) plastic bottle.
• Paints, brushes, white paper.
• Photographs of Polish cut paper designs (*wycinanki*), colored construction paper, scissors.
• Collection of found objects, such as buttons, stray game or puzzle pieces, dry pasta (brought in by students, if possible).

TEACHING THE LESSON

Getting Started

Motivator. Set up a simple balance scale, using a long piece of cardboard or plywood balanced across the corner of a desk or on a quart-sized plastic bottle. Ask volunteers to select various objects to place on the two sides of the scale. Encourage students to explore ways in which they can balance different objects—as well as pairs of identical objects—on the scale. Then explain that students will learn more about balance and its application in works of art.

Vocabulary. Ask volunteers to check the definitions of *symmetrical*, *asymmetrical*, and *radial* in a dictionary and to give familiar examples of the uses of each word. Then explain the meanings of these words in art, when used to modify *balance*.

LESSON 1

The Language of Design

You know that speakers of any language follow rules of grammar. These rules govern the way words can go together to form sentences. The language of art also has rules. They are called **principles of art**, *guidelines that govern the way elements go together*.

The principles of art are: balance, variety, harmony, emphasis, proportion, movement, and rhythm. Like the elements, the principles in a work of art are hard to single out.

In this lesson you will meet the first of the principles of art, balance.

▲ **Figure 5–1 What kind of feelings might the formal balance of this church suggest? In what direction does the building seem to point? Why is this important?**

Monastery of Oliva. Late 12th century. Oliva, Spain.

THE PRINCIPLE OF BALANCE

When you ride a bicycle and lean too far to one side or the other, what happens? You fall over. In riding a bike, balance is important.

Balance is important in art, too. In art, **balance** is *arranging elements so that no one part of a work overpowers, or seems heavier than, any other part*. In the real world, balance can be measured on a scale. If two objects weigh the same, the two sides of the scale will balance. If they do not, one side of the scale will tip. In art, balance is seen or felt by the viewer. A big, bold splotch of color off to one side of a painting pulls the viewer's eye there. It can

▲ **Figure 5–2 How different would this work have been if the artist had spread the figures around the picture?**

Michel Sittow. *The Assumption of the Virgin*. c. 1500. Wood; painted surface. 21.3 x 16.5 cm (8⅜ x 6½"). National Gallery of Art, Washington, D.C. Ailsa Mellon Bruce Fund.

Cooperative Learning
Divide class into groups of six. Assign each group one kind of balance—formal, informal, or radial. Each student will take a piece of paper measuring 6 x 6 inches (15 x 15 cm) and, using marking pens, create a design illustrating the type of balance their group has been assigned. When the pieces have been completed, the group will mount the six examples on a 12 x 18 (30 x 46 cm) sheet of paper. Display the works and ask students to help identify the type of balance illustrated.

Background Information
The way we use the elements and principles of art comes largely from the ideas developed in a German school of design known as the Bauhaus. By 1926 it had secured a worldwide reputation for design research and education. Master craftspeople were hired to teach there and students participated in an introductory program of creative experiments that stressed free manipulation, originality, and sensitivity to the individual qualities of different materials.

make the work seem lopsided. It can make the viewer feel uncomfortable.

Artists speak of three kinds of balance. These are formal balance, informal balance, and radial balance.

Formal Balance

Formal balance happens when one half of a work is a mirror image of the other half (Figure 5–1). Also called symmetrical balance (suh-**meh**-trih-kuhl), formal balance is the easiest type to notice. Because it is so predictable, using formal balance sometimes makes a work seem less interesting. This is not always the case. Look at the painting in Figure 5–2. Notice how the formal balance adds a feeling of quiet dignity to the work.

Informal Balance

In informal balance, two unlike objects are made to seem to have equal weight. The weight is suggested by the hues, values, intensities, and shapes of those objects. Also called asymmetrical balance (**ay**-suh-**meh**-trih-kuhl), informal balance often shows up in the way the artist has used color and shape. A small shape painted bright red will balance several larger shapes painted in duller hues. (See Figure 5–3.)

▲ **Figure 5–3** Where does your eye move first when you look at this picture? Why do you think this is so?

William Glackens. *Family Group.* 1910–1911. Canvas. 182.9 x 213.4 cm (72 x 84"). National Gallery of Art, Washington, D.C. Gift of Mr. & Mrs. Ira Glackens.

Informal balance is often used to create more interesting compositions. Arranging objects or elements informally can be very complicated, but can create visual interest when used skillfully.

Radial Balance

Radial balance happens when elements or objects in an art work are positioned around a central point. A flower with its petals spreading outward from the center is an example of radial balance in nature. The stained-glass rose window in Figure 5–4 is an example of radial balance in art.

▲ **Figure 5–4** An identical pattern is repeated several times in this cathedral window, nevertheless it holds our eye. Why?

Rose Window, Burgos Cathedral. 14th century. Burgos, Spain.

✔ CHECK YOUR UNDERSTANDING

1. Define principles of art.
2. List the principles of art.
3. What is balance?
4. Describe the three kinds of balance.

Lesson 1   *The Language of Design*   📖   **81**

Formal Balance Cityscape

Objectives

After completing this lesson, students will be able to:
- Draw a night cityscape, using formal balance.
- Describe and analyze their own work.

Supplies
- Old magazines that include photographs of cities, scissors, glue, sheets of colored construction paper.
- Pencils; sketch paper; white chalk; gum erasers; sheets of black construction paper, 12 x 18 inches (30 x 46 cm); oil pastels.
- Scrap blocks of wood in various shapes and sizes, sandpaper, glue.
- Sheets of colored construction paper, scissors.

> **TRB Resource**
> - 5-1 *Georgia O'Keeffe,* (artist profile)

TEACHING THE LESSON

Getting Started

Motivator. To help students consider and discuss city scenes, distribute old magazines that include photographs of cities. Have students work in groups to select and cut out several city photos. Then let the members of each group arrange their photographs and glue them onto a sheet of construction paper. Have each group present its arrangement of photos to the rest of the class, and encourage all students to discuss and compare the city scenes featured in each work.

Vocabulary. Review with students the meanings of the terms *formal balance* and *informal balance.* Then ask students to define the word *approximate.* Let volunteers look the word up in a dictionary and explain the meaning of the Latin word from which *approximate* is derived.

Formal Balance Cityscape

Look at the painting in Figure 5–5. This cityscape of New York City was painted by Georgia O'Keeffe. In many of her works she uses formal balance to give them a sense of dignity. To avoid boring the viewer, she uses approximate symmetry. That means that both sides of the work are not a perfect mirror image of each other.

The center of this painting is the Radiator Building. Notice that the top of the skyscraper is symmetrical. However, the symmetry at the middle of the painting is not quite perfect. Do you see how the bright red rectangle catches your attention? It is balanced by the white and blue-green smoke on the opposite side.

▶ **Figure 5–5   How is color used to achieve balance in this cityscape? How is shape and line configuration used?**

Georgia O'Keeffe. *Radiator Building — Night — New York.* 1927. Oil on canvas. 121.9 x 76.2 cm (48 x 30″). Carl Van Stieglitz Gallery of Fine Arts at Fisk University. Alfred Stieglitz Collection.

82 Lesson 2   *Formal Balance Cityscape*

Note

Tell students that sometimes artists become well-known once their works are recognized. In the case of Georgia O'Keeffe, the artist who painted Figure 5–5, it was the other way around. Her husband, Alfred Stieglitz, a well-known photographer, photographed her 500 times. Americans knew O'Keeffe's face long before they knew her paintings. Can students find Stieglitz's name in the painting above?

WHAT YOU WILL LEARN

You will create a night cityscape or a city scene, using formal balance. To make your work more interesting, you will use approximate symmetry. To create the nighttime effect that O'Keeffe captured, you will work with oil pastels on black paper.

WHAT YOU WILL NEED

- Pencil and sketch paper
- White chalk, gum eraser
- A sheet of black construction paper, 12 x 18 inch (30 x 46 cm)
- Oil pastels

WHAT YOU WILL DO

1. Do visual research. Study photographs of interesting city buildings, including skyscrapers. Make sketches of the buildings with the most interesting shapes. As you sketch the buildings, make changes that you think will make them more interesting. See how another student achieved formal balance in Figure 5–6.
2. Plan your composition. On your sketch paper make several plans for arranging your own city buildings using symmetry. Vary the sizes and shapes of your buildings. You may use one large building in the center, or you may have two almost equal shapes on either side of the center.
3. Choose your best plan and change it so that it becomes a design using approximate symmetry. Remember, to achieve approximate symmetry, your work must be almost symmetrical. Study O'Keeffe's painting in Figure 5–5 for ideas. Notice how she uses the dark blue rays of light to balance the large gray arched window. What effect is created by the yellow in some windows?

EXAMINING YOUR WORK

- **Describe** Identify the sources you used for your inspiration. Describe how you changed the original shapes to make your own building shapes. Tell what colors you used to achieve a nighttime effect.
- **Analyze** Tell how you created symmetry in your work. Identify the changes you made to achieve approximate symmetry.

4. Using the white chalk, draw your composition on the black paper. Press very lightly so that you can erase, if necessary, with the gum eraser without tearing the surface of the paper. If you press hard, the chalk may make a dent in the paper.
5. Add color with oil pastels. To keep the night effect, let the brightest colors come from the window shapes. (See Technique Tip **3**, *Handbook* page **271**, for oil pastel techniques.)
6. Display your finished cityscape.

▲ **Figure 5–6   Student work. A formal balance cityscape.**

OTHER STUDIO IDEAS

- Use the same instructions to create a daytime effect on white or yellow paper.
- ●● Do a nighttime landscape using informal balance and the same materials.

Developing Concepts

Exploring Aesthetics. Guide students in discussing the balance in Figures 5-5 and 5-6: How has approximate symmetry been achieved? What changes would be needed to create true formal balance? If those changes were made, how would they affect the impact the work has on the viewer?

Developing Studio Skills. Let students form small groups in which to assemble non-objective sculptures. Give each group a supply of scrap wood blocks in a variety of shapes and sizes. Have group members select and sand the blocks to be used in their sculpture. Then ask them to assemble their blocks (using glue) into a work that demonstrates approximate symmetry.

Following Up

Closure. Have students work in small groups to discuss their cityscapes, following the steps in "Examining Your Work." Then have each student write a short response to the "Analyze" instructions.

Evaluation. Review students' cityscapes and read their analyses of their own work.

Reteaching. Let pairs of students work together to cut out ten squares of construction paper in various sizes and colors. Then have them arrange their rectangles in various designs to show true formal balance and formal balance with approximate symmetry.

Enrichment. Have pairs of students look for and study reproductions of other works by Georgia O'Keeffe. Then help students work together to discuss what they have learned about O'Keeffe from studying her art works. Present this quotation from O'Keeffe: "Painting is my language. It is the way I speak." Then ask: What do you think Georgia O'Keeffe says in her language, painting? Encourage students to present and support various responses.

Classroom Management Tip

An overhead projector is a valuable teaching aid for any art teacher and, if at all possible, should be a permanent part of the art room equipment. Information can be presented on transparencies and kept on file for future review. Printed illustrations can be lifted from clay coated magazine pages by adhering the printed side to a sheet of clear, adhesive-backed acetate and soaking off the paper from the back. In addition to projecting all kinds of prepared materials, the overhead pro-

vides a good way to illustrate the visual elements and to experiment with composition. Cut shapes and found objects can be projected onto a screen and moved around to create various types of balance. Yarn, string, and rods become lines, and color experiments can be added by the use of gels and colored acetate. Line and texture drawing may be demonstrated with markers on a sheet of plexiglass or acetate placed on the projector.

LESSON 3

Variety, Harmony, Emphasis, and Proportion

LESSON PLAN
(pages 84–87)

Objectives
After completing this lesson, students will be able to:
- Define the principle of variety and explain how artists use it.
- Define the principles of harmony, emphasis, and proportion and explain how artists use them.

Supplies
- Colored pencils or markers, drawing paper.
- Drawing paper, markers, colored construction paper.
- Collection of reproductions of paintings from various periods (or several art books with color reproductions).
- Reproductions of paintings by Henri Matisse.

> **TRB Resource**
> - 5-2 *Pictoral Time Line*, (cooperative learning)

TEACHING THE LESSON

Getting Started

Motivator. Have students draw pictures of themselves sitting in their favorite places, wearing their favorite outfits, reading their favorite magazines, and eating their favorite foods. Then let the students share and discuss their pictures. Ask: How would you feel if you could spend the next hour doing what you are doing in your picture? How would you feel if that's all you could do for the next week? How would you feel if you had to do that every day for a month? Encourage all the students to contribute to this discussion; then help them recognize and discuss the importance of variety.

Variety, Harmony, Emphasis, and Proportion

You may have heard it said that "variety is the spice of life." Variety is also the spice of art. The principle of variety and three others, harmony, emphasis, and proportion, make works of art interesting and pleasing to view. In this lesson you will learn how these principles are used by the artist to create art.

THE PRINCIPLE OF VARIETY

Imagine that you had to eat the same food every day for a whole year. Even if the food were your absolute favorite, after a while you would grow tired of it. You would long for other things to eat—even things you disliked—just for the change of pace.

▶ **Figure 5–7** Point to the different colors in this painting. How many kinds of lines can you count? How many shapes? How many textures?

Henri Matisse. *Woman in a Purple Coat.* 1937. Oil on canvas. 81.3 x 64.1 cm (32 x 25¼"). The Museum of Fine Arts, Houston, Texas. John A. and Audrey Jones Beck Collection

Background Information
Henri Matisse (France, 1869–1954) first gained recognition around 1905 as a member of the Fauves. These painters earned their name, which means "wild beasts," because their use of brilliant colors and their bold handling of the media were considered wild.

Matisse moved beyond Fauvism, searching for his own personal style. He felt that art should express a nearly religious feeling toward life. Art—like life—should be active, not static.

Matisse experimented with different styles, but his aim was always harmony. He felt that art should avoid being distressing; instead, it should be "like a good armchair." His colors were bold and strong, his lines unexpected. Matisse never attempted to copy nature, only to interpret it. He believed that order and unity would be brought about without rules, and he used his art work to demonstrate the validity of his belief.

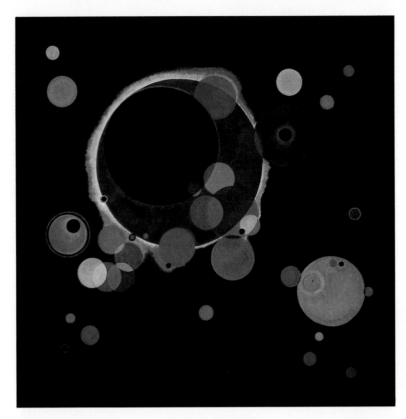

◀ **Figure 5–8   Which shape brings harmony to this work?**

Wassily Kandinsky. *Several Circles*. 1926. Oil on canvas. 140.3 x 141 cm (55¼ x 55⅜"). Solomon R. Guggenheim Museum, New York, New York. Gift of Solomon R. Guggenheim.

Vocabulary. Help students consider the meaning of *harmony* by asking: What is musical harmony? What do we mean when we speak of people living or working in harmony? Based on these meanings of the word, what do you think harmony in a work of art might be? Then ask students to define familiar uses of the words *emphasis* and *proportion* before checking the art-related meanings in the Glossary.

Developing Concepts

Exploring Aesthetics. Let students spend some time reacting to the art works reproduced in this lesson: What do you see in each painting? How does it make you feel? Why? Encourage students to discuss which of the paintings they consider to be successful works of art and the reasons for their choices. Then present this quotation from American philosopher and educator John Dewey: "As long as art is the beauty parlor of civilization, neither art nor civilization is secure." Ask students what they think Dewey meant; then ask whether they agree with his idea. Encourage a lively exchange of opinions.

To extend this discussion, present the following statements, one at a time:

If it is not beautiful, it is not art.

Art can be ugly.

If it is too ugly to hang in my living room, it is not good art.

Beauty is in the eye of the beholder.

Art is made to decorate our world with beauty.

Let students show by voting whether they agree or disagree with each statement. Then encourage them to express their opinions in response to each statement, presenting as many persuasive supporting details as they can.

People need change to keep their lives interesting. The same goes for art. In art, **variety** is *combining one or more elements to create interest*. By giving a work variety, the artist heightens the visual appeal of the work.

Variety may be brought into play in many different ways. Light values of a color may be used to break the sameness of mostly dark values of that color. Straight lines can be a welcome change in a work made up mainly of curved lines. Which elements show variety in the work in Figure 5–7?

THE PRINCIPLE OF HARMONY

On the opposite side of the coin from variety is harmony. **Harmony** in art, as in music, is *blending elements in a pleasing way*. Harmony is uncomplicated and soothing. Often artists use a small number of the same elements again and again, or in repetition, to bring harmony to a work of art. (See Figure 5–8.)

Skilled artists use the principles of harmony and variety together in different amounts to bind the parts of a work to the whole. Too much variety and too little harmony in a work can make it complicated and confusing. Focusing only on harmony, on the other hand, can make a work humdrum and uninteresting. Notice how the artist of the work in Figure 5–8 combines harmony and variety.

Developing Perceptual Skills

In order to help students understand the concept of harmony, let them play the Harmony Game. Divide the class in half by rows or tables. As you call out a category, a student from group 1 volunteers an example showing harmony. Student from group 2 has to give an answer from the same category that is an example of disharmony. For instance, if the category is "people talking," the harmony example could be "agree-ment."—the opposite would be "disagreement, or arguing." Categories suggested could include clothing (suit and tie/suit jacket and running shorts), garden (flowers and shrubs/weeds and trash), interior decor (beige walls, brown carpet/beige walls, purple carpet). The Variety Game could be substituted using examples of variety and monotony. Close the exercise by stressing the definition of harmony: blending elements in a pleasing way.

THE PRINCIPLE OF EMPHASIS

When people want to call attention to an important word in a sentence, they will underline it. Underlining a word makes that word stand out from the rest of the words in the message. It gives it emphasis.

Artists also use emphasis in their messages to viewers. In art, **emphasis** is *making an element or object in a work stand out*. The use of this principle helps the artist control what part of a work the viewer looks at first. It also helps the artist control how long the viewer will spend looking at each of the different parts. Emphasis can be created by contrast, or extreme changes in an element.

In the painting in Figure 5–9 several groups of figures are shown. One of these groups seems more important than the others. Can you identify that group? Can you tell why it caught your attention?

THE PRINCIPLE OF PROPORTION

Have you ever tried on a piece of clothing and found that it made you look shorter or taller than you actually are? Perhaps the problem was one of proportion. In art, **proportion** is *how parts of a work relate to each other and to the whole*.

▲ Figure 5–9 Besides value contrast, what techniques call attention to the group of people that includes the girl in white?

Jean-Baptiste-Joseph Pater. *Fête Champêtre*. 1730. Canvas. 74.6 x 92.7 cm (29⅜ x 36½"). National Gallery of Art, Washington, D.C. Samuel H. Kress Collection.

Look at the painting in Figure 5–10. Notice how the artist points out the main figures in the work by making them larger than the rest.

Proportion as an art principle is not limited to size. Elements such as color can be used in differing proportions. What is the key color in the work in Figure 5–11? What do you think was the artist's reason for using this color as he did?

▲ **Figure 5–11** What has the artist done to make the element of color stand out? What one color is used most?

Alexei von Jawlensky. *Portrait of a Woman*. 1910. Oil on panel. 53 x 49.5 cm (20⅞ x 19½"). The Museum of Fine Arts, Houston, Texas. John A. and Audrey Jones Beck Collection.

▲ **Figure 5–10** Which figures are the largest? Why are they larger than the other figures? Who are they? Who are the figures in the "supporting roles"?

Bernardo Daddi. *Madonna and Child with Saints and Angels*. 1330. Wood. 50.2 x 24.1 cm (19¾ x 9½"). National Gallery of Art, Washington, D.C. Samuel H. Kress Collection.

✔CHECK YOUR UNDERSTANDING

1. Name two ways artists can achieve variety in works of art.
2. How do artists achieve harmony in works of art?
3. What is emphasis? What two things does using this principle enable an artist to do?
4. What is proportion? How do artists use proportion?

Lesson 3 *Variety, Harmony, Emphasis, and Proportion* 📖 **87**

Abstract Painting

Look at the painting in Figure 5–12. Notice how Robert Gwathmey has used the principles of variety, harmony, emphasis, and proportion. He has used a red color scheme to create harmony. Variety is introduced through different sizes and different shapes. Notice that the land, sky, and church are simple rectangles. The people are composed of geometric and free form shapes. Hands and feet are very small, arms are thin, and the shapes of the bodies vary.

As you study the painting you will notice that all the busy shapes in the foreground lead your eyes to the dark simple church on the horizon. Gwathmey emphasizes the church by isolating it and making it a different shape and a different value.

▲ **Figure 5–12   How does the use of proportion give depth and variety to the painting?**

Robert Gwathmey. *Country Gospel Music.* 1971. Oil on canvas. 101.6 x 127 cm (40 x 50"). Terry Dintenfass Gallery.

88   Lesson 4   *Abstract Painting*

LESSON PLAN
(pages 88–89)

Objectives

After studying this lesson, students will be able to:
• Describe abstract painting.
• Explain how color can be used to create harmony.
• Create an abstract painting.

Supplies

• Pencil and sketch paper.
• Sheet of white paper, 12 x 18 inches (30 x 46 cm).
• Colored construction paper and scissors.

TEACHING THE LESSON

Getting Started

Motivator. To help students think about how to create an abstract work of art, show them a large sheet of white paper and explain that it represents a space to be used in organizing a picture or design. Ask them to write short descriptions of pictures they might make on the paper. Discuss the descriptions and add as many details as possible. List on the chalkboard all examples of visual elements that are mentioned in the description. Have students suggest ways that they could alter the visual elements to create an abstract work of art.

Building Vocabulary. Discuss the term *abstract art* and help students understand the differences between non-objective and abstract art. Tell them that non-objective art occurs when there is no recognizable subject. Abstract art occurs when the subject is non-realistic. Discuss techniques that the artist could employ to create abstract works, such as distortion or exaggeration.

Developing Concepts

Exploring Aesthetics. Have students compare Figure 5-12 to the chapter opening reproduction on page **14.** Ask students to describe how the two works are similar. *(Both are abstract pieces and both use color to create harmony in the work).* Have students review the aesthetic viewpoints as presented in Chapter 2 and ask: What aesthetic viewpoint would be most appropriate when judging abstract works of art?

Note

Before students proceed with the abstract studio lesson, you may wish to list the following on the chalkboard: (1) You are alone in a dark cave with no idea how to get out. (2) After walking a long distance on a cold winter evening you finally see the lights of your warm home. (3) You are falling through space and your parachute will not open. Have students use one of these ideas for the subject of the abstract work.

Background Information

"Reduce, reduce, reduce" was the admonition of Marcel Duchamp (France, 1887–1968). His words were taken to heart by a number of post-Modern artists who reduced their art works to monochromatic paintings. This reductionist tendency is central to Minimalism. Minimalists were concerned with the surface of the canvas and the material applied to it, not with the meaning or message, which is left up to the viewer.

WHAT YOU WILL LEARN

You will create an abstract painting using the principles of harmony, variety, and emphasis. You will use a variety of lines to draw shapes that vary in size from very large to very small. You will add harmony to your work by using different light and dark values of a single hue to paint the shapes and the negative spaces. You will emphasize a center of interest by painting one small shape the complement of the hue used.

WHAT YOU WILL NEED

- Pencil and sketch paper
- Sheet of white paper, 12 x 18 inch (30 x 46 cm)
- Colored chalk, gum eraser
- Tempera paints and thick and thin brushes
- Newspaper

WHAT YOU WILL DO

1. Make several sketches on your sketch paper to plan your composition. Decide how you will use a variety of lines to divide your paper into shapes. Using vertical, horizontal, diagonal, curved, and zigzag lines, vary the shape from large to small.

EXAMINING YOUR WORK

- **Describe** What hue did you choose for your monochromatic color scheme? What hue was the complement of that hue? Identify the lines you used to create shapes.
- **Analyze** How did you create a variety in your painting? Tell how color was used to create harmony. Identify the object of emphasis.

---

2. Select your best plan. Draw it, freehand, on the large white paper with a piece of colored chalk. If you need to make corrections, use the soft gum eraser so that you don't tear the paper.
3. Select one hue. Use black and white paint to create a variety of tints and shades of that hue. Select one shape to be the center of interest. Leave it white for now. Paint the rest of the shapes with your hue and tints and shades of that hue. See Technique Tip **12**, *Handbook* page **274** on mixing colors.
4. Paint the center of interest with the complement of the hue you used in your painting.
5. Place your work on display with your classmates. Can you find similarities and differences in the works?

OTHER STUDIO IDEAS

- Create a design for your painting using objects you like instead of abstract shapes. Harmonize the colors and introduce variety through size. Use a complementary color to create emphasis.
- ●● Create an abstract composition in construction paper using warm colors for your shapes. Select a sheet of colored construction paper that works well with the other colors. Cut as many shapes as you think you will need, varying the size of the shapes. Repeat some of the sizes for both shapes to create harmony. Arrange your shapes in several different positions until they balance and then glue them to the background sheet.

Developing Studio Skills. Have students select a site that they will observe at different times of the day and night in order to gain a vivid sense of how changing light affects the quality of the scene. They may choose either an indoor or an outdoor scene, as long as the illumination (artificial or natural) changes during a 24-hour period. Allow a few days for them to complete the assignment so that they will be able to schedule observations at various odd hours. Have them record in their sketchbooks the times that they made their observations, the quality of light present at each time, and how it altered the mood or character of the scene. Encourage them also to sketch the differently lit scenes, using color to create harmony with the work. Have them present their art work to the class.

Appreciating Cultural Diversity. Explain to students that the use of visual elements is universal but they are used in various ways and with different emphases in particular cultures. These are the differences that help establish the distinctive character of a culture's art. Have students research art works from another culture and report on the use of elements. Guide them with questions including: What color schemes are typical of the culture? What kinds of line are used? How are textures developed?

Following Up

Closure. Have students work in small groups to discuss their abstract painting, following the steps in "Examining Your Work." Have students write a short response to the "Analyze" section.

Evaluation. Review the definition of abstract art and have students read their analysis of their own work.

Reteaching. Let pairs of students work together to cut out shapes of construction paper in various sizes and colors. Have them arrange their shapes in various designs to create an abstract work that uses proportion and creates harmony with the use of color.

Enrichment. Have groups of students research one of the artists in this text who produced abstract works of art. Ask them to report back to the class and explain what visual elements were favored in these works.

Classroom Management Tip

Remind students that, when mixing tempera colors and white to create a variety of tints, they can conserve paint by starting with several blobs of white. Clean brush, wipe on edge of water container, and blot brush on paper towel. Then take a brushful of the hue they have chosen and drop one dot of color on the first, two dots of color on the second, and three on the third. Wash, wipe and blot brush. Mix color in first dot, move to second and mix, then on to the third. Brush can be scraped against edge of pan to remove excess paint, but doesn't have to be *cleaned* between mixing. In making a darker shade of the hue, start with two or three blobs of the *hue*. Clean brush and add black, one dot to first blob, two to the second, three to the third. Mix. Remind students to clean brush after applying different tints and shades to keep mixed paints clean and clear.

Movement and Rhythm

LESSON PLAN
(pages 90–91)

Objectives

After completing this lesson, students will be able to:

- Explain how artists use the principles of movement and rhythm.
- Draw their own patterns of movement and rhythm.

Supplies

- Colored markers or pencils, newsprint, drawing paper.
- Reproduction of *Starry Night* by Vincent van Gogh.
- Collection of buttons or other small objects.
- Copy of the poem *The Raven* by Edgar Allen Poe.

TRB Resources

- 5-3 *Comparing the Principles,* (art history)
- 5-4 *The Principles in Your Life,* (aesthetics/art criticism)

TEACHING THE LESSON

Getting Started

Motivator. Begin by having students close their eyes; ask them to see in their minds a perfectly calm, still lake—nothing is moving. Give them a moment of quiet to visualize the lake. Then tell them that a sudden storm has come to the lake; choppy, irregular waves move across the surface, and the water seems to twist and turn around branches and rocks. After a moment or two, suggest another change: The storm is over, but now small, regular waves lap against the sandy beach in a quiet, steady rhythm. Again, allow a moment or two for students to visualize this. Then explain to students that they have been seeing movement and rhythm.

Vocabulary. Ask volunteers to give familiar definitions of the nouns *movement* and *rhythm*. Then let students discuss what they think these terms might mean as principles of art. Finally, have volunteers read aloud the definitions from the Glossary.

Have you ever thrown a rock in a pond and watched the concentric circles that followed? Have you traveled down the highway and watched the telephone lines passing by? These are two examples of movement and rhythm.

In this lesson you will learn about the principles of movement and rhythm.

THE PRINCIPLE OF MOVEMENT

You live in an age of special effects. When you go to the movies nowadays, you see strange life forms arriving from different galaxies. You see humans traveling backward in time or dancing with cartoon figures. These amazing sights and others like them are possible only through creative imaginations and special effects.

In art, special effects are nothing new. Artists have been using them for a long time. One of these effects is movement. **Movement** is *the principle of art that leads the viewer to sense action in a work or it can be the path the viewer's eye follows throughout a work.* Artists create movement through a careful blending of elements like line and shape. (See Figure 5–13.)

Through the principle of movement, the artist is able to guide the viewer's eye from one part of a painting to the next. Notice how the lines in Jean-Baptiste-Joseph Pater's painting in Figure 5–9 on page **86** carry your eye toward the girl in white. The trees and the people seem to be leaning toward her.

THE PRINCIPLE OF RHYTHM

Have you ever found yourself tapping your fingers or feet to the beat of a song? Songs can have catchy rhythms. Sometimes it seems as though we can feel these rhythms as well as hear them.

► **Figure 5–13 By repeating lines and shapes, the artist helps us see the movement of a speeding cyclist.**

Umberto Boccioni. *Study for Dynamic Force of a Cyclist I.* 1913. Ink wash and pencil on paper. 20.5 x 30.5 cm (8¹⁄₁₆ x 12″). Yale University Art Gallery, Connecticut. Gift of Societe Anonyme.

Background Information
Umberto Boccioni (Italy, 1882–1916) was one of the leading artists of the Futurist movement, which began as an extension of Cubism. The emphasis of Futurism was on the dynamic quality of life. As one Futurist wrote, "The splendor of the world has been enriched by a new form of beauty, the beauty of speed."

The Futurists announced the end of the art of the past and the beginning of the art of the future. In 1910, Boccioni and other Futurists published a manifesto that included this statement: "All things move and run, change rapidly, and this universal dynamism is what the artist should strive to represent."

A sculptor as well as a painter, Boccioni discussed the possibilities of including ready-made objects in sculptures and even of using motors to set sculptures in motion. The artist did not live to try these new approaches to art; he was killed during World War I.

In art, we feel rhythms as well as see them. To the artist, **rhythm** is *the repeating of an element to make a work seem active*. Look at Figure 5–14. The artist uses rhythm to make his painting come alive. By carefully mixing shapes and colors, he gets your eye to move to the painting's "beat."

Sometimes, to create rhythm, artists will repeat not just elements but the same exact objects over and over. When they do this, a pattern is formed.

✔CHECK YOUR UNDERSTANDING

1. What is movement?
2. What is rhythm?
3. What does an artist create by repeating an object again and again?

▼ **Figure 5–14** **Which element creates rhythm? Which element does the artist incorporate with the rhythm to give the painting a "beat"? How?**

Jasper Johns. *Between the Clock and the Bed*. 1981. Encaustic on canvas. 183.2 x 321 cm (72⅛ x 126⅜"). Museum of Modern Art, New York, New York. Given anonymously.

Developing Concepts

Exploring Aesthetics. Have students work in small groups to compare and discuss the paintings shown in Figures 5–13 and 5–14. How are color, line, and shape used in each painting? What principles of art emphasize those elements in each work? What is the subject of each work? What response to that subject does the artist want to create in the viewer?

Using Art Criticism. Display a reproduction of *Starry Night* and ask: What rhythm is created by this painting? How is it created? What feeling does the rhythm give you? What message or idea do you think van Gogh wanted to communicate with this painting? Do you think he succeeded? Why, or why not? After a class discussion, ask students to write brief descriptions of the work.

Following Up

Closure. Let the students work in small groups to discuss and evaluate their own "Studio Experience" patterns of movement and rhythm.

Evaluation. 1. Review students' written responses to the "Check Your Understanding" questions. 2. Check students' patterns of movement and rhythm, and consider their own evaluations of their work.

Reteaching. Let students work in pairs to arrange buttons or other small objects into various patterns. Let the partners share each of their patterns with another pair of students. Ask the students who are viewing: What rhythm does each pattern create? How does it create that rhythm?

Enrichment. Read *The Raven* aloud to the class, or ask a volunteer to prepare and then read the poem. Help students discuss the work: What patterns of movement and rhythm do you hear in the poem? How do those patterns relate to visual art? Then have students draw or paint pictures to evoke the feeling of the poem.

Answers to "Check Your Understanding"
1. Movement is the principle of art that leads the viewer to sense action in a work.
2. Rhythm is the repeating of an element to make a work seem active.
3. By repeating an object again and again, an artist creates a pattern.

Creating Visual Movement

STUDIO   LESSON 6   STUDIO

Creating Visual Movement

This painting by Jacob Lawrence has a strong sense of visual movement. The artist has used several special effects to create the feeling that the soldiers are surging forward. (See Figure 5–15.) First he used diagonal lines to form arrow-like movement to the right. Notice how the guns and hats slant down to the right, while the bodies of the soldiers slant up to the right. Second, he has repeated lines and shapes to create a visual rhythm that makes your eye move through the painting from left to right. The repetition of the waving vertical grasses balances the strong movement. This helps to rest the viewers' eyes.

WHAT YOU WILL LEARN

You will create a construction paper design using repeated silhouettes of one action figure. You will use visual rhythm to create a sense of visual movement. Use a cool color for the background and warm colors for the figures.

WHAT YOU WILL NEED

- One whole action figure cut from a magazine (sports magazines are good sources)
- Scissors and fine-tip marker
- One sheet of cool-colored construction paper, 12 x 18 inch (30 x 46 cm)
- Several pieces of warm-colored construction paper, 9 x 12 inch (23 x 30 cm)
- Pencil, eraser, and glue
- Envelope to hold cutouts, 9 1/2 x 4 inch (24 x 10 cm)

▶ **Figure 5–15   What are the elements used in repetition? How do they also provide harmony?**

Jacob Lawrence. *Toussaint L'Overture Series*. 1938. Tempera on paper. 46.4 x 61.6 cm (18¼ x 24¼"). Fisk University.

LESSON PLAN
(pages 92–93)

Objectives
After completing this lesson, students will be able to:
- Create construction paper designs that express visual movement.
- Describe their own designs.

Supplies
- Small pieces of construction paper: red, yellow, orange, blue, green, and violet.
- Sports magazines or other magazines from which students can cut action figures; scissors; fine-tip markers; sheets of cool-colored construction paper, 12 x 18 inches (30 x 46 cm); sheets of warm-colored construction paper, 9 x 12 inches (23 x 30 cm); pencils; erasers; glue; envelopes, 9 1/2 x 4 inches (24 x 10 cm).
- Reproductions of Marcel Duchamp's *Nude Descending a Staircase*, Umberto Boccioni's *Dynamism of a Cyclist*, and/or Giacomo Balla's *Dynamism of a Dog on a Leash;* sheets of drawing paper; colored pencils.

> **TRB Resource**
> - 5-5 *Expressing Movement*, (studio)

TEACHING THE LESSON

Getting Started

Motivator. Begin by having students form small groups, and give each group six small pieces or scraps of construction paper in these colors: red, yellow, orange, blue, green, violet. Ask students in each group to categorize the colors: warm and cool. Then let them experiment with different combinations of warm and cool colors.

Vocabulary. Help students review the definitions of *movement* and *rhythm*. (Refer them to pages **90** and **91** if necessary.) Then let volunteers suggest several specific techniques for creating movement and rhythm in works of art.

Background Information
Jacob Lawrence (United States, born 1917) is an African American painter who first became famous during the Harlem Renaissance of the 1920s and 1930s.

Lawrence produced graphic images of urban life. As a Social Realist, he has used his art as a means of expressing his social values. Major themes in his work include violence and in-

justice. The uprootedness of African Americans is the subject of a series of paintings entitled *The Migration of the Negro* (1940–41). There are 60 individual works in this series.

A prolific artist, Lawrence has completed series of paintings on several different themes, including *War, Coast Guard, Sanitarium,* and *Life in Harlem.*

WHAT YOU WILL DO

1. Look through magazines and newspapers to find a whole body of an action figure. Be sure the figure is complete with both hands and feet.
2. Using a fine-tip marker, outline the figure. Then carefully cut out the figure by cutting along the outline. You will use this figure for the motif of your design.
3. Select a sheet of cool-colored construction paper. This will be used for your background. Select several sheets of smaller pieces of warm-colored construction paper. These will be used for the figures. (See Figure 5–16.)
4. Place the magazine cutout figure on a piece of construction paper and trace around it. Conserve paper by arranging the tracing on one side of the paper and using the other half for another cutout. Cut out five, seven, or nine figures or silhouettes. Keep them in the envelope until you are ready to use them.
5. Experiment with several arrangements of the silhouettes on the background. You may want to include the original magazine cutout to create a center of interest. The figures may overlap. When you have an arrangement that shows visual movement, glue it to the background piece of construction paper.
6. Display your design. Compare the designs with those of your classmates, and look for different rhythmic beats. Which designs have a strong sense of movement?

EXAMINING YOUR WORK

- **Describe** Identify the action figure you selected. Did you cut it out carefully? What colors did you choose for the background? What colors did you choose for the cutout figures? Tell why, or why not, you chose to use the magazine cutout. Explain what kind of rhythm you created and how you achieved a feeling of visual movement.

▲ **Figure 5–16** Student work. An action figure.

OTHER STUDIO IDEAS

- Do the visual movement problem above, but use complementary colors for the color scheme.

- •• Create a rhythmic design, using geometric shapes, that has a strong sense of movement. Use cool colors for the shapes and a warm color for the background.

Lesson 6 *Creating Visual Movement* **93**

Developing Concepts

Exploring Aesthetics. Let students work in groups to discuss their responses to Lawrence's painting shown in Figure 5-15: How does this work make you feel? What aspects of the work evoke that response? How do you account for different responses among group members?

Understanding Art History. Let students use historical almanacs or other reference works to research the social and political climate during the time Jacob Lawrence painted *Toussaint L'Overture Series.* Then help them discuss how that climate may have influenced Lawrence's work.

Following Up

Closure. Let students work in small groups to discuss their designs, following the instructions in "Examining Your Work." After the group discussion, have each student write a short description of the rhythm and movement in his or her work (following the final step in the "Examining Your Work" instructions).

Evaluation. Review students' construction paper designs, listen to their contributions to group discussions, and read their descriptions of their work.

Reteaching. Work with small groups of students. Ask them to browse through this text (or other books with reproductions of art works). Have each group member identify and share several works that show the use of movement and rhythm.

Enrichment. Show students reproductions of Marcel Duchamp's *Nude Descending a Staircase,* Umberto Boccioni's *Dynamism of a Cyclist,* and/or Giacomo Balla's *Dynamism of a Dog on a Leash.* All these works show human figures in motion, using repetition, overlapping, and/or extensions of natural boundaries. Guide students in discussing and analyzing the movement in each painting. Then ask a volunteer to model a motion (such as walking or jumping rope); have the other students draw the movement of the model, using the techniques they have discussed.

Cooperative Learning

Divide students into groups of three. Tell them the object of this lesson will be to create visual movement by showing the arc a ball takes when thrown through the air. Distribute a 9 x 12 (23 x 30 cm) piece of colored construction paper and a 12 x 18 (30 x 46 cm) piece of plain paper to each group. One student will draw 10 circles decreasing in size from about 3 inches (8 cm) to about 1 inch (2.5 cm). The second student will cut out the circles, starting with the smallest. The third will draw a curved line on the large piece of plain paper. The line will start in the lower left corner, travel up to the top middle of the page, and drop down toward the right center. The third student will arrange the circles, placing the smallest at the end of the line and ending with the largest circle at the lower left corner where the line began. The circles can be adjusted for best position and then glued down. Let students display work and compare. Ask if using different tints of the color would have helped to make the ball disappear into the distance.

Unity in Art

LESSON PLAN
(pages 94–95)

Objectives
After completing this lesson, students will be able to:
- Explain what unity does for an art work.
- Identify and practice using a design chart.

Supplies
- Two or more eggshells with the eggs blown out—eggshells may be decorated with watercolors, markers, glitter, dye, and the like.
- Recording of a short piece of familiar music (selected by students, if possible).
- Photographs of Navajo rugs.

> **TRB Resources**
> - 5-6 *The Principles of Art*, (reproducible master)
> - 5-7 *Analyzing the Principles*, (appreciating cultural diversity)
> - 5-8 *The Design Chart*, (reproducible master)

TEACHING THE LESSON

Getting Started

Motivator. Display the eggshells, and allow students to comment on them. Then break one of the shells. Let the students compare the broken shell with the whole shells. Be sure they recognize that even if the broken pieces of shell were glued back together, the separate pieces would still be visible.

Vocabulary. Write on the board the names of the principles of art: balance, variety, harmony, emphasis, proportion, movement, rhythm. Add to this list the word *unity*, and define it for the class (the blending together of elements and principles with media to create an unbroken whole). Help students review the meanings of the principles of art. Then ask them to explain how the words listed on the board can be used to describe and explain music. After a short discussion, play a short musical recording; encourage the students to discuss and describe the music, using the terms listed on the board.

Unity in Art

When something breakable shatters—a vase, for example—it can never again be as it was. The pieces can be glued together, but the object will never be truly the same. The jagged seams will always be a reminder that the item is made up of separate parts.

When the pieces of an art puzzle are put together by a skilled artist, the seams do not show. The viewer cannot tell where one part ends and the next begins. The work has a oneness. It has unity.

UNITY IN ART

Unity is *the arrangement of elements and principles with media to create a feeling of completeness*. Unity in an art work is like an unseen glue. You cannot point to it as you can an element or principle, but you can sense it. You can also sense when it is missing. Look at Figure 5–17. The landscape below shows unity for many reasons. It seems to display a sense of completeness. Can you name the principles shown in this art work that make it have unity?

▲ **Figure 5–17** Van Gogh usually painted in brilliant colors with strong, passionate brush strokes. What do you think makes the painting show such a feeling of calmness?

Vincent van Gogh. *Garden of the Rectory at Nuenen.* Oil on canvas, mounted on panel. 53 x 78.2 cm (20⅞ x 30¾"). The Armand Hammer Foundation.

> **Note**
> In order to further illustrate the concept of unity, ask the class if everyone has put together a picture puzzle. Ask students to visualize the puzzle pieces as they are dumped out of the box onto the table. Imagine putting all the pieces right side up, separating those with a straight edge from the others. Take students through the stages of sorting and assembling the puzzle until each piece has been put in its proper place and interlocked to form a whole. Once the last piece has found its home, the puzzle has been put together and unity achieved. Ask for other examples of objects that need to be assembled to form a whole. They might include the pieces of a garment that are sewed together to form a dress, the parts of a car that are put together in an assembly plant. Finish by reviewing the definition of unity: blending together elements and principles with media to create an unbroken whole.

DESIGN CHART	PRINCIPLES OF ART					
	Balance	Variety	Harmony	Emphasis	Proportion	Movement/ Rhythm
ELEMENTS OF ART Color: Hue						
Intensity						
Value						
Line						
Shape/Form						
Space						
Texture						

UNITY

Note: Do not write on this chart.
▲ Figure 5–18 Design chart.

PLOTTING UNITY ON A CHART

Explaining how the parts of an art work fit together can be difficult. Using a design chart (Figure 5–18) makes the task easier. Notice that the chart shows the elements along the side and the principles along the top. Think of each square where an element and principle meet as a design question. Here, for example, are some questions that might be asked about hue.

- Is the balance of the hues formal, informal, or radial?
- Do the hues show variety?
- Is a single hue used throughout to add harmony?
- Is hue used to emphasize, or highlight, some part of the work?

- Is the proportion, or amount of hue greater or lesser than that of other elements?
- Does hue add to a sense of movement?
- Do hues repeat in a rhythmic way that adds action to the work?

Think about what questions you might ask about each of the remaining five elements.

✔CHECK YOUR UNDERSTANDING

1. What is unity in art?
2. What does a design chart help you do?

Developing Concepts

Exploring Aesthetics. Monroe Beardsley, an American aesthetic philosopher, identified unity as one of the components of praiseworthy art. In contrast, the German philosopher Immanuel Kant stated that we cannot use rules or definitions to judge art; in his view, art that moves us is, by definition, good. Present these two different philosophies to the class, and help students discuss them.

Appreciating Cultural Diversity. Display photographs of Navajo rugs or blankets. Explain that the Navajos, who constitute the largest tribal group in this country, are probably the best known of all Native American weavers. Navajo weaving is traditionally done by women at upright looms. The woven rugs present unusually fine examples of unity. Let volunteers describe how the photographed rugs demonstrate the use of elements and principles to create unity.

Following Up

Closure. Have students write short statements of their own ideas about the importance of unity.

Evaluation. 1. Review students' written responses to the "Check Your Understanding" questions. 2. Read students' statements about unity.

Reteaching. Work with small groups of students. Let the group members select one of the works of art reproduced in this chapter. Then guide the group in using a design chart to describe how the parts of that work fit together.

Enrichment. Have each student bring in an object found in nature, such as a leaf, a rock, or a blossom. Then have students form small groups, and let each group member describe his or her natural object as if it were a work of art. Encourage students to identify and discuss the elements of art and the principles of art as evidenced in these natural objects.

Lesson 7 *Unity in Art* 95

Answers to "Check Your Understanding"
1. Unity in art is a blending together of elements and principles with media to create an unbroken whole.
2. A design chart helps you explain how the parts of an art work fit together.

ANSWERS TO "CHAPTER 5 REVIEW"

Building Vocabulary
1. principles of art
2. balance
3. variety
4. harmony
5. emphasis
6. proportion
7. movement
8. rhythm
9. unity

Reviewing Art Facts
10. Symmetrical balance is shown when one half mirrors the other.
11. Another name for asymmetrical balance is informal balance. Another name for symmetrical balance is formal balance.
12. Radial balance can be thought of as a complicated form of formal balance.
13. The work can become monotonous when an artist overuses harmony.
14. The artist will use emphasis to control what part of a work a viewer's eye sees first.
15. Proportion in art is not limited to the relationship to size of objects. It could also be used as the proportion of one element to another, for example the amount of color can be used in differing proportions.
16. The artist will use the principle of movement to lead the viewer's eye from one part of the work to the next.
17. Pattern occurs when objects are repeated over and over.
18. Another name for oneness is unity.
19. A design chart is used to help identify how the elements and principles are used in an art work.

Thinking About Art
1. Radial balance is demonstrated by a design viewed in a kaleidoscope.
2. The element of line can give emphasis to an object by pointing towards the object.
3. An artist may choose not to use the principle of proportion in order to show exaggeration or distortion.
4. Both the elements of movement and rhythm create action in a work of art. Movement also is used to move the viewer's eye throughout the work. Rhythm is used by repeating an element to make the work seem active.

CHAPTER 5 REVIEW

BUILDING VOCABULARY

Number a sheet of paper from 1 to 9. After each number, write the term from the box that best matches each description below.

balance	proportion
emphasis	rhythm
harmony	unity
movement	variety
principles of art	

1. The rules that govern how the elements of art go together.
2. What a work has when no one part overpowers any other.
3. Mixing one or more elements for contrast.
4. Blending elements in a pleasing way.
5. Making an element or object in a work stand out.
6. The way parts of a work relate to each other.
7. The principle that leads a viewer to sense action in a work.
8. The repeating of an element again and again to make a work seem active.
9. Combining elements, principles, and media into an unbroken whole.

REVIEWING ART FACTS

Number a sheet of paper from 10 to 19. Answer each question in a complete sentence.

10. What kind of balance is shown in a work where one half mirrors the other?
11. What is another name for asymmetrical balance? For symmetrical balance?
12. Some artists think of radial balance as a complicated form of what other type of balance?
13. What can happen to a work when an artist overuses harmony?
14. What principle will an artist use to control which part of a work a viewer's eye sees first?
15. Is proportion in art limited to size of objects? Explain.
16. What principle will an artist use to carry the viewer's eye from one part of a work to the next?
17. What is a pattern?
18. What is another name for oneness?
19. What is a design chart used for?

THINKING ABOUT ART

On a sheet of paper, answer each question in a sentence or two.

1. **Extend.** What kind of balance is demonstrated by a design viewed in a kaleidoscope?
2. **Interpret.** How might an artist give emphasis to an object by using the element of line?
3. **Analyze.** Why might an artist choose to disobey the principle of proportion?
4. **Compare and contrast.** What do the principles of movement and rhythm have in common? How are they different?

MAKING ART CONNECTIONS

1. **Science.** Find examples from nature that represent formal, informal, and radial balance. Draw each example. Try looking at natural objects through a microscope and draw what you see. Group your drawings according to the type of balance. Think about the different principles of art. How do they relate to the designs found in nature?
2. **Industrial Arts.** Boccioni created *Study for Dynamic Force of a Cyclist I* (Figure 5–13, page 90) in 1913. That same year Henry Ford introduced the conveyor belt assembly line. Find out what kinds of transportation were used at that time. Use repeated lines and shapes to create your own speeding vehicle from the same period.

CHAPTER 5 REVIEW

LOOKING AT THE DETAILS

The detail shown below is from Hale Woodruff's *Poor Man's Cotton*. Study the detail and answer the following questions.

1. Would you describe this work as realistic? Why or why not?
2. The figures' garments are smooth and flowing and some of the faces are obscured and without detail. Why do you think the artist chose to omit certain details? For what purpose?
3. There is continuous, deliberate movement in this painting. How did Woodruff achieve this?
4. Which element or elements create rhythm in this work?
5. Do you feel a sense of unity in Woodruff's work? Why or why not?

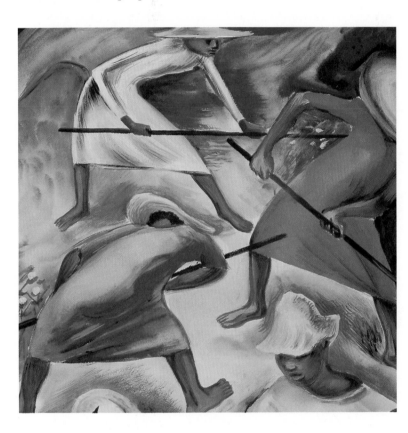

Hale Woodruff. *Poor Man's Cotton.* 1944. Watercolor on paper. (Detail.) 77.5 x 57.2 cm (30½ x 22½"). The Newark Museum, Newark, New Jersey. Sophronia Anderson Fund.

ANSWERS TO "LOOKING AT THE DETAILS"

1. No, the work is not realistic. Responses will vary. Students might note that the environment, the colors, and the sense of depth are not realistically portrayed; the human forms are void of realistic detail; and the forms are stacked in an unrealistic composition.
2. Responses will vary. Students might mention the following: The movement and action in the work is the primary message; therefore the personalities of the figures are not essential to the work. Woodruff may have omitted the detail to focus the viewer's attention on the movement, rhythm, color, and overall feel of the work. Because his intent was not to portray realism, the detail in the figures is not crucial.
3. Responses will vary. Students might note these possibilities: by his use of harmony in the curved lines of the figures, through his use of alternating straight dark lines of the hoes, and through composition.
4. Line and shape create rhythm. Students might also mention color because all the hoes are dark.
5. Yes. Allow students to express their opinions. Students might mention the following: His use of the same hue with different tonal qualities adds a sense of unity. The zigzag pattern of the hoes seems to go together with the hats and figures. All the figures are curved and flowing, creating the same feeling.

Chapter Evaluation

The goal of this chapter is to introduce students to the principles of art and to apply these principles, when evaluating works of art and creating works of art. Possible methods of evaluating results include:

1. Use separate slips of paper and label each principle. Put the slips of paper in a brown paper bag. Have students select a slip from the bag. Have them define the principle that they have chosen and explain how the principle has been used in a work of art within the text.
2. Write the phrase, "Unity in art means . . ." on the chalkboard. Have students write a paragraph using this phrase as the opening sentence.
3. Have students complete Chapter Test (TRB, Resource 5–9).

97

You, the Art Critic

Chapter Scan

Lesson 1 Describing Art Works
Lesson 2 Using Descriptive
          Techniques
Lesson 3 Analyzing Art Works
Lesson 4 Interpreting Art Works
Lesson 5 Mood Chalk Painting
Lesson 6 Judging Art Works
Lesson 7 Using Art Criticism

TRB Resources
• 6-10 Chapter Test
• Color Transparency 11
• Color Transparency 12

TEACHING THE CHAPTER

Introducing the Art Work

Direct students' attention to Berthe Morisot's *In the Dining Room*. Inform students that Berthe Morisot was a French Impressionist painter in the nineteenth century. In her time it was unusual for a woman to train as a painter. However, Berthe Morisot was the daughter of wealthy and prominent parents who astonished their society by encouraging their daughter's painting.

Morisot was dedicated to Impressionism, and she produced Impressionist still lifes, landscapes, and scenes of women in various settings. Her models were primarily close family members and friends.

Examining the Art Work

Tell the students that Berthe Morisot uses loose, undisguised brush strokes in her work. Explain how the artist blurs shapes in this painting. Have students look at the far door of the cupboard and note how it blends with the background and the colors of the woman's skirt. Point out the window and how the pane and the scene beyond it seem to meld together. Yet the viewer still gets the impression that a grassy area is outside and a red house is in the distance. Explain that this could suggest that the setting could be in the country.

▲ Would you view this painting differently if you knew when and where it was painted? Would knowing something about the artist make a difference?

Berthe Morisot. *In the Dining Room*. 1886. Canvas. 61.3 x 50.0 cm (24⅛ x 19¾"). National Gallery of Art, Washington, D.C. Chester Dale Collection.

You, the Art Critic

Life is full of new and enjoyable experiences. You hear a new song. You taste a food you have never before eaten. You see a piece of art that gives you a feeling of joy and excitement.

However, have you ever had the feeling, even after looking closely at a work of art, that you may be missing something? For example, when you look at the painting at the left, what do you see? Is there more you can learn about it to add to your understanding and appreciation of the work?

In this chapter you will learn about the steps you can take to answer these questions.

OBJECTIVES

After completing this chapter, you will be able to:

- Name the four steps used in art criticism.
- Explain how to describe objective and non-objective works of art.
- Define analyzing, interpreting, and judging.
- Apply art criticism to a work of art.

WORDS YOU WILL LEARN

analyzing	describing
applied art	interpreting
art critic	judging
art criticism	non-objective art

ARTISTS YOU WILL MEET

Pieter de Hooch	Berthe Morisot
Richard Estes	Raphael
El Greco	Milton Resnick
Grace Hartigan	Albert Pinkham Ryder
Barbara Hepworth	Andrew Wyeth

Tell students that Morisot asks the viewer to acknowledge the process of painting, by exposing brush strokes and avoiding well-defined silhouettes.

Suggest that Morisot doesn't use strong contrasts of color; instead, she strives for an overall quality of color. This work exhibits a brown, earthy tone, even further suggesting a country setting.

Discussing the Art Work

Ask students to think about the mood of the painting. Ask: Do the colors or the scene suggest noise, or urgency? Do they suggest nature and serenity? Point out the subtle hues, the expression on the woman's face, the furnishings and quality of the room, and the scene outside the window.

Ask students if Morisot's technique adds a sense of movement to the scene. Explain that as a result of the visible brush strokes and blurred shapes, the viewer experiences color and pigment as gesture. Explain that the movement is in the viewer's eye and in the sense of light in the room.

Ask students to look at some of the details in the painting. Point out the bowl of fruit on the table and how the viewer is able to interpret the bowl by its placement, color, and general shape. Refer students to the clock on the wall, and how the viewer can assume it is a clock by its placement, color and general shape, even though no clock face is shown.

Tell students that in this chapter they will learn to describe, analyze, interpret and judge a work of art through applying the steps of art criticism. Then they will be able to apply the steps of art criticism to their own works of art.

99

Building Self-Esteem

Tell students that in Chapter 6 they will learn how an art critic gathers and examines evidence about an art work. Then ask them to look at *Christina's World* by Andrew Wyeth. Ask if, when they first looked at the work, they felt sorry for Christina. After discussing the picture, they may have changed their minds. Instead of feeling sorry for Christina, they may admire her for her bravery and the strength she showed by not giving up. Ask if they have ever met someone who they felt sorry for at first but later admired. Most of us have. Sometimes we might even wonder if we could be so strong under similar circumstances. Ask students to think of someone they know who has qualities they admire, even though that individual might be limited in some way. That person could be an acquaintance or a character in a TV program they watch. Ask students to tell how that person has overcome the limitation and what quality it took to do so.

Describing Art Works

What do you think of when you hear the words art criticism? Do you think of someone saying they like a painting because the colors are vivid or the scenery is realistic? It is more than saying you like or do not like a piece of art. **Art criticism** is *the process of studying, understanding, and judging art works*.

A person who practices art criticism is called an **art critic**. Art critics learn as much as possible from all kinds of art work. They carefully study and examine works of art. They search for a meaning or message in the work. They gather facts that add to their understanding about the art work. Then this information is used to help them form judgments that can be supported with solid reasons.

You, too, can practice art criticism. You will find that it can help you:

- Examine and understand the art works of others.
- Study your own art works to determine how to improve them.
- Gain a better understanding and appreciation for all types and styles of art.

Every art critic has his or her way of doing things. By using the following four steps, you, also, can become an art critic. The four steps are:

- **Step 1:** Describing what is in the art work.
- **Step 2:** Analyzing how it is designed or put together.
- **Step 3:** Interpreting its meaning.
- **Step 4:** Judging its success.

In this lesson you will learn about the first of these steps, describing.

DESCRIBING OBJECTIVE ART WORKS

When you describe a work of art, you ask yourself the question "What do I see?" **Describing** is *making a careful list of all the things you see in the work*. In describing a work, you identify:

- The size of the work, the medium and process used.
- What people and objects you see and what is happening.
- The elements of art used.

In the describing stage, you report only the facts. You do not mention, for example, if the artist's use of many colors makes the painting confusing. That will come later in the judging stage.

Size, Medium, and Process

Describing the size and medium of a work is easy. You learned about credit lines in Chapter 2. The credit line gives the size, medium, and process used. In museums, this information appears on a card or paper near the work. Remember that the height of a work is always the first of the two numbers listed.

What is the size of Figure 6–1? What medium was used? What process was used?

Subject, Objects, and Details

Look again at the painting in Figure 6–1. A critic describing this work might begin by listing the people and other objects in it. Now it is your turn to be the art critic. How many figures do you see? Are all the figures the same distance from the viewer? Do some figures seem close to the viewer while others seem further away?

Objectives

After completing this lesson, students will be able to:

- Understand the goals of art criticism.
- List the four steps of art criticism.
- Describe objective and non-objective art works.
- Understand the information provided in a credit line.

Supplies

- Sheets of white paper, 18 x 24 inches (46 x 60 cm).
- Crayons and objects of a similar use from several different cultures.
- A variety of small objects to view under a microscope, such as leaves, bits of fabric, and onion skins.
- Drawing pencils.
- Several microscopes.

TRB Resource

- 6-1 *Content in a Work of Art*, (aesthetics/art criticism)

TEACHING THE LESSON

Getting Started

Motivator. Have students select a large, clear reproduction of a painting in a book or view a painting at a local art museum. First have them write down what they notice in their chosen art work. Then have them draw their paintings on plain paper. Ask them to list at the bottom of their sketches the things that they noticed only after sketching the work. Did they see details that they had initially overlooked? Discuss the importance of careful observation in art criticism.

Vocabulary. Discuss what the word *criticism* means in everyday usage. How is the meaning of *art criticism* different? Point out that although artists may sometimes be offended by what an *art critic* says about their work, art criticism does not necessarily entail a negative evaluation.

100

Note

It is easy for students to forget that the art works in their textbook are almost always reproduced much smaller than the original piece. For example, Figure 6-3 is 90 x 65.5 inches (228.6 x 166.4 cm), over four times as high as Figure 6-1, which students may have assumed was the larger work. Encourage students to mentally picture each work according to its true scale. If necessary, draw a rectangle or simple outline on the board to help students keep the correct proportions in mind.

Background Information

During the second half of the seventeenth century, mother and child scenes became an increasingly popular subject among Dutch painters. These scenes almost always feature a daughter, not a son. Some scholars have said that this is because the mothers in these works are acting as models for their daughters to imitate. According to a seventeenth-century Dutch manual, these daughters were supposed to learn how to be even tempered, obey a future husband, and keep an immaculate house.

▲ Figure 6–1   What time of day or night is it? How are the figures dressed? What might this tell you about them?

Pieter de Hooch. *The Bedroom.* c. 1660. Oil on canvas. 50.8 x 59.7 cm (20 x 23½"). National Gallery of Art, Washington, D.C. Widener Collection.

The critic would next tell what each figure was doing. The critic would note that the child has her hand on the door as though she has just entered. What other details might the critic mention? The critic might notice the quality of light entering the scene from the open door behind the child.

Finally, the critic would make a list of the furniture and other objects in the painting. What familiar pieces or objects do you see? Are there any that are unfamiliar?

Developing Concepts

Exploring Aesthetics. Have students browse through the textbook illustrations. Discuss whether any of the art works seem more difficult to describe than others. Have students explain their opinions. Ask: Is sculpture harder to describe than other types of art? Are realistic paintings easier to describe than non-objective art? Are modern art works easier to describe than older ones, or art from other cultures?

Using Art Criticism. Write on the board the headings that appear on the lefthand side of Figure 6-2 on page **102**, and familiarize students with systematic description by using the terms as a basis for describing Figure 6-1.

Understanding Art History. Have students research other paintings by Pieter de Hooch. Compare all of the reproductions of de Hooch paintings that the students find. Have them describe the size, medium, process, subject, objects, details, and art elements of each painting. Discuss which of these features are often repeated in de Hooch's art, such as open doorways, children, and intense coloration.

Appreciating Cultural Diversity. Explain to students that non-objective art is not just a twentieth-century phenomenon. Both Eastern and Western art traditions include many fascinating and beautiful examples of non-objective art works. Divide students into groups. Have each group explore one of the following categories of non-objective art: Amish quilts, African textiles, geometric mosaics by Arab artists, and pages in medieval Irish illuminated manuscripts such as the *Book of Kells.* Have students report their findings to the class. Their presentations should include careful descriptions of the type of non-objective art that they explored.

Background Information
Pieter de Hooch (Netherlands, 1629–1688) is best known for his colorful paintings of well-to-do townspeople and their servants. These works, created in the years from 1655 until the early 1660s, feature carefully constructed interior and exterior spaces, rectangular shapes that frame the figures, and doors left ajar to permit the viewer to see into other rooms or a courtyard. De Hooch's lighting is typically warm and sunny. He also used light sources to create deep shadows in sunlit homes and open air scenes alike. De Hooch's genre scenes are particularly charming when they represent a mother or maid and a child involved in a simple task. They are quietly absorbed in their chores and the routine activities of a Dutch housewife are imbued with a poetic dignity. According to art historians Jakob Rosenberg and Seymour Slive, in de Hooch's paintings "all of the virtues of the Dutchwoman, her care and love of a neat and proper arrangement of things, are brought out with touching sincerity."

Appreciating Cultural Diversity. Present to students objects of similar use from different cultures and have students write a description of each. For example, have students compare eating utensils—a set of common wooden chopsticks from China, elegant mother-of-pearl inlay chopsticks from Japan, and early American coin silver or pewter utensils. A comparison of clothing might include a Japanese kimono, an Indian silk sari, and a full length veil worn in Saudi Arabia. Have students read their favorite descriptions aloud.

Developing Studio Skills. Present students with a variety of objects that yield interesting images when magnified. Have students draw an object and write a careful description of it. Then have students examine their objects under a microscope and write a second description. Have them look at their first drawing and ask them if they see the object differently. Does the experience of seeing the item magnified make it look different in its unmagnified state?

DESIGN CHART		PRINCIPLES OF ART						
		Balance	Variety	Harmony	Emphasis	Proportion	Movement/ Rhythm	
ELEMENTS OF ART	Color: Hue							UNITY
	Intensity							
	Value							
	Line							
	Shape/Form							
	Space							
	Texture							

Note: Do not write on this chart.

▲ **Figure 6–2 Design Chart.**

Describing the Elements

The critic would next describe the way elements of color, line, texture, shape, and space are used in the work. To make it easier, the critic might make a checklist such as the one in Figure 6–2. On a sheet of paper, the critic would write the name of each element found in the work. Then next to each element, he or she would write a brief statement describing it.

As a critic, what hues can you identify in Figure 6–1? List them on the checklist. Then ask yourself what is the lightest value in the painting. Where is it found? Turning next to the element of line, you might ask whether the lines are thick or thin. You might then question the shapes. Are they flat two-dimensional shapes or are they solid, three-dimensional forms?

DESCRIBING NON-OBJECTIVE ART WORKS

How would you describe the painting in Figure 6–3? Would it make you feel uncomfortable because you cannot identify any objects? This type of work is called non-objective art. **Non-objective art** is *a work with no objects or subjects that can be readily identified*. Are such works passed over by critics?

Not at all! The critic's job, you will recall, is to describe what he or she sees. Since this work has no people, places, or objects, the critic will focus attention on the art elements. This is what the critic — or anyone else — will see in the work. This is called describing the formal aspects of a work.

How would you, the critic, describe the elements in this work? How many hues can you identify? Are the lines thick or thin? Are any straight lines used? What kinds of shapes are found?

Background Information
The history of Grace Hartigan's bold, gestural, and colorful paintings reflects the tension between her natural artistic impulses and the prevailing aesthetic fashions of the 1950s and later. During her childhood, Hartigan spent long hours observing the itinerant gypsies who camped near her house. After arriving in New York City in 1946, she saw a strong similarity between the caravans, bonfires, and flashy clothing of the gypsies and the colorful world of pushcart peddlers and pickle barrels on the city's Lower East Side. She initially took New York street life as her subject, but in the 1950s she allowed herself to be persuaded by successful abstract artist colleagues who told her that she wasn't selecting sufficiently serious subject matter. Hartigan did not return to the realist material for which she had such an affinity until the late 1960s.

The next time you look at a non-objective work of art and someone asks, "What do you see in that work?," point to the colors, lines, shapes, and other visual elements. Those were the concern of the artist. Concentrating on them will help you understand and appreciate the work.

▲ **Figure 6–3** How did the artist use the element of space?

Grace Hartigan. *The Far Away Places*. 1974. Oil on canvas. 228.6 x 166.4 cm (90 x 65½"). McNay Art Museum, San Antonio, Texas.

✔CHECK YOUR UNDERSTANDING

1. What are the four steps of art criticism?
2. Describe one benefit of learning art criticism.
3. How can the credit line help you in describing art works?
4. What do you use to describe a non-objective work?

Lesson 1   *Describing Art Works*   📖   **103**

Using Descriptive Techniques

Objectives
After completing this lesson, students will be able to:
• Observe and describe details in a painting.
• Draw the components of a section of a painting in a manner consistent with the style of the original work.

Supplies
• Sheets of lined notebook paper and pencils.
• Sheets of sketch paper.
• Large sheets of white drawing paper.
• Variety of drawing materials.

TRB Resource
• 6-2 *Art Criticism Past and Present*, (aesthetics/art criticism)

TEACHING THE LESSON

Getting Started
Motivator. Ask students to write down a fantastic image from a dream they have had. Then have students quickly sketch the dream image based on their written descriptions alone. Discuss whether the sketch is enough to convey the dream itself to other viewers. Relate this dilemma to Raphael's task of imagining and illustrating the story of *St. George and the Dragon.*

Developing Concepts
Exploring Aesthetics. Have students research other paintings by Raphael and make sketches of various elements that are rendered similarly in the different paintings, such as trees, faces, horses, or even particular poses. Have students share their findings with the rest of the class. Discuss Raphael's treatment of these details.

104

Using Descriptive Techniques

Look at the painting by the Italian artist Raphael (**raf**-ee-l) in Figure 6–4. The man on horseback is Saint George. He is rescuing the woman in the red dress from a ferocious dragon. Do the figures and objects in the painting look real? What techniques has the artist used to get this result?

WHAT YOU WILL LEARN
In this studio lesson imagine that part of Raphael's painting is missing at the right side. Begin by making a description of this painting using the information on describing in Lesson 1. Then make a pencil drawing that continues the landscape in the painting at the viewer's right. Details of your drawing will reflect the ones in your description.

▶ **Figure 6–4   How is the element of space used differently in Raphael's painting than the one in Figure 6–3? What is the result?**

Raphael. *Saint George and the Dragon*. c. 1506. Oil on wood. 28.5 x 21.5 cm (11⅛ x 8⅜"). National Gallery of Art, Washington, D.C. Andrew W. Mellon Collection.

Background Information
Raphael was born in the northern Italian city of Urbino, which was an important cultural center. His father was employed as a court painter at the palace of Urbino. This palace, with its fine library, art work, architecture, and rich cultural surroundings, was an important influence on the boy, whose father died when he was eleven. Later, Raphael apprenticed with Pietro Perugino, an early Renaissance master. After gaining proficiency in Perugino's style and technique, Raphael went to Florence and Rome, where he learned from other artists. From Leonardo, he learned ways to paint the human form in a sculptural and idealized fashion. From Michelangelo, Raphael saw how to infuse solid human form with the spirit of life and drama. Raphael also benefited from the heightened social position that enabled Renaissance artists to mix easily with nobles. Other developments important to his life were the discovery of linear perspective, and the invention of the printing press.

WHAT YOU WILL NEED

- Sheet of lined notebook paper and pencil
- Sheets of sketch paper
- Large sheet of white drawing paper

WHAT YOU WILL DO

1. Imagine that the right half of Raphael's painting of *St. George and the Dragon* is missing.
2. On your sheet of lined paper, describe what you see in this painting. Identify the figures and tell what each is doing. Pay special attention to details of the landscape. Notice how the artist used the elements of line, shape, and space.
3. Imagine the landscape as it might appear on the missing half. On sketch paper, practice sketching the half of the picture as you feel it would appear.
4. Use only lines and outlines of shapes in your drawing. Do not use shading. Create a feeling of deep space by having objects overlap. Distant objects should also be made smaller and with little detail.
5. Draw your completion of the landscape on a large sheet of white paper. Use your rough sketches and your description to guide you. Refer to the painting in the textbook. Match your sky, trees, flowers, and plants as carefully as you can. If you like, add another view of the city in the distance (Figure 6–5).
6. Share your work with your classmates. Look for differences and similarities between your own landscape and those of other students.

EXAMINING YOUR WORK

- **Describe** Identify the trees, plants, rocks, and other objects in your work. Point to the place in your drawing where your trees and ground blend into the trees and ground in the painting.
- **Explain** Referring to your description, identify the kinds of lines, shapes, and space found in the painting. Show examples of the same kinds of lines, shapes, and space in your drawing.

▲ **Figure 6–5** Notice the city in the distance. What kinds of buildings would the city be made of?

Raphael. *Saint George and the Dragon*. c. 1506. Oil on wood. (Detail.) 28.5 x 21.5 cm (11⅛ x 8⅜"). National Gallery of Art, Washington, D.C. Andrew W. Mellon Collection.

OTHER STUDIO IDEAS

- Do a pencil sketch of a landscape you know well. Use at least two of the elements from the description you made for this lesson.
- Look through a magazine and find a picture of an outdoor scene which empha-

sizes one of the seasons. Cut out the picture and then cut the picture in half. Glue or tape the left half of the picture to your paper and continue the missing part using crayons or colored pencils.

Lesson 2 *Using Descriptive Techniques* 105

Developing Studio Skills. Prepare a description of a painting. Read it to the students and have them draw it. Then display a reproduction of the art work and compare it to the students' drawings. Discuss which parts of the description could be changed to more clearly communicate the details of the painting.

Following Up

Closure. Have students briefly state whether they enjoyed drawing a scene in the manner of Raphael. Ask: Did Raphael's way of rendering figures and landscape come naturally? Were they tempted to draw it differently than Raphael did? Have students explain their responses.

Evaluation. 1. Assess students' contributions to class discussions on description and Raphael's style. 2. Evaluate paragraphs on different artists' treatment of the same theme. 3. Review students' responses to "Examining Your Work."

Reteaching. Have students page through their textbooks and identify several works that required the artist to describe the subject without the benefit of a model. Discuss whether it is easier or more difficult to paint the details of a scene without being able to actually see it. Point out that artists who imagine an entire composition often take details from past painted versions of the story and set up models to help them visualize it better.

Enrichment. Invite a professional art conservator from a local museum or art restoration business to speak to the students. Have him or her discuss the profession and the experience of filling in decomposed or otherwise missing parts of an art work.

Background Information
St. George is a legendary warrior saint and martyr who is thought to have died near the end of the third century. He typically appears in Christian art either undergoing martyrdom or slaying a dragon. In the latter version, the symbolic key is the dragon. Early Christians associated the dragon with evil and paganism. Hence, an illustration of a saint who converted a pagan nation to Christianity might be rendered as that saint spearing a dragon. St. George has been represented by this convention to signify his role in bringing Christianity to Cappadocia in Asia Minor. The place itself is symbolized by a maiden in these scenes. Later ages lost the original meaning of the dragon and maiden and reinterpreted the images. According to the later version, St. George was said to have fought a dragon in order to rescue the king's daughter.

LESSON 3

Analyzing Art Works

LESSON PLAN
(pages 106–107),

Objectives

After completing this lesson, students will be able to:
• Describe how color, line, texture, shape, form, and space are used in an art work.

Supplies

• Sports magazines and other popular magazines.
• Pencils and sketch paper.
• Sunday comics.
• Garments of different styles.
• Cameras and film.

TRB Resource
• 6-3 *Artistic Styles*, (reproducible master)

TEACHING THE LESSON

Getting Started

Motivator. Ask students to bring in copies of the comics from the local Sunday newspaper and have extra copies on hand. Select one of the action-oriented strips, which usually feature the dramatic use of the art elements, and discuss how line, color, shape, and space direct the viewer's eye and create strong visual impact. If you like, show reproductions of paintings by the Pop artist Roy Lichtenstein, who based his aesthetic approach on comic strips.

Vocabulary. Discuss how people in different fields *analyze* or break down their object of study in order to better understand it. For example, a chemist analyzes a compound to discover its ingredients. A stock broker analyzes the stock market to find out which factors cause the market to rise or fall. Relate these practices to that of art critics, who analyze an art work to figure out how it is organized.

Analyzing Art Works

Have you ever taken something apart to see how it works? In a way, that is what an art critic does in the second stage of art criticism. During this stage the critic analyzes by looking at the parts of the work to see how the whole was made.

ANALYZING ART WORKS

When you analyze a work of art, you ask yourself the question "How is the work organized?" **Analyzing** is *noting how the principles are used to organize the elements of color, line, texture, shape, form, and space*. Remember that some of the principles of art are balance, variety, and harmony. Can you name the other principles?

Look at the painting of *St. Martin and the Beggar* in Figure 6–6. To analyze this work, a critic might use a design chart like the one shown in Figure 6–2 on page **102**. The critic might notice the following:

• The painting is divided in half by an imaginary vertical line beginning with the right front leg of the horse (Figure 6–7). Trace the line upward with your finger from the right front leg of the horse, along the saddle blanket, through the center of St. Martin's breastplate, to his head. The different shapes are balanced on either side of this center line.
• Different values, textures, and shapes have been used to add variety to the picture. Can you point to different uses of each? How do these differences increase your visual interest?
• Other elements have been repeated to bring harmony to the work. What kinds of hues — warm or cool — has the artist used most? What kinds of lines are repeated more often — vertical or horizontal? What would happen if harmony had not been used?

▲ **Figure 6–6   How does texture and choice of color contribute to the realism in this painting? How do the shapes display proportion? Is there any movement in the painting? Where?**

El Greco. *Saint Martin and the Beggar*. 1597/1599. Canvas. 193.5 x 102.8 cm (76⅛ x 40½″). National Gallery of Art, Washington, D.C. Widener Collection.

• The imaginary vertical line dividing the picture in half leads the viewer's eye directly to a single round shape. Can you find this shape? What else is done to emphasize the shape?

106   ▨   Lesson 3   *Analyzing Art Works*

Background Information

St. Martin of Tours, who lived from 315 to 397 B.C., was a preacher and the founder of the earliest French monasteries. He is often pictured cutting his cloak in half. These images refer to an event that took place when Martin was a Roman soldier serving in Gaul. Encountering a poor man suffering in the cold weather, Martin divided his cloak and gave part to the man. That night, Martin had a dream in which Christ appeared wearing the cloth that Martin had given away.

▲ **Figure 6–7 (left) and Figure 6–8 (right)** What kind of balance is displayed on the left? What other technique did the artist use to emphasize the head of St. Martin?

El Greco. *Saint Martin and the Beggar.* 1597/1599. Canvas. 193.5 x 102.8 cm (76⅛ x 40½"). National Gallery of Art, Washington, D.C. Widener Collection.

STUDIO EXPERIENCE

Look back at Figure 6–4 on page **104**. Notice that the line of Saint George's lance leads the viewer's eye to the dragon. An imaginary line following the gaze of the saint also directs attention to the dragon. Look through a sports magazine for a photograph that shows action. Do a rough pencil sketch of the action scene. In your sketch, include lines that would lead a viewer's eye from one part of the scene to another. Your lines may be real (for example, the outstretched arm of a football player) or imaginary. Share your sketch with your classmates. See if your viewers can trace the lines in your sketch with their fingers.

- Many of the lines are used to direct the viewer's eye from one important point to another. Notice that one of the lines begins at the left side of the picture at the corner of St. Martin's cloak. It carries the eye upward, first to the head of the saint and then to the head of the beggar. (See Figure 6–8.)

You can use this same process for analyzing non-objective works. Look at the non-objective painting in Figure 6–9. Develop a design chart, and point out how the artist has used balance, variety, harmony, and the other principles to organize the elements in the painting.

✔CHECK YOUR UNDERSTANDING

1. What is the second step in art criticism?
2. What does an art critic do in the analysis stage of art criticism?
3. Why is a design chart helpful during analysis?

▲ **Figure 6–9** Which hues are used for balance? Which ones for emphasis? Do they overlap? Which element provides harmony? Does it also add movement?

Milton Resnick. *Genie.* 1959. Oil on canvas. 264.2 x 177.8 cm (104 x 70"). Whitney Museum of American Art, New York, New York.

Developing Concepts

Using Art Criticism. Discuss the design principles of the Roman suit of armor pictured in Figure 6-6. Ask students how the line, balance, texture, and emphasis combine to present St. Martin's garb. Compare this outfit to that of other dress styles, such as a flowing and ruffled dress, jeans and a tee shirt, and a black leather motorcycle outfit. Ask: How does the design of each garment influence the way its wearer is perceived? If possible, bring in examples of the different garments.

Developing Studio Skills. Provide students with cameras and have them each select a site and take five shots of it from different angles and distances. After the film has been developed and printed, have students compare the different arrangements and write a few paragraphs on how the compositional elements differ in each view. Their essays should also comment on which composition was the most effective.

Following Up

Closure. Review the first two steps of art criticism. Make sure that students understand the difference between description and analysis.

Evaluation. 1. Review students' written responses to the "Check Your Understanding" questions. 2. Evaluate student essays comparing different photographic compositions.

Reteaching. Print advertisements often demonstrate a highly sophisticated understanding of design principles. Have students examine full page ads in popular magazines. Ask the students to identify how the principles of art are used in each layout.

Enrichment. Invite someone versed in the art of Japanese flower arrangement to visit your class. Have him or her discuss the formal design principles involved in Japanese flower arrangement. If possible, have examples of both Japanese and North American floral arrangements so that students can appreciate the vast formal differences between the two aesthetic views.

Note

The Dover Pictorial Archive Series, published by Dover Publications, is an excellent source of material on two-dimensional, abstract design. The books are well-researched, the material is copyright free, and each book in the series is a quite inexpensive but well-bound paperback edition. The series is being expanded every year and already includes books on Japanese, Arab, African, Chinese, Pueblo, Pre-Columbian, Coptic, Hopi, and Celtic design, among other design traditions.

Answers to "Check Your Understanding"

1. The second step in art criticism is analyzing the work of art.
2. In the analysis stage an art critic notes how the principles of art are used to organize the elements of color, line, texture, shape, form, and space.
3. A design chart is helpful because it suggests a design question about each element in terms of each principle.

Interpreting Art Works

No two people see things exactly the same way. One person looks at a glass of water and sees it as half empty. Another person looks at the same glass and sees it as half full. What appears to be orange to you may look red to someone else.

People may, and often do, argue over their different views, or interpretations. In art, it is not unusual for two people to have different interpretations of the same art work. Since each interpretation can be based on different things found in the work, both can be right. When people share their opinions with other people, they learn something new about the work.

Interpreting is the third stage of art criticism. For the art critic, **interpreting** is *determining and explaining the meaning, mood, or idea of the work of art.* You will find that interpreting is the most exciting and creative part of art criticism.

INTERPRETING ART WORKS

When you interpret a work of art, you ask yourself two questions. One is "What do I believe is happening?" The other is "What idea, mood, or feeling does it suggest?"

Interpreting makes use of the facts and clues you gathered in the first two steps of criticism. But it also relies heavily on your ability to think things through and use your imagination. What you have done and seen in your life can also be important to your interpretation.

Look back at the painting in Figure 6–1 on page **101**. The artist has placed two people in the foreground. In step two of art criticism, a critic might have speculated this was done to emphasize these people. Now, in step three, the critic would ask questions that begin with who, what, where, when, why, or how. The answers to these questions help the critic arrive at an interpretation of the work.

INTERPRETING OBJECTIVE ART WORKS

Look at the child in the painting more closely (Figure 6–10). You be the critic. Who would you guess she is? How old would you suppose she is? What would you guess her feelings are? What clues can you find in the details to back up your theory?

Next, look back at the whole painting (Figure 6–1) on page **101**. Where is the woman looking? What does she seem to be looking at? (To answer this question, follow the line of her eye.) What is her expression?

Having answered these questions, a critic might give the following interpretation:

• The little girl in the work could be the daughter of the woman. (The woman is the right age to be the child's mother. They are in a bedroom of a house. The mother is looking fondly at the child.)
• The child is aglow with anticipation. (She looks as though she has just run in the house to tell her mother something.)
• She is carrying a ball and her cheeks are flushed. (She has been playing outside.)
• The background shows green trees and bushes in bloom. (A clue to the time of year, making it seem even more possible that the child has been playing outside.)
• The house is well-furnished and clean. The mother and child are well-dressed. (This indicates a certain level of social and economic status.)

In order to reach these conclusions, the critic would have to know about the customs and the way people lived in that period of history. Knowing clothing and architectural styles would also be important for interpreting art works.

◄ Figure 6–10   A subject's clothes can indicate what period in history they are a part of, and often where they lived. What do the girl's clothes tell you about her?

Pieter de Hooch. *The Bedroom*. c. 1660. Canvas. (Detail.) 50.8 x 59.7 cm (20 x 23½"). National Gallery of Art, Washington, D.C. Widener Collection.

INTERPRETING NON-OBJECTIVE ART WORKS

Pictures without subjects can also express ideas and feelings. Look at the painting in Figure 6–9 on page 107. Notice how the overall pattern of lines and splashes of color creates a feeling of action and excitement in Milton Resnick's painting. Compare this with the feeling of calm stillness in the non-objective painting in Figure 6–3.

✔ CHECK YOUR UNDERSTANDING

1. Define interpreting, as the term is used in art criticism.
2. What two questions do you ask yourself when you interpret a work?
3. Name three different sources of information a critic might use in an interpretation of an art work.
4. What words identify the six questions critics try to answer when interpreting a work of art?

Developing Concepts
Developing Studio Skills. Have the students use markers and magazine illustrations to create a composition that subtly expresses a single message or emotion. Glue the torn shapes on paper and use the markers to enhance or obscure parts of the composition. See if classmates can determine its intended message. Discuss why art critics may not always interpret an art work in the way that the artist had in mind.

Appreciating Cultural Diversity. Explain to students that it is easy to misinterpret or dislike art from another culture if that culture's aesthetic views are unfamiliar. For example, the smiles found on Cameroon figurative sculptures don't represent happiness—they are a convention that is meant to give the statue a sense of life. Have students find pictures of Cameroon or other Ivory Coast art. Brainstorm a list of things that an art critic would need to know before interpreting it.

Following Up
Closure. Have students state what they think is the most important clue leading to an interpretation of Figure 6-1 on page **101**. Have students explain their reasons.

Evaluation. 1. Review students' written responses to the "Check Your Understanding" questions. 2. Evaluate students' contributions to discussions on interpretation and African art.

Reteaching. Have students show Figure 6-1 on page **101** to three people outside of class and find out what they think the painting means. Then have students write two or three sentences that summarize what each person said. Compare the results. Did the interpretations differ? Were the differences related to any particular factor, such as the age or gender of the respondent?

Enrichment. Have students read short art reviews that you have gathered from local newspapers or national magazines such as *Art In America, ArtNews, New Art Examiner, Arts,* and *Artforum.* Select the simplest and most clearly written examples and, if possible, choose reviews that are accompanied by an illustration of the art under discussion. Have the students try to identify the first three steps of art criticism in each review.

LESSON PLAN
(pages 110–111)

Objectives
After completing this lesson, students will be able to:
- Describe, analyze, and interpret a seascape.
- Create a seascape that expresses a particular mood.

Supplies
- Pencils and notepads.
- Sketch paper and sheets of rough sandpaper, 10 x 12 inches (25 x 30 cm).
- Colored chalk.
- Simple still life or diorama.
- Several hand-held light sources, such as flashlights.
- Several colored gels.

TEACHING THE LESSON

Getting Started
Motivator. Tell students how Albert Pinkham Ryder attended an opera performance and was so caught up in its mood that he went home and excitedly painted for a 48-hour stretch without food or sleep. Ask your students to describe times when they have been possessed with a strong emotion that they directed toward creative expression.

Exploring Aesthetics. Ask students to identify the sources of lighting in Figure 6-1 on page **101** and Figure 6-11. Discuss the expressive quality of de Hooch's and Ryder's lighting. Set up a simple still life or diorama. Darken the room and demonstrate how different degrees and angles of illumination can dramatically change the mood of a subject. Use colored gels to demonstrate the effects of different colors of light.

110

Mood Chalk Painting

Look at the work in Figure 6–11. This seascape, or painting of the sea, was done by the American artist Albert Pinkham Ryder. Notice that the work is made up of simple shapes and few colors. No object is clearly shown. There is hardly any detail. Yet the quiet, calm mood of this moonlit scene is almost impossible to miss.

WHAT YOU WILL LEARN
You will use colored chalk to create another version of the seascape in Figure 6–11. Your version will include simple shapes of sailboats, the sea, the moon, and clouds. Repeat some of these shapes throughout the work to give it harmony. Your seascape, too, will fo-

cus mainly on mood. Yours, however, will express a mood opposite that of the original. Look at Figure 6–12 to see how a student captured an opposite mood from the original painting (Figure 6–11). You will choose four colors that help capture that mood. Repeating these colors will also add harmony to your work.

WHAT YOU WILL NEED
- Pencil
- Notepad
- Sketch paper
- Sheet of rough sandpaper, 10 x 12 inch (25 x 30 cm)
- Colored chalk

▶ **Figure 6–11 The artist who did this work lived as a hermit in New York City and only went out at night. He painted mostly from his imagination.**

Albert Pinkham Ryder. *The Toilers of the Sea.* 1880s. Oil on wood. 29.2 x 30.5 cm (11½ x 12"). The Metropolitan Museum of Art, New York, New York. George A. Hearn Fund.

Background Information
Albert Pinkham Ryder (United States, 1847–1917) was born in New Bedford, Massachusetts when it was still a thriving fishing port. When he was a young man, his family moved to New York City, where an older brother helped pay his expenses to art school. At first Ryder lived in Greenwich Village, but later he moved to a humble rooming house on the city's West Side. There he slept beneath piles of old overcoats on a floor littered with stacks of newspapers, empty cans, and other trash.

Troubled with poor eyesight, he remained indoors during the day and roamed the streets of the city alone at night. Passersby must have wondered about the big bearded man dressed in tattered clothing, especially when they observed him staring for long periods of time at the moon. Perhaps, during those walks alone down dark city streets, ideas formed which Ryder eventually expressed in his paintings.

WHAT YOU WILL DO

1. After looking at Ryder's seascape in Figure 6–11, brainstorm with your classmates to come up with words meaning the opposite of quiet and calm. Two possibilities are stormy and rough. Try to come up with at least four more words. Write these on your notepad.
2. On a sheet of sketch paper, lightly draw shapes of sailboats, the sea, the moon, and clouds. Keep your shapes simple, like those in Figure 6–11. Add no details beyond those in the original work.
3. Review the list of terms you copied. Think of colors that capture the mood expressed by these terms. Write the names of four of these colors on your notepad. Look back at your sketch. Think of changes you could make in line and shape that would help express the new mood. Make those changes. Again, do not add any new objects or details.
4. Transfer your sketch to the sandpaper. Color in your shapes with the four colors of chalk you chose. Limiting your colors to four will help add harmony to your work.
5. Compare your finished seascape with those of your classmates. Can you guess the mood of each work? Which most successfully expressed a mood?

━━━━━━━━━ **SAFETY TIP** ━━━━━━━━━

Chalk, which creates dust, should be used in a room with good ventilation. Those with breathing problems should wear a dust mask or avoid using chalk altogether. Crayon or oil pastels can be used instead.

OTHER STUDIO IDEAS

- Create another mood seascape. This time, lightly wet the sandpaper before applying color. Explain what difference this technique makes in the look of the work.

EXAMINING YOUR WORK

- **Describe**   Point out the shapes of sailboats, the sea, the moon, and clouds in your work. Tell whether you added shapes and details that were not in the original. Identify the four colors you chose. Explain how you used colored chalk to obtain different effects in your work.
- **Analyze**   Explain how your use of the same simple shapes in your work gives it a feeling of harmony. Tell how your use of four colors repeated throughout the work added to the feeling of harmony.
- **Interpret**   Tell what mood your work communicates to the viewer. Explain what you did to communicate a mood opposite that communicated by Ryder's painting.

━━━━━━━━━━━

▲ **Figure 6–12   Student work. A mood chalk painting.**

- ●● Create a city skyline using chalk on sandpaper. Decide what objects you will need to include. The work should be made up of simple shapes and colors. It should also express the same mood found in Figure 6–11.

Lesson 5   *Mood Chalk Painting*   **111**

Note
Sandpaper is less expensive when purchased by the box. Since it is rarely sold in boxes, you will need to go to a store that specializes in woodworking equipment or order it from a company that advertises in periodicals such as *Fine Woodworking.* So-called 220 grit sandpaper will disintegrate if it gets too wet, but you can also purchase a black "wet-dry" sandpaper. A low-cost alternative would be to place a sheet of ditto paper over sandpaper and clip it with paperclips.

LESSON PLAN
(pages 112–113)

Objectives
After completing this lesson, students will be able to:
• Describe three aesthetic views.
• Understand the steps involved in judging fine art and applied art.

Supplies
• A variety of examples of applied art.

TRB Resources
• 6-5 *Art Form,* (appreciating cultural diversity)
• 6-6 *The Class Critic,* (cooperative learning)
• 6-7 *Richard Estes,* (artist profile)

TEACHING THE LESSON

Getting Started
Motivator. Ask students to consider the aesthetic qualities of their school building. If necessary, take a walk and view the building's exterior from all sides. Then have students assess the school's architecture. How might the building's design be altered to improve its appearance or function?

Vocabulary. Show the class a broad range of examples of *applied art,* such as textiles, flatware, ceramics, jewelry, and well-designed consumer goods. Discuss with the class how each item can be considered and judged as an art work. Ask the students to think of other examples of applied art.

LESSON 6

Judging Art Works

It is the responsibility of every judge to be fair and open-minded. This is true of judges who rule over courts of law. And it is equally true of critics who judge works of art. Neither type of judge would ever hand down a ruling without first looking at all the facts. Neither would ever pass judgment without giving reasons.

In this lesson you will learn what goes into the final step of art criticism, judging.

JUDGING ART WORKS

When you judge a work of art, you ask yourself two questions. The first of these is: "Is this a good or successful work?" The second is: "Why is it good or successful?" **Judging** means *making a decision about a work's success or lack of success and giving reasons to support that decision.*

Ways of Judging a Work

Do you remember the three aesthetic views on art that you learned about in Chapter 2? Some art scholars, you will recall, feel art should imitate the real world. For them, a work succeeds if it looks real.

Others believe that what is most important about a piece of art is its composition. For them, a work succeeds if the artist has used the principles of art to combine the elements of art into an interesting whole.

Still others hold that what counts most is the mood or feeling a work expresses. For them, a work succeeds if the viewer shares this feeling or mood when seeing it.

The judgment that an art critic makes will depend on the aesthetic view he or she accepts. Look at the painting of the telephone booths (Figure 6–13). A critic from the first aesthetic view might praise the work because it is true to life. A critic from the second aesthetic view might admire the work for the

► **Figure 6–13   Would you consider this painting successful? Why or why not?**

Richard Estes. *Telephone Booths.* 1968. Oil on canvas. 121.9 x 175.3 cm (48 x 69"). Allan Stone Galleries, New York. Tissean-Bornemisza.

Cooperative Learning
Have the students write down which local building they think is most impressive. Have them pass the sheets to you so you can list the buildings on the board. Was one building mentioned more frequently? What characteristics made students identify this building and think it was impressive? Select several of the buildings and have groups of students choose one of them to visit and write a study of it based on the four steps of art criticism. Later, have the groups present their findings. Encourage the students to include slides, photos, and drawings as part of their presentations. Now ask everyone to list on separate sheets the building they believe is most impressive. Does this list differ from the first one? If some students selected different buildings, what made them change their minds? Was there agreement on a single building, or was the class divided?

way the artist has created visual movement through the repetition of lines, shapes and color. A critic from the third aesthetic view might say the painting captures the existing mood of a busy city.

Not all critics limit themselves to one view of art. Many feel that accepting a single view carries the risk of missing some exciting discoveries. If a person accepts all three views, what judgments might he or she make about the sculpture in Figure 6–14? How would you personally judge the work?

JUDGING APPLIED ART

Art criticism can be applied to the study of all areas of art, not just paintings, sculptures, and other kinds of fine art. One other area that can be, and often is studied, is applied art. You may recall that **applied art** is *art made to be functional, as well as visually pleasing.* Designing details for jewelry or making decorative furniture are examples of applied art.

▲ **Figure 6–15** Does the chair's appearance make you want to sit in it? Why or why not?

Verner Panton. *Stacking Side Chair.* 1967. PU-foam Baydur. 83.6 x 48.9 x 59.7 cm (32⅝ x 19¼ x 23½"). Museum of Modern Art, New York, New York. Gift of Herman Miller AG.

In using art criticism for works of applied art, critics use the same four steps: describing, analyzing, interpreting, and judging. At the final step, however, the rules change. The critic no longer evaluates a work purely in terms of its appearance. It must also be judged on how well the work does its job. A chair may look beautiful, but if it is uncomfortable to sit in, it is not successful. (See Figure 6–15.)

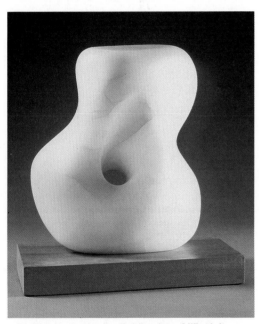

▲ **Figure 6–14** Is this a "realistic" sculpture? What is its visual texture? What images does it evoke in your mind?

Barbara Hepworth. *Merryn.* 1962. Alabaster. 33.0 x 29.2 x 20.3 cm (13 x 11½ x 8"). National Museum of Women in the Arts, Washington, D.C. Wallace & Wilhelmina Holladay.

✔CHECK YOUR UNDERSTANDING

1. Define *judging*, as the term is used in art criticism.
2. What two questions do you ask yourself when you judge a work?
3. Describe briefly the three ways a critic can aesthetically view an art work.

Lesson 6 *Judging Art Works* 📖 **113**

Developing Concepts

Understanding Art History. Explain to students that Richard Estes was one of a number of American painters who worked in the Photo Realist style, which began around 1963. Have groups of students investigate other Photo Realist painters, such as Don Eddy, Audrey Flack, Alfred Leslie, Malcolm Morley, and Janet Fish. Ask the groups to present to the class basic information on their chosen artist and a critical review of one work by that artist.

Appreciating Cultural Diversity. Present to students examples of Tibetan mandala paintings, statues of the Buddha, and Japanese paintings or other Asian art works. Have students write a short review of any one of these works. Then have the students read about the aesthetic views of the culture that produced the art work. Ask them to write a paragraph on how an increased understanding of Asian aesthetics changed their view of the art work.

Following Up

Closure. Have students briefly state to the class what they think is most important in a work of art. Is there one aesthetic view that best expresses their outlook on art?

Evaluation. 1. Review students' written responses to the "Check Your Understanding" questions. 2. Evaluate student presentations on Photo Realist painters. 3. Assess student paragraphs on an Asian art work.

Reteaching. Have students select a studio project that they completed in this class and write a short art critical review of it. Have them clearly label the four steps of art criticism in their review.

Enrichment. Invite an industrial designer to speak to the class about how he or she evaluates the design of goods that are being considered for mass production. Make sure the designer discusses how he or she balances the cost considerations, consumer preferences, functionalism, and aesthetic appeal of a potential product. Try to find a designer who works for a company that produces goods used by the age group of your students.

Background Information

Verner Panton's stacking chair was the first plastic chair that consists of a single form, bearing a strong resemblance to Gerrit Rietveld's 1934 Zig-zag chair. Panton's design is both comfortable and structurally strong. Its fluidity of line and the somewhat disconcerting way in which it emerges out of the floor is slightly reminiscent of Art Nouveau forms. Panton's chair takes advantage of advances in plastics and mold-forming technology.

Answers to "Check Your Understanding"

1. *Judging* means deciding about a work's success or lack of success and giving reasons to support that decision.
2. When you judge a work of art, you ask yourself these questions: Is this a successful work? Why is it successful?
3. A critic may feel that a work of art should imitate what we see in the real world, that the most important aspect of a work is its composition, or that the mood or feeling expressed is the most important aspect of a work.

Using Art Criticism

LESSON 7

Using Art Criticism

You have probably heard it said that experience is the best teacher. In this lesson you will discover the truth behind that saying. You will have the experience of using all four steps of art criticism on a single work.

The work you will criticize is the painting in Figure 6–16. Its title is *Christina's World*, and it was painted by an American artist, Andrew Wyeth.

DESCRIBING THE WORK

First, notice the size of the work and its medium. Try to imagine the full-size painting as it would look if it were in front of you right now. How might that affect the way you see the work?

Next, study the painting carefully. On a sheet of paper, write down every fact and detail you see. Use the following questions as a guide:

Subject

- What details about the girl's dress can you note?
- How would you describe the color and fabric of the girl's dress?
- Look at the folds in the dress. What do they tell you?
- Describe the color of the girl's belt.
- Look at the girl's hairdo. Notice the detail with which each hair is shown.
- Look closely at the girl's legs. What color are they? Is the color the same as that of her arms?
- Do you notice anything unusual about her arms or hands? Where is her left hand positioned?
- Look closely at the girl's posture. Where is all her weight resting?

Foreground

- Describe the girl's surroundings.
- In what direction do the blades of grass bend?
- How is the area where the girl is sitting different from the top of the hill?
- Describe the road.

Background

- How many buildings do you see and of what are they made?
- What facts can you gather from the background and grass? What colors are they?
- How are the buildings different?
- What color are the buildings? Do they look well-kept?
- How many chimneys do you see? Is there any smoke coming out of them?
- Do all the windows look the same?
- What color is the sky? How much of the picture is sky and how much is ground?
- What point of view do you think the artist is giving the viewer?

Design Elements

- What kinds of lines has the artist used for the buildings and for the line between the ground and sky?
- What lines are used for the girl?
- Describe the texture of the girl's dress, the grass, and the buildings?
- What kinds of colors do you see?

Try not to make guesses about the meaning of this work. Save your clues for later use.

LESSON PLAN
(pages 114–115)

Objectives

After completing this lesson, students will be able to:
- Use their knowledge of art criticism to describe, interpret, and judge *Christina's World* by Andrew Wyeth.
- Apply their knowledge of art criticism in a related design activity.

Supplies

- Construction paper in various colors.
- Magazines, scissors, and white glue.
- Large sheets of white paper.

> **TRB Resources**
> - 6-8 *The Influence of Primitive Art*, (studio)
> - 6-9 *An Interview with an Art Critic*, (reproducible master)

TEACHING THE LESSON

Getting Started

Motivator. Have students examine Figure 6-16. Encourage them to enter imaginatively into Christina's experience. If possible, have students sit on the floor or outdoors and imitate Christina's exact posture. Have students share how they feel in that position, and discuss what thoughts Christina may be having. Write this information on the board to use later in the class's interpretation of *Christina's World*.

Developing Concepts

Using Art Criticism. Have each student show Figure 6-16 to three people and ask them whether they like the work or not and why they like or dislike it. Students should classify their answers according to the three aesthetic views. Discuss the results in class. Was one of the theories preferred by most people or by a particular subgroup of those interviewed?

114

Background Information
Born in Chadds Ford, Pennsylvania, Andrew Wyeth gained a knowledge and appreciation of art and draftsmanship from his father N. C. Wyeth. Because Wyeth was born during World War I, some of his childhood memories are stories of war. He experienced the Depression, which was followed by World War II. All of these events must have had a sobering effect on the artist, but none affected him as much as the death of his father in 1945, after which he turned to art with greater seri-ousness. Wyeth spends winters in Chadds Ford and summers in Maine. In these familiar locales, he finds and paints his subjects, all of whom he knows well, in a realistic manner. Sometimes he expresses their character by painting the objects that are a part of their lives. Other times he creates an atmosphere that tells a great deal about the person. He does this by simplifying details until he finds those that reveal the most. Wyeth also often uses an unusual perspective and strong light to express a sense of his subject.

◄ **Figure 6–16 The vast area of grass is essential to the mood of the painting. Why? Where is the emphasis? Do you feel a sense of urgency?**

Andrew Wyeth. *Christina's World*. 1948. Tempera on gessoed panel. 81.9 x 121.3 cm (32¼ x 47¾"). Museum of Modern Art, New York, New York.

ANALYZING THE WORK

What kind of balance has the artist used? What has been done to give the work variety? How is harmony achieved? Is anything in the painting emphasized? If so, what?

How does the artist control the way your eyes move through the work? Hold a ruler along the left slope of the roof on the biggest building. Where does the line lead your eye? Does the artist use accurate proportion to represent objects?

INTERPRETING THE WORK

Reread the clues you have gathered. What might the artist be telling you about the girl and about the world she lives in? When you imagined yourself in the girl's pose, did you feel the weight on your arms? Were your legs carrying your weight?

Why do you think the artist includes such a large area of ground in the work? Why has he shown separate blades of grass? How do you think the girl feels? Why do you think she feels this way? Whose house is it?

Do you think the title is appropriate? How does it help you interpret this work? Can you think of several adjectives that describe this work? What title would you give it?

JUDGING THE WORK

Tell whether the painting succeeds. Give the reasons why you feel as you do. Does the painting make you think? Why, or why not? Does it succeed in one of the following ways?

- It is lifelike.
- It uses the elements and principles to create an unusually interesting whole.
- It communicates a feeling or mood to the viewer.

Does the work succeed in more than one of these ways? Which ones? Explain your answer.

✔CHECK YOUR UNDERSTANDING

1. List the four steps of art criticism.
2. List the three ways a critic could aesthetically view *Christina's World*.

Developing Studio Skills. Point out to students that Andrew Wyeth's painting expresses Christina's yearning to be back in her home. Have students think of something that they yearn for that is out of reach at this time and create a design using abstract shapes or magazine cutouts that includes the student and his or her dream. Students should use the shapes and the negative space to show the relationship between themselves and their dreams. Is their dream within grasp, above them, or beyond their reach?

Following Up

Closure. Have each student briefly state whether *Christina's World* is a painting that they would like to have on their wall at home. Do they identify with Christina in any way or does her condition and experience seem entirely foreign?

Evaluation. 1. Review students' written responses to the "Check Your Understanding" questions. 2. Assess students' ability to categorize peoples' comments on an art work according to the three aesthetic views.

Reteaching. Have students use the four steps of art criticism to study one of their favorite possessions. Ask them to write down whether this process changed their perception of that object and explain in what way.

Enrichment. Have students write a critical review of a chair. They may select a chair in their environment or base their discussion on a picture of a chair seen in a home furnishings or interior design magazine. Then have the students compare their experiences of critiquing Wyeth's painting and critiquing a chair. Is it easier to apply the four steps of art criticism to fine art than to applied art?

Background Information
Christina Olson, the subject of Figure 6-16, was a friend of the Wyeth family. Christina was disabled from polio, and her legs were paralyzed. One day Wyeth saw her out in the field gathering vegetables. She pulled herself back to the house with her arms. The memory of what Wyeth saw haunted him and he had to paint it. Because he was afraid to ask Christina to pose, Wyeth's wife modeled instead to help him get the position right.

Answers to "Check Your Understanding"
1. The four steps of art criticism are describing the work, analyzing the work, interpreting the work, and judging the work.
2. A critic would ask these three questions: Is the work lifelike? Does the work use the elements and principles of art to create an unusually interesting whole? Does the work communicate a feeling or idea to the viewer?

ANSWERS TO "CHAPTER 6 REVIEW"

Building Vocabulary

1. art criticism
2. art critic
3. describing
4. non-objective art
5. analyzing
6. interpreting
7. judging
8. applied art

Reviewing Art Facts

9. The four steps in art criticism are describing the art work, analyzing it, interpreting it, and judging it.
10. In describing an art work, you also describe the size of the work, the medium and process used, and the elements of art used. (Students may identify any two of these.)
11. In a credit line, the height of the work is given first.
12. The second step of art criticism, analyzing, answers the question "How is the work organized?"
13. A design chart comes in handy during the analyzing stage of art criticism. A design chart suggests a design question about each visual element in terms of each principle of art.

Thinking About Art

1. Responses will vary. Students should recognize that Figure 6-3 is a non-objective work and thus it should be considered in terms of its composition or perhaps its content.
2. Responses will vary; they should show students understand that size and medium can affect the impact—and thus the content—of a work.
3. Responses will vary; they should indicate an understanding of the importance of description within the process of criticism and an understanding of individual differences even among trained critics.
4. Responses will vary; they should show that students understand that critics may have different aesthetic views and that individual differences may affect the interpretations and judgments critics make.

CHAPTER 6 REVIEW

BUILDING VOCABULARY

Number a sheet of paper from 1 to 8. After each number, write the term from the box that best matches each description below.

analyzing	describing
applied art	interpreting
art critic	judging
art criticism	non-objective art

1. The process of studying, understanding, and judging works of art.
2. One who practices the four steps in art criticism.
3. Making a careful list of all the things you see in a work of art.
4. A work with no objects or subjects that can be readily identified.
5. Noting how the principles in a work are used to organize the elements.
6. Explaining the meaning or mood expressed by an art work.
7. Telling if and why a work of art succeeds or fails.
8. Art made to be functional as well as visually pleasing.

REVIEWING ART FACTS

Number a sheet of paper from 9 to 13. Answer each question in a complete sentence.

9. Name the four steps of art criticism.
10. In addition to describing the people, objects, and events shown in a work of art, name two other things you could identify in a description.
11. In a credit line, which is given first—the height of a work or the width?
12. Which step of art criticism answers the question "How is the work organized?"
13. In which part of art criticism does a design chart come in handy? Briefly tell how it is used.

THINKING ABOUT ART

On a sheet of paper, answer each question in a sentence or two.

1. **Analyze.** Look at Figure 6–3 on page **102**. Which aesthetic view would you use when judging this work? Explain your answer.
2. **Analyze.** Why do you think it might be important to take the size of a work into account in a criticism? Why might the medium be important?
3. **Extend.** What problems could arise if one critic used another's description in his or her criticism of a work?
4. **Interpret.** Explain how two critics using the same four steps could come up with different interpretations and judgments of a work.

MAKING ART CONNECTIONS

1. **Social Studies.** The works of Andrew Wyeth (Figure 6–16) and Milton Resnick (Figure 6–9) were produced only 11 years apart, yet they are very different from each other. Investigate this period in history to determine how each artist's work may have been influenced by current events.
2. **Language Arts.** Select an object from nature. Look at it closely and write a description of the object as if you were describing a work of art. Use each element and principle of art at least once in your description. Try reading your description to a classmate without telling what it is you are describing. Have your classmate draw the object as you describe it.
3. **Social Studies.** Use a world map to locate where each of the artists in the chapter lived. Tell when they lived and what was happening in the world at that time.

LOOKING AT THE DETAILS

The detail shown below is from Berthe Morisot's *In the Dining Room*. Study the detail and answer the following questions.

1. Describe the objects you see here. What do the surroundings tell you about the young woman?
2. Examine Morisot's brush strokes and use of color. How would you describe the artist's style?
3. Is the artist successful in creating a mood? If so explain what kind of mood you sense.
4. In interpreting the work, you may want to know where this woman lives. Does this detail assist you in answering that question? Why?

Berthe Morisot. *In the Dining Room*. 1886. Canvas. (Detail.) 61.3 x 50.0 cm (24⅛ x 19¾"). National Gallery of Art, Washington, D.C. Chester Dale Collection.

Chapter Evaluation

The goal of this chapter is to have students understand the process of art criticism and to apply the four steps of art criticism to their own works of art. Possible methods of evaluation include:

1. Divide the class into four groups with each group representing one of the four steps of art criticism: describing, analyzing, interpreting, and judging. Display one work of art and have each group apply their step of art criticism to the work of art.
2. Have students apply the four steps of art criticism to one of their completed student art works.
3. Distribute the Chapter 6 Test (TRB, Resource 6-10).

Art History and You

Chapter Scan

Lesson 1 Describing—Who, When, and Where
Lesson 2 Making a Mixed Media Self-Portrait
Lesson 3 Analyzing Artistic Style
Lesson 4 Painting in the Fauve Style
Lesson 5 Interpreting Time and Place
Lesson 6 Time and Place Collage
Lesson 7 Judging Historical Importance

TRB Resources

- 7-9 Chapter Test
- Color Transparency 13
- Color Transparency 14

TEACHING THE CHAPTER

Introducing the Art Work

Direct students' attention to Pablo Picasso's *Three Musicians.* Inform students that Pablo Picasso was a dominant figure in the art world during most of the twentieth century. Picasso was born on the southern coast of Spain and had extraordinary talent in painting, drawing, sculpture, graphics, and ceramics. At the age of 19, Picasso went to Paris to study art styles and to experiment with the techniques of other artists. By the time he was 24 years old, Picasso was a successful artist. Instead of continuing to paint and sell his popular paintings of tranquil scenes, he created a style that revolutionized the art world—Cubism. Picasso's work was not only daring for his time but also shocking to those who saw it because this style shattered almost every perception of Western painting known up until that time. Picasso created an entirely new approach to art.

▲ What objects or elements does the artist emphasize in this work? What elements does he use to bring harmony to the work?

Pablo Picasso. *Three Musicians.* 1921. Oil on canvas. 200.7 x 222.9 cm (6'7 x 7'3¾"). Museum of Modern Art, New York. Mrs. Simon Guggenheim Fund.

Art History and You

As you have seen, you can discover a lot by looking closely at works of art. When you look at the painting on the left, what do you see? You might notice the geometric angles. You might also comment on the use of line and color.

As you look at art works, you may also have questions. For example, you may wonder whether the work is similar to others done around the same time. You may ask who painted it and when. These questions are among many you will learn about in this chapter. These questions explore the whys, whens, and wheres of art.

OBJECTIVES

After completing this chapter, you will be able to:
- Define *art history*.
- Tell what is revealed through each of the four parts of the art historian's job.
- Define *style*.
- Tell how time and place influence a work of art.
- Create works of art in the styles of different art movements.

WORDS YOU WILL LEARN

analyzing	interpreting
art history	judging
art movement	Madonna
collage	Renaissance
describing	style
Fauves	

ARTISTS YOU WILL MEET

Georges Braque	Claude Monet
Jasper Francis Cropsey	Pablo Picasso
Edgar Degas	Raphael
André Derain	Pierre Auguste Renoir
Sir Jacob Epstein	Georges Seurat
Giotto	Élisabeth Vigée-
George Inness	Lebrun
Judith Leyster	Maurice de Vlaminck
Fra Filippo Lippi	Clarence H. White
Henri Matisse	

119

Examining the Art Work
Tell students that *Three Musicians* represents Picasso's developed Cubist style. Explain to students that in this work, as in many of his others, Picasso takes the human form apart, then puts it back together again in startling ways. Explain how the figures do not occupy a rational position in space, thus challenging the viewer's perspective. The perspective in this work is flat, and the bodies are fragmented with angular planes of color. Tell students that this work is both simple and complex at the same time. Although the figures have a flat quality, there is also a sense of depth, which Picasso achieves by creating several planes on top of each other. Point out how he creates different planes, not only by overlapping shapes but also in the way he uses color. Have students notice how the blue color allows the figure to the left and the sheet music to move one level up toward the viewer. Refer to the animal stretched out on the floor. Explain that the viewer gets the impression that the animal's back leg is one level underneath its body.

Discussing the Art Work
Ask students if they can identify the forms and what they are doing. Explain that Picasso's arrangement of shapes enables the viewer to identify his subject. He also uses familiar shapes—round for eyes, guitar, notes, mustache—in conjunction with unusual ones and unrealistic proportions to help the viewer understand the scene. His unusual sense of proportion is consistent, therefore more acceptable as a whole.

Tell students that in this chapter they will learn how art history influences a work of art and affects the way it is judged. They will also learn about different styles and art movements and create their own works in those styles.

Building Self-Esteem
Tell students that in Chapter 7 they will be learning about art history and how time and place affect an artist's choice of subject matter. Ask them to imagine being stranded on a desert island with only one other person. Of course, they would all like for the other person to be as handsome or beautiful as possible. But ask what *personality* characteristics they would hope to find in this person. Stress that the two of them would have to rely completely upon one another to survive. Tell them to discuss the personal qualities they value in others as well as those qualities they *do not* like in others. Ask if they possess the same qualities they value in others. Suggest they choose one quality they value and think about how they might develop it in themselves. Discuss what media might be used most effectively if they were to paint a desert island. What kinds of colors would they choose to emphasize the mood one would feel if stranded there.

LESSON 1

Describing— Who, When, and Where

LESSON PLAN
(pages 120–121)

Objectives
After completing this lesson students will be able to:
• Explain the goals of art history.
• Understand how art historians describe a work.
• Distinguish art history and art criticism.

Supplies
• Postcard reproductions of well-known art works.

> **TRB Resource**
> • 7-1 *Time/History Board Game*, (cooperative learning)

TEACHING THE LESSON

Getting Started

Motivator. Have students bring in a photograph of themselves. Discuss what someone might think about a person in a photograph if that were the only information available about the subject. Ask: What if a series of photographs were available that ranged from a person's infancy through adulthood? Point out to students that questions would still remain unanswered. Ask students how they could collect more information on the subject of a photo. Relate their responses to an art historian's use of interviews, letters, diaries, and knowledge of the culture in which an art work was made.

Vocabulary. Have students compare the activities of a historian with those of an art historian. List on the board the kinds of questions, documents, and objects that each uses.

Developing Concepts

Understanding Art History. Tell students that Renoir once said painting ". . . should be something pleasant, cheerful and pretty, yes pretty!" How might this information help an art historian confirm whether Renoir painted Figure 7-2? Ask students whether they can think of any artists who would not have described their goal this way.

120

Describing—Who, When, and Where

In a very real sense, no artist works totally alone. To understand any art work fully, you need to do more than just look at it. You need to look beyond it. You need to know when and where the work was done. You need to know something about the artist who did it. You need to know about his or her style of making art.

These and other kinds of information are the subject of art history. **Art history** is *the study of art from past to present*. Art history looks at changes that take place in the field of art over time. It also looks at differences in the way art is made from place to place. People who work in the field of art history are called *art historians*.

Like art critics, art historians use many different approaches when they study art. Art historians, however, go outside the art work for many of their clues. Their goal is not to learn *from* a work, as art critics do. Rather, it is to learn *about* a work.

▲ **Figure 7–1** This painting was originally done as an advertisement for the Delaware Lackawanna & Western Railroad. The artist was hired by the company's first president. Is it similar to advertisements you see today? Explain.

George Inness. *The Lackawanna Valley*. 1855. Canvas. 86.0 x 127.5 cm (33⅞ x 50¼"). National Gallery of Art, Washington, D.C. Gift of Mrs. Huttleston Rogers.

Background Information

George Inness was one of the best known American artists of the nineteenth century. Although he painted in a realist style, his two trips to Europe between 1850 and 1855 acquainted him with pictures by Jean-Baptiste-Camille Corot, and he learned to add a romantic touch to his otherwise realistic scenes. Inness's work, *The Lackawanna Valley*, reflects his romantic temperament, despite the intrusion of the railroad that must have caused him some discomfort to include in his landscape. The work reflects the tension between the growth of nineteenth-century industry and the serene beauty of the Pennsylvania countryside. Much to Inness's dismay, the railroad company president who had commissioned the work demanded that Inness include the four or five tracks that were expected to be built in the future, instead of the lone track that existed in 1855. After completing this prophetic picture of industry's advent, Inness developed a style that was even more romantic, and he omitted any allusions to the modern world.

ART HISTORY

In doing their jobs, art historians may use the same four-step system you read about in the last chapter. They describe, analyze, interpret, and then judge. As you will see, however, each of these terms has a different meaning to the art historian.

In this lesson, you will look at the first of these steps.

DESCRIBING A WORK

To art historians, **describing** is *telling who did a work, and when and where it was done.* Look at the painting in Figure 7–1. To begin, the art historian would look to see whether the artist had signed the work. Check the lower left corner. What name do you see there? Suppose the historian had never heard of G. Inness. He or she would then turn to an art history book. This source would reveal that George Inness was the name of two painters, a father and a son. It would also tell that both men lived and worked in America in the 1800s.

A little further exploration might turn up these facts:

- This painting was done by the father.
- It was painted in 1855.
- The painter was 30 years old at the time.
- He had studied landscape painting on his own in both America and Europe.

The historian might also come across this one especially interesting and important detail: George Inness had been taking formal art lessons for only one month when he began work on this picture.

Now it is your turn to be an art historian. Study the painting of the child with the watering can (Figure 7–2). But before you do, cover up the credit line with your hand.

Now can you identify the artist who painted this picture? Can you find his or her name on the work? It starts with the letter *R*.

▲ **Figure 7–2** Why do you suppose art historians are not lucky enough to have credit lines to help them?

Auguste Renoir. *A Girl with a Watering Can.* 1876. 100.3 x 73.0 cm (39½ x 28¾"). National Gallery of Art, Washington, D.C. Chester Dale Collection.

Can you make out the two numbers after the name? These are the last two figures of the year the work was painted. Where could you go to find out the artist's full name or to find out the century when this work was done? What other things would you try to find out?

✔CHECK YOUR UNDERSTANDING

1. What is art history?
2. What four steps do art historians use in their work?
3. Where might an art historian find details about an artist's life?

Making a Mixed Media Self-Portrait

Making a Mixed Media Self-Portrait

LESSON PLAN
(pages 122–123)

Objectives

After completing this lesson, students will be able to:
- Examine self-portraits for clues about the artist.
- Create a self-portrait that emphasizes the student's strongest personality trait.

Supplies

- Pencils and scrap paper.
- Sheets of white paper, 10 x 12 inches (25 x 30 cm).
- Found objects, such as buttons, string, yarn, stones, cardboard, feathers, ribbon, shells.
- Scissors and glue.
- Crayons, colored pencils, markers.
- Instamatic camera and film.
- Sketch paper.

> **TRB Resources**
> - 7-2 *Judith Leyster,*
>   (artist profile)
> - 7-3 *You, the Portrait Painter,*
>   (studio)

TEACHING THE LESSON

Getting Started

Motivator. Have students snap quick self-portraits with an instamatic camera. Make sure that students consider in advance the angle from which the shot is to be taken, the distance between subject and camera, and the facial expression that they wish to document. Have students write a short paragraph that explains their aesthetic choices and how well the result captures their personality. Explain that self-portraits can also be painted to reflect one's personality.

Developing Concepts

Using Art Criticism. Have students examine Figure 7-3 and write a short description of the artist's personality. Read some of the descriptions aloud and discuss how the art elements and principles are used to convey each personality trait.

As you study art history, you will find that many artists painted portraits of themselves. These portraits are called self-portraits. By studying self-portraits, you can find out what the artist looked like, what kind of personality the artist had, and something about when and where he or she lived.

Look at the painting below (Figure 7–3). What can you tell about the artist? When and where do you think she lived? How would you describe her personality? What other things in the picture give you insight into the artist's life?

▶ **Figure 7–3 How would you describe the personality of this woman? Identify things in the painting that tell you where she lived and when she painted.**

Judith Leyster. *Self-Portrait.* c. 1635. Canvas. 74.4 x 65.3 cm (29⅜ x 25⅝"). National Gallery of Art, Washington, D.C. Gift of Mr. & Mrs. Robert Woods Bliss.

Background Information

Judith Leyster (Netherlands, 1609–1660) is one of the few historical women artists who was not the daughter of an artist, the usual way for a woman to obtain art training that was otherwise very difficult to receive. She apprenticed at the studio of Frans Hals around 1629 and had become a member of the Haarlem guild of painters by 1633. Unusually versatile for a Dutch artist, who tended to specialize, Leyster executed portraits, still lifes, and flower paintings. Her most original and successful works, however, are scenes of domestic interiors. Leyster was painting pictures of the daily lives of women decades before such themes caught the attention of such painters as Pieter de Hooch and Nicolaes Maes. Nevertheless, after Leyster married the genre painter Jan Molenaer in 1636 her domestic responsibilities seem to have prevented her from devoting herself to painting with the same fervor. Her works dated from that period are few and of lesser quality than those executed between 1629 to 1635.

WHAT YOU WILL LEARN

In this lesson you will imagine you are a famous artist. You will create a self-portrait using mixed media. Your self-portrait can be realistic or abstract. You will organize colors, lines, shapes, and textures to depict your personality and interests. The self-portrait should identify when and where you live and what your interests are. You will use the principle of emphasis to call attention to your strongest personality trait.

WHAT YOU WILL NEED

- Pencil and scrap paper
- Sheet of white paper, 10 x 12 inch (25 x 30 cm)
- Found objects: buttons, string, yarn, stones, cardboard, feathers, ribbon, shells
- Scissors
- Glue
- Crayons, colored pencils, or markers

WHAT YOU WILL DO

1. On a sheet of scrap paper, write down some of your personality traits, such as outgoing, confident, shy, unpredictable, athletic, or boisterous. List traits that give you a distinctive personality.
2. Determine if you will make a realistic or an abstract self-portrait. Think about a point of emphasis in the self-portrait. For example, you may wish to emphasize your eyes because you have an expressive and warm personality. Your smile might be a point of emphasis if you have a happy, outgoing personality.
3. On another sheet of paper, if you're making a realistic portrait, sketch an outline of your face. You may use a side or front view. Think of lightweight found objects

EXAMINING YOUR WORK

- **Describe**   Explain how your portrait tells something about your appearance. Point to the objects that show when and where you live and what your interests are.
- **Analyze**   Identify whether the self-portrait is realistic or abstract. Explain how color, lines, shapes, and textures have been used to express your personality and interests. Explain how emphasis has been used to highlight your strongest personality trait.
- **Interpret**   Explain how a viewer might describe your personality and interests.
- **Judge**   Tell whether you feel your work succeeds. Explain your answers.

that can be added to the picture that represent when and where you live and your interests.
4. Choose your best sketch and transfer it to the sheet of white drawing paper. Your portrait may run off the edges of your paper if you wish.
5. Take found objects and arrange them on the paper so they tell the viewer more about you. Using a small amount of glue, attach them to the paper.
6. When the glue is dry, add colors, shapes and lines using crayons, colored pencils, or felt markers.
7. Share your finished work with your classmates.

OTHER STUDIO IDEAS

- Create a mixed media portrait of a favorite friend.

- ●● Create a mixed media portrait of a famous person, portraying some of the skills, events, or organizations the person is noted for.

Lesson 2   *Making a Mixed Media Self-Portrait*   **123**

Note
You may wish to discuss with students the special difficulties that art historians encounter when researching a female artist. For example, name changes associated with marriage make it difficult to trace a woman's name in various kinds of records, such as auction lists and censuses. Unscrupulous dealers, collectors, and art professionals have been known to obscure a woman's signature and replace it with a more prominent name. Women artists, who frequently obtained their training from their fathers or brothers, have had their work incorrectly attributed to those men. Those who apprenticed in an artist's studio, such as Judith Leyster, have also suffered a loss of recognition for their accomplishments. It was only after modern cleaning techniques revealed Leyster's characteristic signature and star that many paintings once credited to her teacher Frans Hals have been reattributed to Leyster.

LESSON PLAN
(pages 124–127)

Objectives

After completing this lesson, students will be able to:
• Define *style*.
• Understand how an art historian analyzes an art work.
• Describe the artistic style shared by the Fauves.

Supplies

• Pencils and sketch paper.
• Crayons, oil pastels, colored chalk.
• Similar objects manufactured in different styles, such as flatware.
• Several prints of paintings from a variety of art historical periods.
• Inexpensive reproduction of an Impressionist painting.

TRB Resource

• 7-4 *A War of Styles,*
  (art history)
• 7-5 *Looking at Style*
  (reproducible master)

TEACHING THE LESSON

Getting Started

Motivator. Have students analyze the artistic style of either their class notebook covers or the decor of their school lockers. Ask them to describe the style of these items, which reflect an aesthetic sensibility whether they are adorned or not. Ask students whether they can discern any similarities between the styles of different students' notebook covers or lockers. Relate such similarities to the stylistic closeness of members of an *art movement*.

Vocabulary. Guide the students to a working definition of *style*. Relate the everyday association of style and fashion to the text definition of style as a personal approach to using the art elements and the art principles as a method of expression. Ask students whether an art work can ever be said to lack a style.

Analyzing Artistic Style

No two people have exactly the same handwriting. Their writing styles may be similar, but one may use a slightly bigger loop on the *j*'s or cross the letter *t* using a line that is slightly longer.

The same is true of artists. Each artist works in a way that is at least slightly different from any other artist. These differences are the key to stage two of the art historian's job—analyzing.

ANALYZING A WORK

You will recall that in the describing stage the art historian looks for a signature on a work. Sometimes there is no signature. Sometimes the historian does not need one because the artist's style speaks as clearly as any signature. **Style** is *an artist's personal way of expressing ideas in a work.* You may remember that many times artists develop their style by studying the work of others. *Noting the style of a work,* or **analyzing**, is what the art historian does during the next stage.

▲ **Figure 7–4   How are lines and hues combined to show depth? How does the mood in this painting differ from the mood in Figure 7–5?**

Jasper Francis Cropsey. *Autumn on the Hudson River.* 1860. Canvas. 152.5 x 274.3 (60 x 108″).
National Gallery of Art, Washington, D.C. Gift of the Avalon Foundation.

Background Information
Art historians often struggle to discern the most basic information about an art work—who made it, when, and where. Artists such as Rubens, for example, may have only designed, sketched, or touched up a particular painting. It was understood in his time that that was enough to credit him with the entire work, but art historians are eager to know exactly which faces or costume details the master actually executed and which parts were done by students or assistants. To date a work, art historians must take into account the possibility that an artist was copying one of his or her earlier works, or that the artist started a work, abandoned it, and then finished it much later. Art historians, when carefully assessing a work, also need to consider that the pigments may have changed radically over time and that the work may have been touched up by a restorer or a later owner.

▲ **Figure 7–5** Which element do you think was most important to this artist? Which do you think was the least important?

André Derain. *The River Seine at Carrieres-sur-Seine.* 1905. Oil on canvas. 70.7 x 110.7 cm (27⅞ x 43½"). Kimbell Art Museum, Fort Worth, Texas.

Look back at the landscape by George Inness on page **120** (Figure 7–1). An art historian might note that the painting shows a lifelike, or realistic style. Which of the landscapes shown in Figure 7–4 and 7–5 also shows a realistic style? What words might you use to describe the style of the other work?

ART MOVEMENTS

Sometimes *a group of artists with similar styles who have banded together* form an **art movement**. One of these had its beginnings early in this century in France. It was known as the Fauve (**fohv**) movement. Fauves is a French word meaning "wild beasts," and artists who developed the new artistic style were known as the Fauves. **Fauve** refers to the art movement in which the artists used *wild intense color combinations in their paintings*. The Fauves were not interested in doing realistic art. Instead, they emphasized the colors in their works as a way of increasing the visual and emotional appeal. The landscape in Figure 7–5 is an example of a work in the Fauve style.

In analyzing a work, art historians will try to decide if it fits into a movement. Look at Figures 7–6 and 7–7 and be the art historian. Which of these paintings is done in the Fauve style? What details can you point to that support your decision?

Lesson 3   *Analyzing Artistic Style*   📖   **125**

Using Art Criticism. Have students imagine that they are art critics writing a review of landscape paintings that include all of the works reproduced in this lesson. Make sure that their reviews evaluate each of the works according to the three aesthetic views presented in Chapter 2.

Developing Studio Skills. Find an inexpensive poster-size reproduction of a painting by Renoir or another Impressionist. Cut it into as many squares as there are students and give each student one square. Have the students use oil pastels to enlarge their square onto a piece of paper. They should imitate the brush strokes and colors found in the original version. Assemble the finished squares into a whole. Discuss the key features of Impressionist style that were discovered through completing this exercise.

Appreciating Cultural Diversity. Have students browse through books that have good reproductions of art works from non-Western cultures. Ask each student to select an image executed in a style that is as different as possible from that of Figure 7-4 on page **124**. Have them write a paragraph that characterizes the style of their non-Western art work and then contrasts it to the style of Jasper Francis Cropsey. You may wish to simplify this exercise by pre-selecting several examples of art works that provide readily apparent differences, such as Japanese inkbrush landscapes or Chinese watercolor landscapes.

▲ Figure 7–6 Compare this work with Figure 7–2 on page 121. Both paintings were done by the same artist. What similarities and differences can you find between the two works?

Auguste Renoir. *Regatta at Argenteuil*. 1874. Canvas. 32.4 x 45.6 cm (12¾ x 18″). National Gallery of Art, Washington, D.C. Ailsa Mellon Bruce Collection.

▶ Figure 7–7 Does this sailboat scene have a different feel from the one in Figure 7–6? Compare the use of elements in each painting. How do they contribute to the overall effect?

Maurice de Vlaminck. *Sailboats on the Seine*. Oil on canvas. 54.6 x 73.7 cm (21½ x 29″). Metropolitan Museum of Art, New York. Robert Lehman Collection.

Background Information
Art historians have adopted some scientific techniques to analyze and date the art that they study. For example, chemical analyses of paint samples can identify a painting based on the materials used at a particular time and place. Ultra-violet rays reveal where paint surfaces have deteriorated. Infra-red rays can penetrate to just below the varnishes and glazes and can occasionally reveal signatures that are invisible to the naked eye. X-rays are also sometimes useful. Artists including Leonardo da Vinci and Van Eyck used paint materials that are opaque to x-rays, but when radiography is possible it provides valuable information for those who try to conserve and restore art works. The method permits one to see the preliminary sketches and strokes that an artist made when starting a painting. It is as though one can see the private side of a painting as well as the public face it usually presents.

Look again briefly at Figures 7–6 and 7–7. Study the work in this pair that you decided was *not* in the Fauve style. This work also came out of a movement. The movement, called Impressionism, also had its start in France in the late 1800s. This painting was done by a leader of the movement, Pierre Auguste Renoir (pee-**air** oh-**goost** ren-**wahr**).

As an art historian, how would you describe this style of Impressionist painting? What kinds of colors do you think its members liked to use? What kinds of lines do you think they liked? Can you see how they tried to show the effects of sunlight on the subject matter? Did you notice how the choppy brush strokes were used to reproduce the flickering quality of sunlight? As you practice the skills of an art historian, you can turn to your school or community library to help you find the answers.

▲ **Figure 7–8** The artist used dabs and dashes of paint in an attempt to show the flickering effect of sunlight on trees, shrubs, and other objects. Do you think the painting captures the look of a bright summer afternoon?

Claude Monet. *The Artist's Garden at Vetheuil*. 1880. Canvas. 151.4 x 121.0 cm (59⅝ x 47⅝″). National Gallery of Art, Washington, D.C. Ailsa Mellon Bruce Collection.

STUDIO EXPERIENCE

Study the painting in Figure 7–8. The work, by Claude Monet, is another example of the Impressionist style. Look closely at the painting. What do you notice about the use of color and of line?

Imagine that you are Monet, getting ready to do this work. Make a rough pencil sketch of a simple landscape. Use crayons, oil pastels, or chalk to color your sketch. Imitate Monet's Impressionist style by using short dashes and dabs of color. Begin in the center of the objects and work outward. Use complementary colors to make hues look dark. Compare your sketch with those of your classmates. Decide which sketches come closest to imitating the Impressionist style. Discuss what coloring techniques give the best result.

✔CHECK YOUR UNDERSTANDING

1. Define *analyzing*, as the term is used by an art historian.
2. What is style as it relates to art?
3. Describe the features of an art work done in the Impressionist style.

Lesson 3   *Analyzing Artistic Style*   ▦   **127**

Following Up

Closure. Ask students to briefly state whether there is an artist whose style they wish they could imitate. Have students explain their responses and state which elements of their own art would need to change in order for it to resemble the chosen artist's style.

Evaluation. 1. Review students' written responses to the "Check Your Understanding" questions. 2. Assess students' landscape show reviews. 3. Evaluate student paragraphs on Cropsey and non-Western art.

Reteaching. Have students consider the style of their own art work. Have them characterize its style in a paragraph, making sure that they refer to specific pieces that they have made in this class. Is there any resemblance between the style of their work and the style of an artist studied in this class so far?

Enrichment. Invite an artist or craftsperson to speak to the class about the development of his or her artistic style. Have the speaker bring in examples of slides that demonstrate his or her stylistic evolution. The speaker should also be encouraged to show slides of art works that he or she found particularly inspiring or influential and to discuss the relationship between those works and his or her own art.

Background Information
Claude Monet (France, 1840–1926) is known as the father of Impressionism. He studied at the Paris Academy. The Academy controlled the sale of art works and required artists to follow strict rules in order to exhibit there. Tired of the Academy rules, Monet and his friends banded together to hold their own show in 1874. The show shocked the public, and a critic said Monet had created his work by loading a pistol with paint and firing it at the canvas.

Answers to "Check Your Understanding"
1. For an art historian *analyzing* means noting the style of a work.
2. Style is an artist's personal way of expressing ideas in a work.
3. Works in the Impressionist style are created in short dashes and dabs of color.

Painting in the Fauve Style

LESSON PLAN
(pages 128–129)

Objectives

After completing this lesson, students will be able to:
• Describe the style of a Fauve painting.
• Create an art work in a Fauvist style.

Supplies

• Pencils, erasers, and sheets of scrap paper.
• Sheets of white paper, 9 x 12 inches (23 x 30 cm).
• Watercolor paint in bold hues and large watercolor brushes.
• Watercolor brushes with very fine bristles.
• Jars of water and paper towels.
• Oil pastels or crayons and colored chalk.

TEACHING THE LESSON

Getting Started

Motivator. Discuss the following quote from Matisse: "What I dream of is an art of balance, of purity and serenity devoid of troubling or depressing subject matter, an art which might be for every mental worker, be he businessman or writer, like a mental soother, something like a good armchair in which to rest from physical fatigue." Ask students why Matisse compares his art to resting in an armchair. Do they think that Figure 7-9 fulfills Matisse's goal?

Developing Concepts

Using Art Criticism. Have students use the four steps of art criticism to compare Figure 7-9 and Figure 6-1 on page **101**. How does the information gained from this process tell them that de Hooch was not a Fauve? What do you think might have been each artist's purpose in painting an interior?

Painting in the Fauve Style

Look at the painting in Figure 7–9. This was done by Henri Matisse (ahn-**ree** mah-**tees**), the leader of the Fauves whom you met in the last chapter. Notice that the room in the work is free of corners and shadows. What else can you observe from this style?

▲ Figure 7–9   Which objects in the painting are painted in the most detail? Which are painted in the least detail? What reason might the artist have had for leaving certain objects less finished than others?

Henri Matisse. *The Red Studio*. 1911. Oil on canvas. 181 x 219.1 cm (71¼ x 7′2¼″). Museum of Modern Art, New York. Mrs. Simon Guggenheim Fund.

Background Information
Nothing in the early life of Henri Matisse (France, 1869–1954) indicated the fame he was to achieve in the world of modern art. He showed no interest in art in high school, and he later received a law degree. Confined to bed after an appendicitis attack at the age of twenty-one, however, Matisse became bored and experimented with a paint box his mother bought him. The experience changed his life. He went back to school to study art and by 1905 had found a style of his own. He wanted to create works using flat shapes and simple colors, and he wanted to flatten out Renaissance space. He was not comfortable with shading and perspective. To many people Matisse's work looks childlike, but this kind of simplicity is difficult to accomplish. It is the result of his ability to look at a complex subject and reduce it to its simplest elements using line, shape, and color.

WHAT YOU WILL LEARN

Paint an interior scene in the Fauve style of Matisse. Start with a rough sketch and choose a single bold color for the background and paint shapes in the room in other bold colors. Create harmony in your work by repeating certain line and colors throughout.

WHAT YOU WILL NEED

- Pencil and eraser
- Sheets of scrap paper
- Sheet of white paper, 9 x 12 inch (23 x 30 cm) or larger
- Watercolor paint in bold hues
- Two watercolor brushes, one large and one with very fine bristles
- Jar of water
- Paper towels

WHAT YOU WILL DO

1. On a sheet of scrap paper, do a pencil sketch of an interior scene, such as your bedroom, living room, or classroom. (Notice how much detail Matisse gives to the chair in the right foreground in Figure 7–9.) For other objects, sketch only the outline. (Notice the grandfather clock against the back wall in Figure 7–9.) Do not worry about proportion or whether your shapes seem realistic.
2. Using pencil, lightly copy your sketch onto the sheet of white paper. Sign your name in pencil to the back of the paper.
3. Choose three special hues of watercolor paint. Do not use brown or black. One color is to be the background of your work. The other two are to be used for

EXAMINING YOUR WORK

- **Describe**   Tell what bold hue you have used as a background color. Identify the objects you have included in your interior scene.
- **Analyze**   Tell how your use of line and color adds harmony to your work.
- **Interpret**   Identify the adjectives a viewer might use to describe the colors in your work.
- **Judge**   Tell whether you feel your work succeeds. What aesthetic view would you use to support your judgment?

---

the details. Soften the paint by adding a few drops of water to each.
4. Load your large brush with the color you have picked for the background. Using broad strokes, cover the sheet of paper with color. Do not worry about leaving streaks. Set your paper aside to dry.
5. When the paint is totally dry, begin to add objects using the remaining two colors. Use less water to make your colors as strong as possible. Use one of the colors to paint outlines. Use your small brush to make narrow lines. (See Technique Tip **4**, *Handbook* page **271** for information on how to make thick and thin lines with a brush.) Use the other color to fill in shapes. Refer to your sketch as you work.
6. Allow your painting to dry totally. Share your finished work with your classmates.

OTHER STUDIO IDEAS

- Create another work in the Fauve style showing an interior scene. Do this work using oil pastels or colored markers and a sheet of construction paper in a light value of a primary or secondary color.

- ●● Do an oil pastel of an interior scene. This time, work in the style of the Impressionists. (See page **127**.) In preparing your pencil sketch, use the technique that seemed to give the best result in the studio experience on page **127**.

Background Information

Fauvism only lasted a few years, but it was one of the most important artistic movements of the twentieth century. Fauve works are exciting in themselves, and they were highly influential among many contemporary painters. Among the earliest inspirations of the Fauves was Gustave Moreau, a teacher of Henri Matisse. According to Moreau, "Nature itself is of little importance. It is merely a pretext for artistic expression. Art is the relentless pursuit of the expression of inward feeling by means of simple plasticity." Matisse and other Fauves melded this attitude with an optimistic temperament and a preference for bright colors and free forms. Most critics were hostile to Fauve art, but this may not explain why the movement declined so suddenly and ceased to exist by 1908. One expert has hypothesized that the age range of the Fauves, most of whom were in their late twenties and early thirties, is one during which vivid enthusiasms are apt to cool as one takes leave of one's youth and embarks on a fully adult life.

Interpreting Time and Place

Interpreting Time and Place

LESSON PLAN
(pages 130–133)

Objectives
After completing this lesson, students will be able to:
- Understand how an art historian interprets a work.
- Explain the influence of photography on painting.
- Describe how portraits were used in the past.
- Explain how the status of artists changed during the Renaissance.

Supplies
- Inexpensive scrapbooks.
- Drawing materials.
- Camcorder and videotape.
- Popular women's magazines.
- Sketch paper and pencils.
- Oil pastels.
- Sheets of white drawing paper.

> ### TRB Resources
> - 7-6 *When Japan Reached Europe*, (appreciating cultural diversity)
> - 7-7 *A Matter of Taste*, (aesthetics/art criticism)

TEACHING THE LESSON

Getting Started
Motivator. Select a popular television series and discuss how its subject matter gives clues that it is a late twentieth-century American show. List on the board topics and characters from various episodes. Have students explain how someone watching the show would know that it described life in late twentieth-century North America. Ask students to explain why television reruns often seem outdated.

Our lives are shaped by when and where we live. Today we take cars and televisions for granted. People living a hundred years ago had neither of these inventions.

In art, too, time, place, and world events can have a great influence on an artist. Artists living in wartime may create works very different from those done in peacetime. Ethnic background often influences an artist's work as well. In art, time and place are central to the art historian's interpreting of works.

INTERPRETING A WORK

Do you remember the three questions art historians ask when describing a work? Two of those questions are "when?" and "where?" In stage three, art historians follow up on their answers to those questions. **Interpreting** is *noting how time and place affect an artist's style and subject matter.*

Sometimes historians interpret a work by studying the impact of time and place on its style. At other times, they focus mainly on the subject matter used. At still other times, an interpretation takes both style and subject matter into account.

Interpreting for Style

In the late 1800s a new branch of art was born. This branch was photography. Thanks to photography, familiar subjects could now be viewed from new and unusual angles.

The art of photography opened new doors for painters and other artists. Some began experimenting with new rules for making art. Figures in paintings were now pushed off to the side, as they were in photos. Parts of objects were sometimes cut off by the edges of the work. Compare the works in Figures 7–10 and 7–11. What words might an art historian use in interpreting the style of the painting?

Interpreting for Subject Matter

Today when people make news, their pictures often appear in the newspaper. If the news is big enough, their pictures may appear on television. Where do you think pictures of famous people appeared before there was photography or television?

▲ **Figure 7–10   This photograph originally appeared in a magazine called *Camera Work*. The magazine was run by Alfred Stieglitz (steeg-luhts), an important American photographer.**

Clarence H. White. *Ring Toss*. 1903. Photograph. International Museum of Photography at George Eastman House, Rochester, New York.

Background Information
The invention of the camera was a technological development that gave artists new ways to observe and think about light. Monet's use of flickering light paralleled the instant impressions of light captured by the shutter of the camera. The camera also made it possible to study movements that artists pre-

viously had difficulty observing. Prior to the invention of photography, people argued about the number of feet a horse had off the ground when running. Photographs solved the question and revealed that many equestrian paintings had depicted horses in impossible poses.

◄ **Figure 7–11** How would you describe the artist's use of the principle of balance? What do you think art critics at the time may have said when they saw this work?

Edgar Degas. *Four Dancers*. 1899. Canvas. 151.1 x 180.2 cm (59½ x 71″). National Gallery of Art, Washington, D.C. Chester Dale Collection.

▼ **Figure 7–12** Among this painter's subjects were queens and other famous people. These days we know what leaders and famous people look like from photographs. Where else do we see their faces?

Marie-Louise-Élisabeth Vigée-Lebrun. *Theresa, Countess Kinsky*. 1793. Oil on canvas. 137.4 x 99.8 cm (54⅛ x 39⅜″). Norton Simon Art Foundation.

They appeared in paintings and other works of art. Figure 7–12 is a painting of one such person who was famous in the 1700s. The artist herself was well-known as a painter of portraits. These facts would be uppermost in the mind of an art historian interpreting this work. As an art historian, what questions might you ask about the subject in the painting? Where would you go for answers?

Portraits are not the only example of art that keeps records of people and events. Look once again at the landscape by George Inness (Figure 7–1 on page **120**). The work is a reminder of what railroads were like in the 1800s. It is also a record of an event in the artist's own life. This was the first time George Inness was paid for a painting. It marked a turning point in his career. An art historian might note both these facts in an interpretation of the painting. What other facts might an historian want to note?

Vocabulary. Divide the class into groups that will research the Renaissance. Each group should assemble a scrapbook of information about the Renaissance, including a list of famous people and artists, sketches of clothing worn by Renaissance people, notes on how people lived and entertained themselves, sketches of buildings erected, and any other findings that the students wish to include.

Developing Concepts

Exploring Aesthetics. Discuss with students the impact of photography on artists' perceptions of motion. Then have the class tape a high-speed action video. Replay the tape in slow motion and discuss whether the actual sequence of movements is different than they anticipated.

Using Art Criticism. Have students examine Figure 7-12. Explain that commissioned portraits often represent the sitter as he or she would ideally want to be perceived. Ask students how Vigée-Lebrun presented the countess in a flattering manner. If possible, display other portraits by Vigée-Lebrun. Then have the students find and study images of women in magazine ads, such as those that promote cosmetics. Help students see how the ads reflect modern notions of beauty and glamour, just as Vigée-Lebrun's society portraits show how women wanted to look in the late eighteenth century.

Understanding Art History. Have students find out what subject matter Degas typically painted. List the results on the board. Then discuss how an art historian might use this information to get a sense of life in nineteenth-century France. Ask students whether they think that de Hooch or Raphael might ever have painted similar subject matter. Have students explain their responses.

Lesson 5 *Interpreting Time and Place* 📖 **131**

Background Information
Marie-Louise-Élisabeth Vigée-Lebrun (France, 1755–1842) is one of history's most celebrated women artists. Before she was twenty, she had studied in a convent and had received private art lessons from colleagues of her artist father. She had also painted portraits of important members of the French aristocracy. By the age of twenty-five, she was employed by Queen Marie-Antoinette, whose portrait she painted some twenty times. On the night the queen and king were arrested, Vigée-Lebrun escaped from Paris. The French Revolution did not stop her career, however. She continued to work in other European capitals and was flooded with commissions. She earned a huge sum of money, the great majority of which was devoted to paying off her husband's gambling debts. Vigée-Lebrun's easy, charming portraits present sitters to their best advantage. They also preserve for posterity a picture of the aristocratic way of life as it faded from history.

Interpreting for Style and Subject Matter

A period of great awakening in the arts in Europe in the 1500s is known as the Renaissance (ren-uh-sahns). **Renaissance** is a *French word meaning "rebirth."* Before the Renaissance, artists were thought of as skilled craftspeople. Their work was no more important than that of carpenters or stone cutters. During the Renaissance, however, artists suddenly gained new prestige. This was partly because of the enormous talents of many artists of the period. You have probably heard of Michelangelo (my-kuh-**lan**-juh-loh) and Leonardo da Vinci (lee-uh-**nahr**-doh duh **vin**-chee). Both of these highly gifted artists worked during the Renaissance.

Another artist of the period whom you already met was Raphael. (In Chapter 6, you studied his painting *St. George and the Dragon* page **104**.) Look at the painting in Figure 7–13. An art historian interpreting this work

▶ **Figure 7–13** This is thought to be the most beautiful of the many Madonnas Raphael painted. It was painted shortly before Raphael began work on *St. George and the Dragon*.

Raphael. *The Small Cowper Madonna*. c. 1505. Wood. 59.5 x 44.0 cm (23⅜ x 17⅜"). National Gallery of Art, Washington, D.C. Widener Collection.

would notice two things. First, like most of Raphael's paintings, this one has a religious subject. Do you know the figures in the work? Reading about the Renaissance, an art historian might learn the following:

- The Catholic Church was a great patron of the arts.
- The Catholic Church hired artists to paint and sculpt scenes from the Bible.
- The art works were used to decorate churches.
- Most people living in the 1500s were unable to read.

Through these church paintings, the people were able to understand the story of Christ without reading about him.

The second thing an art historian might notice is that the painting has a religious figure as a central theme or subject. During the Renaissance, the Madonna became a theme for many works of art. A **Madonna** is *a work showing the mother of Christ*. The word madonna means "my lady." Raphael alone painted over 300 Madonnas. Figure 7–14 shows a Madonna by another Renaissance painter. Compare it with Raphael's Madonna (Figure 7–13). Notice the circles, or bands, framing the figures' heads. Do you know what these are called? How might you describe the looks on the faces of the figures? What other style features do the two works share? In what ways are the works different?

▲ **Figure 7–14** What differences do you see in the use of art elements and art principles between the two paintings shown on these two pages?

Fra Filippo Lippi. *Madonna and Child*. 1440/1445. Wood. 80 x 51 cm (31⅜ x 20⅛"). National Gallery of Art, Washington, D.C. Samuel H. Kress Collection.

 ## CHECK YOUR UNDERSTANDING

1. Define *interpreting*, as the term is used by an art historian.
2. What use did portraits have in the past?
3. What is a Madonna?
4. What and when was the Renaissance? How were artists thought of before the Renaissance and during the Renaissance?

Closure. Ask students to briefly state which artist or art historical period they think is the most fun for an art historian to research. Which might be the most boring? Have students explain their responses.

Evaluation. 1. Review students' written responses to the "Check Your Understanding" questions. 2. Evaluate student scrapbooks on the Renaissance. 3. Assess student paragraphs about a non-Westerner's interpretation of a Madonna painting.

Reteaching. Have students pretend that their research into Figure 6-4 on page **104** revealed that sixteenth-century Italians used dragons as symbols of good, not evil or paganism. Have students first recall the correct interpretation of this painting and then state how the different information might change an art historian's understanding of this painting.

Enrichment. Have students visit a public or museum library and meet with a librarian who can show examples of the various materials that art historians consult while researching an art work. The materials might include primary sources such as letters, diaries, and old sketchbooks, and secondary sources such as a dictionary of symbols, art magazines and journals, and artist biographies.

Classroom Management Tip
Be sure to use a high quality video tape and to follow camcorder instructions carefully when doing the stop-action film exercise. The tape feed should be set at the slowest possible setting to obtain an image that will still be clear when it is later played in slow motion.

Answers to "Check Your Understanding"
1. For an art historian *interpreting* means noting how time and place affect an artist's style and subject matter.
2. In the past portraits recorded people and events.
3. A Madonna is a work showing the mother of Christ.
4. The Renaissance was a period of great awakening in the arts in Europe around the 1500s. Before the Renaissance, artists were thought of as skilled craftspeople. During the Renaissance artists gained prestige.

Time and Place Collage

Time and Place Collage

LESSON PLAN
(pages 134–135)

Objectives

After completing this lesson, students will be able to:
• Define the term *collage*.
• Produce a collage that provides information about contemporary American life.

Supplies

• Magazines and newspapers.
• Scissors, pencils, and sketch paper.
• Poster board.
• Slightly thinned white glue and small brushes.
• Reproductions of art works executed in a variety of media.

> **TRB Resource**
> • 7-8 *Time Line of Arts and History*, (cooperative learning)

TEACHING THE LESSON

Getting Started

Motivator. Have students empty the class trash basket. Sift through the items found there and discuss whether a collage that incorporated these items would provide an accurate and interesting account of life in that classroom. Discuss why Braque and other so-called collage Cubists may have turned to the scraps of their daily life for art materials.

Vocabulary. Tell students that collage is the French word for "paste-up" and briefly review the technique of collage. Then display reproductions of art works executed in a variety of media including, if possible, fabric appliqué. Ask students to identify the media used in each work and make sure that they can distinguish collage from other forms of two-dimensional design.

Look at Figure 7–15. This type of art work is called a collage. A **collage** (kuh-**lahzh**) is *art arranged from cut and torn materials pasted to a surface.* Some of the materials in this collage are clues to the time and place in which it was created. Look at the piece of newspaper on the left side. Can you read any of the words? Do you know what language they are? Can you guess? Where might you go to find out when this newspaper was first printed? What would these facts reveal about when the artist worked?

WHAT YOU WILL LEARN

You will make a collage out of scrap paper (Figure 7–16). The principles of art will be used to combine the colors, textures, and shapes into a visually interesting whole. Your collage will give clues about life in America today.

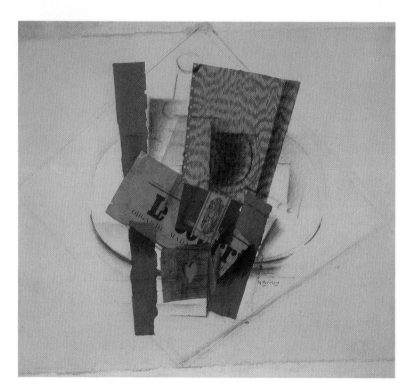

 Figure 7–15 How many of the bits and pieces in this work can you identify? Do they add up to an interesting whole? Why or why not?

Georges Braque. *Le Courrier*. Charcoal, gouache and printed paper collage. 50.6 x 57.8 cm (20¼ x 22¾"). Philadelphia Museum of Art. A. E. Gallatin Collection.

Background Information

Georges Braque (France, 1882–1963) is credited with making the first paper collage. The act freed artists to arrange strips of paper according to a pattern and color design that had no reference to realistic illusions, even while the same papers included information about the items that were represented. By inventing a technique that did not involve oil paints or brush strokes, Braque and his artistic colleague Picasso had made an almost clean break with the traditional methods and assumptions of art. Cubist paper collages were initially composed of a wide range of wallpapers. Soon Braque and Picasso experimented with sheet music, scraps of newspapers and posters, cigarette and tobacco wrappers, bottle labels, cards, postage stamps, and strips of imitation wood graining. Eventually they realized that they could obtain the same sense of pictorial space without pasting materials. They needed only to paint flat forms, such as are found in Picasso's *Three Musicians,* that mimicked paper collage elements.

WHAT YOU WILL NEED

- Magazines and newspapers
- Scissors
- Pencil and sheets of sketch paper
- Poster board
- Slightly thinned white glue
- Small brush

WHAT YOU WILL DO

1. Turn through pages of newspapers and magazines. With scissors, clip out images that might depict life in America today. Use images of different sizes. You can use pictures or words from advertisements. Be as imaginative as you can in your choices.
2. Decide what materials will fill the spaces around your images. Again, be creative in choosing visually interesting colors, textures, shapes, and sizes. Clip the pieces out and set them aside.
3. Experiment with the pieces by arranging them on your poster board using the art principles. Pieces can overlap.
4. With the thinned glue and small brush, glue the pieces of your collage in place. Set your collage aside to dry.
5. *Optional.* You may want to use watercolor or tempera paint to help unify your composition. To do this, use a thin layer of paint to cover over some parts and accent others.

▲ Figure 7–16   Student work. A time and place collage.

EXAMINING YOUR WORK

- **Describe**   Point to the images you clipped from newspapers or magazines. Tell what colors, textures, and shapes you chose.
- **Analyze**   Tell what principles you used to organize the elements into an interesting whole.
- **Interpret**   Tell what the images you chose reveal about life in America today. Point to images that show time, place, or both. Tell what overall feeling the viewer will have when seeing your work.
- **Judge**   Tell whether you feel your work succeeds. Explain your answer.

OTHER STUDIO IDEAS

- Make a collage of things having to do with new food trends or your favorite food. Again, use magazine and newspaper clippings.

- ●● Make a collage of items promoting or representing your city or town.

Lesson 6   *Time and Place Collage*   **135**

Developing Concepts

Using Art Criticism. Have students use the four steps of art criticism to compare Figure 7-15 on page **134** and the Picasso work pictured in the Chapter 7 opening on page **118**.

Understanding Art History. Have students research the place and period of time during which Braque worked and identify other artists who made art in a similar style. Have them select one of these artists and write a paragraph that explains why their choice is considered a Cubist artist. Discuss the stylistic traits that the Cubists shared.

Following Up

Closure. Ask students to describe how an art historian would go about researching the collages that they just made. List all of the steps on the board. Discuss whether an art historian who studied all of the student collages would develop a consistent picture of modern American life. Ask students whether any single picture can ever completely express the society in which it was made.

Evaluation. 1. Review students' collages. 2. Evaluate student paragraphs on a Cubist artist.

Reteaching. Have students decide what activities and what kinds of people are suggested in Figure 7-15 on page **134** and then write a story or a description of a person based on this information. Invite students to read their works aloud and explain how it relates to Braque's collage.

Enrichment. Have students investigate the different kind of collage that was invented by Jean Arp soon after Braque's experiments with collage. Once students are familiar with Arp's collages, which were "arranged according to the laws of chance," discuss the differences between spontaneous and arranged collages. If you wish, have students use Arp's method to create their own torn paper collages.

Background Information
Collage was first used by early Cubists and Dadaists. The Cubists were concerned with the essence of an object and painted a subject from various perspectives to express the idea of that object. In later phases of Cubism, a decorative and ornamental sensibility is evident. During this period, Picasso introduced elements other than paint onto the canvas. The Dada movement saw collage as an expression of their own theories of art. They intended to outrage and shock the art world, and one way to do this was to make use of non-paint media in the context of a painting. Marcel Duchamp was the most famous of the Dadaists. He eventually abandoned oil painting altogether to make art out of objects that he had found. His role as an artist was to bring these elements together and arrange them at random.

Judging Historical Importance

Judging Historical Importance

LESSON PLAN
(pages 136–139)

Objectives
After completing this lesson, students will be able to:
• Name several ways in which an art work may be considered important in the history of art.
• Describe what was new about the style of Giotto's paintings.
• Describe the technique that Seurat introduced.

Supplies
• Sheets of drawing paper, 9 x 12 inches (23 x 30 cm).
• Oil pastels.
• Color-aid paper, or other pieces of colored paper to illustrate simultaneous color contrast.
• Variety of painting and drawing materials.

> **TRB Resource**
> • 7-9 *Salon des Refuses*, (reproducible master)

TEACHING THE LESSON

Getting Started

Motivator. Ask students to bring in any collections that they work on as a hobby. Have the students present their collections and explain how they judged whether certain items were worthy additions to their collection.

Vocabulary. Discuss what the term *judging* means in different contexts. For example, explore the different kinds of judgments that are made by a court judge, a medical doctor, and a sports referee. Compare these judgments with those made by art historians. Ask students whether art historical judgments are always final or if there is room for an art historian to change his or her mind or to differ with art historians of a previous generation.

What is the most important accomplishment that happened to you during the past week? What happened to you in the past month that was important? What event was an accomplishment during the past year? It is not likely your answer was the same for all three questions. For a few days doing well on a test or earning 20 extra dollars may seem like a big accomplishment. However, as days turn into months, your idea of what is important changes.

The same is true for art historians in the last stage of their work. In judging a work of art, they look at all aspects of the artist's work.

JUDGING A WORK

To art historians, judging is determining if a work of art makes a lasting contribution to the history of art. **Judging** is *deciding whether a work introduces a new style or if it is an outstanding example of an existing style*. It can also involve deciding whether a work makes a contribution to art by introducing a new style, technique, or a new medium.

Judging for Style

There are many ways in which pieces of art can make a contribution. One is by introducing a new style. Look again at Henri Matisse's painting of his studio (Figure 7–9) on page **128**. An art critic judging the painting would praise its bold colors. An art historian judging the painting would look beyond it. The historian would note how Matisse's use of bold colors influenced other artists and changed ideas about what is art. Do you remember the name of the art movement Matisse led? Do you remember what its members believed?

Look at the painting in Figure 7–17. It is a Madonna painted in the 1300s by an artist named Giotto (**jah**-toh). Is there anything in this work a historian would call new or striking? Is there any reason why the work should be judged important?

To the untrained eye today, Giotto's painting might seem stiff and awkward. To the art historian, however, there is more here than meets the eye. The historian would try to imagine himself or herself living in Giotto's time. Back then most Madonnas were like the one in Figure 7–18 on page **138**. True, this work does not look very realistic. But in the 1300s paintings seldom did. Pictures of religious figures were not meant to look real. They were painted to remind people of saints and prophets and to teach religious values. The golden lines in the drapery in Figure 7–18 were painted as a decorative pattern. No effort was made to make them look like real folds in real cloth.

The people in Giotto's day were shocked by Figure 7–17. His figures, compared with those in the typical Madonna, are lifelike. They are not flat figures painted on a gold background. They give the impression of being rounded three-dimensional forms that stand out in space.

Now look again at Figure 7–18. The child in the work does not look or act like a real child. He seems to be giving his mother a lecture. Giotto's child, on the other hand, is more believable. He holds one of his mother's fingers as a real baby might.

Consider these points and tell how an art historian might judge this work. How would you judge it?

> **Note**
> Explain to students that art historians sometimes disagree with each other about the interpretation or importance of particular art works and movements. Art historians may even change their own mind during the course of their career in art history. For example, it wasn't until a decade or two ago that works by women artists were given the same kind of scholarly attention that was accorded art made by their male peers. Major textbooks on the history of Western art were published without a single mention of female artists, even in chapters that discussed art after World War II, a period during which over half of art school graduates have been female. Other art that has recently received increased respect from art historians includes medieval art, which was once thought to be childish and unsophisticated, and Third World art, which used to be relegated to museums of natural history instead of art museums.

▲ Figure 7–17   This painting may have been one of several that were joined together to decorate the altar of a church.

Giotto. *Madonna and Child*. c.1320/1330. Wood. 85.5 x 62.0 cm (33⅝ x 24⅜"). National Gallery of Art, Washington, D.C. Samuel H. Kress Collection.

Lesson 7   *Judging Historical Importance*   📖   **137**

Developing Concepts

Exploring Aesthetics. Demonstrate Chevreul's law of simultaneous color contrast, on which Seurat's work was based. Place paper squares of various hues on top of larger sheets of contrasting colors to show how the perception of any given color will change according to the color that is placed next to it.

Using Art Criticism. Have students choose a picture from this chapter. Have them imagine that they are professional art critics and, using the four steps of art criticism, write short reviews of their chosen art work. Read aloud the different critical evaluations of each picture. Discuss how critics, like art historians, may legitimately arrive at different opinions of a given art work. Then discuss whether an art critic might declare a particular work to be successful while an art historian might call the same piece historically insignificant.

Understanding Art History. Have students select an artist whose work is illustrated in this text. Students should figure out what style this artist used and write a paragraph that explains why the work pictured in the text is, or is not, an outstanding example of that style or whether it introduces a new style or technique.

Note
Teachers will find a box of silk screened "Color-aid" papers very useful in the art classroom, particularly for demonstrations of the properties of various color combinations. Color-aid comes in sets of 202 sheets that include a systematic array of twenty-four hues, four tints of each hue, three shades of each hue, eight gray sheets, and black and white sheets. The set is exceptionally well produced and can be used for years.

Judging for Technique

Another way a work of art can make a contribution is by introducing new techniques. Techniques are the ways an artist chooses to use a medium. This can be explained by taking a look at Figure 7–19. This painting was done by a French artist named Georges Seurat (suh-**rah**).

You can see by looking at Figure 7–19 that the technique used here differs from the technique used by other artists. Georges Seurat took a more scientific approach by combining thousands of dots of color. This made his paintings seem to shimmer with light. This is an example of how artists who use the same medium develop individual techniques.

◀ **Figure 7–18** Paintings like this were thought to have great power. One famous Roman emperor carried one like it when he went into battle. These works were also thought to heal the sick and give sight to the blind.

Byzantine XIII Century. *Enthroned Madonna and Child*. Wood. 131.1 x 76.8 cm (51⅝ x 30¼"). National Gallery of Art, Washington, D.C. Gift of Mrs. Otto H. Kahn.

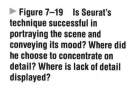

▶ **Figure 7–19** Is Seurat's technique successful in portraying the scene and conveying its mood? Where did he choose to concentrate on detail? Where is lack of detail displayed?

Georges Seurat. *Sunday Afternoon on the Island of La Grande Jatte*. 1884–86. Oil on canvas. 207.6 x 308.0 cm (81¾ x 121¼"). The Art Institute of Chicago. Helen Birch Bartlett Memorial Collection.

Background Information
Seurat's painting, *Sunday Afternoon on the Island of La Grande Jatte*, speaks both of past traditions and the coming age of industry and progress. In one sense it resembles the numerous nineteenth-century utopian images of a blessed land. It also has an affinity with Realist works that attempted to portray a cross-section of modern society. According to one art historian, the mongrel and pug dogs that Seurat placed in the foreground may symbolize different social classes. Despite its Realist references and Impressionist subject and technique, Seurat's work presents a new world that is dominated by science and the machine. The people scattered on the banks appear to be robots and their placement is fantastically well ordered and even regimental.

▲ Figure 7–20 How would you describe the looks in the eyes of the two figures? What do these people seem to be feeling? Notice the mother's big feet. What other features has the sculptor used to make his subjects seem real?

Sir Jacob Epstein. *Madonna and Child*. Riverside Church, New York.

THE ART HISTORIAN AND HISTORY

If the historian's job is to look beyond works, should the historian look forward? Study the Madonna in Figure 7–20. This sculpture was done in the 1920s. It was finished 600 years after Giotto made his painting. Notice that this one is much more lifelike than Giotto's Madonna. The mother and child look like real people. They are similar to a mother and child you might meet on the street.

Does a work like this take away from the importance of Giotto's work? No. Changes in art happen little by little. Each age learns from and builds on advances made by earlier artists. A sculpture like this is made possible by the contributions of Giotto and others. Its creation is a testimony to the sensitivity and skill of artists who went before.

STUDIO EXPERIENCE

Many great artists were also teachers. They were called masters. Their students were known as apprentices. Many times the way apprentices learned art was to copy the works of their masters. Apprentices often became more skilled than their teachers. They would start new art movements and schools of their own.

Choose a favorite work of art from this chapter or a work by one of the artists listed below. Use other art books for reference if you need to.

On drawing paper, 9 x 12 inch (23 x 30 cm) sketch as accurate a copy of the art you have chosen as possible. Then using oil pastels, fill in the colors, following the original work of art for style and shading. See how close you can come to creating a piece that looks like the art work you used as a model.

Share your finished work with your classmates. Did you achieve the effect you wanted? If you were an apprentice what changes would you like to make in the art work you just finished?

Michelangelo da Caravaggio (1573–1610)
Antoine Watteau (1684–1721)
Francisco Goya (1746–1828)
Wassily Kandinsky (1866–1944)

✔CHECK YOUR UNDERSTANDING

1. Tell what the term judging means to an art historian.
2. What are two ways a work of art can make a contribution to the world of art?
3. How do changes in art happen?
4. Do artists learn from those who have created long before them?

BUILDING VOCABULARY

Number a sheet of paper from 1 to 11. After each number, write the term from the box that best matches each description below.

analyzing	interpreting
art history	judging
art movement	Madonna
collage	Renaissance
describing	style
Fauves	

1. The study of art from past to present.
2. Identifying who did a work of art, and when and where it was done.
3. Noting an art work's style.
4. An artist's personal way of expressing ideas.
5. A group of artists with a similar style.
6. French art movement in which artists used wild blends of strong colors.
7. Noting the way that time and place affect an artist's style and subject matter.
8. A period of great awakening in the arts in Europe in the 1500s.
9. A work showing the mother of Christ.
10. A work made up of bits and pieces of objects pasted to a surface.
11. Deciding upon a work's place in art history.

REVIEWING ART FACTS

Number a sheet of paper from 12 to 20. Answer each question in a complete sentence.

12. In what ways is an art historian's approach to art different from an art critic's?
13. In describing a work of art, where does an art historian look first for an answer to the question "who"?
14. Why is style like a person's signature?
15. What did the Fauves believe in? When and where did they work?
16. What did the Impressionists believe in? Where did they work?
17. Where did pictures of famous people appear before the invention of photography?
18. Name two great artists of the Renaissance.
19. Name one way in which an art work might be judged as making a contribution to art history.
20. Explain how art works today often build upon the art works of the past.

THINKING ABOUT ART

On a sheet of paper, answer each question in a sentence or two.

1. **Extend.** Where else in a library besides art history books might you turn for information on an artist's life?
2. **Analyze.** Give an example of how time and place can affect style. How do time and place affect an artist's choice of subject matter?
3. **Compare and contrast.** How are describing and interpreting similar for an art historian? How are the two tasks different?

MAKING ART CONNECTIONS

1. **Home Economics.** Art history provides a look into the past to show us what people did, the things they used, and the clothes they wore. Look at the Renoir painting of the little girl on page **121**. Compare her clothing styles with the styles children wear today.
2. **Science.** Research methods used to date ancient artifacts and ways in which the art works contributed to a better understanding of the culture from which they came.

LOOKING AT THE DETAILS

The detail shown below is from Pablo Picasso's *Three Musicians*. Study the detail and answer the following questions.

1. At the turn of the century in Paris, Spanish born Pablo Picasso studied the works of the masters of his time, which included the Fauve artists and Impressionists. However, instead of merely imitating them, Picasso created a radically new and bold style, referred to as Cubism. Most of his fellow artists including Henri Matisse, disliked his work. What do you think are some of the reasons for this?
2. Compare this detail with the work of Henri Matisse on page **128**. What differences do you see? Would you consider Picasso's work as daring?
3. Does Picasso successfully organize the elements of art to create human forms? Explain.
4. Does it disturb you that the hands and faces are not realistically proportioned? Why or why not?
5. How does Picasso's Spanish heritage enter into this work?
6. As an art critic, how does knowing the time and place Picasso painted assist you in judging his work? What might be some other important considerations?

Pablo Picasso. *Three Musicians*. 1921. Oil on canvas. (Detail.) 200.7 x 222.9 cm (6'7 x 7'3¾"). Museum of Modern Art, New York. Mrs. Simon Guggenheim Fund.

Chapter 7 Review **141**

Drawing

Chapter Scan

Lesson 1 The Art of Drawing
Lesson 2 Gesture Drawing
Lesson 3 Contour Drawing
Lesson 4 Presentation Drawing
Lesson 5 Fantasy Jungle

TRB Resources
- 8-8 Chapter Test
- Color Transparency 15
- Color Transparency 16

TEACHING THE CHAPTER

Introducing the Art Work

Direct students' attention to Paul Calle's drawing *Gemini VI Astronauts.* Inform students that Paul Calle is an American artist who uses a variety of media but is best known for his works in pencil. Many believe that Calle's most important work was as an artist with the NASA Fine Art Program, which was initiated in 1962 to help document and interpret America's space program. The administrators felt that although thousands of photographs had been taken of the space program, photographs could not convey the human element and emotional impact that artists could express.

Examining the Art Work

Tell students that Calle's drawing of astronauts McDivitt and White is a realistic interpretation of two astronauts who have just completed suiting up and are about to board the spacecraft. Explain how Calle's hasty yet deliberate pencil strokes seem to enhance the sense of urgency and importance of the astronauts' task ahead. Point out that Calle uses a strong contrast of value as well as variation in the direction of his straight pencil lines to create the shiny and crinkled texture of the astronauts' space suits. This drawing asks the viewer to think about the astronauts' mission as opposed to the personalities of the men themselves.

Point out how Calle shows only the crucial details—American flag, watch, life support system, and the like—and omits any background or miscellaneous objects that would interfere with his message.

▲ NASA hired artists to make records of humans' first steps off the planet Earth. Do you know where those steps were? Why do you suppose NASA wanted artists to prepare such records?

Paul Calle. *Gemini VI Astronauts.* Pencil on paper. 55.9 x 76.2 cm (22 x 30"). NASA.

Drawing

Ask students where they think the focus is in this drawing. Point out the face mask and headgear of the first astronaut and how it seems to lunge forward. Ask: What are some of the reasons for this? Explain how Calle used the darkest values of the work here. The movement of the work is forward, toward the viewer. Have students discuss what kind of feeling this motion suggests. Ask: Does the astronauts' gear seem heavy and cumbersome? Why? Suggest that students consider the posture of the men as well as the hoses, straps, size of the helmets, and other details.

Ask students to think about what the lack of background might suggest in this work. Relate it to the astronauts' mission and feeling of the infinite quality of space.

Ask students why they think Calle chose drawing as his medium. Point out the limited amount of time he had to capture the astronauts in their various tasks, and suggest that color is not a crucial element in communicating Calle's message.

Tell students that in this chapter they will learn the different ways drawing is used in art. They will also learn various shading techniques and make their own drawings.

Have you ever heard someone say, "I can't draw"? Perhaps you have said it yourself. What you may not realize is that drawing is a skill. It can be learned just as dancing or playing a sport can be learned. With practice, you can use your drawing skills to express what you see in the world.

Look at the sketch on the left. What do you think the artist saw? With nothing more than a blank sheet of paper and a pencil, Paul Calle has created a detailed sketch. In this chapter you will find out how he made the astronauts and their equipment look so real.

OBJECTIVES
After completing this chapter, you will be able to:
- Name the three ways in which drawing is used in art.
- Define *shading*, and name four shading techniques.
- Make gesture drawings.
- Make contour drawings.

WORDS YOU WILL LEARN

blending	hatching
contour drawing	perception
crosshatching	shading
gesture drawing	stippling

ARTISTS YOU WILL MEET

Paul Calle	Henri Rousseau
Natalia Goncharova	Élisabeth Vigée-
Juan Gris	Lebrun
Rembrandt van Rijn	Leonardo da Vinci

143

Building Self-Esteem
Introduce the subject of a "Success Still-Life" by saying that everybody has things that he or she is good at doing. Some might be good at fishing or dancing; others may be really good singers or athletes. Perhaps some are excellent students or belong to a church group in which they are leaders. Maybe their special job at home is roasting hot dogs on the barbecue grill because no one else can do it better. Stress that whatever it is, everybody is good at something. Ask students to look around at home and find two or three small objects that represent something they do well. Tell them to ask their parents for permission to bring the objects to school so they can make a personal still-life. See Technique Tip 6, *Handbook* page **272** about shading techniques. After the students have finished their drawings, let them share their art, tell about the objects they chose, and explain how they represented some of the things they do well.

The Art of Drawing

You have probably seen people doodling with a pencil. You may have done it yourself. If you have, you are not alone. Ever since you took a crayon in your hand and scribbled on paper, you have been drawing.

You can learn certain skills to help you improve your ability to draw. Look again at the drawing of the astronauts on page **142**. Notice how the artist, Paul Calle (**kal**-ee), using just a pencil, made such dark shadows. Notice how he made some surfaces look soft and others smooth and shiny.

▶ **Figure 8–1** Does this drawing tell you simply how these people looked? How did da Vinci perceive this group of men? How does he convey this perception?

Leonardo da Vinci. *Five Grotesque Heads*. c. 1494. Pen on white paper. Windsor Castle, Royal Library of Her Majesty the Queen.

LESSON PLAN
(pages 144–147)

Objectives
After completing this lesson, students will be able to:
• Name the three ways in which drawing is used in art.
• Define *shading* and name four shading techniques.
• Use and compare those four shading techniques.

Supplies
• Collection of common objects that have distinct descriptive characteristics, such as rulers, chalk, brushes, and the like; sketch paper and pencil.
• Index cards, markers.
• White paper, 9 x 12 inches (23 x 30 cm); rulers; pencils; fine-tipped pens.
• Variety of surfaces for drawing, such as construction paper, tissue paper, brown paper bags, scraps of cardboard; variety of media for drawing, such as crayons; chalk; markers; ink with pens, sticks, or twigs.
• Photocopies of drawings that show multiple drawing techniques, colored markers.

TRB Resources
• 8-1 *The Drawing Tool,* (aesthetics)
• 8-2 *An Analysis of Self-portrait,* (art criticism)
• 8-3 *Use All of Your Brain to Draw,* (cooperative learning)
• 8-4 *Shading,* (studio)
• 8-5 *Drawing—The First Language,* (appreciating cultural diversity)

TEACHING THE LESSON

Getting Started
Motivator. Let students work with partners to practice using their skills of perception. Have students in each pair sit back to back, and give one of the partners a common object with distinct descriptive characteristics. Let that partner describe the object as fully as possible without naming it. Suggest that students describe such details as size, shape, texture, and color. Have the listening partners ask questions to

Background Information
Many painters, sculptors, and other artists use drawings both to improve their perception and to plan their art works. For example, Michelangelo (Italy, 1475–1564) used sketches to discover how to represent the body in motion. His drawings make it evident that he was interested only in the human form itself; they show his close attention to the shapes and movements of muscles. The realism of Michelangelo's representations of the human form surpasses that of all other artists of the period.

Art historians frequently use preliminary sketches as an aid in attributing art works. The Maison de Renoir, for example, houses a collection of the materials left by Pierre Auguste Renoir (France, 1841–1919). If someone "discovers" a painting by Renoir, these documents can be used to establish the authenticity of the work.

In this lesson you will learn about some of the uses of drawing. You will also learn a few drawing techniques. In later lessons you will get a chance to use these techniques.

THE USES OF DRAWING

Drawing has a great many uses in art. The three most important are to develop perception, to help plan projects, and to make a finished art work. **Perception** is *the ability to really see and study an object*.

Improving Perception

To an artist, looking and seeing are not the same thing. Looking is simply noticing an object as you pass by it. Seeing, or perceiving, is really studying the object. It is picking up on every line and shadow. It is observing all the details.

Through drawing, artists become better at perceiving. Many artists use sketchbooks to record their surroundings and to study objects. They use drawing to make preliminary studies for finished works. The Renaissance artist Leonardo da Vinci filled over a hundred sketchbooks with drawings. The drawings in Figure 8–1 come from one of them.

Planning Projects

Drawing is usually the first step in completing many art works and other projects. Rough sketches, or studies, are almost always done before creating a work in another medium, such as painting or sculpture. Design drawings for this year's fashions were made long before any fabric was cut. (See Figure 8–2.) Many creative people, such as stage designers, graphic designers, and architects must show presentation drawings for a client's approval. Once the drawing is approved, work can begin on the project.

▲ Figure 8–2 Can you envision how this drawing would translate into an actual piece of clothing? What feeling do you think a viewer gets when looking at this work? Explain your answer.

elicit more details. Then have each listener draw the object his or her partner has described. Encourage students to share their drawings and discuss the process.

Vocabulary. Have students work in groups to prepare sets of eight index cards. On each of four cards, have them write the name of one shading technique: *hatching, crosshatching, blending,* or *stippling*. On each of the other four cards, have them draw an example of one shading technique. Then let students work individually, in pairs, or in small groups with sets of the cards. Have them mix up the cards, turn the cards face down, and then turn pairs of cards over, trying to match the names and examples of shading techniques.

Developing Concepts

Exploring Aesthetics. Guide students in discussing Leonardo da Vinci's sketches shown in Figure 8-1: What is the subject of each sketch? How would you describe the use of line in each sketch? Which other visual elements can you identify? How would you describe their use in each work? What feeling or idea does each sketch seem intended to communicate? Are these sketches works of art? Why, or why not?

Using Art Criticism. Help students compare and contrast the types of lines used in Figures 8-1, 8-2, and 8-3. Help students identify and discuss such characteristics of the lines as thick/thin, long/short, rough/smooth, curvy/angular, sharp/blurry, heavy/light, constant/variable. Ask students to identify lines that are fast (moving incisively in one direction or another) and others that are slow (full of small changes of direction, breaks, and variations in weight or density). Following the discussion, have each student write a paragraph describing the lines used in one of the drawings.

▲ **Figure 8–3** Why do you think color was an important element for the artist? What guidelines did the artist have to consider before beginning this work?

Natalia Goncharova. *The City Square*. Design for scenery for the ballet Le Coq d'Or. Produced by Ballets Russes, Paris, 1914. Gouache, watercolor and traces of pencil on cardboard. 46.7 x 61.6 cm (18⅜ x 24¼″). Museum of Modern Art, New York, New York. Acquired through the Lillie P. Bliss Bequest.

Making a Finished Art Work

A third use of drawing is to make finished art works. These are sometimes used to illustrate books and magazines. The drawing in Figure 8–3 originally was used to show a stage design for a ballet. Now it is considered fine art. The picture of the astronauts on page **142** was done for the National Aeronautics and Space Administration (NASA).

Look more closely at Figure 8–3. Notice the fine detail the artist has chosen to show. Why do you think she made such a detailed drawing?

SHADING TECHNIQUES

Look once again at the drawing of the astronauts on page **142**. Here the artist creates a work so real it looks almost like a photograph. Do you know how this is done? One technique he uses to get this result is shading. **Shading** is *the use of light and shadow to give a feeling of depth.*

There are four basic shading techniques.

- **Hatching** is *drawing a series of thin lines all running parallel, or in the same direction.* Look at the shapes in Figure 8–4. Which show hatching?

- **Crosshatching** is *drawing lines that criss-cross each other.* Which shapes in Figure 8–4 show crosshatching?
- **Blending** is *smoothly drawing dark values little by little by pressing harder on the drawing medium.* Which shapes in Figure 8–4 show blending?
- **Stippling** is *creating dark values with a dot pattern.* Which shapes in Figure 8–4 show stippling?

(For more on how to use these shading techniques, see Technique Tip **6**, *Handbook* page **272**.)

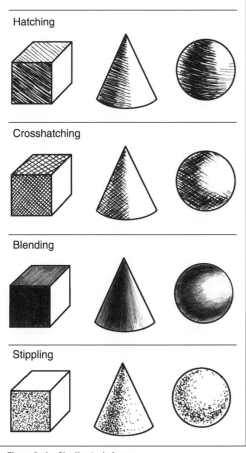

▲ **Figure 8–4** Shading techniques.

STUDIO EXPERIENCE

On a sheet of white paper, 9 x 12 inch (23 x 30 cm), make six rectangles. Each should be 1 inch by 5 inches (2.5 cm by 12.5 cm). Using a pencil, shade four of the rectangles with a different shading technique for each one. In each rectangle demonstrate your control of shading by changing values from pure white on the left to deep black on the right. Then shade the two remaining rectangles using a fine-tipped pen. Use crosshatching for one and stippling for the other.

✔CHECK YOUR UNDERSTANDING

1. What are three ways in which artists use drawing?
2. What is shading?
3. Name four techniques for shading. Describe each.

Closure. Have students work in small groups to compare and discuss their shading exercises. Then ask each student to write a few sentences answering these questions: Which shading technique were you able to use most successfully? What was good about your use of that technique? Which shading technique was most difficult for you? What can you do to improve your use of that technique?

Evaluation. 1. Review students' written responses to the "Check Your Understanding" questions. 2. Read students' evaluations of their own shading exercises.

Reteaching. Have the students work with partners to review the four shading techniques. Give each pair of students a photocopy of a drawing in which several shading techniques have been used. Ask the partners to identify and discuss the different techniques. Then let them outline all the areas that have been shaded, using a different color around each shading technique. As a follow-up, encourage the partners to work together to make an original drawing of the classroom or another familiar scene, using at least two different shading techniques.

Enrichment. Talk briefly with the students about Leonardo da Vinci (1452–1519), whose drawings are shown in Figure 8-1. Point out that the artist also had many other interests, including anatomy, botany, astronomy, physics, geology, architecture, and engineering. He filled many notebooks with thousands of scientific observations, notes, and ideas for inventions—including a flying machine, a parachute, and a movable bridge. Have students work in small groups to research Leonardo's inventions and to compare his sketches with actual machines in use today. Give each group an opportunity to share its findings with the rest of the class.

Answers to "Check Your Understanding"
1. Artists use drawing to improve their own perception, to help plan projects, and to make finished works of art.
2. Shading is the use of light and shadow to give a feeling of depth.

3. These are four basic techniques for shading: hatching, which is adding a series of thin parallel lines; crosshatching, which is adding lines that crisscross each other; blending, which is adding dark values little by little by pressing harder on the drawing medium; stippling, which is creating a dot pattern.

LESSON 2

Gesture Drawing

LESSON PLAN
(pages 148–149)

Objectives

After completing this lesson, students will be able to:
- Define the term *gesture drawing*.
- Practice focusing on the movement of a figure, not simply on what the person looks like.
- Make and examine their own series of gesture drawings.

Supplies

- Sketch paper, pencil.
- Sticks of charcoal, soft graphite, or wrapped crayon; sheets of sketch paper, 12 x 18 inches (30 x 46 cm); pencils with sharp points; erasers.
- Collection of students' drawings (or reproductions of drawings), only some of which are gesture drawings.

TEACHING THE LESSON

Getting Started

Motivator. Have students brainstorm a list of body movements, such as running, jumping, bending, kicking, and so on. Then let each student choose one kind of movement and draw a quick sketch of a person making that movement. Encourage students to share and discuss their drawings: What kinds of lines did you use to express movement? Which lines communicate the sense of movement most effectively? Then explain to students that they will learn more about specific drawing techniques for showing movement.

Vocabulary. Have volunteers look up the word *gesture* in dictionaries and read the definitions to the rest of the class. Then help students discuss the term *gesture drawing*. What kinds of gestures does the term refer to? When and how can gesture drawing be used?

Artists are able to freeze movement in a picture using a technique called gesture drawing. **Gesture drawing** is *drawing lines quickly and loosely to capture movement.* Look at Figure 8–5. This was done by the great Dutch painter Rembrandt van Rijn (**rem**-brant van **ryn**). Notice how the lines appear to have been made quickly to catch the action of the figure.

Using gesture drawing will help you break the habit of outlining everything you draw. In gesture drawing you use your whole arm, not just your hand. (See Technique Tip **2**, *Handbook* page **271**.)

▲ **Figure 8–5   What appears to be in motion? How does detail enter into this?**

Rembrandt van Rijn. *Jan Cornelius Sylvius, The Preacher.* c. 1644–1645. Pen and brown ink on laid paper. 13.3 x 12.2 cm (5¼ x 4¹³/₁₆"). National Gallery of Art, Washington, D.C. Rosenwald Collection.

WHAT YOU WILL LEARN

You will make a series of 30-second gesture drawings using charcoal, graphite, or crayon. You will focus on the *movement* of the figure, not on the likeness of the person. Then you will make a large, slower sketch of a seated figure. Select one area of this figure to emphasize with details and shading. (See Figure 8–6.)

WHAT YOU WILL NEED

- Sticks of charcoal, soft graphite, or un-wrapped crayon
- Sheets of white paper, 12 x 18 inch (30 x 46 cm)
- Pencil with a sharp point, and an eraser

WHAT YOU WILL DO

1. You and your classmates will take turns acting as the model. Models should pretend to be frozen in the middle of an activity. This may be an everyday action, such as sweeping the floor, or tying a shoelace. Dancing or acting out a sport are other possibilities. Each model will hold the pose for 30 seconds.
2. Using charcoal, graphite, or a crayon, begin making gesture drawings. You can fit several sketches on one sheet of paper. Make loose, free lines that build up the shape of the person. Your lines should be quickly drawn to capture movement.
3. After many 30-second drawings, make a slower gesture drawing of a seated model. Fill a sheet of paper. Select one area of the figure to emphasize with details and shading. Try a hand, a shoe, or a sleeve. (See Figure 8–7.)
4. When you are done, display your last drawing. Did your classmates choose the same detail to emphasize?

Background Information
Artists are particularly aware of the importance of movement. One popular artist, Carole Katchen, explained her use of gesture drawing this way: "I saw this woman at a ballroom dance competition. The way her head was tilted . . . typified her whole attitude. I drew a quick sketch of her on the spot. Rather than laboring over proportion and anatomy, I let myself draw quick contours that would give some sense of gesture and personality."

Movement in a work of art allows an artist to direct the observer's eye. It also helps indicate mood. Thus Gothic architecture uses vertical movement to draw our eyes heavenward. We perceive horizontal movement to be safe. Diagonal movement gives us a sense of action—flowers bending in the wind, an athlete running. Spiral movement gives us a sense of depth and space. Artists use gesture drawing to imply all these kinds of movement.

▲ Figure 8–6 Which areas are strongly shaded? Which are not? Why?

Marie-Louise-Élisabeth Vigée-Lebrun. *La Princesse Barbe Gallitzin.* c. 1801. Graphite and chalk. Approximately 17.8 x 11.1 cm (7 x 4⅜″). National Museum of Women in the Arts, Washington, D.C. Gift of Wallace & Wilhelmina Holladay.

▶ Figure 8–7 Student work. A gesture drawing with a detailed left foot.

EXAMINING YOUR WORK

- **Describe** Show the series of gesture drawings you made using charcoal, graphite, or crayon. Identify the action or pose you tried to capture in each.
- **Analyze** Point to the loose, sketchy lines in your gesture drawings. Explain why your lines were drawn this way. Tell how movement is shown.
- **Interpret** Explain how viewers will be able to recognize that your figures are involved in some kind of action.
- **Judge** Tell whether you feel your drawings succeed in showing figures in motion. Explain your answer.

OTHER STUDIO IDEAS

- Pretend you are a fashion illustrator for a local newspaper. Look through catalogs and do gesture drawings of the models in different action poses.

- ●● Look through a sporting magazine and find a picture of an athlete in motion. Tape the picture at eye level and do a gesture drawing of the athlete. Do the same drawings of the same athletes in different poses.

Lesson 2 *Gesture Drawing* **149**

Developing Concepts

Understanding Art History. Ask volunteers to work individually or in small groups to read about and study reproductions of the gesture drawings of famous artists. Suggest that each volunteer or group of volunteers research the work of one of the following: Michelangelo, da Vinci, Goya, Rubens, Toulouse-Lautrec, van Gogh, Degas, Picasso, Käthe Kollwitz, Henry Moore. Then have the volunteers share their findings with the rest of the class, showing reproductions of gesture drawings, if possible.

Developing Studio Skills. Have students start keeping their own sketchbooks. Encourage students to carry their sketchbooks with them and to make gesture drawings of many different subjects. Remind them that many artists do gesture drawings while in a standing position to allow for free, loose movements. They can capture quick images of people, animals, and objects and then refer to these sketches as they plan and create future art works. Remind the students to try working with various media—pens, pencils, markers, colored pencils, crayons, and so on—in their sketchbooks. At first they may not be able to finish each drawing in 30 seconds. Encourage them to keep trying; with practice their skill and speed will improve.

Following Up

Closure. Have students work in small groups to discuss their own gesture drawings, as directed in "Examining Your Work." Then have the students write one or two sentences describing what they have learned—either about themselves or about art—from their studio experiences.

Evaluation. Review students' series of gesture drawings, and read their descriptions of what they have learned.

Reteaching. Help small groups of students go through the collection of drawings, identifying the gesture drawings and explaining how those drawings differ from the others.

Enrichment. Have a local artist (professional or aspiring) visit the class to display and discuss his or her sketchbooks.

Handbook Cross-Reference
Be sure students understand that gesture drawings do not have outlines or details; they are intended to depict the movement of a figure rather than the figure itself. For specific help in making gesture drawings, refer students to Technique Tip 1, *Handbook* page **271**.

Classroom Management Tip
Let students take turns acting as the "action model" either for the entire class or for a group of classmates. Arrange desks or work tables in a circle or semicircle around each modeling area, so that all the students will have a good view of the table. Keep the drawing materials handy at each table so students will not need to search for supplies during the activity.

LESSON PLAN

(pages 150–151)

Objectives

After completing this lesson, students will be able to:
• Define the term *contour drawing*.
• Practice drawing by moving their eyes and hands together.
• Make and examine their own series of contour drawings.

Supplies

• Overhead projector, photograph of a person, perhaps in a draped or elaborate outfit.
• Fine-point felt-tipped pens; sheets of sketch paper, 12 x 18 inches (30 x 46 cm), or newsprint, 18 x 24 inches (46 x 61 cm); a variety of objects, such as shells, pots and pans, flowerpots, driftwood, houseplants, draped fabrics, baskets, kitchen utensils, tools, pens, crayons, and so on.
• Long pieces of wire that can be easily bent.
• Long pieces of yarn or string.

> **TRB Resource**
> • 8-6 *Line in Art History*, (art history)

TEACHING THE LESSON

Getting Started

Motivator. Use an overhead projector to enlarge and display a photograph of a person. (Select a photograph that includes interesting contours; a flowing gown, for example, may add interest.) Let students discuss and comment on the photograph. Then help them recognize how the edges and ridges define the image. Let students trace, either on the projector or (using a pointer) on the screen, the defining lines. Help them imagine how a drawing composed only of these lines would portray the figure.

Vocabulary. Ask volunteers to use the word *contour* in sentences, showing several different uses of the word. Then help students brainstorm a list of synonyms and near-synonyms for *contour*.

150

Contour Drawing

Look at Figure 8–8. Notice how lifelike the subject looks for a drawing made almost totally of line. A first step toward doing work like this is learning to do contour drawing. **Contour drawing** is *drawing an object as though your drawing tool is moving along all the edges and the ridges of the form*. This technique helps you become more perceptive. You are concerned with drawing shapes and curves.

In contour drawing, your eye and hand move at the same time. Imagine that the point of your pen is touching the edge of the object as your eye follows the edge. You never pick up your pen. When you move from one area to another, you leave a trail. Look at the model and not at the paper.

WHAT YOU WILL LEARN

You will make a series of contour drawings with a felt-tipped pen. First, you will draw different objects. Second, you will use your classmates as models. Finally, you will make a contour drawing of a classmate posed in a setting. (See Technique Tip **1**, *Handbook* page **271**.)

WHAT YOU WILL NEED

• Felt-tipped pen with a fine point
• Sheets of white paper, 12 x 18 inch (30 x 46 cm)
• Selected objects provided by your teacher

WHAT YOU WILL DO

1. Take one of the items from the collection on the display table. Place it on the table in front of you. Trace the lines of the object in the air on an imaginary sheet of glass. As you look at the object, you must concentrate and think. Notice every detail indicated by the direction and curves of the line.

▲ **Figure 8–8**   Notice how the artist gives a feeling of form by changing the thickness of the line. What ways do you know of making lines thicker and darker?

Juan Gris. *Max Jacob.* 1919. Pencil on paper. 36.5 x 26.7 cm (14⅜ x 10½″). Museum of Modern Art, New York, New York. Gift of James Thrall Soby.

2. Make a contour drawing of the object on a sheet of paper using a felt-tipped pen. Do several more drawings on the same sheet of paper. Turn the object so you are looking at it from a different angle. Make another contour drawing. Keep working until your drawings begin to look like the object. (See Figure 8–9.)
3. Next, exchange objects with your classmates. Do a contour drawing of your new object. Work large, letting the drawing fill the page. Do not worry if your efforts look awkward. Complete several drawings of different objects.

Cooperative Learning

In step three of this lesson, students are asked to exchange items and to do a contour drawing of the new object. After these new drawings have been completed, ask students who have exchanged to compare their drawings of the same item. Let them notice which details of the object they have included, and which ones they have missed or handled differently. If the students have drawn the object from a different angle, let them compare the drawing with the object itself and together analyze what might have been included. Ask them to focus on detail. Give them a maximum of five minutes to compare and contrast with the goal of further developing their perceptual skills.

4. Work with a partner. Take turns posing for each other. Each model should sit in a comfortable pose. The first contour will look distorted. Remember, you are drawing the pose. Work large and let the drawing fill the page.

5. Finally, make a contour drawing of one person sitting in a setting. Include background details. (See Figure 8–10.) You may stop and peek at the drawing. When you do, do not pick up the pencil. Do not take your eyes off the model while drawing.

6. Display the final drawing. Discuss how contour drawing has improved your perception.

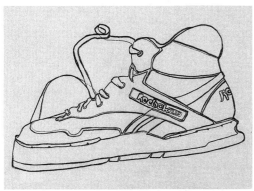

▲ Figure 8–9 Student work. A contour drawing of a shoe.

EXAMINING YOUR WORK

- **Describe** Show the different kinds of contour drawings you did. Identify the media you used.
- **Analyze** Compare your first contour drawing to your last. Explain how using contour drawing has changed your perception skills.
- **Judge** Evaluate your final contour drawing. Tell whether you feel your work succeeds. Explain your answer.

▲ Figure 8–10 Student work. This is an example of a contour drawing that shows background details.

OTHER STUDIO IDEAS

- Make a contour drawing of a chair in your classroom using crayons.

- ●● Use a piece of wire that bends easily and make a three-dimensional contour "drawing" of a foot or hand.

Lesson 3 *Contour Drawing*   **151**

Developing Concepts

Using Art Criticism. Help students discuss the drawing shown in Figure 8-8. Ask: How would you describe the line in this art work? How does it change? What effect do those changes have? What other drawing techniques could Gris have used for this work? Why do you imagine he chose contour drawing?

Developing Studio Skills. Have students use wire to experiment with three-dimensional "contour drawing." Let students choose an object in the classroom—or an object they can remember distinctly—and then try bending pieces of wire to depict the contours of that object. You may want to start by demonstrating the process of bending and shaping the wire; then encourage students to work together and discuss their ideas.

Appreciating Cultural Diversity. Ask volunteers to find and share with the class reproductions of several traditional Japanese woodcuts. Help students discuss these works and their relationship to contour drawings: What similarities and differences can you identify?

Following Up

Closure. Give each student a turn to answer these questions: What is the most challenging part of contour drawing? What do you hope to learn from practicing contour drawing?

Evaluation. Review students' series of contour drawings, and consider their responses to the "Closure" questions.

Reteaching. Have students use long pieces of yarn or string to create the contours of specific objects. Let students shape the yarn or string directly on the tabletop. Encourage students to compare and discuss their work.

Enrichment. Ask one or more volunteers to serve as models for the rest of the class. Let students give the model directions for posing for both gesture drawings and contour drawings. Then have each student make two different drawings of the model. Ask: How are the two kinds of drawings different? What similarities are there?

Classroom Management Tip
Remind students that, whenever they work with long pieces of material (such as wire), they must be especially careful. Students must always be aware of others working near them. Loose ends of wire can quite easily be flipped up, possibly injuring someone's eye. Have students try to keep one foot on top of the free end of wire as they work. Also remind them to be careful in making any necessary cuts with wire snips, keeping fingers well out of the way.

Handbook Cross-Reference
Contour drawing can help students develop the feel of a subject, but making these specialized drawings may seem awkward at first. For help in developing the skill of contour drawing, refer students to Technique Tip 2, *Handbook* page **271**.

Presentation Drawing

LESSON PLAN
(pages 152–153)

Objectives

After completing this lesson, students will be able to:

• Define the term *presentation drawing*.

• Make and examine their own presentation drawings.

Supplies

• Sheets of scrap paper; sheets of sketch paper, 12 x 18 inches (30 x 46 cm); pencils; rulers; colored pencils or fine-line markers.

• Examples or reproductions of presentation drawings for various kinds of projects, such as architectural designs, landscaping projects, stage and costume designs, and product designs.

• Sketchbook and paper.

• *Optional:* camera

TEACHING THE LESSON

Getting Started

Motivator. Display and identify several presentation drawings for various kinds of projects. Guide students in discussing what they see in the drawings and in considering how and why such drawings might be used. Ask: What kinds of projects might require presentation drawings? Who would probably evaluate the drawings? What requirements and limitations would the artist have to consider? Why is it especially important for presentation drawings to be clear and accurate?

Vocabulary. Ask volunteers to identify the verb (*present*) from which *presentation* is formed. Then ask: What does a presentation drawing present? What other verbs have about the same meaning as *present*? What other terms can you make up to use in place of the term *presentation drawing*?

152

Presentation Drawing

Sometimes artists are called upon to do presentation drawings. Such drawings show a possible idea or design for a project. Figure 8–11 is a presentation drawing for the Washington Monument in Washington, D.C. It is one of many that were done by different artists. As you can see from the finished building (Figure 8–12), this design idea was not used.

Imagine you have been asked to design a set of wrought iron gates for the entrance to a zoo, botanical garden, or a playground.

WHAT YOU WILL LEARN

You will create a presentation drawing of a gate with two sides. The outside shape of the gate will be symmetrically balanced. To unify your design within the shape of the gate, create a symmetrical or asymmetrical design using lines and symbols that represent the place. Use the principles of rhythm and harmony to organize the lines.

▲ **Figure 8–11** How would you describe the mood of this design? What features help create that mood?

Robert Mills. Rejected Sketch of Washington Monument. The National Archives.

▲ **Figure 8–12** What features does this work have in common with the presentation drawing in Figure 8–11? In what ways is it different? Does it convey the same mood? Which of the two design ideas do you like better? Explain.

Washington Monument. Washington, D.C.

152 Lesson 4 *Presentation Drawing*

WHAT YOU WILL NEED

- Sheets of scrap paper
- Sheet of white paper, 12 x 18 inch (30 x 46 cm)
- Pencil and ruler
- Colored pencils or fine-line markers

WHAT YOU WILL DO

1. Choose a theme for your gates. Make some rough sketches of designs that symbolize the theme. On scrap paper, do rough pencil sketches showing different possible outline shapes for the symmetrical gate. Choose your best design, and set it aside.
2. Do rough pencil sketches of possible designs within the shape of the gate. Decide if the interior part of the gate will represent symmetrical or asymmetrical balance.
3. With a pencil, carefully develop your best idea. Use a ruler to make all the straight lines. (For information on the right way to hold a ruler, see Technique Tip **9**, *Handbook* page **273**.)
4. Fill in the two sides of your gate with your best designs. Again, use the ruler in drawing the design for the left side. Remember that repeating symbols can produce harmony.
5. Using the colored pencils or markers, add color to your presentation drawing. Use color to help give balance to the design.
6. Display your work. Discuss how students took different approaches to the assignment.

EXAMINING YOUR WORK

- **Describe**   Show your presentation drawing. Show where you used the elements of line and color. Tell what other elements you used.
- **Analyze**   Explain how you used the principles of harmony, movement, and rhythm. Show where you used them. Tell how your use of symmetrical or asymmetrical balance helped unify your gate design.
- **Interpret**   Can a viewer tell what your gates represent? Explain your answer.
- **Judge**   Tell whether you feel each of the gates succeeds as a design when viewed individually. Do they work together when they are closed?

SAFETY TIP

When a project calls for the use of markers, always make sure to use the water-based kind. Permanent markers have chemicals in them that can be harmful when inhaled.

OTHER STUDIO IDEAS

- Make a presentation drawing for a new front door for your school. What mood do you want to capture in the finished work? Create the presentation drawing using colored pencils or fine-line markers.

- ●● Make a presentation model of a door using wire that bends easily. Do the decorations for the two sides separately. Fasten them to the outline of the door with transparent tape.

Lesson 4   *Presentation Drawing*   **153**

Developing Concepts
Exploring Aesthetics. Help students discuss the differences between the rejected design (Figure 8-11) and the completed Washington Monument (Figure 8-12). Then ask: Which elements of the rejected design do you prefer to those in the design that was used? Why? Which elements of the completed monument do you prefer to those in the rejected design? Why?

Using Art Criticism. Have students write paragraphs about their own gate designs, answering these questions: What mood or feeling is the gate intended to convey? What specific elements help convey that mood or feeling? What changes could you make in your design to communicate that mood or feeling more clearly?

Developing Studio Skills. Have students walk through their own neighborhoods, using cameras or sketchbooks to record decorative architectural details, such as windows, doorways, gates, fountains, columns, and so on. (If the neighborhoods do not offer appropriate examples, have students sketch from magazines featuring architectural work.) Encourage the students to share and discuss their work.

Following Up
Closure. Lead a brief discussion on what students have learned from this lesson on presentation drawing; encourage everyone to participate.

Evaluation. Review students' presentation drawings, and consider their contributions to the "Closure" discussion.

Reteaching. Discuss the presentation drawings with individual students, using "Examining Your Work" as a guide. Let the students describe, analyze, interpret, and judge their own work.

Enrichment. Have students work individually or with partners to find photographs of three examples of interesting architectural detail from the culture and the period of their choice. Let them photocopy and then share and discuss the examples.

Classroom Management Tip
Encourage students to make several thumbnail sketches of various ideas for each art project they work on. Making these sketches can help them understand that there are usually many different ways of "seeing" a given subject. Students will often find that their fourth or fifth idea is better than their first. Help students compare and, if possible, discuss the ideas represented by their sketches before they begin final work on their projects.

Note
In order to stimulate creative design ideas, help students focus on the concept of choosing a theme that utilizes symbols. In a theme *park*, many decorative elements are organized around a central theme—such as fantasy, future world, or past age. If designing a gate for a zoo, stylized animal outlines could be used. Ask what design elements might be used for gates to other facilities. Urge students to select a theme and appropriate symbols to use in designing their gates.

Fantasy Jungle

LESSON PLAN
(pages 154–155)

Objectives

After completing this lesson, students will be able to:
• Recognize imagination as an important source of artists' inspiration.
• Plan, create, and examine their own drawings of fantasy jungles.

Supplies

• Pencils; sheets of sketch paper or other plain white paper; sheets of colored construction paper, 12 x 18 inches (30 x 46 cm); white chalk; soft erasers; oil pastels.
• Reproductions of art works showing realistic scenes by artists such as Audubon, Wyeth, Homer, Constable, Eakins, and Millet; reproductions of art works showing surreal and imaginary scenes by artists such as Bosch, Rousseau, Chagall, Magritte, Dali, and Miro.
• Houseplants and cut flowers, or photographs of plants and flowers; photographs of birds, reptiles, and other animals.

> **TRB Resource**
> • 8-7 *Henri Rousseau*, (artist profile)

TEACHING THE LESSON

Getting Started

Motivator. Display the reproductions of art works showing various scenes. Let volunteers describe what they see in each work, and encourage students to discuss their responses to the works. Then have students work together to identify several different moods created by the art works and to group the reproductions according to those moods.

Vocabulary. Guide students in discussing the meaning of *fantasy* as "imagination". Then display the plants and the photographs of animals. Let volunteers describe first the actual appearance of each plant or animal and then their own fantasy versions of those plants and animals.

Fantasy Jungle

Look at the painting in Figure 8–13. It was done by Henri Rousseau (aan-**ree** roo-**soh**), a French painter famous for his imaginary jungles. The artist used real plants and other life forms as models in all his works.

WHAT YOU WILL LEARN

You will create your own imaginative fantasy jungle. You will study real leaves and plants as models for those in your work. Images of birds, animals, or reptiles will be based on photographs. You will do your finished work with oil pastels on colored construction paper. (See Figures 8–14 and 8–15.)

WHAT YOU WILL NEED

• Pencil and sheets of sketch paper or other plain white paper
• Sheet of colored construction paper, 12 x 18 inch (30 x 46 cm)
• White chalk and soft eraser
• Oil pastels

WHAT YOU WILL DO

1. With pencil on sketch paper, make detailed contour drawings of plants. These may be houseplants, flowers, or weeds.
2. On other sheets of sketch paper, make drawings of imaginary animals. They may be based on real birds, reptiles, and animals.
3. Using chalk, sketch the plan for your jungle on construction paper. Use the principles of harmony, informal balance, and emphasis. Pick a color of paper based on the mood your work will have. (Keep in mind differences of hue, intensity, and value.) Arrange your shapes and planned colors using informal balance. Keep other

▶ **Figure 8–13** The artist loved to spend time copying plants and animals from books. His finished works were a mixture of real-life images and images from his imagination. Which elements and techniques do you think give this painting the quality of a fantasy? Which ones display a sense of realism?

Henri Rousseau. *The Waterfall (La Cascade)*. 1910. Oil on canvas. 116.2 x 150.2 cm (45⅞ x 59"). Art Institute of Chicago. Helen Birch Bartlett Memorial Collection.

154 Lesson 5 *Fantasy Jungle*

Background Information

"In its present state," wrote the Expressionist artist Paul Klee, "this is not the only possible world." This idea was vividly demonstrated by Henri Rousseau (France, 1844–1910), who became famous for his fantastic drawings and paintings.

Rousseau served in the army and then worked as a toll inspector until he was 40. Then he retired to devote himself to art. He seemed to have a vision that he wanted to share; as a French poet understood it, Rousseau wanted us to see what he saw, and he wanted us to understand that he loved what he saw.

Rousseau was not a trained artist; he learned to paint by copying the paintings he saw in the Louvre. His lack of formal training allowed him to paint as a child might—from imagination. His use of simple colors and clear details captured the attention of Picasso, Toulouse-Lautrec, and many other artists, who hoped to emulate this "primitive art." From Rousseau's example grew Surrealism.

elements and principles, such as rhythm, in mind. As you draw, press lightly. That way, you will not tear the paper if you need to erase. Don't draw details so small that they can't be drawn with oil pastels.

4. Color your jungle. Use color contrast to create a strong center of interest or area of emphasis. Use different oil pastel drawing techniques. (See Technique Tip 3, *Handbook* page **271**.)

5. Display your work. Can you recognize what plants and animals your classmates used as models?

▲ Figure 8–14 Student drawing. A fantasy jungle.

- **Describe** Identify the different plants in your fantasy jungle. Explain what real plants you used as sources. Explain what the imaginary animals were based on.
- **Analyze** Show where you used informal balance to organize colors and shapes. Tell what principles you used to organize other elements.
- **Interpret** Explain what kind of mood your work expresses. Tell what role background and foreground colors play in this mood. Tell whether your work has the look and feel of a fantasy jungle. Give your jungle a title.
- **Judge** Tell whether you feel your work succeeds. Explain your answer.

▲ Figure 8–15 Student drawing. A fantasy jungle.

OTHER STUDIO IDEAS

- Do a second jungle scene using brush and ink only. Explain how you were able to capture the mood of an imaginative jungle without using color.
- ● Draw your jungle with fine-line felt pens. Leave everything plain except your center of interest. Call attention to it by creating a strong contrast. Color it with bright colors, or give it the illusion of a three-dimensional form by shading it with one of the techniques you learned on page **147**.

BUILDING VOCABULARY

Number a sheet of paper from 1 to 8. After each number, write the term from the box that best matches each description below.

blending	hatching
contour drawing	perception
crosshatching	shading
gesture drawing	stippling

1. The use of light and shadow to give a feeling of depth.
2. A shading technique using thin lines all running in the same direction.
3. A shading technique using lines that crisscross each other.
4. A shading technique in which dark values are added little by little.
5. A shading technique in which tiny black dots are accumulated.
6. Drawing lines quickly and loosely to show movement in a subject.
7. Drawing an object as though your drawing tool is touching the edge.
8. The ability to really see and study an object.

REVIEWING ART FACTS

Number a sheet of paper from 9 to 14. Answer each question in a complete sentence.

9. What are three main ways in which drawing is used by artists?
10. To an artist, how is looking at an object different from seeing it?
11. How does drawing help artists "see" better?
12. Name three ways in which drawing might be used to plan a project.
13. What is a name for the rough sketch an artist uses to plan a painting?
14. Name one place where drawings of finished works of art are used.

THINKING ABOUT ART

On a sheet of paper, answer each question in a sentence or two.

1. **Analyze.** Suppose someone said to you, "Drawing isn't real art. Anyone can pick up a pencil and make a drawing." How would you answer?
2. **Extend.** Why might the publishers of a book choose drawings rather than photographs as illustrations?
3. **Compare and contrast.** Which of the shading techniques you studied do you think gives the most realistic result? Which gives the least realistic result? Explain your answers.
4. **Interpret.** In what ways is using a rough or a thumbnail sketch similar to doing an outline for a piece of writing?
5. **Analyze.** Why do you think it is important to work quickly when doing gesture drawing? Why is it important to work slowly when doing contour drawing?

MAKING ART CONNECTIONS

1. **Science.** Scientists rely on photographs and detailed drawings to record and learn about the natural world. They sketch from observation and include unique features of their subjects. Study the work of scientific illustrators shown in science books, field guides, and magazines to see the type of images they use. Would Rousseau's paintings be useful to scientists studying plant and animal forms? Why or why not?
2. **Social Studies.** Starting with a drawing of your house and school, make a contour map showing the pathway of a short imaginary journey you plan to make. Include pictorial images to represent important landmarks. Show where you turn and how many blocks or miles you travel.

LOOKING AT THE DETAILS

The detail shown below is from Paul Calle's *Gemini VI Astronauts*. Study the detail and answer the following questions.

1. Calle used predominantly one shading technique. How does it relate to the sense of movement you see here?
2. Is Calle's organization of line successful? Why?
3. The window of the astronaut's headgear is dark and the viewer is unable to see a human face. Why do you think Calle avoided using the astronaut's face?
4. How do you think Calle perceived this astronaut?
5. How does the gear of the astronaut in front differ from the same gear worn by the astronaut behind him?
6. Can you think of some reasons for this difference?

Paul Calle. *Gemini VI Astronauts.* Pencil on paper. (Detail.) 55.9 x 76.2 cm (22 x 30"). NASA.

ANSWERS TO "LOOKING AT THE DETAILS"

1. Responses will vary. Students might mention the following: By shading the face mask and some headgear of the first astronaut darker than the rest of the drawing, Calle focuses attention there. The movement of the figures is toward the viewer. Calle creates movement by showing how the suit crinkles as the man walks.
2. Yes. Students might suggest the following reasons: The viewer can easily identify Calle's subject and can sense the movement he is portraying. The viewer gets a feeling of urgency and importance from the way Calle organized line.
3. He avoided using the face to keep the viewer focused on the mission and sense of urgency rather than on the personalities of the men.
4. Responses will vary. Students might suggest the following: courageous, bold, strong, determined, focused, intense, skillful.
5. The astronaut's gear in the background has less detail, is lighter in contrast, and the lines are less bold.
6. Responses will vary. Students might note that the difference allows the viewer to focus on the one in front, to create the sense of forward motion and immediacy. Because the first astronaut is shown in detail, the viewer assumes that the second astronaut is similarly equipped and doesn't miss the lack of detail. The lack of detail only enhances the sense of depth and movement.

Chapter 8 Review **157**

Chapter Evaluation
The purpose of this chapter is to identify the ways that artists use drawings, and to help students develop their own drawing skills. Methods of evaluation include:
1. Have students divide a sheet of paper into four squares. In each square have them demonstrate the shading techniques of hatching, crosshatching, blending, and stippling.
2. Ask students to list three ways that artists use drawing skills.
3. Show students pictures that represent contour and gesture drawings. Ask students to identify which type of drawing is being represented.
4. Have students complete the Chapter 8 Test, (TRB, Resource 8-8).

Printmaking

Chapter Scan

Lesson 1 The Art of Printmaking
Lesson 2 More About Printmaking
Lesson 3 Monoprints
Lesson 4 Glue Prints
Lesson 5 Linoleum Block Prints
Lesson 6 Silk Screen Prints

TRB Resources
• 9-9 Chapter Test
• Color Transparency 17
• Color Transparency 18

TEACHING THE CHAPTER

Introducing the Art Work

Direct students' attention to Albrecht Dürer's woodcut, *Four Horsemen of the Apocalypse.* Inform students that Albrecht Dürer was the first German artist to travel to Italy, in the late 1400s and early 1500s, to study the art and theories of the Renaissance. His art reflects his interest in the science, biology, and philosophy of his time. Dürer was trained as a goldsmith, and this background was a contributing factor to his skill in depicting minute detail. Tell students that Dürer created some 70 paintings, more than 1000 drawings, 250 woodcuts, and more than 100 engravings during his lifetime. Dürer became the first non-Italian artist to reach international fame, because of his diversity and mastery of graphic arts.

Examining the Art Work

Tell students that this woodcut is one of a series of 15, which Dürer finished in 1498, depicting events from the last book in the Bible, the Book of Revelation. Explain that in this work Dürer was communicating St. John's vision of war, pestilence, famine, and death, as trampling over a helpless humanity.

▲ The artist made a series of 15 woodblock prints to show scenes from the Bible. Do you know the story of the Four Horsemen of the Apocalypse? Notice the small letter D inside an *A* at the bottom. This is how Albrecht Dürer signed all his works.

Albrecht Dürer. *The Four Horsemen of the Apocalypse.* 1498. Woodcut. 30.9 x 20.8 cm (12 x 8″). Reproduced by courtesy of the Trustees of the British Museum, London.

158

Printmaking

Artists are curious innovators. They never tire of looking for new challenges — new ways to create. Study the picture at the left. Notice the attention the artist has paid to detail. Notice the fierce looks on the faces of the riders. Notice how the horses seem to gallop across the picture.

The work would be remarkable if the artist had drawn it. But it was made using a technique far more technically involved than drawing with a pen or pencil. In this chapter you will learn more about the technique of printmaking and the media used in this process.

OBJECTIVES

After completing this chapter, you will be able to:
- Explain what printmakers do.
- Identify the three steps in printmaking.
- Name the four main methods for making prints and describe each of the methods.
- Make your own art work using different printmaking methods.

WORDS YOU WILL LEARN

brayer	printing plate
edition	printmaking
intaglio	registration
lithograph	relief printing
lithography	screen printing
monoprinting	serigraph

ARTISTS YOU WILL MEET

Albrecht Dürer	Pablo Picasso
Katsushika Hokusai	Janet Stayton
Doris Lee	Andy Warhol
Edvard Munch	

Point out how the composition of this work organizes the horsemen and the fallen people on imaginary diagonal lines. This helps create depth.

Explain that Dürer was a master at using many lines to follow and create the form of an object. Dürer's groups of lines are so fine that they resemble pen-and-ink drawings. Point out the similarities between drawing and woodcut and the importance of the element of line.

Discussing the Art Work

Ask students to think about the mood of the work. Point out how the woodcut can create severity in the lines of the work. This, along with the high contrast of black and white, provides a harshness to the scene and causes the viewer to focus on the action of the message.

Ask students what elements Dürer used to create movement in this scene. Point out how the riders are set against rolling clouds and how the horizontal lines in the background also run through and behind the clouds. Have students look at the slanting posture of the men with their arms raised in action. Also discuss the horses hooves, how the curved lines of the hats of the two riders and the horse's tail flow to the left, and how the trampled people slant, falling to the right.

Have students look at the small details Dürer chose to include: belts, cuffs, bridles, facial expressions, muscle tone, bone, and the like. Ask them to think about the skill involved in carving this detail from a block of wood.

Tell students that in this chapter they will learn about the different methods of printmaking and will make their own prints.

159

Building Self-Esteem

Tell students that in this chapter they will learn about a number of printmaking techniques. In this lesson they will draw the cover of an invitation to an award ceremony. Tell them, "The ceremony will honor someone very special, YOU!" Perhaps they are being honored for some real or imaginary act of heroism, for being an outstanding student, or doing a great job of cleaning their room at home, for being nice to a brother or sister, or for being a great baseball player or ballerina. Urge them to use their imaginations, and tell them that they can even use a sense of humor in deciding what they are being honored for. On the cover of the invitation they can draw a picture of themselves doing what they are being honored for. The words "HONORING *(name)*" could be included. Discuss the various printing methods and what method might be best to use for duplicating an announcement of this kind.

The Art of Printmaking

LESSON PLAN
(pages 160–161)

Objectives

After completing this lesson, students will be able to:
- Explain what printmakers do.
- Identify the three steps in printmaking.
- Explain the method for numbering prints within an edition.

Supplies

- Thread spool or other small object, tempera paint in a shallow bowl, index cards or small pieces of construction paper.
- Sketch paper.

> **TRB Resources**
> - 9-1 *Critiquing Prints,* (aesthetics/art criticism)
> - 9-2 *The Aesthetics of Everyday Printing,* (aesthetics/art criticism)

TEACHING THE LESSON

Getting Started

Motivator. Review with students the basic steps in printmaking by dipping a thread spool or other small object in tempera paint and making prints on several index cards. As you demonstrate (or as a volunteer demonstrates), help students identify the printing plate, the process of inking the plate, and the final step, transferring the image.

Vocabulary. Help students review the terms *printmaking* and *edition* by asking these questions: What process was used to make these cards? What specific steps identify this process as printmaking? What do we call this complete set of prints?

Developing Concepts

Exploring Aesthetics. Have students work in groups to examine and discuss Hokusai's print shown in Figure 9-1. Let group members share their responses to these questions: What is the subject of this print? How would you characterize the artist's use of color and line? What feeling or idea does this work communicate to you?

160

When you think of printing, newspapers might come to your mind. But printing has its place in art, too. In art, printing, or **printmaking**, is *transferring an inked image from one prepared surface to another*. Often the surface to which a printed image is transferred is paper.

THE HISTORY OF PRINTMAKING

Printmaking is nearly 2000 years old. The Chinese were among the first people to make prints. Later the Japanese developed printmaking into a fine art. (See Figure 9–1.) The remarkable work on page **158** is a print made toward the end of the 1400s. The artist was a German named Albrecht Dürer (**ahl**-brekt **dure**-uhr).

▲ **Figure 9–1 Do you think carving an image into wood may be more time consuming than painting it? What advantages do you think this artist may have seen in choosing wood as his medium?**

Katsushika Hokusai. *View of Mt. Fuji from Seven-Ri Beach*. 1823-29. Colored woodcut. 25.7 x 38.1 cm (10⅛ x 15"). Metropolitan Museum of Art, New York, New York. Rogers Fund.

Background Information

Woodcuts (sometimes called wood blocks or wood engravings) are one of the most familiar and popular forms of relief printing. Their development can be traced back to ancient Babylonia, Egypt, and China, where carved wooden stamps were used to create decorative patterns in clay or wax. During the second century A.D., paper was developed in China, and woodcuts were first used to produce book illustrations. These kinds of illustrated books were introduced in Japan several hundred years later, and during the 1600s Japanese artists developed highly refined techniques of creating woodcuts.

Hishikawa Moronobu (Japan, c. 1618–1694) was a central figure in the development of woodcuts. He was the first artist to produce large editions of a single print and to show that printmaking could be financially rewarding. His subjects included love scenes, historical events, and other topics of interest to the general public.

Prints may be made with many different media and techniques. Dürer's print began as an image carved in a wooden block. Ink was applied to the block, which was then pressed onto a sheet of paper. With the invention of the printing press in 1438, block prints were used for book illustrations.

THE PRINTMAKING BASICS

All prints are made using three basic steps. These steps, in the order in which they take place, are:

- **Making a printing plate.** A **printing plate** is *a surface onto or into which the image is placed*. In making a plate, the artist makes a mirror image of the final print. (See Figure 9–2.)
- **Inking the plate.** The artist applies ink. Often this is done with a **brayer**, *a roller with a handle*. For a multi-color print one plate is made for each color.
- **Transferring the image.** The paper is pressed against the inked plate. Sometimes this is done by hand. At other times a printing press is used.

Usually more than one print is made from a given plate. *A group of identical prints all made from a single plate* is called an **edition**. The artist will determine how many prints are made in an edition.

Creating a Print Edition

As each print in an edition is made, the artist studies it carefully. Each one that meets with his or her approval is signed and numbered in pencil. The number has this form: 11/50. The number on the right tells how many prints are in the edition. The number on the left tells that this particular print is the eleventh print made.

When an edition has been completed, the artist cancels or destroys the plate. This is done by disfiguring the plate so it can no longer be used.

▲ **Figure 9–2** The invention of the printing press changed our world. Can you name some of the advantages?

CHECK YOUR UNDERSTANDING

1. Define the term *printmaking*.
2. Name the three basic steps of making a print.
3. What does the number that appears on a print mean?

162

LESSON 2

More About Printmaking

Printmaking is a popular art technique in today's world. Because prints are usually made in multiples, they are less expensive than paintings. People who might not be able to afford an original painting are often able to buy prints. Figure 9–3, a print by Edvard Munch, shows how stylized some prints can be.

PRINTMAKING

There are four main techniques artists use for making prints. They are relief printing, intaglio, lithography, and screen printing.

Relief Printing

You are probably already familiar with relief printing. If you have ever made a stamp print you have made a relief print. In **relief printing**, *the image to be printed is raised from a background* (Figure 9–4).

▶ Figure 9–3 Does allowing the wood grain to show affect the feeling of the work? How? Does the title help you interpret the image?

Edvard Munch. *The Kiss*. 1902. Woodcut, printed in grey and black, block. 46.7 x 46.4 cm (18⅜ x 18⅝"). Museum of Modern Art, New York, New York. Gift of Abby Aldrich Rockefeller.

Background Information
One of the most famous American lithographers of the nineteenth century was a company. The printing firm of Currier and Ives was created in 1857 by Nathaniel Currier (United States, 1813–1888) and James Merritt Ives (United States, 1824–1895). The firm, which ceased to exist in 1907, printed more than 7000 lithographs. The names of the individual artists are not known. The works were printed in black and white and then hand-painted by hundreds of people working on an assembly line.

Currier and Ives obviously understood that Americans were searching for a national identity; they chose for their prints scenes that reinforced popular notions about American culture. Many of their prints depicted the individual, independent spirit of Americans. Important historical figures, such as George Washington, were popular. Other Currier and Ives prints showed the Wild West or such rugged activities as whaling, hunting, and fishing.

A popular medium in relief printing is carved wood. A print made by carving an image in a wooden block is called a woodcut. The print of the fierce riders on horseback on page **158** is a woodcut. Often woodcuts are done in color. When they are, a separate block, or plate, is made for each color. The blocks must be very carefully lined up during the printing process. If this is not done, the colors in the prints may overlap in the wrong places. This *careful matching up of plates in prints with more than one color* is called **registration**. How many blocks do you think were carved for the woodcut in Figure 9–3?

▲ **Figure 9–4** This drawing shows a woodcut being made. In the upper left corner you will see a detail that shows where the ink contacts the paper during the printing process.

Intaglio

A second technique for making prints is, in a way, the reverse of relief printing. **Intaglio** (in-**tal**-yoh) is *a printmaking technique in which the image to be printed is cut or etched into a surface* (Figure 9–5), rather than being

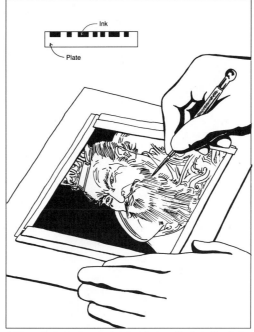

▲ **Figure 9–5** Look at the detail of the intaglio plate. How is it different from the woodcut detail?

raised from a background as in relief printing. In intaglio, paper is forced into the grooves that have been cut and scratched and which hold the ink. If you touch the surface of an intaglio print you can feel the buildup of the printmaking ink. One intaglio technique favored by many printmakers is engraving. In engraving, lines are scratched deep into a metal plate with an engraving tool.

Etching is another printing technique used by many artists. To make an etching, a metal printing plate is covered with a thin protective coating. The drawing is scratched through the coating with an etching needle. The plate is given an acid bath. The lines of the drawing are etched into the metal by the acid while the rest of the plate is protected by the protective covering.

Lesson 2   *More About Printmaking*   📖   **163**

Finally, help students compare the different techniques: What kinds of lines do you see? How would you characterize the shapes, the colors, and the textures in each kind of print?

Vocabulary. Ask students to recall the definition of *relief sculpture* (a form of sculpture in which forms or figures are projected from the front only—in other words, raised). Help them use this definition as a basis for developing their own definition of the term *relief printing*.

You may also want to introduce some etymology to help students remember and understand the names of two other printmaking techniques. *Lithography* comes from two Greek word parts: *lith-* meaning "stone" and *-graphy* meaning "writing." *Intaglio* comes from an Italian word meaning "to engrave or cut."

Developing Concepts

Exploring Aesthetics. Have students examine the reproductions of prints they discussed in the "Motivator" activity and compare those prints with commercially printed pictures from magazine ads and articles. Let students work in groups to discuss the similarities and the differences between the two sets. Ask: Which are works of art? Why are those works art? How would you classify the other works? Were artists engaged in the production of those works? If so, what was their role? After the group discussions, let a representative of each group summarize the results of each discussion for the rest of the class.

Using Art Criticism. Guide students in discussing Doris Lee's print shown in Figure 9-8 on page **164**. Help students describe the colors, lines, shapes, and other visual elements in the work. Then ask: Which elements provide balance in this work? Which elements have been used to add variety? Which elements have been combined to bring harmony to the work? How is emphasis used? Then help students analyze the print by asking: What feeling or message does this work communicate to you? How does the title affect your understanding of the work? Finally, let students choose one aesthetic view as a basis for judging the work.

Classroom Management Tip
To provide students with a record of the special terms and materials presented in conjunction with printmaking, prepare a classroom display including tools, materials, definitions, and illustrations. Have students help organize the display and select new items for inclusion as the lessons progress. Encourage students to refer to the display during class discussions and chapter review sessions.

Cooperative Learning
Many of the Currier and Ives prints have been reproduced on greeting cards and postcards, as well as in magazines and books. Have a group of volunteers work together to find various examples of Currier and Ives prints. Then have them plan and present a visual display—perhaps using an overhead projector or a bulletin board—of the sample prints they have selected.

Understanding Art History.
Have students examine and compare the print by Albrecht Dürer on page **158** and the print by Edvard Munch in Figure 9-3. Encourage students to discuss the differences between these works. Then have them do research to discover some of the reasons for these differences. When was each work created? What were the major events in Europe during those times? What was the social environment in which each artist worked? What materials did each artist use? What message did each artist intend to convey in his work?

Developing Studio Skills.
Explain to students that one relatively simple way to understand the printmaking process is to compare the printing plate to a low relief sculpture. Ask students to remember interesting relief designs on buildings, walkways, gates, fences, and other structures. Tell them to imagine rolling an inked brayer over the surface of these objects and then applying the paper and transferring the ink.

Appreciating Cultural Diversity. Tell students about an Indonesian printing technique used to decorate fabric. Several different designs are carved into wooden blocks. These blocks are then inked and pressed onto the cloth in a repeat pattern, alternating the designs for variety. The decorated fabric is made into clothing. Ask volunteers to learn about other printing techniques used to decorate fabrics. Let them research the tradition and development of silk-screen printing. Suggest they bring information on how India prints are made and what items are being sold using this method. Ask volunteers to find photographs of clothing made from printed fabrics to share with the class.

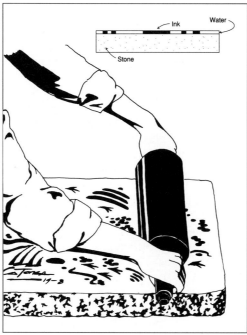

▲ Figure 9–6   The illustration above shows a lithography stone as ink is being applied with a brayer.

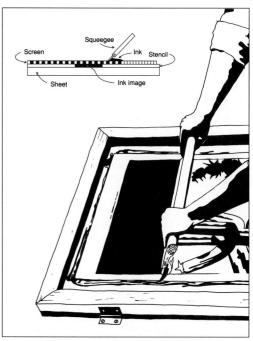

▲ Figure 9–7   Notice the detail of a screen print. How does it differ from the other printing plate details shown in Figures 9–4, 9–5, and 9–6?

▲ Figure 9–8   In this serigraph do you think some screens overlapped? Explain.

Doris Lee. *Untitled*. Serigraph on paper. 55.9 x 76.2 (22 x 30″). National Museum of Women in the Arts, Washington, D.C. Gift of Wallace and Wilhelmina Holladay.

164   📖   Lesson 2   *More About Printmaking*

Handbook Cross-Reference
Encourage students to learn more about the life and the works of Albrecht Dürer, one of whose woodcuts is reproduced on page **158**. They can begin by reading the Artist Profile on Dürer in the *Handbook,* page **283**.

Classroom Management Tip
To let the rest of the school know what the art department is doing, arrange a printmaking display in a showcase or other suitable spot. Have students help select materials and information that will help explain the printmaking process; also ask volunteers to arrange the display itself. Include student-made plates and prints, which can be replaced at regular intervals to represent as many different students as possible.

Lithography

Have you ever noticed that grease and water don't mix? This fact is at the root of the printmaking technique called lithography. **Lithography** (lith-**ahg**-ruh-fee) is *a printmaking method in which the image to be printed is drawn on limestone, zinc, or aluminum with a special greasy crayon.* When the stone is dampened and then inked, the greased area alone holds the ink (Figure 9–6). Paper is pressed against the plate to make the print. *A print made by lithography* is called a **lithograph** (**lith**-uh-graf).

By using separate stones for each hue, lithographs may be printed in several colors. Lithography also allows the artist to use fine lines and blend values little by little.

Screen Printing

You have probably used lettering stencils at one time or another. The same basic idea is at work in **screen printing**, *a printmaking technique in which the artist transfers the design to the screen through various processes.* The area not to be printed is covered up with a special glue or sticky paper. (See Figure 9–7.) Ink is forced through the screen onto paper to make a print. *A screen print that has been handmade by an artist* is called a **serigraph** (**ser**-uh-graf).

Screen printing is the newest method for making prints. It was developed in the United States in this century.

To make a color serigraph, the artist makes one screen, or plate, for each color. Some serigraphs may have as many as 20 colors. How many colors can you find in the serigraph in Figure 9–8?

STUDIO EXPERIENCE

One of the hardest tasks facing a printmaker is thinking backwards. The printing plate, you will recall, must be a mirror image of the final print.

Each student in the class is to select a different letter of the alphabet. Once you have chosen a letter, place a thin sheet of paper over a thick pad of newspaper. Pressing down hard, draw your letter on the thin sheet of paper. Turn the paper over, and you will see your letter in reverse. Using the image as a model, carve a stamp from a cube of modeling clay. Apply paint to your stamp with a brush. On a sheet of paper, make a pattern by pressing your stamp several times. Does each image in your pattern look the same, or do they differ? Does this make your pattern more or less interesting? Explain your answers.

✔ CHECK YOUR UNDERSTANDING

1. Name the four main techniques used for making prints.
2. Define the term *registration*.
3. Explain the difference between a lithograph and a serigraph.

Monoprints

Objectives

After completing this lesson, students will be able to:
• Define the term *monoprinting.*
• Make monoprint drawings of a person.
• Describe, analyze, interpret, and judge their own work.

Supplies

• Simple costume: depending on what you have available, this might be a floppy hat and a big bow tie or scarf; a complete outfit, such as a costume from the drama department.
• Pencils; sheets of sketch paper; water-based printing inks; brayers; squares of smooth vinyl flooring; sheets of white paper, the same size as or larger than the squares of flooring.
• Embossed greeting cards or children's alphabet blocks, newspaper, straight pins, India ink, brushes, sheets of thin paper.

TEACHING THE LESSON

Getting Started

Motivator. Let the students look at and discuss the model (or student volunteer) in costume (see "Supplies"). Ask: How does the costume help make this subject interesting? What special lines and shapes do you see? Lead students to the conclusion that costumes provide surface adornment and can stimulate ideas for printmaking projects.

Vocabulary. Help students define the prefix *mono-,* which means "one" or "single." Then ask students to brainstorm a list of words that begin with the prefix *mono-* and write their words on the board. Review the meaning of each listed word, focusing on the prefix. Finally, ask students to suggest their own definitions of the word *monoprint.*

166

Monoprints

Look at Figure 9–9. This is an example of a type of art print called a monoprint. **Monoprinting** is *a printmaking technique in which the image to be printed is put on the plate with ink or paint and then transferred to paper by pressing or hand-rubbing.* A monoprint plate can be used only once. The paint is absorbed into the paper, and the original image is gone.

WHAT YOU WILL LEARN

You will use a contour drawing process to make a monoprint drawing of a person. The image quality of the monoprint will help you understand the reversal process of printmaking. Create a mood within your work using the elements of line and color. The difference in line quality of a pencil line and a line made in a monoprint will become apparent. (See Figures 9–10 and 9–11.)

WHAT YOU WILL NEED

• Pencil and sheets of sketch paper
• Water-based printing ink
• Brayer
• Square of smooth vinyl flooring to be used as the printing plate
• Sheet of white paper the same size as or larger than the square of flooring

► **Figure 9–9** Notice how much this print looks like a painting. What differences can you see between finished monoprints and finished lithographs?

Janet Stayton. *Yellow Promenade.* 1983. Oil on linen. 151.1 x 181.6 cm (59½ x 71½″). Pat Heesy Museum.

166 Lesson 3 *Monoprints*

Background Information
The monoprint form of printmaking was probably invented by Giovanni Benedetto Castiglione (Italy, c. 1610–1665). In spite of the name, monoprint plates may be used twice, the first time to create a strong, initial image and then the second time to create a weaker impression.

During the nineteenth century, several artists experimented with monoprints. Edgar Degas (France, 1834–1917) and Paul Gauguin (France, 1848–1903) were the best-known mono-printmakers. Degas experimented with many graphic media. Degas also tried etching, drypoint, and lithography. His work exerted a strong influence on Gauguin, who became a pioneer in the field of graphic arts. Gauguin concentrated on design; working with monoprints helped him experiment with different design ideas.

WHAT YOU WILL DO

1. Using pencil and sketch paper, make blind contour drawings of the model. When you are happy with your drawing, move on to the next step.
2. Squeeze ink onto the square of vinyl flooring. This is to be your printing plate. Spread the ink evenly with your brayer.
3. Place the sheet of white paper very lightly on your plate. Don't move it once it is down.
4. Supporting your hand so that it doesn't rest on the paper, use your pencil to draw a contour drawing that fills the paper. Be careful not to let anything but the pencil touch the paper. If a line looks wrong, draw it again. Do not, however, try to erase a line.
5. Starting at two corners, pull your paper carefully from the plate. Do not stop once you begin pulling. Place your paper, image side up, in a safe place to dry.
6. When the print has dried, display your work.

▲ Figure 9–10 Student work. A monoprint.

EXAMINING YOUR WORK

- **Describe**   Show where you used contour drawing to create an image of a person. Explain how the monoprint came out the reverse of your pencil drawing.
- **Analyze**   Explain how the quality of the monoprint line is different from a pencil line. Tell how you created contrast between the line of the print and the paper.
- **Interpret**   Tell what mood your work creates. Explain how the mood is different from one a simple line drawing would create.
- **Judge**   Tell whether you feel your work succeeds. Explain your answer.

▲ Figure 9–11   Student work. A monoprint.

OTHER STUDIO IDEAS

- Make an expressive drawing of a human head and face. Use a paper towel wrapped around your finger to draw this face on a plate. The removed ink will leave white lines on your print. Rub out solid areas for the cheeks, forehead, and chin. Make an impression of the print on a sheet of white paper.

- •• Create a series of three expressive faces and repeat the steps listed above. Try the first print of the face. Check and make any corrections. When you are satisfied, continue with the other two drawings. Compare your prints to see if they work well as a series.

Lesson 3   *Monoprints*   **167**

Developing Concepts

Exploring Aesthetics. Help students discuss and compare the various kinds of prints shown in this chapter: What differences do you see in the quality of the lines? How do these differences affect the content of the prints?

Appreciating Cultural Diversity. Introduce the Japanese art of making monoprints directly from fish, called gyotaku. The word *gyotaku* comes from *gyo*, which means "fish," and *taku*, a shortened form of the word for "rubbings." Explain that this art began as a form of record keeping; samurai warriors were required to ink and print the fish they caught. Ask a group of volunteers to learn more about the history and development of gyotaku and to find reproductions of these prints. Then let the volunteers plan and make a presentation to the rest of the class.

Developing Studio Skills. Let the students work in small groups to make their own monoprints. Give each group an embossed greeting card or a child's alphabet block, and encourage students to examine and discuss its texture. Then have students lay the card or block on a pad of newspapers, brush India ink onto the card or block and gently press a sheet of thin paper onto the inked surface, making a print. Each student in a group can re-ink the card or block and make his or her own monoprint.

Following Up

Closure. Let students work in small groups to discuss the most successful aspects of their own monoprints.

Evaluation. Review students' monoprints, and listen to their evaluations of their own work.

Reteaching. Help students review the process they used in making their monoprints. Ask: Why can a strong image be created only once?

Enrichment. Encourage students to find and discuss reproductions of monoprints created by other well-known artists (see "Background Information").

Classroom Management Tip
If vinyl flooring is not available, students can make their printing plates on any smooth, non-absorbent surface. If printing ink is not available, have students mix tempera paints with liquid starch and use the mixture to ink their plates.

Classroom Management Tip
To reduce smudges and smears, have helpers dispense printing ink when students have finished their practice drawings and are ready to work on their monoprints. Set up individual work stations in advance, if possible; otherwise, organize supplies on trays for groups of students sitting at the same table or in the same work area. Assign clean-up duties in advance, and allow plenty of time for cleaning up.

Glue Prints

Objectives

After completing this lesson, students will be able to:

- Make a printing plate from cardboard and dried glue and use the plate to print an edition.
- Describe, analyze, interpret, and judge their own work.

Supplies

- Several rubber stamps, ink pads, paper.
- White glue; newsprint; toothpicks, rulers; pencils; sheets of sketch paper; squares of corrugated cardboard; water-based printing inks; brayers; squares of vinyl flooring; sheets of white paper, the same size as or slightly larger than the cardboard squares.
- Crayons, white paper.
- One or more octoscopes (kaleidoscope-like instruments usually available in toy stores or gift shops).

> **TRB Resource**
> - 9-6 *Printing Around the World,* (appreciating cultural diversity)

TEACHING THE LESSON

Getting Started

Motivator. Let students work in groups to experiment with a familiar form of relief printing. Give each group a few rubber stamps, one or two ink pads, and a sheet of paper; have group members work together to print a design on the paper. Then let all the groups share their designs with the rest of the class, and help students discuss the process they used to make relief prints. Explain that they will make another kind of relief print in this lesson.

Vocabulary. Let volunteers recall the definition of the term *radial balance* (the balance created by elements or objects positioned around a central point). Then help the students list and discuss examples of radial balance.

168

Glue Prints

The techniques for making relief prints are almost endless. Did you know, for example, that you could make a printing plate from dried white glue? The work in Figure 9–12 was made using such a plate.

WHAT YOU WILL LEARN

You will make a printing plate from cardboard and dried glue. Lines and dots arranged in a radial design will be used. You will print an edition of three prints using water-based inks. Give your finished print a descriptive title.

▲ **Figure 9–12 Student work. A glue print.**

WHAT YOU WILL NEED

- White glue and newsprint
- Toothpicks and ruler
- Pencil and sheets of sketch paper
- Square of corrugated cardboard
- Water-based printing ink
- Brayer and vinyl floor square
- 3 sheets of white paper the same size or larger than the square of cardboard

WHAT YOU WILL DO

1. For practice, squeeze a thin line of glue onto a sheet of newsprint. You will notice that as it dries, it shrinks to form a line of fat dots. By pulling a toothpick from one to another, the dots can be connected again. This forms a new line. (See Figure 9–13.)
2. Using sketch paper, pencil, and ruler, plan a design with radial balance. Use straight lines and dots. Plan your design to fit your printing plate.
3. Transfer your design to the square of cardboard. Go over your lines with glue. Where your design shows lines, connect the shrinking dots to form them. Some lines may need a second coat of glue. When the glue has become clear, it is completely dry and the plate is ready to print.
4. Squeeze a small amount of ink onto a corner of the square of vinyl flooring. Roll your brayer into the ink, first in one direction, then in the other. Be sure that the brayer is well-coated and sticky with ink.
5. Transfer the ink to the cardboard print plate by rolling the brayer across your design in all directions.

Classroom Management Tip

Printmaking is messy! In any printmaking activity it is difficult to keep the work area clean and the prints free of smudges and fingerprints. To help deal with these problems, have students work in pairs. Partners can take turns being the "clean hands" person—the one who handles clean paper and does the pressing. If necessary, remind students that both partners should participate in all the stages of printmaking.

6. With clean hands, place the sheet of white paper very lightly on your plate. Press it to the plate with the heel of your hand or a clean brayer. Pull the paper carefully from the plate. Set the print aside. If the plate is dry, add more ink. Make a second print, and then a third print.

7. When the prints are dry, use a pencil to write the title in the lower left corner of the white paper below the print. Sign your name in the lower right corner. In the center, record the number of the edition (3/3 means the third print in an edition of three).

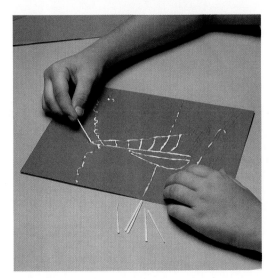

◀ Figure 9–13 The photo at the left shows the technique used to connect the dots as the glue dries.

EXAMINING YOUR WORK

- **Describe** Point out the lines in your print and show what parts of the design were made with dots. Identify each print in the edition. Show where you signed and numbered each print.
- **Analyze** Tell what kind of balance your design has. Explain how the drawing and glue print are different. Identify what is unusual about the lines and surface textures of the glue print.
- **Interpret** Explain what your title tells others about your print. Describe what type of mood or feeling you hoped to express in your print.
- **Judge** Tell whether you feel your work succeeds. Explain your answer.

OTHER STUDIO IDEAS

- Ink your plate and press a sheet of aluminum foil over it to create a relief design. Then carefully remove the foil from the plate. Explain how this print differs in appearance from the paper print.

- ●● Team up with a friend and plan a composition using two glue plates to make one print. Print each plate with a different color.

Lesson 4 *Glue Prints* **169**

Developing Concepts

Using Art Criticism. Help students discuss the print shown in Figure 9-12: What element creates the balance in the print? What kind of balance is it? How does the balance in the print help communicate a feeling or mood? What other elements in the work contribute to that feeling or mood? Is the print successful in communicating a message?

Developing Studio Skills. Have students make crayon rubbings from their glue-print plates. Then let them work in groups to compare and discuss their prints and rubbings. How are the prints and rubbings similar? How are they different?

Appreciating Cultural Diversity. Explain that printmaking is a relatively new form for Inuit art. Inuit artists now use relief and stencil techniques to create sensitive images of birds and other animals in their environment. Ask students to research Inuit prints, and have them try to find reproductions to share with the rest of the class.

Following Up

Closure. Have each student write a paragraph about another student's glue print. The paragraph should include a description of the print and an evaluation of the title. Ask: Does the title match the mood of the work? If not, what title might be better?

Evaluation. Review students' glue prints, and read their evaluations of one another's work.

Reteaching. Ask students to bring in natural objects (such as leaves) and ink them to make prints. Then help them discuss the balance exhibited in each print.

Enrichment. Octoscopes are kaleidoscope-like instruments that multiply segments of viewed images into complex radial designs. Let students look through octoscopes and sketch some of the designs they see. Encourage students to make new glue prints based on some of these sketches.

Classroom Management Tip
Wet prints can take up an amazing amount of classroom space. To save space and prevent smudging, string a clothesline or other small rope across a corner of the room. Then use drilled-spring clothespins to hang the prints until they are dry enough to take down, sign, and display.

Linoleum Block Prints

Linoleum Block Prints

LESSON PLAN
(pages 170–171)

Objectives
After completing this lesson, students will be able to:
• Design and make a linoleum block print.
• Describe, analyze, interpret, and judge their own work.

Supplies
• Colored markers, drawing paper.
• Scrap pieces of linoleum; linoleum cutting tools with different sizes of blades; pencils; sheets of sketch paper; pieces of linoleum, 4 x 6 inches (10 x 15 cm); carbon paper; crayons; inking plates; brayers; colored water-based printing inks; sheets of white paper.

> **TRB Resources**
> • 9-7 *What a Relief!*, (studio)
> • 9-8 *Pablo Picasso,* (artist profile)

TEACHING THE LESSON

Getting Started
Motivator. Begin by letting students draw lines to reflect different moods. Identify a specific mood, such as melancholy, joyous, angry, or peaceful. Ask students to choose a marker in a color that suggests the mood and then to draw a line that expresses the mood. Let volunteers show their lines for each mood, and help students compare and discuss the different color choices they made and the different kinds of lines they drew.

Vocabulary. Ask students to explain what linoleum is and what use of linoleum is most familiar to them. Ask interested students to find out how linoleum is made.

Developing Concepts
Exploring Aesthetics. Let students work in groups to discuss their responses to Figure 9-14. Ask group members to consider these questions: How does the work make you feel? Why do different students have different reactions?

Look at the print in Figure 9–14. This was done by the Spanish artist Pablo Picasso (**pah**-bloh pee-**kahs**-oh). The print was made from a relief carved in a section of linoleum. This material is softer than wood to cut. Notice the thin black lines in the gold area in the upper left corner. These show ridges left from cutting linoleum away in long strips. The artist has left them in to add to the visual interest of the work.

WHAT YOU WILL LEARN
You will create a linoleum block print using a clown as the subject. The main purpose of the print, however, will be to suggest a mood. You will use the elements of line and color to express this mood.

WHAT YOU WILL NEED
• Scrap pieces of linoleum
• Linoleum cutting tool with different sizes of blades
• Pencil and sheets of sketch paper
• Piece of linoleum, 4 x 6 inch (10 x 15 cm)
• Dark-colored marker and tape
• Carbon paper and crayon
• Inking plate and brayer
• Colored water-based printing inks
• Sheets of white paper

WHAT YOU WILL DO
1. Using a linoleum scrap, experiment with the different blades. Practice cutting thin lines and carving out large areas.
2. Using pencil and sketch paper, make rough sketches of a clown design. As you work, experiment with different moods. Remember that color and line can affect

▲ **Figure 9–14   Linoleum is softer than wood. This makes it easier to cut. Compare this work with the woodcut on page 158. What differences between the two types of print can you find?**

Pablo Picasso. *Seated Woman (After Cranach).* 1958. Color linoleum cut, composition. 65.4 x 54.1 cm (25¹¹⁄₁₆ x 21⁵⁄₁₆"). Museum of Modern Art, New York, New York. Gift of Mr. & Mrs. Daniel Saidenberg.

mood. (See Chapter 4, Lessons 2 and 4.) Select the color ink you will use. Set aside your best design sketch.
3. Trace the outline of your linoleum block on a sheet of sketch paper. Draw your final design so that it touches all four edges of the block. Leave some shapes a solid color. Do not draw thin lines. Draw only the main lines of your clown face for now. You will add details later.

Background Information
Pablo Picasso (Spain, 1881–1973), one of the twentieth century's best-known artists, is most famous for his paintings. He was also a gifted sculptor, collagist, ceramicist—and printmaker. Picasso was very active in the art of printmaking, producing hundreds of lithographs during his lifetime.

Picasso created a number of etchings during his Rose Period (1904–1906). The sentimentality of these prints is similar to

that seen in the paintings created during his Blue Period (1901–1904).

Picasso abandoned printmaking when he began developing the Cubist style (around 1907). Lithography then went into a decline, as it had during the mid-1800s, when other forms of printing became popular. In 1944, however, Picasso created another series of prints, which caused a resurgence in the popularity of lithography.

4. Hold your sketch up against a window. With a colored marker, trace over the lines you see through the page. (See Figure 9–15.) This will allow you to make a print that faces in the same direction as your drawing. Otherwise, you will end up with the mirror image of your design.

5. Place a piece of carbon paper on the linoleum. Place your design face down over the carbon paper. Trace over the lines with a pencil. Lift a corner of the carbon paper to be sure the image is transferring to the block. To keep the paper from slipping, tape the paper down.

6. Using the colored marker, color in all the areas on the linoleum that will not be cut away.

7. Using different blades, cut away the background. Remember that the background ridges can add interest to your print. As you cut, stop from time to time and make a crayon rubbing of your plate. This will help you identify areas that need further cutting.

8. Squeeze out some ink on the inking plate, and load the brayer. Roll the brayer over the linoleum block. Place the printing paper carefully on the block, and press the paper to the plate by rubbing it by hand or running it through a press.

9. Make an edition of five prints. Sign and number your prints and display one of them.

SAFETY TIP

Linoleum blades are very sharp and can cause serious cuts. Always cut away from your body and your other hand.

OTHER STUDIO IDEAS

- Make a colored tissue collage on a sheet of white paper. (See Technique Tip **27**, *Handbook* page **281**.) Print your clown design on the collage. Describe the new mood of your print.

EXAMINING YOUR WORK

- **Describe**   Point out the details you used to give the idea of a clown. Identify the details you included in the background. Explain why you used these details.
- **Analyze**   Note which kinds of lines (horizontal, vertical, diagonal) and colors (warm, cool, dark, light) you used.
- **Interpret**   Identify the mood of your print. Explain how the lines and colors you used helped to express this mood.
- **Judge**   Tell whether you feel your work succeeds. Explain your answer.

▲ **Figure 9–15**   This student is transferring the art image to the reverse side of the paper.

●● Hand color one print with crayons or oil pastels. Do not use paints, because your ink is water based and it will run.

Lesson 5   *Linoleum Block Prints*   **171**

Using Art Criticism. Have the class choose two prints shown in other lessons of this chapter. Then help students compare those prints and the Picasso print shown in Figure 9-14: What mood do you think each artist was trying to create? How did each artist use line and color to help develop that mood? How do shape, space, and texture contribute to that mood? Which print do you consider most successful in communicating a mood? Why? After the discussion, have each student write a short analysis of the print he or she likes best.

Understanding Art History. Ask a group of volunteers to find three or more reproductions of art works that were created in different centuries and that have clowns as their subject. Have the volunteers share these reproductions—and a few facts about each artist and the period in which each art work was created—with the rest of the class. Then help students discuss these various art works, noting differences in treatments of the same subject by different artists.

Following Up

Closure. Let students work in small groups to discuss their own block prints, using "Examining Your Work" as a guide. Then have each student write a short explanation of the lines and colors he or she used: How were they successful? How might they have been changed to improve the work?

Evaluation. Review students' block prints, listen to their group discussions, and read their evaluations of the lines and colors they used.

Reteaching. Let students work with partners to plan and make new printing plates with simple designs. Encourage students to experiment with all the available blades.

Enrichment. Let students research the history of the traditional character of French mime, Pierrot, and find reproductions of paintings and other art works representing Pierrot. Encourage them to draw their own Pierrot characters.

Classroom Management Tip

Linoleum cutting tools are sharp; help students learn to use them safely so they can avoid injury. They must keep hands and other parts of the body out of the path of the gouge, and they must never cut toward anyone. To improve control and avoid slipping, try to have students use bench hooks. These simple tools can hold the linoleum block firmly, leaving students with both hands free to manipulate the cutting tool. Simple bench hooks can be purchased through art supply companies or made from scraps of wood.

Silk Screen Prints

Objectives

After completing this lesson, students will be able to:
- Make a screen plate, block out a design on the plate, and use the plate to print an edition.
- Describe, analyze, interpret, and judge their own work.

Supplies

- Recording of "Rhapsody in Blue" or another work by George Gershwin, photograph of George Gershwin.
- Small pieces of construction paper, scissors.
- Pencils, rulers, shoe box lids, utility knives or scissors, sheets of sketch paper, masking tape, nylon net fabric, wax crayons, colored water-based printing inks or school acrylic paints, squeegees or pieces of heavy-duty cardboard, sheets of white paper.
- Reproductions of several art works created by screen printing.

TEACHING THE LESSON

Getting Started

Motivator. Begin by playing a short section of "Rhapsody in Blue" or another Gershwin work. As the music plays, display a photograph of George Gershwin. Then have students look at the Andy Warhol screen print of Gershwin. Ask: How are the photograph and the print different? How do you think this art work was created? What mood or idea does it communicate to you? How do you think the technique used to create the print contributes to that mood or idea?

Vocabulary. Review with students the definitions of *rhythm* and *shape*. Let each student cut out several shapes and try arranging them in different ways to create a rhythmic design.

Silk Screen Prints

Screen printing is the easiest technique to use when making a print using many colors. Study the screen print in Figure 9–16. This was done by American artist Andy Warhol. How many different colors of ink do you think the artist used? How do the colors affect the mood of the work?

WHAT YOU WILL LEARN

You will make a screen plate out of cardboard, masking tape, and net fabric. You will block out a design with a wax crayon. The design will use the principle of rhythm to organize the element of shape. Give your print a title that describes the mood or feeling you want to capture. You will print an edition of three prints.

WHAT YOU WILL NEED

- Pencil and ruler
- Shoe box lid
- Utility knife and scissors
- Sheets of sketch paper
- Masking tape and nylon net fabric
- Wax crayon
- Colored water-based printing ink or school acrylic paint
- Squeegee or a piece of heavy-duty cardboard the size of the screen opening
- Sheets of white paper

▶ **Figure 9–16** What do we learn from the artist's mixing and matching of bold color? What does this tell you about the way color affects shape?

Andy Warhol. *George Gershwin from Ten Portraits of Jews of the 20th Century.* 1980. Silk screen. 50.8 x 81.3 cm (40 x 32"). Ronald Frieman Fine Arts, New York.

Background Information

Andy Warhol (United States, 1927–1987) was probably the best-known American Pop artist. He illustrated popular culture by mass-producing art.

Warhol was trained at the Carnegie Institute of Technology, and during the 1950s he worked as an advertising illustrator. In 1960 he created his first enlarged comic strip figures to be used in window displays. During the next decade he used innovative silk screening techniques to create images of such subjects as Campbell's soup cans, Coca-Cola bottles, and the faces of Hollywood celebrities.

Warhol mass-produced representations of mass-produced consumer goods, and called his work art. He defended his creations by pointing out that mechanical reproduction was an important part of American society and a legitimate means of creating art. His use of the idea of duplication—along with his use of duplication itself—conveys the message of coolness and detachment that is a distinct feature of modern life.

WHAT YOU WILL DO

1. With pencil and ruler, measure a 3 x 5 inch (8 x 13 cm) square on the shoe box lid. Using the utility knife, carefully cut out the rectangle. Protect the table with a thick piece of cardboard.

2. Trace the size of the opening in the shoe box lid on sheets of sketch paper. Experiment drawing rhythmic designs that lead the eye around the space. One way to do this is by repeating shapes. Change the size, however, to add interest to these shapes. (See Figure 9–17.) Choose the best of your designs. Shade the space between the shapes with a pencil. Set your sketch aside.

3. Cut a rectangle of net fabric slightly larger than the opening. With masking tape, fasten the fabric securely to the inside of the lid. Cut a piece of cardboard that will fit inside the lid but cover the opening. The cardboard will act as a squeegee later.

4. Place the screen over your design. Hold it firmly in place. Pressing heavily with the crayon, plug the holes in the net over the shaded areas.

5. Place the screen over a sheet of white paper. Choose a color of ink. Squeeze a small amount of ink at the top of the screen. With your cardboard squeegee, pull ink from the top of the screen to the bottom. As you do, press down heavily.

6. Lift the screen carefully off the paper so as not to smear the ink. Make a second and third print.

7. Display one of your finished prints. Discuss any interesting textures you created.

EXAMINING YOUR WORK

- **Describe**   Tell how this print technique is different from the others you used. Tell how the finished work is different. Show how you repeated the same shape in different sizes.
- **Analyze**   Explain how you used the principle of rhythm to organize the shapes. Tell whether the element of texture plays an unplanned role in the finished work. Discuss what this reveals about printmaking.
- **Interpret**   Tell how the title describes the mood you wanted to express in your work.
- **Judge**   Tell whether you feel your work succeeds. Explain your answer.

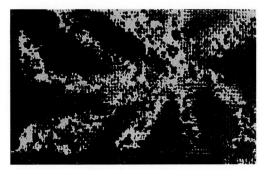

▲ Figure 9–17   Student work. A serigraph.

OTHER STUDIO IDEAS

- Make a screen print using crayon to draw a line design on the screen.

- ●● Borrow a classmate's plate. Using a second color of ink, add a second color to one of your dried prints. Line up the outlines of your print and the plate opening. Describe the result.

Lesson 6   *Silk Screen Prints*   **173**

Cooperative Learning
Encourage interested students to explore these questions together: What other materials can be used to block the screen and create stenciled images? How might school acrylics be used? What effects can be created with white glue? How might liquid wax resist be used? How long must each material dry before you try to print from the screen? Let these students present their ideas—and their new silk screen prints—to the rest of the class.

Note
To help students review the element of shape, you may want to go over Chapter 4, Lesson 5, "Shape, Form, and Space" on pages **66–69**. To help them review the principle of rhythm, you might return to Chapter 5, Lesson 5, "Movement and Rhythm" on pages **90–91**.

Developing Concepts

Exploring Aesthetics. Help students identify some of the commercial products—such as their own T-shirts—that are created through silk screening. Then display reproductions of several art works created by silk screening. Ask: Are the silk screen prints shown here art? Why, or why not? Are your silk screened shirts art? Why, or why not? What makes the difference between a silk screened work of art and a silk screened product?

Understanding Art History. Ask students to read about Andy Warhol and look at reproductions of his work. Then present these two quotations from Warhol: "I like boring things." "I think it would be terrific if everyone looked alike." Help students identify and discuss any relationships they can see between these quotations and Warhol's works.

Developing Studio Skills. Let students experiment with gluing paper shapes onto the bottom side of their screens. The paper blocks the screen completely and produces sharp images.

Following Up

Closure. Ask students to review all the prints they have made in the Studio Lessons of this chapter. Let them discuss their responses to these questions: Which of your prints do you like best? Why? What do you like most about each of your other prints?

Evaluation. Review students' silk screen prints, and consider their evaluations of their own work as printmakers.

Reteaching. Work with small groups of students to review the different printmaking techniques the students have used. Display examples of students' prints, and ask group members to explain how each print was made.

Enrichment. Have groups of students plan and make silk screened posters promoting events such as plays or concerts sponsored by the school or by a local community organization.

BUILDING VOCABULARY

Number a sheet of paper from 1 to 12. After each number, write the term from the box that best matches each description below.

brayer	printing plate
edition	printmaking
intaglio	registration
lithograph	relief printing
lithography	screen printing
monoprinting	serigraph

1. The art of transferring an inked image from a prepared surface to another surface.
2. The surface onto which an image is placed.
3. A roller with a handle.
4. A group of identical prints all made from a single plate.
5. A technique in which the image to be printed is raised from the background.
6. The careful matching of plates in prints with more than one color.
7. A technique in which the image to be printed is cut or scratched into a surface.
8. A technique in which the image to be printed is drawn on limestone with a special crayon.
9. A print made by lithography.
10. A technique in which the image to be printed is drawn on a screen made of silk.
11. A screen print that has been handmade by an artist.
12. A technique in which the image to be printed is put on the plate with ink or paint and then transferred to paper by pressing or hand-rubbing.

REVIEWING ART FACTS

Number a sheet of paper from 13 to 18. Answer each question in a complete sentence.

13. What is inking? What tool is often used in inking?
14. What is meant by the numbers an artist writes on each print in an edition?
15. How does an artist "cancel a plate?"
16. What is a woodcut? What method of printmaking is used to make a woodcut?
17. Name one type of intaglio printing.
18. Which printmaking technique gives an edition size or number as 1?

THINKING ABOUT ART

On a sheet of paper, answer each question in a sentence or two.

1. **Analyze.** What reasons might artists have for canceling a plate at the end of an edition?
2. **Summarize.** Why is being able to "think backwards" important to a printmaker?
3. **Extend.** What problems might there be in making a glue print with an edition of 500?

MAKING ART CONNECTIONS

1. **Social Studies.** Look at the colored woodcut by Hokusai on page **160**. Mount Fuji, a volcano in Japan, appears in many works by Hokusai and other Japanese artists. Look for other art works showing the volcano and share them with the class. Why do you think this image plays such an important part in Japanese works of art?
2. **Science.** The printmaking technique called lithography is based on the fact that oil and water do not mix. What other substances don't mix? Find out why.

LOOKING AT THE DETAILS

The detail shown below is from Albrecht Dürer's woodcut *Four Horsemen of the Apocalypse*. Study the detail and answer the following questions.

1. Albrecht Dürer included many details in his work. What techniques did he use to make objects look like three-dimensional forms?
2. How does Dürer's choice of technique affect the mood of the work?
3. How do you think this image would change if the artist painted it in watercolor?
4. If you were to look at the original woodcut of this image, would it look the same? Explain.
5. What would you think about this image if you were told that it was done by a contemporary artist?

Albrecht Dürer. *The Four Horsemen of the Apocalypse.* Woodcut. (Detail.) 30.9 x 20.8 cm (12 x 8"). Reproduced by courtesy of the Trustees of the British Museum, London.

CHAPTER 10

Painting

Chapter Scan

Lesson 1 The Art of Painting
Lesson 2 Watercolor Painting
Lesson 3 Non-objective Painting
Lesson 4 Expressive Painting

TRB Resources

- 10-1 *Alma Thomas,* (artist profile)
- 10-9 Chapter Test
- Color Transparency 19
- Color Transparency 20

TEACHING THE CHAPTER

Introducing the Art Work

Direct students' attention to *Iris, Tulips, Jonquils and Crocuses* by Alma Thomas. Inform students that Alma Thomas was a painter, teacher, and gallery director who is considered one of the leaders of African-American abstract art. Alma Thomas began creating art in the 1920s, using the media of sculpture. Then in the 1950s she began painting, but it wasn't until the 1960s and at the age of 74 that she developed her own personal style. She chose abstract art as her form of expression. Abstract art is a style created in the twentieth century. Alma Thomas's designs are abstracted from nature and express a unique use of color.

Examining the Art Work

Tell students that the title of this work helps the viewer identify the abstract images as flowers. Explain that the flat rows of bright colors painted with short brush strokes give the viewer an illusion of these three kinds of flowers.

Point out that Alma Thomas establishes a visual rhythm by repeating strokes in the same direction and by using the white background to clearly define a series of repeating columns. Explain how the white background also allows the viewer's eye to rest between the bright patches of color and helps the viewer move in and out of her design.

▲ The strong colors in the bands move up and down as well as across. They show the artist's strong feelings toward nature. Can you see a breeze moving over a sunlit garden? If not, what does the work say to you?

Alma Thomas. *Iris, Tulips, Jonquils and Crocuses.* 1969. Acrylic on canvas. 152.4 x 127 cm (60 x 50″). National Museum of Women in the Arts, Washington, D.C.

Painting

The goal of writers is to make their words speak to the reader. The goal of artists is to make their images "speak" to the viewer. Look at Alma Thomas's painting at the left. Notice the size of the work. How big does that make each of the dabs of color? What hues has she used? Has she used any neutral colors? Has she changed the value of any hues? Can you relate the dabs of paint in her work to the title?

In this chapter you will learn about the many different techniques painters use. You will learn to use some of those techniques yourself.

OBJECTIVES

After completing this chapter, you will be able to:

- Name the basic ingredients of paint.
- Describe six important painting media.
- Make paintings using watercolors, school tempera, and school acrylic.

WORDS YOU WILL LEARN

acrylic	palette
binder	pigment
encaustic	solvent
fresco	synthetic paints
glaze	tempera
impasto	transparent
oil paint	watercolor
opaque	

ARTISTS YOU WILL MEET

Sonia Delaunay	Alice Neel
Lavinia Fontana	Diego Rivera
David Hockney	David Alfaro Siqueiros
Winslow Homer	Alma Thomas
Dong Kingman	Andrew Wyeth

Tell students that Alma Thomas used the vivid colors in acrylic paints to communicate a feeling about the nature of these flowers. The viewer senses the flowers' brilliance and vitality. She uses the bright yellow rows to give the work a slow, irregular beat. The bright yellow is the first color to jump out and attract the eye.

Discussing the Art Work

Ask students to think about other abstract paintings or works they may have seen. Explain to them that abstract painting is a style of expression that does not present objects as they appear to the eye; instead, it presents arrangement of forms and colors as imagined by the artist.

Ask students how this painting makes them feel. Ask them if they might feel something similar if they saw these real flowers arranged in rows. Explain that abstract art is the artist's vision or interpretation of a particular thing and many times abstract art gives the viewer a new way of looking at that thing. Now ask students if they were to see these flowers in real life, would they think of the painting and perhaps begin to see the flowers in a new way.

Suggest other forms in nature: trees, rocks, streams, leaves in the spring, leaves in autumn, and so on. Ask students to think about how they might want to paint some of these forms.

Tell students that in this chapter they will learn about paint and its ingredients as well as various techniques painters use. Then they will create their own paintings using several different painting media.

177

Building Self-Esteem

Explain to the class what the term "Expressive" painting means. Ask if anyone has seen the masks of comedy and tragedy. Tell the class that in this exercise they will be using tempera or watercolors to paint two faces. In the first, they should show someone who is very happy about something. Ask them to think about what the person was doing or what happened that made him or her happy. What colors can be used to show happiness? Next to the first, paint a second face, but this time, show a person who is angry or sad. Tell students to imagine something that could have caused the anger or sadness. Ask what colors can be used to emphasize mood. Should the color be natural or invented? Remind students that they can exaggerate the features of the face to show feeling and that paint can be applied to emphasize the mood. When the paintings have been completed, ask for volunteers to share what they have tried to convey and what action might have been taken to bring on the happiness or sadness they have illustrated.

The Art of Painting

LESSON PLAN
(pages 178–181)

Objectives
After completing this lesson, students will be able to:
• Name the basic ingredients of paint.
• Describe six important painting media.
• Experiment with and compare various kinds of paint in a single hue.

Supplies
• Examples of original student art in each of the six painting media (or as many as possible).
• Painting media, tools, and support media for each of the six painting media (or as many as possible).
• Different kinds of paint of the same hue, brushes, white paper.
• Display-sized color wheel (if available).

> **TRB Resources**
> • 10-2 *Types of Paints,* (reproducible master)
> • 10-3 *The Painted Word,* (art history)

TEACHING THE LESSON

Getting Started

Motivator. Display previous student art done in various painting media. With the paintings, display the media, the tools, and the support material. Give students an opportunity to examine and discuss the displays. Ask: How was each painting created? Which painting medium was used? Which tools do you think were used? How are these paintings alike? How are they different? How would you describe the characteristics of each different kind of paint? Which kind of paint would you most like to try using? Why?

Vocabulary. Help students review the basic vocabulary of paint ingredients by asking these questions: How many parts do all kinds of paints have? What are those parts called? What is pigment? What is binder? What is solvent?

The Art of Painting

Most artists have stories about their first experiences with paint. They tell of blending beautiful, brilliant colors—and of ending up with a muddy mess! They tell of learning little by little how to make paints "behave."

In this lesson you will learn some of their secrets. You will learn to speak about color using the language of art.

THE HISTORY OF PAINTING

Do you remember reading about cave paintings in Chapter 4? Figure 4–1 on page **54** shows one such painting. Works like these date back as far as 15,000 B.C. Humans have been painting for nearly 17,000 years!

In the time since, many paint media and methods have been discovered. A large number of them are still in use.

PAINTING MEDIA

The basis of all paintings is, of course, the paint. Paint, you will recall, has three parts:

• **Pigment** is *a finely ground powder that gives every paint its color.*
• **Binder** is *a liquid that holds together the grains of pigment.*
• **Solvent** is *a material used to thin the binder.*

Every painting medium has its own unique quality. The best-known of these media are encaustic, fresco, tempera, oil paint, acrylic, and watercolor.

Encaustic

Some of the early paintings by the ancient Greeks and Romans were done using **encaustic** (in-**kaw**-stik), *a painting medium in which pigment is mixed into melted wax.* The wax, which is the binder, is kept liquid by heat. Heat is the "solvent." Works that are painted with encaustic seem to glow with light.

Fresco

Another technique of applying paint, which also was developed long ago, is the one called fresco. **Fresco** (**fres**-koh) is *a painting medium in which pigment is applied to a wall spread with wet plaster.* The fresh plaster is applied to a small area of a wall and water-based pigments are painted quickly on the wet plaster. The paint bonds with the plaster, and when the plaster dries, the painting is part of the wall.

In fresco painting, the plaster itself is the binder. There is no solvent. Fresco painting was refined by Italian Renaissance painters and "rediscovered" in this century by Mexican mural painters (Figure 10–1).

▲ **Figure 10–1   How would you describe the looks on the faces of these men? What part does the medium play in the artist's "statement"? Explain.**

Diego Rivera. *Detroit Industry.* 1923–33. Fresco. North wall central panel. (Detail.) Founders Society, Detroit Institute of the Arts, Detroit.

Background Information
Diego Rivera (Mexico, 1886–1957) was the most famous of several twentieth-century Mexican muralists. Rivera trained first in his native Mexico and then in Europe. After experimenting with Cubism, he returned to Mexico—and to the traditions of Mexican art. He painted large murals depicting contemporary Mexican life and reflecting his interest in social and political themes.

During the 1930s Rivera was invited to paint frescoes on several important buildings in the United States. Here he gained fame—and a bit of notoriety. He was commissioned to paint a mural at Rockefeller Center, but the work was later destroyed because Rivera had included a portrait of Lenin.

In addition to his murals, Rivera created easel paintings and portraits. He also designed and built his own house, which he named Anahuacalli. The house is now a museum housing the collection of pre-Columbian art that Rivera left to the people of Mexico.

▲ **Figure 10–2** Why do you think this artist chose tempera as his medium? How might this same image differ if he had used watercolor?

Andrew Wyeth. *Christina's World.* 1948. Tempera on gessoed panel. (Detail.) 81.9 x 121.3 cm (32¼ x 47¾"). Museum of Modern Art, New York, New York.

▲ **Figure 10–3** What is the visual texture of this work? How do you think the artist's application of oil paint contributes to its realism?

Lavinia Fontana. *Portrait of a Noblewoman.* c. 1580. Oil on canvas. (Detail.) 115.6 x 89.5 cm (45½ x 35¼"). National Museum of Women in the Arts, Washington, D.C. Gift of Wallace and Wilhelmina Holladay.

Tempera

Another very old medium is **tempera** (tem-puh-ruh), *a painting medium in which pigment mixed with egg yolk and water is applied with tiny brush strokes.* Tempera does not spread easily or blend well. Because of this, **transparent**, or *clear*, layers of color must be built up little by little. This can take time. Once dry, tempera is waterproof.

Tempera allows a painter to capture the details of a subject. Look at the portion of a painting, or detail, in Figure 10–2. Note how the artist shows highlights in the hair and in the individual blades of grass.

Notice, by the way, that this use of tempera is not the same medium as the tempera paint you use in school. The paint you use in your work is a poster paint.

Oil Paint

Oil paint is *paint with an oil base.* Oil paint was first used in the 1400s and has continued to be one of the most popular mediums used today.

Linseed oil is the binder for oil paint, and its solvent is turpentine. Oil paint dries slowly. This allows artists to blend colors right on the canvas.

Oil paint can be applied in *thick, buttery layers*, called **impasto** (im-**pahs**-toh), to make interesting textures. When applied thickly, oil paint is opaque. **Opaque** (oh-**pake**) means *that it does not let light pass through.* It can also be applied in a *thin, transparent layer*, called a **glaze**. A glaze allows dry color underneath to show through. Some painters make their works glow with light by building up layers of glaze. Look at Figure 10–3. Notice how the artist has blended the colors of the face so that they seem to melt together.

Developing Concepts

Exploring Aesthetics. Help students examine, discuss, and compare the paintings shown in Figures 10-1, 10-2, 10-3, 10-4, 10-5, and 10-6. Be sure students understand that each reproduction shows a detail from a larger painting. Ask: How would you characterize the use of color in each painting? How do you think the choice of medium affects the color? How would you characterize the use of line and texture in each painting? Are these elements also affected by the artist's choice of medium? Then let students discuss the subject of each painting and the idea or feeling they feel each communicates. You may want to have volunteers find and display reproductions of each work in its entirety; ask students whether seeing the whole painting changes their ideas about its subject or its content.

Using Art Criticism. Have students form six groups, one to discuss each of the paintings reproduced in this lesson. Let students in each group discuss stories suggested by their painting: What is happening in the painting? What may have just happened? What will happen next? After the group discussion, have each student work independently to write an original story suggested by the painting.

Understanding Art History. Have groups of students do research to learn more about the fresco paintings of the Italian Renaissance. Ask each group to find and examine reproductions of at least four different frescoes. Also have students read to find answers to questions such as these: How did members of a shop work together in creating a fresco? What were the master's responsibilities? What did the assistants do? Who are the most famous fresco painters of the thirteenth, fourteenth, and fifteenth centuries? Where can their frescoes be seen? When the groups have finished their research, let them discuss their reactions to what they have learned.

Note

The ingredients and directions for mixing plaster are given in "Carving a Plaster Relief," pages **212–213**. Only a small amount is needed for the "Developing Studio Skills" activity. Pouring plaster into a round plastic lid will provide an appropriate shape for the fresco color wheel. When plaster is set, wrap it in plastic to keep it damp until students are ready to use it.

Classroom Management Tip

Caution is needed when mixing plaster for the fresco painting activity. Avoid breathing plaster dust, and avoid mixing plaster when students are present.

Remember that plaster must be kept away from sinks and drains to avoid clogging the plumbing. Rinse your hands and the mixing equipment thoroughly in a bucket of water before washing at the sink. Then dispose of the rinse water without pouring it down the drain.

Watercolor

Once used only for sketches, watercolor has become a favorite medium of serious painters. **Watercolor** is *a painting medium in which pigment is blended with gum arabic and water.* Watercolor takes its name from its solvent. For the best results, watercolors are applied to good quality white paper. Blended colors are usually mixed on a palette before painting. A **palette** can be *any tray or plate where paints are mixed before use.* A white palette allows you to see what new mixed hues will look like against white paper before painting. A piece of white scrap paper can also be used to test colors for value and intensity before painting on good quality paper.

Watercolor can give a light, misty feel to paintings or they can be intense and brilliant.

Look at Figure 10–4. The artist, Winslow Homer, was among the first to use watercolor in finished works. Notice the amount of white paper he allows to show through. How do you think this affects the look of the work?

Acrylic

Advances in technology in the twentieth century have given artists new media choices. **Synthetic paints** are *manufactured paints with plastic binders.* They came onto the scene in the 1930s. The first artist to use a synthetic paint was a Mexican mural painter. His name was David Alfaro Siqueiros (dah-**veed** al-**far**-oh see-**care**-ohs). Figure 10–5 shows a detail from one of Siqueiros's early experiments. The work was done with quick-drying duco (**doo**-koh) paint.

▲ **Figure 10–4** Is there any movement in this work? How does it feel? Compare the visual texture of this painting with Figure 10–3.

Winslow Homer. *Return From the Hunt.* 1982. Watercolor. (Detail.) 40.6 x 53.3 cm (16 x 21"). Los Angeles County Museum of Art, Los Angeles. Paul Rodman Mabury Collection.

▲ **Figure 10–5** Do you find the look on this child's face troubling? Why? How do you think the medium helped the artist capture this mood?

David Alfaro Siqueiros. *Echo of a Scream.* 1937. Enamel on wood. (Detail.) 121.9 x 91.4 cm (48 x 36"). Museum of Modern Art, New York, New York. Gift of Edward M. M. Warburg.

180   Lesson 1   *The Art of Painting*

One of the most widely used paints today is **acrylic** (uh-**kril**-ik), *a quick-drying water-based synthetic paint.* Acrylic paint first appeared in the 1950s. Not only does acrylic offer the artist a wide range of pure, intense colors (Figure 10–6) but it also is versatile. Like oil paint, it can be applied both thickly and in thin glazes. Acrylic paints can even be thinned enough to be sprayed in a thin mist with an airbrush. Acrylic is less messy to use than is oil paint because the solvent used for acrylic paint is water.

▲ **Figure 10–6** How does the artist's choice of color contribute to the mood of this painting?

David Hockney. *Les Mamelles des Tiresias*. 1980. Oil on canvas. (Detail.) 91.5 x 122 cm (36 x 48").

✔ CHECK YOUR UNDERSTANDING

1. What are the three main parts of paint?
2. How is encaustic different from fresco? How is it different from tempera?
3. How is oil paint different from watercolor? How is it different from acrylic?
4. What is impasto? What is a glaze?
5. What is a synthetic paint? When did synthetic paints first appear?

Lesson 1 *The Art of Painting* **181**

Watercolor Painting

Look at the painting in Figure 10–7 by the artist Dong Kingman. He has captured a day in the life of an American city. Do you know what city it is? Is this just an ordinary day? How can you tell?

Take another look at the painting. What kind of paint did the artist use to create this work? What is unusual about his use of white paper?

▲ **Figure 10–7   What is the mood of this work? How does the medium help set the mood? How does the artist's attention to small details help?**

Dong Kingman. *Cable Car Festival.* 1988. Watercolor on paper. 76.2 x 55.9 cm (30 x 22"). Conacher Gallery San Francisco.

WHAT YOU WILL LEARN

You will make a watercolor painting in the style of Dong Kingman. The subject will be a festival that includes people and a setting. Pick an event similar to the one in Figure 10–7. Use bright colors to emphasize some part of the event in which people are having fun. Use lines and color to create a feeling of excitement. You will leave areas of your work unpainted.

WHAT YOU WILL NEED

- Pencil and sheets of sketch paper
- Watercolor paints
- Palette for mixing colors
- Container for water
- Thin and thick watercolor brushes
- Sheet of good quality white paper, pressed board, or watercolor paper, 12 x 18 inch (30 x 46 cm)
- Paper towels

WHAT YOU WILL DO

1. Brainstorm with your classmates to develop ideas for your work. Choose a festive occasion that is important to you, your school, or your community. Think of the particular part of the festival that represents the excitement. Think of special colors tied to the occasion and how those colors add to the festive mood.
2. Make pencil sketches to plan your work. Use line movements to create excitement. Choose your best idea.
3. Remember to set up all your supplies before you begin. Watercolor is a quick-drying medium.
4. Mix a light value of a watercolor paint on your palette. (You create light values with watercolors by adding more water to the

---

Objectives

After completing this lesson, students will be able to:
- Make watercolor paintings in the style of Dong Kingman.
- Describe, analyze, interpret, and judge their own work.

Supplies

- Old magazines with color photographs, scissors, large sheets of colored construction paper, glue.
- Pencils; sheets of sketch paper; watercolor paints; palettes for mixing colors; water and containers; thin and thick watercolor brushes; sheets of good quality white paper, pressed board, or watercolor paper, 12 x 18 inches (30 x 46 cm); paper towels.

> ### TRB Resources
> - 10-4 *Get Into the Act,* (cooperative learning)
> - 10-5 *Ideas for Watercolor Painting,* (reproducible master)

TEACHING THE LESSON

Getting Started

Motivator. Let students work in groups to find and discuss photographs of festive occasions. Have the students in each group go through magazines to select and cut out photos showing people who are celebrating. Then ask the group members to select their favorite photos and glue them onto a large sheet of construction paper. Encourage them to use construction paper in a color that helps develop the sense of a festive occasion. Finally, let each group present its display to the rest of the class, describing the photographs and noting especially how the lines and colors contribute to the festive mood in each photo.

Vocabulary. Help students review the definitions of *watercolor* and *palette,* noting the particular uses of each. (Refer students to page **180,** if necessary.)

Background Information

Paints made with water and gum arabic have been used since ancient times. One form of water paint was used on the illuminated manuscripts of the Middle Ages. Albrecht Dürer (Germany, 1471–1528) used another form of water paint as a wash. Watercolor as we know it now, however, did not develop until the late eighteenth century. The medium became especially popular in Great Britain, where several outstanding landscape artists painted with watercolor.

Watercolor has its own characteristics that demand a certain ability and knowledge to handle. The art of watercolor relies on glazing thin layers of transparent colors on each other, allowing the paper to give light to the painting. Watercolorists usually use special papers that have grains ranging from smooth to rough and weights ranging from heavy and thick to light and thin. Each kind of paper allows the artist to produce different effects of light and color. See Technique Tip 14, *Handbook* page **275.**

▲ Figure 10–8 Student work. A watercolor painting.

color you choose. This will allow more white from the paper to show through.) With the thin brush, draw your final sketch onto the sheet of good white paper. (See Technique Tip **4**, *Handbook* page **271**.)

EXAMINING YOUR WORK

- **Describe**   Identify the festive occasion you chose to paint. Tell what part of the event you focused on. Tell what colors and kinds of lines you used.
- **Analyze**   Point to areas in which bright colors are used. Explain how these colors emphasize these areas. Explain how you created contrast.
- **Interpret**   Tell what words a viewer might use to describe the mood of your painting. Explain how color and line are used to create this mood. Give your work a title based on its mood.
- **Judge**   Tell whether you feel your work succeeds. What views of art would you use to defend your answer?

─────────

5. Decide which area of your work you will emphasize and paint this area with your brightest colors. Paint other areas in contrasting dull colors. Leave large areas of the white paper showing. Do not paint in all your drawn objects. If you like, draw over some of your light lines with darker paint with a thin brush.
6. When your work is dry, display it. Discuss various ways classmates have achieved contrast and shown excitement using line and color.

OTHER STUDIO IDEAS

- Try drawing your work with colored pencil or crayon. Then wet the whole paper and paint it wet on wet. When it dries, add stronger color.

- ●● Notice how Kingman has used comedy in the work. Look at the little mice in the lower right corner. Notice the figure that is white, except for the brown legs. Find something you have finished, and add some unexpected things to it to create humor.

Lesson 2   *Watercolor Painting*   **183**

LESSON PLAN
(pages 184–185)

Objectives

After completing this lesson, students will be able to:
• Use repetition of geometric shapes to produce paintings showing rhythmic movement.
• Describe, analyze, interpret, and judge their own work.

Supplies

• Tempera paints, brushes, white paper, recording of music with several different rhythms.
• Pencils; sheets of sketch paper; rulers; different-sized objects with round shapes, such as jar lids and empty cans, or round, pre-cut cardboard patterns in various sizes; paper towels; yellow chalk; sheets of white paper, 12 x 18 inches (30 x 46 cm); tempera paints; thin and thick bristle brushes.
• Construction paper in primary and secondary hues, scissors.

> **TRB Resource**
> • 10-6 *Painters and Fashion,* (aesthetics)

TEACHING THE LESSON

Getting Started

Motivator. Begin by helping students explore the relationship between rhythmic movement in paintings and musical rhythm. Play a short piece of music, and ask students to respond to the music by choosing a paint color and then moving the brush in time with the rhythm. After several minutes, change the music and encourage the students to change paint colors and begin responding to the new rhythm. Use two or more musical selections, as time permits. Then encourage students to share their paintings and to discuss their reactions to this activity.

Vocabulary. Help students review the definitions and uses of the terms *non-objective* and *rhythm* by having them re-examine a familiar work, Piet Mondrian's *Blue Tree,* Figure 4-26 on page **74.**

184

Non-objective Painting

Look at the painting in Figure 10–9. The artist, Sonia Delaunay, believed color was the most important art element. With her artist-husband, Robert, she explored the expressive quality of color. Notice the rhythmic movement of the shapes along diagonal lines. Notice also the soft edges of the shapes.

WHAT YOU WILL LEARN

You will make a painting that, like Delaunay's, is made up of the repetition of geometric shapes. Also like hers, yours will show rhythmic movement. You will use a primary- or secondary-color scheme. The background will be painted in black. (See Figure 10–10.)

WHAT YOU WILL NEED

• Pencil, sketch paper, and ruler
• Round shapes of different sizes, such as jar lids, or pre-cut cardboard patterns
• Paper towels
• Yellow chalk
• White paper, 12 x 18 inch (30 x 46 cm)
• Tempera paints, thin and thick brushes

▶ **Figure 10–9 Does your eye start at the top of this painting or at the bottom? Is the beat of the work a fast one or a slow one? Explain your answers.**

Sonia Delaunay. *Colored Rhythm No. 698.* 1958. Oil on canvas. 114.3 x 87 cm (45 x 34¼"). Albright Knox Art Gallery, Buffalo, New York. Gift of Seymour H. Knox.

184   Lesson 3   *Non-objective Painting*

Background Information
Sonia Delaunay (Russian-born, France, 1885–1979) and her husband Robert Delaunay (France, 1885–1941) were both important non-objective painters who became known for their use of color.

Robert Delaunay is considered the creator of Orphism, a development of Cubism. A contemporary French critic who gave the movement its name defined it as "the art of painting new structures out of elements that have not been borrowed from the visual sphere, but have been created entirely by the artist himself and endowed by him with the fullness of reality."

Sonia Delaunay (sometimes known as Sonia Terk or Sonia Delaunay-Terk) participated with her husband in the development of this movement. She created abstract art that depended on color for a decorative effect as well as to suggest movement. In addition to her painting, Sonia Delaunay created designs for books and for clothes; in all areas of her art, she used bright colors and abstract forms.

WHAT YOU WILL DO

1. Using pencil and sketch paper, plan your work. Using the ruler, draw a diagonal line across the paper from top to bottom. With the ruler, make squares and/or rectangles so that their sides rest on the diagonal. Use the circle patterns to make a series of circular shapes in different sizes. These should meet and cross the lines of the four-sided shapes. Repeating the different shapes will give a feeling of rhythm and movement to the design.

2. Using yellow chalk, draw your design on the sheet of white paper. Use the ruler and circle pattern. The edges of your shapes do not have to be perfect. Draw your design so that it touches at least three sides of the paper.

3. Choose a primary- or secondary-color scheme for the work. You may also use white. Repeat your colors in a way that adds to the sense of rhythmic movement.

4. Using the thin brush, paint the outline of each shape. Switch to the thick brush to fill in each shape with the same color you used for its outline. Since poster paints will run, be sure that one shape is dry before you paint a wet color next to it. (For more on using poster paints, see Technique Tip **13**, Handbook page **275**.)

5. When your work is dry, display it along with those made by other members of the class. Do any of the paintings look like yours? Are some completely different?

▶ Figure 10–10   Student work. Non-objective painting.

EXAMINING YOUR WORK

- **Describe**   Identify the diagonal line that organizes the shapes in your work. Point out and name the different geometric shapes you used. Explain which color scheme you chose.
- **Analyze**   Tell what colors and shapes you repeated to create rhythmic movement. Tell whether the "beat" of your work is steady or irregular. Show the path the viewer's eye follows through your work. Explain how you created contrast.
- **Interpret**   Tell what mood your work expresses. Give your work a title based on this mood.
- **Judge**   Tell whether you feel your work succeeds. Explain your answer.

OTHER STUDIO IDEAS

- Do the same project, but limit yourself to the repetition of one geometric shape, and vary the sizes.

•• Do the same project but limit the colors to a pair of complementary hues and black and white.

Lesson 3   *Non-objective Painting*   **185**

Developing Concepts
Using Art Criticism. Help students examine and discuss Sonia Delaunay's painting shown in Figure 10-9. Ask: What do you see when you look at this work? Which hues can you identify? How are those hues related? What kinds of lines are used in this painting? What kinds of shapes do you see? What evidence can you identify to show the principles of rhythm, variety, and balance? After this discussion, have students write a short interpretation of the painting, answering this question: What feeling does this painting communicate to you?

Developing Studio Skills. You may want to refer the students to Technique Tips 12 and 13, *Handbook* pages **274** and **275** respectively.

Understanding Art History. Ask students to work with partners to find reproductions of other non-objective art works in this text (or in other sources) and to note the year in which each was created. Then ask: When was the earliest of these non-objective works created? Why do you think artists began creating non-objective art around that time?

Following Up
Closure. Let the students work in groups to compare and discuss their non-objective paintings: What are the most important differences between the works? Why are the paintings different?

Evaluation. Review students' non-objective paintings, and listen to their group discussions.

Reteaching. Have students work with partners to cut a series of geometric shapes from construction paper in primary and secondary hues. Then, using the diagonal lines described in the lesson, let the partners experiment with different arrangements of the shapes to show rhythmic movement.

Enrichment. Ask students to pay special attention to their environment: Which objects and scenes show repetition? Have students record their observations by making sketches, writing notes, or taking photographs. Then encourage students to compare and discuss their observations.

Expressive Painting

Expressive Painting

Sometimes artists use their works to speak about problems of the day. Look at the painting in Figure 10–11. It was done in 1940 by an American painter named Alice Neel. The patient in the painting is suffering from "T.B.," or tuberculosis. At the time of the painting, cases of tuberculosis were widespread in inner city ghettos. Its victims were, like the person in the painting, poor.

What statement about ghetto life and about being poor might the artist be making in this work? Which elements and principles has she chosen to punctuate her statement?

WHAT YOU WILL LEARN

You will learn to use social issues as content for a work of art. A social statement can be subject matter for art works. Select a social issue that faces the world today. You will paint a close-up view of people to illustrate this issue. Colors and heavy lines will be used to emphasize the mood of your work. Distorting the proportions of shapes will also add to this mood. Free-flowing, loose brush-strokes will be used to show movement and add texture. (See Figure 10–12.)

WHAT YOU WILL NEED

- Pencil and sheets of sketch paper
- School acrylic paints
- Shallow tray with sides to mix paints
- Water (as a solvent)
- Bristle brushes, varied sizes
- Sheet of heavy white paper, 12 x 18 inch (30 x 46 cm)
- Water (to clean brushes) and paper towels

▶ **Figure 10–11** What is the patient in the picture feeling? How does the artist help you feel the suffering? How does the medium help?

Alice Neel. *T. B. Harlem.* 1940. Oil on canvas. 76.2 x 76.2 cm (30 x 30"). National Museum of Women in the Arts, Washington, D.C. Gift of Wallace & Wilhelmina Holladay.

LESSON 4

Expressive Painting

LESSON PLAN
(pages 186–187)

Objectives

After completing this lesson, students will be able to:
- Paint close-up views of people to illustrate social issues.
- Describe, analyze, interpret, and judge their own paintings.

Supplies

- Collection of photographs and drawings that illustrate current social issues, such as poverty, family abuse, violent crime, and pollution (ask volunteers to cut photos and drawings from old newspapers and magazines provided by the school, or have each student bring in at least one clipping).
- Pencils; sheets of sketch paper; school acrylic paints; shallow trays with sides to mix paints; water; bristle brushes in various sizes; sheets of heavy white paper, 12 x 18 inches (30 x 46 cm); paper towels.
- Long sheet of butcher paper or other mural paper, tempera paints, brushes.

TRB Resources

- 10-7 *Native American Painters*, (appreciating cultural diversity)
- 10-8 *Thematic Mixed Media*, (studio)

TEACHING THE LESSON

Getting Started

Motivator. Display photographs and drawings from newspapers and magazines that illustrate current social issues (see "Supplies"). Have students point out the photos or drawings that seem to tell most vividly about a condition or conflict. Ask: What messages do these photographs and drawings communicate? What details help make the messages clear?

Vocabulary. Direct students' attention to the title of the lesson, and help them explore the meaning of the work *expressive*: When you "express yourself," are you more likely to deal in facts or in emotions? How do you think you might express emotions in a painting?

186

WHAT YOU WILL DO

1. Brainstorm with your classmates, and list social issues of the day. Some possibilities include pollution, teenage pregnancy, drug abuse, the homeless, and acid rain. Choose one that you know about and that truly concerns you.
2. Think about a way that you can create a painting that will make people think about the problem. How can you show its effect on people?
3. Make several pencil sketches for your composition. Use distortion and exaggeration to make your message strong. This is a painting, not a poster. Do not put any words in balloons for your people to speak. The visual image must carry the message. Select the best sketch.
4. Decide on a color scheme. Think about what colors will help express your feelings. How can you use strong contrast?
5. Pour a little of a light-value paint into the shallow tray. Add enough solvent to make a thin paint. Using your 1/4-inch (0.6-cm) brush draw the main shapes of your work on the sheet of white paper.
6. Paint your composition. Using your 1-inch (2.5-cm) brush, add deeper hues to the shapes. Do not try to smooth over the brush strokes. Let them show movement and create different textures. Use strong colors to emphasize the outlines of your shapes.
7. Put your work on display. Can you and your classmates read the themes in each others' statements?

► Figure 10–12 Student work. An expressive painting.

EXAMINING YOUR WORK

- **Describe** Identify the person or persons in your work. Tell what problem you chose to speak about. Tell what statement you decided to make. Identify the colors and lines used. Identify places where different textures are used.
- **Analyze** Point to places where free-flowing, loose brushstrokes are used to show movement. Explain how the heavy lines and brush strokes add to the distortion, exaggeration, and contrast. Show where the proportions of shapes have been distorted.
- **Interpret** Tell what mood your painting expresses. Explain how the colors you chose help express this mood. Tell how distortion adds to the mood. Give your work a title that sums up its meaning.
- **Judge** Tell whether you feel your work succeeds in making a social statement. Tell whether it succeeds as a work of art. Explain your answers.

OTHER STUDIO IDEAS

- Carry out this project combining magazine cutouts and paint.
- ●● Choose one hue, and paint your work using a monochromatic color scheme.

Lesson 4   *Expressive Painting*   **187**

Developing Concepts

Exploring Aesthetics. Help students examine Alice Neel's painting in Figure 10-11. Next have each student write a short answer to this question: How does *T. B. Harlem* make you feel? Then ask students to share and discuss their reactions to the work.

Understanding Art History. One of the best-known art works dealing with social issues is Pablo Picasso's *Guernica*, which he painted in 1937. The work was inspired by the bombing of Guernica during the Spanish Civil War. Have students find reproductions of *Guernica* and read about both the work itself and the events that led Picasso to create it.

Developing Studio Skills. Let students work together to select an issue of concern at their school. Then have them plan and paint a large mural that expresses a statement about that issue. Display the completed mural in a school hallway.

Following Up

Closure. Display all the students' paintings. Have each student choose one work (other than his or her own) to examine closely. Then ask students to write short paragraphs, using words to communicate the message they feel that painting communicates.

Evaluation. Review students' expressive paintings, and read their paragraphs based on others' expressive paintings.

Reteaching. Work with small groups of students to review the subject and the content of Neel's painting, Figure 10-11. Then have the group members look through the text (or other sources) to find art works depicting other expressive faces. What different messages and moods can they identify?

Enrichment. Have small groups of students select a social problem, such as poverty or the horrors of war. Ask the group members to find at least eight different art works (by different artists) dealing with that issue.

Classroom Management Tip
Help students consider the use of distortion and exaggeration to create expressive visual statements. Refer them to Alice Neel's painting (Figure 10-11) and to David Alfaro Siqueiros's painting on page **180** (Figure 10-5). Encourage them to try using various forms of distortion and exaggeration in their sketches. To help them experiment with these techniques, suggest they draw closer views of their subject and that they enlarge the image of the subject, making it fill the entire work.

Cooperative Learning
Let students work in groups to consider one of the social issues depicted in their expressive paintings. What are possible solutions to the problem inherent in that issue? Which of those solutions do group members think should be adopted? How can they paint a work that promotes that solution? Then have group members work together to plan, execute, and display that painting.

ANSWERS TO "CHAPTER 10 REVIEW"

Building Vocabulary

1. pigment
2. binder
3. solvent
4. encaustic
5. fresco
6. tempera
7. oil paint
8. impasto
9. transparent
10. glaze
11. watercolor
12. synthetic paints
13. acrylic
14. opaque
15. palette

Reviewing Art Facts

16. The three parts of paint are pigment, which gives the paint its color, binder, which holds together the grains of pigment, and solvent, which thins the binder.
17. In encaustic the solvent is heat. In fresco there is no solvent.
18. Tempera can be hard to use because it does not spread easily or blend well and because layers of color must be built up little by little. Two advantages of tempera are that it is waterproof and that it allows a painter to capture the details of a subject.
19. Because oil paint dries slowly, an artist can blend colors on the canvas.
20. Oil paint can be applied in thick, buttery layers, called impasto, which makes interesting textures. It can also be applied in a thin, transparent layer, called a glaze, which allows dry color underneath to show through.

Thinking About Art

1. Responses will vary; they should show students understand that cave dwellers probably used materials they found in nature—in soil, rocks, and plants, for example.
2. Responses will vary; they should indicate an understanding of some difficulties in working with melted wax.
3. Responses will vary; they should indicate an understanding of some problems associated with working quickly on wet plaster.

CHAPTER 10 REVIEW

BUILDING VOCABULARY

Number a sheet of paper from 1 to 15. After each number, write the term from the box that best matches each description below.

acrylic	palette
binder	pigment
encaustic	solvent
fresco	synthetic paints
glaze	tempera
impasto	transparent
oil paint	watercolor
opaque	

1. A finely ground powder that gives every paint its color.
2. A liquid that holds together the grains of pigment.
3. A material used to thin the binder in paint.
4. A medium in which pigment is mixed into melted wax.
5. A medium in which pigment is applied to a wall spread with wet plaster.
6. A medium in which pigment mixed with egg yolk and water is applied with tiny brush strokes.
7. Paint with an oil base.
8. Thick, buttery layers of paint.
9. Clear.
10. A thin, clear sheet of paint.
11. A painting medium in which pigment is blended with gum arabic and water.
12. Manufactured paints with plastic binders.
13. Quick-drying water-based synthetic paint.
14. Does not allow light to pass through.
15. Light colored tray where paints are mixed before they are used for painting.

REVIEWING ART FACTS

Number a sheet of paper from 16 to 20. Answer each question in a few words.

16. What are the three parts of paint? What is the purpose of each part?
17. What is the solvent in encaustic? In fresco?
18. Why is tempera paint hard to use? What is an advantage of using it?
19. What fact about oil paint allows an artist to blend colors on the canvas?
20. Name two different techniques for applying oil paint. Tell what kind of results you get with each technique.

THINKING ABOUT ART

On a sheet of paper, answer each question in a sentence or two.

1. **Interpret.** What sort of paint do you think cave dwellers used to make their paintings? What sorts of tools do you think they painted with? Explain your answers.
2. **Analyze.** Do you think encaustic was an easy medium to use? Why, or why not?
3. **Compare and contrast.** Name some problems of doing frescoes that would not be true of other painting techniques.

MAKING ART CONNECTIONS

1. **Language Arts.** Discuss how artists use their art work to speak about problems or social issues. Write a paragraph describing what the artist was trying to say in *Echo of a Scream* on page **180**.
2. **Science.** Explore an interesting color illusion called an afterimage. Stare at a bright shape for a minute and then look away. What do you see? It's an afterimage of the same shape and size but a different color. Read about this occurrence and report to the class.

LOOKING AT THE DETAILS

The detail shown below is from Alma Thomas' *Iris, Tulips, Jonquils and Crocuses.* Study the detail and answer the following questions.

1. Do you think Alma Thomas could achieve the same effect in her painting if she used watercolors? Explain.
2. Which color draws your eye first? How does this color contribute to the "beat" of the painting?
3. In what way does the white background affect the image?
4. No two shapes in this painting are exactly the same, yet the image is organized. How did the artist achieve this effect?

Alma Thomas. *Iris, Tulips, Jonquils and Crocuses.* 1969. Acrylic on canvas. (Detail.) 152.4 x 127 cm (60 x 50"). National Museum of Women in the Arts, Washington, D.C.

Chapter 10 Review **189**

ANSWERS TO "LOOKING AT THE DETAILS"

1. No. In watercolor, the colors are more subtle and the paint wouldn't allow for the same thick application and brush stroke that is the basis for Thomas's image. Students might also note that the painting wouldn't be as bright or have the same contrast.
2. Yellow draws the viewer's eye first. Students might note that the yellow rows draw the eye to a repetitive pattern of a long row, a short row, and vice versa. This creates a slow, irregular beat.
3. Responses will vary. Students might suggest the following: The white background provides contrast for the rows of colors. It allows the viewer's eye to rest between colors. It helps the viewer move in and out of the design.
4. Responses will vary. Students might note that the artist achieves this effect by allowing the white background to show equally between the rows, by having all the rows going in the same downward direction, by having the rows be basically the same width, and by using color to organize the shapes within the rows.

Chapter Evaluation
The goal of this chapter is to develop students' understanding of painting media and methods. After completing the chapter, students should be able to describe painting media and create works of art using different painting media. Some possible evaluation techniques include:

1. On separate index cards write the definitions of the various types of painting media, such as encaustic, fresco, tempera, oil paint, watercolor, and acrylic. Give each student a card. Have the student read aloud the definition and identify the correct term.
2. Divide the chalkboard into six sections and title each section with one of the painting media. Have students list terms, characteristics, and advantages associated with the individual painting media.
3. Have students complete Chapter 10 Test (TRB, Resource 10-9).

Graphic Design

Chapter Scan

Lesson 1 The Art of Graphic
            Design
Lesson 2 Designing a Logo
Lesson 3 Drawing a Comic Strip
Lesson 4 Designing a Poster
Lesson 5 Illustrating a Story

TRB Resources

- 11-1 *Henri de Toulouse-Lautrec*, (artist profile)
- 11-10 Chapter Test
- Color Transparency 21
- Color Transparency 22

TEACHING THE CHAPTER

Introducing the Art Work

Direct students' attention to Henri de Toulouse-Lautrec's poster of Jane Avril. Inform students that Henri de Toulouse-Lautrec was a French artist from a noble family, who worked during the late 1800s. During childhood he broke both his legs, and as a result, he never grew to an adult height. Lautrec's favorite subject matter for his art was the dancehall and the Paris nightlife of the 1890s. Through his art, Lautrec gives the viewer an experience of this subject, but his vision of reality is presented from the point of view of an outsider.

Tell students that Lautrec brought the printed poster to the level of a work of art. He insisted that the poster have a design that could be absorbed in a single glance and that the images and lettering be part of the same design style.

Examining the Art Work

Tell students that this poster was an advertisement for the singer Jane Avril. Explain to students that Lautrec used flat areas of color to define form. Have students note how Lautrec's beautifully curved lines have the ability to create the illusion of a third dimension. Point out the curved yellow snake on the woman's dress and how it accentuates her shape. it gives the viewer the impression of three dimensions as it seems to wrap around behind her, creating the sense of a dimension the viewer doesn't see.

▲ The artist was very careful about his work. He was even known to go into the print shop and mix his own colors.

Henri de Toulouse-Lautrec. *Jane Avril*. 1899. Color lithograph. 68.3 x 47 cm (26⅞ x 18½″). Free Library of Philadelphia.

CHAPTER 1

Graphic Design

Artists, as you have seen, work and create in many different areas. Some artists paint. Others draw or sculpt. Others make prints.

The poster at the left is an example of yet another area in which artists work. This poster was done by a famous French painter, Henri de Toulouse-Lautrec. He was the first artist to create posters for commercial use. Most of his posters were used to advertise musical performances.

Artists working in commercial art use various art media and techniques to communicate their messages. In this chapter you will learn about this field.

OBJECTIVES

After completing this chapter, you will be able to:
- Explain what graphic design is.
- Describe jobs of different graphic artists.
- Identify layout and typeface.
- Design a logo, a comic strip, a concert poster, and a story illustration.

WORDS YOU WILL LEARN

editorial designers   layout
graphic artists   logo
graphic design   typefaces
illustrators

ARTISTS YOU WILL MEET

Victor Moscoso   Henri de Toulouse-
Jeff MacNelly   Lautrec
Beatrix Potter   N.C. Wyeth
Theophile-Alexandre
   Steinlen

Point out the hat the woman is wearing and the way its color gives the viewer the impression that it is not perfectly smooth and elegant, rather a bit eccentric. This gives the viewer some insight into Lautrec's impression of the singer. Suggest that Avril seems apart from the ordinary, playful, and even humorous.

Discussing the Art Work
Inform students that Lautrec preferred asymmetrical composition. Point out the way the woman's upper body as well as her legs tilt to the left. Ask students whether they think this is an inviting pose or whether it distances the viewer. Explain how the woman is absorbed in her own action and that Lautrec uses the elements in a way that would block the viewer from being part of the action. Ask students to think about how different the point of view might be if the woman were looking out at the viewer and kicking up her legs, creating a more balanced composition. Suggest that if that were the case, the viewer might feel more involved, as if Jane Avril were addressing in some way or even performing for the viewer.

Ask students to think about why Lautrec chose such an unusual composition. Suggest that perhaps the unusual tends to be more eye-catching and that for an advertisement, the attention of the viewer is an essential element.

Tell students that in this chapter they will learn about graphic design and some careers associated with it. They will also design their own logos, comic strips, posters, and a story illustration.

191

Building Self-Esteem
Discuss the definition of the word "logo" as it appears in the Glossary. Ask the students to suggest personal qualities or virtues they consider admirable in others. List them on the board. Tell students to choose three qualities they would like to develop in themselves or that represent their own best qualities. They will take the initial of each quality and make a design utilizing those three letters. They can use capitals or lower-case letters; the letters could be overlapped, intertwined, or stacked. This exercise could utilize drawing materials, or the letters could be cut out of colored construction paper and glued on a piece of manilla paper. As the logos are completed, they should be displayed and discussed with the rest of the class. Suggest to students that these personal logos could be mounted in their rooms at home as an inspiration and reminder of those areas in which they want to develop personally.

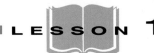

The Art of Graphic Design

LESSON PLAN
(pages 192–195)

Objectives
After completing this lesson, students will be able to:
- Explain what graphic design is.
- Describe the work of editorial designers, illustrators, advertising designers, and sign makers.
- Define the terms *layout* and *typefaces.*
- Design and make a collage using a single letter of the alphabet in a variety of type styles and sizes.

Supplies
- Examples of the work of graphic designers, such as illustrated books, instructional manuals, children's picture books, newspapers, magazines, posters, distinctive packaging, and the like.
- Old newspapers and magazines; scissors; drawing paper; white glue; watercolors, crayons, or pastels.
- Strips of cardboard, 3/8 inch (10 mm) wide, to be used as lettering guides; pencils; sheets of white drawing paper; various colored waterbased markers.
- Book, magazine, or other publication in Japanese (if available).
- Several state maps.

TRB Resources
- 11-2 *Signs of Your Time,* (reproducible master)
- 11-3 *Critiquing Your Commercial Environment,* (art criticism)
- 11-4 *Television Advertising and Technology,* (art history)
- 11-5 *Hanging Your Shingle,* (appreciating cultural diversity)

TEACHING THE LESSON

Getting Started
Motivator. Have students form groups, and give each group several examples of the work of graphic artists—illustrated books and pamphlets, textbooks, magazines, newspapers, small posters, signs or pictures of signs. Give the members of the groups time to examine and discuss the materials.

LESSON 1

The Art of Graphic Design

There are artists at work all around you. Artists create the television commercials you view and the billboards you read. Some of the art work they create includes posters, packaging, magazine advertisements, and corporate symbols. There were even artists responsible for the graphic design of this book.

Artists who work in these areas are known as graphic artists. **Graphic artists** *work in the field of art known as graphic design.* **Graphic design** is the *field of art that uses pictures and words to instruct, or to communicate a specific message.* Look around your classroom. What graphic design symbols and images do you see?

GRAPHIC ARTISTS

Graphic artists work in a great many areas. Each area has its own special tasks and job title. Some of these areas are editorial design, illustration, advertising design, and sign making. Sometimes graphic artists work together as members of a larger creative team.

Editorial Design

The field of graphic design flourished in the 1500s. That was when the printing press was invented, making it possible to produce multiple copies of printed material at one time. People who arranged the words and pictures were similar to today's graphic artists.

Today these people are called editorial designers. **Editorial designers** are *graphic artists who arrange words and illustrations and prepare the material for printing.* Some editorial designers work on books, while others work on magazines and newspapers.

Planning the **layout**, or *the arrangement of words and pictures on a page,* is only one task of the editorial designer. Another is selecting the **typefaces**, or *styles of lettering for the printed material.* Figure 11–1 shows a typeface design based on an early typeface used many years ago in Europe. Today's editorial designers can choose from hundreds of typefaces. How many different typefaces can you find on this page? What differences can you spot among these styles?

abcdefghijklmnopqrstuvwxyz
ABCDEFGHIJKLMNOPQRSTUVWXYZ
1234567890 (&.,:;!?'“”-*¢%/$£)

▲ **Figure 11–1 Before Gütenberg invented the printing press, books were handwritten. Where do you think some of the first typeface styles came from?**

Background Information
Henri de Toulouse-Lautrec (France, 1864–1901) was schooled in the academic tradition and was exposed to the Impressionists and their work early in his career as an artist. While he incorporated many of the Impressionists' techniques and principles in his work, Toulouse-Lautrec was always more concerned with the human figure than with landscapes.

In 1891 Toulouse-Lautrec, commissioned by the Moulin Rouge cabaret to create his first poster, reached his full artistic range. Creating these advertising posters allowed him to use his vigorous style and simple, brilliant colors imaginatively. Because of his interest in time and motion, his posters were innovative and fascinating. The viewer of each poster seems to be participating in the action.

Toulouse-Lautrec began creating lithographs in 1899. Though he was by then in poor health, he did some of his most exciting work during this period. The effectiveness of a poster depends on how quickly the viewer understands the subject.

▲ Figure 11–2   Do you know this story? You may have heard it when you were small. How do illustrations like this help you visualize the personality of the characters?

Beatrix Potter. *Jemima Puddle-Duck*. 1908. Pencil, pen and ink, watercolor. Frederic Warne & Co., London.

Illustration

Have you ever used step-by-step drawings to put something together? If you have, you have used the same work habits of an illustrator. **Illustrators** are *graphic artists who create printed materials that explain or teach.* Many times illustrators work closely with editorial designers.

The color wheel on page **56** of this book (Figure 4–4) was drawn by an illustrator. So were the shaded shapes on page **147** (Figure 8–4). The drawing in Figure 11–2 was made to illustrate a children's book. When you look at Figure 11–3, you see the drawing of a technical illustrator. Notice the fine details that are included in the drawing.

Did you notice that each illustration listed above used a different art medium? Illustrators may use an airbrush, pen and ink, colored pencils, or watercolors to achieve the look they want. Today illustrators often use computers and other technology to create art.

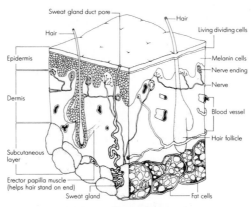

▲ Figure 11–3   This is a drawing from a health textbook. How do drawings like this one help explain the lessons being taught?

Advertising Design

Other graphic artists specialize in advertising design. In this area the graphic artist communicates and creates a message in words and pictures to help sell or promote products or services.

Look again at the lithograph on page **190**. This was done by Henri de Toulouse-Lautrec to promote a concert by a well-known performer. Figure 11–4 shows an ad by another French printmaker of the 1800s. This one was for a company that made teas and chocolates. Notice that both artists used a combination of words and pictures. This is true of the work of graphic artists today.

Like editorial designers, advertising designers are concerned with layout and type styles. Some advertising designers work on newspaper or magazine ads. Others design commercials for television. The success of their work is measured by the impact the message has on the receiver. Can you think of an advertisement that has left an impression in your mind?

Lesson 1   *The Art of Graphic Design*   📖   **193**

Then ask: What examples can you identify of pictures and words intended to instruct or to communicate a specific message? What message or instruction is intended?

Vocabulary. Let students identify the kinds of graphs with which they are familiar—line graphs, bar graphs, circle or pie graphs. Then point out that the English word *graph* comes from an ancient Greek word meaning "to write." Ask: How are graphs like a form of writing? (*They are intended to instruct or to communicate a specific message.*) Help students recognize that *graphic* in the terms *graphic artists* and *graphic design* comes from the same Greek word. Then refer students to the materials they examined in the "Motivator" activity. Explain that these are the work of graphic artists, and ask: In what sense do you think the work of graphic artists is like a kind of writing?

Developing Concepts

Exploring Aesthetics. Ask students to form groups, and have the members of each group choose and discuss one of the illustrations on display (see "Motivator"). Ask: What is the subject of this work? Which visual elements can you identify and describe in this illustration? What message is this work intended to communicate? Is this illustration a work of art? Why, or why not?

Using Art Criticism. Help students examine and discuss the technical illustration shown in Figure 11-3. Begin by asking: What objects do you see in this illustration? How are color, line, texture, shape, and space used in the illustration? Then ask: How have the visual elements been combined and used to achieve balance? Which elements add variety? How have harmony and emphasis been achieved? Finally, help students decide why the work was produced and judge how well the illustration serves the purpose for which it was made.

Cooperative Learning

Have students work in cooperative groups to collect examples of typefaces that reflect specific moods or ideas. The members of each group should work together first to select a mood or idea they believe can be reflected in a typeface and then to look through books and magazines to find various examples of such typefaces. Let students make photocopies of the typefaces or, if appropriate, cut them out. Then have the students in each group plan and prepare an effective display of their collection.

Cooperative Learning

Graphic communication began with simple materials and hand-drawn images. Many cave paintings may be records and teaching aids for young hunters. Petroglyphs, etched into rock, represent records and messages. Native American groups have traditions of storytelling by symbolic drawings in soft earth; sand painting is graphic ritual for others. Have students work in groups to learn more about one of these forms of graphic communication.

Understanding Art History.
Explain to students that the history of European typefaces began with the introduction of movable type, around the middle of the fifteenth century. Those earliest typefaces were based on the style of handwriting commonly used in Germany. Then an Italian designer began creating typefaces influenced by the writing used for classical Roman texts—and roman typefaces were first used. Around the year 1500 italic typefaces were developed, based on a style of cursive handwriting. These basic type styles remained the only choices until the eighteenth century, when designers such as Baskerville began creating new typefaces. Ask students to work with partners to research the history of typefaces. Each pair of students can investigate either the history of a given typeface or the new typefaces designed during a given century.

Developing Studio Skills.
Distribute cardboard strips (3/8 inch [10 mm] wide), and show students how to use the strips as lettering guides. Each simple block letter should be three lettering-guide widths wide (except *M* and *W*, which should be four widths wide) and five lettering-guide widths high. Show students how to draw guidelines marking the top and bottom of a letter. Then help students analyze the letter forms: How do the vertical, horizontal, diagonal, and curved components fit together? Have each student sketch one of his or her initials and then draw a final copy, using waterbased markers on white paper.

Appreciating Cultural Diversity.
Display a Japanese-language publication (not Romanized) if you have one available, and let students examine the various characters. If no publications are available, explain that the Japanese writing system is unusually complex; to achieve a minimal level of literacy, a person must recognize 1850 different characters. Guide students in discussing how this complexity might affect editorial designers and other graphic artists in Japan.

▲ Figure 11–4   What mood does the artist convey? Is it appealing? Is it appropriate for the company he is promoting? Why?

Theophile-Alexandre Steinlen. *Compagnie Française des Chocolats et des Thés.* 1899. Color lithograph. 76.2 x 101.6 cm (30 x 40″). Metropolitan Museum of Art, New York, New York.

▲ Figure 11–5   These are international signs intended to help travelers. Do the pictures quickly convey their messages? How does the artist's choice of color contribute to the sign's effectiveness?

▲ Figure 11–6   Notice how much information the designer has packed into these few words and symbols. Could a person unable to read tell what kind of business this was?

Rendered by John Sullivan. *Tailor's Shears* (Shop sign). c. 1935. National Gallery of Art, Washington, D.C.

194   Lesson 1   *The Art of Graphic Design*

Background Information
Poster art has always been an effective way of communicating with an audience at a street level. Shakespeare alludes to its power when Bottom argues for the top billing in "Pyramus and Thisby" during *A Midsummer Night's Dream*. Likewise, the creators of political campaign signs and advertisement billboards bank on the persuasiveness of posters. With a smaller audience, but perhaps purer intentions, exists the concert flyer artist.
    Effective posters utilize art work to convey a message that

distinctively characterizes the band and its music. It is no coincidence that among Los Angeles' most noted concert flyer artists, Raymond Pettibon and *los hermanos Hernandez* have the graphic and narrative skills necessary to publish their own comic books. These artists present social and psychological messages to criticize social and moral decay. Like all artists, the successful flyer artist does not merely create an image; he or she communicates an idea.

Sign Making

You may not think of Figure 11–5 as an art work. Yet it was someone's job to choose a type style and size for the letters. Someone had to design the figures and pick a color combination for the signs.

The "someone" behind these choices was a graphic artist with the job title of sign maker. The art of making signs traces its roots to the earliest times. The sign in Figure 11–6 was made back during America's Colonial period. Can you tell what this sign is made of? Can you tell what kind of business the sign advertised?

▲ **Figure 11–7 Student work. Letter collage.**

STUDIO EXPERIENCE

Choose one of the 26 letters of the alphabet. Search through newspapers, magazines, and books. See how many different typefaces and sizes for this letter you can find. Cut examples of the letter from newspapers and magazine headlines. On a sheet of paper, make a collage based on the examples of your letter. To add interest to your collage, turn some of your letters upside down and some sideways. Try overlapping some of your letters. When you have an interesting arrangement, glue the letters to the background with white glue. If possible, photocopy your finished collage. Then add color using watercolors, crayons, or pastels. (See Figure 11–7.) (For more information on making a collage, see Technique Tip **28**, *Handbook* page **281**.)

✔ CHECK YOUR UNDERSTANDING

1. What does an editorial designer do?
2. What is a layout? What is another term meaning "type style"?
3. What is the job title of a graphic artist who makes step-by-step drawings?
4. What are three art tools that an illustrator might use?
5. What do graphic artists who specialize in advertising do?

Designing a Logo

LESSON 2

Designing a Logo

A **logo** is *a special image representing a business, group, or product*. All logos are one-of-a-kind shapes or pictures. Some contain letters or words as well. Figure 11–8 shows some well-known logos. How many of these have you seen? Do you know the business, group, or product each stands for?

Imagine you are a graphic artist for an advertising agency. You have been asked to create a logo for a space colony on a newly discovered planet. Imagine you were also asked to come up with a name for the colony.

PLAN INTERNATIONAL USA

American Red Cross

childreach
S P O N S O R S H I P

▲ Figure 11–8   What do you think makes a logo successful? Why? What other logos can you think of that you see often? What companies or products do they stand for?

Logos courtesy of American Red Cross, Childreach Sponsorship, and Plan International USA.

WHAT YOU WILL LEARN

Working in a small group, you will create a logo for a new space colony. The logo should contain the name of the colony (or at least the name's initials). The logo should capture the idea that the space colony is a pleasant place to live. It should create a feeling that the settlers are living in their own backyard rather than out in space. You will use a variety of colors, lines, and shapes to help show this. These elements must be arranged using either formal or informal balance. See Figure 11-9.

WHAT YOU WILL NEED

- Pencil, eraser, and ruler
- Sheets of sketch paper
- Sheet of white paper, 9 x 12 inch (23 x 30 cm)
- Watercolor markers

WHAT YOU WILL DO

1. You have been selected to design a logo. The logo must include the name or initials of the space colony. Brainstorm with the class about what life might be like on the space colony. Will the colony be divided into neighborhoods? Will the colony be under a temperature-control dome? What kinds of jobs will the people have? What will they do for entertainment? Will they have TV?
2. Working by yourself, make rough pencil sketches for your logo. Think about different ways of showing the letters you chose to use. Think about what images you might use to stand for a space colony. Choose different lines and shapes to show that life in the colony is pleasant and comfortable.

LESSON PLAN
(pages 196–197)

Objectives

After completing this lesson, students will be able to:
- Design and draw logos.
- Describe, analyze, interpret, and judge their own work.

Supplies

- Examples of various familiar logos, cut from ads or packages and glued onto index cards or small pieces of paper (prepared by two or three student volunteers, if possible).
- Pencils; erasers; rulers; sheets of sketch paper; sheets of white paper, 9 x 12 inches (23 x 30 cm); watercolor markers.
- Drawing paper, pencils, markers.

> **TRB Resource**
> - 11-6 *Universal Symbols*, (aesthetics)

TEACHING THE LESSON

Getting Started

Motivator. Give each student or pair of students a familiar logo mounted on a card (see "Supplies"). Let students describe their logos and identify the products, groups, or companies the logos represent. Then encourage students to describe and identify other familiar logos. Ask: How are these logos used? How do you and people you know react to logos?

Vocabulary. Ask volunteers to look up the definition of *logo* in a dictionary. Then help students use a dictionary to understand the derivation of the word. Ask: *Logo* is a shortened form of what longer word? What word form from ancient Greek is one of the bases of *logotype*? What is the meaning of the Greek word form *log-* or *logo-*? How does that meaning help you understand our English word *logo*?

Background Information

For centuries artisans and craftspeople have used logos to distinguish their products. In fact, logos have been in use longer than brand names have. Hundreds of years ago a potter would make his mark on the bottom of his pot—and customers would look for that mark when choosing their pots.

More widely known were the national and international logos used by kings. Many European peasants recognized symbols of current rulers wherever they appeared.

During the seventeenth and eighteenth centuries royal patronage of a company meant that the company was a respectable, quality enterprise. Still, the widespread use of logos as we know them did not develop until the late nineteenth century. Improvements in mass production and mass marketing allowed brands to become known nationally and internationally.

3. Working neatly, draw your best idea onto the sheet of white paper. Use a ruler to draw the straight lines.
4. Color in your logo with the watercolor markers. Use colors that suggest the spirit of adventure experienced by people living in the colony.
5. Display your work. Look for similarities and differences between your work and those of classmates.

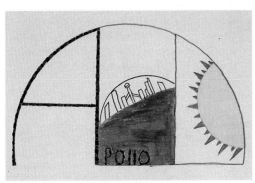

▲ Figure 11–9   Student works. Space colony logos.

OTHER STUDIO IDEAS

- Create pencil sketches for a logo for yourself. Include both type and visual elements. Select your best sketch and neatly draw it on paper 9 x 12 inch (23 x 30 cm).

•• Do a logo for your school. Try to give depth to the logo. Use techniques of shading you have learned about to create the look of deep space.

EXAMINING YOUR WORK

- **Describe**   Point to the image you created for your logo. Explain why you chose that image. Show where the name or initials of the space colony appear in your design. Name the colors you chose for your logo.
- **Analyze**   Point to the variety of colors, lines, and shapes used in your logo. Explain why you chose these elements. Tell what kind of balance you used. Explain why you decided to use that type of balance.
- **Interpret**   Explain how the colors, lines, and shapes in your logo suggest comfort and pleasant living conditions.
- **Judge**   Tell whether you feel your work succeeds. Identify the best feature of your design. List ways you could improve your design.

SAFETY TIP
When a project calls for the use of markers, always make sure to use the water-based kind. Permanent markers have chemicals in them that can be harmful when breathed in.

LESSON PLAN
(pages 198–199)

Objectives
After completing this lesson, students will be able to:
• Create original comic strips with five or more frames.
• Describe, analyze, interpret, and judge their own work.

Supplies
• Several different comic strips cut apart, with each frame glued onto a separate index card or small piece of paper (prepared by two or three student volunteers, if possible).
• Notepads; pencils; sheets of sketch paper; erasers; rulers; sheets of white paper, 12 x 18 inches (30 x 46 cm); black fine-line felt-tip markers; colored pencils, markers, or crayons; transparent tape.

> **TRB Resource**
> • 11-7 *A La Lichtenstein*, (studio)

TEACHING THE LESSON

Getting Starting
Motivator. Give each student a card with one frame from a comic strip (see "Supplies"). Let students organize themselves into groups with frames from the same comic strip. Then have the members of each group put their frames in order and discuss the complete comic strip: What kinds of characters are involved? What do they say and do? Is the strip intended to be funny or thought-provoking—or both?

Vocabulary. Ask students to recall (or use a dictionary to check) the meaning of the adjective *comic*. Then ask: Are all comic strips funny? What other kinds of moods or messages—in addition to humor—can be communicated by a comic strip? Guide students in developing a definition of the term *comic strip*; ask a volunteer to check a dictionary definition of the term.

Drawing a Comic Strip

Some graphic artists are storytellers. They tell their stories in connected boxes, or frames, made up of words and pictures. We know these strings of frames better as comic strips. Like a play, every comic strip has a cast of characters. When characters speak, their words often appear in outlined white spaces called balloons. (See Figures 11–10 and 11–11.)

Most "comic" strips are funny. Some, however, are not. Some are satirical, meaning that they poke fun at public figures and world events. Others are adventure stories or show suspense in some other way. Look again at Figure 11–10. Which kind of strip is this box from?

WHAT YOU WILL LEARN

You will create a comic strip made up of five or more boxes, or frames. Each box will be at least 5 inches (13 cm) square. The characters in your strip may be drawn in either a humorous or realistic way. Your strip may be funny, action-packed, or have a serious subject. If your strip is funny, the last frame should have the punch line. The lines and shapes will be used to add rhythm or movement to your strip.

WHAT YOU WILL NEED
• Notepad and pencil
• Sheets of sketch paper
• Eraser and ruler
• Sheets of white paper, 12 x 18 inch (30 x 46 cm)
• Black fine-line felt-tip marker
• Colored pencils, markers, or crayons
• Transparent tape

WHAT YOU WILL DO

1. Think about the people and situations you could include in your comic strip. Possibilities are school activities, fun with friends, or fantasy. Decide whether you will make your comic strip humorous or adventurous.

2. On your notepad, plan out your story. Identify the characters you will use. Decide what you will show them doing in the strip. Write out what you will have them say. Decide how many frames you will need to show the action.

▼ **Figure 11–10   How does the illustration help you in interpreting the words?**

Jeff MacNelly. *Shoe.* © 1989. Tribune Media Services, Inc.

Background Information
Cartoons, complete with speech balloons, were published as early as the eighteenth century. The drawings were often caricatures of well-known personalities and were sometimes published as political commentary. Many books were illustrated with cartoons.

The first successful comic strip began appearing in the *New York World* in 1895. It was "Hogan's Alley" by Richard Outcault, and it featured a young character known as "The Kid." The following year, the newspaper printers began tinting the character's oversized nightshirt, on which his comments were lettered, with yellow ink, and he became "The Yellow Kid." Outcault's use of action and dialogue set the pattern for the classic comic strip form.

Speech balloons were introduced to comic strips in 1897, with "The Katzenjammer Kids" by Rudolf Dirks. In 1908 "Mutt and Jeff" by Ham Fisher became the first successful daily comic strip.

3. Make rough pencil sketches of your characters. Use lines and shapes to show movement. Sketch the background. Practice drawing word balloons. Do a rough sketch for each one of the boxes that will be in your strip. Carefully print out the words each character will say. Number each frame.

4. Divide a sheet of paper, 12 x 18 inch (30 x 46 cm) into as many squares or rectangles as you will need. How many will you use? Will all the boxes be the same size, or will some be larger for emphasis? Use your ruler and pencil to draw the boxes. (See Technique Tip **22**, *Handbook* page **278** for information on measuring squares and rectangles.) Use extra sheets as needed. Use repetition of characters and environments to give the strip unity.

5. Working lightly in pencil, carefully draw your final sketches into the boxes. Print out your characters' words in balloons.

6. Go over all the lines and letters with the black fine-line marker. Color in your shapes with colored pencils, markers, or crayons. If you used more than one sheet, join the pages together with transparent tape.

EXAMINING YOUR WORK

• **Describe**   Identify the characters in your strip. Tell who they are and what they are doing. Show that you used at least five boxes. Point to the different lines and shapes.

• **Analyze**   Explain how the lines and shapes create rhythm or movement in your strip.

• **Interpret**   Identify the mood of your strip. Tell what clues help the viewer understand this mood. If your strip was humorous, was the punch line in the last box effective?

• **Judge**   Tell whether you feel your work succeeds. Explain your answer.

7. Display your work. Notice how classmates completed the assignment. Ask your classmates to read your strip. Can they understand your story? Can they recognize the theme?

◄ **Figure 11–11** **What kind of balance does the comic strip at the left display? Explain.**

Charles Schulz. *Peanuts.* © 1989. United Feature Syndicate, Inc.

OTHER STUDIO IDEAS

• Redraw your strip. This time, instead of adding color, use different values of India ink. Different values can be obtained by adding small amounts of water to India ink. Apply the India ink with a small brush. Does this change the mood of the work? Explain.

•• Have the whole class work together to plan a whole comic book. Each student will create one story for the book. When it is finished, protect the pages with lamination, and bind them into a book.

Lesson 3 *Drawing a Comic Strip* **199**

Using Art Criticism. Let each student choose and analyze a cartoon strip (using either the cartoon strips from the "Motivator" activity or favorite cartoon strips brought from home). Have the student identify the use of visual elements—especially line, color, and shape—and of art principles—especially balance, emphasis, and movement. Then help students discuss how lines and shapes can work together to create action and to lead the reader from one frame to the next.

Understanding Art History. Have students read about the history of comic strips in the United States, and encourage them to ask their parents, grandparents, or other adults about the comic strips they remember. Then ask volunteers to find reprints of early comic strips and to report on changes in characters, drawing styles, and themes.

Following Up

Closure. Let students work in groups to identify and discuss the mood created in the comic strips each one has executed. What is the mood? How is it developed? What aspects of the strip—if any—do not contribute to that mood?

Evaluation. Review students' comic strips, and consider their discussions of the moods developed in one another's works.

Reteaching. Help groups of students focus on the process of planning a comic strip. They should begin by agreeing upon a familiar story or by making up an original story. Help them plan the frames: What are the most important events in this story? How can those events be shown in comic strip frames? Then help them discuss the characters: How does each character feel and look? What—if anything—does each character say?

Enrichment. Ask students to research the use of language in comic strips. What new words have come into use from comic strips? How have comic strips affected our general use of the language?

Classroom Management Tip
Comic strip artists often rough in their panels lightly with non-reproducing blue or brown pencil. When the sketch is complete, the final lines are carefully drawn with black drawing ink. You may want to have students use ordinary colored pencil (in light tones) to try this technique when they draw their own comic strips.

Cooperative Learning
Animals have always been popular comic strip characters. Some of the animal characters have been humanized stars, while others have played supporting roles. Let students work in cooperative groups to collect and discuss examples of comic strip animals. What mood or personality does each animal represent? What does the animal contribute to the comic strip? Then have group members work together to create and draw a new comic strip animal.

LESSON PLAN
(pages 200–201)

Objectives

After completing this lesson, students will be able to:
- Design and make concert posters appropriate to chosen styles of music.
- Describe, analyze, interpret, and judge their own work.

Supplies

- Recordings of music in several different styles, such as rock, country, classical, and folk; drawing paper; colored pencils or markers.
- Notepads; pencils; sheets of sketch paper; erasers; rulers; broad-line and fine-line colored markers; crayons; collage materials, including old magazines and newspapers, scissors, white glue, small brushes; sheets of heavy white paper; transparent tape.
- Musical instruments, sketch paper, pencils.
- Packages for albums, tapes, and/or compact discs.

> **TRB Resource**
> - 11-8 *Design a Television Commercial*, (cooperative learning)

TEACHING THE LESSON

Getting Started

Motivator. To help students recognize the relationship between music and visual images, play short selections of several different kinds of music. During each selection, have students close their eyes and try to "see" what they hear. Let volunteers describe the colors, shapes, and movements they visualized. After all the selections have been played, ask each student to create a drawing suggested by one of the kinds of music. Can the other students identify the kind of music from the drawing?

Vocabulary. Help students use a dictionary to find the meaning of the word *post* as it is used in *poster*. Then encourage students to describe posters they have noticed and/or made.

200

Designing a Poster

In music, as in art, different artists have different styles. The style of today's most popular rock group is different from that of yesterday's. Both are very different from the musical style of Mozart.

When graphic artists design concert posters for musical groups, they try to capture the musician's style. Their works often reflect one of the three views of art you have learned about. Look at the concert posters in Figure 11–12. Which of these is realistic? Which uses design composition alone to make its statement? Which expresses a feeling?

WHAT YOU WILL LEARN

You will invent a musician or musical group and choose the style of music your imaginary artist makes. Then you will design a concert poster for that artist. Decide on a title for the group. The poster will include the title of the concert and name of the artist. You will choose the medium or media to carry out the assignment. You will use the principles of balance, rhythm, and emphasis to organize the elements of colors, lines, shapes, space, and texture in your design. (See Figure 11–13.)

WHAT YOU WILL NEED

- Notepad and pencil
- Sheets of sketch paper
- Eraser and ruler
- Any or all of the following: broad-line and fine-line colored markers, crayons, collage materials (magazines, newspapers, scissors, white glue, small brush)
- Sheet of heavy white paper
- Transparent tape

▲ **Figure 11–12** Describe the style of music of the top poster. If you were interested in rock and roll, would this poster interest you? What does the guitar symbolize to you? Explain.

(TOP) Victor Moscoso. *Junior Wells and His Chicago Blues Band.* 1966. Offset lithograph. Poster. 50.5 x 35.6 cm (19⅞ x 14"). The Museum of Modern Art, New York, New York. Gift of the designer.
(BOTTOM) Ernie Friedlander Studios. 1990. Offset lithograph. 91.5 x 61 cm (36 x 24"). Portal Publications Ltd.

WHAT YOU WILL DO

1. Think of a musical style and name for your imaginary musician or group. Write the name on your notepad. Create a title for the concert poster. Write a short description of your group.
2. Create your own style or choose a style of lettering for the concert title and the artist's name. Decide where on the poster

---

Background Information

The English word *poster* was first used around 1838, but precursors of the modern poster date back many centuries. Commercial and electioneering signs were painted on the walls of buildings—especially popular gathering places—in ancient Rome; these can be considered early forms of posters. The excavations of Pompeii and Herculaneum uncovered more than 1600 election posters.

Because few people could read, posters were apparently little used during medieval times. As literacy rose during the Renaissance, so did the use of commercial posters. The first poster using printed illustration was produced in 1491.

Posters in their familiar form—such as those by Toulouse-Lautrec on page **190** and Steinlen on page **194**—were made possible by two important developments: the invention of lithography during the 1790s by Alois Senefelder (Germany, 1771–1834); and the development of high-speed presses, which by 1848 could print up to 10,000 sheets per hour.

each will appear and decide how large each will be. Sketch them in.

3. Plan how you will fill the remaining space. If you plan to use collage materials, find and clip images found in magazines and newspapers. Choose which aesthetic view of art you will take. Decide if you wish your work to look realistic, to make a statement with design alone, or to express a feeling or mood.

4. Working lightly in pencil, place your title lettering, artist's name and any other images on the poster. (See Technique Tip **5**, *Handbook* page **271**, which gives instructions on using a grid to enlarge letters and images.)

5. Using markers or crayons, color in the letters and images you have drawn. Using glue and brush, paste down any magazine or newspaper clippings you have chosen to add to your design.

6. Display your concert poster. Take a poll among your classmates. How many can tell the style of music your imaginary artist plays?

EXAMINING YOUR WORK

- **Describe** Point out the artist's name and the concert title. Tell what media you chose to make your concert poster. Identify the elements of art used in your design.
- **Analyze** Tell which principles you used to organize the elements. Explain why you chose to use those principles.
- **Interpret** Explain how your design helps a viewer understand the style of music of this group.
- **Judge** Tell whether you feel your work succeeds. Identify the view or views of art you used when making this decision.

▶ **Figure 11–13 Student works. Music concert posters.**

OTHER STUDIO IDEAS

- Create a compact disc cover for a real group or musician you like. Invent a title for the compact disc and individual song titles. Use a style that differs from the one you used above.

- ●● Design a poster for an amusement park or a sporting event.

Lesson 4 *Designing a Poster* **201**

Illustrating a Story

Illustrating a Story

Look at Figure 11–14. This is an illustration by N.C. Wyeth, a famous American story illustrator. Wyeth's illustrations made the stories he illustrated come alive for the readers. Do you know what famous story this Wyeth illustration comes from?

WHAT YOU WILL LEARN

Select an action story or poem you have recently read and liked. You will paint an illustration for an incident that took place in the story or poem. Your illustration will capture the setting, mood, and style of the whole work. You will decide whether your illustration will have formal or informal balance. You will decide whether to use realistic proportions for your figures or distortion. (See Figure 11–15.)

WHAT YOU WILL NEED

- Notepad, pencil, and eraser
- Sheets of sketch paper
- Paper towels
- Sheet of white paper, 12 x 18 inch (30 x 46 cm)
- School acrylic paint
- Bristle brushes, varied sizes
- Water

▶ **Figure 11–14** Would you describe the artist's style as realistic? What elements does he use to get this result? What principles does he use to organize those elements?

N. C. Wyeth. *Blind Pew.* 1911. Illustration from *Treasure Island* by Robert Louis Stevenson, Charles Scribner's Sons, Macmillan Publishing Company.

LESSON 5

Illustrating a Story

LESSON PLAN.
(pages 202–203)

Objectives

After completing this lesson, students will be able to:
- Paint illustrations for incidents in stories or poems.
- Describe, analyze, interpret, and judge their own work.

Supplies

- *Treasure Island*, by Robert Louis Stevenson.
- Notepads, pencils, erasers, sheets of sketch paper, paper towels, sheets of white paper, school acrylic paints, bristle brushes in various sizes, water.
- Drawing paper, colored markers.

> **TRB Resource**
> - 11-9 *The Dot and the Photograph*, (art history)

TEACHING THE LESSON

Getting Started

Motivator. Before students open their books, read aloud a selection from Robert Louis Stevenson's *Treasure Island* describing the blind villain, Pew. Encourage students to visualize the character. Then have them look at the illustration by N. C. Wyeth (Figure 11-14). Ask: Is this the way you imagined the character? How does this illustration affect your understanding of the selection?

Vocabulary. Have students look up the words *illustrate* and *illustration* in a dictionary. Then ask: What is the meaning of the Latin word from which these words come? How are illustrations different from other kinds of drawings or paintings?

Developing Concepts

Understanding Art History. Explain that illustrations usually reflect developments both in other areas of art and in society. Ask volunteers to find and share book illustrations from 50 and 25 years ago. What changes do they reflect? How are they different from current illustrations?

Background Information

N. C. (Newell Convers) Wyeth (United States, 1882–1945) became famous for his narrative paintings and, especially, for his book illustrations. His crisp, realistic style and his tough, individualistic tone helped him capture the spirit of the stories he illustrated. An unusually prolific illustrator, Wyeth used his brush to give life to the heroes in adventures such as *Treasure Island, Robin Hood,* and *Robinson Crusoe*. Wyeth's greatest skill lay in choosing the most gripping moment of a story and rendering it clearly.

While engaging in a lifelong career as an illustrator, Wyeth felt his limitations acutely. To him, the drawing of heroes for storybooks was not "true" art. He further suffered because his naturalistic style of painting was unacceptable to the art world of his time, which engaged itself with abstraction and expressionism. He was not viewed as a serious artist, yet his illustrations have been seen and loved by generations.

▲ Figure 11–15   Student work. A story illustration.

WHAT YOU WILL DO

1. Think about a short story, novel, or poem you have read and liked. Decide what scene from this work you want to illustrate using the main characters.
2. On the notepad, describe what the characters are doing. Write down information about their expressions, moods, and actions. List ways you will use color and the other elements of art in your painting. Decide whether the proportions of your figures will be realistic or exaggerated. Decide if you will use emphasis to

EXAMINING YOUR WORK

- **Describe**   Tell what story you have chosen to illustrate. Tell what is happening in the part of the work you have illustrated. Explain who the characters are. List the elements and principles used.
- **Analyze**   Tell whether your work has formal or informal balance. Point to and describe the proportions of your figures. Tell whether these proportions were used to make these figures look realistic or cartoon-like.
- **Interpret**   Explain how your illustration captures the setting, mood, and style of the story. Give your illustration a title and explain why you chose the title.
- **Judge**   Tell whether you feel your work succeeds.

make a figure or object stand out. Balance your illustration using either formal or informal balance.
3. Make rough pencil sketches for your painting.
4. Lightly sketch your plan on the good paper. Use your 1/4-inch (0.6 cm) brush and a light-value paint to draw the main shapes of your illustration on the sheet of white paper. Use your larger brushes to fill in shapes. Complete your painting.
5. Display your painting. Notice similarities and differences in the way you and classmates completed the assignment. Try to guess the titles of the different stories and poems illustrated.

OTHER STUDIO IDEAS

- Illustrate something you have written.
- Work with the whole class. Choose one children's story and turn it into an illustrated book. Each student select a differ-

ent scene to illustrate. Protect the pages by laminating them, and bind them into a storybook for the little children to read at the library.

Developing Studio Skills. Present a sentence with few details, such as the following: The girl went down the road with her dog. Then, to help students consider the kinds of details they might add, ask questions such as these: How old is the girl? How does she feel? How is she moving—running, strolling, riding a bike? What kind of road is it? How big is the dog? Encourage students to create complete, detailed images of the scene. Then have each student use markers to draw an illustration of the scene he or she has imagined. Let students compare and discuss their finished illustrations.

Following Up

Closure. Have students form small groups in which to discuss their story illustrations. As students present their illustrations, have other group members suggest possible titles; then let the student read—and, if necessary, explain—the title he or she gave the work.

Evaluation. Review students' illustrations, and listen to their discussions about the titles of their illustrations.

Reteaching. Ask students to bring in, either from home or from a library, picture books for young children. Help them examine and discuss the illustrations in these books: What story do the pictures in each book tell? How are words used (if at all) in telling the story? How does the subject of the illustrations help tell the story? How does the style of the art contribute to the story?

Enrichment. Point out that photographers are illustrators, too. Newspapers and many magazines rely on photographers to illustrate their articles; textbooks are often illustrated with photographs. Have students bring in articles, pamphlets, or books illustrated with photographs. In addition, if students have access to cameras, ask them to choose or write a story or nonfiction article and then take a series of photos to illustrate it.

Classroom Management Tip
To help students understand and appreciate the work of illustrators, encourage them to learn about another well-known American illustrator, Norman Rockwell (United States, 1894–1978). Ask students to read about his life and to find reproductions of his work. How are his illustrations similar to those of N. C. Wyeth? What are the most important differences? What can students learn about illustrating by comparing the works of these two artists?

Cooperative Learning
In this lesson students have painted illustrations to accompany stories. Now have them write stories to accompany pictures. Let students form cooperative groups, and have the members of each group work together to select a painting or other art work. What story can they tell to go with that art work? Together, students should plan and write a story—or, if they prefer, a poem or play—and then present it to the rest of the class.

BUILDING VOCABULARY

Number a sheet of paper from 1 to 7. After each number, write the term from the box that best matches each description below.

editorial designers	layout
graphic artist	logo
graphic design	typefaces
illustrators	

1. The field of art that uses pictures and words to instruct, or communicate.
2. Graphic artists who arrange words and illustrations and prepare the material for printing.
3. The arrangement of words and pictures.
4. Styles of lettering.
5. Graphic artists who create printed materials that explain, teach, or decorate.
6. A special image connected with a business, group, or product.
7. People who work in the field of art known as graphic design.

REVIEWING ART FACTS

Number a sheet of paper from 8 to 14. Answer each question in a complete sentence.

8. Name four main areas of graphic design.
9. What invention spurred the beginning of the field of graphic design?
10. Name two tasks of an editorial designer.
11. What were lithographs by artists like Toulouse-Lautrec used for in the 1800s?
12. Name two places besides TV where you can see the work of advertising designers.
13. What kinds of graphic artists make step-by-step drawings?
14. Besides shapes or pictures, what do logos often contain?

THINKING ABOUT ART

On a sheet of paper, answer each question in a sentence or two.

1. **Analyze.** What kinds of products have you seen advertised both on TV and in printed form? In what ways are the two kinds of ads different?
2. **Extend.** How do you think the invention of the printing press affected the work of the sign maker?
3. **Extend.** In which kinds of books, science or history, do you think technical illustrations would be more useful? Explain your answer.

MAKING ART CONNECTIONS

1. **Drama.** Find out all you can about the theme and character of an upcoming play in your school or community. Design a poster advertising the play. Develop visual images that show what the play is about. Include information such as where and when the show will be given, the name of the organization producing it, the author, and how much tickets cost.
2. **Home Economics.** Collect an assortment of favorite recipes. Design and illustrate a cookbook. Work from direct observation of subject matter such as fresh fruits and vegetables, pots and pans, china, and cooking utensils.
3. **Physical Education.** Design a logo representing your favorite sport, create a poster design advertising an upcoming event, or design a school spirit T-shirt. Learn as much about the subject as possible. Observe and draw athletes in action, cheerleaders, mascots, and equipment used. Develop original imagery. Do not use existing images.

CHAPTER 11 REVIEW

LOOKING AT THE DETAILS

The detail shown below is from a poster of the performer *Jane Avril*, done by the artist Henri de Toulouse-Lautrec. Study the detail and answer the following questions.

1. Examine the woman's hat. How do the elements of line and color affect the mood?
2. Knowing that this is only part of the work, where or how might you imagine to find the woman's legs, if you were told the image was symmetrically balanced?
3. Why do you think the artist chose this lettering style as opposed to a more formal one?
4. Imagine that you are walking down the street and you see several posters of advertisements, but only one catches your eye. What elements of art and principles of art would you expect to find in that one?

Henri de Toulouse-Lautrec. *Jane Avril.* 1899. Color lithograph. (Detail.) 68.3 x 47 cm (26⅞ x 18½"). Free Library of Philadelphia.

Sculpture

Chapter Scan

Lesson 1 The Art of Sculpture
Lesson 2 Carving a Plaster Relief
Lesson 3 Modeling in Clay
Lesson 4 Abstract Sculpture

TRB Resources

- 12-9 Chapter Test
- Color Transparency 23
- Color Transparency 24

TEACHING THE CHAPTER

Introducing the Art Work

Direct students' attention to Henry Moore's sculpture *Family Group.* Inform students that Henry Moore was an English sculptor of the twentieth century whose sculptures explored the problems of humanity and human relationships. His sculptures represented the human form in various situations and interactions. Henry Moore studied works of art in English and European museums, which provided him with the greatest immediate influence on his art. He was attracted to classical, pre-classical, African, and Pre-Columbian art; these influences can be seen in some of his early sculptures. In the 1930s Moore was influenced by Picasso and Surrealist sculpture. He explored various sculpture media and began to create abstract forms. Most of Moore's latest works are in bronze.

Examining the Art Work

Tell students that *Family Group* represents Henry Moore's personal feelings about the idea of family. Explain that Moore created this sculpture just before the birth of his first child.

Point out the smooth texture of the work and the lack of detail in the faces, clothes, and bodies. Suggest that this creates a feeling of a universal statement because specific personalities are not introduced. Explain to students that Moore combined round abstract forms with openings and holes to create unique human images. Tell students that by his lack of detail, the artist quickly focuses the viewer's attention on the action of the figures, where his message lies.

▲ The artist sculpted the work just before his first child was born. Notice the name of the work. What clues tell you how he felt the child would affect his relationship with his wife?

Henry Moore. *Family Group.* 1948–49. Cast 1950. Bronze. 150.5 x 118.1, base 114.3 x 75.9 cm (59¼ x 46½, base 45 x 29⅞"). Museum of Modern Art, New York, New York. A. Conger. Goodyear Fund.

Sculpture

Like other artists, sculptors begin new projects by asking themselves questions. Here are some questions that faced the sculptor of the work at the left.

- What medium will I use?
- Will I create by adding to or taking away from?
- Will the work be realistic?
- Will the figures appear smooth or rough?

In this chapter you will learn about the different choices sculptors have when they create their art work.

OBJECTIVES

After completing this chapter, you will be able to:
- Name the four basic methods used by sculptors.
- Describe each method of sculpting.
- Define the terms *freestanding* and *relief.*
- Tell which sculpting methods are additive and which are subtractive.
- Create sculptures of your own using carving, modeling, and assembling.

WORDS YOU WILL LEARN

additive	high relief
assembling	low relief
carving	modeling
casting	relief
freestanding	subtractive

ARTISTS YOU WILL MEET

Jean Baptiste Carpeaux	Henry Moore
Clodion	Louise Nevelson
Naum Gabo	Georgia O'Keeffe
Alexandre Hogue	David Smith

Point out how the figures' arms are intertwined and how the woman has both arms around the baby. The man seems to be trying to hold onto the child, while at the same time trying to maintain contact with the woman. Explain that Moore shows detail on the man's hand resting on the woman's shoulder to take the viewer's eye there and indicate that it is significant.

Discussing the Art Work
Ask students to think about the message Moore is trying to communicate in this work. Point out that the man's hand rests on the woman's shoulder rather than around her, indicating a certain distance. Point out how the man's legs lean toward the woman, while her legs are straight. Note that the man is looking at the woman and child, while both of them are looking out. Suggest that perhaps Moore is communicating the idea that the relationship between the man and woman has changed. It has distanced them in one way, while providing a common bond at the same time. Perhaps the man is feeling left out, while he sees the woman as having a new preoccupation. Ask students how else they might interpret this work. Suggest concepts such as envy, fear, curiosity, and change.

Tell students that in this chapter they will learn about the methods of sculpting and create their own sculptures using several of these methods.

Building Self-Esteem
Remind students that all artists must make important decisions when they begin to plan a new project. Two of the most basic will be, "What will I choose as my subject," and "What style will I use to depict it?" In this chapter there are photographs of people who look like us and others who look like mythological characters, surfaces that are smooth and others that are textured, sculptures made from clay, bronze and celluloid. One of the lessons uses clay as a medium to model an animal. Ask the class to think about the question, "What will I choose as my subject?" Will they plan to sculpt a recognizable animal or create a new form of animal life? What options does the second choice give them? Help the class to think about creative decision-making and how to select a subject and style best suited to their skills and interests.

LESSON 1

The Art of Sculpture

LESSON PLAN
(pages 208–211)

Objectives

After completing this lesson, students will be able to:
• Name and describe the four basic techniques used by sculptors.
• Tell which sculpting techniques are additive and which are subtractive.

Supplies

• Large photographs of sculptures in various styles from different periods in history (including, if possible, at least one photograph of a local sculpture).
• Large bars of white soap, knives in several sizes.

TRB Resources
• 12-1 *Louise Nevelson*, (artist profile)
• 12-2 *Sculpture and Architecture*, (art history)
• 12-3 *The Process of Bronze Casting*, (reproducible master)

TEACHING THE LESSON

Getting Started

Motivator. Display photographs of various sculptures. Try to include sculptures representing the four different sculpting techniques and sculptures created during various periods of history and by members of different cultures. Also try to include at least one photo of a sculpture students may have seen in the local community—a statue in a nearby park, for example. Let students discuss the photographs: What do you see in each work? What do all these works have in common? (Students should recognize all as sculpture from their introduction to art media in Chapter 3.) How are the sculptures alike? What distinguishes each work from the others? Explain to students that they will learn more about how these works and other sculptures were created.

When artists work with paints, they create the illusion of space in their works. It is the job of sculptors to create their works in space. Look at the painting in Figure 12–1. The objects in it seem to have roundness and depth. If you try to grasp one, however, your hand will bump up against flat canvas. The boy in Figure 12–2, on the other hand, has *real* roundness and depth. The work casts *real* shadows. It invites you to move around it. It invites you to see it from every side.

In this lesson you will learn about the many tools and methods sculptors use to create their art work. In later lessons you will use some of these tools and methods yourself.

THE BEGINNINGS OF SCULPTING

You may recall that the earliest artists, the cave dwellers, were painters. But did you know they were also sculptors? Stone, horn, ivory, and bone were some media used by these early sculptors. The sculpture in Figure 12–3, completed in 2600 B.C., is regarded by many to be one of the wonders of the world. Do you know in what country this remarkable work is found? Do you know what it is called? What medium was used to construct it?

▶ **Figure 12–1** Does this painting seem lifelike? How many different ways does the artist create a feeling of space?

Alexandre Hogue. *Drouth Stricken Area*. 1934. Oil on canvas. 76.2 x 107.9 cm (30 x 42½"). Dallas Museum of Art.

Classroom Management

If your community has any examples of public sculpture, arrange a field trip to view one or more works—or encourage students to go on their own to view the sculpture. Have students write descriptions of a favorite sculpture and/or draw several sketches of it. Then have students research the sculptor who created the work to find out more about the sculptor's life and work, including where other works by this artist can be seen.

Cooperative Learning

Have students work together in cooperative groups to explore the relationships between sculpture and dance. Both sculptors and dancers work in three-dimensional space and must be aware of balance in all three directions. What experiments can students devise to represent sculpture in dance forms? How can they try interpreting dance as sculpture?

Jean Baptiste Carpeaux. *Neopolitan Fisherboy*. 1857. Bronze with light brown patina. 34.6 cm (13⅝"). Allen Memorial Art Museum, Oberlin College, Oberlin, Ohio. Gift of Charles F. Olney.

▼ Figure 12–3 At its highest point this sculpture is 65 feet (19.8 m) tall. The head is that of an ancient Egyptian king. The body is that of a lion. What statement could the Egyptians have been making?

Great Sphinx, Giza. c. 2600 B.C.

Lesson 1   *The Art of Sculpture*   📖   **209**

Vocabulary. Help students use dictionaries to examine the words *sculpt, sculpture,* and *sculptor.* Ask: What is the meaning of the old Latin word from which our word *sculpt* is derived? What are the meanings of the word endings *-ure* and *-or*?

Developing Concepts

Exploring Aesthetics. Help students discuss Jean-Baptiste Carpeaux's sculpture shown in Figure 12-2: What is the subject of this work? How would you characterize the sculptor's use of form, space, and texture in this work? How have the principles of balance and harmony been used to organize the visual elements? What other principles of art can you identify in the sculpture? What idea or feeling do you think the sculptor intended to communicate?

Using Art Criticism. Let students work with partners to examine one of the sculptures shown in this lesson. Ask the partners to go through the four stages of art criticism together: describing the sculpture, analyzing it, interpreting it, and judging it. Then have them work together to write a one-paragraph judgment of the sculpture they have chosen.

Understanding Art History. Have students examine and learn more about the Great Sphinx of Giza, shown in Figure 12-3. Begin by asking: What do you see in this work? What idea or feeling does it communicate to you? Let students discuss their ideas, and then have them research this sphinx and others created by the ancient Egyptians. Where and when were sphinxes created? Which familiar figures are usually combined to create a sphinx? What purpose were the sphinxes intended to serve? How large were most of the carved sphinxes? After students have researched these and related questions, let them meet again to compare and discuss what they have learned.

Background Information

The sphinx is a mythical creature—part beast (usually a lion) and part human. This creature originated in ancient Egypt, but its image also appears among the cultures of ancient Greece, Mesopotamia, and Etruria.

The most famous Egyptian sphinx is the one shown in this lesson, near Giza, which is now a suburb of Cairo. There were three pyramids constructed by three different pharaohs at this site. The second was built by Khafre, the fourth king of the Fourth Dynasty, who ruled during the first half of the twenty-sixth century B.C. Khafre had this famous sphinx built to guard his pyramid. Most monumental sphinxes were built with the heads of ruling pharaohs, so it can be assumed that this sphinx shows the features of Khafre. Later the sphinx came to be worshiped as a representation of the god Ra of the Two Horizons.

▲ Figure 12–4 Do you know the Biblical story in this carving?

The Annunciation. Estella San Miguel, Spain.

SCULPTING TECHNIQUES

Sculptors use four basic techniques in their work. These are carving, casting, modeling, and assembling. Some of these techniques are **additive**, *produced by adding to or combining materials*. Other techniques are **subtractive**, *produced by removing or taking away from the original material*.

Carving

Carving is *a sculpting method in which material is cut or chipped away*. The very first carvings were probably nothing more than figures scratched into a flat rock. Since then sculptors have learned ways of freeing images from great blocks of stone. Study the carving in Figure 12–4. It decorates the doorway of a church in Spain. The work has a religious subject. Do you remember any other art works you studied that have religious subjects?

In carving, sculptors end with less material than they start with. For this reason, carving is known as a subtractive method of sculpting.

Casting

Casting is *a sculpting method in which melted material is poured into a mold*. When the material cools it hardens and the mold is taken off. Often the material used is a metal such as bronze in a liquid form.

The art of casting bronze figures is over 3000 years old. The first people to do it were the Chinese. The Greeks and Romans later showed great skill in their bronze castings. Look again at Figure 12–2 on page **209**. Notice how lifelike the boy looks. Today artists still cast in bronze. The bronze statue that opened this chapter (page **206**) was cast by a leading sculptor of our century.

Modeling

Painters start off with blank canvases. Sculptors sometimes start off with blank space. By adding together bits of material, they create something where nothing was before. Such methods of sculpting are called additive methods.

Modeling, *a sculpting method in which a soft or workable material is built up and shaped*, is an additive method. The material used most often in modeling is clay. Like carving and casting, modeling is a very old method.

Assembling

Not all sculpting methods are old. A second additive method, known as assembling or constructing, came into being only recently. **Assembling** is *a sculpting method in which different kinds of materials are gathered and joined together*. Wood, plastic, wire, string, as well as found objects are some of the materials used to assemble sculpture. Glue, screws, and nails are a few of the materials used to join the objects together. Study

▲ **Figure 12–5   What elements and principles are blended to create a feeling of action in this work?**

David Smith. *Cockfight-Variation.* 1945. Steel. 86.3 x 34.9 x 15.2 cm (34 x 13¾ x 6"). Whitney Museum of American Art, New York, New York.

Figures 12–5 and 12–6. What materials were used to assemble each work of art? What tools did the artists use to construct their sculptural pieces? What does Figure 12–5 look like? How would you describe Figure 12–6?

▲ **Figure 12–6   The artist's father ran a lumberyard. How might that have affected her life's work?**

Louise Nevelson. *Atmosphere and Environment.* 1970. Cor-Ten steel. 640.1 x 487.7 cm (252 x 192"). The Art Museum, Princeton University. John B. Putman Jr. Memorial Collection.

✔ CHECK YOUR UNDERSTANDING

1. Name the four basic techniques of sculpting. Define each method.
2. Which technique of sculpting is called a subtractive technique? Why is it called this?
3. Who were the first people to do bronze casting?
4. Which two techniques of sculpting are called additive techniques? Why are they called this?
5. Name three media that can be used in assembling.

Following Up

Closure. In a short class discussion, let students share their responses to sculpture: How is it like other forms of art? What makes sculpture different? What particular appeal does sculpture have for you as a viewer and as a creator of works?

Evaluation. 1. Review students' written responses to the "Check Your Understanding" questions. 2. Consider students' contributions to the "Closure" discussion.

Reteaching. Work with small groups of students to compare and discuss the sculptures shown in Figures 12-2, 12-3, 12-4, 12-5, and 12-6. Be sure students can identify the sculpting techniques used to create each work. Ask: Is each an additive technique or a subtractive technique? Then have students use the credit lines to identify the date in which each sculpture was created and to organize the works chronologically. Help them identify and discuss differences in subject, composition, and content. Ask: How might these differences be related to the time during which each sculpture was created?

Enrichment. Help students explore some of the boundaries of the art of sculpture. Explain that a well-known contemporary artist, Michael Brewster, has created a series of art works that he calls sculptures; the medium he uses is sound. Brewster sets up speakers that emit various tones in a gallery room. The tones are designed to interact and produce different sounds in different areas. Let students discuss their responses to these questions: Do you think these works can be called sculpture? Why, or why not? After a group discussion, have students write paragraphs expressing their own ideas about Brewster's work.

Answers to "Check Your Understanding"

1. These are the four basic techniques of sculpting: carving, in which material is cut or chipped away; casting, in which melted material is poured into a mold; modeling, in which a soft or workable material is built up and shaped; and assembling, in which different kinds of materials are gathered and joined together.
2. Carving is called a subtractive technique of sculpting because carvers end with less material than they start with.

3. The first people to do bronze casting were the Chinese.
4. Modeling and assembling are called additive techniques of sculpting because they involve adding to or combining materials.
5. Wood, plastic, wire, string, and found objects are some of the media that can be used in assembling. (Students may identify any three of these media.)

Carving a Plaster Relief

Objectives

After completing this lesson, students will be able to:

- Use the technique of carving to make relief sculptures of flowers.
- Describe, analyze, interpret, and judge their own sculptures.

Supplies

- Display-sized reproductions of several flower paintings by Georgia O'Keeffe (if available).
- Real flowers or photographs of flowers; pencils; sketch paper cut into sheets, 7 inches (18 cm) square; plastic bowls; cold water; mixing sticks; pie pan, 9 inches (23 cm), lined with plastic; molding plaster; vermiculite; assorted carving tools, such as knives, nails, and files; fine-grain sandpaper.
- Excess plaster, paper cups, damp sand in shallow containers.

> **TRB Resources**
> - 12-4 *The Lighter Side,* (reproducible master)
> - 12-5 *Locating Public Art,* (aesthetics/art criticism)

TEACHING THE LESSON

Getting Started

Motivator. Display reproductions of Georgia O'Keeffe's flower paintings (if available), or have students examine *The White Calico Flower* by O'Keeffe, shown in Figure 12-7. As students study her painting, read aloud this quotation from Georgia O'Keeffe: "Everyone has many associations with a flower—the idea of a flower. Still, in a way, nobody sees a flower. It is so small—we haven't time, and to see takes time. If I could paint a flower exactly as I see it, no one would see what I see, because I would paint it small like the flower is small. So I said to myself—I'll paint what I see—what the flower is to me, but I'll paint it big and they will be surprised into taking time to look at it. I will make even busy New Yorkers take time to see what I see of flowers." Encourage students to share their responses to the ideas expressed in the quotation and to the painting.

212

Carving a Plaster Relief

Sometimes sculptures are only partly enclosed by space. Such sculptures are called relief. **Relief** is *a type of sculpture in which forms and figures are projected from the front only*. Relief sculptures are flat along the back. They are meant to be viewed only from the front.

Sculptors speak of two kinds of relief sculpture. *Relief that stands out in space only slightly* is **low relief**. *Relief that stands out boldly from its background* is **high relief**.

In this lesson you will make a low relief sculpture using the method of carving.

WHAT YOU WILL LEARN

Using the method of carving, you will make a relief sculpture of a flower. Your work will show the flower close up. You will not try to make your flower realistic. Instead, you will concentrate on creating a unified design. Use radial balance and rhythm to organize the shapes and lines suggested by the flower. Use a variety of textures to make your design more interesting. Use line directions to make your flower express a certain mood, such as twisting wildly or swaying gently.

WHAT YOU WILL NEED

- Real flowers or photographs of flowers
- Pencil and sketch paper cut into sheets, 7 inches (18 cm) square
- Plastic bowl, cold water, mixing stick
- Molding plaster and vermiculite (vuhr-**mik**-yuh-lite)
- Pie pan lined with plastic, 9 inch (23 cm)
- Paper clip; assorted carving tools, such as knives, nails, files; fine sandpaper

▶ **Figure 12–7 How would you describe this flower? What elements and principles can you identify?**

Georgia O'Keeffe. *The White Calico Flower.* 1931. Oil on canvas. 76.2 x 91.4 cm (30 x 36"). Whitney Museum of American Art, New York, New York.

Background Information

In the ancient world low relief was used as a form of narrative art; examples can be found all over the world. In Java the temple Borobodur devotes more space to narrative relief than does any other known building. The reliefs illustrate the life of Buddha and depict possible terrors in the afterlife. Persian reliefs at Persepolis depict the celebrations of the New Year Festivals, and Assyrian reliefs at Assur depict a famous king as a skilled and successful hunter. In Thebes ancient Egyptians carved reliefs on the walls of temples to commemorate the lives of the pharaohs. Battles are depicted, as are scenes from everyday life.

Early Christians in Rome also carved narrative reliefs. Church authorities feared that sculpture in the round might lead to idolatry, so artists carved low-relief depictions of Bible stories to be used as teaching tools.

WHAT YOU WILL DO

1. Study the painting by Georgia O'Keeffe in Figure 12–7. It is one of many close-up looks at flowers the artist has painted. Notice that O'Keeffe has left out realistic details. Instead, she has focused on the flowing lines and curved surfaces to create an abstract design.

2. Using real flowers or photographs of flowers as models, make pencil sketches in the style of O'Keeffe. Focus on creating rhythm with the lines and shapes of stems and petals. Look for places where different textures can be used. Choose your best sketch. Set it aside.

3. Pour 3 parts cold water into a plastic mixing bowl. Mix in 3 parts molding plaster and 2 parts vermiculite. Using the stick, stir the mixture until it is smooth and creamy. When the mixture thickens slightly, pour it carefully into the plastic-lined pie pan. (See Technique Tip **19**, *Handbook* page **276**.)

4. After a few minutes you will notice the mixture begin to dry and set. Place a bent paper clip in it near the top center. Leave the looped end of the paper clip sticking out to serve as a hanger. When the mixture is dry and hard, grasp the plastic liner. Carefully lift the dried plaster mixture from the pan. Turn it so the clip side is down. Another name for your relief is a plaque (**plak**). A plaque is an ornamental tablet that is meant to be hung on a wall.

5. Transfer your flower design onto the flat part of the plaque. Using the knife, begin scraping away the plaque surrounding your design. The flower design should

EXAMINING YOUR WORK

- **Describe** Point to the areas around your flower relief that you carved away. Show the petal shapes and lines you carved, and describe the texture you added.
- **Analyze** Show where you used the principle of rhythm to organize the lines and shapes. Point to the variety of textures in your relief. Explain how you used the elements and principles to make a design that has unity.
- **Interpret** Tell what mood your work captures. Explain which elements and principles help the viewer understand the mood.
- **Judge** Tell whether you feel your work succeeds. Explain your answer.

stand out from the background. Use smaller tools to carve the petals so they appear to overlap. Add texture to the leaves using the nail and other pointed tools. When you have finished carving, lightly sand the relief to give it a clean, smooth look.

6. Using the paper clip as a hook, hang your relief. Compare your work with those of your classmates.

SAFETY TIP

If you have breathing problems, tell your teacher. Dry dust from plaster and clay can be harmful. Wear a dust mask if necessary.

OTHER STUDIO IDEAS

- Do the above activity using corrugated cardboard. This time use the additive sculpture method to build your relief up from the flat base.

- ●● Make a plaster plaque as directed above and carve a relief design using symmetrical balance.

Lesson 2 *Carving a Plaster Relief*   **213**

Vocabulary. Review with students the definition of *relief* (from Chapter 3, Lesson 5, "Sculpture") and help them distinguish between low relief and high relief.

Developing Concepts

Exploring Aesthetics. Let students continue their discussion of O'Keeffe's painting in Figure 12-7. Ask: What kind of balance did O'Keeffe use? What other art principles can you identify in this work? What mood or idea do you feel this painting expresses?

Developing Studio Skills. Pour any excess plaster into paper cups and let students use it to create plaster reliefs in sand. Have students mold depressions in damp sand and then pour the plaster into their molds. Encourage them to discuss their reactions to working with the damp sand and the plaster—it should be fun!

Following Up

Closure. Hang all the flower reliefs for display in the classroom. Let each student identify and discuss his or her work, responding to the directions in the "Judge" section of "Examining Your Work."

Evaluation. Review students' flower relief plaques, and listen to their evaluations of their own work.

Reteaching. Work with small groups of students to review the process and techniques they used in creating their flower reliefs. Ask: Which steps did you find most difficult? What approaches might have made those steps easier? Did you use additive or subtractive techniques of sculpture?

Enrichment. Let groups of students work together to examine and read about examples of low relief and high relief. Suggest that about half the students in each group research the low-relief sculpture on the walls on ancient Egyptian structures; have the other half research the high-relief sculpture on the walls of European cathedrals built during the Middle Ages and Renaissance. Then have the group members meet to discuss and compare what they have learned.

Classroom Management Tip
If you would like to have students experiment with color, you can add bluing or other liquid dyes to plaster in its liquid state.
Remember that special caution is needed when mixing plaster and when cleaning up. See the "Classroom Management Tip" on page **179** and Technique Tips, *Handbook* page **276**.

Modeling in Clay

Modeling in Clay

Objectives

After completing this lesson, students will be able to:

• Use the technique of modeling to make freestanding sculptures of animals.

• Describe, analyze, interpret, and judge their own sculptures.

Supplies

• Samples of as many kinds of clay as possible—naturally produced clay in different colors and commercially produced clay.

• Pencils, sketch paper, pieces of muslin or other smooth cloth, clay (one ball about the size of a grapefruit for each student), forks, slip (a liquid mixture of clay and water), clay modeling tools.

• Leftover clay, toothpicks, strong thin cord or fishing line.

TRB Resource

• 12-6 *Design a Sculpture,* (cooperative learning)

TEACHING THE LESSON

Getting Started

Motivator. Display as many different kinds of clay as possible. Give students an opportunity to examine and handle the different clays. Then ask: How are all the kinds of clay alike? What makes each kind look different from the others? What is special about the feel of each kind?

Vocabulary. Help students recognize *freestanding* as a compound word: What are the two main parts of this compound word? How does understanding those two parts help you understand the meaning of *freestanding*?

Developing Concepts

Exploring Aesthetics. Help students examine and discuss *The River Rhine Separating the Waters* by Clodion, Figure 12-8: What is the subject of the work? How would you characterize the sculptor's use of art elements and principles? What idea or feeling does the work communicate to you?

Sculpture, you have read, uses space. Some sculptures use more space than others. Some are **freestanding**, or *surrounded on all sides by space*. Such works are also said to be "in the round."

The lively work in Figure 12–8 is a sculpture in the round. It was done by the French sculptor Clodion (**kloh**-dee-onh). When creating it the artist did not conform to limits of working on it from any one side. Instead, the artist kept turning the sculpture as work progressed. That way, Clodion was able to give equal attention to all sides. Study the work. Do you see the marks of the artist's fingers and tools on the surface? These help make the sculpture seem fresh and alive.

WHAT YOU WILL LEARN

Using the method of modeling, you will make a freestanding sculpture of an animal. You will build up the sculpture from a simple egg form. You will use texture to add harmony to the sculpture. Try to capture the personality of your animal by making it look gentle, friendly, or vicious.

WHAT YOU WILL NEED

• Pencil and sketch paper
• Piece of muslin or other smooth cloth
• Clay (a ball about the size of a grapefruit)
• Fork and slip (a liquid mixture of clay and water)
• Clay modeling tools

▶ **Figure 12–8** The figure in the sculpture is a river god from mythology. Does the work give you a sense of water? Do you know any other characters from mythology? Which ones? How do you think they would be best shown in a sculpture?

Clodion (Claude Michel). *The River Rhine Separating the Waters.* 1765. Terracotta. 27.9 x 45.7 x 30.5 cm (11 x 18 x 12"). Kimbell Art Museum, Fort Worth, Texas.

Background Information

Clodion (France, 1738–1814) was known as Claude Michel to his contemporaries. He studied sculpture in Rome, as did many other French sculptors of the seventeenth and eighteenth centuries.

French sculptors as a group developed a distinctive style, different from the main art movements in the rest of Europe. For example, though they studied in Rome, they did not generally work in the Baroque style that dominated Italian art.

The portrait bust was the most common type of French sculpture during this period. Ordinary people, as well as state leaders, were portrayed. Equestrian statues were also popular, though many of these did not survive the French Revolution. Equestrian statues are essentially studies in torsion. This can be clearly seen in the passionate work *Bacchanates* by Clodion; the subjects all appear to be alive.

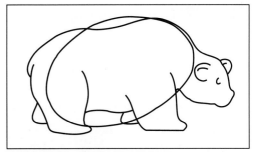

▲ **Figure 12–9** Notice the oval shape of the bear's body. What other shapes do you see in this sketch?

WHAT YOU WILL DO

1. Look at the sketch of a bear in Figure 12–9. Notice how the rounded body of this animal has the form of an egg. Draw an egg outline similar to this one on a sheet of sketch paper. This will be the starting point for your own sculpture of an animal. Add legs, a head, a neck, and a tail to make an animal. Experiment with different animals. Begin each with an egg form. Choose your best sketch. As you sculpt, look back at the sketch from time to time.

2. Read the Technique Tip **17**, *Handbook* page **275**, about joining clay pieces. Working on a piece of burlap, divide your clay in half. Use one half to shape your egg form. Use the other half to make legs, neck, head, and tail. Using the fork, scratch lines on each part where it is to be attached to the egg. Wet each scratched surface with slip. Attach the parts firmly to the egg. Keep turning your sculpture as you work. Freestanding sculpture

EXAMINING YOUR WORK

- **Describe**   Tell what animal you sculpted. Point out details that make it easy to identify your animal. Point to the texture you used. Explain how this was done to suggest hair or fur. Explain what you learned about the strengths and weaknesses of clay as a sculpture medium.
- **Analyze**   Show how texture has been used to give harmony to your sculpture.
- **Interpret**   Show what features in your work would help a viewer understand the personality of your animal — friendly, fierce, gentle.
- **Judge**   Tell whether you feel your work succeeds. Explain your answer.

---

must look right when viewed from all angles. Avoid any fine details of clay that stick out. Keep your sculpture compact.

3. Finish your sculpture with a clay modeling tool. Do not use your fingers. Add details to your animal. Add an overall texture to give harmony to your sculpture. (*Hint*: A comb pulled or twisted across the surface will give a look of hair or fur.)

4. When your sculpture is firm but not dry, make a hole in the bottom. Hollow out the sculpture with a clay tool. This will keep it from cracking or exploding when it is baked, or fired.

5. Display your finished sculpture in a class "zoo."

OTHER STUDIO IDEAS

- Do a second clay sculpture, this time of an animal with a completely different personality. Compare it with your first sculpture. Are the different personalities easily identified?

- ●● Do another clay sculpture, this time using a different geometric shape for the body. Use a cube, cone, sphere, or other shape.

Lesson 3   *Modeling in Clay*   **215**

Abstract Sculpture

Sculptures created through the method of assembling are often unique and daring. Look at Figure 12–10. Can you tell what materials the sculptor used? Can you tell what this sculpture is supposed to be?

This sculpture, by Naum Gabo, is abstract. Art work is abstract if you can recognize the subject of the work, but the object is portrayed in an unrealistic way. You probably can see that this sculpture represents a human head, but does it look real?

Imagine that this sculpture has been taken apart, and all of its pieces are laid in a pile in front of you. Would you be able to tell that these shapes represent the parts of a face? Imagine now that you are a sculptor. Could you assemble these same shapes to represent another kind of object?

WHAT YOU WILL LEARN

You will create an abstract sculpture using the method of assembling. You will use cardboard as a building material and glue as a joining material. Your sculpture will not be realistic. It will use a variety of geometric shapes and forms to express the idea of a bird, reptile, or amphibian. Design your sculpture with either a vertical or horizontal emphasis. When finished, paint the sculpture with a coat of black or white paint to give it harmony. (See Figure 12-11.)

WHAT YOU WILL NEED

• Pencil and sheets of sketch paper
• Sheets of corrugated cardboard cut from boxes
• Large scissors and white glue
• Tempera

▲ **Figure 12–10** The sculpture shows a human figure. Can you identify any features of this figure? Which ones? Why do you think this work was considered to be so daring when it was first seen?

Naum Gabo. *Constructed Head No. 2.* 1916. Sculpture celluloid. 43.2 x 31.1 x 31.1 cm (17 x 12¼ x 12¼"). Dallas Museum of Art.

WHAT YOU WILL DO

1. Look through nature books to see the many variations of birds, reptiles, and amphibians. Choose one that has a variety of interesting shapes.
2. Make pencil sketches of your creature. Do several sketches until you have one that pleases you. You may want to combine the features of different types of birds, reptiles, or amphibians.

3. Make a revised pencil sketch of your creature using simple geometric shapes to symbolize the real shapes. Decide whether your sculpture will be horizontal or vertical.
4. Using scissors, cut a large cardboard shape as a base. Refer to your sketch to cut out smaller geometric shapes to form the body and features of your creature. You may cut the shapes in half, or in eighths. Think about different action poses. Is your creature standing still or twisting and turning? Is it sitting, lying down, or involved in some activity?
5. Assemble your work by gluing shapes and forms to each other. Work carefully. To see which angle works best, look at your sculpture from different angles before joining each new piece.
6. Paint your sculpture using either white or black. The use of a single color will add harmony to the work. Spray paint works especially well in this case.

═══ **SAFETY TIP** ═══
Use spray paint outdoors or in a room with good ventilation. Before spraying, place your sculpture inside a large cardboard box. This will contain some of the harmful fumes.

OTHER STUDIO IDEAS

- Create a second sculpture, this time combining found objects to represent an animal, bird, reptile, or amphibian. These odds and ends might include plastic spoons, soda straws, old door hinges, or other mechanical parts. Paint your sculpture black, white, or grey to emphasize the overall form of the sculpture.

EXAMINING YOUR WORK

- **Describe** Identify the bird, reptile, or amphibian you chose as a starting point for your sculpture. Name the different shapes and forms you used in your work. Show shapes with different textures or patterns.
- **Analyze** Tell whether you used vertical or horizontal emphasis in your work. Point to the variety of shapes and forms you used. Explain how these add interest to your work. Explain how the use of a single black or white color adds to the harmony of the work.
- **Interpret** Give your work a title. Explain how the shapes you combined suggest a bird, reptile, or amphibian.
- **Judge** Tell whether you feel your work succeeds. Explain your answer.

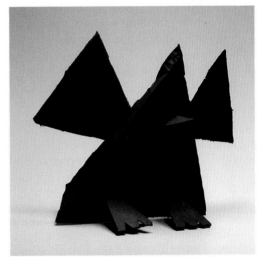

▲ Figure 12–11   Student work. An abstract sculpture.

Lesson 4   *Abstract Sculpture*   **217**

Background Information
In 1912 Pablo Picasso (Spain, 1881–1973) constructed a sculpture that looked similar to a guitar. He made it of metal and wire. The sculpture was not carved or cast or modeled—it was assembled. The work had a profound effect on other sculptors.

Vladimir Tatlin (Russia, 1885–1953) visited Picasso's studio, saw the assembled sculpture, and began using the new technique to create non-objective reliefs.

Other sculptors took these ideas and techniques in different directions. For many sculptors, however, assembling replaced carving and modeling, and non-objective subjects replaced objective.

The techniques of assembling were especially interesting to Constructivists, including Naum Gabo (Russian-born, 1890–1977). They usually worked in such media as wood, glass, and plastic, and restricted colors to those inherent in the media.

Developing Concepts
Exploring Aesthetics. Let students work in groups to discuss what they see in Naum Gabo's sculpture (Figure 12-10) and how they respond to it: What is the subject of this work? Do you need the title of the sculpture to help you recognize or understand the subject? What idea or feeling does this sculpture communicate to you?

Developing Studio Skills. Working from the photographs on display (see "Motivator"), have students make realistic drawings of the animals on which they based their abstract sculptures. Display the drawings and the sculptures together. Ask: How are they alike? How are they different?

Appreciating Cultural Diversity. Ask students to explore the animal carvings created by African artists. What differences in style distinguish the carvings created by different African groups? How are the carvings similar? What purpose are these carvings intended to fulfill? Have students read to find answers to these and other questions about African sculpture; also have them look for photographs of African sculptures. Then help students share and discuss their findings.

Following Up
Closure. Let students work with partners to discuss their abstract sculptures, using "Examining Your Work" as a guide. Then have each student write a short explanation of the title given to his or her sculpture.

Evaluation. Review students' abstract sculptures, and read their explanations of their works' titles.

Reteaching. Work with small groups of students. Help them browse through this text and/or other books with reproductions of art works: Which paintings and sculptures are abstract? How are those works different from realistic art works and non-objective art works?

Enrichment. Have students work with partners or in small groups to research and report on one of these classes of animals: birds, reptiles, or amphibians.

CHAPTER 12 REVIEW

BUILDING VOCABULARY

Number a sheet of paper from 1 to 10. After each number, write the term from the box that best matches each description below.

additive	high relief
assembling	low relief
carving	modeling
casting	relief
freestanding	subtractive

1. A sculpting method in which material is cut or chipped away.
2. A term describing a sculpting method that takes away or removes material.
3. A sculpting method in which melted material is poured into a mold.
4. A term describing a sculpting method that adds together or joins bits of material together.
5. A sculpting method in which a soft or workable material is built up and shaped.
6. A sculpting method in which different kinds of materials are gathered and joined.
7. Surrounded on all sides by space.
8. Sculpture that is partly enclosed by space.
9. Sculpture that stands out in space only slightly.
10. Sculpture that stands out boldly from its background.

REVIEWING ART FACTS

Number a sheet of paper from 11 to 18. Answer each question in a complete sentence.

11. Name three sculpting media that have been in existence for thousands of years.
12. What are four sculpting techniques?
13. How old is the art of casting in bronze?
14. Who were the first people to do bronze castings?
15. What material is used most often in modeling?

16. Which method of sculpting is the most recent?
17. Name two building materials used in assembling. Name two fastening materials.
18. What is slip? What is it used for?

THINKING ABOUT ART

On a sheet of paper, answer each question in a sentence or two.

1. **Extend.** What kinds of materials do you think might be found in sculptures of the future? Explain your answer.
2. **Analyze.** Which two methods of sculpting could be used to create an ice sculpture? Describe how you would use each method. Tell why the two methods you didn't name would not work as well.
3. **Compare and contrast.** In what ways are the methods of modeling and assembling alike? In what ways are they different?
4. **Extend.** The term *terra cotta* means "baked earth." In which method of sculpting would you expect to find terra cotta used as a medium?

MAKING ART CONNECTIONS

1. **Science.** In this chapter you learned that early cave painters were also sculptors. In 1912 a cave, Tuc' d' Audoubert, was discovered in the French Pyrenees. Research more about this discovery and the artifacts associated with it.
2. **Social Studies.** Find examples of relief and freestanding sculptures in your community. Find out who or what the sculptures represent. Using a sketchbook and pencil, record what you see and take photographs of the works of art. Put together a journal using your drawings, photographs, and notes.

LOOKING AT THE DETAILS

The detail shown below is from Henry Moore's sculpture, entitled *Family Group*. Study the detail and answer the following questions.

1. This sculpture was made out of bronze. How can knowing the materials in a sculpture help you identify the technique the artist used?

2. The faces of the figures have little detail. How does this affect the visual texture of the work? How does it influence the interpretation of the work?

3. Do the positions of the figures' arms express a relationship? Explain.

4. Why do you think Moore chose to show detail in the fingers of the hand on the shoulder, but omitted detail in the child's feet?

Henry Moore. *Family Group.* 1948–49. Cast 1950. Bronze. (Detail.) 150.5 x 118.1, base 114.3 x 75.9 cm (59¼ x 46½, base 45 x 29⅞"). Museum of Modern Art, New York, New York. A. Conger. Goodyear Fund.

ANSWERS TO "LOOKING AT THE DETAILS"

1. With some materials there are only specific techniques that can be used. Knowing the material can tell you its limits and the technique it lends itself to. For example, bronze is cast, clay is usually modeled because it is soft, odd materials are assembled, and wood is usually carved.

2. The visual texture is smooth. Students might note that the lack of detail focuses the viewer on the action of the figures rather than their personalities. The lack of detail suggests universal statement, since specific personalities are not introduced.

3. Yes. Responses will vary. Students might mention the following: The figures' arms are intertwined around the baby; thus the baby is portrayed as both a common bond as well as something between them. The man's hand on the woman's shoulder shows a unity; yet at the same time it shows distance because the arm is not around her.

4. Moore did this to emphasize the hand, to show its importance in terms of the message he is trying to communicate. The baby's feet do not represent an issue in the message of the relationship between the man and the woman.

Chapter Evaluation

The goal of this chapter is to help students analyze the four methods of sculpture, differentiate between relief and freestanding sculpture, and create works of art using various sculpting methods. Possible methods of evaluating results include:

1. Show students various reproductions of fine art pieces which include different sculpting methods. Have students identify whether the work is a relief or freestanding sculpture, and list the sculpting method used to create the work.

2. Have students use the sculpting medium of their choice and demonstrate the additive and subtractive process.

3. Have students complete Chapter 12 Test (TRB, Resource 12-9).

Crafts

Chapter Scan
Lesson 1 The Art of Crafts
Lesson 2 Clay Bowl
Lesson 3 Slab Container
Lesson 4 Making a Weaving
Lesson 5 Jewelry Art

TRB Resources
• 13-10 Chapter Test
• Color Transparency 25
• Color Transparency 26

TEACHING THE CHAPTER

Introducing the Art Work

Direct students' attention to the photograph of the *Chilkat Blanket*. Inform students that this blanket was woven by a North American Indian tribe called the Tlingit. The Tlingit tribe lives on the upper Skeena River in British Columbia. This tribe practices no agriculture. They live off of fishing and some hunting. They have a ranked society, consisting of chiefs, the upper class, the commoners, and the slaves, who are not owned but are workers. This culture is organized into different clans, and each clan has a particular animal associated with it. The designs in much of the art work of the tribe incorporate the clan's animal in a stylized form.

Examining the Art Work

Tell students that this blanket and others like it are used as robes and are a sign of high status. Inform students that the blankets were woven by the women of the tribe, based on designs from their husbands or fathers. The men would draw or carve their designs on boards; then the women would use the boards as guidelines for their weaving. These Chilkat blankets were commissioned by other tribe members who had the money to pay for the women's time in weaving. The blankets were woven on an upright loom using shredded cedar bark

▲ Notice the materials mentioned in the credit line. What do you know about these materials? Can they be easily obtained? What challenges face the craftsperson who works with materials such as these?

Unknown. Chilkat Blanket. c. 1900. Woven cedar bark, mountain goat wool, fur. American Museum of Natural History, New York, New York. Courtesy of Department of Library Services.

Crafts

Have you ever made or bought a special, hand-crafted item? Look at the blanket at the left. What materials did the artist use to create it? What details do you see in the work? All over the world there are people who make items that are not only functional, but are also works of art.

In this chapter you will learn what art works of this type are called. You will learn how — and by whom — they are made.

OBJECTIVES

After completing this chapter, you will be able to:
- Define the terms *crafts* and *craftsperson.*
- Describe the crafts of weaving, glassmaking, and ceramics.
- Identify the different conditions of clay.
- Make a clay bowl, a slab pot, a woven wall hanging, and paper jewelry.

WORDS YOU WILL LEARN

crafts
craftsperson
fibers
fired
glassblowing
glazed
kiln

loom
pottery
slab
slip
warp
weaving
weft

ARTISTS YOU WILL MEET

Elizabeth Garrison
Kim Keats
Kimiko
Dextra Q. Nampeyo
Bob Owens
Jane Pleak

Tommye M. Scanlin
Pat Steadman
Margaret Tafoya
Louis Comfort Tiffany
Ann Renee Weaver
    and Tony Mann

and mountain goat wool. Explain to students that it took the women much time and precision to create these designs. Point out the precise lines and the symmetrical balance of the design. Explain how the colors create harmony in the work. Refer to the shape, and suggest to students that the shape is designed to wrap around the shoulders, successfully enveloping the body and providing warmth.

Discussing the Art Work
Ask students if they can define the animal being depicted in this blanket. Explain that this is a stylized version of the animal and an abstract design. Suggest that they may get some clues from some of the other shapes in the work. Point out the two long gray shapes in the center of the work; propose that they may represent wings, suggesting that the animal is a bird, perhaps an eagle or falcon. Explain that the way to find this information would be to research which clan the blanket came from and which animal represented that clan.

Ask students to think about why the craftsperson chose these particular colors. Suggest that the tribe's lifestyle consisted of living in nature, so the earth tones may represent the way of life. The earth tones represent the colors of the animal shown in the work and its environment. In addition, the dyes available to the craftsperson may have been limited. Another consideration may be how the materials themselves respond to certain dyes.

Tell students that in this chapter they will learn about various crafts and their relationship to art. Tell them that they will make their own crafts, including a clay bowl and paper jewelry.

Building Self-Esteem
Tell students that artists of many cultures decorate the outside of their pottery with pictures and symbols of important events from the past. Sometimes the stories are about important heroes and their deeds. Tell students they are going to be planning the design for the outside of their own "achievement" pot. The shape of the pot can be drawn as a flat-sided box, the top of a box, or a traditional open bowl or bottle shape. Remind students that if they were decorating an actual clay pot, they would be using relief, incising, and stamping. Ask students to draw two or three memorable events in which they finally achieved a goal; events that made them feel good about themselves. They can even include important events they hope to achieve in the future: learning to drive a car, earning an award for a sports or scholastic competition, or mastering a new skill. Let students share their drawings with classmates and tell about their most important achievements.

The Art of Crafts

LESSON PLAN
(pages 222–225)

Objectives

After completing this lesson, students will be able to:
• Define the terms *crafts* and *craftsperson.*
• Describe the crafts of weaving, glassblowing, and pottery.
• Identify the different conditions of clay.

Supplies

• Handcrafted items, including, if possible, weavings, blown glass, and pottery; media and equipment used in making those handcrafted items (if available), such as loom, fibers, glassblowing tools, clay, clay tools.
• Manufactured mugs and/or drinking glasses.
• Drawing paper, colored pencils.

TRB Resources

• 13-1 *Patterns in Quilts,* (reproducible master)
• 13-2 *Handmade vs. Mass Produced,* (aesthetics/art criticism)
• 13-3 *Crafts in Ages Past,* (art history)

TEACHING THE LESSON

Getting Started

Motivator. Display as many handcrafted items as you have available; if possible, also display some of the media and equipment used in creating such handcrafted items. Give students an opportunity to examine and discuss the display informally. Then let volunteers describe each handcrafted item and identify the media and equipment used in creating it. Then help students explore their responses to the crafts, and ask: Which of these items do you consider art works? Why?

The Art of Crafts

Before there were machines, everything that people used was made by hand. Fabric to make clothing was woven by hand. Plates, bowls, and pots to cook with were made by hand. At that time, artists worked not only out of a wish to create, but also out of necessity. These artists considered the useful function of the item. They also considered the beauty or the aesthetic qualities of the object. In many cases, their items were works of art.

An artist who made such useful and aesthetically pleasing goods was—and still is—called a craftsperson. A **craftsperson** is *someone who has become an expert in an area of applied art. The different areas of applied art in which craftspeople work* are called **crafts**.

▶ **Figure 13–1   This quilt was created to celebrate Georgia's 250th birthday. Everything on the quilt symbolizes one part of the state. Can you tell which part by studying the symbols?**

Elizabeth Garrison. *Georgia.* 1983. Quilt. 120 x 157.5 cm (48 x 63"). Private collection.

Classroom Management Tip
Encourage local craftspeople to demonstrate and display their work. Invite a craftsperson to visit the class, or arrange to take the class on a field trip to a craftsperson's studio. Help students prepare by learning about the person—the craft he or she practices and the specific works he or she has created.

CRAFTS

Today there is a renewed interest in all types of crafts. Look at the quilt in Figure 13–1. It was not made to cover a bed. Instead, it was designed and created by a craftsperson to hang on a wall. Crafts have increased in popularity because people appreciate the one-of-a-kind, well-made product.

Today, as in the past, craftspeople use many different media. Some work in wood (Figure 13–2). Others work in metals, (Figure 13–3). Still others work in fibers, fabrics, glass, and clay.

▲ **Figure 13–2** What makes these blocks special? How are they different from the kind made in factories?

Ann Renée Weaver and Tony Mann. *Alphabet Blocks in Case*. Brazilian Mahogany, non-toxic paints and finishes and brass hardware. Case, 7 x 41.3 x 15.2 cm (2¾ x 16¼ x 6"). Blocks, 4.8 x 4.3 x 4.4 cm (1⁷⁄₁₀ x 1⁷⁄₁₀ x 1¾").

▲ **Figure 13–3** How would you imagine it would feel to wear this helmet? In what ways would it be different if it were made out of fabric?

Unknown. *Parade Sallet in the Form of a Lion's Head*. Steel, gilt bronze, silver, semi-precious stones. 28.3 cm (11⅛"). Metropolitan Museum of Art, New York, New York. Harris Brisbane Dick Fund.

▲ **Figure 13–4** This one-of-a-kind basket is made of natural materials. How does the craftsperson create unity in the work?

Kim Keats. *Banded Tulip Basket*. 1986. Wisteria and dyed reeds. 33 x 68.6 x 35.6 cm (13 x 27 x 14").

Weaving

Weaving is *a craft in which fiber strands are interlocked to make cloth or objects*. The basket in Figure 13–4 and the mask in Figure 13–5 are examples of the weaver's art.

▲ **Figure 13–5** The Iroquois wove these masks from corn husks. What does this fact reveal about the habits of the tribe?

Iroquoian. *Husk Face Mask*. National Museum of American History, Smithsonian Institution.

Lesson 1 *The Art of Crafts* **223**

Vocabulary. Help students review the distinction between fine art and applied art. (Refer them to "Examining Art Works," pages **4** and **5**, if necessary.) You may also want to review the definition of the term *artist* and ask students to compare this with the definition of *craftsperson* given in the text: Are all craftspeople artists? Are all artists craftspeople? Encourage students to present and support differing points of view.

Developing Concepts

Exploring Aesthetics. Display several manufactured mugs (or drinking glasses), and help students compare them with the handcrafted items of pottery or glass. Ask: How are these items alike? How are they different? What difference does it make that one was created by a craftsperson and another was manufactured by a machine? Is there any difference between the purpose the handcrafted item is intended to serve and the purpose of the manufactured item? If so, what is that difference? What approaches can you suggest for distinguishing handcrafted items from manufactured items? Should everyone be prepared to make such distinctions? Why, or why not? As students respond to these questions, help them focus on the most basic aesthetic question: What is art?

Using Art Criticism. Have students form eight groups, and assign each group one of the works shown in Figures 13-1, 13-2, 13-3, 13-4, 13-5, 13-7, 13-8, and 13-9. Ask the group members to examine and discuss the work: What do you see here? Which visual elements—color, line, texture, shape, form, space—can you identify? How would you describe the use of each element? How are the principles of art used to organize those elements? What idea or feeling does the work suggest? What purpose do you think the work is intended to serve? How successfully does it serve that function? Then let one member of each group summarize the discussion for the rest of the class.

Classroom Management Tip

Making, owning, and using fine handcrafted items can be very rewarding; encourage students to explore this idea. Ask whether students and their families have craft objects that they have made, inherited, or purchased—basketry, weaving, quilting or other stitchery, woodworking projects, jewelry, and so on. Ask those students to describe—or to bring in and share—their handcrafted items. What makes each handcrafted item especially meaningful to its owner or owners?

Cooperative Learning

Have students work in cooperative groups to learn more about other crafts—quilting, basketry, glassblowing, jewelry making, knitting, stained glass making, wood carving. Ask the members of each group to select a specific craft and then work together to learn about its development and about people who practice that craft now. Students should also find examples of the craft, either actual objects or pictures of them and prepare a visual display that shares what they have learned.

The first weavers used twigs, reeds, and grasses as fibers. **Fibers** are *any thin, thread-like materials*. Today fibers are spun from animal hairs, such as wool, plant materials, such as cotton, and manufactured materials.

Cloth weaving is done on a loom. A **loom** is *a frame or machine that holds a set of threads that run vertically*. These are called the warp threads. The weaver passes threads from a second set under and over the first set. These threads are called the weft. This creates a pattern and locks the threads together. Today some artists work on computerized looms. In factories computers are programmed to control the weaving machines (Figure 13-6).

▲ Figure 13-6   What are the advantages of using a loom as opposed to hand weaving?

Courtesy of American Weaving Association.

Glassmaking

The practice of melting sand to make glass is thousands of years old. So is the art of glassblowing. **Glassblowing** is *the craft of shaping melted glass by blowing air into it through a tube*. One of the most famous glassmakers of the recent past was Louis Comfort Tiffany. The son of a New York jeweler, Tiffany found a way of making unusually handsome glass patterns. Notice how the luminous color swirls seem to flow through the vase in Figure 13-7. Today glassblowers experiment with designs that, like much art of the day, are daring.

▲ Figure 13-7   Tiffany set up a glass factory in 1885. The goal of the company was to make stained glass windows. The company began making pieces like this one from leftover glass.

Louis Comfort Tiffany. *Vase*. c. 1900. Favrile glass. 52 x 13 cm (20½ x 4¾"). Museum of Modern Art, New York, New York. Gift of Joseph H. Heil.

Ceramics

Ceramics is another craft. Ceramic pieces are any objects made from clay and hardened by fire. Clay is a natural material found in the ground all over the world. **Pottery** is *the craft of making objects from clay*. You may think of pottery as bowls and dishes, but it can also be statues, masks, or anything else made out of clay.

The making of clay pots goes back to ancient times. Today craftspeople use many of the same techniques that were used many centuries ago.

Making pottery starts with preparing the clay. Water is added to the clay so that it is wet enough to be worked easily. Potters have special words for the different conditions of the clay:

- **Plastic clay** is clay that is wet enough to be worked but firm enough to hold its shape.
- **Leather hard clay** is clay that is still damp but is too dry to shape. It can be carved or joined together with slip.
- **Slip** is *clay that has so much added water that it is liquid and runny.* It is used as glue to join pieces of clay together. It is also used in decorating a finished work.

When working clay by hand, there are special methods that have been developed to shape the clay. Some of these are called pinching, coiling, and slab building. In the studio lessons that follow you will have a chance to try these techniques.

Clay can also be shaped by throwing it, which means turning it on a rapidly spinning wheel called a potter's wheel. This helps make a smooth, symmetrical piece. Some works combine both methods.

After the clay is shaped, it must be **fired**, or *hardened by heating in a kiln.* A **kiln** is *a special piece of equipment used to fire ceramics.* It can get as hot as 3000°F (1650°C). Before clay

▲ **Figure 13–9** How would the mood and feel of this work be different if it were not glazed? Why do you think the artist chose to glaze it?

Kimiko. *Vase.* 1990. Ceramic glazeware. 46 cm (18"). Private collection.

has been fired in a kiln, it is called greenware. After it has been fired, it is called bisqueware (**bisk**-ware).

Sometimes bisqueware is **glazed**, or *coated with a mixture of powdered chemicals that melt during firing into a hard, glasslike finish.* The glaze is spread on the pottery and the item is fired a second time.

Pottery does not always have to be glazed. Some of the best pottery, like terra cotta, is unglazed (Figure 13–8). However, if it is to hold food or liquid, it must be glazed with nontoxic glazes to keep the clay from absorbing the moisture. (See Figure 13–9.)

▲ **Figure 13–8** This piece is terra cotta. Do you think this piece would have been more effective in a different medium? Explain.

Bob Owens. *Alpha Wolf.* 1990. Terra cotta sculpture. 36 x 41 x 30 cm (14 x 16 x 12"). Home Federal Savings, Gainesville, Georgia.

CHECK YOUR UNDERSTANDING

1. What is a craftsperson? Define the term *craft.*
2. What is weaving? What is the name of the machine on which cloth is woven?
3. What is glass made of? What is glass-blowing?
4. How is slip used?
5. Describe the difference between plastic and leather hard clay.
6. What is the difference between greenware and bisqueware?

Answers to "Check Your Understanding"

1. A craftsperson is someone who has become an expert in one area of applied arts. A craft is one of the areas of applied art in which craftspeople work.
2. Weaving is a craft in which fiber strands are interlocked to make cloth or objects. The machine on which cloth is woven is a loom.
3. Glass is made from sand. Glassblowing is the craft of shaping melted glass by blowing air into it through a tube.
4. Slip is used to join pieces of clay together or to decorate a finished work.
5. Plastic clay is wet enough to be worked but firm enough to hold its shape. Leather hard clay is still damp but too dry to shape.
6. Before a shaped piece of clay has been fired, it is greenware. Once it has been fired, the piece of clay is bisqueware.

Following Up

Closure. Have each student write a short answer to these questions: What do you find most interesting about crafts? Why does that aspect of crafts interest you?

Evaluation. 1. Review students' written responses to the "Check Your Understanding" questions. 2. Read their statements about their own interests in crafts.

Reteaching. Many artists known for their fine art works have also created crafts. Examples include the Italian painter and architect Raphael, who designed tapestries, and the American painter Georgia O'Keeffe and the Spanish painter and sculptor Pablo Picasso, both of whom created pottery works. Work with small groups of students to explore the crafts interests of one of these well-known artists. Try to discover how the design of the craft related to the artist's other work.

Enrichment. Like painters and other artists, craftspeople have shows. Organizations such as the National Craft Museum display crafts and sponsor competitions and traveling exhibitions. The Museum of Contemporary Crafts in New York City features the work of modern craftspeople; other big cities also have permanent crafts museums. Local crafts shows often offer an opportunity to see—and even buy—the handmade work of skilled craftspeople. Have students explore these resources for seeing and learning more about crafts. Are there any crafts museums in the area? Are there—or will there be—any local crafts shows? Encourage students to visit any museums or shows they discover. If local museums or shows are not available, have students read more about the exhibits at crafts museums in major cities; this project may involve writing to several museums for information and catalogs.

LESSON PLAN
(pages 226–227)

Objectives
After completing this lesson, students will be able to:
• Use the pinch method to make a small container from clay.
• Describe, analyze, interpret, and judge their own clay containers.

Supplies
• Sheets of newspaper or cloth; clay and slip; containers of water; clay tools; clay scoring tools; plastic sheets or bags; found objects, such as buttons, weeds, pieces of broken toys (optional).
• Lengths of string, small sticks.
• Recordings of music in various rhythms.

> **TRB Resource**
> • 13-4 *Art Is Everywhere*, (appreciating cultural diversity)

TEACHING THE LESSON

Getting Started
Motivator. Begin by giving each student a lump of clay with which to work. Have students hold the clay in their hands and gently squeeze it. Ask: How does it feel? Then have them roll it into balls. Ask: How does this feel? What shapes does the clay suggest to you? What forms would you like to create with this clay? Encourage students to share their responses to this medium.

Vocabulary. Review with students some of the ceramics-related terms introduced in Lesson 1. Ask: What is pottery? What examples of pottery can you name? What is slip? How do potters use slip? What is a kiln? What happens to clay in a kiln? What is glazed pottery? What examples of glazed pottery can you point out? What examples of unglazed pottery can you point out?

Clay Bowl

Look at Figure 13–10. This is a piece of pottery that was handbuilt by Margaret Tafoya. Her work was done without the use of a potter's wheel. You also can make a container, such as a glass, mug, or bowl in the same way. Before you begin, concentrate on the form of the object. Identify the rim, body, and foot of the vase. Notice how the area lifts from the bottom to give shape and support to the container.

WHAT YOU WILL LEARN
You will make a small container by the pinch method. Make all the sides with even thickness and smooth the rim of the bowl and add a foot to the base. You may decorate it by pressing found objects into its surface. You may add pieces and coils of clay to create rhythmic, repeated patterns. (See Figure 13–11.)

WHAT YOU WILL NEED
• Sheets of newspaper or cloth
• Clay and slip
• Container of water
• Clay and clay scoring tools
• Plastic sheet or bag
• *Optional:* found objects, such as buttons, weeds, and pieces of broken toys

WHAT YOU WILL DO
1. Spread sheets of newspaper or cloth over your work area. Pinch off a small piece of clay. Dip one finger in the water and wet the piece. Set it aside for later. It may be used for decorating.
2. Form your clay into a ball by rolling it.
3. Hollow out the ball of clay by pressing your thumbs into the center while gently squeezing the clay between your thumbs on the inside and your fingers on the outside. Form it into the shape you want your container to have.
4. Gradually thin the sides and bottom of your pot with your thumbs and fingers. Make the walls and bottom smooth and even. Fix any small cracks in the clay by pressing and smoothing it out with your fingers and thumbs.

▲ **Figure 13–10** This piece is a reflection of a Native American style. How might this vase be different if the artist created it on a potter's wheel?

Margaret Tafoya. *Jar.* Santa Clara Pueblo, New Mexico. c. 1965. Blackware. 43 x 33 cm (17 x 13"). National Museum of Women in the Arts, Washington, D.C. Gift of Wallace & Wilhelmina Holladay.

Background Information
Pottery is an ancient craft practiced in every part of the world where clay deposits are found. Many tools and methods have been developed to make clay products, but the unique plastic quality of the moist material makes hand forming techniques the most satisfying.

Peter Voulkos (United States, born 1924) is one craftsperson who stopped using the wheel and began to shape pottery by hand. Voulkos is interested in the expressiveness of clay as handled by the artist. While the potter's wheel allows symmetry and formality, Voulkos believes the art of hand building allows the sculptural aspects of the craft to dominate. He often uses modern painting materials instead of the usual glazes on his works. As a sculptor, painter, and potter, Voulkos has crossed the lines separating various kinds of artists.

5. Wet your fingertips or use a damp sponge to smooth the top rim of your bowl.

6. Roll out a coil, or rope, of clay about 1/2 inch (13mm) thick. Turn your bowl upside down. Join your coil to the bottom to make a foot, or stand, for your work.

7. Decorate the surface of the bowl with a rhythmic pattern while the clay is still damp. Press your found objects into the surface of the bowl to create a pattern. Use your fingers to support the inside of the bowl while you make your impression. Add a second pattern by joining some small pieces of clay to your work. (See Technique Tip 17, *Handbook* page 275, for hints on joining clay pieces.)

8. Cover the piece loosely with a plastic sheet or bag. This will help it dry evenly and keep it from cracking. Remove the plastic when the clay is leather hard. When your work is completely dry, it is ready to fire.

9. *Optional*: Apply glaze and fire your work a second time. Do not apply glaze to the bottom of your piece. If you do, it will stick to the shelf in the kiln.

SAFETY TIP

Some older glazes are made with lead, which is poisonous. Be sure to use a nontoxic glaze on your work. If you're not sure whether or not a glaze is nontoxic, check with your teacher before using it.

OTHER STUDIO IDEAS

• Use the pinch method to make a clay bell. Poke a small hole in the top of the bell big enough to thread a string through. Form a small bead with a hole going through the center. Then make a thin clay clapper with a small hole at the top for the string. Dry and fire these clay pieces. See your teacher for assembling instructions.

EXAMINING YOUR WORK

• **Describe** Show that the sides of your container have an even thickness and that the rim is smooth. Point out the ring of clay you added to the bottom to create a foot. Point out the found objects and pieces of clay rope you added as a design.

• **Analyze** Describe the texture of your bowl's surface, and explain what you did to change the surface texture. Tell whether you used found objects and strips of clay to create a feeling of rhythmic repeated pattern.

• **Interpret** Tell whether your bowl is functional or a purely decorative item.

• **Judge** Tell whether your bowl succeeds as art. Explain your answer.

▲ Figure 13–11 What kind of balance is displayed by the design on this piece?

Dextra Q. Nampeyo. *Jar.* c. 1920. Hopi polychrome pottery. 22.2 x 35 cm (8¾ x 13¾"). The Thomas Gilcrease Institute of American History and Art, Tulsa, Oklahoma.

Lesson 2 *Clay Bowl* **227**

Developing Concepts

Using Art Criticism. Guide students in discussing Margaret Tafoya's work shown in Figure 13-10. Ask: What visual elements can you identify? How have the principles of balance and harmony been used to organize those elements? What other principles can you observe in the work? What is the purpose of the work? How well does it serve that purpose?

Developing Studio Skills. Have students make clay bells, as directed in "Other Studio Ideas." You may want to suggest that students can add small clay handles to the tops of their bells before firing; remind them to use the method they have learned to join clay pieces using slip. Then help them assemble their dried and fired clay pieces. Have each student tie a small stick to the center of a length of string. Then show students how to place the stick inside the bell and thread one end of the string through the top of the bell. Have them knot the small bead to the string outside the bell to keep the string from pulling through, and then untie the stick and remove it. Finally, have students tie the other end of the string to the clapper so that it hangs partly below the bell to catch the wind.

Following Up

Closure. Let students work in groups to discuss their clay bowls, following the directions in "Examining Your Work." Then have each student write a brief response to the "Judge" section of the activity.

Evaluation. Review students' clay bowls, and read their judgments of their own work.

Reteaching. Have students respond to music while manipulating lumps of plastic clay. Stamping and pinching the clay in time to musical rhythms can create interesting visual patterns.

Enrichment. Have students read about and, if possible, try techniques of working with clay on a potter's wheel.

Classroom Management Tip
Most commercial glazes sold for school use are lead-free, but you should still read labels and check specifications before using ceramic materials or ordering supplies.
Remind students to wash their hands thoroughly after handling clay and glazes.

Classroom Management Tip
You will need to plan on devoting several class sessions to this lesson; students need time to build, fire, and glaze their clay projects. Once their greenware is dry, demonstrate the use of the kiln. Show students how the heat is controlled and clearly identify the temperature at which the clay and glazes are fired. After their projects have been fired, students will need class time for glazing their bisqueware. At the end of each session, allow plenty of time for cleaning up.

Slab Container

LESSON PLAN
(pages 228–229)

Objectives

After completing this lesson, students will be able to:
- Use the slab method and proper joining techniques to make cylindrical containers.
- Describe, analyze, interpret, and judge their own clay containers.

Supplies

- Sheets of newspaper or cloth; guide sticks, each about 1/2 inch (13 mm) thick; clay and slip; rolling pins, pipes, or smooth jars; rulers; needle tools or open paper clips; containers of water; scoring tools or forks.
- Craft magazines that show various pieces of handcrafted pottery.
- Swedish cookie stamps, made either from clay or from wood, or pictures of the stamps (if available).

TEACHING THE LESSON

Getting Started

Motivator. Let students begin by working with the clay, noticing and discussing how it feels. Show them how to use a rolling pin (or similar equipment) to roll the clay out from the center. Explain that the roller should be kept dry to keep the clay from sticking to it. Also show them how to use a needle tool to puncture any bubbles that rise in the clay; after being punctured, bubbles can be smoothed with a damp finger. Let students experiment and enjoy these techniques; encourage them to discuss their responses to the medium and the techniques.

Vocabulary. As students participate in the "Motivator" activity, point out several of their rolled sheets of clay and identify them as slabs. Then ask students to develop their own definition (based on these examples) of the term *slab*.

An easy way to make ceramic objects is by using clay slabs. A **slab** is *a slice or sheet of clay*. The slab method works especially well when you are building an object with straight sides. Figure 13–12 shows a work made from slabs.

Slabs can be cut into any shape. The slab method can also be used to make cylinders. In this case, the slab must be curved while the clay is still flexible to avoid cracking. If you want to build a straight-wall rectangular box, the slabs must be dry, but not quite leather hard.

WHAT YOU WILL LEARN

You will use the slab method and proper joining techniques to make a container shaped like a cylinder. This can be used as a vase, pencil holder, or jar. You will decorate the surface of the container with designs cut from another slab. The designs may be flowers, animals, letters, or other objects made with geometric forms and shapes. (See Figure 13–13.) Be sure that the decorative designs are in proportion to the size of the container. Your container will be glazed inside and out.

WHAT YOU WILL NEED

- Sheets of newspaper or cloth
- Two guide sticks, each about 1/2 inch (13 mm) thick
- Clay and slip
- Rolling pin, pipe, or smooth jar
- Ruler
- Needle tool or open paper clip
- Container of water
- Scoring tools or fork

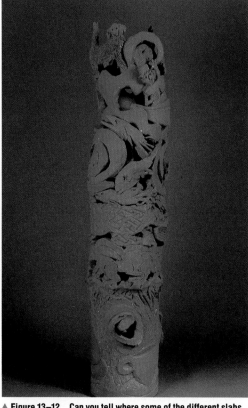

▲ **Figure 13–12   Can you tell where some of the different slabs come together?**

Jane Pleak. *Summertime Totem.* 1987. 129.5 x 35.6 x 35.6 cm (51 x 14 x 14"). Ceramic redware. Private collection.

WHAT YOU WILL DO

1. Spread sheets of newspaper or cloth over your work area.
2. Place the guide sticks on the cloth 6 inches (15 cm) apart. Place the clay between the guide sticks. Flatten it with the heel of your hand. Resting the rolling pin, pipe, or jar on the guide sticks, roll out the clay. This will help keep the thickness of the slab even.

Background Information
Slab building is used in sculpture as well as in pottery. The qualities of clay and the kind of firing sculptors do require that forms be hollow rather than solid. Thus one of the best techniques for this type of sculpture is slab building. The sculptor begins by preparing slabs of the appropriate thickness and then assembles the slabs in a chosen shape. For some sculptures the artist may incorporate the processes of molding, coiling, and throwing in addition to the process of slab building.

Note
The best way to fire student work is to "soak" it in heat before raising the temperature. Set the temperature on low and leave the lid cracked open for 6 to 12 hours. This allows moisture to evaporate from the clay. Then close the lid and continue firing according to the directions of the kiln.

3. Using the ruler and needle tool, measure and lightly mark two rectangles on the slab. One should be 6 x 10 inches (15 x 25 cm), the other, 5 inches (13 cm) square. Any mistakes can be wiped away with your fingers. Cut out the rectangles using the needle tool. Save the scraps. Keep them damp.

4. Bend the longer slab into a cylinder. Join the edges by scoring and using slip. (See Technique Tip **17**, *Handbook* page **275**.) Wet your fingers and wipe away any cracks in the surface of the cylinder.

5. Using the needle tool, trim one end of the cylinder so it will stand straight. Stand the cylinder, trimmed end down, on the 5-inch (13 cm) square slab. With the needle tool, lightly and carefully trace around the base of the cylinder. Remove the cylinder, and cut out the circle you have drawn. Join the cylinder and circle to form your container.

6. Cut design shapes of your choice from the leftover clay slab. Using the joining techniques you used to form the cylinder, apply the slab designs to the surface of the container. Allow the container to dry slowly. When it is at the greenware stage, fire it.

7. Apply glaze to every surface but the bottom, and fire the container a second time. If you want the container to hold water, pour a small amount of glaze in the container. Swirl it around the bottom and sides. Keep turning the container as you pour the excess glaze out so that it will cover the inside completely.

EXAMINING YOUR WORK

- **Describe**   Show that the surface of your container is smooth and free of cracks. Tell whether your container is glazed inside and out. Describe the designs you added.
- **Analyze**   Point out the shapes you used to decorate your container. Tell whether your decorations are in proportion to the size of your container.
- **Interpret**   Tell how you would use the container.
- **Judge**   Tell whether your work succeeds as applied art. Explain your answer.

▲ Figure 13–13   Student work in progress. A slab container.

OTHER STUDIO IDEAS

- Use the slab method to make a container shaped like a rectangle. You will need four slabs, two measuring 10 x 3 inches (25 x 8 cm), and two measuring 10 x 2 inches (25 x 5 cm).

Lesson 3   *Slab Container*   **229**

Developing Concepts

Exploring Aesthetics. Ask students to look through crafts magazines and select pieces of hand-crafted pottery they would like to own. Then have them work in groups to share and discuss their choices: Why did you choose this piece? How is it similar to the pieces chosen by other students? How is it different? Which particular visual elements and art principles evident in this work make it especially attractive?

Appreciating Cultural Diversity. If possible, display Swedish cookie stamps or pictures of the stamps. Explain that these stamps were probably first made and used early in the sixteenth century and that they are familiar in other European countries as well. Traditionally, each Swedish family had a set of carved clay or wooden stamps to use for special occasions. The designs were round or diamond- or square-shaped with animal figures, hearts, or geometric patterns carved into them. Let students cut their own stamps from clay slabs and join a clay handle to one side. After the clay has dried to the leather hard stage, have students cut designs into the bottom. Remind them that their stamps will create mirror-image designs. Let the stamps dry, and then fire them in a kiln.

Following Up

Closure. Let each student show and describe his or her clay container to the rest of the class. What do they like best about their own work?

Evaluation. Review students' clay containers, and listen to their descriptions.

Reteaching. Help groups of students discuss the slab containers shown in Figures 13-12 and 13-13. How were they made? What is the purpose of each? How well does each serve its purpose?

Enrichment. Have students research the uses of clay slabs in pictographic and cuneiform writing. Ask: When, where, and how were clay slabs used for writing?

Classroom Management Tip
Fabric-backed wall vinyl works well as a base on which to work clay and roll slabs. Thick dowel rods can be used as rolling pins. If clay tools are not available, many household items can be useful—silverware and other kitchen utensils, paper clips, wire, nails, old paintbrush handles, damaged pen points, and so on.

Classroom Management Tip
To make guide sticks, tape two rulers together. This will result in an even thickness.

Making a Weaving

LESSON PLAN
(pages 230–231)

Objectives

After completing this lesson, students will be able to:
• Make fabric wall hangings, using cardboard looms and yarns, strings, and found fibers.
• Describe, analyze, interpret, and judge their own weavings.

Supplies

• Small scraps of woven fabric, in various textures; if possible, include pieces of burlap, straw hats, and so on.
• Small loom already warped (or use a cardboard loom like those students will make).
• Rulers; pencils; scissors; transparent tape; sheets of heavy cardboard, 12 x 18 inches (30 x 46 cm); spools of strong, thin thread; different colored yarns and strings; found materials that can be used as fibers, such as grass, strips of paper, and used film; tapestry needles; combs; wooden dowels.
• One or more examples of handwoven fabric and manufactured fabric.

TRB Resources

• 13-5 *The Art of Quilting*, (cooperative learning)
• 13-6 *Tommye Scanlin*, (artist profile)

TEACHING THE LESSON

Getting Started

Motivator. Distribute several different scraps of fabric to each pair or small group of students (see "Supplies"). Have students examine and compare the fabrics: How do they look? How do they feel? Let them try to determine how the fabrics were made. Then have them unravel edges of the scraps to discover how they were constructed, and ask them to count the threads in each direction.

230

Look at the tapestry weaving in Figure 13–14. It was woven on a floor loom. The craftsperson dyed the threads before weaving. She wanted to control the color scheme, as well as the shape and texture.

Like all work done on a loom, this one is made by interlocking fibers. *The threads attached to the loom* are known as **warp** threads. *The threads pulled across the warp* are the **weft** threads. The weft threads are passed over and under the warp threads to lock the two sets of fibers together.

WHAT YOU WILL LEARN

You will make a fabric wall hanging using a cardboard loom and yarns, strings, and found fibers. You will use a variety of textures and limit the colors to a monochromatic or analogous color scheme.

WHAT YOU WILL NEED

• Ruler, pencil, scissors, and transparent tape
• Sheet of heavy cardboard, 12 x 18 inch (30 x 46 cm)
• Spool of strong, thin thread
• Different colored yarns and strings
• Found materials that can be used as fibers, such as grass, strips of paper, and used film
• Tapestry needle
• Comb
• Wooden dowel

WHAT YOU WILL DO

1. To make your loom, hold the ruler along the top edge of your cardboard. With the pencil, mark off every 1/4 inch (6 mm).

▲ **Figure 13–14** Describe some of the elements and principles of art the artist incorporated into her weaving.

Tommye M. Scanlin. *Cat Dreams.* 1988. Hand dyed wool tapestry. 55.9 x 86.4 cm (22 x 34"). Private collection.

Using the scissors, make a cut about 1/2 inch (13 mm) deep at each mark. Do the same thing along the bottom of the cardboard.

2. Tape the end of your thread to the back of the cardboard. Bring the spool to the front, passing the thread through the top left notch. Pull the spool down to the bottom of the loom. Pass the thread through the bottom left notch and around to the back. Move one notch to the right. Pull the thread through and up the front

---

Background Information

The nomadic Bedouin of the Middle East travel with tents, which are traditionally handwoven. They use a very simple ground loom to weave the cloth for their tents. Pegs driven into the ground hold two posts, which hold the warp taut. The heddle bar, used to lift alternate threads so that the weft can pass through, is supported on each side by whatever happens to be handy. A metal hook or animal horn is used to help put the weft in position. With this simple equipment, the Bedouin produce incredibly complex designs. The simplicity of the loom allows the Bedouin to roll up unfinished weavings, strike camp, and continue the work later at another camp.

The Bedouin use such fibers as goat hair, camel hair, and sheep wool. The hair and wool are gathered from the ground or brushed from the animals. Then the yarns used for weaving are spun on a traditional spindle, which, like the loom, is easily carried from camp to camp.

of the loom. Keep working until you reach the last notch. (See Figure 13–15.) Bring the spool to the back. Cut the thread, and tape the end.

3. Decide which color scheme you will use. Select fibers you will use for your weft. Choose textures to add interest to your wall hanging.

4. Thread one of your thinner yarns through the eye of the tapestry needle. Start to weave at the bottom of your loom. Move the yarn across the warp, passing over one thread and under the next. (Figure 13–16.) Keep working in this over-and-under manner. When you reach the end of the warp, reverse directions. If you wove over the last thread, you must weave under when you start the next line of the weft. Do not pull the weft too tight. Curve it slightly as you pull it through the warp. This is called ballooning.

5. After weaving a few rows, pack the weft threads tightly with the comb. The tighter the weave, the stronger the fabric will be. Experiment with different weft fibers.

EXAMINING YOUR WORK

- **Describe**   Describe how you made the loom. Explain how you attached the warp threads to your loom. Explain ballooning. Why did you use it? List the weaving techniques you used.
- **Analyze**   What color scheme did you choose? Explain how you added a variety of textures to your weaving.
- **Interpret**   In what setting might you hang this weaving?
- **Judge**   Tell whether you feel your work succeeds. Explain your answer.

6. Be sure to end with another inch (2.5 cm) of thin, tightly-packed fiber. Break the tabs of your loom to slip the weaving off the cardboard. Fold the weaving over the dowel and stitch your weaving together, using a long piece of yarn and a tapestry needle.

7. Make a hanging loop by tying the ends of a piece of string to each end of the dowel.

▲ Figure 13–15   Notice the series of vertical lines. These are the warp threads.

▲ Figure 13–16   These are the threads that will display your image. What are these threads called?

OTHER STUDIO IDEAS

- Make a table placemat for a favorite holiday. Choose the colors that best symbolize that holiday.

●● Experiment with weft and warp materials of differing textures and weights, incorporating found objects as you go to create a wall hanging.

Lesson 4   *Making a Weaving*   **231**

Vocabulary. Introduce the terms *warp* and *weft*, and use the warped loom to demonstrate the difference. In addition, you may want to help students review terms related to color: What is a monochromatic color scheme? What is an analogous color scheme? (Refer students to Chapter 4, page **59,** if necessary.)

Developing Concepts

Exploring Aesthetics. Help students examine examples of handwoven fabric, and guide them in discussing the visual elements, especially texture, color, and line. Then ask them to compare the handwoven fabrics with manufactured fabrics: How are they similar? What are the most important differences? Which can be considered an art work? Why?

Appreciating Cultural Diversity. Explain to students that the Inca of Peru have a weaving tradition that extends as far back as 1500 B.C. The yarn for weaving was hand-spun from cotton or from the wool of alpacas, llamas, or vicunas; the subjects usually included mythological creatures, animals, and humans. Ask one group of volunteers to find and share photographs of these Inca weavings; ask another group to read and report on their history.

Following Up

Closure. Let students work in groups to display and discuss their weavings, using "Examining Your Work" as a guide. Then have students answer this question about each group member's weaving: Which visual element is used most successfully in this weaving?

Evaluation. Review students' weavings, and listen to their group discussions of their work.

Reteaching. Help groups of students examine and discuss Tommye M. Scanlin's weaving shown in Figure 13-14: Can you identify the warp threads and the weft threads? What can you learn from this work that will help you plan and create your own weavings?

Enrichment. The basic techniques of weaving were probably first used in basketry, one of the oldest and most widespread crafts. Ask volunteers to read about and report on basket weaving among ancient peoples.

Classroom Management Tip
It will be difficult for a large class to see a weaving demonstration that involves small detail. To provide a clearer demonstration, fasten wide paper strips (representing warp threads) to a large piece of cardboard. Prop the board in front of you and demonstrate the weaving of the weft threads by using wide paper strips of a contrasting color.

Note
The difference between fiber and fabric artists is clearly defined. Fiber artists construct fabrics, rugs, baskets, and other goods by weaving fibers together. Fabric artists work with the finished fabric by dying it as with batik, or cutting and sewing, as with quilting.

Jewelry

Objectives

After completing this lesson, students will be able to:
- Make pieces of paper jewelry with particular wearers in mind.
- Describe, analyze, interpret, and judge their own jewelry.

Supplies

- Books and magazines with photographs showing real people from around the world.
- Pencils; sheets of sketch paper; sheets of heavy watercolor paper, 9 x 12 inches (23 x 30 cm); sheets of scrap paper; scissors; watercolor paints and brushes; white glue; pin or earring backs; straight pins; polyurethane spray.

> **TRB Resource**
> - 13-7 *Wearable Art*, (studio)

TEACHING THE LESSON

Getting Started

Motivator. Provide groups of students with books or magazines that show real people in real-life situations around the world. (*National Geographic* is a good source.) Ask students in each group to find as many pictures as possible showing ways in which people adorn themselves. Then ask: Which forms of adornment do you consider jewelry? Which do you consider works of art? Why? Encourage students to present and support various points of view.

Vocabulary. Have students use a dictionary to distinguish the meanings of *jewel* and *jewelry*. Ask: Do you need jewels to make successful jewelry?

Developing Concepts

Using Art Criticism. Help students examine and discuss the three pieces of jewelry shown in Figures 13-17, 13-18, and 13-19. Let volunteers pose questions that will help the class describe, analyze, interpret, and judge each work.

Jewelry

Some art is made to be worn. An example of this kind of art appears in Figure 13–17. We call this art, and the craft of making it, jewelry.

Cave dwellers wore jewelry made of colorful shells and feathers. Today people wear jewelry made of precious stones and metals. Look once more at the necklace in Figure 13–17. From what stones and metals is this item made?

WHAT YOU WILL LEARN

You will make a piece of paper jewelry with a particular wearer in mind. You will paint your jewelry with watercolors. You will choose either geometric or free-form shapes for your design. You will make a pendant, a pin, or a pair of earrings (Figures 13–18 and 13–19). The item must harmonize with the size and clothing style of the person for whom it is intended.

WHAT YOU WILL NEED

- Pencil and sheets of sketch paper
- Sheet of heavy watercolor paper, 9 x 12 inch (23 x 30 cm)
- Sheets of scrap paper
- Scissors
- Watercolor paints and brushes
- White glue
- Pin or earring backs
- Straight pin
- Polyurethane spray

WHAT YOU WILL DO

1. Identify the person for whom the piece is intended. Decide whether you will make a pin, a pendant, or a pair of earrings. Make pencil sketches experimenting with different shapes for your jewelry.

▲ **Figure 13–17   What kind of balance is displayed in this work? Why does this kind of balance work for creating a necklace?**

L. L. Lee. *Native American Necklace*. 1990. Turquoise and silver. From the collection of John and Sue MacLaurin.

You may use either geometric or free-form shapes. Transfer your best sketches to the sheet of heavy watercolor paper. Set the paper aside.

2. On scrap paper, experiment with different colors and techniques for applying watercolor paints. (To review the different techniques, see Technique Tip **14**, *Handbook* page **275**.) If you are making the jewelry for yourself, think of your favorite colors. If the jewelry is to be a gift, think about the tastes of the person you have in mind.

3. Tear or cut out the paper shapes.

4. Paint your finished shapes. Make sure the colors you choose work together to create a feeling of harmony.

Background Information

Between the fourteenth and eighteenth centuries in Europe the art of the jeweler achieved great importance. Skills in cutting, polishing, and setting gems were highly prized. The uses of cloisonné and other methods of embellishment were developed during this period.

Both the men and the women of the European aristocracy decorated themselves with as much jewelry as they could afford and wear. In addition to wearing chains, bracelets, and rings, wealthy people had jewelry sewn into their clothing. Thus the jewelers of the time competed to produce more and more impressive works.

Some of the jewelry created in Europe during this period shows the influence of West African artists, whose jewelry usually came into the rest of Europe through Spain and Portugal. The West Africans produced sophisticated, finely detailed jewelry with imaginatively embellished forms.

5. When the paint is dry, attach the pieces to a pin or earring backs with glue. If you are making a pendant, poke a hole near the top with the straight pin.

6. If you want to waterproof the jewelry, use polyurethane (pahl-ee-**your**-uh-thane) spray. *Make sure your teacher is present during this step*.

7. Display your finished jewelry. Note ways in which it is like and different from jewelry made by your classmates.

EXAMINING YOUR WORK

- **Describe** Tell what type of jewelry (pin, pendant, earrings) you have made. Identify the materials you used to create the jewelry. Tell what colors you have chosen.
- **Analyze** Tell whether you have chosen geometric or free-form shapes. Explain whether the colors and shapes you chose will harmonize with the size and clothing style of the wearer.
- **Interpret** Tell whether the jewelry will appeal to the individual for whom it was made. Explain why.
- **Judge** Explain whether you feel your work succeeds as applied art. Explain your answer.

▲ Figure 13–19   Student work. Three sets of paper earrings.

▲ Figure 13–18   What shape and kind of balance is shown in this piece?

Ann Renee Weaver. *Paper Jewelery Pin*. 1989. Paper towels, white glue, opalescent acrylic, and textile paint. 7.6 cm (3") diameter. Private collection.

OTHER STUDIO IDEAS

- Add other materials to your paper jewelry. Try fabric, buttons, string, or feathers, for example.

 Make a pin out of clay using the clay working techniques in Lesson 3.

Lesson 5   *Jewelry*   🎨   **233**

Understanding Art History. Explain that people have been making and wearing jewelry since prehistoric times. Though jewelry may always have been an adornment, at first its primary purpose was probably as a charm or amulet, to protect the wearer against the forces of evil. Later the primary purpose of jewelry became to distinguish rank; in some societies laws defined who could wear certain kinds or forms of jewelry. Ask: What is the most important purpose of jewelry in modern times? Do people sometimes still wear jewelry as an amulet or as a sign of rank? What specific examples can you cite?

Appreciating Cultural Diversity. Help students brainstorm a list of cultural groups, including as many as possible. Then have students work in groups to find photographs and information about traditional jewelry from each cultural group.

Following Up

Closure. Display all the finished jewelry. Have students choose works they consider different from their own and write descriptive paragraphs about those pieces of jewelry.

Evaluation. Review students' paper jewelry, and read their descriptions of other students' work.

Reteaching. Help groups of students discuss the jewelry that they and their contemporaries wear: Which media are used? Which visual elements are emphasized? Which art principles are used to organize the elements? What are the purposes of the jewelry? Then ask students to sketch new pieces that would serve those purposes.

Enrichment. Help students discuss ways they might combine this form of jewelry making with one or more techniques used in other lessons of this chapter. For example, students might try weaving parts of their jewelry. What other ideas do they have? What other new techniques for making paper jewelry can they suggest? Encourage students to experiment and then display and discuss the results of their work.

Cooperative Learning
Let students work in groups to experiment with other methods of coloring or decorating paper jewelry. Students in each group might work together to explore one of these techniques: dipping paper shapes into water stained with watercolors; dripping paints onto paper shapes; splattering paints onto paper shapes; pressing damp paper shapes against textured surfaces. Then have each group explain the technique and demonstrate their results to the rest of the class.

BUILDING VOCABULARY

Number a sheet of paper from 1 to 14. After each number, write the term from the box that best matches each description below.

crafts	loom
craftsperson	pottery
fibers	slab
fired	slip
glassblowing	warp
glazed	weaving
kiln	weft

1. Someone who has become an expert in an area of applied art.
2. The areas of applied art in which craftspeople work.
3. A craft in which strands of fiber are interlocked to make cloth or objects.
4. A frame used for weaving threads.
5. The craft of shaping melted glass by blowing air into it through a tube.
6. The craft of making objects from clay.
7. Hardened by heating in a kiln.
8. Any thin, threadlike materials.
9. Clay that has so much added water that it is liquid and runny.
10. A slice or sheet of clay.
11. Coated with a mixture of powdered chemicals that melt during firing into a hard, glasslike finish.
12. A special oven used to fire ceramics.
13. Threads attached to a loom.
14. Threads pulled across those already on the loom.

REVIEWING ART FACTS

Number a sheet of paper from 15 to 21. Answer each question in a complete sentence.

15. What kinds of things did the first weavers use as fibers?
16. What is glass made of?
17. Who is Louis Comfort Tiffany? For what is he famous?
18. What are ceramics?
19. What are the different conditions of clay called?
20. Describe how clay pieces are joined in making pottery.
21. What method of claymaking is best for designing objects with straight sides?

THINKING ABOUT ART

On a sheet of paper, answer each question in a sentence or two.

1. **Interpret.** What information would you need to have before accepting a drink out of a homemade ceramic cup?
2. **Extend.** Name two ceramic objects that would be best made using the slab method. Name two that would be best made using the pinching method. Give reasons for your choices.

MAKING ART CONNECTIONS

1. **Science.** Clay is the result of a certain type of rock decomposition. Research where clay is found and find out what is added to make it easier for artists to use. Report your results to the class.
2. **Industrial Arts.** Choose one of the products discussed in this chapter and find out how a similar product might be produced in industry. Explain how the industrial methods differ from those of an individual craftsperson.

LOOKING AT THE DETAILS

The detail shown below is from a Chilkat Blanket woven by a member of the Tlingit, a tribe of Native Americans who live in British Columbia. Study the detail and answer the following questions.

1. Notice the precision of line and well-displayed harmony in this detail. Knowing that it was woven entirely by hand, what does this tell you about the craftsperson who created it? Would you consider this person an artist? Why or why not?
2. We discussed visual movement in painting. In sculpture and in crafts, physical movement is also a possibility. Where did this artist create the feeling of movement?
3. Consider the historical information of this work found in the credit line. What do you think might be some reasons for the artists' choice of these colors? How might a particular craft determine some of your creative choices?
4. Do you think this blanket was successful as applied art? Explain.

Unknown. Chilkat Blanket. c. 1900. Woven cedar bark, mountain goat wool, fur. (Detail.) American Museum of Natural History, New York, New York. Courtesy of Department of Library Services.

---

1. Responses will vary. Students might note that the person was precise and took much time to create this work and that the person was a skilled weaver. Yes, this person would be considered an artist because the design displays an organized use of the principles and elements of art.
2. The artist created movement in the fringe.
3. Responses will vary. Students might note that the environment, the subject, and the materials used could all be considerations in the choice of colors.

   The applied use of the craft and its materials would limit some of the choices to suit the craft's purpose and make it successful in its applied use. For example, if a pitcher is to serve its purpose of holding liquid, it can't be full of holes or made out of materials such as porous cloth.
4. Yes, it is successful as applied art. Its intent was to wrap around the shoulders of a person and keep the wearer warm; its shape and the materials, which are good insulators, are conducive to that purpose. Responses will vary as to the work's success as art. Students might note that it is successful as art because it displays the principles and elements of art in an aesthetically pleasing way and communicates a message to the tribe it is intended for.

Chapter Evaluation

The goal of this chapter is to develop students' understanding and appreciation of different types of crafts and to create works of art using the crafts of weaving, pottery, and jewelry making. Some possible evaluation techniques include:

1. On the chalkboard list the following pottery terms: plastic clay, leather hard clay, slip, kiln, fired, and so forth. Have students write definitions for each term.
2. Have students write a paragraph explaining how crafts can be classified as applied arts and fine arts.
3. Have students complete Chapter 13 Test (TRB, Resource 13-8).

CHAPTER 14

Architecture

Chapter Scan

Lesson 1 The Art of Architecture
Lesson 2 Building a Clay Model
Lesson 3 Drawing Floor Plans
Lesson 4 Clay Entrance Relief

TRB Resources

• 14-8 Chapter Test
• Color Transparency 27
• Color Transparency 28

TEACHING THE CHAPTER

Introducing the Art Work

Direct students' attention to the photograph of the Temple of Athena Nike. Inform students that the Greeks constructed this temple between 427 and 424 B.C. Its architect was Callicrates, who carefully supervised the temple's construction.

Tell students that this temple is one of seven buildings known as the Acropolis, which is built on a rocky hilltop overlooking the city of Athens, 500 feet below. At that time Athens was the most powerful of the city-states of Greece, and the Acropolis was meant to show the world that the Athenians considered their city to be the strongest and most beautiful on earth.

Examining the Art Work

Tell students that *Athena Nike* means "Athena Victorious." The Temple of Athena Nike was built to honor Athena, the goddess of wisdom, art, and the intellectual aspects of warfare.

Explain to students that the Greeks, and especially the Athenians, thought that logic and reason were the most important of human qualities, and they wanted their art to reflect this belief. Therefore their buildings were always clearly balanced in both the parts of the building and the building as a whole.

▲ This shrine has long been admired for its beauty. If you were asked to design a shrine how might it be different from this one?

Temple of Athena Nike. 427–424 B.C. Acropolis, Athens, Greece.

Architecture

Note for students the proportions of the temple and how the slim columns, the walls, and the borders are gracefully proportioned, exhibiting symmetrical balance. Point out how the detail in the building is more like a sculpture than just a building. Explain how the top border of the temple, detailing the figures in action, is done in relief sculpture form. Note also that the columns are precisely carved stone.

Discussing the Art Work

Ask students to think about why the Greeks included the detailed border with the figures. Explain how they were exhibiting their devotion to Athena by displaying the things she stood for on the temple designed for her worship. The figures are shown as carefully preparing and strategically planning for battle in which they will be victorious. This displays Athena's wisdom and her intellectual outlook on warfare. The art is displayed by the sculpture itself as well as by the entire construction of the building. The building was constructed without mortar or cement; thus the architect relied on the precision of order, reason, and logic for its construction. Ask students to point out some of the elements of art as portrayed in the temple. Suggest that the elements of line, shape, and form are dominant in the temple's construction. Point out the precisely cut stones, the straight lines on the columns. Point out the texture in the relief border and the carved columns as well as the smooth texture of the stone walls.

Tell students that in this chapter they will learn about how architects work and the main uses of architecture. They will also design a clay model of a house, a relief of a mall entrance, and a floor plan for a shopping mall.

When you look around any city, you notice many kinds of buildings. Houses, schools, churches, and office buildings are just a few of the different types of buildings. Each of them serves a different purpose.

What do you think the building on the left was used for? Who do you think used it? It was built in the fifth century B.C. in Athens, Greece. In this chapter you will explore the different purposes of buildings. You will also discover that buildings of the past still influence structural designs of today.

OBJECTIVES

After completing this chapter, you will be able to:

- Define architecture and explain what architects do.
- Describe three main uses of architecture.
- Explain how architects use floor plans and elevation drawings.
- Design a clay model of a house, a floor plan for a shopping mall, and a clay relief of a mall entrance.

WORDS YOU WILL LEARN

amphitheaters	elevation
architect	facade
architecture	floor plan
basilicas	post and lintel

ARTISTS YOU WILL MEET

Louis Sullivan
Frank Lloyd Wright

237

Building Self-Esteem

In Chapter 14, students are asked to plan and create a clay model for a vacation home. Tell them they will now be doing a floor plan of their "Dream House." This should be a house in which each room is designed for one of the student's special interests. Each room might also show a different quality of their personalities. Tell students to let the size of each room show how important that activity or personal quality is to them. For instance, if listening to music and dancing are most important, then the house can have a room planned just for that purpose, and it will be the biggest room in the house. Other floor plans might include libraries, gymnasiums, or maybe even a secret room for the quiet side of their personalities. Draw the layout of the house first. Then label each room. After students have completed their plans, let them share and discuss their favorite rooms. Do others have some of the same favorite rooms? After viewing other dream house plans, were ideas for new rooms stimulated?

The Art of Architecture

LESSON PLAN
(pages 238–241)

Objectives
After completing this lesson, students will be able to:
- Define *architecture* and explain what architects do.
- Describe three main uses of architecture.
- Draw a building in an ideal setting.

Supplies
- Sketch pads; pencils; sheets of drawing paper, 12 x 18 inches (30 x 46 cm); colored pencils or markers.
- Drawing paper; pencils; various small objects, such as boxes of several sizes, balls, jars, pencils, tacks, cups, and the like.

TRB Resources
- 14-1 *Architectural Features,* (reproducible master)
- 14-2 *The Shape of Your Environment,* (aesthetics/art criticism)
- 14-3 *Back to the Future,* (art history)
- 14-4 *Louis Henri Sullivan,* (artist profile)

TEACHING THE LESSON

Getting Started
Motivator. Introduce the lesson with a class discussion about the classroom: How else could our classroom be used? Could a family live here? Would it be a practical living space? Why, or why not? Could it be used as a meeting hall, a place of business, an artist's studio, or a storage location? Encourage students to consider the space arrangements and facilities that would make the room practical—or impractical—for other uses. Then let students suggest what they might include in designs for an ideal classroom.

238

LESSON 1

The Art of Architecture

Have you ever made a house out of playing cards or designed a sand castle? Maybe you have built a fortress from craft sticks. All these activities borrow ideas from the field of art called architecture. **Architecture** is *the planning and creating of buildings*. An **architect** is *an artist who works in the field of architecture*.

Architecture is considered to be both a fine art and an applied art. Like painters and sculptors, architects use color, line, shape, form, space, and texture. Like craftspeople, architects make works that are functional.

In this lesson you will look at the many uses of architecture. In later lessons you will try out some of the methods architects use in their work.

THE BEGINNINGS OF ARCHITECTURE

The first architects were cave dwellers who left their caves to build shelters from tree branches. Sun-dried mud and clay were some other materials used by early architects.

None of these materials, of course, could stand up long to wind or rain. In time, the buildings crumbled. Architects were faced with the task of finding or making stronger building materials. The early Egyptians found the solution by using stone. The most famous of their buildings are the pyramids. These amazing structures were built as tombs for the most important person in

▲ Figure 14–1   This wonder of the world had only two rooms. What do you suppose those rooms might have been filled with? Explain your answer.

Parthenon. Acropolis, Athens, Greece. Begun 447 B.C.

Background Information
"Form follows function" was the creed of Louis Sullivan (United States, 1856–1924), who is often considered the first modern architect. Sullivan skillfully combined the functional and decorative elements of his work, creating buildings that please the eye and serve their function admirably and efficiently.

Sullivan studied briefly at the Massachusetts Institute of Technology and trained both in the United States and in Paris before setting up an independent practice in Chicago. There he was one of the founders of the Chicago School of Architecture, a style of commercial architecture centered in, but not limited to, Chicago. The Chicago Fire of 1871 had created a need for many new buildings, and the price of land made the need for taller buildings acute. At the same time, steel frames and electric elevators became practical—and the skyscraper became a reality. Sullivan's work in designing functional yet aesthetic skyscrapers impressed his contemporaries and has influenced the work of modern architects.

Egyptian society, the Pharaoh. The Pharaoh was not only a king but also, in the eyes of his subjects, a god.

USES OF ARCHITECTURE

Because people need shelter to protect them from the weather and to provide privacy, creating dwellings has been a main purpose of architecture since earliest times. Other purposes were to create structures for prayer, business, and recreation. These remain key concerns of architects today.

Structures for Prayer

Because religion was central in their culture, the single most important building made by early Greek architects was the tem-

▲ Figure 14–2   Does this building appear delicate and charming to you? Does it appear strong and solid? Explain.

Cathedral of Leon-Outside. 13th-14th centuries. Leon, Spain.

ple. The building on page 236 is an example of a Greek temple.

The Greeks did not gather inside their temples to worship. The temples were built as houses for their gods. Only priests and a few helpers were allowed inside. Everyone else prayed in front of the temple. For this reason Greek temples did not have to be large, nor provide areas for seats. Instead, Greek architects concentrated on making the temples perfectly proportioned. Their success is evident in the most famous Greek temple, the Parthenon (Figure 14–1).

In Europe in the 1200s and 1300s larger churches were built. Architects also began exploring new ways of using line and balance. Figures 14–2 and 14–3 show two views of the same church. Notice how the architect created a feeling of lightness and openness whether one is viewing the church from the inside or the outside. Colored light pouring into the interiors through the stained glass windows added to the drama of this church.

Think of the churches you've seen in your neighborhood. Can you tell by their architectural style when they were built? In what ways are they different from churches of old? How are they similar?

▲ Figure 14–3   Stained glass windows in churches like these were used to color the light inside. Does looking at the church from the inside communicate the same feelings as those in Figure 14–2? Why or why not?

Cathedral of Leon-Inside. 13th-14th centuries. Leon, Spain.

Vocabulary. Have students use dictionaries to find the meanings and derivations of these words: *architect, architecture, basilica, amphitheater.* Ask: From what two Greek words does the work *architect* come? How are the two words *architect* and *architecture* related? What is the meaning of the ancient Greek word from which *basilica* comes? From what two Greek words does our word *amphitheater* come?

Developing Concepts

Exploring Aesthetics. Guide students in discussing their personal responses to the buildings shown in this lesson. Help the class discuss Figures 14-1, 14-2 and 14-3, 14-4, 14-5, and 14-6 in turn. Ask: What message or feeling does this work communicate to you? What aspects of the building help communicate that message or feeling? Then go on to help student discuss the central question of aesthetics: Is this building a work of art? In what ways do you think it is a work of fine art? In what ways do you think it is a work of applied art? Encourage students to express and support various points of view.

Using Art Criticism. Remind students that the first task of an art critic is to describe the art work. Have students recall the art elements they have studied—color, line, shape, form, space, and texture—and list them on the board. Then help them examine Louis Sullivan's skyscraper shown in Figure 14-5. Ask: What colors can you identify in this work? How would you describe the lines here? Are they vertical, horizontal, diagonal? Can you identify any repeated shapes? Are the shapes geometric or organic? Do you see open areas or recesses allowing for the feeling of deep space, or does the space appear more shallow? How would you describe the texture on the surface of the building? After a class discussion, have each student write a short description of the work.

Classroom Management Tip
To help students appreciate the various styles of architecture used around the world, make available magazines and books that feature photographs of dwellings and other structures. Ask students to browse through these resources, and have each student select one photograph to share with the rest of the class. Then guide students in discussing these structures: How are they alike? How are they different? What do the structures show about the cultures in which they were built?

Cooperative Learning
Share the following quote with students: "No house should ever be *on* any hill or *on* anything. It should be *of* the hill, belonging to it, so hill and house could live together, each the happier for the other."

—Frank Lloyd Wright
Working in small groups have students find examples of structures that are good examples of the quote and share their findings with the class.

Structures for Business

The ancient Romans, like the Greeks before them, built temples. But Roman architects were also called upon to create many
other kinds of buildings. Figure 14–4 shows
a public arena used for sports contests and
entertainment. *Huge meeting halls* called **basilicas** (buh-**sil**-ih-kuhs) were also built.

After the time of the Romans, other kinds
of business buildings began appearing in cities. Banks were designed. Schools and government buildings were built.

In our own time, buildings used for business have taken a new direction—up. Strong
metals such as steel have allowed architects
to use space efficiently. The modern skyscraper can be found in major cities throughout the world. Buildings today are built on
skeletons, or frames, of steel. One of the first
buildings to use this technique is shown in
Figure 14–5. It was designed by Louis Sullivan, a pioneer of modern architecture. How
is this "skyscraper" different from the ones
of today? How is it similar?

▲ **Figure 14–5   Rows of brick were used to cover the steel
skeleton in Sullivan's building. Can you think of some coverings
used today?**

Louis Sullivan. Wainwright Building. 1890–1891. St. Louis,
Missouri.

▲ **Figure 14–4   Over the centuries, conquering rulers carried off stones from the Colosseum
to build new buildings. Many of the great palaces of the 1500s are made from these stones.**

Colosseum. Rome. A.D. 72–80.

240   📖   Lesson 1   *The Art of Architecture*

Structures for Recreation

In addition to temples and buildings for business, the Romans designed amphitheaters (**am**-fuh-thee-uht-uhrs) for sporting events. **Amphitheaters** are *circular or oval buildings with seats rising around an open space.* The famous open-air amphitheater shown in Figure 14–4 could seat 50,000 people. Structures like this were early models of our modern sports arenas.

Sports arenas, of course, are not the only kinds of buildings designed for recreation. Concert halls and theaters are two others. Museums are a third. Figure 14–6 shows a museum by twentieth-century architect Frank Lloyd Wright. The building has one large main windowless room. The art works are hung on walls along a ramp that spirals upward. Would you know at a glance that this building is a museum? Why, or why not?

THE CHALLENGE OF ARCHITECTURE

Like other applied artists, architects are faced with a double challenge. That challenge is creating works that are both useful and pleasing to the eye. Since architecture is so much a part of everyday life, the search for new solutions is never-ending. These solutions show up not only in new styles but also in new and exciting building materials.

Take a close look at buildings going up in your town or city. There you are likely to see how architects combine a knowledge of engineering with an understanding of design to create buildings that are *both* attractive and functional.

✔CHECK YOUR UNDERSTANDING

1. What is architecture?
2. What are three main purposes of architecture?
3. What is an amphitheater?
4. Describe the double challenge facing every architect.

STUDIO EXPERIENCE

The buildings around us can become so familiar we don't even notice them. This studio experience will help you appreciate local architecture as an art form.

Choose a building in your community you believe is interesting. Sketch the building as accurately as you can. In class, draw your building in the center of a sheet of 12 x 18 inch (30 x 46 cm) paper. In the space around your building, draw a new, imaginary setting. This should be an *ideal* setting that allows your building to look its best. Without telling the name of your building, see if your classmates recognize it. Can you identify theirs?

▲ **Figure 14–6**   Not everyone liked Wright's design. Some said it looked like a giant cupcake. What do you think of it? Do you think it is an appropriate design for a museum?

Frank Lloyd Wright. Solomon R. Guggenheim Museum, New York, New York. 1988. Guggenheim Museum, New York, New York.

Lesson 1   *The Art of Architecture*   📖   **241**

Following Up

Closure. Have students meet in groups to share and discuss their "Studio Experience" drawings. Have them discuss responses to these questions: Which building is shown in this drawing? What is the actual setting of that building? How is ideal setting in the drawing different from the actual setting? How do the different settings affect your response to the building itself?

Evaluation. 1. Review students' written responses to the "Check Your Understanding" questions. 2. Listen to their group discussions of the "Studio Experience" drawings.

Reteaching. Work with small groups of students to help them examine and discuss the Parthenon, Figure 14-1. Guide students in identifying and characterizing the use of visual elements in the work. Let one of the group members record the ideas about each element. Then help students compare their description of this work with their description of Louis Sullivan's work, Figure 14-5 (see "Using Art Criticism"). Ask: How are the two buildings similar? What are the most important differences? What do you think accounts for those differences?

Enrichment. New materials and new technologies have greatly expanded the possibilities for architects. The development of reinforced concrete in the late nineteenth century has enabled architects to give form to dramatic new ideas. Have students research modern structures that are built from reinforced concrete. Examples include the Opera House in Sydney, Australia, and the Guggenheim Museum in New York City (Figure 14-6). Ask students to find answers to these questions about the buildings they choose: When and where was it constructed? Who designed it? What purpose is it intended to serve? How has it been accepted by the public and by critics? Why was reinforced concrete chosen for this building? What materials were used to reinforce the concrete? Then ask students to make brief oral presentations to the rest of the class.

Cooperative Learning

Have students form cooperative learning groups, and ask each group to learn more about one of the structures shown in this lesson (Figures 14-1, 14-2, 14-3, 14-4, 14-5, 14-6). The students in each group should begin by deciding what aspect of the building they want to explore; examples include the building's architect, the style of the building, the building materials used, the specific purposes of the building, and so on. Then have group members work together to find answers.

Answers to "Check Your Understanding"

1. Architecture is the planning and creating of buildings.
2. Purposes of architecture include creating dwellings, creating structures for prayer, creating structures for business, and creating structures for recreation.
3. An amphitheater is a circular or oval building with seats rising around an open space.
4. Architects face the double challenge of creating works that are both useful and pleasing to the eye.

LESSON PLAN
(pages 242–243)

Objectives
After completing this lesson, students will be able to:
• Design and build three-dimensional models for vacation houses.
• Describe, analyze, interpret, and judge their own models.

Supplies
• Several decks of playing cards (or, if you prefer, flash cards or other small pieces of stiff paper).
• Pencils; sheets of sketch paper; sheets of cloth, 14 inches (36 cm) square; wood strip guides, each about 1/2 inch (13 mm) thick; clay; rolling pins; rulers; containers of water; slip.

TRB Resource
• 14-5 *Eclectic America*, (appreciating cultural diversity)

TEACHING THE LESSON

Getting Started

Motivator. Let students form small groups, and give each group a supply of playing cards (or flash cards or other small pieces of stiff paper). Tell students that the groups will have five minutes to build the largest houses of cards they can. Remind them that *large* does not necessarily mean just *tall*. After five minutes, let students decide which group has built the largest construction. Encourage students to comment on different approaches that made the construction more solid, and ask them to describe any difficulties they encountered. Then explain to students that they have been using the post and lintel method of construction; point out examples of "post" cards and "lintel" cards.

Vocabulary. Let volunteers use dictionaries to find the meanings of *elevation* and *facade*; have them read the definitions to the rest of the class. Then let students discuss the various meanings and identify those used in the text.

Building a Clay Model

To make a house of cards, you stand two cards on end and lay another across them. A similar approach was used by the architect of the temple in Figure 14–7. **Post and lintel** (**lint**-uhl) is *a building method in which a cross-beam is placed above two uprights*. The posts in this temple are the ridged columns. The lintels are the connected slabs of stone held up by the pillars. How many posts can you count in the picture? How many lintels?

WHAT YOU WILL LEARN

You will design and build a three-dimensional clay model for a vacation house. You will use the clay slab method you learned in Chapter 13 to cut and assemble a variety of square and rectangular shapes. Your house will have a porch built using the post and lintel method.

WHAT YOU WILL NEED

• Pencil and sheets of sketch paper
• Sheet of cloth 14 inches (36 cm) square
• 2 wood strip guides, each about 1/2 inch (13 mm) thick
• Clay
• Rolling pin and ruler
• Clay modeling tools and fork
• Container of water
• Slip

WHAT YOU WILL DO

1. Make pencil drawings to plan your house. Begin by drawing a floor plan. A **floor plan** is *a scale drawing of how a room or building would appear without a roof as if seen from above*. Floor plans show how the space inside a building is to be used. Don't forget to show the porch in your floor plan. Clearly label each room.

▲ **Figure 14–7** Which elements and principles of art do you think this architect was most concerned with?

Parthenon. Acropolis, Athens, Greece. Begun 447 B.C.

2. Make a second drawing. This time, draw the front of the house as it would appear from outside. Such *a drawing of an outside view of a building* is called an **elevation**. An elevation can show any outside view. This one is of the **facade** (fuh-**sahd**), *the front of a building*. Your elevation should show a second view of your porch using posts and lintels.

3. To achieve a slab of clay of uniform thickness, place the wood strip guides on the cloth 8 inches (20 cm) apart. Place

---

Background Information
The post and lintel structure of windows and doors has been used since the earliest buildings were erected. The Egyptians used post and lintel structures in tombs; the ancient Greeks and Romans used them in temples; Europeans used them in churches. Today this is still the most common way of building an opening without losing structural strength or stability.

There is, however, a problem with post and lintel structures: the stress on the lintel can cause it to crack. This problem was solved by Roman and European architects, as well as Eastern architects, through the use of arches. The arch allows the weight of a building to be distributed differently, and so is inherently stronger. The rounded arches common to the Romanesque style of architecture presented another problem: Rounded arches of different widths must start their curve at different points in order to support the weight of a building, so arches of different widths could not all be of the same height. This construction difficulty was overcome by the use of the pointed arch.

the clay between the wood strips. Flatten it with the heel of your hand. Resting the rolling pin on the wood strips, roll out the clay.

4. Using the ruler and a needle tool, lightly mark off a large rectangle. This is to be the floor. Using the measurements from the length and width of your large rectangle, mark off two pairs of rectangles. One pair is to be the front and back walls. The second pair is to be the side walls. If you wish to have a house with a sloping or gabled roof, cut the front and back slabs so they come to a point. You will also need slabs for the roof. Carefully mark off windows and doors. Cut along the marks you have made and remove the clay rectangles. Keep each slab damp until you are ready to use it.

5. Using the fork to score the ends of the walls and some slip, attach the back wall and a side wall. Make sure they form an *L*. Carefully attach the joined walls to the floor. Then add the second side wall and the front wall.

6. Attach the floor, or deck, of the porch to the front wall. Attach the posts to the deck. Carefully add crossbeams, between posts and to the front wall.

7. Measure and cut additional clay slabs to be used for the roof and the porch. Attach these securely with slip after scoring.

8. Add decorations and details to your house by cutting into slabs or adding other details.

9. Fire your house in a kiln. Consider color schemes and glaze to add color and texture.

EXAMINING YOUR WORK

- **Describe**   Display the floor plan with your model house and the elevation drawing you used in planning your house. Identify the different rooms on your floor plan. Tell how each is to be used. Point out the posts and lintels you used in designing the porch. Tell how the slabs were tightly joined before your model was fired.
- **Analyze**   Show how your model is made from a variety of square and rectangular shapes. What forms have you created?
- **Interpret**   Tell how a viewer would know that your model represents a vacation house. What word would you use to describe the feeling your house gives — comfortable, peaceful, unusual? List ways in which the family living in your house could use the porch.
- **Judge**   Tell whether your work succeeds as architecture. Explain your answer. If you were to do another, what would you do differently?

10. *Optional*: Your house may be glazed and fired again, or you may wish to paint your model with acrylic paint. One or two coats of polymer resin coating will give acrylic colors a great luster.

OTHER STUDIO IDEAS

- Design a garage for the vacation house. Decide how many cars will be kept in the garage. Make a clay model of the garage.
- ●● Make a pencil drawing of a place of worship to be used today similar to the one in Figure 14–7. Use the post and lintel method. Decide what kinds of designs you will use to decorate your place of worship. Use cardboard and make a model based on your drawing.

Lesson 2   *Building a Clay Model*   **243**

Understanding Art History. Divide the class into five groups, and have each group research one of these methods of construction: post and lintel, arch, barrel vault, groin vault, dome. Ask: Which civilization first used the method of construction? What materials were used? What are the advantages of the method? How do architects still use the method (if at all)? Have each group make a presentation, including drawings to illustrate the method of construction.

Developing Studio Skills. To provide students with practice before they construct their models for houses, have students use the slab method to make clay cubes. Ask them to make their cubes 2 inches (5 cm) on a side, and remind them that their goal is to make the sides of the cubes meet at 90-degree angles. Be sure students poke holes in their cubes before firing; without these holes, the cubes may explode in the kiln.

Following Up

Closure. Have students work in the same groups they formed for the "Motivator" activity. Distribute cards again, and give groups only three minutes to enclose as large a space as possible. Then help students discuss their constructions: How have their approaches changed? How were they able to use what they had learned about building with the post and lintel method?

Evaluation. Review students' clay models, and evaluate their contributions to the "Closure" activity and discussion.

Reteaching. Help groups of students discuss their use of color on their vacation home models: Which have complementary, analogous, or monochromatic color schemes? On which models has the use of color been organized by the principle of emphasis, of variety, of harmony, or of balance?

Enrichment. After creating clay cubes, some students may want to try making hollow spheres of clay. Help students brainstorm possible approaches to this problem in construction; then let them experiment with clay. Remind students to poke holes in their spheres before firing.

Classroom Management Tip
Before beginning the studio portion of this lesson the teacher may ask students to walk around their community to identify buildings exhibiting the post and lintel form of construction. These could then be discussed in class in preparation for the studio activity.

Explain that the floor plans and elevations called for in this lesson need not be detailed or in scale. Students will have an opportunity to prepare these plans to scale in later lessons. Rough drawings are intended here to introduce students to these kinds of architectural plans.

LESSON PLAN
(pages 244–245)

Objectives

After completing this lesson, students will be able to:

• Design and draw a floor plan for a one-story shopping mall.

• Describe, analyze, interpret, and judge their own floor plans.

Supplies

• Pencils; rulers; erasers; sheets of sketch paper; sheets of white graph paper, 18 x 24 inches (46 x 61 cm); transparent tape.

> **TRB Resource**
>
> • 14-6 *Your Dream House,* (studio)

TEACHING THE LESSON

Getting Started

Motivator. Have students brainstorm a list of their ideas about an ideal shopping mall. What types of stores would they like to find there? Record their ideas on the board. Then ask them to extend the list: What types of stores would their parents, older adults, or children want to find? The list should be quite long. Then help students condense and organize it: Which types of stores can be combined into one? Which types of stores should be located beside or near each other? Who are the customers you want to attract to this mall? Which stores on the list will not interest those customers? What extra facilities will those customers hope to find?

Vocabulary. Students are probably very familiar with the word *mall*; they recognize it as a place to shop. However, the word has several other meanings. Have students use dictionaries to find its other meanings. Ask: What are the various meanings? How do they seem to be related?

Drawing Floor Plans

Today in many places bits of crumbled stone, brick, and adobe stand alone as reminders of past cultures. In its day, the Forum in Rome (Figure 14–8) was a busy public square and marketplace. Here people gathered to chat or do business. Visitors standing before these grand ruins today can almost hear the echoes of ancient voices and footsteps. It is a powerful reminder of the past.

The design idea behind the Forum—many shops clustered together—lives on. Today we call such groupings of stores shopping malls (Figure 14–9).

Imagine that your community needs a new shopping mall. You are one of many architects community leaders have asked to design plans for a unique new mall. Leaders want to be sure there will be space inside the mall for businesses and for large groups of people to move about freely. They also want a large parking area for mall visitors. Most important, they want people of the community to find the mall useful.

WHAT YOU WILL LEARN

You will design a floor plan for a one-story shopping mall. Your mall will have one department store, 10 smaller shops, and two restaurants. The department store should be emphasized as the most prominent place of business in the mall. Divide the space in your mall so that large and small shops are cre-

▲ 14–8   At first, the Forum was used strictly for business. Later, temples were built around it. Today, only a few ruins remain to tell of its former beauty.

Forum of Julius Caesar. Begun 46 B.C.

▲ Figure 14–9   How is this building different from the one in Figure 14–8? Which do you like better, the new or the old? Why?

Modern Shopping Mall. Fashion Island, Newport Beach, California.

Background Information

The history of the marketplace—beginning with the bazaars of Northern Africa and the Middle East—goes back centuries, but the history of the American shopping mall does not begin until after the Industrial Revolution. Mass merchandising began in 1826, when Lord and Taylor's department store opened in New York City.

Although the concept of the urban mall has its roots in the nineteenth century, the enclosed suburban shopping mall is only a generation old. Initially, shopping malls were huge, with large, spacious center courts. The recent trend in design is to reduce this open space, and the average mall store is now half the size it was when the first suburban malls opened.

The development of the shopping mall has been strongly influenced by a social factor—the mall has become entertainment. Shopping itself is now a form of entertainment. But people don't frequent malls only to shop. They go for walks, they meet friends, they sit and "people watch."

ated. Your mall will also have a wide, roomy public walkway linking the different stores. Finally, it will have a large parking lot for mall visitors.

WHAT YOU WILL NEED

- Pencil, ruler, and eraser
- Sheets of sketch paper
- Sheets of white graph paper, 18 x 24 inch (46 x 61 cm)
- Transparent tape

WHAT YOU WILL DO

1. Using pencil, ruler, and sketch paper, create different possibilities for floor plans. (You may use malls you have visited for ideas. The final design, however, should be your own.) A large department store will be the focal point of the mall. Decide what kinds of businesses you will have among the 10 shops. Decide which businesses will be next to each other along the walkway. Decide whether either or both of the restaurants will serve fast food. Decide how much floor space each business will need. Provide a large parking lot. Use the foot as a unit of measurement. Develop a scale for your design, such as 1/4 inch equals 1 foot.
2. Carefully line up two sheets of the white graph paper so their long sides touch. Fasten them where they meet with transparent tape. Turn the paper over. Neatly transfer the final design of your floor plan to the large sheet. Use your ruler. Neatly label each store. Label the walkway and parking area.

OTHER STUDIO IDEAS

- Design a detailed floor plan for one of the stores in your mall. Decide whether the store will have wide or narrow aisles. Decide whether it will have counters or shelves. Draw your plan.

EXAMINING YOUR WORK

- **Describe**   Tell which store in your mall received the most floor space. Explain why. Tell what other kinds of shops you placed in your mall.
- **Analyze**   Explain how you divided the space in your mall. Point out why some shops received more space than others. Explain how the department store is emphasized in your plan. Tell whether the walkways in your mall are wide and roomy. Tell whether there is enough parking space for times when the mall is busy.
- **Interpret**   Show what features you added to make your mall inviting to visitors. Tell whether the stores and restaurants will appeal to many different tastes. Tell whether visitors would find your mall pleasant to visit. Explain why.
- **Judge**   Tell whether you think your work succeeds as applied art. Explain your answer.

3. Show where the entrance to the mall will be. Add any details that will be used as decoration.
4. Display your floor plan alongside those of your classmates. How are the plans different?
5. *Optional*: Select one plan from the class and construct it out of cardboard as a group project.

- ●● Draw two elevations for your mall — one from the front and the second from any angle you choose. Add details such as arched windows, floor tiles, skylights, and landscaping. Use colored pencils, watercolors, pen and ink, or crayons.

Lesson 3   *Drawing Floor Plans*   **245**

Clay Entrance Relief

LESSON PLAN
(pages 246–247)

Objectives
After completing this lesson, students will be able to:
- Build three-dimensional elevations of shopping mall entrances.
- Describe, analyze, interpret, and judge their own work.

Supplies
- Slabs of clay carved and modeled with a variety of textures (prepared by students, if possible), a single-bulb light fixture that can be easily moved.
- Pencils; sheets of sketch paper; rolling pins; rulers; sheets of cloth 14 inches (36 cm) square; wood strip guides, each about 1/2 inch (13 mm) thick; clay; modeling tools.

> **TRB Resource**
> - 14-7 *Eyes on the Future,* (cooperative learning)

TEACHING THE LESSON

Getting Started
Motivator. Display several clay slabs with a variety of textures. (If possible, have several student volunteers help you prepare these.) Be sure the texture of at least one slab consists of deep curves or cuts as well as attached decorations in high relief. After students have examined the slabs, use the single-bulb light fixture to represent the sun; move it slowly past each slab to show how the sun throws shadows on buildings at different times of day. Help students compare and contrast the shadows created by the different textures. Ask: Which decorations or textures create shadows with sharp edges? Which create shadows with fuzzy edges? Which create shadows with a gradual change in value, and which create shadows with a sharp contrast of value? Encourage students to keep these differences in texture in mind as they design their shopping mall facades.

Vocabulary. Help students review the meaning of *facade.* Then ask: What—or who—has a facade? What can you learn from facades?

246

Clay Entrance Relief

As with people, the faces, or facades, of buildings tell something about their personalities. Look at Figures 14–10 and 14–11. Both are entranceways to churches. Which church would you describe as simple and quiet? Which would you describe as bold and proud? What details of line support your guess in each case? What other elements or principles play a part?

Imagine that you have been called upon to design a second mall. This time, you are to begin by designing a model of the mall entrance. The design you create should give the mall a definite personality.

WHAT YOU WILL LEARN
You will create a three-dimensional elevation of a mall entrance out of clay. Using the slab method, you will carve and model details to create a variety of light and dark values. A variety of different actual textures will be used. Your relief will give the mall a personality.

WHAT YOU WILL NEED
- Pencil and sheets of sketch paper
- Rolling pin and ruler
- Sheet of cloth, 14 inches (36 cm) square

▲ **Figure 14–10** How would you describe the mood of this church? Why?

Valle de Bohi-Romanesque.

▲ **Figure 14–11** Compare this church entrance with the one in Figure 14–10. How are they different? How are they the same?

Mission San Jose. 18th century. San Antonio, Texas.

Background Information
During the twelfth century the services of the Catholic Church were marked by pageantry and splendor, and the church buildings of the period reflect that style. Romanesque architecture flourished from around 1050 until around 1200 throughout most of Europe. The style borrowed heavily from the late Roman buildings (thus its name, meaning "in the Roman manner"), but it is also incorporated aspects of style from Byzantine and Islamic architecture.

Romanesque architecture is characterized by the use of carved stone; before this time, most churches were made of wood. These massive structures use semicircular arches for support, and the arches contribute to a sense of light and spaciousness. Many Romanesque churches also have a number of stained glass windows, which further enhance the feeling of openness within the building.

- 2 wood strip guides, each about 1/2 inch (13 mm) thick
- Clay and modeling tools

WHAT YOU WILL DO

1. Make pencil sketches of different mall entrance designs. As you work, think about the personality you would like the mall to have. Is the mall going to have a fun-filled look or a classic, expensive look? Think about what features would help capture the mood you prefer. Select your best drawing.
2. Place the wood strip guides on the cloth about 6 inches (15 cm) apart. Flatten the clay between the guide sticks, and roll out the clay. Measure and cut out a 6 x 8 inch (15 x 20 cm) rectangle.
3. Arrange the rectangle so a long side is facing you. Working from your elevation drawing, carve and model details of your mall entrance. These details should stick out or be cut into the clay to create a variety of dark and light values. As you work, consider the effects of gradual and abrupt value changes created by carving or adding rounded and angular details. (See Figure 4–12.) Use a needle tool to show the brick or other surface textures. Carve out doors and any details above or to the sides. If you like, include the name of the mall.
4. Using the pencil, poke a small, shallow hole in the back of your relief. The hole should be at the center and about an inch from the top, made at an upward angle.
5. When your relief is dry, fire it. Hang your finished relief from the hole you made in the back on a nail or hook.

OTHER STUDIO IDEAS

- Create your dream home. Draw four views of your dream house (front, back, both sides). Design the outside view to include a porch, garage, trees, and/or bushes. Color your views with colored pencils.

EXAMINING YOUR WORK

- **Describe** Point out the doors and other details of your mall entrance. Show the places in your relief where you carved. Show the places where you modeled. Point out the different actual textures you added to your relief. Show where light and dark values are created.
- **Analyze** Explain how a variety of textures makes your mall more interesting. Explain why a variety of values was needed.
- **Interpret** Identify the personality of your mall. Explain what you did to express this personality in your design of the mall entrance.
- **Judge** Tell whether your work succeeds as applied art. Explain your answer.

▲ **Figure 14–12** Student work. Clay entrance relief work in progress.

- ●● Create a city block viewed from the front. Include shops, office buildings, museum, movie theater, and other buildings of your choice. Create exteriors that reflect the kind of activity that goes on inside each building.

Lesson 4 *Clay Entrance Relief* **247**

Developing Concepts

Exploring Aesthetics. Encourage students to share and discuss their responses to the two entranceways shown in Figures 14-10 and 14-11: What feeling does each create in you? What art elements and principles contribute to that feeling?

Understanding Art History. Have students form cooperative learning groups, and let each group choose one of these architectural styles: Art Deco, Art Nouveau, Colonial, Corinthian, Gothic, Romanesque, Victorian. Have each group research its chosen style and then give a presentation, including photographs or drawings of facades characteristic of that style.

Developing Studio Skills. Have students use clay to make stamps they can use to create decorative motifs or textures on wet clay. Remind students that these stamps must be fired before they can be used. Then encourage students to use their stamps to add texture to their shopping mall elevations.

Following Up

Closure. Ask each student to write a brief description of another student's mall entrance. The description should include a statement identifying the "personality" of the mall. Then have students share and discuss their descriptions with those who created the mall entrances. Does the creator feel the other student understood his or her work?

Evaluation. Review students' three-dimensional elevations of mall entrances, and read their descriptions of one another's work.

Reteaching. Some students may feel awkward working with clay. Encourage students to share tips on rolling out clay evenly, cleaning up, judging when clay is leather hard, and other areas of concern.

Enrichment. Have students discuss the "personality" presented by the facade of their school building or of another local public building. How would they like the message of that facade to be changed? What changes in the facade itself would be required to express that change? Then let students sketch new facades for the building they have discussed.

CHAPTER 14 REVIEW

BUILDING VOCABULARY

Number a sheet of paper from 1 to 8. After each number, write the term from the box that best matches each description below.

amphitheaters	elevation
architect	facade
architecture	floor plan
basilicas	post and lintel

1. The field of art dealing with the planning and creating of buildings.
2. An artist who works at planning and creating buildings.
3. Huge meeting halls.
4. Circular or oval buildings with seats rising around an open space.
5. A building method in which a crossbeam is placed above two uprights.
6. A scale drawing of how a building would appear as if seen from above and there were no roof.
7. A drawing of an outside view of a building.
8. The front of a building.

REVIEWING ART FACTS

Number a sheet of paper from 9 to 18. Answer each question in a complete sentence.

9. Who were the first architects? What did they build? What media did they use?
10. What building material was used by the early Egyptians? What was an advantage of this material over ones used before it?
11. What are four main uses for architecture?
12. Why was it not important that Greek temples be large?
13. In what ways were churches of the 1200s and 1300s different from earlier temples?
14. What made it possible for architects to start building upward?
15. For what modern structures did early amphitheaters pave the way?
16. Name three kinds of buildings used for recreation.
17. What challenge faces every architect?
18. What kind of drawing reveals how the space inside a building is to be used?

THINKING ABOUT ART

On a sheet of paper, answer each question in a sentence or two.

1. **Compare and contrast.** What does architecture have in common with the other visual arts, such as painting and sculpture? In what ways is it unlike those arts?
2. **Analyze.** Why are both floor plans and elevations important in planning works of architecture?
3. **Extend.** From what you learned in this chapter, what other subjects besides art do you suppose architects study? Explain your answer.

MAKING ART CONNECTIONS

1. **Community Affairs.** A zoning law specifies what type building may be built in a certain part of a city. In teams, research whether there are laws that keep certain types of buildings away from schools. When research is complete, prepare reports to give to the class.
2. **Social Studies.** Research famous walls around the world. Tell about the way these walls affected the people who lived near them. Explore the structure of these walls.

LOOKING AT THE DETAILS

The detail shown below is from the Temple of Athena Nike on the Acropolis in Athens, Greece. Study the detail and answer the following questions.

1. The name of the temple means "Athena Victorious." Look at the figures on top of the building. What kind of victory did these people worship?
2. Does any part of this temple remind you of sculpture? If so, how and, what kind?

3. This temple was constructed without mortar or cement. Study the way the elements and principles of art are organized in this detail. Which ones do you think were most important to the Greeks? Why?
4. Consider the building's size. What kind of mood does this temple create?

Temple of Athena Nike. 427–424 B.C. (Detail.) Acropolis, Athens, Greece.

Thinking About Art

1. Architecture, like painting, sculpture, and other fine arts, involves the use of visual elements organized by the principles of art. Architecture differs from other fine arts, however, in that its works must be useful structures.
2. Architects use floor plans and elevations as detailed plans for both the functional and the visually pleasing aspects of their works.
3. Responses will vary. They may include math, engineering, drafting, and others.

ANSWERS TO "LOOKING AT THE DETAILS"

1. They worshiped victory in battle or war over other states or cultures.
2. Yes. The top border, which is relief sculpture, displays a scene with human forms; it communicates a message through the actions of the figures. Other reminders of sculpture are the columns and their three-dimensional form with detailed carving.
3. Line, shape, and form were the most important elements. Responses will vary as to why these were important. Students might mention the following: The stone is laid precisely to form a solid wall. The Greeks had to rely on line and form in construction because they used no other means to force the pieces together. The pieces needed to be exact geometric shapes, which would fit together. The building displays symmetrical balance, which indicates that balance and harmony were important principles. Students might also say that the lines are all vertical on the columns, showing the importance of harmony.
4. Allow students to express their opinions. Responses might include the following considerations: Because of the straight and precise lines and symmetrical balance, it is formal, elegant, and reverential. The temple may be thought to be mysterious, sacred, and distant.

Chapter Evaluation

The purpose of this chapter is to develop students' understanding of architecture. Students learn about the goals of architecture and how architects use floor plans and elevation drawings. Some possible evaluation techniques include:

1. Show students slides or pictures of different phases and styles of architecture such as: amphitheater, basilica,

elevation drawing, facade, floor plan, and post and lintel construction. Have students identify each picture with the correct term.
2. Ask students to develop a scale floor plan for their bedroom, or a room of their choice.
3. Have students complete Chapter 14 Test (TRB, Resource 14-8).

Photography, Video, Film

Chapter Scan

Lesson 1 The Art of Photography
Lesson 2 Making a Photogram
Lesson 3 The Art of Film
Lesson 4 Making a Silent Movie
Lesson 5 The Art of Video
Lesson 6 Designing a Video
          Game

TRB Resources

- 15-10 Chapter Test
- Color Transparency 29
- Color Transparency 30

TEACHING THE CHAPTER

Introducing the Art Work

Direct students' attention to Margaret Bourke-White's photograph *Mahatma Gandhi.* Inform students that Margaret Bourke-White was an American photojournalist who in 1936 was chosen to be the photographer of the first cover of *Life* magazine. With *Life* magazine, she helped pioneer the photo essay and develop the definitive photo, which would tell a story at a single glance. Margaret Bourke-White emphasized the human element and was interested in exposing social injustice through her photography. She traveled to interesting and controversial places where just the scenery alone could have easily overpowered the people in her shots. But with the unfailing eye of a great photographer, she always managed to capture the human essence.

Examining the Art Work

Tell students that this photograph is of Mahatma Gandhi, who was India's leader in its non-violent struggle for independence from Britain. Explain that Gandhi wanted not only political independence for his people but economic self-reliance as well and that he encouraged the growth of the weaving industry for this. Refer to the spinning wheel in the photograph, and explain that Bourke-White chose to photograph Gandhi with the wheel in order to emphasize his belief.

▲ Where would you expect to find photographs like this? Does this photo tell a story?

Margaret Bourke-White. *Mahatma Gandhi.* 1946. Photograph. George Eastman House, Rochester, New York.

Photography, Film, and Video

Throughout this book you have learned about the many different ways that artists express themselves. Painters do this with brushes. Sculptors use clay, wood, or metal. Illustrators use pen or pencils.

Look at the photograph at the left. How is it like other works of art you have studied? How is it different? In this chapter you will learn about artists who use the camera to produce their art works.

OBJECTIVES

After completing this chapter, you will be able to:
- Tell what photography is and describe the history of photography.
- Define *motion picture* and tell how movies are made.
- Talk about the beginnings of video games.
- Make a photogram, a silent movie, and a video game.

WORDS YOU WILL LEARN

camera
cinematographer
daguerreotypes
director
microprocessors
motion picture

negatives
photogram
photography
producer
video game
wet plate

ARTISTS YOU WILL MEET

Margaret Bourke-
  White
Mathew Brady
J. L. M. Daguerre
D. W. Griffith
Fritz Lang

Dorothea Lange
Harold Lloyd
Alfred Stieglitz
William Henry Fox
  Talbot
Orson Welles

251

Explain to students that Bourke-White used backlighting, in which the light is behind the subject rather than on it. This technique outlines the subject, adding emphasis.

Explain that Bourke-White photographed Gandhi sitting in yoga fashion, wearing glasses, and examining newspaper clippings to give the viewer insight into his character. The viewer gets a sense of his self-discipline, focus, education, and patience. Bourke-White also chose to portray him without a shirt, revealing a bony yet healthy frame, perhaps to portray a sense of self-sacrifice.

Discussing the Art Work

Ask students to think about how the element of line is portrayed in this work. Point out how the spokes of the wheel—precise dark lines—point to Gandhi and how the lines of his arms take the viewer's eye downward to the newspaper clippings.

Ask students if they think Bourke-White would have thought to include the spinning wheel in her work if she knew nothing about Gandhi. Explain that for a photographer, understanding the subject is just as important as the equipment used and the organization of the elements of art. Ask students to think about why Bourke-White chose to photograph this scene in black and white. Suggest that perhaps she felt that color would add a dimension that might clutter the message or take away from it; color would soften the lines in this photograph, taking away some of the dramatic contrast and emphasis.

Tell students that in this chapter they will learn about photography, its history, how movies are made, and the beginnings of video games. They will also make their own photogram, silent movie, and video game.

Building Self-Esteem

Ask students to imagine they have chosen still photography as a profession. With their help, list on the board as many categories as they can think of, including portraits, fashion, sports, product advertising, news coverage, travel, interiors. Ask students to select the specialized area that appeals to them most. Give them five minutes to make a written list of as many ways as they can think of to capture the essence of what they have chosen to photograph. For instance, a shot of a sports figure should show the moment of greatest extension as the football is kicked or the moment a runner breaks the ribbon. A food photograph should cause the mouth to water: a bowl of soup steaming, or condensation running down the outside of an ice-cold glass of lemonade. After five minutes, let the students form small groups of those who have chosen the same categories. Let them combine their lists. Share the combined lists with the entire class to increase awareness of ways photographers might perceive and communicate essentials.

The Art of Photography

LESSON PLAN
(pages 252–255)

Objectives

After completing this lesson, students will be able to:
• Tell what photography is.
• Describe and discuss the history of photography.
• Identify the contributions of specific early photographers.

Supplies

• Family and individual photographs (supplied by students).
• Two long pieces of butcher paper; colored markers; scissors, glue.
• Sheets of colored construction paper; photographs (supplied by students); old magazines; scissors; glue; colored markers.

TRB Resources

• 15-1 *Humor in Advertising,* (reproducible master)
• 15-2 *Making vs. Taking Pictures,* (reproducible master)
• 15-3 *Crisis in Aesthetics,* (aesthetics/art crticism)
• 15-4 *Some Interesting Facts,* (art history)

TEACHING THE LESSON

Getting Started

Motivator. Ask all the students to bring in photographs of themselves from the current school year, from elementary school, and from their preschool years. Also ask several volunteers to bring in old family photographs taken at least 25 years ago. Let students talk about their photographs and then post them on a classroom bulletin board. Once all the photos are on display, ask students to describe some of the photographs without identifying or describing the subjects. This will require students to describe the photographs in terms of such visual elements as color, line, and texture; encourage them to use the same kinds of descriptions they might use in discussing a painting.

Vocabulary. Begin by letting students give their own definitions of *photography* and sharing some

252

The Art of Photography

What do all works of art have in common? All try to present an image in a way that makes it special. In recent times artists have discovered new ways of creating special images. In this lesson you will learn about one of those ways — photography. In later lessons you will learn about two others — the arts of film and video.

PHOTOGRAPHY

Today we take photographs for granted. They are all around us. Newspapers, magazines, and books are full of them. It is strange to think that photography was an expensive and difficult process just over 150 years ago. **Photography** is *the art of making images by exposing a chemically treated surface to light.* Photographs are made using *a dark box with a hole controlling how much light enters,* better known as a **camera.**

THE HISTORY OF PHOTOGRAPHY

The idea of capturing an image using light is a very old one. Attempts to do this date back to the time of Leonardo da Vinci (Figure 15–1). It was not until the 1800s, however, that the first true photographs were made. L. J. M. Daguerre (duh-gehr) was the French inventor of an early method of photography. These were called **daguerreotypes** (duh-**gehr**-uh-types), *silvery, mirrorlike images on a copper plate.* Figure 15–2 shows a hand–colored version, taken by an unknown photographer. Notice how worn and scratched the image is. Can you identify the subject of this photograph without reading the credit line?

Daguerreotypes took a long time to make. They were also very costly. The wet plate method, introduced in the 1850s, brought improvements in both these areas. **Wet plate** is

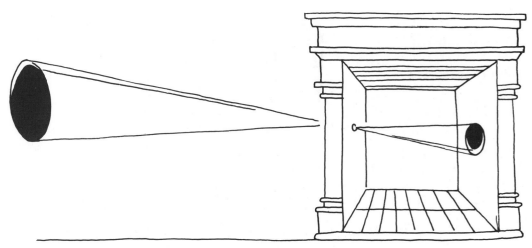

▲ Figure 15–1   The word *obscura* means "dark" and *camera* means "chamber" in Italian. Can you think of other inventions, in which the idea for the invention was around a long time before the invention itself?

Background Information

By the 1870s, when technological improvements had decreased camera size and simplified film developing, photographers were at last free to conveniently shoot pictures outside of their studios. While some photographers documented events and others pursued artistry, photojournalists combined the practices, portraying newsworthy issues with well-composed photos. As an addition to newspaper columns, a photo could be illustrative, informative, and persuasive. Photog-

raphers such as Jacob Riis used their newly-found mobility to take pictures with the goal of instigating societal change.

In collections such as *The Children of the Poor* (1892) and *The Battle with the Slum* (1902), Riis addressed social and economic problems in New York. His photographs profoundly affected his audience. Despite Riis' racist implications in the texts of such publications such as *How the Other Half Lives* (1890), his photos did raise the public's awareness of conditions in the slums, eventually resulting in improvement.

◀ **Figure 15–2** How would you describe the colors in this picture? Consider the technique. What might affect the color?

Unknown/French. *Street Flutists.* c. 1852. Stereograph daguerreotype. 8.7 x 16.8 cm (3.4 x 6.6"). International Museum of Photography, George Eastman House, Rochester, New York.

a method of photography in which an image is created on glass that is coated with chemicals, then transferred to paper or cardboard, as in photography today. Also like photographs today, wet plate photographs used **negatives,** *reverse images of the object photographed.* The wet plate method was used to photograph impor- tant news events through the 1870s. Figure 15–3 was taken by Mathew Brady, a famous Civil War photographer. Figure 15–4 was taken by Dorothea Lange. She was a photo- journalist in the 1930s. What could pictures like these add to a news account that words could not?

▲ **Figure 15–3** In what ways are photographs like these more telling than a drawing would be?

Mathew Brady. *Civil War.* c. 1865. Photograph. National Archives, Washington, D.C.

Lesson 1   *The Art of Photography*   📖 **253**

of their own experiences with tak- ing photographs and being pho- tographed. Then help students use dictionaries to examine the word more closely: What are the two main parts of the word? What is the meaning of the ancient Greek word from which each of those parts is derived? In what sense is photog- raphy "writing with light"?

Developing Concepts

Exploring Aesthetics. Guide students in discussing and com- paring the photographs by Mathew Brady and Dorothea Lange shown in Figures 15-3 and 15-4: What is the subject of each work? Which vi- sual elements can you identify in each photograph? How would you characterize each photographer's use of those elements? Which art principles has the photographer used to organize the visual elements in each work? What mes- sage—that is, what idea or feel- ing—do you think each photogra- pher intended to communicate with this work? Then help students con- sider the central aesthetic question: Are these photographs works of art? Why, or why not?

You may want to extend this dis- cussion by having students select several of their own collected pho- tographs for consideration (see "Motivator"). Have them identify and discuss the subject, composition, and content of these photographs. Then ask: Do you consider any of these photographs works of art? If so, which photographs? How are those you do not consider works of art different from the photographs taken by Brady and Lange? En- courage students to present and support differing points of view.

Using Art Criticism. Help stu- dents examine and discuss the da- guerreotype by L. J. M. Daguerre in Figure 15-2 and the photograph by Alfred Stieglitz in Figure 15-5. First, ask students to describe the two works: What do you see in each? Which visual elements can you identify and characterize? Then, ask students to analyze the works: How are the principles of art used to organize the elements in each work? Next, have them interpret the works: What meaning, mood, or idea do you feel the daguerreotype or photograph creates? Finally, ask students to make decisions about the success of each work: Are both the daguerreotype and the photo- graph successful works of art? If so, how can you account for the differ- ences between the two works?

Understanding Art History.
Divide students into two groups. Have one group research the history of photography; then ask students in this group to work together to plan and make a time line showing major developments and well-known photographers. Encourage students to draw illustrations and photocopy reproductions of important photographs to include in their time line. Have the other group research the three major styles of art being practiced when photography first developed as an art form: Neoclassicism, Romanticism, and Realism. Ask students in this group to work together to plan and make a large chart summarizing these styles and their influences on photography. They can draw illustrations and photocopy reproductions of important paintings to use in their chart. When both groups have finished, display their work in the classroom and let students discuss and explain them.

Developing Studio Skills.
Have students choose some of the photographs they brought for the "Motivator" activity or bring in other photographs of themselves, their family, and their friends. Let students make several photocopies of their chosen photographs; then let students cut the photocopies into interesting shapes. Have students use their cut photocopies to make collages about their families and/or friends. Encourage students to add to their collages, using pictures cut from old magazines and any drawings they might want to make. Let students display and discuss their finished collages.

Appreciating Cultural Diversity.
Ask volunteers to read about and find examples of the work of photographers from other countries, such as Masahisa Fukase and Shomei Tomatsu of Japan, Raghubir Singh of India, Jindrich Styrsky of Czechoslovakia, Manuel Alvarez Bravo of Mexico, and Joao Aristeu Urban of Brazil. Have the volunteers share their findings with the rest of the class.

▲ **Figure 15–4   If this were a painting, would its impact be different from this photograph? Why or why not?**

Dorothea Lange. *White Angel Breadline.* Photograph. Oakland Museum, San Francisco, California.

Background Information
Alfred Stieglitz (United States, 1864–1946) was a leader in establishing photography as a fine art. He was trained in photographic technology in Berlin, where he first established himself as a photographer of technical excellence and penetrating insight. Stieglitz returned to the United States and continued his work as a photographer and as a promoter of other visual artists, both photographers and painters. He published a magazine, *Camera Work,* largely as a vehicle for promoting photography as art. He also helped other American photographers by exhibiting their work in his galleries.

Among Stieglitz's most famous works are his series of portraits of painter Georgia O'Keeffe (United States, 1887–1986), to whom he was married, and his cloud studies, which he titled *Equivalents.*

◀ Figure 15–5 Stieglitz once waited in a New York blizzard for several hours to photograph a horse-drawn carriage. What does this tell you about him as a photographer?

Alfred Stieglitz. *The Steerage.* 1907. Photogravure. George Eastman House, Rochester, New York.

PHOTOGRAPHY AS ART

As picture taking methods improved, some photographers turned to photography for art's sake. You read in Chapter 7 about ways photographs affected painters of the late 1800s. The field of photography also produced some artists of its own. Alfred Stieglitz (**steeg**-luhts) was unusually gifted at capturing moments on film. Figure 15–5 shows a work Stieglitz always believed to be his masterpiece. This moment was captured on a ship taking immigrants from Europe to America. How would you describe the mood of the photograph?

CHECK YOUR UNDERSTANDING

1. Define *photography*. Define *camera*.
2. When were the first real photographs made?
3. What were two methods for making photographs in the 1800s?
4. Name two similarities between the photographs taken in the 1800s and photographs taken today?

Following Up

Closure. Conclude by helping students discuss photography as an art: How is photography similar to painting? How are the two forms different? With what other art forms would you compare photography? What are the similarities and differences? Encourage all students to contribute to the discussion, expressing their personal responses.

Evaluation. 1. Review students' written responses to the "Check Your Understanding" questions. 2. Consider students' contributions to the "Closure" activity.

Reteaching. Work with small groups of students to gather and examine photographs depicting local history. Ask: What do these photographs show? What was the purpose of the photographers who took them? What message do they communicate to you? Do you consider these photographs works of art? Why, or why not?

Enrichment. Photography has developed along with the development of technology. How did the earliest cameras work? How has the camera changed? What are the most recent refinements in cameras and the film used in them? How have the changes in cameras affected photographers and their work? Ask volunteers to work together to research these questions and then summarize their findings in short written or oral reports.

Classroom Management Tip

Find out whether the local community has historic photographs available for public viewing. You may find collections in libraries and archives, but you may also find historic photographs hanging in the hallways and offices of public buildings. Encourage students to view and discuss these photographs, or, if possible, arrange a field trip in which the entire class can see them.

Answers to "Check Your Understanding"

1. Photography is the art of making images by exposing a chemically treated surface to light. A camera is a dark box with a hole controlling how much light enters.
2. The first real photographs were made in the 1800s.
3. The daguerreotype and the wet plate.
4. Like photographs taken today, photographs taken by the wet plate method in the 1800s used negatives and involved transferring an image to paper or cardboard.

STUDIO · LESSON 2 · STUDIO

Making a Photogram

Look at Figure 15–6. This is a calotype (**kal**-uh-type), another early type of photograph. Like daguerreotypes, calotypes were made by transferring images onto materials affected by light.

You can get a glimpse of how these pioneering photographs were made by creating a **photogram**, *an image made on blueprint paper through the action of light and gas fumes.*

WHAT YOU WILL LEARN

You will create a shadow design on blueprint paper using found objects. Add interest to your design by considering each of the elements of art. You will use either formal or informal balance. Your design will show movement or rhythm. It should also express a mood or feeling. If you wish, mount your finished photogram on poster board for display. (See Figure 15–7.)

WHAT YOU WILL NEED

- Found objects, such as keys, coins, lace, pebbles, and small scraps of paper with unusual shapes.
- Sheet of white paper, 9 x 12 inch (23 x 30 cm)
- Blueprint paper, cut into 9 x 12 inch (23 x 30 cm) sheets and stored in a dark place
- Sheet of heavy cardboard
- Small sponge
- Ammonia (sudsy household type)
- Tray with 2 inch (5 cm) sides
- Piece of wire screen slightly larger than the tray
- Sheet of glass slightly larger than the tray
- White glue
- Sheet of poster board, 11 x 14 inch (28 x 36 cm)

▶ **Figure 15–6 Compare this image with Figure 15–2. Which one is the more realistic one? What differences can you name in the way the two images were captured?**

William Henry Fox Talbot. *The Ladder.* 1844. Calotype. George Eastman House, Rochester, New York.

Lesson Plan sidebar

LESSON PLAN
(pages 256–257)

Objectives

After completing this lesson, students will be able to:
- Create shadow designs on blueprint paper.
- Describe, analyze, interpret, and judge their own designs.

Supplies

- Sheets of black construction paper; white chalk; flashlights; found objects.
- Found objects, such as keys, coins, lace, pebbles, and small scraps of paper with unusual shapes; sheets of white paper, 9 x 12 inches (23 x 30 cm); blueprint paper, cut into sheets 9 x 12 inches (23 x 30 cm) and stored in a dark place; sheets of heavy cardboard; small sponges; ammonia (sudsy household type); trays with sides 2 inches (5 cm) high; pieces of wire screen slightly larger than trays; sheets of glass slightly larger than trays; white glue; sheets of poster board, 11 x 14 inches (28 x 36 cm).

> **TRB Resources**
> - 15-5 *Some Interesting Firsts,* (art history)
> - 15-6 *Dorothea Lange,* (artist profile)

TEACHING THE LESSON

Getting Started

Motivator. To help students begin considering shadows and the designs they can make, have them work in groups. Give each group at least one interesting object, such as a piece of lace, a many-petaled flower, or a seashell, as well as a flashlight, a sheet of black construction paper, and several pieces of white chalk. Have group members hold the object above the paper and shine the light above it, and then use chalk to draw the outline of the shadow cast. Ask students to use chalk to fill in the shadow designs. Then have the groups share and discuss their designs.

Background Information

Artists of the Dada movement used photography as a form of art. The camera, mechanical and impersonal, seemed to them a perfect means of expressing their feelings about traditional art. Two different Dadaists developed and used their own forms of photograms.

In 1917 Man Ray (United States, 1890–1976), a painter, filmmaker, and photographer, invented the Rayograph while experimenting with the uses of film apart from a camera. Ray's intention was to create "disturbing images" with his Rayographs, but the results were sometimes whimsical and amusing.

A year later Christian Schad (Germany, born 1894), working independently, developed the Schadograph in an attempt to create abstract images. A friend of Schad's, Tristan Tarza, coined the term Schadograph.

WHAT YOU WILL DO

1. Experiment by arranging different found objects on the sheet of white paper. As you work, keep such art principles as balance and movement in mind. When you have created a design you find interesting, move on to the next step.
2. Place a sheet of blueprint paper on the sheet of cardboard. Carefully transfer your object arrangement to the blueprint paper. Cover the blueprint paper with construction paper.
3. Carefully carry your covered arrangement to a place where there is bright sunlight. Remove the construction paper. Wait about a minute or until the blueprint paper has changed color. Cover the blueprint paper with the construction paper once again. Move your arrangement to a darker part of the room.
4. Soak the sponge in ammonia, and place it inside the tray. Place the wire screen above the tray. Remove the found objects from the blueprint paper. Set the blueprint paper on top of the screen. Cover it with the sheet of glass. After 10 seconds, remove the glass.
5. Mount and display your photogram using white glue and poster board.

SAFETY TIP

Be careful not to inhale the fumes from the ammonia. Work on your photogram in a room that is well ventilated.

OTHER STUDIO IDEAS

● Make a second photogram. This time use transparent objects, such as tissue paper scraps and bits of onion skin. You may tear the tissue paper and onion skin into non-objective shapes. Show movement, rhythm, and harmony in your unified work of art.

EXAMINING YOUR WORK

● **Describe** Identify the found objects you used in your photogram. Identify the elements of art used. Tell how you created the shadow design.
● **Analyze** Tell what kind of balance your design has. Explain how you created movement or rhythm in your design.
● **Interpret** Tell what mood your photogram expresses. Explain how you created this mood.
● **Judge** Tell whether you feel your work succeeds. Explain your answer.

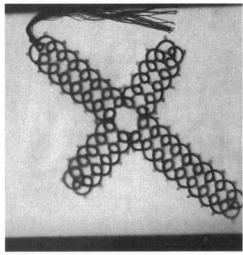

▲ Figure 15–7 Student work. A photogram.

Lesson 2 *Making a Photogram*   **257**

Vocabulary. Have students use dictionaries to check the definition and origin of the word *photogram*. How is it similar to *photograph*? How are the two words different?

Developing Concepts

Exploring Aesthetics. Help students discuss the calotype by William Henry Fox Talbot in Figure 15-6: What is the subject of the work? How did Talbot use the visual elements of art, and what art principles did he use to organize those elements? After the discussion, ask each student to write answers to these questions: Do you consider this calotype a work of art? Why, or why not?

Understanding Art History. Ask volunteers to read about—and, if possible, find examples of—the Schadographs created by Christian Schad and the Rayographs created by Man Ray. Have the volunteers share what they have learned with the rest of the class.

Following Up

Closure. Let students work in groups to display and discuss their photograms. Have each student tell about his or her own work, following the directions in "Examining Your Work" and inviting questions and comments from the rest of the group. Then have each student write a short paragraph in response to the "Analyze" section of the activity.

Evaluation. Review students' photograms, and read their analyses of their own use of balance and other art principles.

Reteaching. Work with groups of students to consider other possibilities for creating photograms. Ask group members to suggest a specific subject for a new photogram; for example, students might choose Native American life. What objects would they use to create the photogram? What other shapes would they include? How would they arrange the objects and shapes? If possible, let group members work together to make the photograms they discuss.

Enrichment. Ask volunteers to share their photograms with older adults who remember the 1920s and 1930s. Do the adults remember seeing calotypes (sometimes called talbotypes)? How did they react to those calotypes? How do the students' photograms compare with the calotypes? Let the volunteers share and discuss what they learned during these interviews.

Classroom Management Tip
When students use potentially dangerous materials (such as ammonia), you may want to have them work with partners. One partner works on his or her project while the other acts as "safety engineer," observing and staying alert to any possible hazards. If you use this arrangement, be sure students understand their responsibilities during each stage; also be sure both partners have time to complete their own projects.

Classroom Management Tip
Ammonia can cause skin irritation; students should be especially careful not to spill it.
Ammonia can also cause injuries if it splashes into eyes; to avoid this possibility, have students wear safety goggles.

LESSON PLAN
(pages 258–259)

Objectives

After completing this lesson, students will be able to:

- Define the terms *motion picture*, *director*, *producer*, and *cinematographer*.
- Describe how movies are made.

Supplies

- A short silent film (if available).
- *Citizen Kane* (or another classic motion picture).

TRB Resources

- 15-6 *Make an Animated Film*, (cooperative learning)
- 15-7 *The Documentary*, (appreciating cultural diversity)

TEACHING THE LESSON

Getting Started

Motivator. If possible, introduce the lesson by showing a short silent film. Then encourage students to discuss their responses to the film: What do you think of this movie? How is it like movies you are used to seeing in theaters today? How is it different? When do you think it was made? How do you think the time when it was made affects the way it was made and the subjects with which it deals? Do you think this film is a work of art? Why, or why not?

If you do not have a silent film available for showing, encourage students to discuss motion pictures they have seen, either in theaters or on television. What black-and-white movies have they seen? What silent movies have they seen? How do these movies help them understand the history and development of motion pictures?

Vocabulary. Ask students to identify the verbs from which the nouns *director* and *producer* are formed. Let volunteers use dictionaries to find the appropriate definitions of those verbs. Then have other volunteers use dictionaries to find the meaning of the word from which *cinema* is derived and to check the definition of *cinematographer*.

258

The Art of Film

"Lights. Camera. Action." These may not be words you would expect to hear spoken in an artist's studio. In some artists' studios, however, the words are spoken nearly every day. These are the kinds of studios where movies are made. The artist who speaks the words is known as the director.

In this lesson you will learn about the art of filmmaking.

THE BEGINNINGS OF FILM

After photographers learned to capture still images using light they began looking ahead to the next form of creative expression. By the end of the 1800s inventors had found a way to capture moving images using light. The **motion picture**, *photographs of the same subject taken a very short time apart and flashed onto a screen*, made the image appear to be moving (Figures 15–8 and 15–9).

▲ Figure 15–8   This film was made by an American. The one in Figure 15–9 by a German. Do you think audiences in either country had trouble understanding the mood and setting of the foreign film? Why or why not?

Directed by D. W. Griffith. Still from *Intolerance*. 1916. Museum of Modern Art, Film Still Archive, New York, New York.

MAKING FILMS

Every motion picture, or movie, is the combined effort of hundreds of people. The three most important of those people are the director, the producer, and the cinematographer.

The Director

The director is the single most important person in the making of a movie. The **director** is *the person in charge of shooting the film and guiding the actors*. He or she also helps with the script.

The director's main job is deciding how every scene should be photographed. To get just the right look, a director may shoot the same scene dozens of times.

▲ Figure 15–9   Compare this with Georgia O'Keeffe's cityscape on page 82. What similarities do you see?

Directed by Fritz Lang. Still from *Metropolis*. 1926. Museum of Modern Art. Film Stills Archive, New York, New York.

Background Information

Several separate factors contributed to the early development of motion picture technology. One of these was a group of popular toys, known then as persistence-of-vision toys; the best remembered was probably the zoetrope. To play with the zoetrope, the viewer fitted a paper strip with many pictures of the same figure inside a circular drum. Then the viewer gave the drum a spin, and, peering through slits in the drum, saw the figure on the paper strip move.

Other important contributions were made by Eadweard Muybridge (England, 1830–1904), Etiennse Jules Marey (France, 1830–1904), Thomas Edison (United States, 1847–1931) and his employee William Dickson (United States, 1860–1935), George Eastman (United States, 1854–1932), and Louis Lumière (France, 1864–1948) and his brother Auguste Lumière (France, 1862–1954).

The Producer

The **producer** is *the person in charge of the business end of making a movie.* The producer is the person who finds the story and hires the director. He or she also figures out how much money it will cost to make the movie. Some producers take part in selecting actors and in writing the script.

The Cinematographer

The **cinematographer** (sin-uh-muh-**tahg**-ruh-fuhr) is *the person in charge of running the camera or cameras.* Like other artists, cinematographers are trained in using light and color.

Before filming, or shooting, the director and cinematographer will go over the script together. They will discuss different camera angles and techniques for shooting each scene.

THE ART OF FILM

The very first films made were silent. Since these films used no words, strong dramatic acting was required. They could be shown to audiences around the world. These films required strong and exaggerated acting.

The arrival of sound in the late 1920s opened up new doors to filmmakers. It also closed doors to actors whose voices did not sound right.

▲ Figure 15–10   The man pictured here was the film's star and director. What problems do you think might exist for a person filling these two positions?

Directed by Orson Welles. Still from *Citizen Kane.* 1941. Museum of Modern Art, Film Stills Archive, New York, New York.

▲ Figure 15–11   How can you tell this scene is not from real life? What is the mood of this scene? Explain

Directed by Tim Burton. Still from *Batman.* 1988. Courtesy of the Academy of Motion Pictures Arts & Sciences.

One of the most inventive motion pictures ever made was *Citizen Kane.* (See Figure 15-10.) Orson Welles' use of camera angles and editing were highly praised and are still imitated today. It, like many old classics, was made before color entered the motion picture industry.

The next advance in film, color, made possible the first colored film classics. These were movies such as *The Adventures of Robin Hood* and *The Wizard of Oz.*

The films of today, of course, use dazzling effects the earliest filmmakers probably never dreamed of. Computers and other high-tech equipment have allowed directors to shoot "the impossible." (See Figure 15–11.) One can only guess what astonishing screen images tomorrow's breakthroughs will bring.

CHECK YOUR UNDERSTANDING

1. What are motion pictures? When was filmmaking invented?
2. What is a director? What are some of the director's tasks?
3. What is a producer? What are some of the producer's tasks?
4. What are two advances that have been made in filmmaking since the days of silent films?

Developing Concepts

Exploring Aesthetics. Help students choose and discuss a current film with which most are familiar: What is the subject of the movie? What is the content—that is, what message does the movie communicate to you? Is this motion picture a work of art? Why, or why not? Then extend the discussion by asking: What other films can you identify that you consider works of art? Why are they art? Are all motion pictures works of art? Why, or why not? Are television programs also works of art? Why, or why not? Encourage students to express and defend various points of view.

Appreciating Cultural Diversity. Ask groups of volunteers to read about the history of films in Japan and in India. Who are the most important filmmakers there? Which films are best known in Japan and in India, and which Japanese and Indian films are best known in the United States? How are Japanese and Indian films similar to and different from films made in the United States? Ask both groups to find answers to these questions and make presentations to the rest of the class.

Following Up

Closure. Have students identify and discuss the "dazzling effects" they have seen in modern movies. Then ask each student to write one or two sentences predicting what "astonishing screen images tomorrow's breakthroughs will bring."

Evaluation. 1. Review students' written responses to the "Check Your Understanding" questions. 2. Listen to their discussion of current movies, and read their predictions for movies of the future.

Reteaching. Show *Citizen Kane* (or another classic film). Let students discuss their reactions to the movie. Then help them identify and discuss the use of camera angles and editing.

Enrichment. Ask students to select and read novels that have been made into movies; then have them watch the movies (on videotape). Help students discuss what they have read and seen: How are the novel and the movie alike? How are they different?

259

Making a Silent Movie

Making a Silent Movie

Objectives

After completing this lesson, students will be able to:

• Participate in making original silent movies.

• Describe, analyze, interpret, and judge their own movies.

Supplies

• Pencils; large notepads divided in half by vertical pencil lines; hand-held video cameras with tripods; sheets of white poster board; black broad-line markers; audio tape recorders.

• Unlined index cards; colored markers.

TRB Resource

• 15-8 *Build a Zoetrope*, (studio)

TEACHING THE LESSON

Getting Started

Motivator. Explain to students that they will be making their own movies. Let them brainstorm a list of all the specific activities that will be involved. Record their ideas on the board. Once the list is complete, help students review their list and put the steps in order. As they organize, they may think of other steps to be added. Then help students divide themselves into two groups, and have each group choose its producer, director, cinematographer, writers, and actors.

Vocabulary. Have students in both groups review all the job titles: producer, director, cinematographer, writer, actor. Ask: What does each term mean? What are the responsibilities of each?

Developing Concepts

Using Art Criticism. Have students read movie reviews in newspapers and magazines. Then have each student bring one review to class, and let students work in groups to discuss the reviews: What aspects of the movie does each critic consider? What questions of criticism are missing from the reviews?

Before the days of sound in movies, the filmmakers had their work cut out for them. They had to rely totally on action to tell the story (Figure 15–12). For those pioneering filmmakers, actions truly spoke louder than words.

WHAT YOU WILL LEARN

You will be part of a group that makes a silent movie. The group will be headed up by a producer and director. A cinematographer for the group will shoot the film using a home video camera. Music will be used to help the audience feel the mood and action. Captions will be used to help the audience understand the action. (See Figure 15–13.)

WHAT YOU WILL NEED

• Pencil
• Large notepad divided in half by a vertical pencil line
• Hand-held video camera with tripod
• Sheets of white poster board
• Black broad-line marker
• Audio tape recorder

WHAT YOU WILL DO

1. The class is to be divided into two groups. Each group is to choose from among its members a producer, a director, a cinematographer, and a three-member writing team. Every other group member is to be an actor.

2. The producer for each group is to meet with the writers. Together, the producer and writers are to agree on a story idea. The story, which is to be original, may be funny, serious, or suspenseful. The story should have parts for as many actors as there are actors in the group. As the writers create, they should tell what each character is doing at any given moment. The final version of the story should be written on the left half of the notepad.

3. While the writers work, the director and cinematographer should test the equipment. At the director's instructions, the cinematographer should take long shots and close-ups. The two should test out indoor shots using the camera's lighting attachment. They should test different uses for the tripod.

► **Figure 15–12   Comedians were especially popular during the silent film era. Do you find this scene funny? Explain your answer. How is movement shown in this picture?**

Directed by Harold Lloyd. Still from *Safety Last*. 1923. Museum of Modern Art, Film Stills Archive, New York, New York.

Background Information

Of the three great comedians of the silent film era, only two remained consistently well known and popular: Charlie Chaplin and Buster Keaton. Harold Lloyd (United States, 1893–1971), the most famous at the time, is not nearly as well remembered. This is because, in the later years of his life, Lloyd refused to make his films available, fearing they would not be shown properly.

Lloyd's film persona was that of a rich, bored young million-aire. His trademarks were his straw hat and his horn-rimmed glasses; they complemented his thin, gaunt figure. Lloyd achieved a reputation as a daredevil, though only three of his films include any dangerous stunts. Probably the most famous is *Safety Last* (1923), in which Lloyd scales the side of a building and then hangs from the hands of a clock, high above the street.

Lloyd's films were "rediscovered" after his death, and in recent years many of his movies have been re-released.

4. When the script is finished, the producer and director should read it. Together, they should decide which scenes need captions to help viewers understand the action. The producer should ask the writers to create these captions with poster board and marker. The producer and director should decide which actors are to play which parts. They should decide what kind of music best fits the mood of the story. The producer should search for and make tape recordings of particular pieces of music.

5. The director should read the script again, this time along with the cinematographer. The two should decide from which angle to shoot each scene or action. They should decide whether a scene calls for a close-up or a long shot. The director should make notes on the right side of the notepad. He or she should also note the points in the shooting where captions are needed.

6. The actors should rehearse the story. They will take their cues on where to stand and what to do from the director. The actors should try to show through their actions and expressions what is happening.

7. When the director feels the group is well prepared, shooting should begin. The finished film should be shown, with music, to the rest of the class.

▶ **Figure 15–13 Students shooting a silent film.**

OTHER STUDIO IDEAS

• Make a silent television commercial. You may use a real product, but the idea should be original. Use captions to help viewers understand the action.

EXAMINING YOUR WORK

• **Describe**   Describe what things the director did before and during shooting. Tell what decisions the director and producer made together. Tell what points the director and cinematographer discussed. Tell what decisions they reached. Tell whether the actors followed the director's instructions. Tell whether they showed what was happening through their actions and expressions.

• **Analyze**   Identify different ways the camera was used. Explain the results.

• **Interpret**   Tell what the story was about. Describe its mood. Explain how the captions helped tell the story and express the mood. Explain how the music added to the mood and emphasized the action.

• **Judge**   Tell whether you feel your work succeeds. Explain your answer.

•• Make a film with a sound track. Rather than have the actors speak, have a narrator tell what is happening. Use sound effects, such as rattling a sheet of lightweight metal to create thunder.

Lesson 4 *Making a Silent Movie*   **261**

Developing Studio Skills. As students prepare to film their movies, have them begin by doing one take—filming a single scene or segment—and then reviewing it. What can each member of the filmmaking team learn from this take? How can each student's contribution to the movie be improved?

Appreciating Cultural Diversity. Television commercials and movie shorts can give students a quick glimpse into the lives of people in other cultures. Check with your school's foreign language department and with local libraries (or have student volunteers check) to see whether videotapes of commercials or movie shorts are available.

Following Up

Closure. Have students keep journals with daily entries about the progress of their movies. Let them refer to these journals as they discuss their completed movies: Which aspects of the project were most difficult? Which do they consider most successful?

Evaluation. Review students' silent movies, read their journal entries, and consider their contributions to group discussions about the work.

Reteaching. Some students may be interested in relating their experiences with making silent movies to the work of movie animators. Encourage these students to experiment with creating their own flip books. Have them draw a cartoon character on an unlined index card. Then have them draw the same character in the same spot on other index cards, changing only one detail in each drawing—the position of an arm or leg, for example. When they flip through the set of index cards, they can see their characters in action.

Enrichment. Have students recall (or watch) *Fantasia*, created by Walt Disney in the 1940s. Encourage students to discuss the visual representations of musical compositions in this work. Then ask each student to select a musical composition and sketch images that could illustrate those sounds in a *Fantasia*-like movie.

The Art of Video

The Art of Video

Objectives

After completing this lesson, students will be able to:
• Explain what video games are.
• Discuss the beginnings of video games.

Supplies

• Any computer games available within the school.
• 5 large sheets of construction paper; pencils, markers, and/or other drawing media.

TEACHING THE LESSON

Getting Started

Motivator. If your school has a computer lab and video games are available there, try to introduce this lesson with a visit to the computer lab. What video games does the lab have? Are *Pong, Space Invaders,* and *Pac-Man* available? Which of these games are familiar to the students? How many students want to try playing them? Encourage everyone to play at least one new game.

If computer games are not available, begin instead by letting students discuss their own experiences playing video games. What do they most enjoy about playing video games? Which games do they like best? Why?

Vocabulary. Divide the class into five groups and assign each group one of these terms: video, microprocessor, light pen, electronic tablet, flow chart. Have the group members use the text, dictionaries, and other sources to develop a definition of their assigned term, and then have them brainstorm ideas for presenting that definition visually. Finally, have group members work together to plan and make a poster illustrating the term. Display the posters in the classroom or in a school hall.

In Lesson 3 you read that computers have opened up new worlds for filmmakers. Computers have also changed forever the face of home entertainment. How? By opening up the exciting and often magical world of video games.

In this lesson you will get a behind-the-scenes glimpse of that world.

VIDEO GAMES

Games have been around for as long as there have been humans. Video games have been around only since there have been computers. A **video game** is *an electronic form of entertainment run by a computer*. The computers that run, or drive, video games nowadays are small enough to fit on a fingertip. Such *tiny computers* are called **microprocessors** (my-kroh-**prahs**-es-uhrs). (See Figure 15–14.)

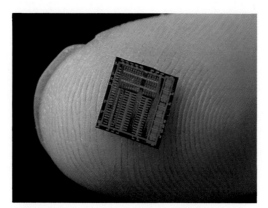

▲ **Figure 15–14** Circuits like these are called chips. Do you know of any other electronic appliances that use chips?

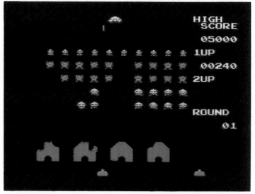

▲ **Figure 15–15** What modern video games do you know of with a space theme?

Screen image from *Space Invaders*.

THE HISTORY OF VIDEO GAMES

Video games take their name from the fact that they use TV, or video screens. The first video game, *Pong*, came out in the early 1970s. The game was modeled on table tennis. It was made up totally of a moving green dot and a center-line "net." In 1979, a highly popular video game was produced called *Space Invaders* (Figure 15–15). This was the first of many video games with a space theme. In the early 1980s, *Pac-Man* gobbled up more video arcade quarters than any other game (Figure 15–16).

Today video games can be found dealing with just about every imaginable fantasy adventure or sport. Technical breakthroughs have led to the use of exciting colors and complicated sound effects.

Background Information

Home and arcade video games made their debut in the early 1970s. It was not until the early 1980s, however, that video games reached their peak of popularity. In 1981 over a quarter billion dollars was spent on this form of recreation. Dozens of books were written, explaining how to "beat the video game." Popular games were pirated as people attempted to cash in on the craze. For example, *Pac-Man*-type games have appeared as *Puck-Man, Gobbler, Cruiser,* and *Packman.*

In response to the popularity of these games, most designers and users point out the benefits: Video games improve memory and reflexes. They also help develop confidence and computer skills. Yet, while these benefits are certainly real, parents, teachers, and other professionals have been alarmed by the distorted perception and desensitization that these games—with their frequent violence—seem to cause in children.

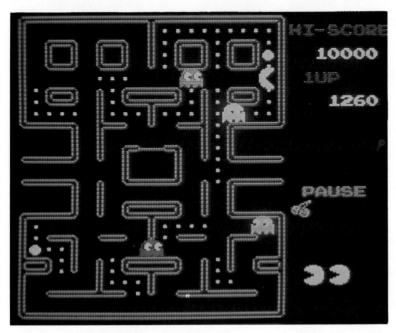

◄ Figure 15–16   How are the art principles of balance, harmony and variety incorporated into this video game?

Screen image from *Pac Man*.

▲ Figure 15–17   Flow chart.

VIDEO GAME DESIGN

Designers of video games draw with space-age tools, such as the light pen and electronic tablet.

Video game designers must do more, however, than just dream up dazzling images. They must also know how to do computer programming. This means creating a set of instructions a computer can follow. A program usually begins with a flow chart, an outline of steps the computer will take. Figure 15–17 shows part of a flow chart.

✔ CHECK YOUR UNDERSTANDING

1. What is a video game? What is a microprocessor?
2. What was the first video game? When did it come out?
3. What tools do video game designers draw with?
4. What is computer programming? How is it tied to video game design?

Lesson 5   *The Art of Video*   263

Developing Concepts

Exploring Aesthetics. Help students discuss the video games with which they experimented in the "Motivator" activity and/or other familiar video games. Ask: Are these games works of art? Are all video games art works? Are the creators of video games artists in the same sense that painters and sculptors are artists?

Using Art Criticism. Ask students to compare various video games with which they are familiar, including, if possible, the games shown in Figures 15-15 and 15-16: What purpose are video games intended to serve? Are some of these games more successful than others in fulfilling that purpose? If so, which games are they? What makes them more successful?

Appreciating Cultural Diversity. Ask volunteers to investigate the popularity of video games in other parts of the world. Ask: Are the games as popular in other countries as they are in the United States? Do people around the world enjoy the same video games, or have different cultures developed their own special video games?

Following Up

Closure. Let students work in groups to discuss their own responses to video games: What do they like most about these games? What do they dislike? Do they know other people—parents or friends, for example—who dislike video games? If so, what facts would they present to change the opinions of those people?

Evaluation. 1. Review students' written responses to the "Check Your Understanding" questions. 2. Evaluate students' contributions to the group discussion.

Reteaching. Work with small groups of students to discuss responses to this question: What kinds of subjects do you think video game designers study in school?

Enrichment. Have students work in groups to brainstorm responses to this question: What do you expect to be the next frontier for video game designers? Then have each student write a paragraph about the future of video games.

Cooperative Learning

Have students work in cooperative groups to explore the subject of video games further. Group members should begin by choosing a question they would like to answer. These are a few examples: How has the cost of purchasing a video game changed since the first games were introduced? Which companies are the major producers of video games, and what are the profits of those companies? What physical problems are associated with video games, and how are they treated?

Answers to "Check Your Understanding"

1. A video game is an electronic form of entertainment run by a computer. A microprocessor is a tiny computer.
2. The first video game was *Pong*. It came out in the 1970s.
3. Video game designers draw with such tools as the light pen and electronic tablet.
4. Computer programming is creating a set of instructions a computer can follow. To make their games work, video game designers must be able to program a computer.

Designing a Video Game

LESSON PLAN
(pages 264–265)

Designing a Video Game

Look at Figure 15–18. This shows a group from a very popular video game of the last few years. These characters star in a cartoon series and are featured in a comic book series. Do you know the name of this group? Do you know who the characters in this scene are?

WHAT YOU WILL LEARN

You will create characters and a story idea for a video adventure. You will write a description of the game that tells what part each character plays. The description will also reveal the goal of the player. You will create illustrations of the characters (Figure 15–19.) Line and color will be used to help show the mood of each character. These characters will be shown in action poses.

WHAT YOU WILL NEED

- Notepad
- Pencil
- Sheets of sketch paper
- Sheets of white paper, 12 x 18 inch (30 x 46 cm)
- Colored pencils

WHAT YOU WILL DO

1. Brainstorm with the class to come up with original ideas for adventures. On the notepad, write the setting of your adventure. Write the types and names of the characters. Make sure at least one of your characters is a villain or evil force. Give your game a title.

Objectives
After completing this lesson, students will be able to:
- Create and describe an original video game.
- Illustrate the characters in their video games.
- Describe, analyze, interpret, and judge their game designs and illustrations.

Supplies
- Notepads; pencils; sheets of sketch paper, 12 x 18 inches (30 x 46 cm); colored pencils.
- Toy figures of characters featured in video games; sheets of sketch paper; pencils.

TEACHING THE LESSON

Getting Started

Motivator. Begin by having students brainstorm a list of ideas for computer games. Write the following headings on the chalkboard: Settings, Characters, Villains, Scoring Methods, Game Goals. Let students suggest as many ideas as possible for each category, including both familiar and original suggestions; record all their ideas on the board. Remind students that during brainstorming they should not stop to evaluate ideas. Suggestions that seem unlikely or even silly at this point may prove interesting and even useful later.

Vocabulary. Help students use the posters they made in the previous lesson to review the terms related to video games. (See "Vocabulary," page 262.)

▶ **Figure 15–18   Are you familiar with the movie that was based on these characters? Are these characters visually appealing? Why or why not?**

Teenage Mutant Ninja Turtles.
New Line Cinema.

Background Information
Video games are, according to designers and manufacturers, here to stay, and their future development will surely prove interesting. Technological advances have made holographic video games a possibility. The player could be literally surrounded by action and sound.

Another possible development is that television manufacturers will begin building video game components into television sets.

With new computer developments, voice units will become increasingly refined and more interactive with the video game player. It is also expected that users will be able to modify existing games or even program their own games.

As the decade progresses, computers and video games will continue to move closer together, eventually merging to form a single medium, capable of producing three-dimensional, life-like, life-size, programmable and realistically detailed adventure games.

▲ Figure 15–19 Student work. An idea for an action video.

EXAMINING YOUR WORK

- **Describe** Identify the different characters you created. Tell the part each one plays in your game. Reveal the setting of your game. Identify the goal of a player. Point to details of background that help emphasize a character's role.
- **Analyze** Explain how the figures are drawn in action poses to show that they are moving. Show where you used line and color to help capture the mood of each character.
- **Interpret** Explain what details of your game make it exciting. Describe how the dangers facing a player add to the excitement.
- **Judge** Tell whether you feel your work succeeds. Explain your answer.

---

2. On another page of the notepad, write notes about the action in your game. Identify the goal of the player. Tell what dangers or problems face the player. Describe different ways in which the player can score points.
3. On sketch paper, do gesture drawings of the characters in different action poses.

Sketch details of background that help emphasize the character's role in the game. Do separate studies of each character's face.
4. Using pencil, transfer the best of your action sketches to sheets of white paper. Lightly sketch details of the characters' faces from the studies you made. Using colored pencils, add detail and shading. Use line and color to capture the mood or personality of each character.
5. Present your finished illustrations to the class. Give a brief talk in which you explain the rules of the game.

OTHER STUDIO IDEAS
- Using watercolors, do a painting of one of your characters. Imagine that this painting will appear on the package in which the game cartridge is sold.
- ●● Use a graphic software program such as MacPaint to draw one of your characters on a computer.

Lesson 6 *Designing a Video Game*   **265**

Developing Concepts

Exploring Aesthetics. Let students discuss the game shown in Figure 15-18: Have you ever played it? What makes this game special? Is this game a work of art? Why, or why not?

Understanding Art History. Ask volunteers to research the background of the Teenage Mutant Ninja Turtles featured in Figure 15-18: Who created the characters? What motivated the creators? In what kinds of shows, games, and toys have the characters been featured?

Developing Studio Skills. Display several toy action figures that are featured in video games (such as the Teenage Mutant Ninja Turtles) or that look as if they might represent video game characters. Set the figures in action poses, and have students sketch each action pose as viewed from two or three different angles.

Appreciating Cultural Diversity. Do any students in the class have firsthand knowledge of the language and traditions of another culture? If they are interested, encourage these students to create video games that reflect other cultures. Be sure these students have an opportunity to explain their game designs to the rest of the class.

Following Up

Closure. Have students work in groups to present their illustrations and explain the rules of their games. Encourage group members to ask questions that will help others expand and clarify their rules. Then ask each student to write a short interpretation of his or her game, following the directions in the "Interpret" section of "Examining Your Work."

Evaluation. Review students' game designs and illustrations, and read their interpretations of their own work.

Reteaching. During the "Closure" discussions, some students may discover that their game rules need to be revised. Ask partners to help these students rework their ideas.

Enrichment. Ask for volunteers who are interested in computer programming. Arrange for these students to work with a computer teacher (if available) to program some of the new video games.

ANSWERS TO "CHAPTER 15 REVIEW"

Building Vocabulary

1. photography
2. camera
3. daguerreotypes
4. wet plate
5. negatives
6. photogram
7. motion picture
8. director
9. producer
10. cinematographer
11. video game
12. microprocessors

Reviewing Art Facts

13. L. J. M. Daguerre was an inventor of one of the earliest forms of photography. He created silvery, mirrorlike images on a copper plate; we now call these daguerreotypes.
14. The wet plate method of photography took less time and cost less than earlier methods.
15. A calotype is an early type of photograph made by transferring images onto materials affected by light.
16. A cinematographer is the person in charge of running the camera or cameras for a movie. Like other artists, cinematographers are trained in using light and color.
17. The first films could be shown to audiences around the world because they used no words.
18. Video games are run by computers, and each game must have a computer program. A flow chart is an outline of the steps that will be included in that program.

Thinking About Art

1. Responses will vary. Students may note that both were early forms of photography and both used light to capture an image. They may note that the wet plate method was less expensive and faster, and that it used negatives.
2. Responses will vary. Students may note that, like studies, takes can be used to practice and explore possibilities.

BUILDING VOCABULARY

Number a sheet of paper from 1 to 12. After each number, write the term from the box that best matches each description.

camera	negatives
cinematographer	photogram
daguerreotypes	photography
director	producer
microprocessors	video game
motion picture	wet plate

1. The art of making images by exposing a chemically treated surface to light.
2. A dark box with a hole controlling how much light enters.
3. Silvery, mirrorlike images made on a copper plate.
4. A photography method in which an image is created on glass coated with chemicals.
5. Reverse images of an object photographed.
6. An image made on blueprint paper through the action of light and gas fumes.
7. Photographs of the same subject taken a very short time apart and flashed onto a screen.
8. The person in charge of shooting a film and guiding the actors.
9. The person in charge of the business end of making a movie.
10. The person in charge of running the camera in the filming of a movie.
11. An electronic form of entertainment run by a computer.
12. Tiny computers.

REVIEWING ART FACTS

Number a sheet of paper from 13 to 18. Answer each question in a complete sentence.

13. Who is L.J.M. Daguerre? What contribution did he make to photography?
14. In what two ways was the wet plate an improvement over earlier methods?
15. What is a calotype?
16. What is a cinematographer? What do they have in common with other artists?
17. Why were the first films made able to be shown to people around the world?
18. What part do flow charts play in the creation of video games?

THINKING ABOUT ART

On a sheet of paper, answer each question in a sentence or two.

1. **Compare and contrast.** In what ways are daguerreotypes and wet plate prints the same? In what ways are they different?
2. **Interpret.** Different shots of the same scene in a movie are called takes. In what way are takes similar to the studies done by painters and sculptors?

MAKING ART CONNECTIONS

1. **Social Studies.** Study the Brady photograph of the Civil War battlefield on page 253. Notice the equipment and uniforms of the military personnel. Find news photos that document events from World War I or World War II. Report to the class how the dress and equipment have changed.
2. **Science.** Research the development of the materials used in photography and find out how the chemical process allows light to be captured on film.

CHAPTER 15 REVIEW

LOOKING AT THE DETAILS

The detail below was taken from Margaret Bourke-White's photograph *Mahatma Gandhi*. Study the detail and answer the following questions.

1. Margaret Bourke-White chose to photograph Gandhi without a shirt, wearing glasses and reading. Why is this important?
2. Mahatma Gandhi was India's leader of nonviolent rebellion for political independence. He encouraged weaving as an industry and for millions of Indians the spinning wheel was the symbol of their fight for independence. How can knowing your subject's historical background help you in taking his or her photograph? How does knowing more about Gandhi and his cause help you in understanding this photo?
3. Does this photograph tell you something about the photographer? Explain.
4. Would the mood of the photograph change if it were taken in color? Explain your answer.

Margaret Bourke-White. *Mahatma Gandhi*. 1946. Photograph. (Detail.) George Eastman House, Rochester, New York.

ANSWERS TO "LOOKING AT THE DETAILS"

1. This is important because it tells the viewer something about the character of the man. It gives the viewer clues as to Gandhi's personality.
2. It can give you insight into what kinds of things you might want to include in the photograph and the best environment for the subject. Also, it might suggest how your subject might best be dressed, what he or she might be carrying, the position of the body, the expression, and the like, in order to best portray the subject's character.

   Responses will vary. Students might note the following: Knowing about Gandhi helps the viewer recognize the spinning wheel and why it is there. It helps in viewing him as a leader instead of confusing his undernourished appearance with poverty and pity. It explains the glasses and newspaper clippings.
3. Yes. Responses will vary. Students might suggest the following explanations: The photograph tells the viewer that the photographer had an understanding of Gandhi's background. She had an interest in photographing people, perhaps even in exposing social injustice. It tells the viewer that she puts thought into her work and she successfully organizes the elements and principles of art to convey a message.
4. Yes. Responses will vary. Students might mention the following: Color might not communicate the message as quickly as black and white. Color would soften the lines; depending on the actual colors, it might create a warmer, softer, brighter, or bluer mood.

Chapter Evaluation

The goal of this chapter is to develop an understanding of the process and history of photography, film, and video. Possible methods of evaluating results include:

1. Have students present a report which traces the history of photography and features the inventors who were responsible for the development of photography.
2. Divide the class into three groups. Each group should represent one of the media described in this chapter: photography, film, and video. Set up a three-way debate in which each group expounds on the advantages of the particular medium.
3. Have students complete Chapter 15 Test (TRB, Resource 15-9).

Using the Handbook

PURPOSE OF THE HANDBOOK

The Handbook is a convenient reference section which offers students step-by-step procedures, additional career and artist profile information, and optional studio lessons. This material is designed to complement and enrich the narrative and studio lessons that appear earlier in the book.

The Handbook is divided into the following sections:

Part 1 Technique Tips
Part 2 Artist Profiles
Part 3 Career Spotlights
Part 4 Additional Studios

▲ Working on group murals is an excellent way to practice artistic skills, gain recognition, and at the same time, have fun.

HANDBOOK CONTENTS

PART 1: Technique Tips

Drawing Tips

1. Making Gesture Drawings   271
2. Making Contour Drawings   271
3. Drawing with Oil Pastels   271
4. Drawing Thin Lines with a Brush   271
5. Making a Grid for Enlarging   271
6. Using Shading Techniques   272
7. Using Sighting Techniques   272
8. Using a Viewing Frame   273
9. Using a Ruler   273

Painting Tips

10. Cleaning a Paint Brush   273
11. Making Natural Earth Pigments   274
12. Mixing Paint to Change
the Value of Color   274
13. Working with Poster Paints
(School Tempera)   275
14. Working with Watercolors   275

Printmaking Tip

15. Making a Stamp Printing   275

Sculpting Tips

16. Working with Clay   275
17. Joining Clay   275
18. Making a Clay Mold
for a Plaster Relief   276
19. Mixing Plaster   276
20. Working with Papier Mâché   277
21. Making a Paper Sculpture   278

Other Tips

22. Measuring Rectangles   278
23. Making a Mat   279
24. Mounting a Two-Dimensional Work   280
25. Making Rubbings   280
26. Scoring Paper   280
27. Making a Tissue Paper Collage   281
28. Working with Glue   281

PART 2: Artist Profiles

Mary Cassatt   283
Albrecht Dürer   283
Winslow Homer   284
Edward Hopper   284
Wassily Kandinsky   285
Henri Matisse   285
Georgia O'Keeffe   286
Pablo Picasso   286
Raphael (Sanzio)   287
Pierre Auguste Renoir   287
Henri de Toulouse-Lautrec   288
Vincent van Gogh   288
Marie-Louise-Élisabeth Vigée-Lebrun   289
Andrew Wyeth   289

- The **Technique Tips** section offers students step-by-step procedures of how to do specific skills related to the areas of drawing, printmaking, painting, and sculpting. General techniques in these areas are described and, when appropriate, illustrated with line drawings. Other general skills, such as making a mat or using glue are included in this reference section.

- The **Artist Profiles** provide students with background information of fourteen artists whose works appear in the text. The information gives a short biographical sketch about the artist and gives the reader an account of world events which occurred during the artist's life. The material is written in a warm, personal tone and will motivate students to seek more indepth outside information about the artist.

- The **Career Spotlights** introduce students to fourteen careers within the art-related fields. Students are presented with an overview of the type of work and personal qualifications required of a person working in the featured occupation. In the Teacher's Wraparound Edition, addresses are provided so that students can research and obtain further information about the careers that interest them.

- The **Additional Studio** section contains nine studio lessons that provide an extension to various chapters. These lessons can be used as independent practice for gifted and talented students, as cooperative learning projects, or as projects to culminate the objectives of specific chapters. In contrast to the lessons which appear within the text, these lessons generally take an extended period of time to complete. Each studio lesson has been reviewed and given an approximate time allotment that should be allowed.

- Within the Handbook you will find the chapter and lesson reference. The Handbook can be used in conjunction with specific chapters and lessons, or you may wish to use each section of the Handbook for independent study. For example, if you want to cover careers or art history in two separate weeks, you can use the Artist Profiles for one week and Career Spotlights for the next week. Regardless of the way you integrate the material, the Teacher's Wraparound Edition offers additional information in the outside column to help you teach, apply, and reinforce these materials.

PART 3: Career Spotlights

Advertising Artist	291
Animator	291
Architect	292
Art Adviser to Corporations	292
Art Director for the Performing Arts	293
Art Teacher	293
Art Therapist	294
City Planner	294
Exhibit and Display Designer	295
Fashion Designer	295
Industrial Designer	296
Interior Designer	296
Landscape Architect	297
Museum Curator	297

PART 4: Additional Studios

Lesson 1 **Print Motifs**	298
• Examining Your Work	299
Lesson 2 **Action Painting**	300
• Examining Your Work	301
Lesson 3 **Group Mural**	302
• Examining Your Work	303
Lesson 4 **Pop-up Cityscape**	304
• Examining Your Work	307
Lesson 5 **Applique Banner**	308
• Examining Your Work	311
Lesson 6 **Wire Sculpture**	312
• Safety Tip	313
• Examining Your Work	313
Lesson 7 **Freestanding Mobile**	314
• Examining Your Work	315
Lesson 8 **A Picture that Tells a Story**	316
• Examining Your Work	317
Lesson 9 **Pinhole Camera Photography**	318
• Safety Tip	318
• Examining Your Work	319

1. Making Gesture Drawings

Gesture drawing is a way of showing movement in a sketch. Gesture drawings have no outlines or details. You are not expected to draw the figure. Instead, you are expected to draw the movement, or what the figure is doing. Follow these guidelines:

- Use the side of the drawing tool. Do not hold the medium as you would if you were writing.
- Find the lines of movement that show the direction in which the figure is bending. Draw the main line showing this movement.
- Use quickly drawn lines to build up the shape of the person.

2. Making Contour Drawings

Contour drawing is a way of capturing the feel of a subject. When doing a contour drawing, remember the following pointers:

- If you accidentally pick up your pen or pencil, don't stop working. Place your pen or pencil back where you stopped. Begin again from that point.
- If you have trouble keeping your eyes off the paper, ask a friend to hold a piece of paper between your eyes and your drawing paper. Another trick is to place your drawing paper inside a large paper bag as you work.
- Tape your paper to the table so it will not slide around. With a finger of your free hand, trace the outline of the object. Record the movement with your drawing hand.

- Contour lines show ridges and wrinkles in addition to outlines. Adding these lines gives roundness to the object.

3. Drawing with Oil Pastels

Oil pastels are sticks of pigment held together with an oily binder. The colors are brighter than wax crayon colors. If you press heavily you will make a brilliant-colored line. If you press lightly you will create a fuzzy line. You can fill in shapes with the brilliant colors. You can blend a variety of color combinations. For example, you can fill a shape with a soft layer of a hue and then color over the hue with a heavy layer of white to create a unique tint of that hue.

If you use oil pastels on colored paper, you can put a layer of white under the layer of hue to block the color of the paper.

4. Drawing Thin Lines with a Brush

Drawing thin lines with a brush can be learned with a little practice. Just follow these steps:

1. Dip your brush in the ink or paint. Wipe the brush slowly against the side, twirling it between your fingers until the bristles form a point.
2. Hold the brush at the beginning of the metal band near the tip. Hold the brush straight up and down.
3. Imagine that the brush is a pencil with a very sharp point. Pretend that pressing too hard will break the point. Now touch the paper lightly with the tip of the brush and draw a line. The line should be quite thin.

   To make a thinner line still, lift up on the brush as you draw. After a while, you will be able to make lines in a variety of thicknesses.

5. Making a Grid for Enlarging

Sometimes the need arises to make a bigger version of a small drawing. An example is when you create a mural based on a small sketch. Follow these steps:

1. Using a ruler, draw evenly spaced lines across and up and down your original drawing (Figure T–1). Count

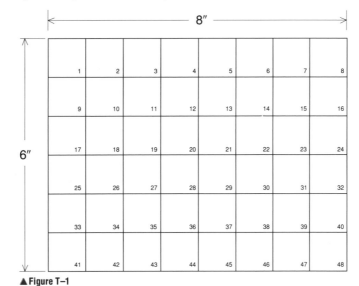

▲ **Figure T–1**

TECHNIQUE TIPS

Using the Technique Tips

The technique tips listed on these and the following pages give students helpful hints for handling different media and tools. There are two types of technique tips. One type offers students step-by-step procedures which should be followed sequentially in order to achieve optimal results. The other type contains procedures and helpful suggestions that students may use as required by their individual studio projects.

USING THE DRAWING TIPS

1. Making Gesture Drawings
   Use with:
   - Chapter 8, Lesson 2, page **148**, Gesture Drawing.
2. Making Contour Drawings
   Use with:
   - Chapter 8, Lesson 3, page **150**, Contour Drawing.
3. Drawing with Oil Pastels
   Use with:
   - Chapter 5, Lesson 2, page **83**, Formal Balance Cityscape.
   - Chapter 8, Lesson 5, page **155**, Fantasy Jungle.
4. Drawing Thin Lines with a Brush
   Use with:
   - Chapter 7, Lesson 4, page **129**, Painting in the Fauve Style.
   - Chapter 10, Lesson 2, page **183**, Watercolor Painting.
5. Making a Grid for Enlarging
   Use with:
   - Chapter 11, Lesson 4, page **201**, Designing a Poster.
   - Handbook, Additional Studio Lesson 3, page **302**, Group Mural.

Classroom Management
Try these suggestions to help stretch your school budget:
- Some drawings look better without a mat. A backing board with a lightweight acetate covering will do the trick. If the drawing is on tracing paper or vellum, however, there needs to be a piece of inexpensive white poster or tagboard between the corrugated board and the drawing. The corrugated board will discolor any drawing in a few years. Thin paper shows the corrugation ridges from the backing.
- Check with the local art club to see if it has a benevolence fund for aid to education. Check with the local art directors' club, designer's association, or society of illustrators (in cities larger than 300,000).
- Tracing vellum and some watercolor papers can be bought less expensively in rolls or by the foot than by the sheet or pads. A 100% rag, twenty-pound vellum is tough—and you can iron the back of it to smooth it after using liquid media.

6. Using Shading Techniques
   Use with:
   • Chapter 8, Lesson 2, page **147**, The Art of Drawing, Studio Experience.
7. Using Sighting Techniques
   Use with:
   • Chapter 1, Lesson 1, page **3**, The Art Experience, Studio Experience.
   • Chapter 4, Lesson 5, page **69**, Shape, Form, and Space, Studio Experience.
   • Chapter 14, Lesson 1, page **241**, The Art of Architecture, Studio Experience.
8. Using a Viewing Frame
   Use with:
   • Chapter 4, Lesson 8, page **74**, Painting a Landscape.
   • Chapter 10, Lesson 2, page **182**, Watercolor Painting.
9. Using a Ruler
   Use with:
   • Chapter 5, Lesson 2, page **82**, Formal Balance Cityscape.
   • Chapter 8, Lesson 4, page **153**, Presentation Drawing.
   • Chapter 11, Lesson 1, page **195**, The Art of Graphic Design, Studio Experience.
   • Chapter 11, Lesson 2, page **196**, Designing a Logo.
   • Chapter 11, Lesson 3, page **198**, Drawing a Comic Strip.
   • Chapter 11, Lesson 4, page **200**, Designing a Poster.
   • Chapter 14, Lesson 3, page **244**, Drawing Floor Plans.
   • Handbook, Additional Studio Lesson 4, page **304**, Pop-up Cityscape.

the number of squares you made from side to side. Count the number of squares running up and down.

2. Measure the width of the surface to which the drawing is to be transferred. Divide that figure by the number of side-to-side squares. The resulting number will be the horizontal measure of each square. You may work in inches or centimeters. Using a ruler or yardstick, mark off the squares. Draw in light rules.

3. Measure the height of the surface to which the drawing is to be transferred. Divide that figure by the number of up-and-down squares. The resulting number will be the vertical measure of each square. Mark off the squares. Draw in pencil lines.

4. Starting at the upper left, number each square on the original drawing. Give the

same number to each square on the large grid. Working a square at a time, transfer your image. (See Figure T–2.)

6. Using Shading Techniques

When using shading techniques, keep in mind the following:
• Lines or dots placed close together create dark values.
• Lines or dots placed far apart, on the other hand, create light values. To show a change from light to dark, start with lines or dots far apart and little by little bring them close together.
• Use care also to follow the shape of the object when adding lines. Straight lines are used to shade an object with a flat surface. Rounded lines are used to shade an object with a curved surface.

7. Using Sighting Techniques

Sighting is a technique that will help you draw objects in proportion.

1. Face the object you plan to draw. Hold a pencil straight up and down at arm's length. Your thumb should rest against the side of the pencil and be even with the tip.

2. Close one eye. With your other eye, focus on the object.

3. Slide your thumb down the pencil until the exposed part of the pencil matches the object's height. (See Figure T–3.)

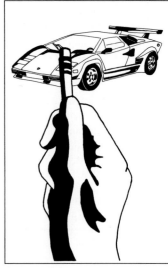

▲ **Figure T–3**

4. Now, without moving your thumb or bending your arm, turn the pencil sideways.

5. Focus on the width of the object. If the height is greater, figure out how many "widths" will fit in one "height." If the width is greater, figure out how many "heights" will fit in one "width."

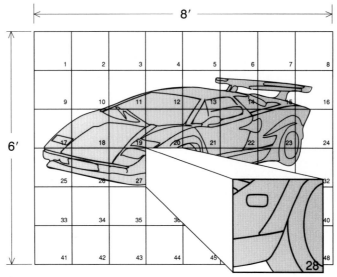

▲ **Figure T–2**

Cooperative Learning

Explain to students that thumbnail sketches are small sketches drawn quickly to record ideas and information for a finished drawing. Tell them that they are called thumbnail because they are almost small enough (5 x 5 inches, [13 x 13 cm]) to have been drawn on a thumbnail. Explain that they are usually done with pen and ink.

Have students think about situations in which the artist would prefer to use thumbnail sketches. For example, graphic artists and illustrators use them to record ideas and also to show ideas to other artists, art directors, and executives. Have students work in small groups and develop a series of thumbnail sketches that could be used to plan a series of paintings of animal totems, or symbols of ancestry. When students have completed their sketches, have them display their work.

8. Using a Viewing Frame

Much in the way a camera is used to focus on one area of a scene, you can better zero in on an object you plan to draw by using a viewing frame (Figure T–4). To make a viewing frame do the following:

1. Cut a rectangular hole in a piece of paper about 2 inches (3 to 5 cm) in from the paper's edges.
2. Hold the paper at arm's length and look through the hole at your subject. Imagine that the hole represents your drawing paper.
3. Decide how much of the subject you want to have in your drawing.
4. By moving the frame up, down, sideways, nearer, or farther, you can change the focus of your drawing.

9. Using a Ruler

There are times when you need to draw a crisp, straight line. By using the following techniques, you will be able to do so.

1. Hold the ruler with one hand and the pencil with the other.
2. Place the ruler where you wish to draw a straight line.
3. Hold the ruler with your thumb and first two fingers. Be careful that your fingers do not stick out beyond the edge of the ruler.
4. Press heavily on the ruler so it will not slide while you're drawing.
5. Hold the pencil lightly against the ruler.
6. Pull the pencil quickly and lightly along the edge of the ruler. The object is to keep the ruler from moving while the pencil moves along its edge.

▲ **Figure T–4**

USING THE PAINTING TIPS

10. Cleaning a Paint Brush
   Use with:
- Chapter 3, Lesson 3, page **41**, Painting, Studio Experience.
- Chapter 4, Lesson 2, page **57**, Color, Studio Experience.
- Chapter 4, Lesson 3, page **61**, Using Color Combinations.
- Chapter 10, Lesson 1, page **181**, The Art of Painting, Studio Experience.
- Handbook, Additional Studio Lesson 1, page **298**, Print Motifs.
- Handbook, Additional Studio Lesson 2, page **300**, Abstract Action Painting.
- Handbook, Additional Studio Lesson 3, page **302**, Group Mural.
- Handbook, Additional Studio Lesson 8, page **316**, A Painting That Tells a Story.

PAINTING TIPS

10. Cleaning a Paint Brush

Cleaning a paint brush properly helps it last a long time. *Always*:

1. Rinse the thick paint out of the brush under running water. Do not use hot water.
2. Gently paint the brush over a cake of mild soap, or dip it in a mild liquid detergent (Figure T–5).

▲ **Figure T–5**

Developing Perceptual Skills

Tell students that seeing the item they are drawing as a whole rather than just a collection of parts results in more successful drawings. Explain that the fact that we naturally see things as a whole was discovered in Germany in 1912 by a psychologist named Max Wertheimer. He founded a branch of psychology called Gestaltism. The German word gestalt means pattern or form. According to Gestalt psychology, we only recognize objects by seeing total patterns or forms, not by adding up the individual parts we see. Tell students that in making most drawings, they should do the large shapes first and add the details later. Encourage them to think in terms of the Gestalt view of life.

11. Making Natural Earth Pigments
Use with:
- Chapter 3, Lesson 4, page **42**, Experimenting with Pigment.

12. Mixing Paint to Change the Value of Color
Use with:
- Chapter 4, Lesson 2, page **57**, Color, Studio Experience.
- Chapter 4, Lesson 3, page **61**, Using Color Combinations.
- Chapter 5, Lesson 4, page **89**, Abstract Painting.
- Handbook, Additional Studio Lesson 1, page **298**, Print Motifs.
- Handbook, Additional Studio Lesson 2, page **300**, Abstract Action Painting.
- Handbook, Additional Studio Lesson 3, page **302**, Group Mural.
- Handbook, Additional Studio Lesson 8, page **316**, A Painting That Tells a Story.

13. Working with Poster Paints
Use with:
- Chapter 3, Lesson 2, page **37**, Printmaking, Studio Experience.
- Chapter 10, Lesson 3, page **185**, Non-objective Painting.
- Handbook, Additional Studio Lesson 1, page **298**, Print Motifs.
- Handbook, Additional Studio Lesson 2, page **300**, Abstract Action Painting.
- Handbook, Additional Studio Lesson 4, page **304**, Pop-up Cityscape.
- Handbook, Additional Studio Lesson 8, page **316**, A Painting That Tells a Story.

14. Working with Watercolors
Use with:
- Chapter 3, Lesson 4, page **43**, Experimenting with Pigment.
- Chapter 4, Lesson 2, page **57**, Color, Studio Experience.
- Chapter 4, Lesson 2, page **59**, Color, Studio Experience.
- Chapter 13, Lesson 5, page **232**, Jewelry.

3. Gently scrub the brush against the palm of your hand to work the soap into the brush. This removes paint you may not have realized was still in the brush.

4. Rinse the brush under running water while you continue to scrub your palm against it (Figure T–6).

▲ **Figure T–6**

5. Repeat steps 2, 3, and 4 as needed.

When it is thoroughly rinsed and excess water has been squeezed from the brush, shape your brush into a point with your fingers (Figure T–7). Place the brush in a container with the bristles up so that it will keep its shape as it dries.

▲ **Figure T–7**

11. Making Natural Earth Pigments

Anywhere there is dirt, clay, or sand, there is natural pigment. To create your own pigments, gather as many different kinds of earth colors as you can. Grind these as finely as possible. (If you can, borrow a mortar and pestle.) (See Figure T–8.) Do not worry if the pigment is slightly gritty.

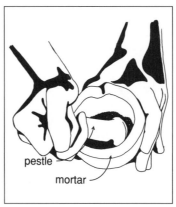

pestle

mortar

▲ **Figure T–8**

To make the binder, mix equal parts of white glue and water. Place a few spoonfuls of your powdered pigment into a small jar. Add a little of the binder. Experiment with different amounts of each.

When you work with natural pigments, remember always to wash the brushes before the paint in them has a chance to dry. The glue from the binder can ruin a brush. As you work, stir the paint every now and then. This will keep the grains of pigment from settling to the bottom of the jar.

Make a fresh batch each time you paint.

12. Mixing Paint to Change the Value of Color

You can better control the colors in your work when you mix your own paint. In mixing paints, treat opaque paints (for example, tempera) differently from transparent paints (for example, watercolors).

- *For light values of opaque paints.* Mix only a small amount of the hue to white. The color can always be made stronger by adding more of the hue.
- *For dark values of opaque paints.* Add a small amount of black to the hue. Never add the hue to black.
- *For light values of transparent paints.* Thin a shaded area with water (Figure T–9). This allows more of the white of the paper to show through.
- *For dark values of transparent paints.* Carefully add a small amount of black to the hue.

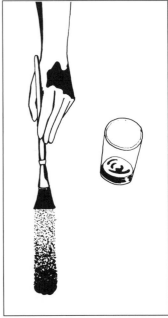

▲ **Figure T–9**

13. Working with Poster Paints (School Tempera)

When using poster paints (school tempera) remember the following:

• Poster paints run when wet. To keep this from happening, make sure one shape is dry before painting a wet color next to it.

14. Working with Watercolors

• If you apply wet paint to damp paper, you create lines and shapes with soft edges.
• If you apply wet paint to dry paper, you create lines and shapes with sharp, clear edges.
• If you dip a dry brush into damp paint and then brush across dry paper, you achieve a fuzzy effect.
• School watercolors come in semi-moist cakes. Before you use them, place a drop of water on each cake to let the paint soften. Watercolor paints are transparent. You can see the white paper through the paint. If you want a light value of a hue, dilute the paint with a large amount of water. If you want a bright hue, you must dissolve more pigment by swirling your brush around in the cake of paint until you have dissolved a great deal of paint. The paint you apply to the paper can be as bright as the paint in the cake.

15. Making a Stamp Printing

A stamp print is an easy way to make repetitive designs. The following are a few suggestions for making a stamp and printing with it. You may develop some other ideas after reading these hints. Remember, printing reverses your design, so if you use letters, be certain to cut or carve them backwards.

• Cut a simple design into the flat surface of an eraser with a knife that has a fine, precision blade.
• Cut a potato, carrot, or turnip in half. Use a paring knife to carve a design into the flat surface of the vegetable.
• Glue yarn to a bottle cap or a jar lid.
• Glue found objects to a piece of corrugated cardboard. Make a design with paper-clips, washers, nuts, leaves, feathers, or anything else you can find. Whatever object you use should have a fairly flat surface. Make a handle for the block with masking tape.
• Cut shapes out of a piece of inner tube material. Glue the shapes to a piece of heavy cardboard.

There are several ways to apply ink or paint to a stamp:
• Roll water-based printing ink on the stamp with a soft brayer.
• Roll water-based printing ink on a plate and press the stamp into the ink.
• Apply tempera paint or school acrylic to the stamp with a bristle brush.

16. Working with Clay

To make your work with clay go smoothly, always do the following:

1. Dip one or two fingers in water.
2. Spread the moisture from your fingers over your palms.

Never dip your hands in water. Too much moisture turns clay into mud.

17. Joining Clay

If you are creating a piece of sculpture that requires joining pieces, do the following:

1. Gather the materials you will need. These include clay, slip, (a creamy mixture of clay and water), a paint brush, a scoring tool, (perhaps a kitchen fork) and clay tools.
2. Rough up or scratch the two surfaces to be joined (Figure T–10).

▲ **Figure T–10**

USING THE PRINTMAKING TIP

15. Making a Stamp Printing Use with:
• Chapter 3, Lesson 2, page **37**, Printmaking, Studio Experience.
• Handbook, Additional Studio Lesson 1, page **298**, Print Motifs.

USING THE SCULPTING TIPS

16. Working with Clay Use with:
• Chapter 12, Lesson 3, page **215**, Modeling in Clay.
• Chapter 13, Lesson 2, page **227**, Clay Bowl.
• Chapter 13, Lesson 3, page **229**, Slab Container.
• Chapter 14, Lesson 4, page **246**, Clay Entrance Relief.

Classroom Management
Remind students to always wipe any remaining ink from a block and brayer after they have finished printing. If they have used a water-based printing ink, they can use water for cleaning. If they have used oil-based ink, however, they should use a solvent such as turpentine. Remember that if they use a solvent, they should be careful not to get the solvent on their skin, or let it come in contact with their eyes.

Classroom Management
Place kilns in a separate room. If that is not possible, locate the kiln in an out-of-the-way part of the room where students are not likely to come into contact when it is in operation. In addition, all kilns should have local exhaust ventilation.

17. Joining Clay
Use with:
- Chapter 12, Lesson 3, page **215**, Modeling in Clay.
- Chapter 13, Lesson 2, page **227**, Clay Bowl.
- Chapter 13, Lesson 3, page **229**, Slab Container.
- Chapter 14, Lesson 4, page **246**, Clay Entrance Relief.

18. Making a Clay Mold for a Plaster Relief
Use with:
- Chapter 12, Lesson 2, page **213**, Carving a Plaster Relief.

19. Mixing Plaster
Use with:
- Chapter 12, Lesson 2, page **213**, Carving a Plaster Relief.

3. Apply slip to one of the two surfaces using a paint brush or your fingers (Figure T–11).

▲ **Figure T–11**

4. Gently press the two surfaces together so the slip oozes out of the joining seam (Figure T–12).

▲ **Figure T–12**

5. Using clay tools and/or your fingers, smooth away the slip that has oozed out of the seam (Figure T–13). You may wish to smooth out the seam as well, or you may wish to leave it for decorative purposes.

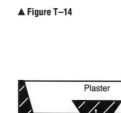

▲ **Figure T–13**

18. Making a Clay Mold for a Plaster Relief

One of the easiest ways to make a plaster relief is with a clay mold. When making a clay mold, remember the following:

- Plaster poured into the mold will come out with the opposite image. Design details cut into the mold will appear raised on the relief. Details built up within the mold will appear indented in the relief.
- Do not make impressions in your mold that have *undercuts* (Figure T–14). Undercuts trap plaster, which will break off when the relief is removed. When cutting impressions, keep the deepest parts the narrowest.
- In carving a raised area in the mold, take care not to create a reverse undercut (Figure T–15).

If you want to change the mold simply smooth the area with your fingers.

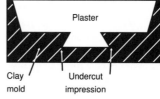

▲ **Figure T–14**

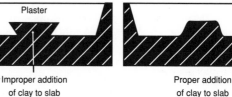

▲ **Figure T–15**

19. Mixing Plaster

Mixing plaster requires some technique and a certain amount of caution. It can also be a very simple matter when you are prepared. Always do the following:

- Use caution when working with dry plaster. Wear a dust mask or work in a well-ventilated room.
- Cover your work space to keep the dust from spreading.
- Always use a plastic bowl and a stick for mixing. Never use silverware you will later eat from.
- Always use plaster that is fine, like sifted flour. Plaster should never be grainy when dry.
- Always add the water to the bowl first. Sift in the plaster. Stir slowly.
- Never pour unused plaster down a drain. Allow it to dry in the bowl. To remove the dried plaster, twist the bowl. Crack the loose plaster into a lined trash can.

Background Information

Pottery is any object made from clay and hardened by fire. Pottery is also the name given to the craft of making such objects. Another word for both is *ceramics*. On its way to becoming finished pottery, clay takes six different forms. These are:
- *Plastic clay*—clay wet enough to be worked but dry enough to hold its shape.
- *Slip*—clay with enough water added to make it runny. Slip is used to glue together shaped pieces of damp clay.
- *Leather hard clay*—clay which is still damp but too hard to model. Pieces of leather hard clay can be joined with slip.
- *Greenware*—very dry clay that will break easily. An object at the greenware stage is ready to be fired.
- *Bisqueware*—fired pottery that is hard but still not ready to use.
- *Glazeware*—pottery coated with powdered chemicals that melt during firing into a hard, glass-like finish.

Most ceramic objects are made hollow. This is so they will not explode or crack during firing.

20. Working with Papier-Mâché

Papier-mâché (**pay**-puhr muh-**shay**) is a French term meaning "chewed paper." It is also the name of several sculpting methods using newspaper and liquid paste. These methods can be used to model tiny pieces of jewelry. They can also be used to create life-size creatures.

In creating papier-mâché sculptures, the paper-and-paste mixture is molded over a support. You will learn more about supports shortly. The molded newspaper dries to a hard finish. The following are three methods for working with papier-mâché:

- **Pulp Method**. Shred newspaper, paper towels, or tissue paper into tiny pieces. (Do not use glossy magazine paper; it will not soften.) Soak your paper in water overnight. Press the paper in a kitchen strainer to remove as much moisture as possible. Mix the mashed paper with commercially prepared papier-mâché paste or white glue. The mixture should have the consistency of soft clay. Add a few drops of oil of cloves to keep the mixture from spoiling. A spoonful of linseed oil makes the mixture smoother. (If needed, the mixture can be stored at this point in a plastic bag in the refrigerator.) Use the mixture to model small shapes. When your creations dry, they can be sanded. You will also be able to drill holes in them.
- **Strip Method**. Tear newspaper into strips. Either dip the strips in papier-mâché paste or rub paste on them. Apply the strips to your support (Figure T–16). If you do not want the strips to stick to your

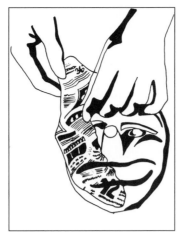

▲ **Figure T–16**

support, first cover it with plastic wrap. Use wide strips for large shapes. Use thin strips for smaller shapes. If you plan to remove your finished creation from the support, apply five or six layers. (Change directions with each layer so you can keep track of the number.) Otherwise, two or three layers should be enough. After applying the strips to your support, rub your fingers over the surface.

As a last layer, use torn paper towels. The brown paper towels that are found in schools produce an uncomplicated surface on which to paint. Make sure no rough edges are sticking up. Store any unused paste mixture in the refrigerator to keep it from spoiling.
- **Draping Method**. Spread papier-mâché paste on newspaper. Lay a second sheet on top of the first. Smooth the layers. Add another layer of paste and another sheet of paper. Repeat until you have four or five layers of paper. Use this method for making drapery on a figure. (See Figure T–17.) If you allow the lay-

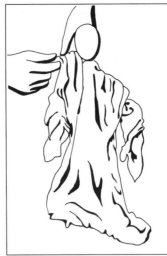

▲ **Figure T–17**

ers to dry for a day or two, they will become leathery. They can then be cut and molded as you like. Newspaper strips dipped in paste can be used to seal cracks.

Like papier-mâché, supports for papier-mâché creations can be made in several different ways. Dry newspaper may be wadded up and wrapped with string or tape (Figure T–18). Wire coat hangers may be padded with rags. For large figures, a wooden frame covered with chicken wire makes a good support.

▲ **Figure T–18**

20. Working with Papier Mâché
Use with:
- Material in the Teacher's Resource Binder.
21. Making a Paper Sculpture
Use with:
- Chapter 3, Lesson 5, page **47**, Sculpture, Studio Experience.
- Chapter 4, Lesson 6, page **70**, Paper Sculpture Forms.
- Chapter 12, Lesson 4, page **216**, Abstract Sculpture.
- Handbook, Additional Studio Lesson 7, page **314**, Free-standing Mobile.

Classroom Management
Most art teachers work with a variety of students who may have physical limitations. Here are some suggestions. At the beginning of each school year or new term, determine if any of your students are asthmatic, visually impaired or hearing impaired, or on prescribed medication. If asthmatic students are enrolled in the art class, they should not be exposed to dusts, fumes, or vapors because of breathing difficulties. Visually impaired students understandably operate very close to their art work, and as a consequence, are more likely to inhale dusts, vapors, and fumes. Students with hearing impairments should not be exposed to activities requiring loud hammering or noisy machinery. This could aggravate their condition. If students are found to be on medication, the teacher should seek a physician's advice regarding the potential harmful interaction between the prescribed medicine and art materials used in the class.

OTHER TIPS

22. Measuring Rectangles
Use with:
- Chapter 11, Lesson 3, page **199**, Drawing a Comic Strip.
- Handbook, Additional Studio Lesson 3, page **302**, Group Mural.
- Handbook, Additional Studio Lesson 4, page **304**, Pop-up Cityscape.
- Handbook, Additional Studio Lesson 7, page **314**, Free-standing Mobile.

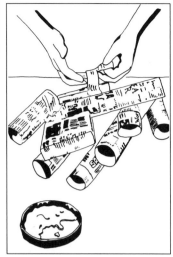

▲ Figure T–19

To create a base for your papier-mâché creations, tape together arrangements of found materials. Some materials you might combine are boxes, tubes, and bowls. (See Figure T–19.) Clay can also be modeled as a base. If clay is used, be sure there are no undercuts that would keep the papier-mâché from lifting off easily when dry. (For an explanation of undercuts, see Technique Tip **18**, *Handbook* page **276**.)

Always allow time for your papier-mâché creations to dry. The material needs extra drying time when thick layers are used or when the weather is damp. An electric fan blowing air on the material can shorten the drying time.

21. Making a Paper Sculpture

Another name for paper sculpture is origami. The process originated in Japan and means "folding paper." Paper sculpture begins with a flat piece of paper. The paper is then curved or bent to produce more than a flat

surface. Here are some ways to experiment with paper.

- **Scoring.** Place a square sheet of heavy construction paper, 12 x 12 inch (30 x 30 cm), on a flat surface. Position the ruler on the paper so that it is close to the center and parallel to the sides. Holding the ruler in place, run the point of a knife or a pair of scissors along one of the ruler's edges. Press down firmly but take care not to cut through the paper. Gently crease the paper along the line you made. Hold your paper with the crease facing upward.
- **Pleating.** Take a piece of paper and fold it one inch from the edge. Then fold the paper in the other direction. Continue folding back and forth.
- **Curling.** Hold one end of a long strip of paper with the thumb and forefinger of one hand. At a point right below where you are holding the strip, grip it lightly between the side of a pencil and the thumb of your other hand. In a quick motion, run the pencil along the strip. This will cause the strip to curl back on itself. Don't apply too much pressure, or the strip will tear. (See Figure T–20.)

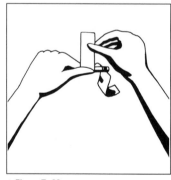

▲ Figure T–20

22. Measuring Rectangles

Do you find it hard to create perfectly formed rectangles? Here is a way of getting the job done:

1. Make a light pencil dot near the long edge of a sheet of paper. With a ruler, measure the exact distance between the dot and the edge. Make three more dots the same distance in from the edge. (See Figure T–21.)

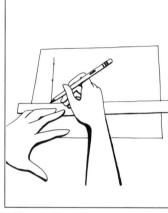

▲ Figure T–21

2. Line a ruler up along the dots. Make a light pencil line running the length of the paper.
3. Turn the paper so that a short side is facing you. Make four pencil dots equally distant from the short edge. Connect these with a light pencil rule. Stop when you reach the first line you drew. (See Figure T–22.)
4. Do the same for the remaining two sides. Erase any lines that may extend beyond the box you have made.
5. Trace over the lines with your ruler and pencil.

The box you have created will be a perfectly formed rectangle.

Classroom Management

The instructional strategy that is probably most familiar to art teachers is demonstration. This is an especially effective method of instruction when applied to studio activities. When preparing for a demonstration always practice beforehand using the same materials students will be expected to use. Include continuous commentary with the demonstration explaining in detail what you are doing and why you are doing it this way. To be of maximum value to students, the demon-stration must be amplified by a detailed explanation of every action. When this is done, students receive information by way of the eyes and ears, increasing the likelihood that this information will be understood and assimilated.

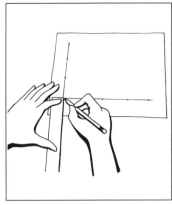

▲ Figure T–22

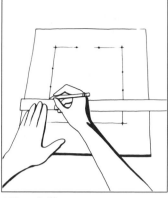

▲ Figure T–23

23. Making a Mat

You can add appeal to an art work by making a mat, using the following steps.

1. Gather the materials you will need. These include a metal rule, a pencil, mat board, cardboard backing, a sheet of heavy cardboard to protect your work surface, a mat knife with a sharp blade, and wide masking tape.

2. Wash your hands. Mat board should be kept very clean.

3. Measure the height and width of the work to be matted. Decide how large a border you want for your work. (A border of approximately 2½ inches on three sides with 3 inches on the bottom is aesthetically pleasing.) Your work will be behind the window you will cut.

4. Plan for the opening, or window, to be ¼ inch smaller on all sides than the size of your work. For example, if your work measures 9 by 12 inches, the mat window should measure 8½ inches (9 inches minus ¼ inch times two) by 11½ inches (12 inches minus ¼ inch times two). Using your metal rule and pencil, lightly draw your

window rectangle on the back of the board 2½ inches from the top and left edge of the mat. (See Figure T–23.) Add a 2½ inch border to the right of the window and a 3 inch border to the bottom, lightly drawing cutting guidelines.

Note: If you are working with metric measurements, the window should overlap your work by 0.5 cm (centimeters) on all sides. Therefore, if your work measures 24 by 30 cm, the mat window measures 23 cm (24 − [2 x 0.5]) by 29 cm (30 − [2 x 0.5]).

▲ Figure T–24

5. Place the sheet of heavy, protective cardboard on your work surface. Place the mat board, pencil marks up, over the cardboard. Holding the metal rule firmly in place, score the first line with your knife. Always place the metal rule so that your blade is away from the frame. (See Figure T–24.) In case you make an error you will cut into the window hole or the extra mat that is not used for the frame. Do not try to cut through the board with one stroke. By the third or fourth stroke, you should be able to cut through the board easily.

6. Working in the same fashion, score and cut through the board along all the window lines. Be careful not to go beyond the lines. Remove the window.

7. Cut a cardboard backing for your art work that is slightly smaller than the overall size of your mat. Using a piece of broad masking tape, hinge the back of the mat to the backing. (See Figure T–25.)

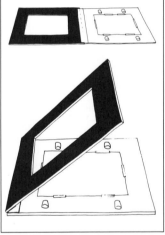

▲ Figure T–25

Technique Tips **279**

23. Making a Mat
Use with:
- Chapter 3, Lesson 2, page **37**, Printmaking, Studio Experience.
- Chapter 3, Lesson 3, page **41**, Painting, Studio Experience.
- Chapter 3, Lesson 4, page **42**, Experimenting with Pigment.
- Chapter 4, Lesson 2, page **57**, Color, Studio Experience.
- Chapter 4, Lesson 2, page **59**, Color, Studio Experience.
- Chapter 4, Lesson 3, page **61**, Using Color Combinations.
- Chapter 5, Lesson 2, page **83**, Formal Balance Cityscape.
- Chapter 5, Lesson 4, page **89**, Abstract Painting.
- Chapter 7, Lesson 6, page **135**, Time and Place Collage.
- Chapter 8, Lesson 2, page **148**, Gesture Drawing.
- Chapter 8, Lesson 3, page **150**, Contour Drawing.
- Chapter 8, Lesson 5, page **155**, Fantasy Jungle.
- Chapter 9, Lesson 2, page **165**, More About Printmaking, Studio Experience.
- Chapter 9, Lesson 3, page **166**, Monoprints.
- Chapter 9, Lesson 4, page **168**, Glue Prints.
- Chapter 9, Lesson 5, page **170**, Linoleum Block Prints.
- Chapter 9, Lesson 6, page **172**, Silk Screen Prints.
- Chapter 10, Lesson 1, page **181**, The Art of Painting, Studio Experience.
- Chapter 10, Lesson 3, page **185**, Non-objective Painting.
- Chapter 11, Lesson 1, page **195**, The Art of Graphic Design, Studio Experience.
- Chapter 11, Lesson 2, page **196**, Designing a Logo.
- Chapter 11, Lesson 3, page **198**, Drawing a Comic Strip.
- Chapter 11, Lesson 4, page **200**, Designing a Poster.
- Chapter 11, Lesson 5, page **202**, Illustrating a Story.
- Chapter 15, Lesson 2, page **256**, Making a Photogram.
- Chapter 15, Lesson 6, page **264**, Designing a Video Game.
- Handbook, Additional Studio Lesson 1, page **298**, Print Motifs.
- Handbook, Additional Studio Lesson 2, page **300**, Action Painting.
- Handbook, Additional Studio Lesson 8, page **316**, A Picture That Tells a Story.

Classroom Management

Always supervise students carefully. Adequate supervision of students is required for both safety and liability reasons. Safety rules should be posted and explained at the start of each term—and these rules should be rigidly enforced. At no time should students be allowed to work in the classroom without direct supervision. Teachers should also make it a rule that students not bring to class and use their own art materials. It is possible that these art materials could contain unknown hazards.

24. Mounting a Two-Dimensional Work
   Use with:
   - Chapter 3, Lesson 2, page **37**, Printmaking, Studio Experience.
   - Chapter 3, Lesson 3, page **41**, Painting, Studio Experience.
   - Chapter 3, Lesson 4, page **42**, Experimenting with Pigment.
   - Chapter 4, Lesson 2, page **59**, Color, Studio Experience.
   - Chapter 4, Lesson 3, page **61**, Using Color Combinations.
   - Chapter 5, Lesson 2, page **83**, Formal Balance Cityscape.
   - Chapter 5, Lesson 4, page **89**, Abstract Painting.
   - Chapter 7, Lesson 6, page **135**, Time and Place Collage.
   - Chapter 8, Lesson 2, page **148**, Gesture Drawing.
   - Chapter 8, Lesson 3, page **150**, Contour Drawing.
   - Chapter 8, Lesson 5, page **155**, Fantasy Jungle.
   - Chapter 9, Lesson 2, page **165**, More About Printmaking, Studio Experience.
   - Chapter 9, Lesson 3, page **166**, Monoprints.
   - Chapter 9, Lesson 4, page **168**, Glue Prints.
   - Chapter 9, Lesson 5, page **170**, Linoleum Block Prints.
   - Chapter 9, Lesson 6, page **172**, Silk Screen Prints.
   - Chapter 10, Lesson 1, page **181**, The Art of Painting, Studio Experience.
   - Chapter 10, Lesson 3, page **185**, Non-objective Painting.
   - Chapter 11, Lesson 1, page **195**, The Art of Graphic Design, Studio Experience.
   - Chapter 11, Lesson 2, page **196**, Designing a Logo.
   - Chapter 11, Lesson 3, page **198**, Drawing a Comic Strip.
   - Chapter 11, Lesson 4, page **200**, Designing a Poster.
   - Chapter 11, Lesson 5, page **202**, Illustrating a Story.
   - Chapter 15, Lesson 2, page **256**, Making a Photogram.
   - Chapter 15, Lesson 6, page **256**, Designing a Video Game.
   - Handbook, Additional Studio Lesson 1, page **298**, Print Motifs.
   - Handbook, Additional Studio Lesson 2, page **300**, Abstract Action Painting.
   - Handbook, Additional Studio Lesson 8, page **316**, A Painting That Tells a Story.

Position your art work between the backing and the mat and attach it with tape. Anchor the frame to the cardboard with a few pieces of rolled tape.

24. Mounting a Two-Dimensional Work

Mounting pictures that you make gives them a professional look. To mount a work, do the following:

1. Gather the materials you will need. These include a yardstick, a pencil, poster board, a sheet of heavy cardboard, a knife with a very sharp blade, a sheet of newspaper, and rubber cement.
2. Measure the height and width of the work to be mounted. Decide how large a border you want around the work. Plan your mount size using the work's measurements. To end up with a 3-inch (8 cm) border, for example, make your mount 6 inches (15 cm) wider and higher than your work. Record the measurements for your mount.
3. Using your yardstick and pencil, lightly draw your mount rectangle on the back of the poster board. Measure from the edges of the poster board. If you have a large paper cutter available, you may use it to cut your mount.
4. Place the sheet of heavy cardboard on your work surface. Place the poster board, pencil marks up, over the cardboard. Holding the yardstick firmly in place along one line, score the line with your knife. Do not try to cut through the board with one stroke. By the third try, you should be able to cut through the board.

▲ Figure T–26

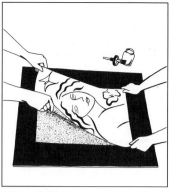

▲ Figure T–27

5. Place the art work on the mount. Using the yardstick, center the work. Mark each corner with a dot. (See Figure T–26.)
6. Place the art work, face down, on a sheet of newspaper. Coat the back of the work with rubber cement. (*Safety Note:* Always use rubber cement in a room with plenty of ventilation.) *If your mount is to be permanent, skip to Step 8.*
7. Line up the corners of your work with the dots on the mounting board. Smooth the work into place. *Skip to Step 9.*
8. After coating the back of your art work, coat the poster board with rubber cement. Be careful not to add cement to the border area. Have a partner hold your art work in the air by the two top corners. Once the two glued surfaces meet, you will not be able to change the position of the work. Grasp the lower two corners. Carefully lower the work to the mounting board. Line up the two corners with the bottom dots. Little by little, lower the work into place (Figure T–27). Press it smooth.

9. To remove any excess cement, create a small ball of nearly dry rubber cement. Use the ball of rubber cement to pick up excess cement.

25. Making Rubbings

Rubbings make interesting textures and designs. They may also be used with other media to create mixed media art. To make a rubbing, place a sheet of thin paper on top of the surface to be rubbed. Hold the paper in place with one hand. With the other hand, rub the paper with the flat side of an unwrapped crayon. Always rub away from the hand holding the paper. Never rub back and forth, since this may cause the paper to slip.

26. Scoring Paper

The secret to creating neat, sharp folds in cardboard or paper is a technique called scoring. Here is how it is done:

1. Line up a ruler along the line you want to fold.
2. Lightly run a sharp knife or scissors along the fold line. Press down firmly enough to leave a light crease. Take care not to cut all the way through the paper (Figure T–28).

280   *Technique Tips*

Classroom Management
Remind students to clean up thoroughly and often. They should make certain to clean up spills immediately to prevent accidents. If dust results, have them use a wet mop or vacuum rather than a broom. Sweeping stirs up dust that could prove harmful to some students, particularly those who are asthmatic.

▲ **Figure T–28**

3. Gently crease the paper along the line you made.
To score curved lines, use the same technique. Make sure your curves are wide enough to ensure a clean fold. Too tight a curve will cause the paper to wrinkle (Figure T–29).

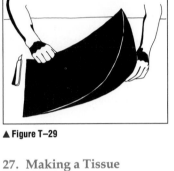

▲ **Figure T–29**

27. Making a Tissue Paper Collage

For your first experience with tissue, make a free design with the tissue colors. Start with the lightest colors of tissue first and save the darkest for last. It is difficult to change the color of dark tissue by overlapping it with other colors. If one area becomes too dark, you might cut out a piece of white paper, glue it over the dark area carefully, and apply new colors over the white area.

1. Apply a coat of adhesive to the area where you wish to place the tissue.
2. Place the tissue down carefully over the wet area (Figure T–30). Don't let your fingers get wet.
3. Then add another coat of adhesive over the tissue. If your brush picks up any color from the wet tissue, rinse your brush in water and let it dry before using it again.
4. Experiment by overlapping colors. Allow the tissue to wrinkle to create textures as you apply it. Be sure that all the loose edges of tissue are glued down.

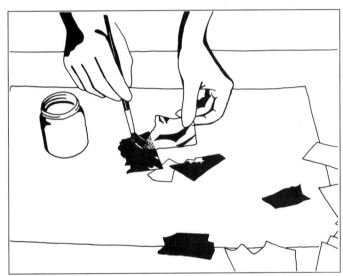

▲ **Figure T–30**

28. Working with Glue

When applying glue, always start at the center of the surface you are coating and work outward.

- When gluing papers together don't use a lot of glue, just a dot will do. Use dots in the corners and along the edges. Press the two surfaces together. Keep dots at least ½ inch (1.3 cm) in from the edge of your paper.
- Handle a glued surface carefully with only your fingertips. Make sure your hands are clean before pressing the glued surface into place.
- *Note:* The glue should be as thin as possible. Thick or beaded glue will create ridges on your work.

25. Making Rubbings
    Use with:
    - Chapter 3, Lesson 2, page **37**, Printmaking, Studio Experience.
26. Scoring Paper
    Use with:
    - Chapter 3, Lesson 5, page **47**, Sculpture, Studio Experience.
    - Chapter 4, Lesson 6, page **70**, Paper Sculpture Forms.
    - Chapter 12, Lesson 4, page **216**, Abstract Sculpture.
    - Handbook, Additional Studio Lesson 7, page **314**, Free-standing Mobile.
27. Making a Tissue Paper Collage
    Use with:
    - Chapter 7, Lesson 6, page **135**, Time and Place Collage.
    - Chapter 9, Lesson 5, page **171**, Linoleum Block Prints.
    - Chapter 11, Lesson 1, page **195**, The Art of Graphic Design, Studio Experience.
28. Working with Glue
    Use with:
    - Chapter 2, Lesson 3, page **25**, Torn Paper Face.
    - Chapter 4, Lesson, 6, page **70**, Paper Sculpture Forms.
    - Chapter 7, Lesson 6, page **135**, Time and Place Collage.
    - Chapter 9, Lesson 5, page **171**, Linoleum Block Prints.
    - Chapter 11, Lesson 1, page **195**, The Art of Graphic Design, Studio Experience.
    - Handbook, Additional Studio Lesson 4, page **304**, Pop-up Cityscape.
    - Handbook, Additional Studio Lesson 7, page **314**, Free-standing Mobile.

Classroom Management

To protect drawings you can spray them with fixative to protect them from smearing. Drawings in just about any medium will be damaged by rubbing against other surfaces if they aren't sprayed.

Spray fixative is sold both in aerosol cans and in small bottles with atomizers. Fixative in a bottle is applied by blowing through the atomizer. Test the spray first on a piece of scrap marked with the same drawing medium used in the drawing.

Avoid getting the spray device too close to the drawing. Hold the spray device 12 to 18 inches (30 to 46 cm) from it. Keep the sprayer moving. Several light coats are better than one heavy one. Fixative dries rapidly. Spray fixative labeled *workable* is best. This term means that after you spray an area of a drawing lightly, you can still draw on it.

When using spray fixative, always use it outside the studio in a well-ventilated area—outdoors, if possible. Breathing the fixative over a long period of time can be lethal.

Using the Artist Profiles

Role playing, games, and bulletin boards can be effective ways to involve students and to help them grasp information about the various artists, the time in which the artists lived, their particular art style and techniques, and their contributions to the world of art. On the following pages are teaching strategies designed to help you introduce, reinforce, and teach students about artists and their works.

▲ Artists, down through the ages, have helped us visualize what we learn about history. Art historians are responsible for much of what we know about the artists who have lived in the past.

Mary Cassatt

1845–1926
American Painter

At the Opera
page 16

Maternal Caress
page 35

The second half of the 1800s was an unparalleled age of discovery. People had learned to harness the power of steam to run locomotives. Streetcars powered by electricity rumbled down cobblestone streets.

For American-in-Paris Mary Cassatt (kuh-**sat**) the age was also one of discovery—bitter discovery. Cassatt had come to Paris to continue the study of painting she had begun in Philadelphia. What she soon discovered was that women had to work twice as hard as men to get noticed in the Paris art world.

Cassatt, however, refused to be beaten. Back home in Pittsburgh, she had overcome her parents' resistance, who were against her becoming an artist. She would not give in now.

One day a painting in a shop window caught her eye. It was by the great artist Edgar Degas (day-**gah**). She was unable to take her eyes off the work. "I used to go and flatten my nose against the window," she later said. "It changed my life."

It also gave direction to Cassatt's career. The soft lines and gentle colors of Degas's Impressionist paintings set the tone for her own works. Works by Cassatt, such as *Maternal Caress*, (page **35**), combine great skill and sensitivity. Much of her work includes women and children as subjects. Today she is widely held to be one of America's finest painters.

The early 1500s were a time of conquest. The Spanish conquistadors had already conquered major parts of North and South America.

The spirit of conquest was being felt in other parts of the world as well. In the world of German art, a bold new conqueror had emerged. His name was Albrecht Dürer (**ahl**-brekt **dure**-uhr).

Dürer was born in Nuremberg, Germany. He was the second oldest in a family of 18 children. When Albrecht was young, his parents assumed he would become a goldsmith, like his father. But the young Dürer showed unusual skill at drawing. At 15, he was sent to study with a local painter.

Like most young German artists of the day, Dürer learned Gothic style. But a trip he made to Italy while in his early twenties changed everything. There the period of artistic awakening known as the Renaissance was in full progress.

Dürer returned to Nuremberg with a fresh view of the world and the artist's place in it. He turned away from his Gothic style and went about the task of becoming a Renaissance artist. Working hard, he learned how to capture the beauty and balance he found in Italian painting. The ideals he taught himself show up in such works as his engraving on page **158**.

Albrecht Dürer

1471–1528
German Painter, Printmaker

The Four Horsemen of the Apocalypse
page 158

Visual Presentation. Divide the class into groups of two or three and assign different time periods to each group. Have each group research that period and report on it to the class. Encourage the students to use as many visual aids as they can, and to use the school media center and local library. Suggest that they use large prints of art works if they are available; the library is a good source of either prints or oversize art books. The media center might have equipment with which the students can make slides from books to use in the report. Slides ensure that everyone in the class can see the works being discussed. Dressing up in costumes, role playing, or presenting a dramatization can also make a report more enjoyable and meaningful for everyone.

Dramatization. A good choice for a dramatization is one event from the artist's life. Dramatizations make stronger impressions than straight reports. For example a debate on style between the Impressionists and Post-Impressionists would be interesting, especially if students took on the roles of real characters, such as Monet, Renoir, Cézanne, or van Gogh.

Artist Profiles **283**

Background Information

Tell students that Dürer was the first artist to complete a true self-portrait. Students may be pleasantly surprised, when you tell them that he was only thirteen years old when he created the work.

After students have read the Artist Profile above, elaborate upon Dürer's life by telling students that he was the second son in a family of eighteen. Explain that he was interested all of his life in reproducing his own sensitive and often troubled features with pencil and paint. Perhaps the worry often seen in his self-portraits was due to the religious conflict between Martin Luther and the Catholic Church. The artist became involved in the controversy. Finally, Dürer sided with Luther and became a strong spokesman for change.

Challenge students to research the Protestant Reformation, Martin Luther, or Dürer to find out more about this time in history. Have them report their findings to the class.

Puzzles. Turn some extra prints found in magazines into puzzles. Dry mount the print on a strong backing, such as poster board or mat board. If you are going to make more than one puzzle, put each on a different color backing so that if the pieces get mixed up they can be separated by color. Laminate the work, if possible, to protect the surface. Then, using a sharp cutting blade, cut the print into puzzle pieces. Try to keep the puzzle pieces large to help students become familiar with the art work. Use a separate storage container for each puzzle. Puzzles can help slower learners, or you can use them to hold a puzzle speed competition. Teams of students can compete to see which team can assemble a puzzle the fastest.

Card Games. Use prints in card games to help students become familiar with the names of artists and the titles of the works. To make a card game, mount medium-size prints on poster board, leaving a small margin around the print. Cut the print in fourths. Print the name of the artist and the title in the margin of each section of the print. Laminate the sections to make them last longer. Using about 10 prints (40 sections), create a deck of cards with which the students can play a variation of the card game, "Go Fish." The students must ask for the cards by artist and/or title. If you have many works by one artist, they must always use titles, but if you only have one print from each artist, they may use just artist. The students should request the work by saying, "Do you have any Picasso?" After a player has collected all four sections of a print, that print must be placed on the table for all to see. This exposes all players and observers to the print. The more times the students hear the names repeated, the more they learn. Use artists and works that you think are worth learning about.

Winslow Homer
1836–1910
American Painter

Right and Left
page 2

Return from the Hunt
page 180

The Fog Warning
page 316

It is hard to think of any good coming out of a war. But for Winslow Homer, the American Civil War — or at least the scenes of the front lines he painted — were his passport to public recognition.

Homer was born in Boston. When he was six, his family moved to Cambridge, Massachusetts. At that time, Cambridge was mostly wilderness, and Homer learned to love the outdoors.

Like his love of nature, Homer's interest in art began early. By the time he was about 10, his talent for drawing was obvious to those around him. At 19, Homer went to work for a large Boston printing firm. There he designed covers for song sheets, a job he soon grew tired of.

For the next 17 years, Homer did magazine illustrations, mainly for *Harper's Weekly* in New York. It was for *Harper's* that he did his Civil War drawings and paintings.

After the war, Winslow traveled abroad. His work had become so much in demand that he paid for his trips with money earned by selling his paintings.

After 1883 he devoted his efforts almost totally to nature paintings. His home on the coast of Maine gave him a chance to study, and paint, the sea. Some of his best works, such as *The Fog Warning*, (page **316**), have the sea as their subject.

If you were going to fill a time capsule with symbols of life in mid-twentieth-century America, what would you include? One possibility might be a baseball. Another might be a photograph of a rock group.

Still another might be a painting by Edward Hopper. His works show the emptiness and loneliness that are as much a part of urban living as skyscrapers and traffic.

Hopper was born in Nyack, New York. He trained to be a graphic artist and worked for a time as an illustrator. Hopper did not turn to painting until he was close to 40.

From 1901 to 1906 he studied with Robert Henri, who headed the Ashcan School. Critics provided this label to describe some artists of this period. They used a stark, realistic treatment in their city scenes, painting ashcans and all. Like other members of the group, Hopper used the city as a setting for his pictures. Unlike other members, he did not focus on the glitter and excitement. Rather, Hopper's works capture the impersonal, unfriendly feeling of the big city. People rarely are seen in his pictures. When they are, they are often seen as alone and lonely.

A notable feature of Hopper's work is his use of color to capture a quiet mood. Such a mood can be seen in the bleak but soothing landscape of his *Cottages at North Truro, Massachusetts* (page **42**).

Edward Hopper
1882–1967
American Painter

New York Movie
page 18

Study for Gas
page 31

Cottages at North Truro, Massachusetts
page 42

Drugstore
page 304

Background Information
Tell students that by the close of the nineteenth century, the United States had become a world leader in art. The country's change and growth were reflected in American art. The art of this period is best represented by three artists—Winslow Homer, Albert Pinkham Ryder, and Thomas Eakins. Explain that these artists were known as the American Realists. Have students compare the works of these three artists.

Note
Edward Hopper worked for twenty years designing book covers, illustrations, and advertisements for an advertising agency in New York City. He was forty-three years old when a gallery owner agreed to exhibit his watercolors. A few months after his first exhibition, which was highly successful, Hopper resigned from the agency. He spent the rest of his life drawing and painting.

Wassily Kandinsky

1866–1944
Russian Painter

Improvisation #27
page 39

Several Circles
page 85

In the early 1900s two brothers named Wright proved that humans could harness the capability of flight. Their pioneering efforts at Kitty Hawk changed aviation history for all time.

Around the same time and a continent away, another person was changing history of a different sort. His name was Wassily Kandinsky (**vahs**-uh-lee kan-**din**-skee). The history he was changing for all time was art history.

Kandinsky was born in Russia in 1866. He studied law and worked as a lawyer through his twenties. In 1885 he visited an exhibit of French Impressionist paintings in Moscow. He was so impressed by the works that he found it hard to leave. In the months that followed, his thoughts drifted back to the paintings he had seen. Finally, he left his legal career and went to study painting in Munich, Germany.

In his early years as an artist, Kandinsky moved from one style to another. Then he spent some time experimenting with more original ideas. Around 1910 he completed an interesting watercolor. The work was bright and may have been based on some earlier landscape studies. What was most important about the work was that it had no recognizable subject. Non-objective art had been born! Today works such as *Improvisation #27* (page **39**) hang in the world's top art museums.

In 1889 the Eiffel Tower was built to celebrate the Paris Industrial Exposition. Around that same time, one of France's great artists began his career.

Henri Matisse (ahnh-**ree** mah-**tees**) had been born some 20 years earlier. Growing up in a small town in northern France, Matisse showed little interest in art. When he graduated from high school, his father sent him to Paris to study law.

When he was twenty-one years old, Matisse suffered an attack of appendicitis. He was forced to stay in bed for a long time. To ease his boredom, his mother bought him some paints. Suddenly Matisse felt as if a weight had been lifted. He had discovered an interest and a talent that changed his direction. He decided to become an artist.

While studying painting, Matisse began to experiment with different styles. By 1905 he had developed a style all his own. It made use of flat shapes and simple bold colors. An example of a work using this style is his painting *The Red Studio*, on page **128**.

While Matisse's paintings were revolutionary in his day, today they are hailed as masterpieces. They are seen as fulfillments of the goal Matisse had set for himself. That goal was to create "an art of purity and serenity without depressing subject matter."

Henri Matisse

1869–1954
French Painter

Woman in a Purple Coat
page 84

The Red Studio
page 128

Artist Profiles **285**

Time–Period Recognition Game.
If you can find individual prints that are small enough, you might organize them into a time-period recognition game. For example, you might set up one deck with four Ancient Egyptian works, four Gothic, four Renaissance, four African-American, four Near East, and so forth. At the beginning of the year you can use stick-on labels that identify the periods. Later you can remove the labels. Be careful that each set of four in a deck is distinctly different from every other set in that deck.

Time–Style Recognition Game.
For a more advanced game than the one above, organize the cards by style. In this deck you might include four Impressionist works, four Cubist works, four Surrealist works, and so forth. Again, be careful not to use two styles that might be confused such as American Regionalist and English Landscape.

Background Information
After students have read the Artist Profile of Wassily Kandinsky, tell them that Kandinsky was part of Der Blaue Reiter. Explain that other artists who participated were Jawlensky, Kubin, Gabriele Münter, Klee, Marc, and Macke.

Georgia O'Keeffe

1887–1986
American Painter

Sunrise
  page 41

The Radiator Building
  page 82

The White Calico Flower
  page 212

The 1920s marked the beginning of a new way of living in our country. The easygoing spirit of earlier times had been crushed by the arrival of the automobile. Americans suddenly found themselves rushing from one place to the next. Few had time to stop and think — to notice the beauty in the world around them.

One who did was the painter Georgia O'Keeffe. O'Keeffe had been raised on a small dairy farm in Wisconsin. Her strong interest in both nature and art had begun early. By the time she was 10, she knew she wanted to become a painter.

O'Keeffe's earliest training was in the styles of the great masters of Europe. Their subjects, however, held little interest for her. She wanted, instead, to paint the rocks, mountains, and wide open spaces around her. When she decided at age 29 to focus totally on nature, she burned her earlier work.

Among O'Keeffe's greatest achievements are the close-ups of flowers she began creating in the 1920s. One of these, *The White Calico Flower*, appears on page **212**. To catch the attention of people too busy to notice, she made the close-ups huge. Each fills its canvas with graceful curved surfaces and flowing lines. The beauty of every petal is seen again and again in the greater beauty of the whole flower.

The 1880s brought the world many wonderful inventions, such as the adding machine, the bicycle, and the car. It also brought the world a painter who would produce some of the greatest art in the history of the Western world. His name was Pablo Picasso.

Picasso was born in Malaga, Spain, in 1881. As a boy, he never stopped drawing. In fact, his mother claimed he could draw before he could talk. Everywhere young Picasso went, his pad and pencil went. He liked betting his friends he could draw anything — in one unbroken line — and he always won.

One day his father, a painter and teacher, came home to a surprise. His young son had finished a portrait. After examining the work, Pablo's father gave the boy all his art materials. So great was the boy's work that the father vowed never to paint again.

In his long and full life, Pablo Picasso passed through many different styles. For some time he created the fractured images that were the hallmark of the Cubist movement. He later returned to paintings of the human figure. The painting of *Seated Woman (after Cranach)* on page **170** shows his mastery of media and technique.

Pablo Picasso

1881–1973
Spanish Painter, Sculptor

Three Musicians
  page 118

Seated Woman (after Cranach)
  page 170

Cooperative Learning
Point out to students that Georgia O'Keeffe and Pablo Picasso lived in different countries but during approximately the same years.

Divide the class into pairs. Have one student represent the works of O'Keeffe and the other represent the works of Picasso. The students should pretend that you, the teacher, are a museum curator who is trying to decide upon purchasing a new painting for the museum. Have each student select one work of art by their artist and explain why it should be added to the collection.

Raphael (Sanzio)

1483–1520
Italian Painter

St. George and the Dragon
page **104**

The Small Cowper Madonna
page **132**

It was the eve of Columbus's voyage of discovery to the New World. It was also the eve of a discovery within the art world. A young boy in Columbus's native Italy showed a gift for art that was rare. The boy's name was Rafaello—or, in English, Raphael.

Raphael was born in a small town in central Italy. His first teacher was probably his father, who was a painter for a noble family. While still a child, Raphael studied with an artist named Perugino (pehr-uh-**jee**-noh). Perugino taught the youth how to use soft colors and simple circular forms. He taught him how to create gentle landscapes. Soon the student's work began to be mistaken for the teacher's. Young Raphael knew it was time to move on.

He went to Florence to study the works of the leading artists of the day. Among his teachers there were the two giants of art, Leonardo da Vinci and Michelangelo. From Leonardo, he learned how to use shading to create a sense of depth. From Michelangelo, he learned how to breathe life into his figures. Both these ideas are present in his masterpiece *St. George and the Dragon* (page **104**).

Raphael died when he was only 37. Yet the works he left behind rank him as one of the great artists of the Renaissance.

Maps. Have world maps and globes available to help students locate cities and countries where the artists lived and worked. This helps students to visualize the geographical features that influenced the artists' work.

Time Line. Display a time line in the class. Have students attach sketches of the masterpieces shown in the text in the proper spot on the time line. They might even add small prints of works that are not in the text or photocopy works from books, color the photocopies, and add the name of the artist and the title of the work. If there is not enough room for all the pieces at one place in time, strings of yarn can be attached to the photocopy and pictures arranged above or below the proper place with yarn leading to the proper place on the time line.

After the Brooklyn Bridge opened in 1883, bridge building would never be the same. After an exhibition of paintings in Paris a year later, art would never be the same. The exhibition contained works by a group who came to be known—at first, jokingly—as Impressionists. One of the group's leaders was a man named Renoir.

Pierre Auguste Renoir (pee-**air** oh-**goost** ren-**wahr**) was born in 1841. His artistic talents became apparent early. By 13, he was already making a living as an artist in a porcelain factory. His job was painting scenes on pieces of china. His earnings helped pay for his education at a famous Paris art school, the Ecole des Beaux-Arts.

It was at school that Renoir met two other young artists, Claude Monet (moh-**nay**) and Alfred Sisley. The three soon became friends. They also began experimenting together by making paintings outdoors in natural sunlight. Their goal was to give objects a shimmering, sunlit quality. At first, their works were scorned by critics. Today they are among the most admired in the history of art.

Unlike most of his fellow Impressionists, Renoir was interested in painting the human figure. His painting, *Girl with a Watering Can* (page **121**) highlights the best features of his own Impressionist style.

Pierre Auguste Renoir

1841–1919
French Painter

Girl with a Watering Can
page **121**

Regatta at Argenteuil
page **126**

Artist Profiles **287**

Note
Much of Raphael's work has a spiritual quality. In fact, one of his most frequent subjects was the Madonna and Child. He, like no other artist, was able to combine subtle shading and rich coloring with life-like forms in a perfectly balanced composition. The blending of all these elements gave the impression of a spiritual harmony, which was in keeping with the many religious subjects that Raphael portrayed. His style shows the Renaissance art at its peak—a balanced unity of forms, at once both natural and ideal.

Henri de Toulouse-Lautrec

1864–1901
French Printmaker, Painter

La Gitane
page 36

Jane Avril
page 190

The year 1864 was one of promising beginnings and promising endings. Union troops marched into Georgia, signaling a swift end to the Civil War. The birth of a baby boy in the town of Albi, France, promised new happiness for the Toulouse-Lautrec (tuh-**loose** low-**trek**) family.

Although no one knew it, baby Henri's arrival also held great promise for the art world. The Toulouse-Lautrecs were an old and wealthy French family. Henri's parents taught their child from an early age to appreciate art. By the age of 10, young Henri was making sketches. This was no surprise since his grandfather, father, and uncle were all draftsmen.

When he was 14, Henri broke both legs in two separate accidents. Although the limbs healed, they never grew properly. All his life he was self-conscious about his deformed legs and dwarf-like appearance.

This did not prevent Toulouse-Lautrec from becoming interested in the dazzling night life of Paris. He loved to sit in cafes and watch the colorful scene. He always carried a sketchpad and often would record what he saw.

Today the remarkable prints he created, many based on his sketches, are thought to be art treasures. One of these, of the performer *Jane Avril*, appears on page **190**.

By the late 1880s trains had become a popular form of transportation. A spirit of restlessness had gripped the Western world. Certainly one of the period's most important artists felt that restlessness. His name was Vincent van Gogh (van **goh**).

You may already know some of the facts of van Gogh's brief life. You have probably heard how he went mad and cut off his earlobe. You may know that he ended his own life at age 37. What you may not know is that this genius left the world 1600 remarkable art works.

Vincent van Gogh was born and raised in a small Dutch village. He spent much of his life contemplating his existence. He tried — and failed at — many different careers, including teaching and the ministry. At last he turned to art, which long had been a passion.

Van Gogh's first paintings were drab and dull. In 1886 he moved to Paris. There he was moved by several artistic forces. One was the color used in Impressionist paintings. Another was the style of Japanese woodcuts.

Van Gogh was not content simply to capture a scene. Instead, he needed to express his deep feelings about it. These feelings come through in short brush strokes of bright, intense color. An example of his unique style may be found in *Cypresses* (page **64**).

Vincent van Gogh

1853–1890
Dutch Painter

Cypresses
page 64

Garden of the Rectory at Nuenen
page 94

Cooperative Learning

Have students select works by van Gogh and Toulouse-Lautrec that contain a similar subject. For example, van Gogh's *The Night Cafe* and Toulouse-Lautrec's *Monsieur Boileau at the Cafe*. Although both paintings have a similar subject (night life), students should work in pairs and make comparisons between the similarities and differences of the two works. Have them analyze the following elements of both paintings:

- Value—How does each artist depict light and shadows? Are shadows realistic or expressive?
- Color—What hues do the artists choose? What effect do the artists' choices of hues have on the works?
- Shape and space—What points of view do the artists choose? How much space does each picture represent?

Marie-Louise-Élisabeth Vigée-Lebrun

1755–1842
French Painter

Theresa, Countess Kinsky
page 131

La Princesse Barbe Gallitzin
page 149

When the French Revolution began in 1789, members of the ruling class fled. So did the woman who had painted many of them, Marie-Louise-Élisabeth Vigée-Lebrun (ay-**lee**-zah-bet vee-**zhay**-luh-**bruhn**).

Élisabeth Vigée-Lebrun's life story reads almost like a novel. She studied art in a convent. Before she was 20, she had painted many important French nobles. By age 25, she was working for Queen Marie-Antoinette. She did some 20 portraits of the queen.

The night the king and queen were arrested, Vigée-Lebrun escaped from Paris. The revolution had temporarily interrupted her career as a portrait painter. Luckily, she was able to continue her work in other capitals of Europe. Everywhere she went, there were requests for portraits. By the time she turned 35, she had earned over a million francs. This was a huge sum of money for an artist to have earned.

Vigée-Lebrun's portraits were very flattering to her subjects. She overlooked any flaws she saw. As in her portrait of *Theresa, Countess Kinsky* (page **131**), she gave all her subjects large eyes.

When Vigée-Lebrun died, a palette and brush were carved on her gravestone as she had asked. It was a fitting tribute to an artist who had completed over 800 paintings in her lifetime.

In the year 1917 the world was politically unsettled. Many of the major powers were at war. Russia was in the midst of a revolution. It was an odd time for an artist devoted to simple, quiet subjects to emerge. Such an artist is Andrew Wyeth.

Andrew Wyeth was the son of N. C. Wyeth, a successful illustrator of adventure stories. As a child, Andrew was sick much of the time. Since his father had little use for public schools anyway, Andrew was educated at home. As a boy, he was constantly drawing and painting with watercolors.

When Wyeth was 20, he had his first exhibit in New York. Every painting in the show was sold.

Several of Wyeth's paintings are based on Christina Olson, a family friend crippled by polio. One of these, *Christina's World* (page **115**), was made after Wyeth watched Christina bravely pull herself home using her arms. As Wyeth himself has explained, the work is more than a portrait. It is a glimpse of Christina's whole life and the things she experienced in it.

Wyeth creates his works by making many, many studies of a subject. For these, he uses both pencil and watercolor. He does his finished works using egg tempera.

Andrew Wyeth

1917–
American Painter

Christina's World
page 115
(detail) page 179

COLOR REPRODUCTION SUPPLIERS

Harry N. Abrams
100 E. 59th Street
New York, NY 10022

Art Education, Inc.
28 E. Erie Street
Blauvelt, NY 10913

Art Extension Press
Box 389
Westport, CT 06881

Associated American Artists
663 Fifth Avenue
New York, NY 10022

Catalda Fine Arts
12 W. 27th Street
New York, NY 10001

Imaginus, Inc.
R. R. 1, Box 552
Lee, MA 01238

Metropolitan Museum of Art
Book and Art Shop
Fifth Avenue and 82nd Street
New York, NY 10028

Museum of Modern Art
11 W. 53rd Street
New York, NY 10019

National Gallery of Art
Department of Extension Programs
Washington, DC 20565

New York Graphic Society
140 Greenwich Avenue
Greenwich, CT 06830

Oestreicher's Prints
43 W. 46th Street
New York, NY 10036

Penn Prints
31 W. 46th Street
New York, NY 10036

Konrad Prothmann
2378 Soper Avenue
Baldwin, NY 11510

Raymond and Raymond, Inc.
1071 Madison Avenue
New York, NY 10028

Reinhold Publishing Company
600 Summer Street
PO Box 1361
Stamford, CT 06904

Shorewood Reproductions
Department S
475 10th Avenue
New York, NY 10018

UNESCO Catalogues
Columbia University Press
562 W. 113th Street
New York, NY 10025

University Prints
21 East Street
Winchester, MA 01890

Note
For additional information about Marie-Louise Élisabeth Vigée-Lebrun you may wish to refer to the Background Information on page **131**.

Note
For additional information about Andrew Wyeth refer to the Background Information on pages **114** and **115**.

Using the Career Spotlights

On the pages that follow you will find teaching suggestions to help you introduce students to the many art-related job opportunities and careers. At the bottom of the page you will find a list of addresses of organizations that students can write for additional information.

▲ There are many careers available in the field of commercial art. This group is discussing a display.

Advertising Artist

Every time you watch a TV commercial, you are experiencing the work of an advertising artist. The same goes for hearing radio commercials as well as reading magazine and newspaper ads. Advertising artists are people whose job is to help sell a product using art.

The field of advertising art dates back at least to ancient Egypt. A papyrus found in an ancient Egyptian tomb offers a reward for a runaway slave. In the Middle Ages, town criers often peppered their news announcements with advertisements for local businesses.

Nowadays advertising artists usually work as members of teams under the leadership of art directors. Some tasks of the ad artist might include designing illustrations and photographs for ads. Advertising artists are also often called upon to pick typefaces.

The success of advertising art is measured by how many people notice the advertisement and how well the product sells.

Animator

When the art of the motion picture was born, a number of fields were born with it. One of these was the field of animation. Animators are artists who create cartoons and cartoonlike figures for film and television.

Animators begin their work by picking a story to tell. They also choose the style of architecture and clothing that will fit the story. They then create the story in the form of storyboards. These are still drawings that show the action in the story. Storyboards are a series of panels that look similar to comic books but are larger. The animator will create about 60 sketches for each board. A short film will need three storyboards. A full-length film will require over 25 storyboards.

Once the storyboards have been created, the animators will create the major poses for each character. Other artists assist by filling in the many drawings that complete each movement.

Analyzing Advertisements.
Divide students into small groups. Select a variety of magazines from different interest areas, such as high fashion, mechanics, photography, architecture, teen life, current events, health, sports, science, science fiction, television, and so forth. Have each group compare such things as the types of advertisements and the types of advertising techniques used to capture the attention of the specific audience. Have them present their findings to the class.

Animation. Have students select their favorite cartoon or comic figure. Ask students to pair up with students who have selected a similar cartoon. Using various comic strips by this artist, have students analyze the style, content, and technique that the artist uses in order to get the message across. Have students present their findings to the class and if possible, provide background information about the artist who creates the cartoon.

Animation Research. If a group cannot decide upon a "favorite" cartoon, you may want them to research the field of animation at the library. Or have them find out how to make a flip book and make one and show it to the class.

Career Spotlights **291**

Note
You may wish to have students write to the following for information about careers in advertising management:
American Advertising Federation
1400 K Street NW, Suite 1000
Washington, D.C. 20025

For information on careers in illustration have students contact:
The Society of Illustrators
128 East 63rd Street
New York, New York 10021

Resource People. Bring in resource people during the time that you are presenting careers to make the material more meaningful to students. Students will be interested in learning from people who work directly in the art-related field being presented. You may also invite the guidance counselor to discuss art-related careers and to talk about the various schools and colleges that specialize in these careers.

If you live in an urban area it will not be difficult to find people who work at some of these careers. Even the smallest newspaper in a rural area needs a layout person. The local television station will also employ someone who fits one of the career categories mentioned in this section. Remember that artists are also hired by industry. Other employees to consider are florists or window display people who can demonstrate how they use the elements and principles of art in their jobs.

If you cannot find a commercial artist, a local art hobbyist or craftsperson may substitute, as well as a college art student who may be home on vacation. If there is a local artist in your area, a field trip to this person's studio can be exciting.

Architect

Do you live in an apartment house or a private home? Whichever you live in, you are in a building designed by an architect. Architects are artists who design buildings of all kinds, including residences, office buildings, and museums.

The architect works with two major goals in mind. One is to make sure the building does what it was planned to do. The second goal is to make sure the building is pleasing to the eye. How a structure fits in with its surroundings is also a concern of the architect.

Architects must know a great deal about building materials. They must also understand how weather and other natural elements act on such materials. Architects are also trained in such matters as ventilation, heating and cooling, and plumbing.

Architects must have a strong background in mathematics and drafting. Most architects nowadays specialize in a particular type of building.

Art Adviser to Corporations

Up until a few years ago, the only art found in a company setting was purely decorative. A painting might be used to dress up a waiting area or conference room. Recently, there has been a growing interest among corporations in starting private art collections. With this interest, a new profession has been born — the corporate art adviser.

Art advisers to corporations have a number of duties and responsibilities. One duty is buying new art for the corporation collection. Another is advising the corporation head about tax laws having to do with art. A third duty is arranging traveling exhibitions and speaking to different groups about the collection.

Corporate art advisers often are hired as employees of the company. Sometimes they work on a free-lance basis and advise several companies at once.

Note
Have students contact the following organization to find out information about education and careers in architecture:
Director, Education Programs
The American Institute of Architects
1735 New York Avenue NW
Washington, D.C. 20006

Art Director for the Performing Arts

In order for a performance to run smoothly, a number of people must do their jobs well. In order for these people to do their jobs well, the show must have a strong director.

The art director oversees all the visual elements of the show and makes sure they fit together. Among the many people with whom the director works closely are scenery, costume, and lighting designers.

Art directors must have a background in art history as well as a knowledge of stagecraft. If a play is set in the past, the setting, furniture, and costumes all need to reflect that period.

Art Teacher

Many people with an interest in art and a desire to share their knowledge become art teachers.

A career in art teaching requires a college education. Part of that education is devoted to methods of teaching. Part is devoted to developing a broad background in art history, aesthetics, art criticism, and the use of art materials and techniques.

Good art teachers guide their students through a wide variety of art experiences. They give students the chance to create their own art and to react to the art of others. They also make sure their students learn about such important art subjects as aesthetics, art criticism, and art history.

Field Trips. Field trips contribute greatly to a course. If class field trips are not possible, individual trips which one or more students may take after school or on weekends might be arranged.

All trips will be more successful if guidelines are set up to help students understand the objectives. Research done prior to the trip and a follow-up evaluation will add to the value of the experience. Students should know what to look for and what to expect to gain from the experience. It might be pointed out that the business people they visit may be possible employers and that appropriate conduct and dress on a trip may make a future interview more likely. Students should know what kind of follow-up will be expected. For example, a written evaluation, a quiz, or participation in a class discussion might be required.

The instructor should make the necessary arrangements well in advance to ensure the students' welcome. A time schedule should be established and carefully followed. While museums, organizations, and industries are happy to conduct tours of their facilities, the staff members usually have other responsibilities, and group tours must be prearranged.

Type of Field Trips. Field trip possibilities vary in each community. The suggested list includes trips which are possible in your area. It may also suggest others to you which are not on the list but which would be valuable. Suggestions for possible field trips: Display rooms in furniture stores; model apartments in new apartment buildings; rug and carpet salesrooms; wallpaper stores; interior design studios; decorator showrooms; historic houses and museums; craft shops (weaving, fabric printing, or pottery); advertising agency.

Career Spotlights **293**

Note
Have students contact the following organizations to learn more about teachers' unions and education-related issues:
American Federation of Teachers
555 New Jersey Avenue, NW
Washington, D.C. 20001

National Education Association
1201 16th Street, NW
Washington, D.C. 20036

Art Therapist

In recent years researchers have learned new ways of helping people with emotional problems. One of these ways is through art.

In the field called art therapy people trained as art therapists use art to open lines of communication with patients. Patients are invited to create images using different media. They are then encouraged to discuss the meanings of their creations. This process often serves to release feelings, allowing the therapists to better help the patients.

Art therapists find work in a number of different settings. Some work as members of teams in large hospitals. Others are employed by community health centers or clinics. Still others work in prisons. Some work in special schools for students with learning disabilities.

A career in art therapy requires professional training in psychology and art education.

City Planner

Have you ever wondered how big cities come to look the way they do? The two-word answer to this question is city planners.

City planners are people whose job is to supervise the care and improvement of a city. Every large American city has a planner.

A main task of city planners is to enforce zoning laws. These are laws controlling what part of a city may be used for what purposes. Thanks to city planners, garbage dumps are not located in residential communities.

A second task of the city planner is to look after the growth and development of the city. The planner works with the mayor and other city officials to create parks, harbors, and shopping malls.

City planners are trained as architects. Their knowledge of design helps them to plan a pleasing cityscape.

City Planner. Have students work in small groups and imagine that they have been hired as a city planner team to improve their town. If they live in a big city, have them limit the area to their own neighborhood. Ask them to prepare a survey to ask people what they like most and what they like least about the town or neighborhood. They should find out which building is considered the most important and which is considered the most attractive. Ask about traffic flow, stores, recreation, entertainment, health services, police protection, and water and sewerage. They can add other questions to the survey. Then they should carry out the survey. Have them talk to students at their school and adults who live in the area. Have them put all of their findings in graph or chart form. Compare adult and teen replies. Do the two groups agree or disagree on each item?

Note
For information on careers, educational requirements, and licensing in all fields of psychology, have students contact:
   American Psychological Association
   Educational Affairs Office
   1200 17th Street, NW
   Washington, D.C. 20036

Note
For additional information on careers in urban and regional planning, have students contact:
   American Planning Association
   1776 Massachusetts Avenue, NW
   Washington, D.C. 20036

Exhibit and Display Designer

The next time you pass a display of clothing or other goods in a department store, look carefully. Somewhere within that display will be a hidden message: "Artist at Work."

Exhibit and display designers work in a number of retail and non-profit settings. Some are trade shows, department stores, showrooms, art galleries, and museums. Such designers plan presentations of collections, exhibits, and traveling shows of all kinds. They are responsible for such matters as deciding what items should be grouped together. They also take into account how displays should be lighted.

The display designer is an important part of the sales team. Displays attract customers. They can affect a customer's decision to buy. The way the display designer does his or her job can make all the difference between "sale" and "no-sale."

Fashion Designer

Some art is made to be worn. Creating art of this type is the work of the fashion designer. Fashion designers draw and plan clothing, hats, handbags, gloves, and jewelry.

Fashion designers must learn about different fabrics, colors, and their uses. Matters such as weight and texture are also important in the designing of clothing. A jacket designed for winter wear, for example, must not only be attractive, it must also be warm and comfortable.

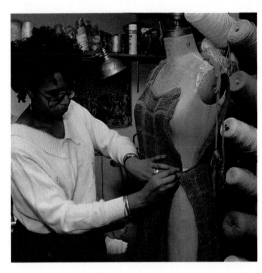

Some fashion designers become involved in high-fashion design. These are the trend-setting fashions that are usually very expensive.

Fashion designers may work either as freelance artists or for clothing manufacturers.

Display Designer. Divide students in small groups and assign them to create either a window display, point-of-purchase display, or exhibit display. Have them select a product of their choice and create a three-dimensional display. Set up criteria for evaluating the display such as: neatness, product identity, eye-catching, informative, and so forth. Set up a panel of students to judge the displays.

Fashion Designer. Tell students that the fashion design industry is a competitive field that requires creativity and originality to continually produce fresh new designs. Have students pretend they are fashion designers for a specific audience, such as: children's clothing, athletic apparel, young teens, special needs, aerobic apparel, dancewear, teen boys, and so forth. Have them sketch a wardrobe for the target audience and include mix-and-match outfits.

Note
Have students contact the following organization for a list of accredited schools of art and design:
   National Association of Schools of Art and Design
   11250 Roger Bacon Drive, Suite 21
   Reston, Virginia 22090

Interior Designer. Divide students into small groups and have each group imagine that they are interior designers who have been asked to plan a student lounge for the school. Before they make their design, they should survey their friends to see what they would like in a lounge. Have them try to think of the lounge as a multipurpose area that could serve as space for a party, a meeting, art exhibits, and so on. What areas will they need to include? Have them use their creativity. Have them make sketches for their lounge and include paint chips, wallpaper and floor covering samples to show the color scheme for the room.

Industrial Designer

What do toys, vacuum cleaners, and cars have in common? All are designed to work easily and have a pleasing look. These and countless other items you see and use each day are the work of industrial designers.

Industrial designers work for makers of products. These artists work closely with engineers who develop the products. Sometimes industrial designers are asked to work on things as simple as tamper-proof caps for medicines. At other times they are asked to work on projects as complicated as space vehicles. Before they begin work, industrial designers need to know how the product is to be used.

Because different brands of the same product are sold, industrial design sometimes crosses over into advertising. The appearance of a design becomes especially important in the case of very competitive products such as cars and entertainment systems, for example.

Interior Designer

Architects give us attractive, functional spaces in which to live, work, and play. Interior designers fill those spaces with attractive and useful furnishings and accessories.

The job of the interior designer is to plan the interior space. This includes choosing furniture, fabrics, floor coverings, lighting fixtures, and decorations. To do this job well, the designer must take into account the wants and needs of the users of the space. In planning a home, for example, the interior designer will learn as much as possible about the lifestyle of the family that lives there.

Interior designers help their clients envision their ideas through the use of floor plans, elevations, and sketches. Once a client has agreed to a plan, the designer makes arrangements for buying materials. He or she also oversees the work for builders, carpenters, painters, and other craftspeople.

Note
For a list of accredited schools of art and design, contact:
   National Association of Schools of Art and Design
   11250 Roger Bacon Drive, Suite 21
   Reston, Virginia 22090
   For information about careers in interior design, contact:
   American Society for Interior Designers
   1430 Broadway
   New York, New York 10018

A brochure that describes careers in industrial design and lists academic programs in the field is available from the Industrial Designers Society of America. For price and ordering information, write:
   Industrial Designers Society of America
   1142-E Walker Road
   Great Falls, Virginia 22066

Landscape Architect

In recent years the role of the landscape architect increasingly has been recognized as very important in making the business and industrial areas of our cities environmentally healthy and aesthetic. Landscape architects are people whose job is to design outdoor areas around buildings. They also create arrangements of shrubs and flowers for playgrounds, parks, and highways.

Landscape architects work closely with architects and city planners to improve the natural setting. Their goal is to make the setting both easy to maintain and beautiful to look at. Landscape architects work with a number of different materials and landforms. These include flowers, plants, trees, rivers, ponds, walks, benches, and signs.

Some landscape architects work independently. Others work for architectural firms, government agencies, or private companies.

Museum Curator

Like universities and libraries, museums have the job of preserving and passing on culture. The person in charge of seeing that the museum does its job is the museum curator (**kyoor**-ayt-uhr).

Curators are part guardian, part restorer, and part historian. The tasks of the curator are many. They include acquiring, caring for, displaying, and studying works of art. The curator makes sure works of art in the museum collection are arranged so the viewer can enjoy as well as learn from museum exhibits.

As holders of advanced college degrees, curators carry on research in their special areas of interest. They report their findings in books, lectures, and journals.

Landscape Architect. Have students imagine that they are landscape architects and they have been asked to redesign the outside area of a local community building, a park, or their school grounds. They should think about how they will be working with color, shape, and form. Ask them to consider what type of plants and construction materials they will use to reshape the environment and integrate buildings with the nature surrounding them.

Note
Additional information, including a list of colleges and universities offering accredited programs in landscape architecture, is available from:
    American Society of Landscape Architects
    4401 Connecticut Avenue NW
    Washington, D.C. 20008

For general information about careers as a curator and schools offering courses in curatorial science, contact:
    American Association of Museums
    1225 I Street NW, Suite 200
    Washington, D.C. 20005

Print Motifs

Using the Additional Studios

LESSON 1

Print Motif

- The Print Motif studio lesson has been provided to give students additional printmaking and design studio experience. This lesson sequentially builds on concepts presented in Chapters 3 and 10.
- The purpose of this lesson is to give students an opportunity to design a motif and use the motif to create a pattern. The pattern will be used for a functional item, such as wrapping paper or a greeting card.
- You may want to use the lesson as an extension of Chapters 3 and 10, as an independent practice for creative and gifted students, as a cooperative learning activity, or as a culminating project. You will need to allow one to two days for students to complete the lesson.
- Suggest that students review the following lessons before beginning the studio lesson:
  Chapter 3, Lesson 2, Printmaking, page **34**;
  Chapter 5, Lesson 6, Creating Visual Movement, page **92**;
  Chapter 9, Lesson 1, Printmaking, page **158**;
  Technique Tip **15**, *Handbook* page **275**.
- Remind students that the definition of motif is a unit that is repeated over and over in a pattern or visual rhythm. Have them look at wallpaper or gift wrapping samples and identify the motifs used in each sample. Point out how the samples used a motif to create a rhythmic pattern.
- Have students practice making different patterns, such as a random pattern, regular pattern, and alternating pattern. Review how each of these pattern schemes can be created (see "Note" page **298**). Give students ample time to sketch and prepare a motif. Have them complete the motif and arrange it in an interesting pattern. Encourage them to think of visual movement as they develop their design.

Artists have always found nature to be a rich source for inspiration. Patterns created by repeated designs can be found in nature all around us. Interesting patterns left in the sand by an insect's tracks can inspire an artist's imagination.

Creating a pattern by repeating a motif can be easily accomplished by using a printing technique. Patterns on fabric, wallpaper, or wrapping paper are often printed. (See Figure S–1.)

WHAT YOU WILL LEARN

You will create a printed pattern to decorate wrapping paper for a special holiday. You will glue bits of styrofoam to a piece of wood to create a relief block for printing. Your wrapping paper will be decorated by a rhythmic pattern created by repeated printing.

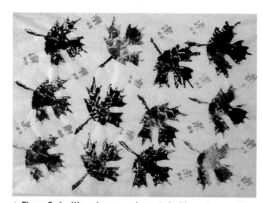

▲ Figure S–1 Wrapping paper decorated with a nature motif.

WHAT YOU WILL NEED

- Scratch paper, pencil, and eraser
- Small piece of wood
- Styrofoam packing trays, or any pieces of reusable styrofoam
- Scissors or cutting knife, glue
- Butcher paper, 12 x 24 inch (30 x 61 cm)
- Printer's ink or tempera paint, brushes
- Newspaper

WHAT YOU WILL DO

1. Consider some of the holidays that are less advertised. You might research a special holiday celebrated in another country. Or you might decide to create wrapping paper that has a personal design for someone special. This person could be someone you know, someone famous or even an imagined character.

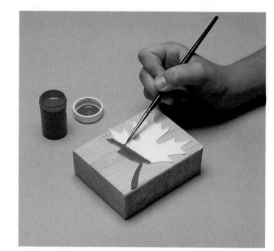

▲ Figure S–2 A student is painting tempera on a styrofoam stamp.

Note

Motifs can be arranged to create interesting designs and different visual rhythms. Here are some possible combinations and ideas:

- **Random pattern.** To create a random pattern, repeat your motif in no apparent order. Draw one motif on the paper. Turn the paper and draw another similar motif. Continue to do this, but vary the space between your prints.

- **Regular pattern.** To create a regular pattern, you will want to place motifs equally spaced. Use a pencil and ruler to draw a grid of equal squares. Place one motif in each square.
- **Alternating pattern.** There are several ways to create alternating patterns. One way is to draw a regular square grid and turn every other motif upside down. An alternate pattern can also be created by using a second motif in every other square.

2. Using pencil and scratch paper sketch some designs that you might use. Remember you will be cutting out a piece of styrofoam to glue on a wood block. Use your pencil to draw the outline of a shape that can be cut out. Keep your design simple. Consider whether your design will have formal or informal balance. Remember even a small motif must have unity or a sense of wholeness to it.

3. Select your best sketch. Draw the shape on the styrofoam and cut it out. If you use more than one shape, carefully determine how they are to be arranged on the wood block. Remember the space between the shapes will be left white. Again think about the unity of your motif. When you are satisfied glue the shape down.

4. Place a pad of newspaper under the butcher paper for better defined prints. Carefully paint the styrofoam shape on your wood block with ink or tempera paint, as shown in Figure S–2, and begin printing. Be sure to add more paint each time you make a print.

EXAMINING YOUR WORK

- **Describe** Point out the shapes in your print. Point out which motifs in your pattern came out most clear. Tell what you did to achieve this clear print. Describe the theme of your wrapping paper.
- **Analyze** Tell whether you used formal or informal balance to create unity in your motif. Tell how you created rhythm with your motif.
- **Interpret** Tell what mood the theme of your motif suggests. Explain how adding different colors to your pattern enhanced the mood.
- **Judge** Tell whether you feel your work succeeds. Explain your answer.

5. You may decide to make prints using different colors. Let the paint dry on your block before adding a new color. Be sure to plan ahead of time when a new color will be added to your pattern.

- Have students display their custom-made wrapping paper or greeting card in a local stationery or giftware store. Ask students to consider a selling price for the wrapping paper and discuss the advantages and value of a custom-made product. Challenge students to consider the entrepreneurial benefits of producing a personalized product such as the wrapping paper. Have them consider the cost of their supplies and their time. Ask them to determine a selling price for the product and estimate their profit.
- You may also wish to use acrylic paints as a medium.
- Instead of painting the medium onto the styrofoam shape, you may want to have the students spread the medium on an inking plate. This way they can work more quickly by pressing the shape into the medium on the plate and transferring it to the receiving material of their choice.

  If they choose to use this technique, they should use styrofoam that is at least a 1/4-inch (6 mm) thick, so that when it is glued to the wooden block, there is enough clearance to keep the medium from touching the face of the wooden block.

OTHER STUDIO IDEAS

- Design a second block print. Create a pattern by printing the two motifs side by side. It will be important that this second wood block be a single shape.
- ● Design a block print that will coordinate with the decor of either the living room of your home, or your bedroom. Choose a color and texture of cloth and color of paint or ink that harmonizes with the room in which it will be displayed. On a piece of cloth about 12 x 18 inches (30 x 46 cm) in size, print a motif using the technique you learned previously. The cloth may be used as a wall-hanging, a place mat, or table runner. It may also be sewn together with another piece of fabric the same size to make a slipcover for a pillow as in Figure S–3.

▲ **Figure S–3** Cloth can also be printed and used for table cloths, napkins, pillow covers, and curtains.

Lesson 1 *Print Motifs* **299**

ADDITIONAL STUDIOS

Action Painting

LESSON 2

Action Painting

- The Action Painting studio lesson has been provided to give students the opportunity to work with paints and to experience some of the expressive qualities of working with paints. This lesson sequentially builds on concepts presented in Chapters 3 and 10.

  In this lesson students will be introduced to the concept of action painting. Some students may want to do additional research to find out more about Jackson Pollock and other Abstract Expressionist painters. As students evaluate Figure S-4, they will develop a sense of the meaning of "action painting." Have students create their own expressive action painting.
- Before students progress with this lesson, you may want them to review the following lessons:
  Chapter 3, Lesson 3, Painting, page **38**;
  Chapter 3, Lesson 4, Experimenting with Pigment, page **42**;
  Chapter 10, Lesson 1, The Art of Painting, page **178**;
  Chapter 10, Lesson 3, Non-objective Painting, page **184**.
- This studio lesson requires close supervision and monitoring by the teacher. Before students begin, remind them to protect their clothing by wearing oversized shirts (or a similar type of coverup) and to protect the area around their painting from splashes of paint. (You may prefer having students work outdoors for this assignment.) Have students consciously think about their feelings as they create their art works. Remind them that the expressive nature of the work is as important as the final product.
- On the chalkboard write the following phrase: "When I paint, I feel. . . ." Ask students to complete the sentence on a separate piece of paper. Collect the anonymous responses and read them to the class. Use these responses as an introduction to the lesson. Tell students that in this lesson they will have the opportunity to combine colors and the process of painting to reflect their own moods and feelings.

300

Look at the painting in Figure S–4. It was created by Jackson Pollock, who created his own technique to accomplish a style of painting, known as *action painting*. The colors in his paintings related to his feelings when he began the work. Notice how the lines appear to move or follow his feelings by being very quickly applied. Sometimes they are slowly dripped and drawn into his canvas. He did not use drawings or color sketches for his works but worked directly on the canvas.

▲ **Figure S–4   Jackson Pollock was known as an action painter. Can you see from this painting why he was called that?**

Jackson Pollock. *Cathedral*. 1947. Enamel and aluminum paint on canvas. 181.6 x 89.1 cm (71½ x 35 1⁄16″). Dallas Museum of Art, Dallas, Texas. Gift of Mr. and Mrs. Bernard J. Reis.

WHAT YOU WILL LEARN

You will create an action painting using tempera on a large sheet of white paper. Choose colors that reflect how you are feeling before you begin to work. Warm colors can be used for feelings of happiness, excitement, or anger. Cool colors can be used to reflect calm, peacefulness, sadness, or serenity.

WHAT YOU WILL NEED

- Sheet of white paper, 12 x 18 inch (30 x 46 cm)
- Tempera paints
- Brushes, varied sizes

WHAT YOU WILL DO

1. Select a color scheme that represents how you feel before you begin to paint. Remember the discussion in Chapter 4, Lesson 2, on the use of monochromatic, analogous, and complementary color schemes. You can create striking art work by combining colors in ways that use tints or shades of the same hue, (monochromatic). You may want to combine colors that share a hue, such as green, blue-green, and yellow-green, (analogous). Or you might choose a third way to combine colors using a complementary color scheme to achieve contrast colors that are opposite each other on the color wheel, for example, yellow and purple.
2. Put a layer or two of newspaper down on the floor and on your work area for protection. Tape the corners of your white paper to the newspaper. Tape the newspaper to the work surface to keep it from moving.

Background Information

Abstract Expressionism is the name of an art movement which occurred after 1950. In this art style, paint is dribbled, spilled, or splashed onto huge canvases to express a feeling. Abstract Expressionist artists steer clear of subject matter in their work. Instead, the act of painting is so tied to their work that the Abstract Expressionists became labeled "action painters."

Other painters, besides Jackson Pollack who excelled in this area, were Arshile Gorky and Helen Frankenthaler.

Frankenthaler's action paintings begin on the floor of her studio. Standing above a blank canvas, the artist pours on layer after layer of thinned color. With each new addition, the work grows. Have students compare the similarities and differences among these Abstract Expressionist painters.

3. Load your brush with the paint. Hold the brush over your paper and let the paint drip from your brush. Let the paint drip to relate to your mood—fast or slow drips. Whether you have fast or slow drips depends on how full your brush is and on the consistency of the paint. A brush full of thin paint will result in fast drips. A brush that is not as full will have slower drips. Also, if the paint you use is thick the drips will be slower.

4. Observe that lines of color will probably dominate your work, but try to create shapes by accident. Be sure to create balance and harmony in your composition.

5. As you examine your art, also check to see if you are achieving balance and harmony. To check for balance look at your entire composition and see if any one area is too overpowering. However, keep in mind that balance need not be symmetrical. Next check for harmony. Make sure the various elements in your work (drip patterns, dark versus light, size of spatters) are blended in a pleasing way to create a harmonious whole.

6. Stop occasionally while you work to look at the parts from every side of the paper.

EXAMINING YOUR WORK

- **Describe** Identify areas in the composition that were a result of fast and slow drips. Point to the way the colors were combined to form a color scheme.
- **Analyze** Tell why you chose the colors you did. Are they warm or cool colors? Do you have fast or slow drips? Does a pattern show in your work? Is there any suggestion of subject in your painting?
- **Interpret** Give your work a title. How do the colors make you feel? Do the drip patterns remind you of anything? Explain why you chose to use fast or slow drips.
- **Judge** Tell whether you feel your work is successful. Explain your answer.

---

7. When you feel your art work is finished, make sure to give the painting enough time to dry in a flat position. If you must move the work to a drying area, carefully carry your painting (still attached to the newspaper) to a flat surface. Let the painting dry and then remove the tape and trim the edges to give a clean professional look to your painting.

8. Show your work to classmates and ask them to interpret your feelings.

OTHER STUDIO IDEAS

- To achieve another effect, you may want to dip strings into different hues of paint. Then holding the string at either end, keeping it taut, lay it down across the paper. Make several lines by redipping the string. Do one hue at a time, giving each a chance to dry before using the next color. By laying the strings across the paper in perpendicular patterns, you can make geometric designs.
- • Marble art is another technique for a different effect. Choose three hues of paint and put each one in a different tin, filling the dish so there is a layer of paint covering the bottom. Put a marble in each tin.

Now fold some paper towels to use as you work. Place your art paper inside a shallow box lid. Take one of the marbles and put it in the lid on top of the paper. Tilt the lid so the marble rolls, causing paint tracks across the paper. Vary the track's shape and direction as you wish. When you are finished with that color put the marble in the extra dish, wipe your hands and start on your next color. Don't make too many tracks the first time because you still have two more marbles to go. Let your art work dry in the lid or on a flat surface.

- You may also want to play an assortment of different types of music, including classical, jazz, hard rock, country, and so forth. Have students close their eyes and think about how the different sounds make them feel and discuss how their body movement would respond to the various styles of music. Explain that this same expressive nature can be experienced while they are painting.
- Students may be uncomfortable with this lesson because they want to create a more realistic piece of art. Remind students that different aesthetic viewpoints can be used to evaluate works of art. Ask them to identify the best aesthetic viewpoint that would be used to evaluate Figure S-4.
- Another technique for varying the design is to lay cut-out paper shapes on the larger sheet of white paper before starting the paint drips or spatters. Paper strips, circles, squares, rectangles, or free-form shapes can add interest. Have the students carefully pick up the cut-out shapes after one or two colors have been dripped and the medium is dry. Then they can continue dripping with other different color paints.
- This studio requires some caution and controlled use of the tools and media so that paint doesn't wind up on everything else in the room besides the paper at which the students are aiming.

Group Mural

LESSON 3

Group Mural

- The Group Mural studio lesson has been provided to give groups of students the opportunity to collaborate on a group project. This lesson builds sequentially on skills presented in Chapters 8, 10, and 11.
- The purpose of this lesson is to have students plan, create, and execute a wall mural. In the process the students will be using mathematical calculations to create a grid and enlarge the picture so that it becomes a wall mural.
- This is one project that must involve the teacher. Based on the experience of many teachers, it is suggested that, although the mural can be planned during class time, it is almost impossible to find the energy to complete one during the school day or after school. It is best to plan a few long weekend sessions rather than daily short sessions. Otherwise, students will tire of the project before it is half completed.
- Before students begin the group mural project, have them review the following lessons:
  Chapter 3, Lesson 3, Painting, page **38**;
  Chapter 3, Lesson 4, Experimenting with Pigment, page **42**;
  Chapter 10, Lesson 1, The Art of Painting, page **178**;
  Chapter 11, Lesson 1, The Art of Graphic Design, page **192**.
- Be sure to consult with administrators or community officials and obtain written permission before beginning a group mural.
- Showing students slides or photographs of murals that have been completed is a great source of inspiration for students. You may also want to introduce students to the works of artists such as Diego Rivera and David Alfaro Siqueiros. Discuss the similarities and differences among paintings that are done on canvas and those that are done as murals.

Have you ever seen large pictures painted on walls of buildings? These pictures are called murals. Look at the mural in Figure S–5. What are the dimensions of the mural? Do you wonder how the artist was able to draw the mural on the wall and keep everything in proportion to one another?

To make murals, artists begin by making a small drawing on paper. They add details and color. Next they create an enlarging grid that is in proportion to the finished product. Using the grid as a guide, the picture is drawn on the wall. (See Technique Tip **5**, *Handbook* page **271**.)

WHAT YOU WILL LEARN

You will work with your classmates to create a wall mural. The mural will be planned for a specific wall in your school or community. Before you begin, get permission from your art teacher and school administrators and determine how the project will be financed. If that is not possible you can paint on butcher paper or plywood and display your art work temporarily in an appropriate area.

WHAT YOU WILL NEED

- Sketch paper, pencil, and eraser
- Ruler, tape measure, yardstick, or meterstick
- Chalk
- Acrylic paints and brushes
- Specific wall to be painted
- Drop cloth
- Safe ladder
- Cleaning materials, such as sponges, soaps, and buckets of water

WHAT YOU WILL DO

1. As a group brainstorm ideas that could be used for a mural. The subject for your mural could be based on native traditions, school or community events, or social statements. Discuss possibilities and as a group decide on a theme for the mural.
2. Develop thumbnail sketches based on the theme. Show these sketches to community officials, school administrators, teachers, and other students. Make adjustments to the plan as needed.

▶ **Figure S–5** This is an example of a wall mural. Wall murals are popular all over the world. Why do you think this is so?

Daniel Alonzo. *A Whale of a Mural.* 1983. Two city blocks long.

Background Information
You may want to refer students to *Detroit Industry* on page **178** by Diego Rivera. Remind students that Diego Rivera worked on murals that depicted the history of Mexico and the life and problems of the people.

Tell students that *Detroit Industry* is one of several commissions which Rivera had in America. Explain to students that when the work was finished, there was much controversy because many felt that all classes of society, not just the working class, should be included. However, despite protests, the murals were allowed to remain.

Rivera saw his murals as a way of teaching the illiterate. Medieval stained-glass windows had served a similar purpose. They instructed the illiterate of that era in the stories of the Bible. Rivera's murals combined a unique use of line, shape, and space to express social themes. In doing so, he brought this teaching tool to new heights.

3. Identify the specific wall where the mural may be painted. Measure the length and width of the area that the final product will take. Determine the materials which make up the wall. Consult with your teacher to find out what pre-treatment is necessary and what medium should be used on the wall.

4. Assign one or two people to render the final composition, which includes ideas and sketches from the entire group. Render the final design in color. Show it to the entire group and make adjustments as needed.

5. Develop an enlargement grid, as shown in Figure S–6, for the drawing and identify a scale for the smaller drawing to the mural. For instance 1 inch = 1 foot (2.5 cm = 1 meter).

6. Place drop cloths on the floor and protect the surrounding area as needed. Divide the wall into squares and number the squares on the wall to match the squares on the paper. Begin to enlarge the plan one square at a time.

7. Continue working until mural is complete.

EXAMINING YOUR WORK

- **Describe**   Explain what medium you used to produce the work.
- **Analyze**   Identify how the work achieved unity.
- **Interpret**   Describe how the mural is a good representation of your school or community.
- **Judge**   Explain why this is a successful work of art.

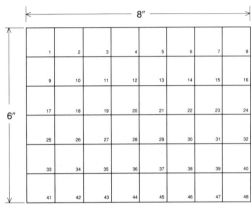

▲ Figure S–6   An enlargement grid.

- In addition to the art-related skills that students will be using in this lesson, they will also be developing others. For example, they will learn how permission and funding are acquired (if appropriate). Students will see the benefit of understanding proportion and mathematical scale. Probably the best benefit, however, will be the interaction of students as they plan, create and execute the project.

- After students have completed the group mural, ask them to assess the success of the project. In addition to the criteria established in "Examining Your Work" have students respond to the following: Did the brainstorming session help the group plan a subject, theme, and content for the mural? Did the group members assemble all of their ideas and, as a team, vote on the best theme? Was everyone involved in some part of the mural? Were the responsibilities divided among the team members? Did the group plan and follow a work schedule? Was the surrounding area protected properly?

  If students agree that they created a successful group mural, encourage them to invite the local newspaper to school to photograph the mural and to feature an article about the group's project.

OTHER STUDIO IDEAS

- On newsprint or butcher paper paint a mural of an imaginary place — perhaps a city of the future, an Old Western town, or a medieval castle, and so forth. Work alone or with a partner. Display your finished work, explain what you wanted to do, and discuss whether you accomplished that aim.

- ● You may want to do a "jigsaw" mural with a group of friends on newsprint. Make a drawing or choose a picture from a magazine. Draw a grid over it, then photocopy it. Cut the photocopy along the grid lines, and put the resulting squares in a container. Pass the container around so each person can choose a square to work from. Make the enlarged grid and begin work. Do not let the participants know what the completed mural should look like. The fun comes from trying to guess what it is as the work progresses. If the group is small, more than one square may be completed by each person.

LESSON 4

Pop-up Cityscape

LESSON 4

Pop-up Cityscape

- The Pop-up Cityscape studio lesson is an ideal project for challenging your creatively gifted students. It serves as an extension to Chapter 11.
- The purpose of the lesson is to have students create a three-dimensional pop-up cityscape based on one of the three aesthetic views presented in Chapter 2.
- In trying to help the students decide what aesthetic style they will choose have them play a short word association game. If you are in a city have the students list words that they would use to describe your city. If you live in a rural area use the word "city" for the game. The words they choose may help them determine what they want to express about their city.
- Before students begin the Pop-up Cityscape studio lesson, have them review the following lessons:
  Chapter 2, Lesson 2, Aesthetics, page **16–19**;
  Chapter 3, Lesson 5, Sculpture, pages **44–47**;
  Chapter 11, Lesson 1, The Art of Graphic Design, pages **192–195**.
- To help the students visualize the real shapes of city buildings, bring in travel magazines, the travel sections of the Sunday papers, or try to borrow posters and brochures from a travel agent. Concentrate on the new, post-modern architecture with its asymmetric forms. Get away from the "glass box" forms of the recent past.
- If possible, have students display their sample cityscapes. Remind students to refer to these cityscapes as they plan their art work.
- Bring to class an assortment of children's books and/or advertising pieces that incorporate a pop-up technique. Have students discuss the visual appeal associated with the pop-up presentation. Have students examine the products and evaluate what aesthetic views has been used in each art work.

Art, as you have learned, may be judged using three different aesthetic views. One of these views holds that what matters most in a work is a realistic subject. A second view states that what is most important in art is form. A third view argues that content is what counts most. Look at the cityscapes in Figures S–7, S–8, and S–9. Which of these would be judged most successful by a critic of the first school, a critic of the second school, or a critic of the third school?

WHAT YOU WILL LEARN

You will create a three-dimensional pop-up cityscape. Your work will be guided by one of the three aesthetic views described previously. The cityscape will have three parts—a foreground, a middleground, and a background. You will use the principle of proportion to organize the element of space.

▲ **Figure S–7   What aesthetic view do you think is best represented by this painting?**

Edward Hopper. *Drug Store*. 1927. Oil on canvas. 73.7 x 101.6 cm (29 x 40″). Museum of Fine Arts, Boston, Massachusetts. Bequest of John T. Spaulding.

304 Lesson 4   *Pop-up Cityscape*

Cross Reference
For more information about Edward Hopper you may wish to refer to Background Information on pages **18** and **43**. The Artist Profile, *Handbook* page **284**, also features this artist.

WHAT YOU WILL NEED

- Pencil and sketch paper
- Four pieces of illustration board: one 3 x 12 inches (8 x 30 cm), one 6 x 12 inches (15 x 30 cm), one 9 x 12 inches (23 x 30 cm), one 10 x 12 inches (25 x 30 cm)
- School tempera paints and several brushes
- Ruler, scissors, masking tape and white glue
- Two scrap pieces of illustration board, 3 x 2 inches (8 x 5 cm)
- Two strips of heavy construction paper, 7 x 2 inches (18 x 5 cm)

- To save time, precut the pieces of illustration board using a large paper cutter.
- If you can't afford illustration board, use precut pieces of corrugated cardboard. Another inexpensive material is grey chip board. Coat all the cardboard with an inexpensive white water base house paint so that the student may draw and paint easily over the white.
- You may substitute watercolor paints or school acrylics for the tempera.
- Students may want to consider making a mixed media of oil pastels and watercolors to achieve an exciting effect.

◀ **Figure S–8 What kind of balance is represented in this painting?**

Stuart Davis. *Place Pasdeloup*. 1928. Oil. 92.1 x 73 cm (36¼ x 28¾″). Whitney Museum of American Art, New York, New York.

◀ **Figure S–9 What is the mood represented in this painting?**

El Greco. *View of Toledo*. Oil on canvas. 121.3 x 108.6 cm (47¾ x 42¾″). The Metropolitan Museum of Art, New York, New York. The H. O. Havemeyer Collection.

Lesson 4   *Pop-up Cityscape*   **305**

- To relate this project to social studies, language arts, or foreign language study, obtain photos of a city that relates to their studies. If they are studying French, use photos and reproductions of paintings about Paris. Show people and trees on a street in the foreground, small buildings in the middle ground, and a cathedral in the background. Even the study of an ancient city can be done, because most cities were built around a hill for protection. The castle or cathedral on the hill could serve as the background.

- If the student is not making a hard edge, realistic, representation of a city it may be impossible to cut the top edge of the rooflines until the painting has been completed. The top of an expressive work may not be finished until the brush strokes have been completed. Even then it may be difficult to determine a definite edge. The student may have to draw an edge that relates to the loose work.

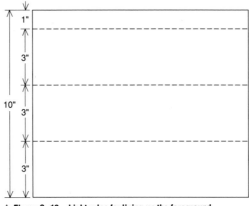

▲ **Figure S–10   Light rules for lining up the foreground, middleground, and background of the cityscape.**

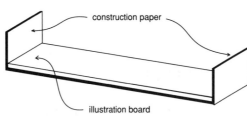

▲ **Figure S–11   This is a connecting U-joint that supports the pop-up portions of the cityscape.**

WHAT YOU WILL DO

1. Look once more at Figures S–7, S–8, and S–9. Decide which of the three paintings you want your cityscape to resemble most. Will it have a realistic subject, like Figure S–7? Will it focus on lines, textures, and shapes like Figure S–8? Will it capture a feeling, like the mood painting in Figure S–9?

2. Once you have chosen a style, make three sets of pencil sketches for your cityscape. One set should focus on the low buildings and shapes that will appear in the foreground. This set should have the most detail and color. A second should focus on the buildings and shapes of medium height that will appear in the middleground. A third should focus on the tall buildings and shapes that will appear in the background. Include details of design. The three sections of illustration board should be cut at the top edge to show the roofline of the buildings on each.

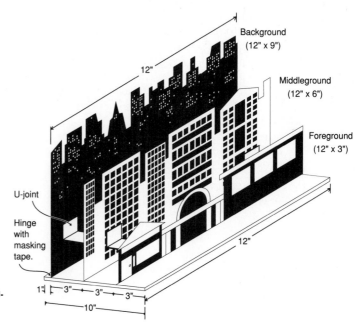

▶ **Figure S–12   Attaching the U-joint to the middleground of the cityscape.**

306   Lesson 4   *Pop-up Cityscape*

3. Use the first three pieces of illustration board and transfer your best sketches to three of the sections of illustration board. Carefully paint the buildings and shapes in each section.

4. Turn the remaining piece of illustration board so the 12-inch (30-cm) side is facing you. Placing the ruler firmly against the near edge, make a pencil mark 3 inches (8 cm) from either end. Make two more pencil dots the same distance from the ends of the opposite side. Connect each pair of parallel dots with a light rule. (See Figure S–10.)

5. Line up the foreground panel (the smallest section) along one rule. Holding the foreground panel upright, attach it along its back to the base panel. Use strips of masking tape for this task. The tape should work as a hinge. Attach the middleground and background to the base in a similar fashion.

6. Center a scrap of illustration board on a strip of construction paper (Figure S–11). Join the two pieces with glue. When dry, bend the flaps up to form a letter U. Apply glue to one flap. Attach the flap to the back of the foreground panel. Be careful about keeping the U-joint out of sight as possible. Apply glue to the other flap. Attach it to the front of the middleground panel. Repeat this task to join the middleground and background panels. (See Figure S–12.)

7. Display your work. Compare it with that of other students. (See Figure S–13.)

- **Describe** Identify the aesthetic view that you chose. How did you express that aesthetic view in the design of your cityscape?
- **Analyze** Tell which art elements and principles you used. Tell how you used the principle of proportion. Explain how you organized the element of space.
- **Interpret** Does your work express a mood or feeling? Why did you choose to express this mood in your cityscape?
- **Judge** Tell whether you feel your work succeeds. Explain your answer.

▲ **Figure S–13 A finished pop-up cityscape.**

OTHER STUDIO IDEAS

- Add to the three-dimensional feel of your cityscape. Create details out of illustration board, such as store awnings and window ledges. Paint these and glue them to your foreground panel.

- •• Create a second pop-up cityscape, this time adding a fourth, near-foreground, panel. This fourth panel should contain cutouts of people, dogs, cars, and so on. The style of these objects should blend with that of the other three panels.

Lesson 4 *Pop-up Cityscape*   **307**

Applique Banner

Applique Banner

- The Applique Banner studio lesson is an extension of Chapter 13. It offers students another optional studio which involves using fibers and fabrics.
- The purpose of the lesson is to have students create a personal banner. Symbolism will be used in the banner to help depict students' interests.
- Before students begin the Applique Banner studio lesson, have them review the following: Chapter 13, Lesson 1, The Art of Crafts, pages **222–225**; Chapter 13, Lesson 4, Making a Weaving, pages **230–231**.
- On a display table put an assortment of objects such as a key chain, mirror, concert ticket stub, baseball, ring (or other jewelry), book, and so forth. Have students list on a sheet of paper the first association that comes into their mind when they see each item. For example, the key might represent their home; the baseball might represent a home run that they hit. Use this simulation to encourage students to think about symbolism and about symbols that have meaning for them.
- This is a studio lesson that all students will have success with. If a few of your students are unable to produce the stitches as described, let them focus on the composition of their work. Have them lightly glue the items to the felt or attach them with an iron-on bonding product.
- If students complete the group project of making a banner to represent their school, community or state, have them choose a site where they can display it and achieve a maximum visibility.

One type of craftsperson uses needle, thread, and fabric to create works of art. The craftsperson who created the tropical birds in Figure S–14 stitched them onto a satin robe using multicolored silk threads. The artist used many different stitches but they are so fine that it is hard to see them in this reproduction.

WHAT YOU WILL LEARN

You will create a personal banner by sewing fibers and fabrics and small found objects onto a shaped piece of fabric. The banner must show objects or designs that are symbolic of you. Include your name or initials on the banner. To give the banner unity use harmony of color and rhythm through repetition

▶ **Figure S–14** This is one example of the art of stitchery. There are many different kinds of art that can be created this way.

Note
Many ancient cultures created applied art that, in some cases, has been preserved well enough for us to see and appreciate the fine quality of the work. Tapestries, embroidered articles of clothing, and weavings impart a great deal of information about the history and lifestyles of the people who created them. For example, Pre-Columbian artists of Central and South America created intricate weavings of wool, cotton, and other materials that depicted deities as well as representations of their own ways of life. Other examples are articles of clothing from Asian countries that display fine silken embroidery.

of line and shape. Use variety in the size of the negative spaces between the shapes and in the textures of fabrics and stitches. See Figure S–15 for an example of a student banner.

WHAT YOU WILL NEED

- Sketch paper, pencil, and ruler
- Large sheet of newsprint
- Fabric scissors and straight pins
- Fabric for the banner
- Thick and thin sewing needles
- Small pieces of fabric
- A variety of fibers
- Small found objects
- *Optional:* A dowel rod or a wire coat hanger

▲ Figure S–15   Student work. Banner in progress.

WHAT YOU WILL DO

1. Plan the symbols you will include in your banner. List and draw them on your sketch paper. Remember to include your name or initials as one of the symbols. Collect a few small found objects that you might sew onto the banner such as a button from a special jacket, a ticket stub, an election button, a dried flower, a blue ribbon, or a stone from the river where you love to fish.
2. Practice some stitches on scrap fabric.
3. Plan the size and shape of your banner. Think about the space where you will hang it, and what you plan to include on it. If you plan to use a coat hanger, the banner can be no wider than the bottom rod of the coat hanger. Then design the way you will arrange the symbols on the shape of your banner. Remember to repeat lines and shapes to create a sense of rhythm. Vary the negative spaces. Make several rough sketches in your sketch book. Select your best design.
4. Make a pattern for the banner. Draw the shape on the newsprint paper. Use the ruler to measure and to make straight lines. Cut out the paper pattern. Pin it to your fabric, and cut the fabric to match the pattern.

- Since it is so difficult to get students to remember to bring in materials for art class, it might be wise for the teacher to collect the fabrics. A heavyweight material that is easy to sew through such as felt, burlap, or monk's cloth would be good for the banner. If the students are going to attach the symbols without sewing, any heavyweight fabric will do. Go to a seamstress or to your friends who sew their own clothes to find a variety of scraps. Students love shiny satins and soft velours.
- The thread you need will depend on the use. Thin threads that match the color of the banner will be best for hemming the banner. Threads that match the shapes being sewn on will not show up and distract from the design. When you want the threads to show, use contrasting colors and thicker fibers such as crochet threads, yarns, and even raffia.
- The found objects the students bring should be their own, and should have special meaning to each individual. They cannot be heavy or they will pull the banner out of shape.
- Do not leave out step 2. The stitches themselves may give the students ideas for creating designs. At one table, have each student do a different stitch. They can compare results.

Lesson 5   *Applique Banner*   **309**

- The couching stitch is very good for attaching thin things such as flower stems to the banner.
- The blanket and the button hole stitch are good for attaching fabric shapes to the banner. If the student uses a matching color of embroidery thread the stitch will seem to be a part of the shape. Contrasting thread will make the shape stand out from the background.
- The running stitch can make a dotted line. A large top stitch and a small, single thread under stitch will look like a line.
- Both the back stitch and the threaded running stitch are good for making lines for letters.
- The outline stitch will make a thicker line.
- The satin stitch is good for making small shapes on the banner.
- The French knot will make a good dot over an "I" or "J."
- Rows of cross stitches will fill in a shape with an unusual texture.

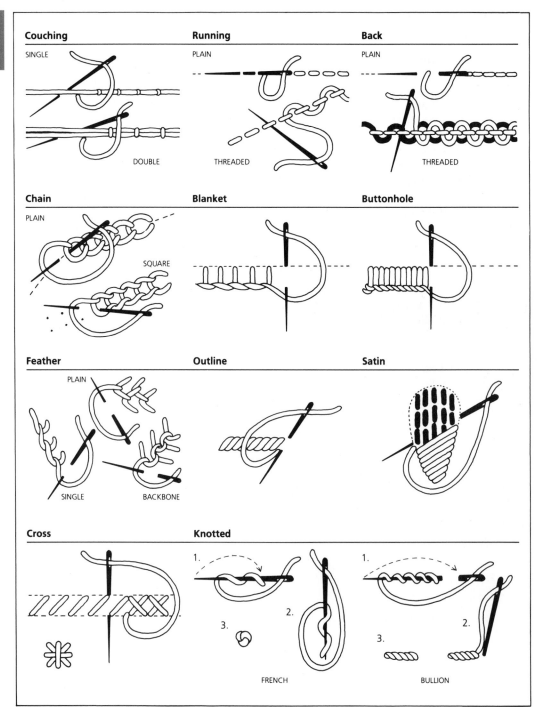

▲ Figure S–16   This chart shows how to do some art stitches.

5. Decide what harmonious color scheme you will use. Select fabrics and fibers to fit the color scheme.

6. Think about texture as you select fabrics and plan stitches. Decide which symbols will be made with fabric and sewn on to the banner, and which will be made with stitches. Draw on the scrap fabric with pencil and cut out the fabric pieces. Pin them in place, and sew them to the banner using the running stitch or the blanket stitch. Study the stitchery chart in Figure S–16. Draw the symbols to be made with stitches onto the banner and stitch them with a variety of fibers.

7. Turn the sides and bottom of your banner under ¼ inch and sew a hem. Sew the top over a thin dowel rod or the bottom rod of a wire coat hanger. Attach string to the rod so that you can hang it up or you may decorate the wire areas of the coat hanger.

8. Place your work on display with your classmates. Can you recognize any by the symbols alone? See Figure S-17 for ideas on different shapes for your banner.

EXAMINING YOUR WORK

- **Describe**   List the kinds of fabrics, fibers, and found objects you used in this project. List the symbols you included. List the stitches you used. Describe how you included your name or initials.
- **Analyze**   Describe the shape of your banner. What harmonizing color scheme did you use? Which lines and shapes did you repeat to create rhythm? Explain how you introduced variety into your design. Did you vary negative spaces? Did you vary textures?
- **Interpret**   Is your banner a symbol of you? Can your friends recognize the banner as your symbol?
- **Judge**   Are you satisfied with the quality of the banner? If not, what could you do to make it better?

▲ **Figure S–17**   Banners have many different uses. Can you name some of those uses?

- The width of the banner is controlled by the size of the wire hanger or the length of the dowel rod.
- The length is determined by the amount of fabric you have for each student. If you can only give each student 24 inches of fabric then give them a piece of newsprint that matches the length and width you want the student to use.
- Keep the shape of the banner itself rather simple so that it does not take away from all the symbols on the banner.
- Encourage the students to experiment with the shapes they are attaching to the banner.
- Have them try different arrangements before they pin them down to be sewn.
- Draw the symbols to be made with stitches on the banner with chalk so the drawing will disappear when the sewing is finished.
- A simple running stitch can be used to sew the hem. If the student does not wish it to be noticed, thin thread in a matching color would be best. If the hem stitches are to be used as an outline, a contrasting color of yarn can be used.
- The student can cover the wire of the hanger with yarn that matches the banner using a half hitch knot. Plain wrapping will also cover the wire.

OTHER STUDIO IDEAS

- Working in groups of three or four, using the above directions, make a large banner, (6 x 2 foot or 183 x 61 cm) to represent your school, community or state.

- •• Working on a square felt piece make a stitchery design as a birthday present for a friend. Be sure to include symbols of that person in your design. Felt is easy to use because it doesn't require hemming. This allows you to make any style bottom edge you choose.

Lesson 5   *Applique Banner*   **311**

Wire Sculpture

LESSON 6

Wire Sculpture

- The Objective Wire Sculpture studio lesson is designed as a low-cost studio lesson which gives students practice in creating three-dimensional objects. The lesson could be a follow-up to Chapter 8 which deals with analyzing contour lines or with Chapter 12 which covers sculpture techniques.

  The purpose of the lesson is to have students create a three-dimensional objective form, which suggests movement.
- You may want to suggest that the students participate in a cooperative effort by forming groups of three or more. Have each student within the group execute one component of a design or structure, keeping in mind that it will be only a part of the finished art work. They will also have to keep in mind how the piece they are working on will attach or be added to those being executed by others in their group. Creating cooperative art work can be a satisfying experience. Junior high students need to work in groups. It encourages cooperation, and gives them an opportunity to interact with others to solve problems.
- If there is time, allow the students to experiment with the wire and pliers so that they can understand the capabilities of the medium. Do this before they make their drawings.

Look at the wire sculpture in Figure S–18. Do you recognize the subject? What is she doing? Notice how the artist has used the principles of movement and rhythm to make the figure seem alive.

WHAT YOU WILL LEARN

You will construct a free-standing wire sculpture. The finished sculpture will be a three-dimensional objective form. It will be created entirely of wire lines. You can bend, curve, and twist the wire to make a variety of large and small shapes. Your figure should show movement. It should also suggest a feeling, such as happiness, sadness, or fright.

WHAT YOU WILL NEED

- Sketch paper, pencil, and eraser
- 14-gauge steel wire, 35 inch (89 cm) piece
- Pair of needlenose pliers
- *Optional:* styrofoam, or wood block for base, 6 x 6 inch (15 x 15 cm)

WHAT YOU WILL DO

1. Study the wire sculpture in Figure S–19. Decide what subject you will use for your true-to-life form. Think of the features and feelings that will be associated with your figure. Identify other objects that may be part of your sculptural form, such as a bike, kite, or balloon.
2. Make a pencil sketch of the form you see in your imagination. Use one continuous line to create this true-to-life form. Keep your form simple and concentrate on the line used. Continue to reshape and re-draw until you are happy with your sketch.

▲ **Figure S–18　Art often displays a sense of humor. Do you think this piece shows humor?**

Alexander Calder. *The Hostess.* 1928. Wire construction. Museum of Modern Art, New York, New York.

3. Grasp your wire at one end. Choose the part of the subject in your sketch where your sculpture will begin. (You will not be cutting the wire; your sculpture will be made of one continuous wire line.) Bend, curve, and twist the wire until it resembles the part you chose. Then move on to the next part. Continue working on one part at a time.

Background Information
Alexander Calder, the son and grandson of sculptors, was born in Philadelphia in 1898. After studying engineering he gradually became interested in art and in 1926 went to Paris where he attracted attention with wire sculptures that moved. Calder's early works were predominantly austere, geometric forms heavily influenced by Piet Mondrian and Naum Gabo, but by the late 1930s he was using free-form shapes reflecting the works of both Joan Miró and Jean Arp, his good friends.

For more information on Calder, see *Handbook,* page **314**.

4. As you work, use a mixture of large, curved twists and small, tight twists. This will give interest and variety to your sculpture.

5. If your sculpture can stand on its own, you won't need to mount it on a base unless you want to. But if your work needs mounting, attach it to a styrofoam or wood block, using wire bent into hooks, or small screws.

6. Display your finished sculpture with those of your classmates in a gallery in front of the class. (See Figure S–19.) Stroll through the gallery, comparing the different sculptures you and your classmates created. It is more important to catch the feeling of life, movement, and uniqueness than to be overly concerned with exact proportions and details.

SAFETY TIP

Before beginning to form your sculpture, cover both ends of the wire with masking tape or electrician's tape. While working, wear protective eye goggles. Both of these tips will help prevent you from scratching or poking your eyes and skin while you work.

EXAMINING YOUR WORK

- **Describe**   Point out the features in your work that identify the subject. Explain what features you added to create a true-to-life sculpture form.
- **Analyze**   Identify the variety of large and small shapes created in your wire line. Explain how your sculpture form shows movement.
- **Interpretation**   Explain how you made the sculpture express a mood.
- **Judge**   Explain why this is a successful work of art.

▲ Figure S–19   Student work. A wire sculpture.

- Be sure that the student remembers that this project is three-dimensional. Remind them to keep turning the wire sculpture and looking at it from all sides. A good piece of sculpture should look interesting from every point of view. Students tend to think of wire as a two dimensional medium.
- If the student wants to change a bend in the wire it is difficult, but it can be done. First smooth the wire with fingers as much as possible. Then use the wider part of the pliers to press it flat. They will need to keep turning the wire and pressing it until it has straightened out.
- Remind the students that they create shapes by outlining them with wire. Once again, a shape may look different from different points of view, so it is very important to keep turning the sculpture as they form different shapes.
- Be very firm about safety in this project. Try to keep the students from working too near each other.

OTHER STUDIO IDEAS

- Create a non-objective wire sculpture. Bend the wire in different directions to create movement and rhythm. Think about how you feel as you bend the wire. Create sharp angles, smooth curves, and straight passages to reflect your feelings. The sculpture can be constructed to stand freely or on a base.

- • Create a relief wire sculpture by attaching the sculpture to a backing for a wall-hanging. Decide if you want the art work to be objective or non-objective. You may want to include washers, rings, bolts, and so forth to give your work extra interest and dimension.

Lesson 6   *Wire Sculpture*   **313**

Freestanding Mobile

LESSON 7

Freestanding Mobile

- The Freestanding Mobile is a studio lesson designed to give students the opportunity to work in a three-dimensional format. The lesson could be used as a follow-up to the introduction of rhythm and movement or it could be used as a culminating project after the coverage of sculpture.
- The purpose of the lesson is to create a freestanding mobile which incorporates either a realistic or abstract subject. The principle of balance will be used.
- Before students begin the lesson have them review the following:
  Chapter 5, Lesson 5, Movement and Rhythm, page **90**;
  Chapter 12, Lesson 1, The Art of Sculpture, page **208**.
- If possible bring an assortment of mobiles to class and hang as many as possible. Have students discuss the visual (and audible) effects of each one. Lead the discussion to include the methods which the artists used to provide balance and harmony in the works.

Artists have always been fascinated with representing motion and movement. Look at Figure S–20. Alexander Calder represents motion by making objects or mobiles that actually sway in the wind. A mobile is made up of objects that are delicately hung and balanced by other objects. Unlike other sculpture pieces, you do not have to walk around them to see them completely.

Figure S–20 is a suspended mobile. The moving objects are suspended from sturdy wire and metal crosspieces that are part of the sculpture.

WHAT YOU WILL LEARN

You will create a freestanding mobile based on natural forms—animals, birds, fish, or plants. The forms will be made from paper and may appear to be realistic or abstract. You will use the principle of balance when constructing your mobile.

▲ **Figure S–20** Do you think mobiles would be successful as art if they were not designed to move?

Alexander Calder. *Untitled.* 1976. Aluminum and steel. 9.1 x 23.2 m (29'10½" x 76'). National Gallery of Art, Washington, D.C. Gift of the Collectors Committee.

WHAT YOU WILL NEED

- Cardboard from boxes, some pieces at least 16 inches (40 cm) long
- Pencil, ruler, and cutting knife
- Glue and string
- Construction paper
- 16-gauge wire, wire cutters, and round-nose pliers
- Paint and brushes

WHAT YOU WILL DO

1. Think of the natural forms—animals, birds, fish, or plants that can be used for your mobile. Decide if your forms will be realistic or abstract. Experiment with constructing the forms, using paper sculpture techniques. (See Technique Tip **21**, *Handbook* page **278**.)
2. Make the base for your freestanding sculpture. Study the diagram (Figure S–21) which shows how two pieces of cardboard can be joined together. Using a pencil and ruler draw the shape for the base. Measure one piece at least 16 inches (40 cm) tall. Make the other piece 3 or 4 inches (7.5 or 10 cm) tall and approximately 10 to 12 inches (25 to 30 cm) long to help make the base sturdy. Cut a slit about 2 inches (5 cm) long at the bottom of the large central piece. Cut a slit 2 inches (5 cm) long at the top of the bottom piece. Slip the cardboard slots together gently connecting the two pieces. Several smaller pieces of cardboard can be joined to the base to make it more interesting or to make it stand more solid. Continue joining them until the base stands alone and then glue the joint. Paint your base using colors that are appropriate to the theme of your mobile.
3. There are several ways that wire can be attached to the base. One way is to cut a small slot in the top of the cardboard and

---

Background Information

Students may be surprised to learn that *mobile* is a fairly new term invented to describe sculptures that move. Calder's first group of hand and motor driven mobiles was exhibited in 1932 at the Galerie Vignon in Paris, France. The work for which Calder is most noted, however, is wind mobiles. These mobiles were made from rods, wires, and delicate shapes made of sheet metal and wire hung from a single point. Air currents set the mobiles in motion, treating the viewer to constantly changing patterns of colors and shapes.

Many of Calder's mobiles are based on natural forms—animals, birds, fish, or plants—and the motions were carefully planned to imitate the movement of the subject. His later works show that he became more interested in shapes and movements that had little to do with natural objects.

then slide the wire down. This leaves both ends of the wire free for balancing objects on either side.

Another way is to poke about 3 or 4 inches (7.5 or 10 cm) of one end of the wire down between the cardboard layers. This leaves only one end free to hang objects.

4. Make your paper sculpture forms and decide how many you will suspend from your mobile. Consider proportion as you make the pieces and think of creative ways to balance the objects. Cut the pieces of wire to the desired lengths and use the round-nosed pliers to turn a small loop at the end. Use string to hang the paper sculptures from the wire loops.

5. Begin assembling your mobile with the lowest hanging pieces and continue working upward from there. After hanging two objects from either end of a piece of wire, locate its balance point by balancing the wire on your finger. Carefully form another loop in the wire to hang it from above.

6. When your work is complete display it in your classroom. (See Figure S–22.)

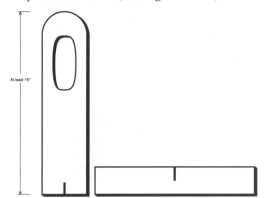

▲**Figure S–21   The base for the freestanding mobile.**

At least 16"

EXAMINING YOUR WORK

- **Explain**   Identify the paper sculpture techniques that you used to create your paper forms. Describe how the base was constructed to give support to your mobile.
- **Analyze**   Tell how balance was achieved in the mobile. Explain whether your mobile creates visual movement.
- **Interpret**   Tell what natural form you had in mind while creating your mobile. Did you portray the form in an abstract or realistic view?
- **Judge**   Tell whether you feel your work succeeds. Explain your answer.

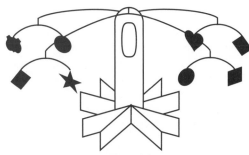

▲**Figure S–22   The completed mobile.**

OTHER STUDIO IDEAS

- Make a mobile that is not freestanding, but is made to hang.
- ●● Work with a partner. Each of you begin a cardboard base for a freestanding mobile. Find ways to connect your cardboard bases so that eventually you have one large base. Then, in cooperation with your partner, create one large mobile on the base.

ADDITIONAL STUDIOS

- If you cannot bring real mobiles to class, large photos of Calder mobiles will show the students how Calder used a series of loops to attach one section of the mobile to another so that there was room for each section to move in both directions. If you can get the students to use three or more wire loops at each joint the work will move freely.
- If possible drip some glue around the wire inserted into the cardboard to hold it in place.
- There are many other ways to create a base for the mobile. Suggest that the shape of the base relate to the theme of the mobile.
- Another way to attach the wire to the base to make it more mobile is to make a small circle of wire and make a loop at the top of the circle. Push the circle into the cardboard so that the small loop is at the top. Then make a small loop in the center of your horizontal wire. Hook that loop into the loop at the top of your circle. That way the horizontal wire will be able to move freely.

Lesson 7   *Freestanding Mobile*   **315**

Handbook Cross-Reference
For additional information on Calder, see *Handbook,* page **312**.

A Picture That Tells a Story

LESSON 8

A Picture That Tells a Story

- This lesson is designed so that students can imagine the entire scene that was taking place when the artist painted the picture. This lesson will require students to use their imagination and painting skills.
- Before students begin the studio lesson, have them review the following:
  Chapter 3, Lesson 4, Experimenting with Pigment, page **42**;
  Chapter 10, Lesson 1, The Art of Painting, page **178**.
- Ask students if they have ever watched a movie and did not see the end. Have students share personal stories of similar situations and ask them to elaborate upon their feelings associated with an unfinished story. Explain that in this lesson they will have the opportunity to visualize the remainder of a scene.

Winslow Homer's painting in Figure S–23 shows a fisherman in a small boat surrounded by signs of danger. Can you identify these signs?

This work is a wonderful example of this artist's skill in arousing the viewer's curiosity. It suggests a great many questions and then allows the viewer to use his or her own imagination to answer these questions. For example, where is the fisherman looking? What does he see? What might he be thinking and feeling at this moment? Where must he go to reach safety?

In this lesson you will give your answer to one of the most important questions about this painting. You will decide the fate of the fisherman.

▲ Figure S–23   Homer's paintings often tell stories. Can you see a story that might be told in this painting?

Winslow Homer. *The Fog Warning*. 1885. Oil on canvas. 76.2 x 121.9 cm (30 x 48"). The Museum of Fine Arts, Boston, Massachusetts. Otis Norcross Fund.

WHAT YOU WILL LEARN

You will complete a painting in which you show what happens to the fisherman in Homer's picture. As in Homer's painting you will use large and small shapes to suggest deep space. You will also use real and imaginary lines to guide the viewer's eyes to the most important objects in your work.

WHAT YOU WILL NEED

- Pencil and sketch paper
- White paper, 9 x 12 inch
- Tempera paint
- Brushes
- Mixing tray

WHAT YOU WILL DO

1. Imagine that Homer completed another painting entitled *Fog Warning II*. In this work he showed what happened to the fisherman. Discuss with other members of your class what this second picture might look like.
2. On your own complete several sketches showing your version of *Fog Warning II*. Include all the facts and details needed by viewers to determine the fisherman's fate. Suggest space by using large shapes in the foreground and smaller shapes in the distance. Use real and imaginary lines to direct attention to the most important features in your work.

- **Describe**   Identify the objects in your picture. Explain how these were suggested by Homer's painting.
- **Analyze**   Show how you used large and small shapes to create an illusion of deep space. Point to real and imaginary lines and explain how these are used to guide the viewer to the important parts of your picture.
- **Interpret**   Determine if others are able to use your picture to learn the fate of the fisherman. Can they identify a happy or a sad ending to the story?
- **Judge**   State whether you think your painting is successful or unsuccessful. What aesthetic view would you suggest to viewers trying to judge your work?

3. Transfer your best sketch to the paper or illustration board. Paint your picture with colors that suggest a happy or sad ending to the story of the fisherman.

ADDITIONAL STUDIOS

- Have students study this work using the four steps of art criticism so that they become deeply involved with the content of the work. That will make it easier for them to imagine what comes next.
- Other materials that could be used to create their scenes are school acrylics or a mixed media combination of oil pastels and watercolors.
- If the students are having difficulty imagining what comes next, bring them together in small groups to brainstorm ideas.
- Go over all the techniques to create depth in a picture emphasizing large and small shapes. Remind them that high and low placement, brightness of color, amount of detail, overlapping and converging lines can also create a sense of depth.
- Remind students that the types of lines they use can also add to the mood of the work. Horizontal lines will create a calm mood, while diagonally curving waves will cause a sense of tension and movement.

OTHER STUDIO IDEAS

- Paint another picture of this same subject. However, do not make this a realistic painting. Instead use colors, shapes, lines, and textures to create a *non-objective* work that suggests a happy or sad ending to the story. Then compare this painting with the first one. Which is most successful? Explain why.

•• Use watercolors on a large sheet of paper to paint a picture showing a storm at sea. Do not include figures or man-made objects. Select colors that suggest water, whitecaps, clouds, and fog. Apply these colors to show the power and fury of the storm. Try to reveal your *feelings* about the storm as you show what it looks like.

Lesson 8   *A Picture That Tells a Story* **317**

Handbook Cross-Reference
For additional background information about Winslow Homer, see page **2** and *Handbook*, page **284**.

ADDITIONAL STUDIOS

LESSON 9

Pinhole Camera Photography

Pinhole Camera Photography

- The Pinhole Camera studio lesson is designed for students to discover the process of photography.
- In this lesson students will build a pinhole camera and then use the camera to create a photographic portrait.
- Before students begin the studio lesson have them review the following:
   - Chapter 15, Lesson 1, The Art of Photography, page **252**;
   - Chapter 15, Lesson 2, Making a Photogram, page **256**;
- The students may want to make a mini painting booth to keep the spray paint from drifting onto something it shouldn't. They can do this by using a medium-sized cardboard box (about the size of an average grocery carton). Turn it on its side and put the object to be painted inside. It is a good idea to have them do this operation outside, if at all possible.

Look at Figure S–24. This is a photograph by American photographer Ansel Adams. As with other works of art, learning to make photographs like this takes skill and practice. It does not, however, take an expensive camera. A simple homemade pinhole camera (Figure S–25) will allow you to test your skills as a photographer. Pinhole cameras work by letting the photographed image enter a darkened box through a tiny hole. The image is captured on a piece of film attached to the inside lid of the box.

WHAT YOU WILL LEARN

You will build a pinhole camera using simple materials found around the house. You will make a photograph using your camera.

WHAT YOU WILL NEED

- Scissors or cutting knife
- Empty round oatmeal box with a lid
- Flat black spray paint
- Square of heavy-duty aluminum foil, 2 inch (5 cm)
- Needle or sharp pin
- Masking tape
- Square of cardboard, 1 inch (3 cm)
- Sheets of Kodak Plus-X film, 4 x 5 inches (10 x 13 cm)
- Sheet of white paper, 12 x 18 inches (30 x 46 cm)

SAFETY TIP

Use spray paint outdoors or in a well ventilated area. Be careful not to inhale the fumes from the paint.

► **Figure S–24** Photography is an art form that can be used in many different ways. What are some ways photography is used?

Photograph by Ansel Adams.

Background Information
Ansel Adams is most noted for his landscape photography of Yosemite National Park. His work shows detail and sharp contrasts of light and dark. He perfected darkroom techniques that emphasized the white of the billowing storm clouds hanging on the dark mountain peaks that he favored as subjects.

Adams also worked in the southwestern states of New Mexico and Arizona, capturing the stark beauty of the desert landscape. In that body of work there are also portraits of Native Americans that show great sensitivity.

He lived and taught for many years in Northern California. Alfred Stieglitz and Georgia O'Keeffe were friends who had some influence on his work. Adams was a proponent of nature preservation long before its importance was widely recognized.

WHAT YOU WILL DO

1. Using the scissors or cutting knife, cut a ½-inch (13 mm) square hole in the bottom of the oatmeal box. The hole should be as close to the center as possible. Paint the inside of the box and the lid with spray paint. Set them aside to dry.
2. Hold the piece of aluminum foil against a hard, flat surface. Using the needle or pin, carefully poke a pin-size hole at the center. Make sure the hole is crisp and sharp. A ragged or too-large hole will produce a blurry image.
3. Place the foil inside the box. Line it up so the pinhole is centered over the hole at the bottom. Using masking tape, attach the foil to the bottom of the box. Place the cardboard square over the hole on the outside bottom of the box. Fasten the square along one side with tape, making a hinged flap. (See Figure S–25.)
4. In a darkroom, cut a piece of film to fit inside the lid of the box. Try to handle the film by the edges only because touching the film may cause blurs on the image. Tape the film in place. Place the lid on the box. Hold the cardboard flap closed until you are ready to shoot a picture.
5. Choose a subject that is outdoors in bright sunlight. Standing about 10 feet away from your subject, set the camera down on a flat unmoving surface. Prop the camera with cloth or crumpled paper towel, so it won't roll or move while you are taking your picture. Aim the bottom of the box at your subject. Lift the flap, and hold it open for about 15 seconds. Close the flap. Holding it in place, return to the darkroom to develop your photo.

- **Describe**   Show that all inside surfaces of your camera are coated with paint. Tell whether you held the camera steady and kept the cardboard flap open for 15 seconds.
- **Analyze**   Tell whether your photograph was blurry or clear. If blurry, explain why. If the photograph is too light or too dark, explain why.
- **Interpret**   Explain how a viewer would recognize your work as a portrait. Give your photograph a title.
- **Judge**   Tell whether you feel your work succeeds. Explain your answer.

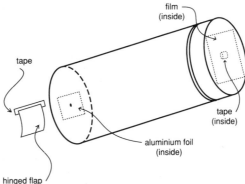

▲ **Figure S–25**   This shows how a pin-hole camera is constructed.

ADDITIONAL STUDIOS

- If you don't have access to a darkroom, a portable darkroom can be devised by acquiring a light-proof black cloth bag from a photo supply store into which the pinhole camera and hands can be inserted while placing the film in the lid. The disadvantage of this is that everything has to be done by touch, which may be a bit difficult for novices.
- Another helpful hint is that the emulsion side which must face the light source can be determined by moistening the thumb and forefinger very slightly and pinching a corner of the film. The side of the film that sticks to a moistened finger is the emulsion side.
- The length of the exposure time varies depending on the intensity of the light source and the size of the pinhole. Each student will have to experiment with exposure times for his or her particular camera.

OTHER STUDIO IDEAS

- Take a second photograph of a subject indoors. Experiment to find out how long the flap needs to be open for indoor light.
- •• Set up an indoor group portrait. Have your subjects strike an interesting pose. Take your photograph.

Adams, Ansel, American, 1902-84, photographer
page 318, *Fig.* S-25

Alonzo, Daniel, American, 1957-
Whale of a Mural, 302, *Fig.* S-5

Boccioni, Umberto, Italian, 1882-1916, painter, sculptor
Study for Dynamic Force of a Cyclist I, 90, *Fig.* 5-13

Bonheur, Rosa, French, 1822-99, painter
Buffalo Bill on Horseback, 7, *Fig.* 1-7

Bourke-White, Margaret, American, 1906-71,
photographer
Mahatma Gandhi, 250, 267, *Chapter 15 Opener,*
Chapter 15 Review Detail

Brady, Mathew, American, 1823?-96, photographer
Civil War, 253, *Fig.* 15-3

Brancusi, Constantin, Rumanian, 1876-1957, sculptor
Mlle. Pogany II, 68, *Fig.* 4-21

Braque, Georges, French, 1882-1963, painter
Le Courrier, 134, *Fig.* 7-15

Burton, Tim, American, 1960-, film director
Batman, 259, *Fig.* 15-11

Calder, Alexander, American, 1846-1923, sculptor
mobile [untitled], 314, *Fig.* S-21
The Hostess, 312, *Fig.* S-18

Calle, Paul, American, 1928-, painter
Gemini VI Astronauts, 142, 157, *Chapter 8 Opener,*
Chapter 8 Review Detail

Cannon, T. C., (Native) American, 1946-1978, painter
Turn of the Century Dandy, 23, *Fig.* 2-7

Carpeaux, Jean Baptiste, French, 1827-75, sculptor
Neopolitan Fisherboy, 209, *Fig.* 12-2

Cassatt, Mary, American, 1845-1926, painter
At the Opera, 16, *Fig.* 2-1
Maternal Caress, 35, *Fig.* 3-9

Cézanne, Paul, French, 1839-1906, painter
The Bay of Marseille, Seen from L'Estaque, 52, 77,
Chapter 4 Opener, Chapter 4 Review Detail

Chernow, Ann, American, 1936-, painter
Lady of L. A., 32, *Fig.* 3-5

Clodion (Claude Michel), French, 1738-1814, sculptor
The River Rhine Separating the Waters, 214, *Fig.* 12-8

Cropsey, Jasper Francis, American, 1823-1900, painter
Autumn on the Hudson River, 124, *Fig.* 7-4

Daddi, Bernardo, Italian, c. 1290-1349/51, painter
Madonna and Child with Saints and Angels, 87, *Fig.* 5-10

Dali, Salvador, Spanish, 1904-89, painter
The Persistence of Memory, 7, *Fig.* 1-6

da Vinci, Leonardo, Italian, 1452-1519, painter, sculptor
Five Grotesque Heads, 144, *Fig.* 8-1

Davis, Stuart, American, 1894-1964, painter
Owh! In San Paõ, vii, bottom
Place Pasdeloup, 305, *Fig.* S-8

Degas, Edgar, French, 1834-1917, painter
Four Dancers, 131, *Fig.* 7-11

Delaunay, Sonia, French, 1885-1979, painter
Colored Rhythm No. 698, 184, *Fig.* 10-9

Derain, André, French, 1880-1954, painter
The River Seine at Carrieres-sur-Seine, 125, *Fig.* 7-5

Dove, Arthur G., American, 1880-1946, painter
Plant Forms, 67, *Fig.* 4-19

Dürer, Albrecht, German, 1471-1528, painter,
printmaker
The Four Horsemen of the Apocalypse, 158, 175, *Chapter*
9 Opener, Chapter 9 Review Detail

Dvorak, Lois, American, 1934, mixed media
The Lizards, 10, *Fig.* 1-10

Edgerton, Dr. Harold, American, 1903-1989,
photographer
Milk-drop Coronet, xiv, top

El Greco, Spanish, 1541-1614, painter
Saint Martin and the Beggar, 106, 107, *Figs.* 6-6, 6-7, 6-8
View from Toledo, 305, *Fig.* S-9

Epstein, Sir Jacob, English (b. New York City), 1880-
1959, sculptor
Madonna and Child, 139, *Fig.* 7-20

Escobar, Marisol, Venezuelan artist, in America since
1950, 1930-, sculptor
Poor Family I, 46, *Fig.* 3-22

Estes, Richard, American, 1932-, painter
Telephone Booths, 112, *Fig.* 6-13

Fontana, Lavinia, Italian, 1552-1614, painter
Portrait of a Noblewoman, 179, *Fig.* 10-3

Gabo, Naum, American, 1890-1977, sculptor
Constructed Head No. 2, 216, *Fig.* 12-10

Garrison, Elizabeth, American, 1914-, quilter
Georgia, 222, *Fig.* 13-1

Giacometti, Alberto, Swiss, 1901-66, sculptor
Man Pointing, 55, *Fig.* 4-3

Giotto, Italian, c. 1266-1337, painter
Madonna and Child, 137, *Fig.* 7-17

Glackens, William, American, 1870-1938, painter
Family Group, 81, *Fig.* 5-3

Goncharova, Natalia, Russian, 1881-1962, painter
Cats, 14, 27, *Chapter 2 Opener, Chapter 2 Review Detail*
The City Square, 146, *Fig.* 8-3

Graves, Nancy Stevenson, 1940-, sculptor
Zaga, 44, *Fig.* 3-18

Griffith, D. W., American, 1875-1948, film director
Intolerance, 258, *Fig.* 15-8

Gris, Juan, Spanish, 1887-1927, painter
Max Jacob, 150, *Fig.* 8-8

Gwathmey, Robert, American, 1903-1988, painter
Country Gospel Music, 88, *Fig.* 5-12

Hanson, Duane, American, 1925-, super-realist
Sunbather, 21, *Fig.* 2-5

Harnett, William, American (b. County Cork,
Ireland), 1848-92, painter
My Gems, 20, *Fig.* 2-4

Hartigan, Grace, American, 1922-, painter
The Far Away Places, 103, *Fig.* 6-3

Harvey, Donald, Amercian, 1947-, sculptor,
ceramicist, art educator
Huaka'i, xii, bottom

Hepworth, Dame Barbara, English, 1903-75, sculptor
Merryn, 113, *Fig.* 6-14

Hockney, David, English, 1937-, painter
Les Mamelles des Tiresias, 181, *Fig.* 10-6
Hogue, Alexandre, American, 1898-, painter, lithographer
Drouth Stricken Area, 208, *Fig.* 12-1
Hokusai, Katsushika, Japanese, 1760-1849, printmaker
View of Mt. Fuji from Seven-Ri Beach, 160, *Fig.* 9-1
Homer, Winslow, American, 1836-1910, painter
The Fog Warning, 316, *Fig.* S-23
Return from the Hunt, 180, *Fig.* 10-4
Right and Left, 2, *Fig.* 1-1
Hooch, Pieter de, Dutch, 1629-after 1684, painter
The Bedroom, 101, 109, *Figs.* 6-1, 6-10
Hopper, Edward, American, 1882-1967, painter
Cottages at North Truro, Massachusetts, 42, *Fig.* 3-16
Drug Store, 304, *Fig.* S-7
Gas (study for), 31, *Fig.* 3-3
New York Movie, 18, *Fig.* 2-3
Houser, Allan, Native American, 1914-, sculptor
Waiting for Dancing Partners, 5, *Fig.* 1-3
Inness, George, American, 1825-94, painter
Lackawanna Valley, 120, *Fig.* 7-1
Jawlensky, Alexei von, Russian, 1864-1941, painter
Portrait of a Woman, 87, *Fig.* 5-11
Johns, Jasper, American, 1930-, painter
Between the Clock and the Bed, 91, *Fig.* 5-14
Kandinsky, Wassily, Russian, 1866-1944, painter
Improvisation Number 27: The Garden of Love, 39,
Fig. 3-13
Several Circles, 85, *Fig.* 5-8
Keats, Kim, American, 1955-, fiber artist
Banded Tulip Basket, 223, *Fig.* 13-4
Kimiko, Japan, 1957-, ceramist
Vase, 225, *Fig.* 13-9
Kingman, Dong, American, 1911-, painter
Cable Car Festival, 182, *Fig.* 10-7
Kiyotoda, Torii, Japanese, printmaker
An actor of the Ichikawa clan, xi, top
Kollwitz, Käthe, German, 1867-1945, painter, printmaker
Death and the Mother, 55, *Fig.* 4-2
Self-Portrait, 46, *Fig.* 3-21
Lange, Dorothea, American, 1895-1965, photo-
journalist
White Angel Breadline, 254, *Fig.* 15-4
Lang, Fritz, American, 1890-1976, film director
Metropolis, 258, *Fig.* 15-9
Lawrence, Jacob, American, 1917-, painter
Toussaint L'Overture Series, 92, *Fig.* 5-15; xi, bottom
Lee, Doris, American, 1905-, printmaker
Untitled, 164, *Fig.* 9-8
Leyster, Judith, Dutch, 1609-60, painter
Self-Portrait, 122, *Fig.* 7-3
Lippi, Fra Filippo, Italian, c. 1457-1504, painter
Madonna and Child, 133, *Fig.* 7-14
Lloyd, Harold, American, 1893-1971, filmmaker
Safety Last, 1923, 260, *Fig.* 15-12
MacNelly, Jeff, American, 1947-, comic strip illustrator
Shoe comic strip, 198, *Fig.* 11-10
Manet, Édouard, French, 1832-83, painter
Gare Saint-Lazare, 24, *Fig.* 2-8

Manguin, Henri-Charles, French, 1874-1949, painter
Port Saint-Tropez, le 14 Juillet, 40, *Fig.* 3-14
Mann, Tony, American, 1950-, woodcraft
Alphabet Blocks in Case, 223, *Fig.* 13-2
Matisse, Henri, French, 1869-1954, painter
The Red Studio, 128, *Fig.* 7-9
Woman in a Purple Coat, 84, *Fig.* 5-7
Michel, Claude. *See* Clodion
Mills, Robert, American, 1781-1855, architect
rejected sketch of Washington Monument, 152, *Fig.* 8-11
Miró, Joan, Spanish, 1893-1983, painter
Three Women, 4, *Fig.* 1-2
Mondrian, Piet, Dutch, 1872-1944, painter
Blue Tree, 74, *Fig.* 4-27
Monet, Claude, French, 1840-1926, painter
The Artist's Garden at Vetheuil, 127, *Fig.* 7-8
Moore, Henry, English, 1898-1986, sculptor
Family Group, 206, 219, *Chapter 12 Opener, Chapter 12
Review Detail*
Morisot, Berthe, French, 1841-95, painter
In the Dining Room, 98, 117, *Chapter 6 Opener, Chapter
6 Review Detail*
Moscoso, Victor, American, born in Spain, 1936-,
graphic artist
Junior Wells and His Chicago Blues Band, 200, *Fig.* 11-12
Motherwell, Robert, American, 1915-, painter
Elegy to the Spanish Republic 108, 17, *Fig.* 2-2
Munch, Edvard, Norwegian, 1863-1944, painter,
printmaker
The Kiss, 162, *Fig.* 9-3
Münter, Gabriele, German, 1877-1962, painter
Staffelsee in Autumn, cover
Murillo, Bartholomé Esteban, Spanish, 1617-82,
painter
The Return of the Prodigal Son, 8, *Fig.* 1-8
Murray, Elizabeth, American, 1936-, painter
Join, 60, *Fig.* 4-8
Nampeyo, Dextra Q., (Native) American, potter
Jar, 227, *Fig.* 13-11
Neel, Alice, American, 1900-1984, painter
T. B. Harlem, 186, *Fig.* 10-11
Nevelson, Louise, American, 1900-, sculptor
Atmosphere and Environment, 211, *Fig.* 12-6
O'Keeffe, Georgia, American, 1887-1986, painter
Radiator Building, 82, *Fig.* 5-5
Sunrise, 41, *Fig.* 3-15
The White Calico Flower, 212, *Fig.* 12-7
Orozco, José Clemente, Mexican, 1883-1949, painter
Zapatistas, 58, *Fig.* 4-6
Owens, Bob, American, 1939-, ceramist
Alpha Wolf, 225, *Fig.* 13-8
Panton, Verner, American, 1926-, designer
Stacking Side Chair, 113, *Fig.* 6-15
Pater, Jean-Baptist-Joseph, French, 1695-1736, painter
Fête Champêtre, 86, *Fig.* 5-9
Picasso, Pablo, Spanish, 1881-1973, painter, sculptor
Seated Woman (After Cranach), 170, *Fig.* 9-14
Three Musicians, 118, 141, *Chapter 7 Opener, Chapter 7
Review Detail*

Periera, William L., American, 1909-, architect
Transamerica Building, San Francisco, xiii, bottom

Pleak, Jane, American, 1949-, sculptor
Summertime Totem, 228, *Fig.* 13-12

Pollock, Jackson, American, 1912-56, painter
Cathedral, 300, *Fig.* S-4

Potter, Beatrix, English, 1866-1943, illustrator
Jemima Puddle-Duck, 193, *Fig.* 11-2

Raphael (Sanzio), Italian, 1483-1520, painter
Saint George and the Dragon, 104, 105, *Figs.* 6-4, 6-5
The Small Cowper Madonna, 132, *Fig.* 7-13

Rembrandt van Rijn, Dutch, 1606-69, painter
Jan Cornelius Sylvius, The Preacher, 148, *Fig.* 8-5

Renoir, Pierre Auguste, French, 1841-1919, painter
Girl with a Watering Can, 121, *Fig.* 7-2
Regatta at Argenteuil, 126, *Fig.* 7-6

Resnick, Milton, American, 1917-, painter
Genie, 107, *Fig.* 6-9

Rivera, Diego, Mexican, 1886-1957, painter
Detroit Industry, 178, *Fig.* 10-1

Rockwell, Norman, American, 1894-1978, painter,
illustrator
Triple Self-Portrait, xvi, 13, *Chapter 1 Opener, Chapter
1 Review Detail*

Rousseau, Henri, French, 1844-1910, painter
The Waterfall (La Cascade), 154, *Fig.* 8-13

Ryder, Albert Pinkham, American, 1847-1917, painter
The Toilers of the Sea, 110, *Fig.* 6-11

Salemme, Attilio, Italian, 1911-1955, painter
Inquisition, 66, *Fig.* 4-18

Scanlin, Tommye M., American, 1947-, weaver
Cat Dreams, 230, *Fig.* 13-14

Schapiro, Miriam, American, 1923-, painter
High Steppin' Strutter I, 57, *Fig.* 4-5

Seurat, Georges, French, 1859-91, painter
Sunday Afternoon on the Island of La Grande Jatte, 138,
Fig. 7-19

Siqueiros, David Alfaro, Mexican, 1896-1974,
Mexican expressionist
Echo of a Scream, 180, *Fig.* 10-5

Sittow, Michel, Flemish, c. 1465/70-1525, painter
The Assumption of the Virgin, 80, *Fig.* 5-2

Smith, David, American, 1906-65, cubist
Cockfight-Variation, 211, *Fig.* 12-5

Stayton, Janet, American, 1939-, printmaker
Ravello, ix, top
Yellow Promenade, 166, *Fig.* 9-9

Steen, Jan, Dutch, c. 1626-79, painter
The Drawing Lesson, 28, 51, *Chapter 3 Opener, Chapter
3 Review Detail*

Steinlen, Theophile-Alexandre, French, 1859-1923,
printmaker
Compagnie Française des Chocolats et des Thés, 194,
Fig. 11-4

Stella, Frank, American, 1936-, sculptor/painter
Agbatana III, 22, *Fig.* 2-6
Saint Michael's Counterguard, 70, *Fig.* 4-22

Stieglitz, Alfred, American, 1864-1946, photographer
The Steerage, 255, *Fig.* 15-5

Sullivan, John, American, active c. 1935, painter
Tailor's Shears (shop sign), 194, *Fig.* 11-6

Sullivan, Louis, American, 1856-1924, architect
Wainwright Building, 240, *Fig.* 14-5

Tafoya, Margaret, (Native) American, potter
Jar, Santa Clara Pueblo, New Mexico, 226, *Fig.* 13-10

Talbot, William Henry Fox, English, 1800-77,
photographer
The Ladder, 256, *Fig.* 15-6

Thomas, Alma, American, 1891-1978, painter
Iris, Tulips, Jonquils and Crocuses, 176, 189, *Chapter 10
Opener, Chapter 10 Review Detail*

Tiffany, Louis Comfort, American, 1848-1933,
painter, stained-glass artist
Vase, 224, *Fig.* 13-7

Toulouse-Lautrec, Henri de, French, 1864-1901,
printmaker, painter
La Gitane, 36, *Fig.* 3-10
Jane Avril, 190, 205, *Chapter 11 Opener, Chapter 11
Review Detail*

van Gogh, Vincent, Dutch, 1853-90, painter
Cypresses, 64, *Fig.* 4-15
The Garden of the Rectory at Nuenen, 94, *Fig.* 5-17

van Rijn, Rembrandt, Dutch, 1606-1669, painter
Portrait of a Lady with an Ostrich Feather Fan, x, top

Vigée-Lebrun, Marie-Louise-Élisabeth, French, 1755-
1842, painter
La Princesse Barbe Gallitzin, 149, *Fig.* 8-6
Theresa, Countess Kinsky, 131, *Fig.* 7-12

Vlaminck, Maurice de, French, 1876-1958, painter
Sailboats on the Seine, 126, *Fig.* 7-7

Warhol, Andy, American, 1928-87, painter,
printmaker
*George Gershwin from Ten Portraits of Jews of the 20th
Century,* 172, *Fig.* 9-16

Weaver, Ann Renée, American, 1955-
Alphabet Blocks in Case, 223, *Fig.* 13-2
Paper Jewelry Pin, 233, *Fig.* 13-18

Welles, Orson, American, 1915-, film director
Citizen Kane, 259, *Fig.* 15-10

White, Clarence H., American, 1871-1925,
photographer
Ring Toss, 130, *Fig.* 7-10

Wilgus, William John, American, 1819-1853, painter
Ichabod Crane, 6, *Fig.* 1-5

Williams, Herbert Andrew, American, 1973-
A Year in the Life of Herbert, 48, *Fig.* 3-23

Willson, Mary Ann, American, active 1810-1825,
painter
The Prodigal Son Reclaimed, 9, *Fig.* 1-9

Woodruff, Hale, American, 1900-, painter
Poor Man's Cotton, 78, 97, *Chapter 5 Opener, Chapter 5
Review Detail*

Wright, Frank Lloyd, American, 1867-1959, architect
Guggenheim Museum, 241, *Fig.* 14-6

Wyeth, Andrew, American, 1917-, painter
Christina's World, 115, 179, *Figs.* 6-16, 10-2

Wyeth, N. C., American, 1882-1945, illustrator
Blind Pew, 202, *Fig.* 11-14

Glossary

Acrylic (uh-**kril**-ik)   A quick-drying water-based synthetic paint. (Ch. 10-1)

Additive   A sculpting method produced by adding to or combining materials. (Ch. 12-1)

Aesthetics (ess-**thet**-iks)   The philosophy or study of the nature and value of art. (Ch. 2-2)

Aesthetic views   Ideas, or schools of thought, on what to look for in works of art. (Ch. 2-2)

Amphitheaters (**am**-fuh-thee-uht-uhrs)   Circular or oval buildings with seats rising around an open space. (Ch. 14-1)

Analogous colors (uh-**nal**-uh-gus)   Colors that are side by side on the color wheel. (Ch. 4-2)

Analyzing   Noting how the principles are used to organize the elements of color, line, texture, shape, form, and space. (Ch. 6-3); Noting the style of a work. (Ch. 7-3)

Applied art   Art made to be functional, as well as visually pleasing. (Ch. 1-2), (Ch. 6-6)

Architect   An artist who works in the field of architecture. (Ch. 14-1)

Architecture   The planning and creating of buildings. (Ch. 14-1)

Art critic   A person who practices art criticism. (Ch. 6-1)

Art criticism   The process of studying, understanding, and judging art works, consisting of four stages: describing, analyzing, interpreting, and judging. (Ch. 6-1)

Art history   The study of art from past to present, consisting of four stages: describing, analyzing, interpreting, and judging. (Ch. 7-1)

Art movement   A group of artists with similar styles who have banded together. (Ch. 7-3)

Artists   People who use imagination and skill to communicate ideas in visual form. (Ch. 1-2)

Assembling   A sculpting method in which different kinds of materials are gathered and joined together. (Ch. 12-1)

Balance   A principle of art concerned with arranging the elements of art so that no one part of a work overpowers, or seems heavier than, any other part. (Ch. 5-1)

Basilicas (buh-**sil**-ih-kuhs)   Huge meeting halls. (Ch. 14-1)

Binder   A liquid to which the dry pigment is added. (Ch. 3-3), (Ch. 10-1)

Blending   A shading technique that involves adding dark values little by little by pressing harder on the drawing medium. (Ch. 8-1)

Brayer   A roller with a handle. (Ch. 9-1)

Camera   A dark box with a hole controlling how much light enters. (Ch. 15-1)

Carving   A sculpting method in which material is cut or chipped away. (Ch. 12-1)

Casting   A sculpting method in which melted material is poured into a mold. (Ch. 12-1)

Cinematographer (sin-uh-muh-**tahg**-ruh-fuhr)   The person in charge of running the movie camera or cameras. (Ch. 15-3)

Collage (kuh-**lahzh**)   Art arranged from cut or torn materials pasted to a surface. (Ch. 1-4), (Ch. 7-6)

Color wheel   An arrangement of colors in a circular format. (Ch. 4-2)

Complementary colors   Colors opposite each other on the color wheel. (Ch. 4-2)

Composition   How the principles are used to organize the elements. (Ch. 2-1)

Content   Message, idea, or feeling. (Ch. 2-1)

Contour drawing   Drawing an object as though your drawing tool is moving along all the edges and the ridges of the form. (Ch. 8-3)

Crafts   The different areas of applied art in which craftspeople work. (Ch. 13-1)

Craftsperson   Someone who has become an expert in an area of applied art. (Ch. 13-1)

Credit line   A listing of important facts about an art work. (Ch. 2-1)

Crosshatching   A shading technique using two or more lines that crisscross each other. (Ch. 8-1)

Daguerreotypes (duh-**gehr**-uh-types)   Silvery, mirrorlike images on a copper plate. (Ch. 15-1)

Describing   In art criticism, making a careful list of all the things you see in the work. (Ch. 6-1); In art history, telling who did a work, and when and where it was done. (Ch. 7-1)

Director   The person in charge of shooting the film and guiding the actors. (Ch. 15-3)

Edition   A group of identical prints all made from a single plate. (Ch. 3-2), (Ch. 9-1)

Editorial designers   Graphic artists who arrange words and illustrations and prepare the material for printing. (Ch. 11-1)

Elements of art   Basic visual symbols artists use to create works of visual art. The elements of art are line, shape, form, space, value, color, and texture. (Ch. 4-1)

Elevation   A drawing of an outside view of a building. (Ch. 14-2)

Emphasis   A principle of art that stresses one element of art or makes an area in a work of art stand out. (Ch. 5-3)

Encaustic (in-**kaw**-stik)   A painting medium in which pigment is mixed into melted wax. (Ch. 10-1)

Facade (fuh-**sahd**)   The front of a building. (Ch. 14-2)

Fauves (**fohvs**)   An art movement begun early in this century in France, in which the artists use wild, intense color combinations in their paintings. (Ch. 7-3)

Fibers Any thin, threadlike materials. (Ch. 13-1)

Fine art Art made purely to be experienced visually. (Ch. 1-2)

Fired Hardened by heating in a kiln. (Ch. 13-1)

Floor plan A scale drawing of how a room or building would appear without a roof as if seen from above. (Ch. 14-2)

Form An object with three dimensions—height, width, and depth. (Ch. 4-5)

Freestanding Surrounded on all sides by space. (Ch. 3-5), (Ch. 12-3)

Fresco (**fres**-koh) A painting medium in which pigment is applied to a wall spread with wet plaster. (Ch. 10-1)

Gesture drawing Drawing lines quickly and loosely to show movement in a subject. (Ch. 8-2)

Glassblowing The craft of shaping melted glass by blowing air into it through a tube. (Ch. 13-1)

Glaze A thin, transparent layer of paint. (Ch. 10-1)

Glazed Coated with a mixture of powdered chemicals that melt during firing into a hard, glasslike finish. (Ch. 13-1)

Graphic artists Artists that work in the field of art known as graphic design. (Ch. 11-1)

Graphic design The field of art that uses pictures and words to instruct or to communicate a specific message. (Ch. 11-1)

Harmony A principle of art concerned with blending the elements of art in a pleasing way. (Ch. 5-3)

Hatching A shading technique that involves drawing a series of thin lines running parallel, or in the same direction. (Ch. 8-1)

High relief Relief that stands out boldly from its background. (Ch. 12-2)

Hue A color's name. (Ch. 4-2)

Illustrators Graphic artists who create printed materials that explain or teach. (Ch. 11-1)

Impasto (im-**pahs**-toh) Thick, buttery layers. (Ch. 10-1)

Intaglio (in-**tal**-yoh) A printmaking method in which the image to be printed is cut or scratched into a surface. (Ch. 9-2)

Intensity The brightness or dullness of a hue. (Ch. 4-2)

Interpreting In art criticism, determining and explaining the meaning, mood, or idea of the work of art. (Ch. 6-4); In art history, noting how time and place affect an artist's style and subject matter. (Ch. 7-5)

Judging In art criticism, making a decision about a work's success or lack of success and giving reasons to support that decision. (Ch. 6-6); In art history, deciding whether a work introduces a new style or if it is an outstanding example of a particular style. (Ch. 7-7)

Kiln A special piece of equipment used to fire ceramics. (Ch. 13-1)

Layout The arrangement of words and pictures on a page. (Ch. 11-1)

Line The path of a dot through space. (Ch. 4-4)

Line quality The unique character of any line. (Ch. 4-4)

Line variation The thickness or thinness, lightness or darkness of a line. (Ch. 4-4)

Lithograph (**lith**-uh-graf) A print made by lithography. (Ch. 9-2)

Lithography (lith-**ahg**-ruh-fee) A printmaking method in which the image to be printed is drawn on limestone with a special greasy crayon. (Ch. 9-2)

Logo A special image representing a business, group, or product. (Ch. 11-2)

Loom A frame or machine that holds a set of threads that runs vertically. (Ch. 13-1)

Low relief Relief that stands out in space only slightly. (Ch. 12-2)

Madonna A work showing the mother of Christ. (Ch. 7-5)

Medium of art A material such as paint, clay, or glass used to create a work of art. (Ch. 3-1)

Microprocessors (my-kroh-**prahs**-es-uhrs) Tiny computers. (Ch. 15-5)

Mixed media The use of more than one medium to create a work of art. (Ch. 3-1)

Modeling A sculpting method in which a soft or workable material is built up and shaped. (Ch. 12-1)

Monochromatic colors (mahn-uh-kroh-**mat**-ik) Different values of a single hue. (Ch. 4-2)

Monoprinting A printmaking method in which the image to be printed is put on the plate with ink or paint and then transferred to paper or cloth by pressing or hand-rubbing. (Ch. 9-2)

Motif (moh-**teef**) A unit that is repeated over and over in a pattern or visual rhythm. (Ch. 4-3)

Motion picture Photographs of the same subject taken a very short time apart and flashed onto a screen. (Ch. 15-3)

Movement A principle of art that leads the viewer to sense action in a work or a path that the viewer's eye follows throughout a work. (Ch. 5-5)

Negatives Reverse images of the object photographed. (Ch. 15-1)

Non-objective Having no recognizable subject matter. (Ch. 2-1)

Non-objective art A work with no objects or subjects that can be readily identified. (Ch. 6-1)

Oil paint Paint with an oil base. (Ch. 10-1)

Opaque (oh-**pake**) Does not let light through. (Ch. 10-1)

Palette Any tray or plate where paints are mixed before use. (Ch. 10-1)

Patrons of the arts Sponsors, or supporters, of an artist or art-related places and events. (Ch. 1-3)

Perceiving Looking at and thinking deeply about what you see. (Ch. 1-1)

Perception   The ability to really see and think deeply about an object. (Ch. 8-1)

Photogram   An image made on blueprint paper through the action of light and gas fumes. (Ch. 15-2)

Photography   The art of making images by exposing a chemically treated surface to light. (Ch. 15-1)

Pigment   A finely ground, colored powder that gives paint its color. (Ch. 3-3), (Ch. 10-1)

Point of view   The angle from which the viewer sees the scene. (Ch. 1-1)

Post and lintel (**lint**-uhl)   A building method in which a crossbeam is placed above two uprights. (Ch. 14-2)

Pottery   The craft of making objects from clay. (Ch. 13-1)

Principles of art   Guidelines that govern the way elements go together. (Ch. 5-1)

Print   An image that is transferred from a prepared surface to paper or fabric. (Ch. 3-2)

Printing plate   A surface onto or into which the image is placed. (Ch. 9-1)

Printmaking   Transferring an inked image from a prepared surface to another surface. (Ch. 9-1)

Producer   The person in charge of the business end of making a movie. (Ch. 15-3)

Proportion   A principle of art concerned with the size relationships of one part to the whole and of one part to another. (Ch. 5-3)

Registration   Careful matching up of plates in prints with more than one color. (Ch. 9-2)

Relief   A type of sculpture in which forms and figures are projected from the front only. (Ch. 3-5), (Ch. 12-2)

Relief printing   A printmaking method in which the image to be printed is raised from a background. (Ch. 9-2)

Renaissance (ren-uh-**sahns**)   A French word meaning "rebirth." (Ch. 7-5)

Reproduction   A photograph of a print. (Ch. 3-2)

Rhythm   A principle of art concerned with repeating an element of art to create the illusion of movement. (Ch. 5-5)

Scoring   Roughing or scratching clay with a clay tool (or fork). (Technique Tip **17** *Handbook,* page **275**)

Screen printing   A printmaking technique in which the artist transfers the design to the screen through various processes. (Ch. 9-2)

Serigraph (**sir**-uh-graf)   A screen print that has been handmade by an artist. (Ch. 9-2)

Shading   The use of light and shadow to give a feeling of depth. (Ch. 8-1)

Shape   An area clearly set off by one or more of the other five visual elements of art. (Ch. 4-5)

Slab   A slice or sheet of clay. (Ch. 13-3)

Slip   Clay that has so much added water that it is liquid and runny. It is used to fasten pieces of clay together. (Ch. 13-1)

Solvent   A liquid that controls the thickness or thinness of the paint. (Ch. 3-3), (Ch. 10-1)

Space   The distance or area between, around, above, below, and within things. (Ch. 4-5)

Stippling   A shading technique achieved by using dots. (Ch. 8-1)

Style   An artist's personal way of expressing ideas in a work. (Ch. 3-3), (Ch. 7-3)

Subject   The image viewers can easily identify. (Ch. 2-1)

Subtractive   A sculpting method produced by removing or taking away from the original material. (Ch. 12-1)

Super-realism   A style of art devoted to extraordinarily realistic works. (Ch. 2-2)

Synthetic paints   Manufactured paints with plastic binders. (Ch. 10-1)

Tempera (**tem**-puh-rah)   A painting medium in which pigment mixed with egg yolk and water is applied with tiny brush strokes. (Ch. 10-1)

Texture   How things feel, or look as though they might feel, if touched. (Ch. 4-7)

Three-dimensional   Having height, width, and depth. (Ch. 3-5)

Transparent   Clear. (Ch. 10-1)

Two-dimensional   Having height and width but not depth. (Ch. 3-5)

Typefaces   Styles of lettering for the printed material. (Ch. 11-1)

Unity   The arrangement of elements and principles with media to create a feeling of completeness. (Ch. 5-7)

Value   The lightness or darkness of a hue. (Ch. 4-2)

Variety   A principle of art concerned with combining one or more elements of art to create interest. (Ch. 5-3)

Video game   An electronic form of entertainment run by a computer. (Ch. 15-5)

Warp   The lengthwise threads attached to the loom. (Ch. 13-4)

Watercolor   A painting medium in which pigment is blended with gum arabic and water. (Ch. 10-1)

Weaving   A craft in which fiber strands are interlocked to make cloth or objects. (Ch. 13-1)

Weft   The crosswise threads pulled across the warp. (Ch. 13-4)

Wet plate   A method of photography in which an image is created on glass that is coated with chemicals, then transferred to paper or cardboard. (Ch. 15-1)

Work of art   Any object created or designed by an artist. (Ch. 2-1)

A

Abstract art
defined, 216
studio lessons
action painting, 300-301
sculpture, 216-217
Acrylic, 180-181, *Fig.* 10-6
applying to a stamp, 275
defined, 181
Action painting
defined, 300
studio lesson, 300-301
Adams, Ansel, 318
Fig. S-25
Additive sculpting techniques, 47, 210
Adventures of Robin Hood, The, 259
Advertising artist, 291
Advertising design, 190, 193-194, 205,
*Chapter 11 Opener, Chapter 11 Review
Detail, Fig.* 11-4
career in, 291
posters, 200-201, *Fig.* 11-12
studio lesson, 200-201
Aesthetics
"big picture" and, 23
defined, 20-21
Aesthetic views, 21-23
"big picture" and, 23
composition and, 22
content and, 22
defined, 21
judging art works and, 112-113
studio experience for, 23
studio lesson, 304-307
subject and, 21
Agbatana III, 22, *Fig.* 2-6
Alonzo, Daniel, 302
A Whale of a Mural, 302, *Fig.* S-5
Alphabet Blocks in Case, 223, *Fig.* 13-2
Alpha Wolf, 225, *Fig.* 13-8
Ammonia, safety tip for, 257
Amphitheaters, 240, 241, *Fig.* 14-4
Analogous color schemes, 59
Analyzing (art criticism), 106-107, 115
defined, 106
design chart for, 106-107, *Figs.* 6-7, 6-8
Analyzing (art history), 124-127
art movements, 125-127
defined, 124
Animator, career as, 291
Annunciation, The, 210, *Fig.* 12-4
AP (Approved Product) paint label, 41
Applied art, 5
architecture as, 241
defined, 4, 113
judging, 113
See also Architecture; Careers; Crafts;
Illustration; Video games; *specific arts
and crafts*
Appliqué banner, studio lesson, 308-
311
Approved Product (AP) paint label, 41
Architect, *Fig.* 3-2
career as, 292
city planner, 294

defined, 238
landscape architect, 297
Architecture, 236-248
beginnings of, 238-239
challenge of, 241
clay model, 242-243
defined, 238
drawing and, 30-31, *Fig.* 3-2
entrance relief, 246-247
floor plans, 242, 244-245
structures for business, 240, *Figs.* 14-4,
14-5
structures for entertainment, 241, *Figs.*
14-4, 14-6
structures for prayer, 239, *Figs.* 14-2,
14-3
studio lessons, 242-247
clay entrance relief, 246-247
clay model, 242-243
drawing floor plans, 244-245
uses of, 239-241
Art adviser to corporations, 292
Art appreciation
architecture, 241
See also Art criticism; Art history
Art critic, 100
Art criticism, 98-116
analyzing, 106-107, 115
defined, 100
describing, 100-105, 114
interpreting, 108-111, 115
judging, 112-113, 115
steps of, 100
Art director for performing arts, 293
Art historians
defined, 120
history and, 139
Art history, 118-140
analyzing, 124-127
architecture, 238-241
defined, 120
describing, 120-121
interpreting, 130-133
judging, 136-139
Art production. *See* Studio lessons
Artist profiles, 283-289
Cassatt, Mary, 283
Dürer, Albrecht, 283
Homer, Winslow, 284
Hopper, Edward, 284
Kandinsky, Wassily, 285
Matisse, Henri, 285
O'Keeffe, Georgia, 286
Picasso, Pablo, 286
Raphael (Sanzio), 287
Renoir, Pierre Auguste, 287
Toulouse-Lautrec, Henri de, 288
van Gogh, Vincent, 288
Vigée-Lebrun, Marie-Louise-
Élisabeth, 289
Wyeth, Andrew, 289
Artists
credit line for, 19
defined, 4
See also Careers

Artist's Garden at Vetheuil, The, 127,
Fig. 7-8
Art movements, 125-127
Ashcan School, 284
Cubism, 286
defined, 125
Fauvism, 125, 128-129, *Figs.* 7-7, 7-9
Impressionism, 126-127, 127, 138, 287,
Figs. 7-6, 7-8, 7-19
Renaissance, 132-133, *Figs.* 7-13,
7-14
Art style. *See* Style
Art teacher, career as, 293
Art therapist, career as, 294
Ashcan School, 294
Assembling, 47, 210-211, *Figs.* 12-5, 12-6
defined, 210
studio lessons
abstract sculpture, 216-217
freestanding mobile, 314-315
objective wire sculpture, 312-313
Assumption of the Virgin, The, 80, 81,
Fig. 5-2
Asymmetrical (informal) balance, 81,
Fig. 5-3
Athena Nike, temple of, 236-237, 239,
249, *Chapter 14 Opener, Chapter 14
Review Detail*
Atmosphere and Environment, 211, *Fig.*
12-6
At the Opera, 16-17, 19, *Fig.* 2-1
Autobiography, 12
Autumn on the Hudson River, 124, 125,
Fig. 7-4

B

Background, describing, 114
Back stitch, 310, *Fig.* S-17
Balance, 80-83
defined, 80
formal (symmetrical), 80, 81, *Figs.* 5-1,
5-2
studio lesson, 82-83
informal (asymmetrical), 81, *Fig.* 5-3
radial, 81, *Fig.* 5-4
Banded Tulip Basket, 223, *Fig.* 13-4
Banner, appliqué, studio lesson, 308-311
Basilicas, 240
Batman, 259, *Fig.* 15-11
*Bay of Marseille, Seen from L'Estaque,
The,* 52, 77, *Chapter 4 Opener, Chapter
4 Review Detail*
Bedroom, The, 100, 101, 102, 108-109,
Figs. 6-1, 6-10
Bell, studio lesson, 227
Between the Clock and the Bed, 91,
Fig. 5-14
Binder, 39, 178
Bisqueware, 225
Blanket, Chilkat, 220-221, 235, *Chapter
13 Opener, Chapter 13 Review Detail*
Blanket stitch, 310, *Fig.* S-17
Blending, 147
Blind contour drawing. *See* Contour
drawing

Blind Pew, 202, *Fig.* 11-14
Block prints
  linoleum blocks, 170-171
  print motifs, 298-299
Blue Tree, 74, *Fig.* 4-27
Boccioni, Umberto, 90
  Dynamic Force of a Cyclist I, 90, *Fig.* 5-13
Bonheur, Rosa, 7
  Buffalo Bill on Horseback, 7, *Fig.* 1-7
Bourke-White, Margaret, 250-251
  Mahatma Gandhi, 250-251, 267, *Chapter 15 Opener, Chapter 15 Review Detail*
Brady, Mathew, 253, 266
  Civil War, 253, 266, *Fig.* 15-3
Brancusi, Constantin, 68, 69
  Mlle Pogany II, 68, 69, *Fig.* 4-21
Braque, Georges, 134
  Le Courrier, 134, *Fig.* 7-15
Brayer, 101
Brush
  cleaning, 273-274
  drawing thin lines with, 271
Buffalo Bill on Horseback, 7, *Fig.* 1-7
Bullion stitch, 310, *Fig.* S-17
Burgos Cathedral, rose window in, 81, *Fig.* 5-4
Burton, Tim, 259
  Batman, 259, *Fig.* 15-11
Buttonhole stitch, 310, *Fig.* S-17

C

c., defined, 19
Cable Car Festival, 182, *Fig.* 10-7
Calder, Alexander, 312, 314
  freestanding mobile [untitled], 314, *Fig.* S-21
  The Hostess, 312, *Fig.* S-18
Calle, Paul, 142-143, 144
  Gemini VI Astronauts, 142-143, 144, 157, *Chapter 8 Opener, Chapter 8 Review Detail*
Calotype, 256, *Fig.* 15-6
Camera, 252
  studio lesson, 318-319
Camera obscura, 252, *Fig.* 15-1
Cannon, T. C., 23
  Turn of the Century Dandy, 23, *Fig.* 2-7
Careers, 291-297
  advertising artist, 291
  animator, 291
  architect, 292
  art adviser to corporations, 292
  art director for the performing arts, 293
  art teacher, 293
  art therapist, 294
  city planner, 294
  exhibit and display designer, 295
  fashion designer, 295
  industrial designer, 296
  interior designer, 296
  landscape architect, 297
  museum curator, 297
Caress, The, 35, 283, *Fig.* 3-9
Carpeaux, Jean Baptiste, 208, 209
  Neapolitan Fisherboy, 208, 209, *Fig.* 12-2
Carving, 47, 210, *Fig.* 12-4
  defined, 210
  studio lesson, 212-213

Cassatt, Mary, 16-17, 19, 35, 283
  artist profile, 283
  At the Opera, 16-17, 19, *Fig.* 2-1
  Maternal Caress, 35, 283, *Fig.* 3-9
Casting, 47, 210
  defined, 210
Cat Dreams, 230, *Fig.* 13-14
Cathedral, 300, *Fig.* S-4
Cathedrals
  Burgos, 81, *Fig.* 5-4
  Leon, 239, *Figs.* 14-2, 14-3
  See also Religious architecture; Temples
Cats, 14-15, 27, *Chapter 2 Opener, Chapter 2 Review Detail*
Cave paintings, 54, 178, *Fig.* 4-1
Ceramics, 224-225
  studio lessons, 214-215, 226-229
  See also Clay; Pottery
Cézanne, Paul, 52
  The Bay of Marseille, Seen from L'Estaque, 52, 77, *Chapter 4 Opener, Chapter 4 Review Detail*
Chain stitch, 310, *Fig.* S-17
Chalk
  mood painting, 110-111
  safety tip for, 111
Checklists
  art criticism questions, 114
  elements, 101, 102, *Fig.* 6-2
Chernow, Ann, 32
  Lady of L. A., 32, *Fig.* 3-5
Chilkat blanket, 220-221, 235, *Chapter 13 Opener, Chapter 13 Review Detail*
Chinese embroidery (parrots), 308, *Fig.* S-14
Christina's World, 114-115, 179, 289, *Figs.* 6-16, 10-2
Cinematographer, 259
Citizen Kane, 259, *Fig.* 15-10
City planner, career as, 294
Cityscape, studio lessons, 82-83, 304-307
City, The, 146, *Fig.* 8-3
Civil War, 253, 266, *Fig.* 15-3
Clay
  architecture model from, 242-243
  bowl, 226-227
  conditions of, 225
  entrance relief, 246-247
  firing, 225
  leather hard, 225
  methods of working, 225, 226-229, 275-276
  modeling, 214-215
  plastic, 225
  safety tip for, 213
  slab container, 228-229
  slip, 225
  studio lessons
    bowl, 226-227
    entrance relief, 246-247
    model (architecture), 242-243
    modeling (sculpting), 214-215
    slab container, 228-229
  technique tips, 275-276
    clay mold for plaster relief, 276
    joining clay, 275-276
    working with clay, 275
  See also Ceramics; Pottery

Cleaning a brush, 273-274
Clodion (Claude Michel), 214
  The River Rhine Separating the Waters, 214, *Fig.* 12-8
Cockfight-Variation, 211, *Fig.* 12-5
Collage, 10-11
  defined, 10, 134
  of letters, 195
  self-portrait, 122-123
  studio lessons, 10-11
    self-portrait, 122-123
    time and place, 134-135
  technique tips, tissue paper, 281
  time and place, 134-135
  tissue paper, 281
Color, 56-61
  combining colors, 59-61
    studio lesson, 60-61
  hue, 57-58
  intensity, 58-59
  proportion in, 87
  studio lesson, 60-61
  traits of, 56-58
  value, 58-59
    technique tips, 274
  wheel, 56, 57, 58, *Fig.* 4-4
Colored Rhythm No. 698, 184, *Fig.* 10-9
Color schemes, 59
  analogous, 59
  complementary, 60-61
  cool, 59
  monochromatic, 59
    studio lesson, 60-61
  warm, 59
Color wheel, 56, *Fig.* 4-4
  complementary colors on, 58
  defined, 56
  primary hues on, 57
Colosseum, 240, 241, *Fig.* 14-4
Combining colors. *See* Color schemes
Comic strips, 198-199, *Fig.* 11-10
  studio lesson, 198-199
Commissioned art, 8
Communication connections, 50
Community affairs connections, 248
Compagnie Française des Chocolats et des Thés, 193-194, *Fig.* 11-4
Complementary colors, 58
Composition, 18-19
  aesthetic view relating to, 22
  defined, 18
Computers
  film and, 259
  video games and, 262, *Fig.* 15-14
Constructed Head No. 2, 216, *Fig.* 12-10
Content, 17-18
  aesthetic view relating to, 22
  defined, 17
  interpreting, 108-111, 115
Contour drawing
  defined, 150
  studio lesson, 150-151
  technique tips, 271
Cool color schemes, 59
Corporate art adviser, 293
Cottages at North Truro, Massachusetts, 42, 43, 284, *Fig.* 3-17
Couching stitch, 310, *Fig.* S-17

Country Gospel Music, 88, *Fig.* 5-12
CP (Certified Product) paint label, 41
Crafts, 220-235
  ceramics, 224-225
    studio lessons, 226-229
  defined, 222
  glassblowing, 224
  jewelry making, 232-233
  media of, 223
  stitchery
    chart of stitches, 310, *Fig.* S-17
    studio lesson, 308-311
  studio lessons, 226-233
    clay bowl, 226-227
    jewelry, 232-233
    slab container, 228-229
    stitchery, 308-311
    weaving, 230-231
  See also Applied art; *specific crafts*
Craftsperson, defined, 222
Credit line
  defined, 19
  reading a credit line, 19
Cropsey, Jasper Francis, 124, 125
  Autumn on the Hudson River, 124, 125,
    Fig. 7-4
Crosshatching, 147
Cross stitch, 310, *Fig.* S-17
Cubism, 286
Curator, career as, 297
Curling paper, 278
Curved lines, 63, *Fig.* 4-14
Cutting, safety tips for, 45, 171
Cypresses, 63, 64, 288, *Fig.* 4-15

D

Daddi, Bernardo, 87
  Madonna and Child with Saints and
    Angels, 87, *Fig.* 5-10
Daguerre, L. J. M., 252, 253, 266
Daguerreotypes, 252, 253, *Fig.* 15-2
  defined, 252
Dali, Salvador, 7
  The Persistence of Memory, 7, *Fig.* 1-6
da Vinci, Leonardo, 132, 144, 145
  Five Grotesque Heads, 144, 145, *Fig.* 8-1
  influence on Raphael, 287
Davis, Stuart, 304, 305
  Place Pasdeloup, 304, 305, *Fig.* S-8
Death and the Mother, 54-55, *Fig.* 4-2
Degas, Edgar, 130, 131
  Four Dancers, 130, 131, *Fig.* 7-11
  influence on Cassatt, 283
Delaunay, Robert, 184
Delaunay, Sonia, 184
  Colored Rhythm No. 698, 184, *Fig.* 10-9
Derain, André, 125
  The River Seine at Carrieres-
    sur-Seine, 125, *Fig.* 7-5
Describing (art criticism), 100-105, 114
  defined, 100
  elements, 102
  guideline questions, 114
  non-objective art works, 102-103
  objective art works, 100-102
  size, medium, and process, 100
  studio lesson, 104-105

  subject, objects, and details,
    100-101
Describing (art history), 120-121
  defined, 121
Design. *See* Graphic design
Design careers. *See* Careers
Design chart
  for analyzing art works, 106-107, *Figs.*
    6-7, 6-8
  elements checklist, 102, *Fig.* 6-2
  unity, 95, *Fig.* 5-18
  video game flow chart, 263, *Fig.* 15-17
Design elements. *See* Elements of art
Detroit Industry, 178, *Fig.* 10-1
Diagonal lines, 63, *Fig.* 4-13
Dimension, three-dimensional art vs.
  two-dimensional art, 44
Director, 258
Display designer, career as, 297
Dove, Arthur G., 67
  Plant Forms, 67, *Fig.* 4-19
Drama connections, 26, 204
Draping method of papier-mâché, 277
Drawing, 30-33, 142-156
  contour drawing
    studio lesson, 150-151
    technique tips, 271
  fantasy jungle, 154-155
  floor plans, 242, 244-245
  gesture drawing
    studio lesson, 148-149
    technique tips, 271
  importance of, 30-31
  improving perception, 145
  making finished art, 146
  media of, 32-33, *Fig.* 3-4
  planning projects, 145
  presentation drawing, 152-153
  shading techniques, 146-147, 272, *Fig.*
    8-4
  space-creating techniques, 69
  studio lessons, 148-155, 244-245
    architecture floor plans, 244-245
    contour drawing, 150-151
    fantasy jungle, 154-155
    gesture drawing, 148-149
    presentation drawing, 152-153
  technique tips, 271-273
    contour drawings, 271
    enlarging using a grid, 271-272
    gesture drawings, 271
    oil pastels, 271
    ruler, using, 273
    shading, 272
    sighting, 272
    thin lines with a brush, 271
    viewing frame, using, 273
  uses of, 145-146
  See also Graphic design
Drawing Lesson, The, 28, 29, 51, *Chapter*
  3 Opener, Chapter 3 Review Detail
Dreams, as inspiration, 7
Drouth Stricken Area, 208, *Fig.* 12-1
Drug Store, 304, *Fig.* S-7
Duco paint, 180
Dürer, Albrecht, 158-159, 160-161, 283
  artist profile, 283

The Four Horsemen of the Apocalypse,
  158-159, 160–161, 175, *Chapter 9*
  Opener, Chapter 9 Review Detail
Dvorak, Lois, 10
  The Lizards, 10, *Fig.* 1-10
Dynamic Force of a Cyclist I, 90, 96, *Fig.*
  5-13

E

Earth pigments, making, 274
Echo of a Scream, 180, *Fig.* 10-5
Edition of prints
  creating, 161
  defined, 35, 161
Editorial design, 192
Editorial designer, 192
Egyptian architecture, 238-239
Elegy to the Spanish Republic 108, 17,
  18, *Fig.* 2-2
Elements of art, 18, 53-76
  analyzing art works and, 106-107, 115
  checklist for, 102, *Fig.* 6-2
  color, 56-61
  describing, 102, 114
  form, 67
  line, 62-65
  shape, 66-67
  space, 68-69
  texture, 72-73
  visual language, 54-55
Elevation, 242
El Greco, 106-107, 304, 305
  Saint Martin and the Beggar, 106-107,
    Figs. 6-6, 6-7, 6-8
  View of Toledo, 304, 305, *Fig.* S-9
Embroidery
  Chinese (parrots), 308, *Fig.* S-14
  See also Stitchery
Emphasis, 86, *Fig.* 5-9
  defined, 86
  studio lesson, 88-89
Encaustic, 178
  defined, 178
Engraving, 163
Enlarging drawings using a grid, 271-
  272
Enthroned Madonna and Child
  (Byzantine), 136, 138, *Fig.* 7-18
Entrance relief, studio lesson, 246-247
Epstein, Sir Jacob, 139
  Madonna and Child, 139, *Fig.* 7-20
Escobar, Marisol, 46, 47
  Poor Family I, 46, 47, *Fig.* 3-22
Estes, Richard, 112-113
  Telephone Booths, 112-113, *Fig.* 6-13
Etching (intaglio), 163, *Fig.* 9-5
Events, as inspiration, 7
Exhibit designer, career as, 295
Expressive painting, studio lesson,
  186-187

F

Facade, 242
Face, torn paper, studio lesson,
  24-25
Family Group (Glackens), 81, *Fig.* 5-3

Family Group (Moore), 206–207, 219, *Chapter 12 Opener, Chapter 12 Review Detail*
Fantasies, as inspiration, 7
Fantasy jungle, studio lesson, 154–155
Far Away Places, The, 102, 103, *Fig.* 6-3
Fashion design
  career in, 295
  drawing and, 30, 145, *Figs.* 3-1, 8-2
Fashion designer, 295
Fauvism, 125, 128–129, *Figs.* 7-7, 7-9
  defined, 125
  studio lesson, 128–129
Feather Stitch, 310, *Fig.* S-17
Fête Champêtre, 86, *Fig.* 5-9
Fibers, 224
Figure of Standing Youth, 45, *Fig.* 3-20
Film, 258–261
  animator, 291
  art of, 259
  beginnings of, 258
  cinematographer, 259
  director, 258
  producer, 259
  studio lesson, 260–261
Fine art
  defined, 4
  See also specific arts
Firing clay, 225
Five Grotesque Heads, 144, 145, *Fig.* 8-1
Floor plan
  for clay model, 242
  defined, 242
  drawing, 244–245
  studio lesson, 244–245
Flow chart, video game, 263, *Fig.* 15-17
Focus, space and, 69
Fog Warning, The, 316, *Fig.* S-23
Fontana, Lavinia, 179
  Portrait of a Noblewoman, 179, *Fig.* 10-3
Foreground, describing, 114
Form, 67
  classes of, 67
  defined, 67
  shape and, 67, *Fig.* 4-20
Formal (symmetrical) balance, 80, 81, 82–83, *Figs.* 5-1, 5-2, 5-5
  studio lesson, 82–83
Forum of Julius Caesar, 244, *Fig.* 14-8
Four Dancers, 130, 131, *Fig.* 7-11
Four Horsemen of the Apocalypse, The, 158–159, 160–161, 175, *Chapter 9 Opener, Chapter 9 Review Detail*
Freestanding, defined, 45, 214, *Fig.* 3-21
Freestanding mobile, studio lesson, 314–315
Fresco, 178, *Fig.* 10-11
  defined, 178

G

Gabo, Naum, 216
  Constructed Head No. 2, 216, *Fig.* 12-10
Gadget print, 37
Garden of Love, The, 39, *Fig.* 3-14
Garden of the Rectory at Nuenen, The, 94, *Fig.* 5-17
Gare Saint-Lazare, 24, *Fig.* 2-8

Garrison, Elizabeth, 222, 223
Georgia Quilt, 222, 223, *Fig.* 13-1
Gas (study for), 31, *Fig.* 3-3
Gemini VI Astronauts, 142–143, 144, 157, *Chapter 8 Opener, Chapter 8 Review Detail*
Genie, 107, 109, *Fig.* 6-9
Geometric shapes, 66, 67, *Fig.* 4-18
George Gershwin from Ten Portraits of Jews of the 20th Century, 172, *Fig.* 9-16
Georgia Quilt, 222, 223, *Fig.* 13-1
Gesture drawing, 148–149
  defined, 148
  studio lesson, 148–149
  technique tips, 271
Giacometti, Alberto, 55
  Man Pointing, 55, *Fig.* 4-3
Giotto, 136–137, 139
  Madonna and Child, 136–137, 139, *Fig.* 7-17
Girl with a Watering Can, 121, 287, *Fig.* 7-2
Giza, Great Sphinx of, 208, 209, *Fig.* 12-3
Glackens, William, 81
  Family Group, 81, *Fig.* 5-3
Glassblowing, 224
Glaze (ceramics)
  defined, 225
  safety tip for, 227
Glaze (painting), 179
Glue
  safety tip for, 11
  technique tips, 281
Glue prints, studio lesson, 168–169
Gogh, Vincent van. *See* van Gogh, Vincent
Goncharova, Natalia, 14–15, 23, 146
  Cats, 14–15, 23, 27, *Chapter 2 Opener, Chapter 2 Review Detail*
  The City Square, 146, *Fig.* 8-3
Graphic artists, 192
Graphic design, 190–204
  advertising design, 193–194, *Fig.* 11-4
  comic strips, 198–199, *Fig.* 11-10
  defined, 192
  editorial design, 192, *Fig.* 11-1
  illustration, 193, *Figs.* 11-2, 11-3, 11-15
  studio lesson, 202–203
  logos, 196–197, *Fig.* 11-8
  posters, 200–201, *Fig.* 11-2
  sign making, 194–195, *Figs.* 11-5, 11-6
  studio lessons, 196–203
    comic strips, 198–199
    illustration, 202–203
    logos, 196–197
    posters, 200–201
  See also Careers; Drawing; Painting
Graves, Nancy, Stevenson, 44
  Zaga, 44, *Fig.* 3-18
Great Sphinx of Giza, 208, 209, *Fig.* 12-3
Greek architecture, 236–237, 238, 239
  Parthenon, 238, 239, 242, *Figs.* 14-1, 14-7
  Temple of Athena Nike, 236–237, 239, 249, *Chapter 14 Opener, Chapter 14*

Review Detail
Greenware, 225
Grid for enlarging drawings, 271–272
Griffith, D. W., 258
  Intolerance, 258, *Fig.* 15-8
Gris, Juan, 150
  Max Jacob, 150, *Fig.* 8-8
Guggenheim Museum, 241, *Fig.* 14-6
Guidelines
  art criticism questions, 114
  elements checklist, 101, 102, *Fig.* 6-2
Gum arabic, 39
Gütenberg, Johannes, 50
Gwathmey, Robert, 88
  Country Gospel Music, 88, *Fig.* 5-12

H

Hanson, Duane, 21
  Sunbather, 21, *Fig.* 2-5
Harmony, 85, *Fig.* 5-8
  defined, 85
  studio lesson, 88–89
Harnett, William, 20, 21, 22
  My Gems, 20, 21, 22, *Fig.* 2-4
Hartigan, Grace, 103
  The Far Away Places, 103, *Fig.* 6-3
Hatching, 146
Health Label (HL) paint label, 41
Helmet, parade, 223, *Fig.* 13-3
Hepworth, Dame Barbara, 112
  Merryn, 113, *Fig.* 6-14
High relief, 212
High Steppin' Strutter I, 57, *Fig.* 4-5
History
  art historians and, 139
  See also Art history
HL (Health Label) paint label, 41
Hockney, David, 181
  Les Mamelles des Tiresias, 181, *Fig.* 10-6
Hogue, Alexandre, 208
  Drouth Stricken Area, 208, *Fig.* 12-1
Hokusai, Katsushika, 160
  View of Mt. Fuji from Seven-Ri Beach, 160, *Fig.* 9-1
Home economics connections, 140, 204
Homer, Winslow, 2–3, 12, 19, 90, 180, 284, 316
  artist profile, 284
  The Fog Warning, 316, *Fig.* S-23
  Return from the Hunt, 180, *Fig.* 10-4
  Right and Left, 2–3, 12, 19, 90, *Fig.* 1-1
Hooch, Pieter de, 100, 101, 102, 108–109
  The Bedroom, 100, 101, 102, 108–109, *Figs.* 6-1, 6-10
Hopper, Edward, 18, 19, 30–31, 42, 43, 284, 304
  artist profile, 284
  Cottages at North Truro, Massachusetts, 42, 43, 284, *Fig.* 3-16
  Drug Store, 304, *Fig.* S-7
  Gas (study for), 31, *Fig.* 3-3
  New York Movie, 18, 19, *Fig.* 2-3
Horizontal lines, 62–63, *Fig.* 4-12
Hostess, The, 312, *Fig.* S-18
Houser, Allan, 4–5
  Waiting for Dancing Partners, 4–5, *Fig.* 1-3

Hue, 57-58
  defined, 57
  intermediate, 58
  primary, 57
  secondary, 58
Husk Face Mask, 223, *Fig.* 13-5

I

Ichabod Crane, 6, *Fig.* 1-5
Idea bank, 9
Ideas. *See* Inspiration
Illustration, 193, 202-203, *Figs.* 11-2,
  11-3, 11-15
  studio lesson, 202-203
Illustrators, 193
Imagination
  as inspiration, 7
  studio lesson, 154-155
Impasto, 179
Impressionism, 126-127, 287, *Figs.* 7-6,
  7-8
  of Seurat, 138, *Fig.* 7-19
*Improvisation Number 27: The Garden
  of Love,* 39, 285, *Fig.* 3-13
Industrial arts connections, 50, 96, 234
Industrial designer, career as, 296
Informal (asymmetrical) balance, 81,
  Fig. 5-3
Ink, applying to a stamp, 275
Inness, George, 120, 121, 125, 131
  Lackawanna Valley, 120, 121, 125, 131,
  Fig. 7-1
Inquisition, 66, 67, *Fig.* 4-18
Inspiration, 6-9
  idea bank, 9
  traditional sources of, 6-8
Intaglio, 163, *Fig.* 9-5
Integrated circuit, 262, *Fig.* 15-14
Intensity of hue, 58-59, *Fig.* 4-7
  defined, 58
  lowering, 58
  space and, 69
Interior designer, career as, 296
Intermediate hues, 58
Interpreting (art criticism), 108-111, 115
  defined, 108
  non-objective art works, 109
  objective art works, 108-109
  studio lesson, 110-111
Interpreting (art history), 130-133
  collage and, 134-135
  defined, 130
  for style, 130, 131
  for style and subject matter, 132-133
  for subject matter, 130-131
In the Dining Room, 98, 99, 117, Chapter
  6 Opener, Chapter 6 Review Detail
Intolerance, 258, *Fig.* 15-8
Iris, Tulips, Jonquils and Crocuses,
  176-177, 189, Chapter 10 Opener,
  Chapter 10 Review Detail
Iroquoian husk face mask, 223,
  Fig. 13-5

J

Jan Cornelius Sylvius, The Preacher,
  148, *Fig.* 8-5

Jane Avril, 190-191, 193, 205, 288,
  Chapter 11 Opener, Chapter 11 Review
  Detail
Jar, Santa Clara Pueblo, New Mexico,
  226, *Fig.* 13-10
Jawlensky, Alexei von, 87
  Portrait of a Woman, 87, *Fig.* 5-11
Jemima Puddle-Duck, 193, *Fig.* 11-2
Jewelry, studio lesson, 232-233
Jigsaw mural, studio lesson, 303
Johns, Jasper, 91
  Between the Clock and the Bed, 91,
  Fig. 5-14
Join, 60, *Fig.* 4-8
Joining clay, 275-276
Judging (art criticism), 112-113, 115
  aesthetic views and, 112-113
  applied art, 113
  defined, 112
Judging (art history), 136-139
  defined, 136
  history and, 139
  for style, 136-138
  for technique, 138
Julius Caesar, Forum of, 244, *Fig.* 14-8
*Junior Wells and His Chicago Blues
  Band,* 200, *Fig.* 11-12

K

Kandinsky, Wassily, 39, 85, 285
  artist profile, 285
  *Improvisation Number 27: The Garden of
  Love,* 39, 285, *Fig.* 3-13
  Several Circles, 85, *Fig.* 5-8
Keats, Kim, 223
  Banded Tulip Basket, 223, *Fig.* 13-4
Kiln, 225
Kimiko, 224-225
  Vase, 224, 225, *Fig.* 13-9
Kingman, Dong, 182
  Cable Car Festival, 182, *Fig.* 10-7
Kiss, The, 162, *Fig.* 9-3
Knotted stitch, 310, *Fig.* S-17
Kollwitz, Käthe, 46, 47, 54-55
  Death and the Mother, 54-55, *Fig.* 4-2
  Self-Portrait, 46, 47, *Fig.* 3-21

L

Lackawanna Valley, 120, 121, 125, 131,
  Fig. 7-1
Ladder, The, 256, *Fig.* 15-6
Lady of L.A., 32, *Fig.* 3-5
La Gitane, 36, *Fig.* 3-10
Landscapes, studio lesson, 74-75
Lange, Dorothea, 253-254
  White Angel Breadline, 253, 254,
  Fig. 15-4
Lang, Fritz, 258
  Metropolis, 258, *Fig.* 15-9
Language arts connections, 12, 50, 76,
  116, 188
La Princesse Barbe Gallitzin, 148, 149,
  Fig. 8-6
Lascaux, cave paintings of, 54, 178,
  Fig. 4-1
Lawrence, Jacob, xi, bottom, 92,
  Toussaint L'Overture Series, 92, *Fig.* 5-15

Layout, 192
Leather hard clay, 225
Le Courrier, 134, *Fig.* 7-15
Lee, Doris, 164, 165
  Untitled, 164, 165, *Fig.* 9-8
Legends, as inspiration, 6
Leon, cathedral of, 239, *Figs.* 14-2, 14-3
Leonardo da Vinci. *See* da Vinci,
  Leonardo
Les Mamelles des Tiresias, 181, *Fig.* 10-6
Leyster, Judith, 122
  Self-Portrait, 122, *Fig.* 7-3
Line, 62-65
  curved lines, 63, *Fig.* 4-14
  defined, 62
  diagonal lines, 63, *Fig.* 4-13
  drawing media and, 33
  drawing thin lines with a brush, 271
  horizontal lines, 62-63, *Fig.* 4-12
  kinds of, 62-63
  movement and, 62
  perspective using, 69
  quality of, 63-65
  vertical lines, 62, *Fig.* 4-11
  zigzag lines, 63, 65, *Fig.* 4-16
Linear perspective, 69
Line quality, 63-65, *Fig.* 4-17
  defined, 63
Line variation, 65, *Fig.* 4-17
  defined, 65
Linoleum block prints, 170-171,
  Fig. 9-14
  studio lesson, 170-171
Linseed oil, 39
Lippi, Fra Filippo, 133
  Madonna and Child, 133, *Fig.* 7-14
Lithograph, 165
Lithography, 164-165, *Fig.* 9-6
  defined, 165
Lizards, The, 10, *Fig.* 1-10
Lloyd, Harold, 260
  Safety Last, 260, *Fig.* 15-12
Logos, 196-197, *Fig.* 11-8
  defined, 196
  studio lesson, 196-197
Loom, 224, *Fig.* 13-6
  cardboard, 230-231
  warping, 230-231, *Fig.* 13-15
Low relief, 212

M

MacNelly, Jeff, 198
  Shoe comic strip, 198, *Fig.* 11-10
Madonna, 132-133, *Figs.* 7-13, 7-14
  defined, 133
  medieval, 136
Madonna and Child, Enthroned
  (Byzantine), 136, 138, *Fig.* 7-18
Madonna and Child (Epstein), 139,
  Fig. 7-20
Madonna and Child (Giotto), 136-137,
  139, *Fig.* 7-17
Madonna and Child (Lippi), 133,
  Fig. 7-14
*Madonna and Child with Saints and
  Angels,* 87, *Fig.* 5-10
Mahatma Gandhi, 250-251, 267, Chapter
  15 Opener, Chapter 15 Review Detail

Manet, Édouard, 24
  Gare Saint-Lazare, 24, *Fig.* 2-8
Manguin, Henri-Charles, 39, 40
  Port Saint-Tropez, le 14 Juillet, 39, 40,
    Fig. 3-14
Mann, Tony, 223
  Alphabet Blocks in Case, 223, *Fig.* 13-2
Man Pointing, 55, *Fig.* 4-3
Markers, safety tip for, 153, 197
Mask, Iroquoian, 223, *Fig.* 13-5
Matisse, Henri, 84, 85, 128-129, 136, 285
  artist profile, 285
  The Red Studio, 128-129, 136, 285, *Fig.* 7-9
  Woman in a Purple Coat, 84, 85, *Fig.* 5-7
Mat making, 279
Max Jacob, 150, *Fig.* 8-8
Media
  of crafts, 223
  in credit line, 19
  defined, 30
  describing, 100
  of drawing, 32-33, *Fig.* 3-4
  of painting, 38-39, 178-181, *Fig.* 3-13
  of printmaking, 34, 35, *Fig.* 3-8
  of sculpture, 45-47, *Fig.* 3-20
  See also Mixed media
Merryn, 113, *Fig.* 6-14
Metropolis, 258, *Fig.* 15-9
Michelangelo, 132
  influence on Raphael, 287
Michel, Claude. *See* Clodion
Microprocessors, 262, *Fig.* 15-14
Mills, Robert, 152
  rejected sketch of Washington
    Monument, 152, *Fig.* 8-11
Miró, Joan, 4
  Three Women, 4, *Fig.* 1-2
Mission San Jose, 246, *Fig.* 14-11
Mixed media
  defined, 30
  studio lessons, 48-49
    self-portrait, 122-123
Mixing paint to change value of color,
  274
Mlle Pogany II, 68, 69, *Fig.* 4-21
Mobile, 314, *Fig.* S-21
  studio lesson, 314-315
Modeling, 47, 210
  defined, 210
  studio lesson
    architectural model, 242-243
    sculpting, 214-215
Mold for plaster relief, making from
  clay, 276
Monastery of Oliva, 80, 81, *Fig.* 5-1
Mondrian, Piet, 74
  Blue Tree, 74, *Fig.* 4-27
Monet, Claude, 127
  The Artist's Garden at Vetheuil, 127,
    Fig. 7-8
  friendship with Renoir, 287
Monochromatic color schemes, 59
Monoprinting, 166-167, *Fig.* 9-10
  defined, 166
  studio lesson, 166-167
Mood chalk painting, studio lesson,
  110-111

Moore, Henry, 206-207
  Family Group, 206-207, 219, *Chapter 12
    Opener, Chapter 12 Review Detail*
Morisot, Berthe, 98, 99
  In the Dining Room, 98, 99, 117, *Chapter
    6 Opener, Chapter 6 Review Detail*
Moscoso, Victor, 200
  Junior Wells and His Chicago Blues Band,
    200, *Fig.* 11-12
Motherwell, Robert, 17, 18
  Elegy to the Spanish Republic 108, 17, 18,
    Fig. 2-2
Motif
  defined, 60
  studio lessons
    color combinations with motif, 60-61
    print motifs, 298-299
Motion picture
  defined, 258
  See also Film
Mounting two-dimensional works, 280
Movement, 90, 91, 92-93, *Fig.* 5-13
  defined, 90
  gesture drawing for, 148-149
  line and, 62
  studio lesson, 92-93
Movements. *See* Art movements
Movies. *See* Film
Munch, Edvard, 162
  The Kiss, 162, *Fig.* 9-3
Mural
  Mexican, 178, *Fig.* 10-1
  studio lesson, 302-303
Murillo, Bartholomé Esteban, 8, 19
  The Return of the Prodigal Son, 8, 19,
    Fig. 1-8
Murray, Elizabeth, 60
  Join, 60, *Fig.* 4-8
Muses, 6
Museum curator, career as, 297
Music connections, 26
My Gems, 20, 21, 22, *Fig.* 2-4
Myths, as inspirations, 6

N
Nampeyo, Dextra Q., 227
  Jar, 227, *Fig.* 13-11
Natural earth pigments, making, 274
Neapolitan Fisherboy, 208, 209, *Fig.* 12-2
Neel, Alice, 186
  T. B. Harlem, 186, *Fig.* 10-11
Negatives, photographic, 253
Nevelson, Louise, 211
  Atmosphere and Environment, 211,
    Fig. 12-6
New York Movie, 18, 19, *Fig.* 2-3
Non-objective art
  defined, 17, 102
  describing, 102-103
  interpreting, 109
  origin of, 285
  studio lessons, 88-89, 184-185

O
Oil paint, 179, *Fig.* 10-3
  defined, 179

glaze, 179
impasto, 179
ingredients of, 39
technique tips
  cleaning a brush, 273-274
  mixing paint to change value of
    color, 274
Oil pastels, technique tips, 271
O'Keeffe, Georgia, 39, 41, 42, 43, 82-83,
    212, 213, 286
  artist profile, 286
  Radiator Building, 82-83, *Fig.* 5-5
  Sunrise, 39, 41, 42, 43, *Fig.* 3-15
  The White Calico Flower, 212, 213, 286,
    Fig. 12-7
Oliva, monastery of, 80, 81, *Fig.* 5-1
Olson, Christina, 289
Opaque, 179
Organic shapes, 67, *Fig.* 4-19
Orozco, José Clemente, 57, 58
  Zapatistas, 57, 58, *Fig.* 4-6
Overlapping, space and, 69
Owens, Bob, 225
  Alpha Wolf, 225, *Fig.* 13-8

P
Pac-Man, 262, 263, *Fig.* 15-16
Paint
  acrylic, 180-181
  encaustic, 178
  fresco, 178, *Fig.* 10-1
  ingredients of, 39
  oil paint, 39, 179
  poster paints (school tempera), 179, 275
  safety tips for, 41, 217, 318
  spray paint, 217, 318
  technique tips
    applying paint to a stamp, 275
    cleaning a brush, 273-274
    making natural earth pigments, 274
    mixing paint to change value of
      color, 274
    poster paints (school tempera),   275
    watercolors, 275
  tempera, 179
  watercolor, 39, 42-43, 180, 182-183, 275
Painting, 38-41, 176-188
  abstract, 300-301
  acrylic, 180-181, *Fig.* 10-6
  action painting, 300-301
  drawing and, 30
  encaustic, 178
  expressive, 186-187
  fresco, 178, *Fig.* 10-1
  history of, 178
  media of, 38-39, 178-181, *Fig.* 3-13
  mural
    Mexican, 178, *Fig.* 10-1
    studio lesson, 302-303
  non-objective, 88-89, 184-185
  oil paint, 39, 179, *Fig.* 10-3
  paint characteristics, 38
  space-creating techniques, 69
  studio lessons
    abstract action painting, 300-301
    color combinations, 60-61
    expressive, 186-187

Painting (Continued)
in Fauve style, 128-129
group mural, 302-303
landscapes, 74-75
mood chalk painting, 110-111
non-objective, 88-89, 184-185
picture that tells a story, 316-317
pigment, 42-43
watercolor, 42-43, 182-183
styles of, 39-41
technique tips, 273-275
cleaning a brush, 273-274
making natural earth pigments, 274
mixing paint to change value of
color, 274
poster paints (school tempera), 275
watercolors, 275
tempera, 179, *Fig.* 10-2
watercolor, 39, 180, 182-183, *Fig.* 10-4
studio lessons, 42-43, 182-183
technique tips, 275
Palette, 180
Panton, Verner, 113
Stacking Side Chair, 113, *Fig.* 6-15
Paper
curling, 278
pleating, 278
scoring, 278, 280
studio lessons
freestanding mobile, 314-315
jewelry, 232-233
pop-up cityscape, 304-307
print motifs on wrapping paper,
298-299
sculpture, 70-71
torn paper face, 24-25
technique tips
papier-mâché, 277-278
scoring, 278, 280
sculpture, 278
tissue paper collage, 281
tissue paper collage, 281
Paper Jewelry Pin, 233, *Fig.* 13-18
Papier-mâché, 277-278
draping method, 277
pulp method, 277
strip method, 277
supports for creations, 277-278
Parade helmet, 223, *Fig.* 13-3
Parthenon, 238, 239, 242, *Figs.* 14-1, 14-7
Pater, Jean-Baptist-Joseph, 86
Fête Champêtre, 86, *Fig.* 5-9
Patrons of the arts, 8
Pattern. *See* Motif
People, as inspiration, 7
Perceiving
defined, 2
drawing and, 145
Perception
defined, 145
improving, 145
Performing arts, art director for, 293
Persistence of Memory, The, 7, *Fig.* 1-6
Personal events and feelings, as
inspiration, 7
Perspective, linear, 69
Perugino, 287

Photogram
defined, 256
studio lesson, 256-257
Photography, 252-257
as art, 255
defined, 252
history of, 252-254
studio lessons
photogram (calotype), 256
pinhole camera, 318-319
Physical education connections, 204
Picasso, Pablo, 118-119, 170, 286
artist profile, 286
Seated Woman, 170, *Fig.* 9-14
Three Musicians, 118-119, 141, *Chapter 7
Opener, Chapter 7 Review Detail*
Pigment
defined, 39, 178
making natural earth pigments, 274
studio lesson, 42-43
Pinhole camera, studio lesson, 318-319
Placement, space and, 69
Place Pasdeloup, 304, 305, *Fig.* S-8
Planning, drawing and, 145
Plant Forms, 67, *Fig.* 4-19
Plaques
defined, 213
studio lesson, 212-213
See also Relief
Plaster
mixing, 276
relief
studio lesson, 212-213
technique tips, 276
safety tip for, 213
Plastic clay consistency, 225
Pleak, Jane, 228
ceramic cylinder, 228, *Fig.* 13-12
Pleating paper, 278
Point of view
defined, 3
studio experience for, 3
Pollock, Jackson, 300
Cathedral, 300, *Fig.* S-4
Polyurethane sprays, safety tip for, 233
Pong, 262
Poor Family I, 46, 47, *Fig.* 3-23
Poor Man's Cotton, 78, 79, 97, *Chapter 5
Opener, Chapter 5 Review Detail*
Pop-up cityscape, studio lesson, 304-
307
Portrait of a Noblewoman, 179, *Fig.* 10-
3
Portrait of a Woman, 87, *Fig.* 5-11
Port Saint-Tropez, le 14 Juillet, 39, 40,
Fig. 3-15
Post and lintel construction, 242
Poster paint
applying to a stamp, 275
technique tips, 275
tempera vs., 179
Posters, 200-201, *Fig.* 11-12
poster paint (school tempera)
techniques, 275
studio lesson, 200-201
Potter, Beatrix, 193
Jemima Puddle-Duck, 193, *Fig.* 11-2

Pottery
defined, 224
See also Ceramics; Clay
Presentation drawing
defined, 152
studio lesson, 152-153
Primary colors, 57
Primary hues, 57
Principles of art, 18, 78-96
balance, 80-83
defined, 80
emphasis, 86
harmony, 85
movement, 90, 92-93
proportion, 86-87
rhythm, 90-91
variety, 84-85
Print
defined, 34
edition of, 35
Printing plate, 101, *Fig.* 9-2
defined, 101
Printmaking, 34-37, 158-174
basic steps for, 101
defined, 160
editions, 35, 101
glue prints, 168-169
history of, 160-161
importance of, 34
intaglio, 163, *Fig.* 9-5
linoleum block prints, 170-171
lithography, 164-165, *Fig.* 9-6
media of, 34, 35, *Fig.* 3-8
methods of, 162-165
monoprints, 166-167
print motifs, 298-299
relief printing, 162-163, *Figs.* 9-3, 9-4
studio lessons, 168-171, 298-299
screen printing, 164-165, *Figs.* 9-7, 9-8
studio lesson, 172-173
silk screen prints, 165, 172-173
stamp printing techniques, 275
steps of, 34-35
studio lessons, 166-173
glue prints, 168-169
linoleum block prints, 170-171
monoprints, 166-167
print motifs, 298-299
silk screen prints, 172-173
technique tips, 275
Print motifs, studio lesson, 298-299
Producer, 259
Profiles, artist. *See* Artist profiles
Proportion, 86-87, *Figs.* 5-10, 5-11
defined, 86
Pulp method of papier-mâché, 277
Pyramids, 238-239

Q
Quilts, *Georgia Quilt,* 222, 223, *Fig.* 13-1

R
Radial balance, 81, *Fig.* 5-4
Radiator Building—Night—New York,
82, *Fig.* 5-5

Raphael (Sanzio), 104-105, 107, 132-133, 287
  artist profile, 287
  Saint George and the Dragon, 104-105, 107, 287, *Figs.* 6-4, 6-5
  The Small Cowper Madonna, 132-133, *Fig.* 7-13
Real-world events and people, as inspiration, 7
Rectangles, measuring, 279
Red Studio, The, 128-129, 136, 285, *Fig.* 7-9
Regatta at Argenteuil, 125-127, *Fig.* 7-6
Registration, 163
Relief
  clay entrance relief, 246-247
  defined, 45, 212, *Fig.* 3-22
  high, 212
  low, 212
  plaques, 213
  plaster relief, 212-213, 276
  studio lessons
    clay entrance relief, 246-247
    plaster relief, 212-213
  technique tips
    clay mold for plaster relief, 276
    mixing plaster, 276
  See also Sculpture
Relief printing, 162-163, *Figs.* 9-3, 9-4
  defined, 162
  studio lessons
    glue prints, 168-169
    linoleum block prints, 170-171
    print motifs, 298-299
Religious architecture, 239
  Burgos Cathedral, 81, *Fig.* 5-4
  Cathedral of Leon, 239, *Figs.* 14-2, 14-3
  Mission San Jose, 246, *Fig.* 14-11
  Parthenon, 238, 239, 242, *Figs.* 14-1, 14-7
  Temple of Athena Nike, 236-237, 239, 249, *Chapter 14 Opener, Chapter 14 Review Detail*
  Valle de Bohi-Romanesque, 246, *Fig.* 14-10
Rembrandt van Rijn, 148
  Jan Cornelius Sylvius, The Preacher, 148, *Fig.* 8-5
Renaissance, 132-133, *Figs.* 7-13, 7-14
  defined, 132
  fresco painting, 178
Renoir, Pierre Auguste, 121, 125-127, 287
  artist profile, 287
  Girl with a Watering Can, 121, 287, *Fig.* 7-2
  Regatta at Argenteuil, 125-127, *Fig.* 7-6
Reproduction, 34
Resnick, Milton, 107, 109, 116
  Genie, 107, 109, 116, *Fig.* 6-9
Return from the Hunt, 180, *Fig.* 10-4
Return of the Prodigal Son, The, 8, 19, *Fig.* 1-8
Rhythm, 90-91, *Fig.* 5-14
  defined, 91
Right and Left, 2-3, 12, 19, *Fig.* 1-1
Ring Toss, 130, *Fig.* 7-10
Rivera, Diego, 178
  Detroit Industry, 178, *Fig.* 10-1

River Rhine Separating the Waters, The, 214, *Fig.* 12-8
River Seine at Carrieres-sur-Seine, The, 125, *Fig.* 7-5
Rockwell, Norman, xvi, 8, 12
  Triple Self-Portrait, xvi, 8, 12, 13, *Chapter 1 Opener, Chapter 1 Review Detail*
Roman architecture, 240, 241, 244
  Colosseum, 240, 241, *Fig.* 14-4
  Forum of Julius Caesar, 244, *Fig.* 14-8
Rousseau, Henri, 154
  The Waterfall (La Cascade), 154, *Fig.* 8-13
Rubbing, 37
  technique tips, 280
Ruler techniques, 273
Running stitch, 310, *Fig.* S-17
Ryder, Albert Pinkham, 110-111
  The Toilers of the Sea, 110-111, *Fig.* 6-11

S
Safety labels, 41
Safety Last, 260, *Fig.* 15-12
Safety tips
  ammonia, 257
  ceramics glazes, 227
  chalk dust, 111
  cutting tools, 45, 171
  glues, 11
  linoleum blades, 171
  markers, 153, 197
  paints, 41
  plaster and clay dust, 213
  polyurethane sprays, 233
  spray paint, 217, 318
  wire, 313
Sailboats on the Seine, 125-127, *Fig.* 7-7
Saint George and the Dragon, 104-105, 107, 287, *Figs.* 6-4, 6-5
Saint Martin and the Beggar, 106-107, *Figs.* 6-6, 6-7, 6-8
Saint Michael's Counterguard, 70, *Fig.* 4-22
Salemme, Attilio, 66, 67
  Inquisition, 66, 67, *Fig.* 4-18
Sallet, parade, 223, *Fig.* 13-3
San Jose, mission of, 246, *Fig.* 14-11
San Miguel, 210
  The Annunciation, 210, *Fig.* 12-4
Satin stitch, 310, *Fig.* S-17
Scanlin, Tommye M., 230
  Cat Dreams, 230, *Fig.* 13-14
Schapiro, Miriam, 57
  High Steppin' Strutter I, 57, *Fig.* 4-5
Science connections, 12, 76, 96, 140, 156, 174, 188, 218, 234, 266
Scoring paper, 278, 280
Screen printing, 164-165, *Figs.* 9-7, 9-8
  defined, 165
  serigraph, 165
  studio lesson, 172-173
Sculpture, 44-47, 206-218
  abstract, 216-217
  additive techniques, 47, 210
  assembling, 47, 210-211, *Figs.* 12-5, 12-6
    studio lessons, 216-217, 312-315
  beginnings of, 208-209, *Fig.* 12-3

carving, 47, 210, *Fig.* 12-4
  studio lesson, 212-213
  casting, 47, 210
  clay modeling
    studio lesson, 214-215
    technique tips, 275-276
  media of, 45-47, *Fig.* 3-19
  methods of sculpting, 47, 210-211
  modeling, 47, 210
    studio lessons, 214-215, 242-243
  paper sculpture
    studio lesson, 70-71
    technique tips, 278, 280
  plaster relief
    studio lesson, 212-213
    technique tips, 276
  relief, 212-213
  studio lessons, 212-217
    abstract sculpture, 216-217
    clay modeling, 214-215
    freestanding mobile, 314-315
    objective wire sculpture, 312-313
    paper sculpture forms, 70-71
    plaster relief, 212-213
  subtractive techniques, 47, 210
  technique tips, 275-278
    clay, joining, 275-276
    clay mold for plaster relief, 276
    clay, working with, 275
    paper sculpture, 278
    papier-mâché, 277-278
    plaster, clay mold for plaster relief, 276
    plaster, mixing, 276
  See also Architecture; Relief
Seashell, 73, *Fig.* 4-25
Seated Woman, 170, *Fig.* 9-14
Secondary hues, 58
Self-Portrait, studio lesson, 122-123
Self-Portrait (Kollwitz), 46, *Fig.* 3-21
Self-Portrait (Leyster), 122, *Fig.* 7-3
Serigraph, 164-165, *Fig.* 9-8
  defined, 165
  See also Screen printing
Seurat, Georges, 138
  Sunday Afternoon on the Island of La Grande Jatte, 138, *Fig.* 7-19
Several Circles, 85, *Fig.* 5-8
Shade, defined, 58
Shading, 146-147
  defined, 146
  techniques, 146-147, 272, *Fig.* 8-4
Shape, 66-67
  classes of, 67
  defined, 66
  form and, 67, *Fig.* 4-20
Shoe comic strip, 198, *Fig.* 11-10
Shopping mall, 244, *Fig.* 14-9
  floor plan for, 244-245
Sighting techniques, 272
Sign making, 194-195, *Figs.* 11-5, 11-6
Silent movie, studio lesson, 260-261
Silk screen printing. *See* Screen printing
Siqueiros, David Alfaro, 180
  Echo of a Scream, 180, *Fig.* 10-5
Sisley, Alfred, friendship with Renoir, 287

333

Sittow, Michel, 80, 81
  The Assumption of the Virgin, 80, 81,
    Fig. 5-2
Size
  describing, 100
  proportion, 86-87
  space and, 69
Slab
  architecture model, 242-243
  container, 228-229
  defined, 228
  studio lesson, 228-229
Slip (clay), 225
Small Cowper Madonna, The, 132-133,
    Fig. 7-13
Smith, David, 211
  Cockfight-Variation, 211, *Fig.* 12-5
Social studies connections, 116, 156,
    174, 218, 248, 266
Solvent
  defined, 39, 178
  studio lesson, 42-43
Space, 68-69
  defined, 69
  space-creating techniques, 69
Space Invaders, 262, *Fig.* 15-15
Sphinx, Great, 208, 209, *Fig.* 12-3
Spray paint, safety tip for, 217, 318
Stacking Side Chair, 113, *Fig.* 6-15
Stained glass windows
  medieval, 5, *Fig.* 1-4
  radial balance in, 81, *Fig.* 5-4
Stamp printing techniques, 275
Stayton, Janet, 166
  Ravello, ix, top
  Yellow Promenade, 166, *Fig.* 9-9
Steen, Jan, 28, 29
  The Drawing Lesson, 28, 29, 51, *Chapter*
    3 Opener, Chapter 3 Review Detail
Steerage, The, 255, *Fig.* 15-5
Steinlen, Theophile-Alexandre, 193-
    194
  Compagnie Française des Chocolats et des
    Thés, 193-194, *Fig.* 11-4
Stella, Frank, 22, 70
  Agbatana III, 22, *Fig.* 2-6
  Saint Michael's Counterguard, 70, *Fig.* 4-
    22
Stieglitz, Alfred, 130, 255
  The Steerage, 255, *Fig.* 15-5
Stippling, 147
Stitchery
  chart of stitches, 310, *Fig.* S-16
  studio lesson, 308-311
Story, picture that tells a, 316-317
Strip method of papier-mâché, 277
Studio experiences
  aesthetic views, 23
  analyzing art works, 107
  architecture appreciation, 241
  art history, 139
  collage of letters, 195
  describing non-objective art, 103
  drawing media, 33
  freestanding sculpture assembly, 47
  hues, 57
  idea bank, 9

impressionism, 127
intensity of hue, 59
line, 65
movement and rhythm, 91
painting media, 41, 181
point of view, 3
printing media, 37
printmaking with reverse images, 165
space-creating techniques, 69
texture, 73
Studio lessons
  aesthetic views, 304-307
  appliqué banner, 308-311
  architecture, 242-247
    clay entrance relief, 246-247
    clay model, 242-243
    drawing floor plans, 244-245
  cityscapes, 82-83, 304-307
  collage, 10-11
    self-portrait, 122-123
    time and place, 134-135
  color combinations with motif, 60-61
  crafts, 226-233
    clay bowl, 226-227
    jewelry art, 232-233
    slab container, 228-229
    stitchery, 308-311
    weaving, 230-231
  descriptive techniques, 104-105
  drawing, 148-155
    architecture floor plans, 244-245
    contour drawing, 150-151
    fantasy jungle, 154-155
    gesture drawing, 148-149
    presentation drawing, 152-153
  Fauvism, 128-129
  formal balance (cityscape), 82-83
  graphic design, 196-203
    comic strips, 198-199
    illustration, 202-203
    logos, 196-197
    posters, 200-201
  mixed media, 48-49, 122-123
  painting
    abstract action painting, 300-301
    color combinations, 60-61
    expressive, 186-187
    in Fauve style, 128-129
    group mural, 302-303
    landscapes, 74-75
    mood chalk painting, 110-111
    non-objective, 88-89, 184-185
    picture that tells a story, 316-317
    pigment, 42-43
    watercolor, 42-43, 182-183
  photography
    photogram (calotype), 256-257
    pinhole camera, 318-319
  pop-up cityscape, 304-307
  printmaking, 166-173
    glue prints, 168-169
    linoleum block prints, 170-171
    monoprints, 166-167
    print motifs, 298-299
    silk screen prints, 172-173
  sculpting, 212-217
    abstract sculpture, 216-217

clay modeling, 214-215
freestanding mobile, 314-315
objective wire sculpture, 312-313
paper sculpture forms, 70-71
plaster relief, 212-213
silent movie, 260-261
torn paper face, 24-25
video games, 264-265
visual movement, 92-93
Style, 124-125
  defined, 124
  interpreting time and place for, 130,
    131, 132-133
  judging for, 136-138
Subject, 17
  aesthetic view relating to, 21
  defined, 17
  describing, 100-101, 114
  in drama and music, 26
  interpreting time and place for, 130-133
Subtractive sculpting techniques, 47, 210
Sullivan, John, 194
  Tailor's Shears (shop sign), 194, *Fig.* 11-6
Sullivan, Louis, 240
  Wainwright Building, 240, *Fig.* 14-5
Sunbather, 21, *Fig.* 2-5
Sunday Afternoon on the Island of La
    Grande Jatte, 138, *Fig.* 7-19
Sunrise, 39, 41, 42, 43, *Fig.* 3-15
Super-realism, 21
Supports for papier-mâché creations,
    277-278
Symmetrical balance. *See* Formal
  balance
Synthetic paints, 180-181, *Figs.* 10-5, 10-6
  acrylic, 181
  defined, 180
  duco, 180

T

Tafoya, Margaret, 226
  Jar, Santa Clara Pueblo, New Mexico,
    226, *Fig.* 13-10
Tailor's Shears (shop sign), 194, *Fig.* 11-6
Talbot, William Henry Fox, 256
  The Ladder, 256, *Fig.* 15-6
T. B. Harlem, 186, *Fig.* 10-11
Teacher, career as, 293
Technique, judging for, 138
Technique tips
  drawing, 271-273
    contour drawings, 271
    enlarging using a grid, 271-272
    gesture drawings, 271
    oil pastels, 271
    ruler, using, 273
    shading, 272
    sighting, 272
    thin lines with a brush, 271
    viewing frame, using, 273
  miscellaneous, 278-281
    glue, working with, 281
    making a mat, 279
    measuring rectangles, 278
    mounting two-dimensional works,
      280
    rubbings, 280-281

tissue paper collage, 281
painting, 273-275
    cleaning a brush, 273-274
    making natural earth pigments, 274
    mixing paint to change value of
        color, 274
    poster paints (school tempera), 275
    watercolors, 275
printmaking, 275
sculpting, 275-278
    clay, joining, 275-276
    clay mold for plaster relief, 276
    clay, working with, 275
    paper sculpture, 278, 280
    papier-mâché, 277-278
    plaster, clay mold for plaster relief,
        276
    plaster, mixing, 276
Telephone Booths, 112-113, *Fig. 6-13*
Tempera, 179, *Fig. 10-2*
    defined, 179
    school poster paint vs., 179
    See also Poster paint
Temples
    Athena Nike, 236-237, 239, 249,
        *Chapter 14 Opener, Chapter 14 Review
        Detail*
    Parthenon, 238, 239, 242, *Figs. 14-1, 14-7*
    See also Cathedrals; Religious
        architecture
Texture, 72-73
    defined, 72
    sight vs. touch for, 72-73
Therapist, career as, 294
Therese, Countess Kinsky, 131, 289,
    Fig. 7-12
Thomas, Alma, 176-177
    Iris, Tulips, Jonquils and Crocuses, 176-
        177, 189, *Chapter 10 Opener, Chapter
        10 Review Detail*
Three-dimensional art, defined, 44
Three Musicians, 118-119, 141, *Chapter 7
    Opener, Chapter 7 Review Detail*
Three Women, 4, *Fig. 1-2*
Tiffany, Louis Comfort, 244
    Vase, 224, *Fig. 13-7*
Time and place, studio lesson, 134-135
Tint, 58
Tissue paper collage, 281
Toilers of the Sea, The, 110-111, *Fig. 6-11*
Torn paper face, studio lesson, 24-25
Toulouse-Lautrec, Henri de, 35, 36,
    190-191, 193, 288
    artist profile, 288
    Jane Avril, 190-191, 193, 205, 288,
        *Chapter 11 Opener, Chapter 11 Review
        Detail*
    La Gitane, 35, 36, *Fig. 3-10*
Toussaint L'Overture Series, 92, *Fig. 5-15*
Transparent, 179
Trees, 73, 74, *Fig. 4-24*
Triple Self-Portrait, xvi, 13, *Chapter 1
    Opener, Chapter 1 Review Detail*
Turn of the Century Dandy, 23, *Fig. 2-7*
Turpentine, 39
Two-dimensional art
    defined, 44

matting, 279
mounting, 280
space-creating techniques for, 69
Typefaces
    defined, 192
    early typefaces, *Fig. 11-1*

U
Unity, 94-95
    defined, 94
    plotting on a chart, 95, *Fig. 5-19*
Untitled, 164, 165, *Fig. 9-8*

V
Valle de Bohi-Romanesque, 246, *Fig.
    14-10*
Value, 58, 59, *Fig. 4-7*
    defined, 58
    mixing paint for, 274
    shade, 58
    space and, 69
    tint, 58
van Gogh, Vincent, 63, 64, 288
    artist profile, 288
    Cypresses, 63, 64, 288, *Fig. 4-15*
    The Garden of the Rectory at Neunen, 94,
        Fig. 5-17
Variety, 84-85, *Figs. 5-7, 5-8*
    defined, 85
    studio lesson, 88-89
Vase (Kimiko), 224, 225, *Fig. 13-9*
Vase (Tiffany), 224, *Fig. 13-7*
Vertical lines, 62, *Fig. 4-11*
Video games, 262-265
    defined, 262
    design, 263-265
    history of, 262-263
    studio lesson, 264-265
Video recording, studio lesson, 260-261
View of Toledo, 304, 305, *Fig. S-9*
Viewing frame technique, 273
View of Mt. Fuji from Seven-Ri Beach,
    160, *Fig. 9-1*
**Vigée-Lebrun, Marie-Louise-
    Élisabeth,** 131, 289
    artist profile, 289
    La Princesse Barbe Gallitzin, 148, 149,
        Fig. 8-6
    Theresa, Countess Kinsky, 131, *Fig. 7-12*
Visual movement, studio lesson, 92-93
Vlaminck, Maurice de, 125-127
    Sailboats on the Seine, 125-127, *Fig. 7-7*

W
Wainwright Building, 240, *Fig. 14-5*
Waiting for Dancing Partners, 4-5,
    Fig. 1-3
Wallpaper paste, safety tip for, 11
Warhol, Andy, 172
    *George Gershwin from Ten Portraits of
        Jews of the 20th Century,* 172, *Fig. 9-16*
Warm color schemes, 59
Warp, defined, 224, 230
Warping a loom, 230-231, *Fig. 13-15*
Washington Monument
    photograph, 152, *Fig. 8-12*
    presentation drawing (rejected), 152,
        Fig. 8-11
Watercolor, 180, *Fig. 10-4*

defined, 180
ingredients of, 39
palette for, 180
studio lessons
    painting, 182-183
    pigment, 42-43
technique tips, 275
Waterfall, The (La Cascade), 154,
    Fig. 8-13
Weaver, Ann Renée, 223, 233
    Alphabet Blocks in Case, 223, *Fig. 13-2*
    Paper Jewelry Pin, 233, *Fig. 13-18*
Weaving, 223-224, *Figs. 13-4, 13-5,
    13-14, 13-15, 13-16*
    loom, 224, *Fig. 13-6*
    studio lesson, 230-231
Weft, 224, 230
Welles, Orson, 259
    Citizen Kane, 259, *Fig. 15-10*
Wet plate photography, 252-253
Whale of a Mural, A, 302, *Fig. S-5*
White Angel Breadline, 253, 254, *Fig. 15-4*
White Calico Flower, The, 212, 213, 286,
    Fig. 12-7
White, Clarence H., 130
    Ring Toss, 130, *Fig. 7-10*
Wilgus, William John, 6
    Ichabod Crane, 6, *Fig. 1-5*
Williams, Herbert Andrew, 48, 49
    A Year in the Life of Herbert, 48, 49, *Fig.
        3-23*
Willson, Mary Ann, 8-9
    The Prodigal Son Reclaimed, 8-9, *Fig. 1-9*
Wire, safety tip for, 313
Wire sculpture, studio lesson, 312-313
Wizard of Oz, The, 259
Woman in a Purple Coat, 84, 85, *Fig. 5-7*
Woodruff, Hale, 78, 79
    Poor Man's Cotton, 78, 79, 97, *Chapter 5
        Opener, Chapter 5 Review Detail*
Works of art, 16-19
    composition of, 18-19
    content of, 17-18
    credit line for, 19
    defined, 16
    subject of, 17
    three-dimensional vs. two-
        dimensional, 44
Wrapping paper, studio lesson, 298-299
Wright, Frank Lloyd, 241
    Guggenheim Museum, 241, *Fig. 14-6*
Wyeth, Andrew, 114-115, 116, 179, 289
    artist profile, 289
    Christina's World, 114-115, 116, 179,
        289, *Figs. 6-16, 10-2*
Wyeth, N. C., 202, 289
    Blind Pew, 202, *Fig. 11-14*

Y
Year in the Life of Herbert, A, 48, 49, *Fig.
    3-23*
Yellow Promenade, 166, *Fig. 9-9*

Z
Zaga, 44, *Fig. 3-18*
Zapatistas, 57, 58, *Fig. 4-6*
Zigzag lines, 63, 65, *Fig. 4-16*

Acknowledgements: The art work executed and submitted by the following students was exemplary. Because of book design constraints, all of the student work could not be included. The authors feel, however, that each student who contributed should be recognized.

Tory D. Almond, Camp Creek Middle School; Justine Altman, Crabapple Middle School; Grace Arbizo, Stanton High School; Brad Ash, Mandarin High School; Juan Atayde, Guillen School; Andre Leon Bailey, Colonial High School; Brett Barnes, Crabapple Middle School; Rob Bass, All Saints Episcopal School; Chad Bates, Burney-Harris-Lyons Middle School; Sonya Beard, Crabapple Middle School; Maria Betancourt, Guillen School; James M. Borwigi, Paxon, Middle School; Wright Branson, Haynes Bridge Middle School; Dennis Bright, Colonial High School; Whitney Brotherton, East Middle School; Lucius E. Burke, Jenkins County Elementary School; Sam Byrd, Burney-Harris-Lyons Middle School; Maurice Calloway, Burney-Harris-Lyons Middle School; Javier Calzadillas, Guillen School; Lamar Kinte Carter, East Middle School; Jason Charles, Magoffin Middle School; Lucy Cobb, Hilsman Middle School; Patrice Cone, Marvin Pittman Laboratory School; Becky Connors, Haynes Bridge Middle School; Josh Cooper, Sandy Springs Middle School; Leticia Corpos, Guillen School; Natasha Cox, All Saints Episcopal School; Forrest Davis, Paxon Middle School; Jason Davis, Paxon Middle School; Paul Davis, East Middle School; Elizabeth Dewey, Marvin Pittman Laboratory School; John Douglass, Jr., Colonial High School; Jessica Drewing, Stanton High School; Julie Drown, Crabapple Middle School; Lisa Duchemin, Tapp Middle School; Nancy Elliot, Hilsman Middle School; Joy Elliott, Hilsman Middle School; Yona N. Ellis, Burney-Harris-Lyons Middle School; Marshall English, Burney-Harris-Lyons Middle School; Melissa Epps, Floyd Middle School; Kim Farmer, Camp Creek Middle School; Christy Farr, Tapp Middle School; Thomas Feeney, Crabapple Middle School; Steven Fisher, Meher High School; Jamie Fraser, Sandy Springs Middle School; Danny Gallegos, Canyon Hills Middle School; Blanca Gandara, Guillen School; Phillip Gatlin, Colonial High School; J. R. Gay, Jenkins County Elementary School; Chris Gibbs, Bassett Middle School; Johnny Gomez, Bassett Middle School; Theodora Gongaware, Savannah Country Day School; Beth Gould, Haynes Bridge Middle School; Erin Graham, East Middle School; Marshall Graham, Hilsman Middle School; Rebekah Hagins, Marvin Pittman Laboratory School; Elsie T. Hall, The Savannah Country Day School; Jason Hall, Crabapple Middle School; Heather Halterman, Stanton High School; Theresa Hanson, Mandarin Middle School; Julie Harper, East Middle School; Billy Harrell, East Middle School; Cornelius Havgabook, Camp Creek Middle School; Elsie Hill, The Savannah Country Day School; Sara Hodgson, Burney-Harris-Lyons Middle School; Tamatha Hudson, Colonial High School; T. J. Hurt, All Saints Episcopal School; Amory Jeffries, Havenview Junior High School; Liza Jensen, Harris Middle School; Leslie Johnson, Treadwell Junior High School; Klay Keiser, Colonial High School; Stephanie Kimbell, Floyd Middle School; Patrick Klenke, Canyon Hills Middle School; Jon Lancaric, Canyon Hills Middle School; Christel Landers, Holcomb Bridge Middle School; Rory Lane, Burney-Harris-Lyons Middle School; Julie Leatherman, Stanton High School; Tommy Lerma, Magoffin Middle School; Tara Liebe, Sandy Springs; Lauren Littlewood, Holcomb Bridge Middle School; Christy Lord, Burney-Harris-Lyons Middle School; Marissa MacCaughelty, Marvin Pittman Laboratory School; Amy Malkey, Haynes Bridge Middle School; Jon Ed Mann, Camp Creek Middle School; Kaia Mapp, Camp Creek Middle School; Henry Martell, Bassett Middle Schoo; Ramon R. Martinez, Canyon Hills Middle School; Carlos Mascorro, Guillen School; Christian Mathis, Colonial High School; Ryan McDowell, Hilsman Middle School; Amy McEntee, East Middle School; Chase McGee, The Savannah Country Day School; Josh McGuire, Tapp Middle School; Justin Miller, Burney-Harris-Lyons Middle School; Torshike Miller, Camp Creek Middle School; Ronald Mitchell, Camp Creek Middle School; Oscar M. Mora, Guillen School; Elizabeth Morales, Guillen School; Gray Morgan, Colonial High School; Katherine Morgenstern, La Pietra School; Marie Mortenson, Meher High School; Riann Munn, Floyd Middle School; Gabriel Myers, Harold Wiggs Middle School; Matt Nall, All Saints Episcopal School; Scott Newman, Marvin Pittman Laboratory School; Michael Ngaujah, Camp Creek Middle School; Jason O'Brian, Mandarin Middle School; Charlie Occhipinti, Burney-Harris-Lyons Middle School; Dana D. Odom, Marvin Pittman Laboratory School; Omar Ontiveros, Bassett Middle School; Julie Parker, The Savannah Country Day School; Alejandro de la Pena, Bassett Middle School; Celena Perkins, Marvin Pittman Laboratory School; Jesus Pinales, Guillen School; Lindsay Podozil, Holcomb Bridge Middle School; Chamera Porter, Bassett Middle School; Maria Rameriz, Bassett Middle School; Juan L. Reyes, Guillen School; Amy Rhoads, Sandy Springs Middle School; Andrew Rippel, All Saints Episcopal School; Danny Roberts, Colonial High School; Ariel Robinson, Havenview Junior High; Joe Rodriguez, Guillen School; Brenda Ross, Burney-Harris-Lyons Middle School; Diego Rothenback, Canyon Hills Middle School; Katherine Sales, La Pietra School; Matt Samuelson, The Savannah Country Day School; Hayden Shore, The Savannah Country Day School; Rebekah Shower, Stanton High School; Chiquita Simmons, Havenview Junior High School; Scarlet Sims, Camp Creek Middle School; Adam F. Skibell, All Saints Episcopal School; Demelia Sloan, Camp Creek Middle School; Lori Slovisky, Crabapple Middle School; Jamie Smallwood, Marvin Pittman Laboratory School; Sok South, Treadwell Junior High; Charlie Stamphill, Crabapple Middle School; Adrian Staton, Crabapple Middle School; Brandi Stratton, Bassett Middle School; Michael Strickland, Paxon Middle School; Momoko Suzuki, La Pietra School; Antonio Taylor, Hilsman Middle School; Alice Thompson, Stanton High School; Kevin M. Thompson, Stanton High School; Lindsey Thompson, Burney-Harris-Lyons Middle School; Larry Townsend, Burney-Harris-Lyons Middle School; Anne Trainer, Colonial High School; Jami Vansant, Haynes Bridge Middle School; Teresa Villalobos, Guillen School; Telisia Wade, Hilsman Middle School; Amanda Walker, Haynes Bridge Middle School; Gerald Walker, Jenkins County Elementary School; Joanna Warchol, Marvin Pittman Laboratory School; Stephen Warneck, The Savannah Country Day School; Walter J. Warneck III, The Savannah Country Day School; Laura Lynn Weber, Glenrock High School; Jason Wheeler, East Middle School; Lakesha Whitaker, Treadwell Junior High School; Abigail White, Sandy Springs Middle School; Melanie Wiggins, Bassett Middle School; Latoya Wiley, Marvin Pittman Laboratory School; Andrew Williams, Jenkins County High School; Jana Williams, Jenkins County Elementary School; John Michael Williams, Colonial High School; Calvin Wilson, Havenview Junior High School; Makana Yasukawa, La Pietra School.